ROBIN LANE FOX

THE
UNAUTHORIZED
VERSION

Robin Lane Fox is a fellow of New College, Oxford,
and a University Reader in Ancient History. He is the
author of a number of widely praised books.

Alexander the Great

Variations on a Garden

Search for Alexander

Better Gardening

Pagans and Christians

THE
UNAUTHORIZED
VERSION

THE
UNAUTHORIZED
VERSION

Truth and Fiction in the Bible

ROBIN LANE FOX

Vintage Books
A Division of Random House, Inc.
New York

Library of Congress Cataloging-in-Publication Data
Fox, Robin Lane, 1946–
The unauthorized version: truth and fiction in the Bible /
Robin Lane Fox. — 1st Vintage Books ed.
p.   cm.
Originally published: London: Viking Penguin, 1991.
Includes bibliographical references and index.
ISBN 0-679-74406-1 (pbk.)
1. Bible—Evidences, authority, etc.   2. Bible—Controversial
literature.   I. Title.
[BS480.L347   1992]
220.6'7—dc20   92-50601
CIP

Contents

Contents

Preface

_____

The Unauthorized Version is a historian's view of the Bible. It is a book about evidence and historical truth, not about faith. It is unauthorized because it addresses questions which the Bible itself obscures: its authors, historical growth and historical truth. It is not an unauthorized version because other people have authorized their own version and wish to suppress the truth in mine. Those for whom the Bible is a book of faith wish to discover the truth, too. I write as an atheist, but there are Christian and Jewish scholars whose versions would be far more radical than mine. They will find this historian's view conservative, even old-fashioned, but there are times when atheists are loyal friends of the truth.

My subject is both Hebrew and Christian scripture, and so I have written with Christian readings most often in mind. I have cited Christians' responses and commentaries more often than Jewish ones because the Bible is a Christian creation. Throughout, I have been aware that its Hebrew texts have had an older life which has not been lived as a Christian Old Testament. That life continues, but it is not the main perspective of my book.

I write, none the less, as an ancient historian who is accustomed to reading the biblical narratives like other narratives which survive from the ancient past. For many readers they are more than that, but they are also that too. I look back on them from outside some of their modern traditions, but my version has evident heroes who have taken on a clearer shape and life as I have written: Israelite piety in the age of Solomon, an unnamed Jewish author in the mid sixth century BC (the Deuteronomist) and Jesus's 'beloved disciple'. Others believe that we know next to nothing about the first of them, nothing about the second,

7

let alone about his work or its revisions, and that the third is not the author of a Gospel. I have weighed the contrary arguments and I disagree.

I do, however, have debts to others whose existence is certain, and I do not wish to be credited with originalities which are theirs, not mine. Most of the points I discuss have been discussed with learning and subtlety by many specialists before me. With their help, I have reached and picked my conclusions with care, aware that I know Greek but not Hebrew. I have not set out all my reasons for rejecting the many alternatives of which I am aware. I have cited some of them in the notes to each chapter, but here, too, there are limits, not only to an outsider's capacity.

When I had almost finished, a friend reminded me that I had once remarked to him that I believed in the Bible but not in God. I had long forgotten this remark, but it must have remained latent in me. Twenty-five years later, this book has turned out to be an explanation of what I meant.

Acknowledgements

My views of the early history of the Hebrew Scriptures have been formed by the insights of J. Wellhausen, more than a century ago. Modern attempts to depart from their main principles have mostly confirmed me in the widely shared acceptance that Wellhausen was right. Like many ancient historians, I have gained much from the distinctive approaches of David Daube and Arnaldo Momigliano, scholars who have moved with authority between the Hebrew and the classical worlds. My final chapter owes an evident debt to published work by the former and my chapters 11 and 12 to the life-long interests of the latter. I am also one of the many beneficiaries of the revised edition and translation of Emil Schuerer's great *History of the Jewish People*, enriched by the scholarship of F. G. B. Millar, G. Vermes, M. D. Goodman and others. My deepest debt, however, is to the clear vision and the exceptional harmony of style and detail in the writings of E. J. Bickerman on so much which I have chosen to discuss. His *Four Strange Books of the Bible* remains an envied example, but my chapters on biblical authorship, Judaism after the Exile and especially the trial of Jesus begin from scholarship and arguments which are his.

Ancient historians sometimes write as if all theologians are an inferior species: I have not shared this belief, least of all while writing this book. There are theologians who can alert ancient historians to a strand of fundamentalism in their own writings and too simple a faith in ancient set texts. The second part of the book, chapters 3–10, is a reflection of what I have learned from them, especially from the writings of J. Barr and E. W. Nicholson. The historical chapters in the third part, especially chapters 14–19, have benefited from Oxford colleagues who spoke to a seminar in 1988 on the Bible and History. During it, P. R. S. Moorey,

Acknowledgements

E. P. Sanders, D. M. Lewis, S. P. Brock and M. D. Goodman acquainted me with evidence which I would probably have missed otherwise. Later, P. R. S. Moorey criticized the chapters on biblical archaeology in the spirit in which they were intended and M. D. Goodman coped perceptively with a penultimate text of the entire book. Jeremy Hughes made acute criticisms of the chapters which mainly concern Hebrew Scripture and argued for plausible alternatives which I had dismissed; the general and particular comments of Tessa Rajak pointed me to many of the places where a sense of perspective had been lost. I owe a special debt to Mark Edwards whose insights, criticisms and grasp of the relevant scholarship have guided me away from my more tenuous or ill-thought views. I was also fortunate in the help of William Eaglestone with the index and the criticisms of my publishers, Peter Carson and Charles Elliott. Without Anne Robinson, there would have been no text at all: she has typed my manuscript in its various forms with exemplary skill and patience.

When I quote the Bible in my text, I usually use the King James version, for reasons outlined in my chapter 10. Where a mistranslation or use of inferior manuscripts seriously affects my argument, I have usually cited the Revised Standard Version instead.

PART ONE

1

As It Was In The Beginning

I

In John's Gospel, Jesus tells Pilate, 'To this end was I born, and for this cause came I into the world, that I should bear witness unto the truth. Every one that is of the truth heareth my voice.' 'What is truth?' asks Pilate and does not receive a reply.

The question is the last of four, none of which Jesus answers directly. On the modern stage we are familiar with dialogue in the discontinuous style in which neither party replies to the other's words. Although there is a wide gap between Pilate and Jesus, their conversation is not quite of this type. Pilate tries three times for a plain answer, but Jesus questions him too, and retains control of the exchange. A direct question about the King of the Jews ends with an open question about truth itself. 'Jesting Pilate,' wrote Francis Bacon, 'would not stay for an answer'; St Augustine suggested that Pilate's mind had already moved on to the custom of releasing a prisoner at Passover, which he then proposes to the Jews. His question is not a jest, but it bears on himself and his predicament. Pilate puts it to the person who has already described himself as the truth (John 14:6); confronting the truth, he goes out to the Jews and prefers their falsehood.

The question leads us on, but it is not truth itself. It is not so much that the dialogue probably involved a third person: Pilate did not know Hebrew or Aramaic and it is highly unlikely that Jesus spoke Greek. It is likely that an interpreter would have been needed, although the Gospels do not mention one. The problem, rather, is that each Gospel gives a different version of what was said and done. An unknown interpreter, or Jesus himself, did not give the authors the exact words of the meeting: the fourth Gospeller's are his own invention.

13

The final question which Pilate asked Jesus has not lacked answers since and is very far from being settled. Philosophers have taken it to levels of ever increasing subtlety, but two types of answer still underlie most of their arguments. On one view, truth consists in correspondence to the facts, the theory of correspondence; on another, truth consists in coherence with a general system of beliefs, the theory of coherence. I intend to take Pilate's question and turn it back on the Bible itself. First, I will explore the view that the Bible's very nature and origin give it a coherence which answers Pilate's question. Then I will explore its narrative to see if there is a level at which it corresponds to fact.

Explorations do not give full answers, least of all through texts as varied as the scriptures. Parts of them would be badly misread if explored only for factual statements: the psalms, the proverbs, the books of Job or Ecclesiastes, parts of the Christian epistles. Here, thought Matthew Arnold, we find 'words thrown out at an immense reality, not fully or half fully grasped by the author, but even then, able to affect us with indescribable force'. They do not refer to factual truth: 'the Bible is literature, and its words are used like the words of common life and of poetry and eloquence, *approximately*, and not like the terms of science, *adequately*'. These parts may affect us, still, with an 'indescribable force' but its causes are not so obvious. Is there an 'immense reality' for which they are somehow straining? Or is it that we enter into what they say because of how they say it, and because we can share as fellow humans in what they are putting into words?

For many people, an answer rests on faith: it does not depend on factual truth. With or without faith, it would be absurd to read these parts of the Bible literally, marking down each sentence for exact truth or falsehood and ignoring its metaphors and wonderfully approximate words. However, the Bible is not always a text of this type. It does also refer to events and persons, from the origin of the world to its imminent end. Here, too, it often interprets what it describes; here, too, its language can be marvellously approximate; but it also narrates, refers, and prophesies. It therefore invites the question of truth. It is as a historian that I will explore it, accustomed to putting Pilate's question to written evidence from the distant past.

Hebrew scripture, the Christian Old Testament, begins with the Creation of the world; two Gospels in Christian scripture, the New

Testament, begin with the story of Jesus's Nativity. These beginnings have their own rich histories, both a history of their origins and a history of their changing interpretations by artists and readers. Nowadays, they conflict with scientific knowledge, which rejects the idea of a virgin birth or a Creation, not evolution, in only six days. Yet without this knowledge they had already engaged historians and careful readers who were testing for truth's two pillars: coherence within the story and correspondence with facts outside it.

I I

The Bible begins with two distinct stories of Creation. From Genesis 1 to 2:4, God creates the world in six days and rests on the seventh. By his word of command, he separates light from darkness, heaven from earth; grass and trees emerge; sun, moon and stars begin to shine; birds and great sea-monsters begin to breed and multiply; the earth brings forth animals and creeping things; God creates human beings in his own image and divides them into man and woman. They are to be fruitful and multiply, rule over the animals, fishes and birds, and eat all the herbs, fruits and trees of the earth. The first Creation is to be vegetarian and remains so until God's orders to Noah in Genesis 9:1–3.

This text does not give a detailed account of how God did it. Like God, it moves mysteriously, from the separation of light to the subsequent creation of stars, from the 'Spirit' which moves, or disturbs, the void to the creation of man in God's image, phrases whose Hebrew meaning is still not pinned down, perhaps because it was never precise, not even to the author himself. Already, approximate language confronts us, thrown out at 'immense reality': the 'Spirit', perhaps, is a wind, not a brooding presence poised above this void. Its movement is almost certainly like the flapping of wings, according to its latest scholars, yet it is not winged itself; it is a moving, unseen force which is left for us to envisage as either gentle or turbulent. My idea of this wind is an unpredictable gust, rousing the void, then blowing over briefly, a wind which would make doors swing and sand fly.

To us, but probably not to the author, the very first verse can be taken in several ways, as the independent sentence of our Bibles ('In the beginning God created . . .') or as an opening clause which is

15

subordinated to the next two verses ('In the beginning of God's creating ... the earth was waste and void'). Language alone does not decide between the alternatives, which have different implications. Did chaos exist already when God went to work or, as usually thought, did God create chaos too? What exactly does the Hebrew word for 'create' mean? The second day has also seemed problematic. On each day God is said to have approved his work ('And God saw that it was good') except on the second, the separation of the waters by a firmament. Here, God is silent in the Hebrew text, a silence which troubled some of his careful Jewish readers. Their answers are known in the early Christian era: God, they suggested, had withheld his approval because the second day was one of division, breaking the unity of the world. The reason was perhaps simpler. At verse 8 the words of approval may have fallen out of the Hebrew text which they used in the second century AD; they are present in earlier Greek translations which perhaps used a better Hebrew manuscript.

On one possible reading of this story, mankind was never solely male but was split into male and female immediately after Creation. At 1:27 Hebrew words which are not specific have been understood as not sexist, allowing a feminist reading in which God first created an 'earth creature' and man did not exist before woman in God's plan. On a separate point, however, the author was quite certain: sabbatical leave, though perhaps not woman, was as old as the history of the world. God, he asserted, did his work in six days and rested on the seventh, blessing it and hallowing it. He was pleased with his work ('behold, it was very good'). He gave mankind some simple orders but no prohibitions. Nothing confused their relationship.

Readers other than Jews, Christians or feminists took a critical view of this story long before Darwin refuted its details. Philosophy was a Greek, not a Jewish, invention, and when its thinkers became aware of Genesis in a Greek translation, they found its Creation quite unconvincing. True Greeks, they complained that the text showed no interest in the materials with which God must have worked and which must have existed before he made them into his world: they agreed with our Bibles' usual Hebrew translation of the book's first verse. The famous doctor and philosopher, Galen, referred in the mid second century AD to objections which Greek thinkers would naturally raise: the author of

Genesis 'believes everything to be possible with God, even if he wishes to make a bull or a horse out of ashes'. The more we discover about other stories of Creation in ancient texts from the Near East, the less unusual this 'creation by word alone' has come to seem. This knowledge has not made it any more credible.

The story, however, is widely believed to have impressed one pagan reader on other grounds. We have an anonymous book of literary criticism, *On the Sublime*, which was written in Greek by a pagan author, 'Longinus', under the Roman Empire, probably in the later first century A D. This book quotes a version of God's opening words in Genesis (in antiquity, texts of it varied) and praises them for their sublime style. 'Let there be light, and there was . . .' This noble imperative suited the noble work of God. Since the seventeenth century, and especially in the eighteenth, this comment has been prized as an outsider's tribute to the power of the Bible as literature. 'The Bible is being ranked among the classics on purely secular grounds,' wrote C. S. Lewis: 'it would be difficult to cite strict parallels from the ages that follow.' However, the passage breaks up the flow of 'Longinus's' text and intrudes oddly between two connected allusions to Homer's poetry. It is arguably a later addition, made by a Christian reader in the text of this pagan book and then passed down, as often happens, in the surviving manuscripts by later copyists. If so, the first praise of the Bible as literature would itself be a cautionary tale: it is an insertion into another man's text.

At Genesis 2:4 scripture's author refers to his own handiwork: 'these are the generations of the heavens and the earth when they were created'. On the usual view, these words refer back to the seven-day Creation which the author has just described, but elsewhere in Genesis, nine times in all, this wording refers to what follows. If they look forwards here, too, they would help to connect the seven-day story to a second story of Creation: from the second part of 2:4 the author gives a second account of Creation which goes on to tell us about Adam and Eve.

Whether the words in 2:4 look forwards or, more probably, backwards, they cannot conceal that this next stretch of narrative flatly contradicts the first. The world exists, we are now told, but as yet there are no plants or herbs or rain (2:5). God takes earth, the 'dust from the ground' (in Hebrew *'adamah*), and fashions man (*'adam*), as if the

17

similarity of two words points to a real connection between two objects. Unlike the Creation at Genesis 1:27, this Creation is specifically male; here, man exists before vegetation, but at 1:12 the grass, herbs and trees had been created on the third day and mankind had had to wait until the sixth.

In a beautiful image, God animates his handful of dust by breathing into it, a puff of divinity which later thinkers connected with each human being's awareness of an inner conscience, our guide from God. God places his animated clod in Eden, whose luxuriance includes two particular trees, the tree of knowledge and the tree of life. God then speaks his first words to his gardener, a genre with a long history; he gives him a command and a prohibition, and he backs them up with a warning of death: 'Of every tree of the garden thou mayest freely eat: But of the tree of the knowledge of good and evil, thou shalt not eat of it: for in the day that thou eatest thereof thou shalt surely die.' Nothing is said here about the tree of life.

Noticing that man is alone, God creates the birds and beasts, and brings them to man for naming: he creates woman to be man's helper from one of his ribs; man calls her 'wo-man' ('out of man'); the text connects her creation with subsequent childbirth and sexual union ('one flesh'). The pair are naked until the serpent tempts the woman by distorting God's prohibition, perhaps in a leading question: 'yea, hath God said, ye shall not eat of every tree of the garden?', as if every tree had been banned, not one or two. In reply, the woman refers to one tree only and strengthens the command: 'God hath said, ye shall not eat of it, neither shall ye touch it, lest ye die', although God had forbidden only eating. The serpent correctly assures her that death will not follow if she disobeys. The human couple eat and are enhanced, and God does indeed go back on his warning. Having threatened his gardener with the death penalty, he relents and expels his couple to a life of hard labour. Like man and woman, God has his freedom and exploits it: when first used as a deterrent, so the Bible tells us, the death penalty fails and deters nobody.

The first story of Creation divides time, from the first day to the seventh; the second story divides space, a garden from the world and two particular trees from the rest of God's arboretum. More than the first story, the second is an Eden of unanswered questions. In Hebrew, its puns proliferate like Eden's greenery, but their plays on words support the story, as if similar names are pointing to connections in the world; the sequence of events raises problems of timing and motive, relations between the sexes, sexuality and death. What exactly was the status of the first woman as man's helper: was she equal or subordinate until they disobeyed? How are we to imagine our first parents' first hours? Were they naked but immortal, so long as they stayed in innocence: childlike, perhaps, as we nowadays so easily picture them, until they discovered the facts of life and fell upwards into adult life? Or were they mortal from the start and always sexually active in their first garden of bliss, as many Jewish rabbis and John Milton presented them? What, then, of the timing: if Adam and Eve had sex in Eden, was Cain, their wicked child, conceived in Paradise? Surely not, but events must then be packed into a single day. April 22 was once a favourite candidate: if Creation occurred at noon and the Fall before dusk, there was not much chance of conception meanwhile. Sex, like the serpent, rears its head behind so many of the details. What exactly was the knowledge which the fruit of the tree bestowed: was it moral, universal or sexual? Why was the serpent so bothersome? On one view, he was thought to be jealous because he had watched the human couple making love in the garden.

Adam's predicament, too, is unclear. If God wished to give him a helper, why did he create a woman? St Augustine wondered why he did not create a helpful male gardener instead. Woman was not even God's first production: when 'for man there was not found a helper', God's first response was to create the birds and beasts. Did he think that an animal might have sufficed? When he did create Eve, Adam welcomed her: 'At last, this . . .' One Jewish scholar suggested that the animals had to come first, so that the sight of them mating would fire Adam to realize what he was missing: 'At last, my turn.' God also brought each beast to him for naming; does not naming presuppose a more intimate 'knowing'? 'And you, I think, shall be called "hedgehog" . . .'

The two stories, the seven-day sequence and Genesis 2:5–3:24, tell of two different Creations, both of which cannot be true because their details contradict each other. Man, beasts and plants are created in two different sequences, and man and woman are made in two different ways. Alert readers in antiquity did notice the contradictions, and in the

Christian era we know of educated Jews who tried to explain them. Like many readers afterwards, they assumed that great problems in scripture must point to a meaning beneath the text which bound it into an inspired whole. Gardens, serpents and double Creations were pointers to a deeper set of hidden truths: Jews who knew Greek philosophy believed that the first Creation of man 'after God's image' was an ideal Creation in God's mind, whereas the second, from earth, was his Creation in the visible world. Some even believed that the first Adam had been a hermaphrodite, and that division into the two sexes had had to wait until God's second attempt.

Literal readers still held to the text's story and opposed these hidden meanings, but many Jewish scholars and readers, many Christian thinkers in the early Church and philosophers in the Renaissance took their non-existent presence for granted. Their reasoning was straightforward: the contradictions in Genesis 1–3 were so obvious that they must be deliberate. The alternative was to believe that the two stories referred to two different Creations, and that both could be true. In the mid seventeenth century, a French Protestant scholar, Isaac La Peyrère (1594–1676), argued that the first Creation had been the work of the non-Jewish peoples, and the second of Adam's particular race, the Jews. This idea of pre-Adamite people made brilliant sense of contemporary problems. It explained the conflict between the Bible's chronology for Adam and the much older and longer chronology of world events which was given in Greek and Egyptian authors and was newly reported in Indian and Chinese texts. It explained why people other than Adam's family were mentioned in the story of Cain and his punishment (Genesis 4). It also solved the origins of life in the Arctic and the Americas which the new age of exploration had recently discovered. Americans, it emerged, were not long-lost children of Adam, tugged west from Eden by continental drift; like the Eskimos, they were pre-Adamites, descended from the first Creation of multiple races who were made in God's image at Genesis 1:27. This pre-Adamite theory was passionately discussed throughout Europe and had a far-reaching impact on theories of history and race. If scripture's story from Eden onwards was only the history of Adam's Jews, the earliest histories of other peoples could be reconstructed and criticized without detracting from the Bible's authority. If there were two Creations, one for the Gentiles, one for the

Jews, it was natural to ask which Creation was superior. Moulded to and fro, La Peyrère's idea of two Creations helped to liberate historians. Despite its author's intentions, it became a support for racial slavery and anti-Semitism which lasted into the nineteenth century.

In fact, the two Creations arose from a much simpler cause: they had been written by two different authors at different times. The truth was first published by a German minister, H. B. Witter, in an academic study in 1711. Nobody paid any attention, and credit usually goes to Jean d'Astruc, doctor to Louis XV, who diagnosed two sources for the opening chapters of Genesis in 1753. Moses, he argued, had edited the book from four separate texts which could still be 'decomposed' by attentive readers. Refined and enlarged, the idea became common currency among scholars by the end of the century.

Since then, we have seen through the belief that Moses wrote or edited the text. The first story, we now know, was the second in time. It was written by a Jewish priestly writer who took the sabbatical view of Creation; other parts of his work are components of Genesis and its succeeding books, Exodus, Leviticus and Numbers. The date and possible revisions of his work are still disputed, but the likeliest view is that it was written as a unity in the later sixth century BC: most of the Jews had been in exile from their homeland, and the Sabbath, their holy day, took on a particular prominence in religious texts of this period. The day which they saw as a focus of Jewish life was seen by the priestly author as a focal point in God's Creation. The second story tells of the Garden, Eve and the Fall, and was written much earlier, probably during the eighth century BC, although some interpreters still look fondly back to an origin *c.* 930–900. Its Jewish author, too, is an identifiable source for other parts of Genesis and its succeeding books. As his work shows no direct knowledge of a great catastrophe, the fall of Israel's northern kingdom in *c.* 722 BC, he probably wrote before it happened. If so, his story of Creation and the Fall belongs in the same age as a famous neighbour, just to the west of it. The first pagan Greek writings on the origins of gods and human hardship survive in the poetry of Hesiod (*c.* 730–700), where they owe an ultimate debt to myths and stories which Greeks had learned through Phoenicians, neighbours to our Creationist's Israel. In Hesiod's poetry, too, a story of origins is combined with a myth of the first woman, Pandora, as the origin of mankind's miseries. In the history of women, the eighth century BC is a dark and all too inventive era.

The achievements of the two authors in Genesis have been variously assessed. On one view, the tale of a seven-day Creation is not story but doctrine, 'ancient sacred knowledge, preserved and handed on by many generations of priests, repeatedly pondered, taught, reformed and expanded'. The author did not create Creation: he simply wrote down what qualified people had been telling each other for years. The special importance of the Sabbath, however, suggests that the story was also a child of its sixth-century times. Unlike the language of Homer's Greek poems, there is nothing in the two stories' language or style which points to their oral composition. For all we know, each story could have begun as the personal version of a single author, writing at odds with many of his contemporaries.

These stories were heirs to other stories, traces of which (especially to great German scholars) show up like secret writing between the lines of what we now read. As heirs, the authors must (on this view) have been self-conscious about this debt: how, then, could they have thought they had written the final truth on their subject when they used or knew older stories which disagreed with them? The author of Genesis 1, being later, was surely aware of the earlier story of Eve and Eden: the story in Genesis 1 is not so detailed, and so 'we have a very clear indication of a gradual development towards extreme reservation about how the process of Creation took place'. This reservation is even claimed to have consequences for ourselves: 'the whole account is permeated by the wish to approach in awe the secret of Creation which is not accessible to the human mind, so we too can research into it, provided we respect this ultimate secret'. But we might know better than an author of the sixth century BC.

Neither of the stories is a straight narrative. They use direct speech; they tell us what God said and thought; their persons utter praises and speak of the future. Did the authors themselves believe that everything happened as they described? It is we, not they, who try to save their credit by calling their stories myths, as if they aimed only to express a general truth, God's involvement in Creation, perhaps, or his gift of moral freedom to humans. The first story and its seven days are not a myth, but a remarkably unmythical beginning, quite different from the myths of gods, creations and battles with chaos which were known in other Near Eastern cultures: God does it all without any struggle or opposition. The second story is harder to judge. Stories of our first parents and a Creation from earth are well known in other cultures, although we do not happen to know of a specific creation of woman in surviving Near Eastern stories: did the author of the second story believe that almost everything happened just as he described? What is myth to us may not have seemed mythical to him. When the early Greek poet Hesiod told of the origins of the gods, and then of woman, he began by telling how the Muses appeared to him, promising truth, not lies; he then told myths, in our opinion. What we call a myth or story, therefore, could seem true to an early author, even when he raised the distinction of myth and truth himself.

We cannot know the authors' intentions, but posterity, certainly, took the stories to be true. Some while after the two stories had been written, almost certainly before 400 BC, a third writer combined the two into one. Probably, with time, the two stories had become too well known for either to be excluded; we now emphasize their contradictions, but perhaps their editor was impressed by their dissimilarities. The first story told of the origin of the universe, whereas the second dwelt on man's predicament, a separate theme. However, their contradictions were blatant; they were even more blatant if the words at 2:4 about the 'generations of heaven and earth' already stood in the first priestly version and rounded off its story. Did the editor, perhaps, see the conflict and begin with it for a reason: to warn us that Creation was a matter on which opinion prevailed, but not fact? If so, it took Darwin to make readers perceive the intention. Those who count the contradictions elsewhere in his edited book, and know the habits of editors with what they receive, will prefer the obvious view. The creator of Genesis inherited two stories of Creation whose general themes looked different, and so he put them one after another as if they were complementary. A few chapters later he did the same with two contradictory stories of the Flood.

His edited text has found many readers ever since, but there are few direct references to its stories of Creation in the books which became Hebrew scripture, the Christians' Old Testament. There is no mention, surprisingly, of Eve's temptation or the drama of the Fall, although these topics did fascinate later Jewish authors. Not until *c*. 200 BC, in the writings of Ben Sira (author of our Ecclesiasticus), do we find Eve's fall cited as the origin of sin and death. It has been pointed out that by Ben Sira's lifetime Jewish women could have rights which they did not enjoy in biblical times. They were married with dowries; they could inherit and bequeath property; personal contracts of marriage might be drawn up on their behalf, setting out terms which the husband should observe. To Ben Sira, good wives were rare, and women of any spirit were the ultimate root of evil.

Inside the Bible the famous references to the story are all Christian. In Mark's Gospel, Jesus alludes to verses in the Creation stories in order to go beyond the Jewish law and support his strong stand against divorce: 'God made them male and female' (Mark 10:6); 'For this cause shall a man leave his father and mother, and cleave to his wife; And they twain shall be one flesh' (Mark 10:7–8). Mark's Jesus quotes from the two contradictory stories as if they hung together and relates them to a topic to which they had not referred. 'God made them male and female' – but why should they therefore not divorce each other? It has even been suggested that Mark's Jesus agreed with those of his Jewish contemporaries who thought that God's 'earth-creature' was a hermaphrodite, uniting both sexes in one. Later, the Christian author of the First Epistle to Timothy cited the Eden story to justify status for Christian women. 'I suffer not a woman to teach, nor to usurp authority over the man' (I Timothy 2:12). Adam was superior because he was formed before Eve; Eve was deceived, whereas Adam was not. Here, the author quoted only from the second story; in the other, it is not clear that man was created first. He also distorted it: Eve was deceived first, but, on a reasonable view, she beguiled Adam, who transgressed too. According to the epistle, woman could be saved through childbearing. However, Genesis does not say anything comparable. Rather, it describes the pangs of childbirth and fertility as a punishment for Eve's disobedience.

These texts were creating new scripture by constructive abuse of the old, a process which reaches a climax in the letters ascribed to Paul. At Ephesians 5:31–2 the author inclined to believe that the union of man and woman ('one flesh') was a mysterious reference to the union of Christ and his Church; this hidden meaning is not at all in Genesis. At Romans 5:12–18 Paul himself tells his Roman Christians how through one man, Adam, sin 'entered into the world' and by the sin of one man death reigned too. These famous verses have inspired whole theories of sin and original sin which have changed many Christians' perspective on human nature. It seems clear that the Fall of Adam and Eve was not just the moral tale of a single couple's fate: the story was meant to be the origin of a change for all subsequent humans. It is not, however, stated that what originated was sin or sinfulness, words which occur nowhere in the Hebrew text. It was St Augustine who ended by arguing that original sin had been transmitted to each of us through Adam, a view which he backed up by Paul's language in Romans 5. However, he followed a mistranslation of it, based only on a Latin version of the text. Paul's Greek had merely said that 'death passed upon all men, because [in that] all sinned'; Augustine followed an author who mistook it to say 'death passed upon all men because of Adam, [in whom] all sinned . . .' Original sin was read unnecessarily into Genesis and was then forced on to Paul by a wrong translation of his writings.

In Genesis, nothing prevents us from thinking that Adam and Eve from the start of their lives had been expected to make love, reproduce and eventually die. After sentencing them, God tells Adam that he will sweat for a living until 'thou return unto the ground; for out of it wast thou taken: for dust thou art, and unto dust shalt thou return'. Toil, not death, is to be his punishment; death had always been part of the couple's dusty nature, and even now, it befalls them only after long years outside Eden. Through Adam toil is added to man's work, the toil of hoeing, weeding and back-breaking labour on every plot of ground. Through Eve come woman's pains of childbirth. The two of them transgress by disobeying and eating from the tree of knowledge: 'disobedience: man's original virtue', remarked Oscar Wilde. They are expelled from Eden not in order to die, but so that they will not go on to further crimes and taste the tree of life (Genesis 3:22). Through Adam and Eve's misconduct, we are not condemned to death. We are condemned to hard gardening and painful childbirth; we are also denied the chance of stealing eternal life.

'Every commentator,' remarked Voltaire, 'makes his own Eden.' In Christian hands, the story looks forward from Adam's sin to Christ's redemption or the parallelisms which are expressed in Christian art, between Adam's naming of the beasts and early Christian miracles, or

Adam and Eve's expulsion and the Annunciation to Mary, the modest second Eve. Sexuality, however, has continued to slip falsely into the story's gaps. The fruit of the tree was an aphrodisiac, in Augustine's opinion, and caused sexual lust to conquer our will. Many artists, including Dürer, placed a cat, about to pounce, beneath the tree from which our parents ate; cats (respected by Muslims) had become symbols of sexual desire in early Christian literature. We have to think away long centuries of later theology to see Adam and Eve in Eden as Rembrandt drew them: earthy, rugged humans, not childlike creatures without any sexual knowledge.

When pressed to the letter, the story is unfair to serpents and women, let alone to cats and apples (the fruit is not specified). 'Who sinned?' wrote John Donne, aware of the paradox. 'T'was not forbidden to the snake/Nor her, who was not then made' (God's prohibition to eat of the tree is not addressed to the serpent; it also occurs before Eve has been created from Adam's rib). Yet a woman's subordinate desire for her husband is one of the punishments for the Fall. In seventeenth-century England, women were encouraged to ask forgiveness in their prayers for the sins of Eve. A similar prayer is still demanded from Jewish women by one minority group in Israel.

The opening chapters of Genesis do not meet the requirement that truth should cohere: they are made up from two contradictory sources. They do not correspond to the facts, for we now know more of the age of the world, the fact of its evolution and the process which stretched beyond six days of work or a garden of greenery near the Euphrates River: our Eve has been traced back to Africa, while Adam is imagined as a pygmy. Totally untrue, the stories have been cited untruly to make yet more scripture, but they continue to be an arena for the imagination. In the sixteenth century Canterbury's cathedral was emptied of its relics and lost its handful of the dust from which Adam was created. But the stories still speak to modern interests, to the relation of mankind and the animals, the rights of men and women, the explanation of stories round pivotal or underlying themes. Ecology, feminism and the structuralist study of myth: each new intellectual interest finds matter in Genesis. For the Bible never says that Eden was destroyed: somewhere, it may be out there, alive in gardens of the mind. In India there is a tree known as Eve's apple which bears yellow fruits with a dent in them, as if someone has taken a bite, then stopped. Gardens, meanwhile, require constant weeding, and childbirth can still be extremely painful.

III

The Creation of the world was an old and uncertain subject, but the New Testament begins with the birth of Jesus, the start of a new era which is very much nearer to its Gospels' date. The details of the first Christmas seem very specific. We hear them each year as Christian lessons, Herod, Bethlehem and that seasonal nightmare, a 'decree . . . that all the world should be taxed': the taxing included a poll tax. The little town of Bethlehem has grown as a place of pilgrimage, and in many Churches the story is read out as the 'word of the Lord'.

The story is not present in every one of the Gospels. Mark's begins with Jesus's baptism and omits any story or dating of the Nativity. John's is equally reticent. Of the other two, Matthew's connects Jesus's birth with the later years of King Herod the Great and locates it in Bethlehem, while Luke's connects the Annunciation with the reign of King Herod and the Nativity with Bethlehem and a specific event. 'And it came to pass in those days, that there went out a decree from Caesar Augustus, that all the world should be taxed. And this taxing was first made when Quirinius was governor of Syria.'

King Herod and Quirinius, Augustus and the taxing of the world, are people and matters which relate to the contemporary Roman Empire and the evidence of its non-Christian histories, coins and inscriptions. Whereas scientists have tested the stories of Creation to see if they correspond to the facts, it is for historians to test the stories of the Nativity to see if they correspond to historical truth. It is not that there was no Nativity or that Jesus was not a historical person. The question is merely whether the Gospels' stories knew when and where he was born. This question was decisively answered by a Christian minister, Emil Schuerer, in his massive *History of the Jewish People* which began to appear in 1885. What Schuerer demonstrated still underlies all informed discussion of the truth. There have been many attempts to evade it since 1885, but when Schuerer's great work was revised in a new English edition in 1973, its two eminent revisers answered these attempts in their supporting notes and correctly left his main discussion of the Nativity unchanged.

The difficulty begins on one small point but spreads from it, like dry rot, to bring larger constructions to the ground. Quirinius, the governor of Syria whom Luke's Gospel mentions, is known from a careful history of affairs in Judaea which was compiled by Josephus, an educated Jew, writing in Greek at Rome between *c.* 75 and *c.* 80. Josephus had his own prejudices and areas of interest, but he worked with a framework of hard facts which were freely available for checking and which he had collected responsibly. According to Josephus, Quirinius was governor of Syria with authority over Judaea in AD 6, when the province was brought under direct Roman control. The year was a critical moment in Jewish history, as important to its province as the year 1972 to Northern Ireland, the start of direct rule. On such a fact, at such a moment, Josephus and his sources cannot be brushed aside. There is, however, an awkward problem. Luke's Gospel links Jesus's birth with Quirinius and with King Herod, but in AD 6 Herod had long disappeared. He had died soon after an eclipse of the moon which is dated by astronomers to 12–13 March 4 BC, although a minority of scholars have argued for 5 BC instead.

The Gospel, therefore, assumes that Quirinius and King Herod were contemporaries, when they were separated by ten years or more. There is no doubt about the Herod in question. When the great King Herod died, his kingdom was split between his sons, two of whom did add Herod to their names. Herod Antipas ruled locally in Galilee as a tetrarch until 39, but Luke 1:5 connects the Annunciation with Herod 'king of Judaea': when he refers to Herod Antipas at 3:1, he correctly calls him tetrarch, not king. Herod Archelaus ruled Judaea until AD 6, but only as an ethnarch: like Matthew 2:22, Luke might have misdescribed him as king, but, like Matthew, he would have called him Archelaus or Herod Archelaus. At 1:5 the Herod must be the great King Herod, just as Matthew's Gospel describes. In Matthew the Nativity coincides with the great Herod, Massacrer of the Innocents, whose death is a reason for the return from the Flight into Egypt.

Luke's Gospel, therefore, assumes that King Herod and the governor Quirinius were contemporaries, but they were separated by ten years or more. The incoherent dating is only the start of the problem. Luke's Nativity story hinges on its 'decree from Caesar Augustus that all the world should be taxed'. 'Caesar Augustus' was the Roman Emperor, but if the Nativity took place in the reign of King Herod the Great, the Jews were still Herod's subjects, members of a client kingdom, not a province under direct Roman rule. The status of client-kings in the Roman Empire left them responsibility for their subjects' taxation. Relations between the Emperor Augustus and King Herod had often been stormy and had even led to threats of Roman interference which Herod and his envoys had had to avert. However, their conflicts never caused the removal of Herod's royal status, although this was the only way in which his kingdom could have been taxed on the Roman model in accordance with orders from the Roman Emperor. It is not just that Herod the Great never coincided with Quirinius the governor: he never coincided with a Roman taxing of Judaea.

It is even doubtful if the Emperor Augustus ever issued a decree to Rome's provinces that 'all the world should be taxed'. Certainly, Romans did take censuses in individual provinces which were ruled directly by their governors. They were not, however, co-ordinated by an order from Augustus to all the world, at least so far as our evidence goes. As that evidence extends through histories, local inscriptions and the papyrus returns of tax-payers in Egypt, it is immensely unlikely that a new edict of such consequence has escaped our knowledge. In AD 6 we do know that Augustus was enacting a new tax on inheritance to help pay for his armies; however, the tax affected only Roman citizens, not Jews of Nazareth, and there was no need for a worldwide census to register their names.

In Judaea under Quirinius, we know from Josephus's histories of something more appropriate, not a worldwide decree but a local census in AD 6 to assess Judaea when the province passed from rule by Herod's family to direct rule by Rome. Although this census was local, it caused a notorious outcry, not least because some of the Jews argued that the innovation was contrary to scripture and the will of God. According to the third Gospel, the census which took Joseph to Bethlehem was 'the first while Quirinius was governor of Syria'. Quirinius's census was indeed the first, but it belonged in AD 6 when King Herod, the story's other marker, was long since dead.

Since the nineteenth century, there have been attempts to evade the meaning of the third Gospel's Greek: 'This census was the first, while Quirinius was governor of Syria' is twisted into 'This census was held before the one which Quirinius, governor of Syria, held'. Nobody has ever entertained this translation for non-doctrinal reasons: it is not true to the Greek, let alone the clear Greek of the third Gospel. An alternative is to try to impugn Josephus. However, he is certainly correct to date Judaea's first census in A D 6: we know independently from the well-informed historian Dio (a Roman senator, writing *c.* 200–220) that the last Jewish ruler in Judaea, Herod's son Archelaus, was banished in that year; the province passed to direct rule by Rome and a census belongs properly with this change in a region's status. Josephus's most detailed account of the census of A D 6 is in his massive work on *Jewish Antiquities* (18:1), a book of great erudition which was published in 93/4 and was not distorted on this detail for any known personal or political end.

The error, so far, might seem rather marginal. The third Gospel has confused a local census in Judaea with a worldwide decree from Augustus; it has tried to date the story by an obscure Quirinius, whereas elsewhere, like Matthew's, its story takes place under Herod the Great. In fact, the trouble goes very much deeper. There is a contradiction in Luke's story: if Quirinius was governor, the Roman census is credible but Herod is a mistake. There is also a contradiction with Matthew's story: if Quirinius or the Roman census is correct, Herod was not king and Matthew's stories of the Wise Men, the Massacre of the Innocents and the Flight into Egypt are all chronologically impossible. If Herod was king, there could have been no census according to Caesar Augustus. Even if there had been such a census, the third Gospel's view of it runs into further problems.

Its decree from Caesar required registration (*apographé*, in Greek). Exactly this word is used for a tax census in contemporary documents which have survived from Egypt under Roman rule. An emperor would not be imagined to have registered his Jewish subjects for any other purpose. He was certainly not planning conscription: Jews were exempt from military service in the Roman army. Tax, certainly, caused the census, but the practices of Roman taxation do not agree with the Gospel's narrative. Correctly, it begins by explaining that 'all went to be taxed, every one into his own city' (Luke 2:3). Joseph's 'own city' is defined in the Gospel by his supposed ancestry, not by his residence and ownership of property. In the Gospel's view, Joseph was descended from David, and so he went to Bethlehem, the 'city of David', a proper birth-place for a future Messiah. However, Roman censuses cared nothing for remote genealogies, let alone for false ones: they were based on ownership of property by the living, not the dead. As the Gospel has already stated at the time of the Annunciation (Luke 1:26), Joseph and Mary were people of Nazareth in Galilee, the home town which later rejected its prophet, Jesus. A Roman census would not have taken Joseph to Bethlehem where he and Mary owned nothing and were therefore assumed to have needed to lodge as visitors at an inn. There was a sound reason for the Romans' type of registration. The census was their base for at least two types of tax: a poll tax and a tax on property of various kinds. There was not even a legal need for Mary to go and register with her betrothed husband. We know from the evidence of Roman tax censuses in Egypt, still surviving on papyrus, that one householder could make the return for everyone in his care. Mary might have chosen to go anyway, in order to give Joseph support, but it was not a necessary journey for a wife who was terminally pregnant.

Above all, it was not a journey which a Galilaean, a man of Nazareth, would have been required to make. In AD 6 Galilee, unlike Judaea, had remained under its independent ruler and would not have been bound by a Roman census or taxing. This ruler's existence is known from Josephus, other histories and his own coins: as a Galilaean, Joseph of Nazareth was exempt from the entire business.

The scale of the Gospel's error is now clear. The first census did occur under Quirinius, but it belonged in AD 6 when Herod the Great was long dead; it was a local census in Roman Judaea and there was no decree from Caesar Augustus to all the world; in AD 6 Joseph of Nazareth would not have registered at Bethlehem: as a Galilaean he was not under direct Roman rule and was exempt from Judaea's registration; his wife had no legal need to leave home. Luke's story is historically impossible and internally incoherent. It clashes with his own date for the Annunciation (which he places under Herod) and with Matthew's long story of the Nativity which also presupposes Herod the Great as king. It is, therefore, false.

Luke's errors and contradictions are easily explained. Early Christian tradition did not remember, or perhaps ever know, exactly where and when Jesus had been born. People were much more interested in his death and its consequences. As the Messiah, Jesus was connected to the line of King David, a connection which was known before the writing of any of our Gospels, as it is mentioned by the Apostle Paul (Romans 1:3). In the Hebrew scriptures, Bethlehem was famous as the home of the young David, the future king; the town was also the subject of a prophecy by Micah in the later eighth century BC: 'But thou, Bethlehem, though thou be little among the thousands of Judah, yet out of thee shall he come forth unto me that is to be ruler in Israel' (Micah 5:2). After the Crucifixion and the belief in the Resurrection, people wondered all the more deeply about Jesus's birthplace. Bethlehem, home of King David, was a natural choice for the new Messiah. There was even a prophecy in support of the claim which the 'little town' has maintained so profitably to this day.

It is easy to sympathize with the third Gospeller's plight. He had not been present at the earliest days of Jesus's mission, as he admits in his opening sentence. He was writing from what he had heard perhaps thirty years or so after Jesus's death, although many scholars would date his books even later. He knew that Joseph and Mary were people of Nazareth, but there were Christians who said that Jesus had been born in Bethlehem, according to the scripture. Why would a man from Nazareth be visiting Bethlehem with his heavily pregnant wife? Somebody, perhaps the Gospeller himself, assumed that the cause was that universal culprit, personal tax. The census of Quirinius was a landmark in Jewish history, and so the Gospel attached the birth in Bethlehem to this well-known fact. The idea had its advantages: the Christian story could begin with Joseph and Mary meekly obeying the orders of Roman government. This origin showed the true nature of a religion which people in the Roman Empire had since misunderstood as a revolutionary movement. The decree, the Gospeller assumed, was not just the edict of a local governor: it was the worldwide decree of the Caesar himself, an exaggeration which was not out of keeping with his misuse of words like 'all' or 'everywhere' at other points in his books. He was writing for a highly placed Gentile, Theophilus, in the Roman world. It was good to begin with connections between his story and Roman government; a higher truth was served by an impossible fiction.

Matthew's Gospel took a different course. Like Luke's, it reported the birth in Bethlehem, but it confined its dating to King Herod's reign and reconciled the story of the birth at Bethlehem with Jesus's known origin in Nazareth by a tax-free route. Joseph, Jesus and Mary, it said, fled into Egypt to escape Herod's Massacre of the Innocents; when they returned, they avoided Bethlehem and Judaea because these places were too unsafe. Instead, they went north into Galilee, took up residence in Nazareth and conformed to the tradition that Nazareth was Jesus's home town. The story is coherent in itself, although it conflicts hopelessly with Luke's. It has, however, attracted historians and scientists by its mention of a curious Star: can we support its birth-date under King Herod by appealing to astronomy and working backwards from the probable date of Jesus's death?

Jesus was crucified under Pontius Pilate, who governed Judaea between 26 and late 36. According to Luke, the 'word of God' came to John the Baptist in 28/9, a date which is given precisely: the Gospel does not, however, say that this year was the beginning of Jesus's own ministry. Rather, it tells how John the Baptist was imprisoned by Antipas, ruler of Galilee: the Baptist had criticized Antipas's marriage to Herodias, his sister-in-law. It was after this arrest that Jesus's ministry began (Mark 1:14 agrees).

The marriage of Antipas and Herodias, therefore, is a key date in Jesus's career. Josephus wrote about it in some detail in his *Jewish Antiquities*. Antipas's brother Philip died in 33/4; Josephus then tells of Antipas's journey to Rome (probably to plead for Philip's territory) and his entanglement en route with Herodias, who can be calculated to have been a mature woman in her forties (Mark's Gospel informs us that Herodias had been married to Philip, a point which Josephus ignores). On Antipas's return, he planned to dismiss his existing wife, a daughter of the powerful King Aretas IV who ruled from Petra beyond the Jordan. The girl fled to her father and told him of Antipas's intention; King Aretas gathered an army, invaded a part of the territory of Philip (presumably because Philip was dead) and won a crushing victory over the army which Antipas sent to oppose him. Reports of the defeat reached Rome, perhaps in dispatches from Antipas himself. Eventually the Emperor Tiberius ordered reprisals against Aretas which were under way in early 37.

Josephus's story assumes that Antipas's marriage followed Philip's death, an event which he dates firmly to 33/4. His account of its sequel is coherent, and its importance has recently been stressed by a historian of Herod's family, Nikos Kokkinos, who has also explored its effects on the dates of Jesus's career. Conventionally, Jesus's Crucifixion is either put in 30 or, more usually, 33. However, if Josephus was right, John the Baptist cannot have been arrested until late 33/4; Mark and Luke connect the arrest with the start of Jesus's public ministry; Jesus, therefore, began to teach early in 34. The fourth Gospel mentions three Passovers during Jesus's ministry, on the third of which Jesus was arrested: we can now see that these three were the only three. Jesus was crucified on Friday, 30 March A D 36 (Passover was fixed by the new moon, and in 36 the dates for it are not an obstacle).

How old was he at the time? According to Luke, Jesus was 'about thirty' when he began his ministry (in A D 34, we now infer). However, John 8:57 suggests something else. After the second Passover of the ministry (A D 35) Jews in Jerusalem reprove Jesus because he implies that he has seen Abraham: 'Thou art not yet fifty years old, and hast thou seen Abraham?' they ask. The number had no special meaning (people over fifty were no more likely to see Abraham than anyone else): here John's Gospel hints that Jesus was aged between forty and fifty, perhaps nearer fifty, in A D 35.

The two suggestions of Jesus's age are contradictory; Luke's also conflicts with a birth-date under Herod (in A D 34, the ministry's first year, Jesus would not be 'about thirty' but at least thirty-eight or 'about forty'). What if John's Gospel is well informed? Then the birth-date would go back to a point between 14 and (say) 10 B C: is there a place here, perhaps, for Matthew's Star? According to the Gospel, it guided the Wise Men and appeared to stand over Bethlehem. It was a single star, therefore, and not a conjunction of planets; it was not strictly a new star, because it was moving, not fixed. If we take Matthew's language literally, it could refer to a single comet, a phenomenon which the ancients observed quite often. In 12 B C we know independently that a comet was seen over the city of Rome during the autumn when Marcus Agrippa, the famous Roman commander, died. We also have Chinese astronomical records which date back to the first century A D and refer to observations in previous years. Here, too, the appearance of a comet has been adduced for 12 B C. Comets can be large and bright; astronomers have fixed the comet of 12 B C as a large and bright appearance of Halley's comet, which was last seen in 1985/6.

In 12 BC Herod's Temple was finished; Halley's comet appeared brilliantly and was seen in Rome; the fourth Gospel (8:57) assumes that Jesus was well into his forties in a year which we can fix as AD 35. Should we, perhaps, equate the Star with the comet, place the Nativity in 12 BC and explain the Wise Men as envoys from Parthia who were visiting Jerusalem for a celebration of the new Temple? At John 2:21 the Jews appeal to their Temple, now forty-six years old: they did not realize, the Gospel tells us, that Jesus had been referring them to his own body. The date was AD 34: was Jesus, like the Temple, aged forty-six at the time?

These attempts are seductive, but they rest on a false view of Matthew's story: it has not grown up from history, and it is not bringing a genuine comet and genuine Eastern envoys on a diversion to Bethlehem during the year of their real appearance in Judaea. The Star was not a comet but a miraculous phenomenon which travelled before the visitors and stood over one 'little town'. Bethlehem was not Jesus's birthplace but was imported from Hebrew prophecies about the future Messiah; the Star itself had a similar origin. At Numbers 24:17 the prophet Balaam predicts that 'a star shall come forth out of Jacob, and a sceptre shall rise out of Israel'. We know that this prophecy was a famous text for a new Messiah: in the 130s a prominent Jew used it to acclaim the Jewish leader in a war against Rome. Nobody had sighted a comet then. Matthew's story is a construction from well-known messianic prophecies (Bethlehem; the Star), and the Wise Men have been added as another legend.

We are left with an uncertain birth-date, an exact day for the Crucifixion and a Jesus who may have been middle aged when he began to teach. Already in the mid second century there were Christian elders in Asia who agreed with the implications of John's Gospel and put Jesus's age nearer fifty than forty: if Jesus was born under Herod, Luke's notion that he began his ministry when 'about thirty' is wrong. Instead, before Jesus's first miracle at Cana stretch long decades of youth and maturity. On our present knowledge, it was most unusual for a Jew to have remained unmarried in his mid forties, except in the inner group of one known sect, the Essenes, who idealized celibacy. Did Jesus's sense of mission dawn on him rather late, and if so, what had he done with the best years of other men's lives? The forties, it seems, are a fertile decade for religious history: it was then, outside Mecca, that an angel began to speak to Muhammad.

A middle-aged Jesus, crucified in his late forties, an expulsion from Eden not for sex but for fear that humans would steal eternal life: these readings are true to texts in the Bible, but they challenge many centuries of contrary interpretation. Yet as they stand, the stories of the Creation and the Nativity are untrue: they do not correspond to the facts or cohere between themselves. We can argue with renewed confidence for the date when Jesus died (March 36), but, like early Christians, we do not know exactly when or where he was born. By *c.* 200 there were Christians who argued that the birth had occurred in November 3 BC (miscalculating the date of King Herod's death), while others argued for mid May or mid April (the date of conception, others maintained).

Not until the mid fourth century AD are Christians known to have been celebrating Christmas on 25 December. Previously, the date had marked a pagan festival, the birth of the sun god at the winter solstice. It was a deliberate retort by Christians in the western parts of the Roman Empire to choose the date as a festival of the birth of their new god, Christ. Not every Christian agreed. In the eastern part of the empire, other Christians fixed the date of the Nativity as 6 January, the time of another great pagan festival. If the pagans were having a huge household holiday, the Christians, still a minority, needed one, too, to keep their members to their own celebrations. Christmas, therefore, settled down in our calendar not through certainty but through conflict, in a battle of festivals between the Christians and the pagan majority among whom they lived.

Where the truth had been lost, stories filled the gap, and the desire to know fabricated its own tradition. Luke told a tale of angels and shepherds, bringing some of the humblest people in society to Bethlehem with news of Jesus's future; shepherds ranked about as low as fishermen in Roman social relations, but they did have the simple charm of a pastoral world. Instead of shepherds, Matthew brought Wise Men, following a Star in the East and bringing gifts of gold, frankincense and myrrh. In one version, there are simple shepherds, in the other, learned Wise Men: the contrast sets our imaginations free, and perhaps like the Wise Men we too should return by 'another way'.

Matthew said little about these Wise Men, but they blossomed through his reticence and took on a life of their own. Their three gifts implied that they had been three in number, but there were Christians in the Eastern Churches who believed that they had been twelve: supporters of the threesome argued that each of the three visitors had had a separate vision, seeing one person each of the Trinity. By *c*. 200 Christian authors had already begun to upgrade the Wise Men from academics into kings or courtiers; early Christian mosaics and wall paintings show their adoration of Jesus on the model of barbarian envoys who offer golden crowns to a Roman emperor. In art, their dress begins to suggest envoys from the Persian Empire, but two of their gifts, myrrh-trees and bushes of frankincense, are native to Arabia; some early Christian readers therefore believed that the Wise Men must have been Arabs who travelled from Arabia up to Jerusalem. Not until the sixth century do we know of names for the three of them: they were found recently in a ruined church of that date at Faras in Egypt. Was their gift of myrrh a medicine or did it look forwards to the myrrh with which Jesus's corpse was embalmed (John 19:39)? As for the gold, was it Arabian gold from the Queen of Sheba's treasures, from the cave, perhaps, of Seth, Adam's son, or the treasure of Alexander the Great? The golden age for Magi-hunters was the century from 1150 to 1250. During it, one king was allotted to each of the world's known continents; the king, therefore, from Africa began to be shown as a black man. At the same time the kings multiplied their known addresses. Bits of their bodies were believed to have been discovered in Milan, but in 1164 they were transported to Cologne: a shrine of the Three Kings is still visible there at the great cathedral's altar. Out in the East, meanwhile, people thought they knew better. In 1272, when Marco Polo made his way to China, he visited one of the Persian towns where the Wise Men of the Orient were said to be buried; at Saveh, south-west of Tehran, they lay, he wrote, 'in three very large and beautiful monuments with a square building above them, carefully maintained. Their bodies are still intact with hair and beards remaining.' Saveh was a great seat of Islamic astronomers, an apt resting-place for Matthew's legendary Magi, who were following their Star. Three days' journey from Saveh lay a castle where one of them was said to have lived. Its village was Zoroastrian, but this claim connected it to the Christian story.

In 1986 two young British travellers checked the tomb-towers of

Saveh, but 'none of the surviving buildings fitted Polo's description'. In the free space around the Wise Men or Eden's tree of life, our minds can continue to wander in approximation, from Persia to Cologne or from Eve's Indian apple to the greenery of Venezuela. In the Christmas story the shepherds and 'no room at the inn' conform to the ideal of humility which belongs with the Christian Messiah. Before the brute facts of death, the image of man as a compound of earth and eternal breath retains its symbolic power: the animating breath ceases while the earthly form remains with the dead. The stories do not confine us, although nothing happened as they narrate.

Believed to be true, they turn out to be false, but the outcome does not ruin religious faith. The inconsistencies in Genesis and the contradictions in Jesus's earthly origin have perplexed readers for centuries without destroying their belief. In his youth, St Augustine was turned away from Christianity, in part because of the contradictions between Luke's and Matthew's family trees for Jesus: he moved to a system of belief which took the stories of Creation as texts which could not be true literally, but had deeper hidden meanings. Yet he returned to the Christian faith and in later life wrote a massive work on Genesis, upholding its truth 'to the letter'.

Instead, these problems concern the Bible, not the presence or absence of faith. It is an unusual book which begins with two contradictory stories and with a narrative whose time and place are false. For centuries that book has been read as the source of truth, the rule of faith, 'holy writ', not merely text. It is the aim of this book to explore the labyrinth which the notion of biblical truth still opens before its readers.

2

The Unerring Word

The truth of the Bible's two beginnings is not a new discovery. In ancient times, people noticed many of these contradictions and tried to explain them; during the nineteenth century, the stories of Creation and the Nativity were shown by Darwin and Schuerer not to correspond to the facts. However, they are still not widely familiar. Most of us know about evolution or problems of the virgin birth, but the making of the book of Genesis is not popular knowledge, let alone the problems of Luke's Roman census and its dates. I now wish to show why these questions are still important. They bear on a misdescription of scripture: that misdescription, in turn, affects the Bible's status, implying that it is no longer special to us if it is anything less. This needs to be cleared up, because its correction opens wider horizons into which we can then move more freely.

Over the ages, many people have believed that scripture is the unerring word of God. Like most Jews of his time, Josephus believed that the Hebrew scriptures were the divinely inspired truth: he even persuaded himself that they were a harmonious whole. It is coincidental, and not part of his purpose, that he gave us details which brought to light errors in the Christians' third Gospel. Christians were also very confident: in the 90s an unknown Christian, author of an epistle from Rome to Corinth, stated that 'the scriptures are true utterances of the Holy Spirit', while the great Christian author and bishop, Irenaeus of Lyons, was even more forthright: 'The scriptures are perfect', he wrote in the 170s, 'because they were uttered by the Word of God and his Spirit.' The belief that as God's word, scripture never errs has been prominent in evangelical Christianity since the nineteenth century, with important consequences for the uses of scripture in Christian missions throughout the world.

As a subtitle for scripture, 'God's unerring word' sounds very impressive, but it becomes awkward as soon as we try to envisage it. The idea that God uses our language, that he dictates like a human and that the process is still with us in an accurate text is not exactly obvious. The 'word of God' might seem a slightly less peculiar description for certain bits of scripture, the prophets, perhaps, or the Gospels. The prophets, after all, do claim to be speaking the word of the Lord in particular verses, while the Gospels do claim to report the sayings of Jesus whom they describe as God's son. However, God's word is a much less apt description of a book like Judges or Ruth or the Song of Songs. The idea that all scripture is not just God's word but his unerring word requires a very close connection between God and our text. As scripture is a text, not a broadcast, there is only one connection which is strong enough: actual dictation by God. During the Reformation, there were Christians in the sixteenth century who did go so far as to champion this extreme idea. It still confronts us in Christian art of the period, where the authors of the Gospels are shown not merely as witnesses at the Ascension, with their books, pens and ink. They are copying down exactly what the Holy Spirit tells them: an angel, even, guides their hand across the page.

Belief in dictation does no justice to the authors, the origins or the contents of biblical books. It also entails that God tells lies: the Bible, as we have already seen, is not always true. Without it, God's word becomes a loose metaphor for the text which we read: if we press the metaphor too closely, it becomes absurd and if we do not press it, the metaphor means no more than 'God's gift' means to some people as a way of referring to twins or a good harvest or an exceptional year for their business. Without 'God's word', 'unerring' is left to stand on its own merits. It, too, might seem a label which is not worth pressing, but it has to be sorted out before we go further because it still has articulate champions. They are nowadays classed as fundamentalists, and they might otherwise overshadow our explorations.

Fundamentalists, in this strict sense, are widely misunderstood. They do not maintain that everything in the Bible is literally true, as if Adam really lived for hundreds of years or the world was created in only six days. Rather, they argue that when properly understood, the Bible is never in error. They attach this view to the belief that the Bible is inspired by God, a belief which they also base on a few texts within it. They cite particular verses about 'inspired scripture' which they interpret to suit their own views and extend them as a description of the entire Bible, as if the Bible is proven to be inspired because one bit of it (arguably) says so. Christian fundamentalists also cite Jesus as their authority, as if the Gospels show him accepting that the entire body of our scripture is inspired and never in error. None of their proof-texts can bear such weight, but strict fundamentalists support them by a further tactic. If the Bible seems incredible, it must mean something else: the hundreds of years of Adam's life must include the years between Adam and the next event in Genesis's story; the six days of Creation are six phases or six long aeons, despite their explicit mention of mornings and evenings.

Confronted with these claims, many people try to explain fundamentalists themselves as something else: they seem to be reactionaries against liberalism or modern change or Western culture or conformists to social or psychological truths about themselves. However, their claims for scripture do attach to a much older pedigree, whatever their motives or reasons for holding them. Unerring scripture requires the acceptance of allegory, the belief that a text may appear to say one thing while meaning another. This belief goes back across two thousand years, when it was also combined with the fundamental belief that scripture is inspired. In the third century A D it was beautifully explained to the great Christian scholar Origen by a Jew who joined his study groups: 'all the divinely inspired writing, because of its obscurity, is like many locked rooms in a house. Beside each room lies a key which does not fit it . . . the greatest task is to find the keys and fit the right one to the room which it can open.' Origen himself was a most assiduous doorkeeper, forcing allegorical keys into some very resistant locks. With their help, he found totally new meanings beneath the literal sense of biblical language.

We now see this search for hidden meanings as a way of saving the credit of an inconvenient text. Allegories, however, are present in our Bible itself: Paul sometimes used them (Galatians 4:24 ff.), and Jesus is credited with a fine one in the parable of the Wicked Tenants who kill the landlord's only beloved son (Mark 12:1–12); the deeper reference, surely, is to himself. Scripture does not always mean what its surface appears to say. It has a rich vein of metaphor, parable and imagery which stretches our imagination; sometimes there is no single meaning to its open-ended language. It is insensitive, then, to object to all allegory on principle and to all uses of it in understanding scripture, although Luther and Christians of the Reformation did object to allegory in this way. The objection, rather, is to allegorical explanations where no allegory exists. Like Origen and many of his heirs, strict fundamentalists look for hidden meanings when the text does not require them. Like Origen, they believe that the entire text is inspired, but they handle it much less delicately. Origen did not deny that often scripture meant what it appeared to say: there might, however, be more to it, the hidden soul in its body whose discernment required God's grace and a pure and faithful heart. Deeper meanings, like God himself, do not appear to everyone: the search for them is part of a serious religious quest, taxing to the participants and questioned, too, by contemporaries.

For Origen, scripture had a deeper meaning even when it made literal sense. For a strict fundamentalist, it has a different meaning only when it does not appear to make literal sense at all. Both types of reading are misguided, because they force on to scripture a type of meaning which it never had. Origen's, however, was part of a consistent mysticism whose search was not merely a defence against common sense: he believed that through it, God brought men closer to himself. God revealed himself in scripture, just as once, he revealed himself to the world in Christ.

Fundamentalists are not concerned with this mysticism but with the question of truth and error. It is here that the old discoveries, the problems of Genesis and Bethlehem, remain acutely relevant. It might seem that they are superfluous because the literal truth of all scripture has been broken once and for all by science. Unerring scripture has foundered on the truth of evolution and on scores of subsequent discoveries, to the point where fundamentalism ought to have joined the fossils as an outmoded relic from the past. Most remarkably, it has survived and re-emerged. The challenge of evolution has become so familiar that it has simply been sidestepped or ignored. In the face of it, fundamentalism has held to its principles and, far from being swept away, has profited from a tide which was set up by science's own success.

Science has its philosophers and alert practitioners, but it has also encouraged belief that authoritative information is true and certain knowledge. Text books set it out; experiments show it, and if any one example conflicts with an accepted experiment, it must be revised, repeated or repositioned in order not to conflict with the accepted truth. In history, a counter-example weakens a generalization, but in science, many generalizations are too secure to be shaken by one freak result: if the water does not boil once when we have switched on the kettle, we assume that there must be something wrong with the kettle or the power-supply, not with the laws of heat. Fundamentalists start with one generalization, that the inspired scriptures never err, and they seem quite scientific when they reinterpret examples which patently do not fit their law.

In our modern house of science there are many mansions, but those who are outside the building, or locked into one small room of it, can easily work with the view that what a reputable text has informed us is simply true. Among philosophies of science, doubt still flourishes marvellously, while the relations of text, truth and reader have never been more disputed among literary critics. However, our general culture lies not in these fields but with practical science, where technology is true because it works; doubt, therefore, has not kept pace with the growth of information in the late twentieth century.

As a result, fundamentalism can still appeal to people who have been brought up in a scientific culture: it is not primitive or medieval or third world. It is also thriving in the technological West. If people assume that science is aiming at certainty, they feel at home with the fundamental view that scripture, too, is never in error. If they are reacting against science's claims, whether out of nationalism or moral conservatism or mental laziness, they are happy to uphold the scriptures as an alternative source of the certainty which science is popularly believed to claim. This way of thinking gives a particular responsibility to the older key to biblical understanding: historical, not scientific, criticism.

Fundamentalists also try to exploit historical types of knowledge. The easiest point of contact is archaeology, where history appears to make most use of science and where the evidence appears to be direct and therefore unambiguous. Archaeology confronts its public without any barrier of language, and as its public grows, fundamentalists find ever more scope for invoking its finds as proof that the Bible's narrative is true. Particular examples are used to spread a general belief that all scripture could be confirmed if only we could dig up its relics. Written evidence is more obstinate. Once again, fundamentalists emphasize those texts outside the Bible which confirm names, places and events in parts of its story. They then imply that these examples hold good for it all. If not, they query the worth of the dissenting evidence: there is less of a popular belief that historians, rather than scientists, can come up with the final truth. This doubt, naturally, is not turned back against the biblical authors themselves.

Historical study, therefore, has a double duty to scripture: it has to assess the use which fundamentalists make of its own evidence and on a wider, more challenging front it has to try to appreciate scripture for what it is. We have already seen its potential value. By itself, historical study refutes fundamentalism and puts one entire wing of modern biblicism out of action. Scripture is not God's word in any strong sense, nor is it unerring, with the possible exception of a few trivial facts. These claims collapse not on tiny details of the age of Methuselah or the possible sacking of Jericho, but on something as central as the story of the Nativity, where neither Matthew nor Luke knew the truth. Strict fundamentalism, therefore, is false, and we can move forward, without being overshadowed by it.

If scripture is not the unerring word, what is it? Beguiling possibilities open beyond this question and are not to be stifled by appealing to the history of a Church of believers and stopping with the view that they have given scripture a binding authority. The texts were written before Church or Bible existed; they can be read, understood and valued by those who belong to no Church or particular nation. It is as a historian that I will explore them here: my answer is unauthorized not because Jewish or Christian scholars have tried to suppress it (some of them would find it decidedly traditional), but because the Bible itself does not proclaim it. If anything, it hides its origins under false clues.

From the history of scripture I will turn to scripture as history: does the truth of the Bible lie in the events to which it refers? We have external evidence, found by archaeologists or preserved in non-biblical writings: samples of it suggest a mutual relationship which is far from fundamental or of one, simple type. If not in events, does the truth lie with biblical authors and the ways in which they have written their narrative? From scripture as history to scripture as story, I will turn to the questions of literary art and human truth in the biblical stories themselves. Unauthorized versions have none of the nobility of the English Authorized Version, but they are not attempts to bypass the texts' authority: they are an attempt to appreciate them for what they were, and are.

PART TWO

3

'Hear, O Israel . . .'

The Bible has its own inner story of creation, quite apart from the two stories of Creation with which it begins. It was not composed as a unity. The texts which we now read as a book between two covers are a collection whose origins span at least seven hundred years, the length of time which divides modern Europe from the age of Dante or the approach of Genghis Khan. The texts of the Hebrew Old Testament were composed at moments between the eighth century BC (some would say the ninth or even tenth) and the mid second century BC. There is a further gap of two centuries until the texts of the Christian New Testament, which were composed probably between AD 60 and 100. Into one book we have gathered texts as far apart in time and type as Dante's *Inferno*, the *Chronicles* of Froissart, prophetic texts from seventeenth-century England and a series of modern letters, memoirs and sermons written since 1945.

This book includes some unexpected candidates. Its Song of Songs is a collection of erotic poetry whose claims to a sacred meaning have been vigorously debated. It gives the Ten Commandments twice (Exodus 20 and Deuteronomy 5) and three differing sets of laws which leave many points unanswered and which contradict each other on particular details (Exodus 20–23; Leviticus 11–27; Deuteronomy 12–26). It includes a historical fiction (Esther), a book which appears to question the attitudes of prophets (Jonah) and a narrative (Chronicles) which retells much of the story in Kings. The New Testament is more compressed in time and length, but even so it includes more than one Gospel: why four, not three or six? We cannot be content with the charming view of an early

49

Christian bishop that there were four Gospels to match the centrality of the number four in the created world, the four winds or four directions. Questions of selection suggest questions about selectors. Were biblical books ever chosen formally from a longer list of candidates, and if so, when, how and by whom?

The question of the Bible's origins is in part a question of history, when each of its books was written and when the collection began to be acknowledged as the only Scripture. These questions are so difficult to answer because no biblical book gives its date of writing, and very few give their authors' names, let alone a name which is authentic. We have to infer the dates, authors and contexts from the texts themselves, many of which, in Hebrew scripture, have been enlarged and updated by later writers. In the next chapters I will map out a broad picture of the books' origins, the problems of their authorship and the nature of the text which we now read. In each case the picture has changed importantly through scholarly work in the past fifty years. We have found vital new evidence about the texts; many uncertainties remain, but the dates of particular books have been defined more clearly, not least because extreme alternatives have been proposed, provoking answers which, in turn, eliminate them. On the question of the Bible's canon, we are also aware of knowing less than was once believed. Here, too, there has been progress by elimination, with important results for our understanding of scripture's growth.

These questions bear directly on the status of scripture and views of its truth. There are still those who believe that the books of the Bible are different in kind from any other book: 'God inspired the canonical books, with no exception, and no non-canonical books are inspired, with no exception.' Their acceptance has been seen as the work of a higher power: 'the early Christians were not exceptionally intelligent people but they did have the capacity to recognize divine authority when they saw it . . . we may well believe they acted by a wisdom higher than their own, not only in what they accepted but in what they rejected'. These views assume that the Bible's own nature answers questions of its truth, so that the question of its correspondence with fact is a secondary distraction.

These special biblical books are sometimes thought to have a special coherence. They make up a canon which marks them off from outsiders:

there are critics and theologians who give great weight to the canon of books as a guide to understanding them. It makes each one into a coherent text, the book of Genesis or Isaiah as we now have it, not Genesis as a web of contradictory sources or Isaiah as a book whose second half is more than a century later than its first. We must look, therefore, for truth and meaning in each book as a canonical whole. This view appeals to literary critics who read the 'Bible as literature' and see attempts to split each book as an obstacle to understanding what they now mean. It also appeals to theological readers who wish to see broader themes in scripture than the tiny fragments into which its critics have ground each verse. The canon, they believe, has a special authority which extends to the form of each book inside it.

It also brings each book into a new relationship with its neighbours. Literary critics tend to believe that these relationships change the way in which a book is read; the canon is a mark of the Bible's coherence as a single work. Coherence, in this sense, is thought to alter meanings: the denial of an after-life in the book of Ecclesiastes might strike some of its readers as unduly bleak, others as realistic when read by itself, but when it is read in the context of other books, especially those in the Christian canon, this aspect takes on a new meaning as only one view in a developing whole. Theologians who are canonical critics agree, but also argue that the canon has a special, religious authority.

This type of criticism uses the canon as a sandbag against the dangers of piecemeal criticism by historians and textual scholars. As a historian, I believe that we cannot appreciate something correctly unless we try to discover what it is. Correct appreciation is a broad band on which we do not only pick up signals from the object before us: we also give them out. However, it is not an open frontier in which anything found is valid. I can illustrate this point by an example. Some years ago, I remember climbing into an abandoned house where a fine pair of cupids from the eighteenth century embraced each other in plaster-work above the door. The mood was one of sensitive discovery; my fellow intruder was a connoisseur of English houses and interiors; we were keen to be discerning and give this find of a house the benefit of every doubt. The walls of its small, well-proportioned sitting-room were covered in faded sacking which excited my companion to new heights of canonical appreciation. There must have been a time, he enthused, in the mid eighteenth century, just at the time of this drawing-room, when owners had used sacking instead of wallpaper, and here, hanging on, was an unspoilt room of it, in keeping with the doors, windows and fireplace. Inquiringly, I turned a piece of the sacking over, afraid that this Georgian unity might disintegrate in my hand. Instead, it dissolved. The words 'King Edward Potatoes' were stamped on the sacking's back. It was a stop-gap against wind and rain which somebody had brought in from the garden and padded on to the cracks within the last five years.

The historical truth of this potato-bag did not exist on a different level from the canonical appreciation to which I had been treated so touchingly: it destroyed it altogether. We were not intruders on a Georgian Eden: we had hit upon a fine old room, botched and padded during the passage of time and no longer a unified capsule, true to attempts to interpret it as a whole. What if the books of Samuel or Jeremiah have their potato-sacking too? What if the Bible is only a unity which we have quite recently constructed? The appreciation of Georgian houses is not correctly served by appreciating the sacks stuffed into their windows. The result can, of course, be appreciated, but it is only the appreciation of something more marginal, sacking and all.

Canonical reading justifies its unified vision by giving particular authority to the Bible as a whole: how significant is this authority? Here, we have been reminded of a simple fact. In biblical times, the Bible or the Old Testament was not a book at all. Its texts were copied on rolls of papyrus, parchment or even leather, each of which would hold only one text or one group of shorter texts. These rolls were often cumbersome. A text of Isaiah which was copied on papyrus and found quite recently in a cave near the Dead Sea unrolls to a length of twenty feet. In Jesus's lifetime, what Christians now call the Old Testament would have had to be gathered up as bulky rolls, rather like the bundles of wallpaper which nowadays wait in a heap to decorate a room. It is harder to control and limit a heap of scrolls than to preserve a book between one pair of covers. It was the Christians who first made the book, or codex, the standard form for biblical texts, and even then they are not known to have copied our Bibles into any one early example. The history of biblical texts runs from scroll to heap, from heap to book-codex, spanning about a thousand years. We need to look beyond our book-binding and try to see when and why, approximately, these texts were written, and what, then, is their authority as a whole.

11

We can be certain of a starting-point: none of the books of our Bible existed in more or less its present form before the eighth century BC. By then at least five hundred years had elapsed since the date at which the Israelites are said to have left Egypt and entered the Promised Land. Many of the great names of the Bible, therefore, had managed without any scripture at all: Solomon, Elijah, David or even Samuel. What, then, was special, if anything, about early Israel's religion?

The Israelites' particular god was Yahweh, whom their older texts connect with a region south of the land of Canaan: the old poetic texts in Judges 5:5 and Psalms 68:8 refer to him in words which probably mean the 'One of Sinai'. We do not know where Mount Sinai was: the Jebel Musa ('mountain of Moses') in the south of the Sinai peninsula is a favourite modern candidate, but the evidence to support it is very late, after A D 300. The Israelites' story was that Yahweh had delivered them from slavery in Egypt and that their leader, Moses, and others had met him and heard from him on Sinai, his home mountain. The stories of this meeting are told in Exodus 19–34, chapters which combine several different sources, laws and notions of God's encounters with his people. They are a wonderful jungle, parts of which are now dated, convincingly, by scholarly argument to the seventh and sixth centuries BC. They contain the famous Ten Commandments, but, typically, 'none of the traditional attempts to divide the text in its existing form into Ten Commandments is wholly above criticism'. There are not ten, and they are patently not original commands which were given to Moses by the mountain god of Sinai. Conservative guesses have recently put their origins in the northern kingdom of Israel during the tenth century BC: perhaps we should come down another hundred years, but not much more, because the prophet Hosea appears to know some of them (Hosea 4:1–6). In the mid eighth century he attacks cursing, lying, murder, stealing, idolatry (8:1–12) and adultery, and blames priests who have forgotten the 'teaching' (*torah*) of God. Most of these sins overlap with some of the commandments, and Hosea's context implies that they are breaches of a well-known way of behaviour. Probably he is thinking of God's commandments, and if so, these particular commandments must go back well before 750 BC. However, the versions which we now read have been enlarged and varied and their final form may be as late as *c.* 550 BC.

In archaic societies it was not unusual for a bundle of laws to be attributed to a single person who had heard them from a god: the Romans, even, had such a story about one of their kings. The Israelite story of Sinai is a majestic tangle of separate stories (Moses and various others go to and fro on the mountain), but it is not unique. Nor are most of the commandments: murder and stealing are anti-social, with or without a god. Historically, the most important commandment is the first, what Bibles traditionally translate as 'Thou shalt have no god but me.' Faith in one god, or monotheism, is such a famous fact about the Jews' religion that we might easily assume that it was present from the start. It is, however, an exceptional belief, not shared by any other peoples known in antiquity, and wherever we are most familiar with it worldwide, it is a Jewish legacy. Among the Jews it was accepted by the first Christians and was passed by contact with both Jews and Christians to the first Muslims, who also looked back to Abraham as their ancestor. It is distinct from acceptance of one special god who is active among lesser neighbours and subordinates. As early as *c.* 900 BC, were the people of Israel being told the strongest version, that their god Yahweh was the only god in existence?

Before we find early monotheism in the first commandment, we have to date it (it might be as late as the seventh or sixth century) and also be sure that we can translate it. Its dating is extremely difficult, although Hosea might seem to presuppose it too: chapter 8 of his book appears to connect idolatry and foreign worship with a blindness to God's law (8:1; 8:12). However, this law seems to be something more general than our First Commandment, and Hosea himself does not deny that other gods exist. If we do not find it stated openly in the early prophets, perhaps we should look to other individuals and consider their choice of personal names. Throughout the Near East, people take names which are based on a particular god. We do not know many early Hebrew names, but in the ninth century we first find a king of Judah who is named after Yahweh (Jehoshaphat, or 'Yahweh judged'), and in the north we find a prophet named likewise (Elijah, or 'Yahweh is God' or 'my God'); this Elijah attacks the rival prophets and the worship of Baal. These two names lead on to many more such 'divine names' known before the Exile in 587 BC. Recent lists have collected 1,058 divine names of Israelites in this period from the Bible and from contemporary inscribed objects, seals and so forth: all but 88 of them are divine names based on Yahweh. Personal names are easily over-interpreted, but the parents who gave them ought to have had some sort of trust in Yahweh. It is also striking how very few names are based on a god other than Yahweh himself, although such names may have been edited out of scripture, our main source. In other Near Eastern societies personal names are based on a much wider range of divinities, not on only one, reflecting people's belief in many different gods at once.

This pattern of naming might seem to be a hint that already in the ninth and eighth centuries there were people who believed that Yahweh was Israel's only God and that the First Commandment was accepted by them. I doubt, however, if it is evidence of anything so extreme: a name based on Yahweh does not prove that the giver or bearer considered Yahweh to be the sole god, rather than a most important god; the sample is small and tells us nothing about most Israelites' beliefs; Yahweh's name is the most frequent, but it is also significant that it is not the only one. As for the First Commandment, the translation of its Hebrew is also not certain. Perhaps originally it meant 'Thou shalt have no other gods before my face' (no idols in Yahweh's temple) or 'before me', in preference to me, but on any view, 'the claim for Yahweh's exclusiveness, in the sense that Yahweh alone has existence, is not contained in the First Commandment'. The text need only have been saying that Yahweh is Israel's Number One among other lesser divinities. Monotheism, the much stronger belief that only one god exists anywhere, was not revealed on Sinai's peaks. At Exodus 34:13, after Moses has gone up to Sinai with a second batch of tablets, the Lord is made to tell him of a covenant which he is now making. It requires the Israelites to be wary of neighbouring peoples and to 'destroy their altars, break their images, and cut down their groves'. These justified vandals must then 'worship no other god: for the Lord, whose name is Jealous, is a jealous God'. This part of the story has now been dated decisively down to the sixth century BC: monotheism was not such an early tradition in Israel, nor was a covenant with God either.

If we could revisit David and Solomon, the first kings in Israel, we would find nothing so fraught. In the mid to late tenth century, these great persons honoured Yahweh, but they would not think that he was the only god in the world. There were vigorous songs and hymns to Yahweh and perhaps a few general laws against murder and adultery which were presented as laws from Yahweh: there were also dozens of bits of law which addressed some of the problems of an archaic society. Yahweh was Israel's Number One. Just as there were prophets of neighbouring heathen gods like Baal, there were prophets who claimed to speak his words: some of them were active in court affairs. From Solomon onwards, there was a temple, or house, for Number One where priests paid him cult by killing and offering animals in order to keep him happy. Male Israelites were circumcised but so were other neighbouring peoples (including Egyptians); Yahweh had his particular shrine, or Ark, in Jerusalem (the gods of neighbouring Gentiles also had little house-sanctuaries); perhaps the priests of Yahweh abstained from particular foods and believed that other Israelites should do the same, but so did the priests of other gods near by (there were cults in Syria which banned the eating of fish; in Israel, priests were against pork). We cannot know how widespread or early these practices were, but they were not at all odd in their surrounding world: diet and men's private parts were frequently victims of religious beliefs.

A visitor to Israel in the tenth or ninth centuries would have found nothing very unusual in this religious practice: as yet, Judaism did not exist. In Moab, the Number One was called Chemosh; in Israel, people looked especially (but not solely) to Yahweh: it is most striking that Saul, the first king, gave one of his sons a name after the god Baal and that his other son, Jonathan, did the same. From time to time Chemosh or Yahweh might be angry with their worshippers, and, as a result (people believed), their wars or weather could be unpredictable. To win Chemosh or Yahweh's favour, they had to offer animals and pay worship in their temples. Eventually, the gods' anger would moderate (in due course people's fortunes improved, if only from bad to less bad), and meanwhile the priests lived off the necessary offerings. All the while, worshippers were realistic about death. At best there might be a ghostly existence for a few people in an underworld, but when they died, they died for ever. Their bodies returned to earth which nobody would judge or bring back to life.

This pattern of worship made religion in early Israel much like religion in Moab, Edom or even one of the Phoenician cities. However, there were two Phoenician tastes which Yahweh did not share. The first was artistic: there were no pictures of Yahweh in stone, wood or paint. At first, perhaps, this gap had been a matter of artistic competence (Israelite art as a whole was a non-event), but it became a religious principle (we meet it, too, in the Ten Commandments). Those in Israel who worshipped other gods did sometimes put up a pillar or a wooden post to symbolize them, but Yahweh himself remained faceless. Even in Solomon's expensive Temple, he was a god without a statue: as time passed, this facelessness came to seem peculiar.

He was also a god who did not demand human flesh. Phoenicians did sacrifice children to gods in some of their cities (although some of their admirers now try to dispute this). At Exodus 22:29 Yahweh does say 'the first-born of thy sons shalt thou give unto me', and years later, the prophet Ezekiel (20:26) understood him to have meant child-sacrifice as a punishment. Probably, the order meant consecration only (at 2 Kings 21:6, however, King Manasseh is said to have 'made his son pass through the fire' in Jerusalem: this was deeply wicked, if true). In Israel, Yahweh reserved a father's right to chastise his people but not to consume them; he loved them like a father; he had chosen the kings who ruled; he upheld order in the world which he had created.

This simple theology was neither new nor special in other literate kingdoms of the Near East (Egypt, perhaps, or Babylon). Like other Near Eastern peoples, the Israelites also told stories about their past, a topic for days by the gate or in the shade of trees, when it rained, when families gathered or when men met and sat, as they sit and converse to this day beneath the chenar trees of Iranian country towns. Once again our earliest datable sources for them are the books of the prophets Hosea, Amos and Micah, which are set in the mid to later eighth century BC: all these prophets were active in the more northerly of the two kingdoms into which the Israelites after Solomon were split. They show us some of the stories which we know in our book of Genesis, but not exactly from the same angle. They take the Exodus from Egypt for granted; they assume that it was God who destroyed Sodom (but Sodom's sins are not said to have been homosexual); they know of the dispossession of the Amorites while the Israelites return towards their land (although Joshua is not named). Stories of a past exile and conquest are known among other Mediterranean peoples (Romans had a story of their flight from Troy to Italy, and the Greeks told tales of the conquering Dorians). They do not survive among the records of Israel's neighbours in the Near East, but similar stories must have existed: the prophet Amos compares the Exodus with similar migrations of the Syrians and the Philistines, also under God's protection (Amos 9:7).

In the earliest prophetic books we also find stories of the artful Jacob. Stories of a trickster are well known in other cultures (Odysseus in Greece or the heroes of South American Indian myths), but Israel's trickster took on the name of the Israelite people themselves (at Genesis 32:28 and 35:10 God changes Jacob's name to Israel). In the books of the first surviving prophets, Jacob is known to have tricked his elder brother Esau in his mother's womb; he strove with a heavenly being; he met God at Bethel; he went to Aram for a wife; at some point, he 'wept' and 'sought God's favour' (we do not know of this event in Genesis). All in all, Jacob, to Hosea, seems rather a rotter.

In none of these prophets do we happen to have a mention of Eve or the Fall, Adam (except, it seems, as a place-name in Hosea 6:7) or even of Abraham. This silence is probably not significant because so little survives of these prophets' sayings: it can also be countered by another source. Behind the biblical books from Genesis to Numbers lie earlier written sources, one of which was a great collection of stories, sightings of Yahweh and tales of origin. Its author is known to biblical critics as the Yahwist (J), but the date and identity of this person are highly disputed: we can only infer them from the biblical compiler's use of bits of J's original text. Dates for it have been proposed at various points from the tenth century BC (under Solomon) to the sixth (in Exile), and the author has even been upheld as a woman (largely on the grounds that we do not know he was male). A date before *c.* 722 BC is likeliest because the author, so far as we know, showed no knowledge of the disastrous fall of the northern of the two kingdoms into which Israel had split. The odds among known authors and scribes in the Bible are heavily against a female prose-writer. The (male) author J seems to have written in the southern kingdom, Judah, probably in the earlier eighth century: it is ultimately to him that we owe the story of Eden, Eve and the Fall which we now read in Genesis. In the Bible, J's book is interwoven with another narrative about the early patriarchs and Moses whose author is known to biblical critics as E (or the Elohist, after E's preferred name for God). Scholars are more inclined to doubt the scale of E's contribution to the biblical books than to turn him into a woman too. To judge from his point of view, E also wrote before *c.* 722, probably in the northern kingdom. We cannot know whether E or J wrote first, but I prefer the view that J is at times reacting to E's earlier stories.

These two authors are the earliest known sources of most of the Bible's earliest tales: they take them back into the eighth century, perhaps earlier, and no doubt many of their characters were already well known in the age of Solomon too. After Solomon's death, the one kingdom of Israel split into two, north and south, and lived through serious political difficulties from the kings of neighbouring peoples and empires. Compared, however, with its sequel, the period from *c.* 950 to 850 BC had the uncomplicated style of a golden age. Number One had his cult, not only in his Temple but at any altar which a worshipper might choose to build for him. Perhaps he was said to have 'chosen' Jerusalem as a dwelling place, and probably he was said to have 'chosen' the line of kings: in some of the early psalms, the king is Yahweh's 'son' (Psalms 2, 89 and 110). With Israel, too, he had a special, natural relationship. He was widely believed to have brought her out of Egypt (already in our earliest prophetic source, Amos 3:1, from the 760s BC). Israel was 'his people', his 'son', perhaps even his 'bride'; these views are criticized by the first prophetic writings in our Bibles, *c.* 760–740 BC, presumably because they were the current views; no doubt they were old and widespread. Like other family relationships, this God's parenting and husbanding were taken for granted. It was not that Yahweh had no interest in anybody else (he was humankind's creator, according to J, and he had punished all the peoples of the world when they became too arrogant with their Tower of Babel). He did, however, love Israel and relate to her specially: 'You only have I known of all the families of the earth,' as Amos 3:2 makes Yahweh say. This view, too, seems to have been widespread in Israel because it is promptly attacked by the prophet: the verb to 'know' here has an intense meaning, almost sexual in its implications of preference and intimacy. Like a father or a patriarchal husband, Yahweh might combine bouts of ill-temper with fundamental love. But he was always there, and Israel could take her Fond Abuser for granted.

Some of the most famous ideas in the Old Testament are the ideas of God's election, promise and covenant: Christians, especially, emphasize them because they look forwards to their own future Gospel. However, the ideas emerged at different times and took on depth at different moments. In the age of Solomon nobody is likely to have thought out such a theology: if people spoke and sang of how Yahweh, their father, had chosen them and loved them, they did not need to dwell on the matter too deeply or think that he might now choose somebody else. They needed no theory of election. They might, perhaps, wonder about their future, on which (before the 720s) we find an optimistic view in bits of the writings of J. From Genesis 12:1–3, we can deduce that J believed that God had promised his blessing to Abraham's descendants and that his people would therefore become great: this blessing would extend beyond Israel and be recognized by other peoples on earth (the translation of Genesis 12:3 is disputed). Genesis 15 begins with a similar promise, also from J's book: Yahweh takes Abraham outside his tent and shows him the myriads of stars in the sky ('So shall thy seed be').

A promise, therefore, of a starry future existed quite early for those whom Yahweh's love had chosen. A 'covenant', or a two-sided contract, was something different. After the promise to Abraham under the night sky, Genesis 15 continues on a new theme; we read of an awesome evening ritual when the 'sun was going down'; Abraham leaves bits of sacrificed birds and animals lying on the ground; 'a smoking furnace and a burning lamp' pass between them; the Lord 'made a covenant' with Abraham about future possession of a huge stretch of Near Eastern territory. This memorable scene has been idealized as J's witness to an ancient element of Israel's theology: a covenant between God and Abraham which pledged the Israelites their land. It is a one-sided covenant, even so: Abraham pledges nothing, but he is in a sleepy trance. Recent scholarly studies have argued convincingly that it was not an old story at all: it was added on to J's story of a promise, probably no earlier than *c.* 620–550 BC. The story of a covenant with Moses on Sinai (at Exodus 34:14 ff.) is also best explained as an invention of the sixth century.

The earlier view had been much simpler. In the earliest psalms and the presuppositions of the first prophetic books, God was thought to have chosen Israel: no doubt David and Solomon were aware of this special relationship, back in the tenth century BC. In J's view (before *c.* 722 BC) he had also blessed her and promised her a big future, but a covenant was not part of the relationship, let alone a covenant which depended on Israel's good behaviour. Rather, Yahweh was a natural fact of life, father, husband and fond abuser, but always there and a focus for pleasant thoughts about Israel's future. Other gods and goddesses existed, and there was no commandment forbidding all Israelites to honour them too. Other women existed too, but no commandment forbade Israelites to marry foreigners: the women of only a few neighbouring peoples were banned, so far as anyone observed the ban strictly. Foreign wives stood outside the parenting of father Yahweh. They brought their own gods with them, seductively and forgivably: might not a husband, or a child, then hedge his bets with the women's gods at times of crisis? To judge from biblical texts, worship for Yahweh among others was still widespread in Israel as late as the eighth century, attracting kings, queens, priests and many individuals.

Even as late as *c.* 750 BC there were very few flies in this congenial ointment: such as they were, they confront us in sayings of Hosea. For the first time we find somebody describing the relation of Yahweh and Israel as a covenant (8:1). This grim idea polarized what most people had taken for granted: fathers are always with you, but covenants, or contracts, exist only so long as both parties adhere to them. Number One was no longer merely the Creator and the ultimate maintainer of order in the world: he had entered into a bargain, and bargains imply that if one party breaks it, so might the other. The metaphor raised the stakes of Israelite piety, but people, after all, could ignore it.

It was perhaps less negligible when some of the prophets began to speak as if a breach of this covenant was inevitable. As seen through their metaphors, the northern kingdom looks like an awful den of sin, but, on closer reflection, it seems no more awful than most other places where men and women have lived together. There were a few murders and thefts; some of the rich were extremely harsh to the poor; adultery was irresistible. However, a few of these prophets looked out on it all and announced a message whose one novelty must have seemed wildly exaggerated and even rather beastly. Because of the sins of a few people, Number One was going to wipe out the entire place.

Societies can live with religious extremists and the intermittent rumble of Seventh Day Adventists. In the north and the south, fondness for

Number One did not preclude worship for Numbers two, three or more. People worshipped Baal; they worshipped a female divinity who was symbolized by posts of wood: 'Thou shalt have no other gods before me': why not, then, have gods beside or below him, and anyway were these commandments known for certain? It was all very well for Hosea to attack the practice of multiple worship: 'They sacrifice on the tops of the mountains and make offerings upon the hills, under oak, poplar and terebinth, because their shade is good. Therefore your daughters play the harlot, and your brides commit adultery' (4:13–14). Perhaps this worship involved free love or the temple-prostitution which is known among some of Israel's neighbours, but even if it did not, it still sounds harmless, perhaps rather charming, for the people on the spot.

Hosea took this type of worship and polarized it too. In a long-lasting metaphor (shared later by Paul) he compared worship of other gods with sexual promiscuity. Promiscuity makes many husbands jealous: Yahweh, people in Israel believed, was Israel's loving husband; if Israel continued to worship around, Yahweh would act on his jealousy and punish her very harshly. Hosea thus introduced not a trinity but an eternal triangle into theology: infidelity, jealousy and the wrath of an aggrieved husband. He also stressed that this marriage might not be permanent, even when made in heaven: might not Yahweh abandon a people who let their husband down?

Hosea's complaints were not merely his own point of view. He alleged that Israel had forgotten God's law and that Israel had rebelled against God's law and covenant (8:1). Plainly, he had some alternative law in mind: this appears to be something more than the many laws of everyday life which we meet in Exodus 20ff. (compare Hosea 8:12). This 'law', or *torah*, cannot be the prophet's own invention: here, he seems to appeal to a standard of conduct shared by others, perhaps even to a written text. Even if it existed in writing, it was not everybody's text, and anyway very few Israelites could read. If it was known by word of mouth, it was not the view of the majority, any more than God's covenant or faithful worship of Yahweh alone. If societies can live with prophets of doom, they can also live with minorities' pamphlets and extremist broadcasts put out on the wavelength of a small intolerant group. 'Hear, O Israel . . .', but life might have gone on indefinitely in the pleasant shade of the terebinths, had foreign politics not intervened. In *c.* 722 the might of the Assyrians destroyed the northern kingdom, resettled its territory with their own colonists, deported some of the Israelites beyond the Euphrates and left the survivors to migrate south to Judah and Jerusalem. The Assyrians took no interest in Israel's prophets of total doom or in those who had broadcast the voice of Yahweh alone. From recently translated texts, we know what Israelites meant to them: not prophets but drivers. We now have the royal horse lists of a contemporary Assyrian king, which show Israelites from the northern kingdom as very high officers in the horse units of the Assyrian army. They were not riders: they were drivers of chariots, a skill in Israel which was internationally famous, at least since the age of Ahab. It was not, however, with chariots that the future lay.

III

Among the survivors, the disaster of Israel in the north cried out for explanation: why had God abandoned this people who worshipped him and thought that he was on their side? In the surviving southern kingdom, after *c.* 722, many people were anxious that they, too, would go the same way. In the south these great events and their aftermath were the setting for the prophet Isaiah.

From the north came refugees and their families; there also came some texts. We have to infer their movements, but I accept that somebody brought to the south the northern version (E) of the stories of the nation's early life, a chronicle of the texts of the northern kings and also, in the hands of its devotees, a text of the 'law', or *torah*, to which Hosea had been referring. The claim that its commands were right and everybody else was wrong had been greatly enhanced by events. In the north, the kingdom which disregarded it had been wiped out and resettled.

The travels of this text might seem pure guesswork, but they connect with the story which first presents holy scripture in a historical setting. It confronts us with spare precision in 2 Kings 22 (written some seventy years later) and slightly differently in 2 Chronicles 34 (written at least as late as the 350s BC).

In the year 622/1 one of the Jewish priests, Hilkiah, is said to have found a scroll in the Temple at Jerusalem which he identified as the 'book of the law of the Lord'. He gave it to a scribe of the Temple who had come down from King Josiah on financial business. The scribe took it back to Josiah, a 26-year-old ruler, and read it aloud. When Josiah heard it, he is said to have torn his clothes in anguish. There is a natural deduction about its identity which was made by the Christian scholars Jerome and John Chrysostom in the late fourth century; in modern scholarship, it was not re-emphasized until 1805. If it is correct, we can well understand the king's reaction. He had heard the core of our book of Deuteronomy, a text of commands and warnings which struck a new and alarming note in the entire history of Hebrew texts.

'Hear, O Israel . . .': the authors of this book had no doubts about their text's importance. They presented it as speeches by Moses which set out God's orders for human behaviour. It was not so much a code of ceremony and ritual as a book of conduct and commandments. It ordered the cult of Yahweh alone, Israel's only god, and, in a ruling of profound historical consequence, it ordered that his cult should be centralized in one place in the world, the only legitimate seat of offerings and sacrifices to the Lord: presumably, this place was thought to be Jerusalem. Other gods might exist, but no Israelite was to worship them or encourage any interest in them on pain of death. For Israelites were 'brothers' whom their God had brought out of Egypt: he had chosen Israel as a holy people, although she was one of the least of nations; with her, he had made a covenant. The book of the law described the proper attitudes of the Israelites in worship, their justified aggression towards their heathen neighbours, their respect for the poor and the defenceless, their festivals, some of their rules of law and the right behaviour of their kings. Yahweh alone was the God of this chosen Israel, and every one of the people must love him with all their heart, soul and might.

This theology of a single, jealous God who required total love from his chosen people had clear, earthly consequences. It distinguished Israel sharply from her Gentile neighbours, to the military discomfort of most of them. Yahweh, lover of his own people, ordered genocide against their unbelieving neighbours: the neighbours had shown no wish to practise it against Israel first. Within Israel, misbehaviour became a matter of public concern. It was not merely that the book of the law approved the choosing of judges and the giving of honest evidence: it appealed repeatedly to the public motive of shame. Those who broke the rules of behaviour were disgraces to Israel and were to be killed by communal punishments. Adulterous couples were to be put to death; women who were discovered to have had sex before marriage were to be stoned, and so were unruly sons who were drunk or dissolute: they were to be publicly denounced and pelted by 'all the men of their city with stones until they die'. 'So shalt thou put evil away from among you' (21:18–21).

Public shame was a sanction for good behaviour, but none the less every person in Israel was responsible for his own good conduct: the law would not punish a son for his father's misdeeds. God, however, could be more arbitrary: if some of his people misbehaved, he might visit his anger on a younger generation. Divine vengeance, as usual, was harsher than human retribution. As a warning, the law book's entire set of commands was hedged about with blessings and curses. Obedient Israel could engage in war against her heathen neighbours, assured of victory and the supporting presence of God; heathen idols must be smashed, and nobody should flirt with their false divinities. Obedient individuals would see their goods multiply, but offenders would be cursed with a range of terrors four times longer than the blessings. They extended from locusts and the 'botch of Egypt' to subjection and perpetual exile, until 'In the morning thou shalt say, Would God it were even! and at even thou shalt say, Would God it were morning!' (28:67).

No wonder Josiah tore his robes: here was God's law and the threats against disobedience, but nobody in Jerusalem had tried to enforce it. This spectacular text united themes with which we still live: war on Israel's neighbours, death to non-believers, personal responsibility and charity for those too poor to protect themselves. Although it ordered that nothing should be added or subtracted from its words, the text grew longer with time, and the command proved no more binding than the others in its book.

What we now read as the book of Deuteronomy has been enlarged by later authors, but an earlier core is still evident, and argument mainly concerns its exact boundaries. It also concerns the degree of truth in the story of the rediscovery, but even if the story in Kings has dramatized the details, it presupposes that such a law book did exist before 620 BC.

On one extreme view, Hilkiah the priest who found it had also forged it: the limiting of cult to only one shrine, the roles and rewards of its priesthood, the reiterated traditions about food and sacrifice, are themes which suggest a priestly source for at least part of the book. However, they are not its only themes, and the book is very different in tone from Leviticus, a priestly blueprint. It also extends the priesthood to all Levites, who were (presumably) priests at many country shrines outside Jerusalem. The offer is not inconceivable from a Jerusalem priest of good family like Hilkiah, but he would have to have been broadminded.

He would also have had to care about more than the observance of traditional rules and due form. When the book of the law discusses some of the great festivals and ceremonies, it emphasizes the scope for inner piety and charity on these occasions. A Temple priest might view his duties in this way: a similar viewpoint is shared by some of the early prophets who also had links with the priesthood and the Temple. Perhaps Hilkiah was both kind to Levites and more sensitive to ethics than to ritual, but perhaps we should look for other collaborators too. What about Shaphan the scribe and Huldah the prophetess to whom the find was submitted? Did they combine, perhaps, with Hilkiah, make up the law book, 'find' it and present it to the young king for his attention? It stated very plainly that even a king must write out a copy of the book, keep it with him and 'read therein all the days of his life'. Priests, meanwhile, had a monopoly of cult at Jerusalem; prophets were highly respected; scribes, perhaps, would like the ethical piety; and even women would not be worse off (accusations of adultery now had to be heard publicly and not merely settled according to a father's or husband's whim).

While the lamps burned low in the Temple, the three of them could have done it, writing the instructions which God and Moses would surely have wanted to be preserved in ink. The idea is tempting, but it is only one guess among all the possibilities. It is clear, however, that the book of the law drew on material older than the interests of anyone in the 620s BC. If we can match its main themes to themes attested elsewhere in our scripture, we can place the book in more of a context. It is an old and compelling view that the most distinctive themes connect with the prophets whom scripture locates in the northern kingdom: Elijah and Elisha, Hosea and Amos. We have already caught a hint of them behind Hosea's reference to a law, where we suspected that the outlines of a text like the core of Deuteronomy were already known to him. We can strengthen the link by appealing to the sayings of Amos and to the stories of Elijah and Elisha, set in the north a century or so earlier, although we now know them from a narrative compiled *c.* 550 B C. Charity and respect for the poor are visible clearly in Amos's sayings and in the stories surrounding Elijah and Elisha. Prophetic support for the destruction of heathen rivals runs like a blood-red stain across the narratives of these prophets, whether in the story of Samuel's horrible anger that Saul had not slaughtered every Amalekite, or in the sons of the prophets' anger at Ahab's mercy to a king of Syria, or in the tale of Elijah's massacre of the prophets of Baal. Cursing, too, remained a natural weapon of the prophet or holy man, and the eighteenth chapter of our Deuteronomy explicitly looks forward to future prophets like the great Moses.

Like the book of the law, these prophets' writings and reported actions are committed to worship of Yahweh alone. I accept, then, that the law book descends ultimately from the heritage of the northern prophets, from the age of Elijah onwards, but this descent does not account for all of it. A priestly element is present too, and any number of guesses can account for it. In my view, heirs of the northern prophets came south with a basic text of such law, composed before 750 B C: it is this 'law', or *torah*, to which Hosea alludes at that date. After the north's catastrophe in 722, its heirs expounded it in Jerusalem and attracted interest from individual members of the Temple priesthood. These priests, too, could interest the heirs of the prophets. They could make them wonder if the practice of sacrificing at any old altar had contributed to northern Israel's many other sins: priests in Jerusalem might very well think that sacrifices should be offered in Jerusalem only. Priestly service ran in families, and there might well be sons of the sons of traditional priests who wanted rather more than their fathers' daily round of rituals and busy performance. Here, the northerners and their text could help them. It had an ethical tone and emphasized the big festivals as a time for good works; it also insisted on Yahweh alone. This insistence was attractive too. According to 2 Kings 21, Josiah's predecessor but one as king in Jerusalem had built 'altars for all the host of heaven' in the two courts of the Lord. The Temple priesthood had been kept extremely busy, but according to the long-lost words of Moses, most of this business was wicked and irrelevant.

Out of these contacts, the main ideas of the book of the law arose. Perhaps they did not take their final form until Hilkiah's own lifetime; perhaps, after all, a threesome wrote the book and then 'discovered' it. Among so much uncertainty, we should perhaps accept that the discovery was genuine, that unknown authors had written a copy of the text, emphasized that all the Levites were priests and left their scroll in the Temple's archives. It was not unusual for authors to deposit a copy of an important book in a temple: there are famous early examples among the Greeks too.

Time passed, and priests who looked no further than priestly duties were not bothered by this minority's ethical law. They were kept particularly busy with their duties because the kings were worshipping so many gods beside Number One; the host of heaven needed a host of sacrifices, and Yahweh alone was not on the daily agenda. The text, meanwhile, the very words of what Moses must have said, was brooding in the Temple archive. In 622 it was rediscovered, curses and all, and its words were taken at face value: here, neglected for centuries, was the law of the Lord. Writing had given it a special power. If it had not been written, nobody would have found it and drawn the conclusion that God's law book had been disobeyed so disastrously: the laws would eventually have been forgotten. Only if they were written could they grow old quietly, gaining the prestige of age, too great an age to those who later found them.

From Israel to Athens, the 620s BC were one of the world's vital eras of written law. In the city of Athens, the first written law code was set up by Draco, author of draconian penalties; in Jerusalem, laws ascribed to Moses were found forgotten in the Temple and were enforced by the king as the law of God. Among the Greeks, a written law code arose through the factional strife of a divided aristocracy and was soon amended; among Jews, the writing of the book of the law owed a debt to the experience of ruin and exile, and was hedged about with curses against those who ignored it. Even so, this law is said to have appealed to only one young king: his successors were less enthusiastic, despite the voices which continued to support it. Among them was the great prophet of this era, Jeremiah; his sayings were worked over after his death by editors who also shared the law book's perspective.

Some modern scholars believe that the finding of the law book encouraged another literary work in circles close to Josiah the king: an unknown author compiled a history of Israel's past, from the last days of Moses to the reign, perhaps, of Josiah himself. He based parts of this work on earlier written sources, but reinterpreted much of the story in the light of the book of the law's main themes: the result is the main source of the books in our Bibles from Deuteronomy to the later part of 2 Kings. It was then worked over in a second edition, at least sixty years later, which brought the story rapidly on beyond Josiah and heightened its warnings and prophecies. I accept that a work of this scope existed, written by an anonymous author, but I agree with those scholars who doubt that there was ever such an early first edition. The arguments for it range from chronology to political outlook and distribution of narrative (it covers events after Josiah in little more than a chapter). They are not conclusive: the author used earlier sources, and I prefer to identify him with the second editor, delaying the book's composition until after 560 BC.

The law book may not have inspired an immediate Josianic history, but it did claim the status of holy scripture for those who read it and accepted it: it claimed to be binding, unalterable and the commandments of God. For the first time among biblical texts and their authors, this claim was being advanced. It was not, however, scripture for everyone, because it was the book of only one particular group. In order for it to become a dominant book, the accidents of politics had to intervene, spread across more than a lifetime.

Within thirty years of the law's rediscovery, it was the southern kingdom's turn for enormous misfortune. It arose purely from international politics, the strength of Gentile armies and wrong choices by Jerusalem's kings. In 597 BC the king of Judah was sent east as a royal captive to Babylon. Some of his subjects went with him and ten years later, in 587, the city of Jerusalem fell to a second invasion by Babylonian troops. The Temple, which the book of Deuteronomy had seen as the sole seat of God's cult, lay in ruins. Its bowls, dishes and sacred vessels were taken as spoils: probably its altar was defiled and the cult of Yahweh ceased.

According to the book of Kings, ten thousand people were exiled in 598 BC and the 'rest of the people', apart from the poorest of the land, in 587. According to a list which now stands in our book of Jeremiah (52:28–30), 4,600 people were exiled in all, only 832 of them in 587. The lower figures are probably nearer the truth: Babylonian colonists were not settled in Jerusalem's surrounds, and the land was not emptied of former inhabitants. The book of Kings sees the Exile as a climactic moment which arises from the people's earlier history; the Exile, therefore, becomes exaggerated, and the exiles are left as the main focus of the people's future. They were important, but not the majority: with them, however, went the salvage of an unknown hero, active (I imagine) with his friends. When faced with fire and destruction, for the first time in history someone had preferred books to basins and precious metals, and saved the contents of a library. Perhaps they were private copies; perhaps they came from the Temple; they survived because the Babylonians wanted silver, not bits of parchment which they could not even read. Naturally the book of the law was among the bundle, but so, too, were old texts of songs, royal deeds and prophetic sayings, from Amos to Isaiah and perhaps some recent words of Jeremiah. There were also the two ancient narratives, the northern and southern versions of E and J which had both been compiled before *c*. 722 BC.

When the exiles headed east, they had a collection of old and unreconciled laws which covered anything from the problems of stampeding oxen to the damage done by hitting a slave; they had a tradition of Ten Commandments; they had sayings of various prophets and a book of the law from Moses which often contradicted the older laws and which not everybody had taken to heart; they also had their psalms, many of which had been sung in the Temple. Enthusiasts for the book of the law did have a text which had the authority of scripture, but theirs was not the only voice among the people. 'How shall we sing the Lord's song in a strange land?' (Psalms 137:4). One answer was to use the library, build on the hero's salvage and preserve the traditions of the past. When the exiles left, very little which is now in our Bible existed. In the span of one long lifetime, much which we now read in it was to be composed. It was not, however, immediately scripture, and once again time, and politics, had to intervene.

4

In Defiance of the Facts

In the ancient world, there was an important connection between exile and writing about the past. The first Greek historians were exiles, men with the leisure to write and the detachment to wish to explain; many of their successors also lived outside their home cities. Among the Jews, the Exile occurred as a shared catastrophe, but it had a similar effect. It left some of them asking why, and what, if anything, was next. Others wished to maintain tradition, to keep alive the past and its practices, to idealize them, even, in order to bridge this great interruption in their lives. In exile, therefore, they wrote; the Jews' songs and writings of this period are the great literary achievements of the mid to late sixth century BC, an age which was one of relative mediocrity among the world's writers elsewhere.

A realistic response to the fall of Jerusalem would have been to accept that the God of the Jews was in fact less strong than his neighbours and that Babylonian troops had been too powerful for minor kings who had rebelled. Those Jews whose writings survive did not take this route: they interpreted events in defiance of the facts. In the book of Lamentations we have several laments over Judah which were probably written in Palestine in the immediate wake of the disaster: 'The elders have ceased from the gate, the young men from their music' (5:14). However, the authors do not blame Yahweh; they blame the Jews' own sins. They appeal to God's mercy in their current plight; and if there is any hope, it lies in their belief that Yahweh will treat others as savagely as he has treated them: are not the Jews' enemies sinning as badly as any among the chosen people? There is only a slight implication and one hint

(Lamentations 4:21) that after their punishment the Jews can look to a better future.

Defiance of the facts was particularly easy for one of the groups in exile: they had a different view of what the facts were. I do not believe that they already had the first edition of a history from Moses to Josiah, but I do believe that in their copy of the book of the law, they had a prediction of disaster and a clear explanation of what had gone wrong. 'Hear, O Israel . . .': Israel had not heard; Yahweh, at best, had been most people's Number One; there had not been Yahweh alone; the laws had been broken and the curses, therefore, had come true.

In exile, people who shared these views began to impose them on the textual salvage which had followed them into captivity. They imposed them on the known stories of Jeremiah and the sayings which had been written down by his faithful scribe, Baruch. There were also the royal chronicles, stories of prophets and traditions about people as distant in time as Joshua. They provoked a remarkable undertaking: it was in exile that one valiant author took them and turned them into a long narrative, propelled by the law book's understanding of events. This astounding effort is still the backbone of six books of our Bible's narrative (from Joshua to 2 Kings). It explained the past in terms of a covenant made by the Lord with his chosen people which, as predicted, they had broken: Solomon or Joshua would have read it with amazement, probably, too, with disbelief. It is 'unparalleled in antiquity that constantly recurrent national apostasy should be made the leitmotif of an entire literature', but the reason is understandable: this narrative arose from a minority who wished to explain disaster and believed that 587 BC had borne out all that they had believed for years. The majority had brought ruin on themselves. Disaster had come from a sinful past which stretched right back to the age of Joshua. This explanation allowed some of the losers to keep their self-respect. It also left open the chance of repentance and a future good from Yahweh.

Why, though, should other Jews listen? The high and mighty book of the law had not laid undue emphasis on priestly ceremonial, even while the Temple still stood. In so far as it mentioned the great festivals, it saw them as a cue for further words on men's duties towards the weak and on the cause of human justice. The book's followers had now composed this great narrative about the past, but even so it was biased. It had a nostalgia for the Temple and its offerings, but it was not punctilious: the great names of the nation, from Joshua to Josiah, were not assessed in it by their degree of adherence to exact ritual and cultic law. In exile there were traditionalists of quite another type: many of the former priests, Temple servants and their families. The covenant and ethical law of the Deuteronomists were all very well, but they were not the only things which mattered in history. There were other traditions too: all the details of priestly ritual and observance of cult. If they were not written down, they might be forgotten, but if they were written, they could be idealized, keeping the past alive and bridging the Exile's gap.

A text with this priestly outlook underlies what are now the first five books of our Bible, and inevitably the dates of its contents are still disputed. There are scholars who wish to date the text early before the Exile, scholars who wish to identify its author with the final editor of the first five books, and scholars who argue for continuing revisions across a hundred years or more. The traditional view, that the main body of its text belongs in or just after the Exile, is still the most compelling: it suits the outlook, chronology and emphasis of what we can trace to one main author. He must, however, have drawn on older rules and traditions for the detailed parts of his work. He was not the only exile in whom these concerns lived on: we find similar details in the book of the prophet Ezekiel who wrote earlier in the years of exile. The priestly author was heir to other like-minded people on whose memories and opinions he could draw.

What he could probably not use was a continuing tradition of cult and Temple service. The Jewish exiles had not been settled in Babylonia as a single group, unlike many of the foreign peoples whom Near Eastern kings transplanted to this area. Many of them were dispersed on the kings' lands round the old city of Nippur, where we encounter them in later local documents: we know of a gardener, a keeper of the king's poultry and a heavily armoured cavalryman. 'The modern idea, expressed originally by Voltaire, that the Jews became tradesmen and usurers in the Babylonian captivity belongs to the professional mythology.' Group solidarity was not at all easy in such a scattered life. They also had their own divisions. Although Jews from the northern kingdom had preceded them to Babylonia in the deportation of the 720s, there is no hint, or particular likelihood, of close friendship between the old exiles from north Israel and the new intake from Judah. There was probably even less friendly contact between the Jews in exile, many of whom were the richer families, and those who had stayed behind on their lands near Jerusalem.

There were also the temptations of life in these immensely old and cosmopolitan cities: Nippur had had a thousand years of history before Jerusalem mattered, and Babylon was the New York of the ancient world. Their countryside was honeycombed with groups of expatriates, none of whom was a monotheist: it was easy in such company to give up such faith in Yahweh alone as any of the '4,600', the Jews in exile, had entertained. When in Babylon, worship with the Babylonians: ancient gods had strong territorial connections (outsiders saw Yahweh, too, in this light), and visitors, even conquerors, would prudently worship the gods of a particular place. For polytheists it was a matter of prudence, not tolerance. Babylon's great temples inspired awe by their size and antiquity; their gods had moral values, and their priests were masters of old and respected rituals. We have no surviving altars or dedications by Jews in this era, but the likelihood is that many, as before, worshipped other gods beside their Number One. Perhaps we can still read the reaction which they provoked. In the 530s an unknown prophet (Second Isaiah) is very insistent that Yahweh is the only god, whereas the heathen gods are not gods at all: they are merely idols, bits of wood or stone. There were Jews, no doubt, who thought otherwise: monotheism, the belief in Only One, was born from tensions in this period.

In Babylonia we know of no temple for Yahweh in which the exiles could honour him: it is unlikely (although some have suggested it) that any cult was kept up at an altar in the remains of Jerusalem. If there were sacrifices, they cannot have been centralized under any one priesthood. Singing, however, was possible anywhere, and hymns, psalms and prayers could be recited to Yahweh outside his land. Unlike the gods of Babylon, he remained faceless, without statues or images. He had his special days and a special dislike of foreskins: in exile, male Israelites were still supposed to be circumcised. Every seventh day, the Sabbath was emphasized, reminding those who observed it that they were special: there were no weekends in the pattern of other ancient peoples' lives. Like their ancestors, the exiles were reminded of God's help for them during the Exodus and were invited to celebrate it yearly in their festival of Passover. A 'day of Atonement' is mentioned, too, for the first time in sources of this period. On it the people were to chasten themselves in order to expiate sins and impurities. Perhaps the day was an older observance which originally marked the start of the New Year, but the disaster of 587 had given it a new point.

Even the extremists, with their heartfelt love for Yahweh alone, confined their hopes to this earthly world only. They did not imagine that when they died they might be graded or one day brought back to life. In the narrative which the Deuteronomists wrote in exile, the heroes of the great speeches retained an admirable realism. 'And now I am about to go the way of all the earth,' says Joshua as death approaches. It would also be excessive to see even the extremists as a scriptural sect. The book of the law ordered them to teach diligently particular words of the Lord to their children: 'And thou shalt . . . talk of them when thou sittest in thine house, and when thou walkest by the way, and when thou liest down, and when thou risest up.' They were to bind the words on their hand, wear them as frontlets between their eyes and write them upon the door posts of their houses and upon their gates. The command, however, did not extend to the entire book of the law: people were expected to learn a mere nineteen verses of the text, the statement that 'the Lord our God is one God', to be loved wholeheartedly, and the promise of the blessings and harm which the Lord would send on those who did or did not serve him. These nineteen verses were very impressive, but they were not a full education.

It is noticeable how the commands of this law were domestic commands: 'And when thy son asketh thee in time to come, saying, what mean the testimonies . . . then thou shalt say . . .', like a father explaining the past world wars. As yet there were no formal schools in Jewish life, and attempts to find them in early Israel or in the Exile have no evidence in their favour. There is no evidence of synagogues, either, at this time, no meeting-places where Jews would pray and listen to readings from scripture. There were, however, various bits of law. Keen Jews were adding new laws to the older laws which had survived from their homeland, but there was no need for other Jews to learn them or even observe the letter of them, especially as they did not cover every eventuality or agree among themselves. Enthusiasts could be left to their own obsessions.

These various writings might have remained the religious texts of a dwindling minority. It was all very well for the prophet Ezekiel, living near the 'grand canal' at Nippur, to insist that God's people had paid their due, that the past had been settled and that the 'dry bones' of dismembered Israel could one day live again as a new people. Yahweh, he suggested, might restore his people in order to win honour for his name among the very peoples who now took it in vain; one day, those same peoples would come flocking to his rebuilt Temple. It was magnificent optimism, and, although the surviving king of the Jews was released and honoured at the Babylonian court in 561 BC, it was still hope in defiance of the facts. There are hints in the psalms and parts of our book of Isaiah that Jews in Babylonia did not find life at all easy: they may even have been persecuted by the king of Babylon, who ruled until 539 BC. It was probably, therefore, the people of Israel whom an unknown prophet (our Second Isaiah) described so memorably as a Suffering Servant in the tribulations of this period.

It took a historical accident to change this Servant's predicament. In 539 BC, as the old Near Eastern kingdoms collapsed like ninepins, Cyrus, king of Persia, captured Babylon and promptly agreed (in Jewish tradition) to return the Jewish exiles to their land and the Temple of their God. Fifty years earlier, the kings of Persia had been nonentities, way beyond the Jews' horizon: nobody had foreseen them, least of all the Hebrew prophets. Like others whom Cyrus allowed to return, the exiled Jews were now to be sent back as a people defined by their particular cult at their former shrine; they were to take back their sacred vessels (basins and all) and go home to worship their god. Cyrus's permission, and its particular form, thus put the worshippers of 'Yahweh alone' in 'the Temple only' at the centre of the Jews' new era. The return and the rebuilding of the Temple were not easy matters, and in each case they raise intriguing problems of timing and opposition. One result, however, was to confirm what the writers in exile had doggedly been saying and writing: Yahweh was indeed the one God, and he had indeed turned back to his people after the long years of punishment. His cult could now resume, in its only permitted place.

Another result was that soon after his conquests, an unknown prophet (again, in our Second Isaiah) hailed Cyrus, the Jews' deliverer, as the Lord's Anointed. These praises cannot have harmed his fellow Jews' chances of favour from the Persian king. Historically, a hope for a new king from David's line had remained alive in Jewish expectations. The Deuteronomists' great narrative still thought of a covenant for ever between their god and David's line; since 597 hope had veered to and fro between the Jewish king in captivity and the substitute king in Judah. After Cyrus, it passed to descendants of the old royal line; during the 520s several years of revolt against Cyrus's successors then threw them into special prominence. From *c.* 550 to 520 the themes of persecution (expressed in Second Isaiah's poems of the Suffering Servant) and an anointed king (whether Cyrus or Jewish leaders in the 520s) were memorably expressed by Jewish prophets and preserved together in writing. They too were to have an unimagined future.

'Bliss was it in that dawn to be alive . . .': to be old, with a memory, was very heaven. Not only had a minority sustained their explanation of history and their hope for the future during some fifty years of life in Babylon, but, against all odds, and to the amazement of their fellow Jews, they had suddenly been proved right by courtesy of a Persian king and returned as worshippers to the very Temple and cult whose memory they had sustained. It was not so unusual that after years of absence, a cult was allowed to be re-established on its former site: we know of other gods whose images were returned from long captivities under the Assyrians, while the goddess of the town of Harran also survived and came home after an absence of over fifty years. What was unusual about these Jews was the extent of their writings about their God's will for them and their insistence that he alone was to be worshipped in one place only. In exile, so far as we know, they had never built Yahweh a temporary shrine.

In Judaea the future belonged with these justified Yahwists and with groups who had kept alive the priestly details of Yahweh's cult. They were helped by an accident of their past. Unlike the old northern kingdom, when destroyed by Assyria in the 720s, Jerusalem and Judah had not been settled with foreign colonists by their Babylonian conquerors in 587. The Temple, therefore, could be rebuilt and the cult of Yahweh could begin again with a priesthood: if there was particular surprise at the return and restoration, it must have been the surprise of those many Jews who had never left Judah. They had hardly expected to see these exiles' children back, with royal approval, in the land.

11

As the Exile ended, God's people had psalms and prophecies, poems, proverbs, the old pair of narratives about their patriarchs (J and E), the long-lost book of the law and the long text of narrative, from our Joshua to the end of Kings, which one of the law book's enthusiasts had composed (not merely edited) in exile after 560 BC. None of these texts constitutes Judaism as many people now imagine it: rather, it is the book of Leviticus which confronts us with the thickest forest of detail about purity, sacrifices, permitted foods and priestly lore. Leviticus is one part of the wider priestly text, now lost, other parts of which have been edited into our Bible's first books, from the sabbatical story of Creation to the covenants with Abraham, from the making of a tent-like shrine for Yahweh in the wilderness and the various laws for priests, rituals and tithes, the priests' income. It is this text (P) whose origin is so hard to date.

One of the best clues is the silence of two other texts, composed in the mid to early sixth century. During the Exile (after 560) the long narrative from Joshua to the fall of Jerusalem was also composed, but it paid no particular attention to the rules and rigmarole which we meet in the priestly writings: it assessed the people's leaders by the book of the law and their fidelity to Yahweh alone, but not by their diet or dress or payments to the Temple and its priests. Perhaps Ezekiel and the author of this narrative could have ignored the entire priestly rules for holiness, even if they had already been written and publicized. It is more likely that they ignored them because a full priestly text did not exist at their time of writing. One obvious time for writing such a text was when the Exile itself was ending, when a new Temple was no longer a dream and people were returning to their promised land. Memories of the old Temple's rules and rituals must have lived on among former priests and their families during the Exile: the author of a new text for the Return could use this older material. Perhaps we should not be too precise, but I suspect that the main priestly text was composed *c.* 530–500 BC. Those returning from Babylon were still an imperilled minority, accustomed to life among a pagan majority: the priestly text's hallmarks are its rules and rituals, guides to behaviour whose social effect is to define and maintain a group's identity. Its clearly defined boundaries between what is permitted and what is not also fit with the social setting of a group whose identity needs to be sustained against other groups.

In Leviticus 11 the most famous boundaries still confront us: 'And the Lord spake unto Moses and to Aaron, saying unto them, Speak unto the children of Israel, saying, These are the beasts which ye shall eat ...' Strict Jews still observe the diet which follows: no pork, no camels, no shellfish, even (to be exact) no sharks. What was the cause of this menu and how was it all worked out?

Israel's neighbours also had rules of diet. There were Syrian cults in which fish were not to be eaten. Egyptians, too, were fastidious. At Genesis 43:31 Joseph orders 'Set on bread' in Egypt, but the Egyptians serve him separately because it was an 'abomination' for Egyptians to eat bread with a Hebrew: after the priestly rules, any law-abiding Hebrew would repay the compliment. Diet was not a new field of divine interest. At Exodus 22:31 (probably no later than the 720s BC) God had already told Israel that they were to be 'consecrated' to him, and that therefore they should not eat 'flesh that is torn of beasts in the field': instead, they must give it to the dogs. In our present text of the book of the law, we also read more general rulings: no pigs, no particular birds, fishes or carcasses, 'For thou art an holy people unto the Lord thy God, and the Lord has chosen thee to be a particular people unto himself, above all the nations that are upon the earth' (Deuteronomy 14:2–21). It might, then, seem that the priestly author of Leviticus was merely repeating what the authors of the book of the law had already commanded before 622 BC. It is, however, more likely that these particular verses on forbidden foods were added to our present Deuteronomy and that they began life in the priestly text: in essence, they summarize the priestly discussion (except Deuteronomy 14:21, which is concerned with 'any thing that dieth of itself': this dead meat was to be given away or sold to foreigners).

The aim in each text is to keep the people in a state of holiness, fit for their God. Before the writing of the priestly text, similar food rules had perhaps applied to the priesthood of Yahweh in his first Temple: perhaps what we now read is an attempt to extend older rules for priests to the entire people as they returned to a new Temple and a restored cult in their homeland. The scope of the rules was very wide: as we read them, they cover all the elements, air, sea and land. Cattle and sheep were permitted, but camels, rock-badgers and pigs were out; fish must have scales and fins; twenty types of bird were forbidden; swarming insects, snakes and creeping things were beyond the pale, as were bats, rats and lizards, with the exception of locusts, which could jump as well as fly.

Whatever had been bothering the Lord and his authors? Were they health-conscious watchers, concerned to ban pork in hot weather: did the rules, perhaps, make ecological sense (a 'foraging strategy' has been divined in them)? Or were they worried by heathen cults, and so they banned all animals which Gentiles offered to Yahweh's inferiors? Or was it all the excusable shudder of minds which found pigs very smelly, liked a fish to look like a fish and hated fast-moving spiders, wriggling snakes and anything which crawled in Near Eastern bedrooms?

None of these old explanations has the necessary scope. Pork, perhaps, might go bad in hot weather, but who are we to say that beef was any better, and where was the health risk in haunches of forbidden camel or prime cuts of unclean horse? As for the heathens, some of them did offer pigs to their gods, but where were the heathen altars which consumed rock-badgers, bits of bats and ostriches or fragments of non-hopping, unclean insects? The priestly author seems to have started from a different line of thought.

From Africa to Burma there are living societies who classify animals in ways which challenge our ideas of diet or species: the anthropologists who study them have suggested a broader approach to the biblical rules. The priestly minds were not guided by concerns about hygiene or heathen practice, but (like their modern contemporaries) by their own mentality and what mattered to it, perhaps because of its social setting. What mattered to priests was a wider concern for wholeness and perfection. These ideals underlie their other rules: priests and their sacrificial offerings must be unblemished, whereas all mixed classes and hybrids were causes of uncleanness. The rules extended to details of clothing and cultivation: robes must not be made of two different stuffs; yokes must not be pulled by two different types of animal; ground must not be sown with two different types of seed. Priests would not tolerate our modern man-made fibres or seventy per cent wools; gardens with mixed borders would seem dreadfully unclean, because they put roses among the rock plants and evergreens among the artichokes. They transgress an ideal of holiness which is 'exemplified by completeness; holiness requires that individuals shall conform to the class to which they belong and that different classes of things should not be confused'.

If a priest with this mentality wished to put animals in classes, he would presumably begin with those animals which people usually offered as sacrifices to his God. If they were unblemished, they were the ideal type of holiness: the most frequent sacrifices were cattle, sheep and goats. What, then, did these species share? What was the lowest common multiple which could easily be seen in other species too? Priests were not zoologists, but even they could look for an animal's food and feet. The hoofs of cattle, sheep and goats were cloven, and all of them chewed the cud: cloven-hoofed, cud-chewing ungulates were therefore fit for the table. Horses and dogs were off the menu, as were donkeys or Samson's unfortunate foxes.

What about the marginal cases – beasts which had more or less cloven feet but did not chew cud, or which chewed the cud and had peculiar claws or hoofs? There were not very many of them, though everyone would think of the cloven pig: it ate roots and grain, but it also ate dung, swill and bits of dead flesh, other pigs (in close confinement) or, many years later in Gaza, the juicy flesh of Christian virgins. Pork, therefore, was out. So were camels (their hoofs were marginal) and so were hares (here, the priests mistook the hare's nibbling and tooth-grinding for chewing a non-existent cud). Perhaps they also thought at once of the little rock-badger; it is more likely that somebody brought it up later. Like a book on the Catholic Church's index, it found itself banned because somebody sent it in for the priests' decision. In the late sixth century BC nobody knew of the problematic llama (it was much too far away). The difficult hippopotamus was known to Job and the Philistines' cities (its bones have been found there), but the priests did not specify it. It was not an animal to study closely or imagine on an Israelite's table.

By starting from what they knew best, the priests could quickly divide the kingdom of beasts into two. It was not that some animals were clean because they were physically whole and perfect: clean feet were split feet, not perfectly round. Nor were they clean because they were vegetarians: on the priestly scheme, some of the hoofed vegetarians were also unclean (horses or donkeys). Rather, they deviated from the ideal type which was defined by the usual victims for sacrifice.

So much for the animals: what about the birds? Here, priests had to follow a different path. The most popular Temple offerings (to judge from later practice) were probably doves and pigeons, but what was so special about either? Like every other bird, they had beaks, wings and feet and so the priests (I think) fell back on what they had already specified for the animals. If there were clean and unclean animals, there could not possibly be clean birds which might feed on unclean animals' flesh. Birds of prey, therefore, were excluded (doves and pigeons were not predators): the book of Leviticus names twenty varieties of bird whose identity is often uncertain, and no doubt there would have been many more if the priests in land-locked Jerusalem had known more about the birds on rivers or sea coasts. An ideal type thus emerged: birds which used wings, had feathers and did not eat flesh. This ideal type defined a few further oddities which transgressed the classes of a tidy mind. Ostriches were out; they did not fly. Bats had wings and flew, but they were out because they did not have feathers; they had baby faces, to a poetic eye, and they also had weird anomalous ears.

Fish and insects were more a matter for pure classification. Neither was offered up to Yahweh, and so the priests relied on their basic principle of perfect, unmixed natures. The ideal type of fish was one which had the most attributes of fishy appearance, with both fins and scales, not one or neither. Particular types of fish were never specified in Hebrew scripture: priestly ignorance thus made the future's diet very strict. As awareness grew the curious catfish was not too much of a loss, but shellfish were serious casualties. Crabs and lobsters crept and could not swim; the priests and their rules banned both, probably without having tasted them. As for insects, they came under a general heading of things which swarm, including snakes and things which move on four feet or more (Leviticus 11:42); they defied all sorts of tidy boundaries, and there were sound reasons for banning the lot. Swarmers flew, but they were not birds; they moved on land, but they did not walk; they might swim, but they lacked fins and scales; swarming lizards and mice had feet like hands; centipedes had far too many feet; weasels did not chew cud. Once again, there was one little problem which was possibly raised by an awkward question later: what about locusts, which hopped on their legs and flew with their wings, moving on land and in air but in each case with the proper parts? Hopping locusts, crickets and grasshoppers were therefore declared clean. In times of locust swarms and famine, it was a very convenient ruling: the poor used to eat these insects who, in turn, were eating their crops.

'I am the Lord your God: ye shall therefore sanctify yourselves and ye shall be holy, for I am holy' (Leviticus 11:44). In the view of her priestly author, Israel must therefore take care what she ate. It was not that some animals were good and some were bad: after P had written his rules, an Israelite could still pat his unclean horse, admire an unclean eagle or keep a hutch full of dirty rock-badgers if he wanted them as pets. It was merely that meat and dead flesh passed on uncleanness. Our present book of Leviticus spends several verses on carcasses (perhaps they were added as a later detail): they follow the main lines of the rules for food with an explicit warning about 'whatsoever goeth upon his paws' (dead cats, therefore, were out; Samson's riddle about the dead lion which swarmed with bees would have seemed extremely unclean to later, priestly readers). There was, however, a difference between eating and touching. Contact with a carcass might pass on temporary uncleanness; anyone who touched a dead mouse remained unclean until nightfall. This type of uncleanness could be cured and made to disappear, like dirt on a skirt or trousers: it was a hazard, not a sin. Unclean food, however, was listed as an absolute prohibition, not as a hazard with a cure or time span; Israelites must please God by never consuming it in the first place.

The effect of these rules was to make Israel special. She had to be special before God because she was his people, and God's people (in the priests' view) should be as clean as priests. Priests' rules also made the priesthood indispensable: somebody had to maintain them, keep up standards, cope with offerings and see to breaches and their remedies. Israel also became special among other peoples: she could not worship their gods, eat their foods or touch their dead animals. How, then, could she marry their women? In the book of the law marriage between Israelites and members of particular neighbouring peoples had been prohibited, although the prohibition had not been a feature of all their earlier history or stories. In priestly company, a strict separation from foreign wives was perhaps already expected; the mentality matched the clear separation of animals, objects and practices which is evident in Leviticus's priestly text. Not all priests, let alone most Israelites, paid any attention, but it is from exactly this priestly milieu that Ezra the priest later comes down to Jerusalem, where he is said to have attacked foreign marriages, going well beyond the letter of the law. Foreign marriage led to foreign practices and often to neglect of Yahweh alone. It is not that one type of separation caused the others, as if priests who already opposed intermarriage now went a step further and grounded their entire idea of holiness in the idea of separate, unmixed kinds. Rather, the mentality was consistent: from wives to food, it separated Israel from other peoples and divided the entire kingdom of nature into separate groups. Life for the dutiful Israelite would never be so free again, but, as the Exile ended, priests were only priests and P was only one voice among them. The text and its rules were far-reaching, but they were only one view of how to live a life before God.

III

Back in their homeland, the Temple to Yahweh was eventually rebuilt; in the closing decades of the sixth century, a priesthood was at last in service: Yahweh was being honoured with animal sacrifices and his worshippers were being told to be very careful what they ate. Diet and history, a growing pattern of festivals, a faceless god and a freely expressed belief that Yahweh was the only god helped to mark off his worshippers from the neighbouring peoples. There is also a simple fact about the priesthood of this second Temple which is almost so large that we miss it: every one of the priests was male. Women might still prophesy, sing or be holy, but they could not serve in this masculine cult. The inner parts of the Temple came to be closed to them.

Among the texts which the exiled minority brought back, the book of the law was special: it alone claimed to be holy scripture. However, for sixty years or more after the return, we lose sight of Israel's history: we do not know what her people read, heard and decided, or how many of them paid any attention to what their priestly author had defined as their diet. Our present text of the book of the law tells how Moses had ordered his law book to be read 'every seven years . . . before all Israel in their hearing . . . men, and women, and children, and the stranger that is within thy gates' (Deuteronomy 31:10–11). When we next have a text of events in Jerusalem, it is far from clear that people had attended carefully to what may, or may not, have been read to them one year in seven.

We know about it from our books of Ezra and Nehemiah, which describe the separate missions of their two namesakes from the Persian king, east of the Euphrates river, to the little region of Judaea. Once again, the impulse to a reformed piety in Israel was to come from outside the homeland, not within it. Yet again the dates are disputed (many prefer 458 for Ezra and 445 for Nehemiah), but when we come later to questions of their correspondence to fact, I will opt for Nehemiah's priority. I share the view that he arrived in 445 and that his mission led not only to a rebuilding of Jerusalem's walls: he made important changes for the poor; he entrenched the whole tribe of Levites as Temple servants, to be maintained by the people; he encouraged a strict enforcement of the Sabbath and attacked marriages to foreigners. Probably, he assumed a broad awareness of Moses's law among his audience, but on none of these topics do our bits of his written memoirs appeal to written scripture: his attack on foreign marriages went beyond the implications of earlier legal texts.

The mission of Ezra, however, involves the law more explicitly: in my view, it is historical and belongs in 398 BC (others opt for 458). Our book of Ezra describes how its hero came down to Jerusalem from the Persian court with a royal letter of support, some splendid gifts for its Temple and a copy of the law of Moses which he read to the assembled Jews. In this book we find for the first time an appeal to 'what is written' (Nehemiah 8:13–15, which was originally part of Ezra's book). It concerns the celebration of the Feast of Tabernacles and appears to allude to our book of Leviticus, chapter 23, although it interprets the details and enlarges on what we now read there. The principle, however, is clear: look up a text of Moses in order to work out what to do; the text has authority.

What exactly was this law of Moses which Ezra brought? Traditionally, it is thought to be the entire Pentateuch, or first five books of the Bible, from Genesis to Deuteronomy, more or less as we now know it. At some point, therefore, between *c.* 540 and 400 BC an unknown editor had amalgamated written traditions and worked older and respected texts into our single body of narrative and law. He used a combination of the old northern and southern versions (E and J). In exile, probably, people with the Deuteronomist outlook had worked over bits of these texts already (it was they who inserted God's promise of a land to

Abraham, a cheering promise for the exiles, into Genesis 15). The unknown editor also took the detailed rigmarole which the priestly author had composed more recently (P); he took the opening section of the Deuteronomist's great narrative because it, too, was a text of law (it amounted broadly to our Deuteronomy, extending to the death of Moses). Out of these four sources, he made what we now read as the first five books with our later titles, based on Greek: Genesis, Exodus, Leviticus, Numbers and Deuteronomy. The editing was not unduly difficult or subtle, although there are modern critics who overrate it.

It is no wonder that the resulting law of Moses needed people to explain it who 'gave the sense and caused them to understand the reading' (Nehemiah 8:8). It included three separate groups of laws, composed by different hands at different dates and enlarged since. Exodus 20–23 went back, in part, to customary law under the pre-exilic kings; Deuteronomy to the authors of the book of the law *c.* 720–620, which had also been expanded since; Leviticus 11ff. to the priestly authors during the sixth century BC. There were serious gaps, obscurities and contradictions in this law, which was never one person's code so much as the amalgamation of disparate earlier writings. Anyone who tried to run his life by its laws and nothing else would find himself in a hopeless muddle. Incoherence was a fact of its origin.

Ezra did not merely read this law to his hearers: by an order to him, the Persian king Artaxerxes is said to have recognized this law of Moses as the law which Persian governors should now apply locally to Jews in their jurisdiction, from Judaea to the Euphrates river. The law which preached Yahweh alone was thus officially imposed, probably through Ezra's petition to the king (I assume this story, too, is historical) rather than through a sudden initiative of the king himself. This unique body of older written texts now had a status and scope which nothing else could rival. It had become the unquestioned centre of Jewish religious writings, a position which it has held ever since. People did not know where it came from: the belief that Moses had written it all (foreseeing the bits after his death) merely confirmed its supremacy.

Back in their land with their new Temple, people also respected the writings of those prophets, from Amos to Zechariah, who appeared to have spoken so truly about their past. It was not that prophecy now ceased: far from it. New prophets, however, could not compete with older texts of such historic importance. To gain credit from the public, it was worth passing off a new prophecy under some ancient person's name: our book of Isaiah is one which gained from this trick. In subsequent Jewish piety, 'the law' and 'the prophets' were to become two special divisions in the people's religious texts: Jesus is made to appeal to them at Matthew 7:12. By 400 BC they were already evident, confirmed in their position by historical changes: the law was the living centre.

Much, then, of what is now our Old Testament had been composed in the years of the Exile and their immediate sequel, but (if we believe Ezra 7:25 ff.) the historical actions of a Persian king had helped to propel the law books into special prominence as a potential national scripture. Life, however, must have been more diverse than the scriptural rules of conduct would imply: there are hints of diversity in the archaeology of Judah in the fourth century BC (its pottery, the images on some of its coins); written scriptures, anyway, were not the main force in religious life. Throughout the years of Persian rule (c. 520–331 BC) Jews had their Temple, whose cult and priesthood mediated between the people and their God. According to the book of the law, this cult was acceptable in only one place, but even on a point of such importance, scripture was ignored. In Egypt during the Persian period we know of one group of Jews (up the Nile at Elephantine) who had a temple of their own to Yahweh, irrespective of the book of the law: they even associated him with other gods. Scripture, therefore, by no means bossed everybody; in relations with Yahweh it did not compare with the calendar of festivals, and the sacrifices and ceremonies of the Temple and its hierarchy.

The existence of older texts certainly did not inhibit the writing of new ones. In the fourth century BC, perhaps c. 350–340, a second block of narrative was formed which tells the stories of Ezra, Nehemiah and the narrative which we know as Chronicles, covering again most of the period which had already appeared in the books of Kings. The authorship of this block is disputed, but the older view is still convincing, that it is the work of a single author, 'the Chronicler'. Possibly he was a Levite, maintained in Jerusalem: near the beginning his book tells us how David installed Levites in the Temple, and at the end of it (assuming the whole block is his) the Levites are firmly back in place, attending Ezra and entrenched with their portions, thanks to Nehemiah. This block of edited story also shares a common concern: to tell which Jews belonged in the true, undivided homeland and to connect their story to the subsequent return and rebuilding of the Temple. These concerns are understandable in an age of shrunken and precarious boundaries, in which the Jews were beset by foreign neighbours and the peril (in some eyes) of intermarriage with foreigners. Their territory was perhaps a tenth of modern Israel, and many Jews already lived scattered outside it, from Egypt to Babylonia. The author was also aware that the Jewish community still lacked a king, promised by God from the ancient line of David.

In an important way, these books of Chronicles are secondary literature: most of their narrative rewrites the story as it was already known in the older books of Samuel and Kings. This rewriting is a mark of respect for the older writings; the author also echoed phrases which we know from books of the prophets, although he never cited them as a source. This rewriting and echoing are far from a sense that these books are holy authorities, fixed and defined by a canon. Such a sense of fixing and limits does not emerge, either, from our increased knowledge of the range of religious writings which continued to be composed in Hebrew or Aramaic *c.* 400–100 BC. We know more because bits of a wider range of texts have been found in caves around the Dead Sea and elsewhere. The book of Jonah (probably written in the fourth century BC) explores the dilemmas of a prophet. The book of Ruth (which might, however, be older) presupposes a different view on foreign marriage (Ruth was a woman of Moab) from the hostility shown to it in Ezra and Nehemiah. The book of Job appeared, possibly, in the fourth century BC; Ecclesiastes followed it, perhaps as a response to Job, stating the 'philosophy of an acquisitive society' in the social and economic setting of the third century BC. In these two fine books we hear a different note from the one-sided outcries of prophets or the rigmarole of priestly codes of holiness. Like the earlier core of the book of Proverbs, the main sections of Job have been seen 'simply as ignoring Judaism ... they do not mention its special practices nor its festivals'. The book (like Ecclesiastes) has even been ascribed to an upper-class author who is 'more interested in the plight of man than the plight of the lower classes'. During these centuries other psalms and proverbs continued to be composed, and in the 160s visions and prophecies were added to older stories, which had gathered about the figure of Daniel: they were combined into a single text in those years of profound national crisis. At a late date, too, perhaps *c.* 250–180 BC, the tale of Esther had been composed (it was translated into Greek as late as 78/7 BC).

These texts are now in our Bibles, but they are only part of a much wider group composed in the period: the cosmopolitan story of Tobit and Tobias, parts of the visionary books of Enoch, the fictions of Judith and many other tales which were attached to the names of Ezra and so forth. The tantalizing questions are how far, if at all, the boundaries of this increasing literature were clearly defined and whether, in the wake of it, we should already think of Jewish piety as based on a fixed bunch of scrolls. In Christian sources we are used to reading of the 'law and the prophets' or 'the Psalms' as if they have a fixed identity: between the fourth century BC and the age of the Gospels, we might well think that the Jews had sorted out something like a Bible of their own.

5
Authors Anonymous

So far, the scriptures have grown with a splendid incoherence. There was no single block of early 'scripture' which was then padded by later users: the analogy of my Georgian room and the potato-sack is too simple. Padding has certainly been added to older writings: it is obvious in the books of particular prophets and has had important effects in the older narratives. A covenant, for instance, with God has been added into the earlier stories of God and Moses on Sinai, or God and Abraham at nightfall in Genesis 15. However, this later padding is not the end of the matter. Some of the texts were compiled from older, separate texts, and, unlike bricks and plaster, these earlier building blocks had led a separate meaningful life. The prospects for one consistent and coherent construction out of this variety were precisely zero.

Brute facts of history continued to intervene, causing yet more texts to be written and older texts to be understood differently. Between the years of Persian rule and the end of the first century AD, the Jews lived through three major historical events. In 332 BC they came under the control of Alexander the Great, conqueror of the Persian Empire; in 167 BC the cult in Jerusalem was interrupted by one of Alexander's successors, Antiochus IV, whose persecution raised up a great war of resistance led by the Maccabees, a heroic Jewish family; from AD 66 to 70 the Jews rose in a war against Rome, the latest power to dominate the Near East. Each of these events affected them differently.

Alexander's conquests caused no new flurry of scripture and no new historical writings. The reason was simple: the Jews exchanged one remote master for another. None of them went into exile and from their

90

point of view, the new rulers continued to govern much like the old. The one change occurred in the old northern kingdom of Israel. Its foreign settlers had taken up worship of Yahweh alone: when Alexander's generals settled heathen colonists in their land, they appealed for permission as Samaritans to build a new shrine to Yahweh on their holy mountain, Gerizim. Permission was granted, and so Yahweh (despite the book of the law's orders) began to receive worship in another site outside the Jerusalem Temple. In the south there were Jews who hated this change: by *c.* 200 BC we find one of them referring to these fellow Yahwists as 'fools'. Their heirs still survive with their own text of the Pentateuch (our Bible's first five books), living 'in the ghetto at Nablus', near their holy mountain.

No heathen colonists were settled in Judah to the south, but the Greek language, culture and economics of the surrounding areas kept up a slow and subtle pressure on Jewish life itself. They also encouraged Jews to migrate and seek their future elsewhere: the Promised Land could be left to fend for itself. In cities and territories of the Gentile world, some of Alexander the Great's successors hired and settled Jews as soldiers, and elsewhere the Gentile cities offered new opportunities. There was, however, a slight awkwardness for Jews who settled abroad. If they still obeyed the book of the law, they must worship Yahweh alone, love him with all their hearts and minds, and disregard everyone else's gods. Yahweh, however, could only be honoured with sacrifices in the Temple at Jerusalem. Expatriates either had to ignore the rule or devise a regular form of worship of their own. Like the Samaritan 'fools in Shechem', some of the Jews in Egypt had long had a little temple of their own, and others in Egypt followed suit. Most of the Jewish expatriates were more obedient: by the 250s BC we know of meeting houses which were places of communal prayer: they were synagogues, attested for Jews in Egypt. The synagogue was probably an innovation of this period which began outside Judaea and then spread back into Judaea itself. Our evidence for its uses is very slim, but by the time of Jesus, Jews met in these synagogues for a bloodless type of worship to which our Western piety is still the heir. They could not sacrifice outside their Temple, and so, like Sunday congregations all over our villages, they met to say prayers and sing psalms. By the time of Jesus, we know that synagogues in Judaea were places where bits of the ancient texts were read aloud. Probably, these lessons from scripture had begun earlier in the Diaspora too. A fixed order of yearly lessons must have become established, but as yet we cannot discover what it was.

Before long, Gentiles began to be curious about these little prayer houses, and some of them attended as sympathetic hearers. At first sight, they would have found the scrolls of the Jews familiar: among the many cults of Gentile gods there were those in which people used texts too. However, their use and scope were rather different. Among Gentiles, texts were either hymns or books of miracles or else they were manuals of worship which set out the correct practice in a religious rite. They were read and used by priests, much as cooks now use a recipe-book, but they were not read widely to other worshippers, let alone as books of education to guide all understanding. Even texts of this limited type were highly unusual in the worship of a pagan god. Pagans knew books of hymns or rituals among small minorities, people who respected wise sayings ascribed to the legendary Orpheus or the Egyptian god Hermes, one of the gods whom they worshipped among many others. The great gods of their own pagan cities were worshipped by offerings of incense and animal victims, not by knowing or reciting scripture.

The new role for old scriptures in the synagogues encouraged a step which increased their appeal way beyond the priests in Yahweh's Temple in Jerusalem: uniquely, Jews began to translate them. Whereas the hymns and holy recipe-books of neighbouring Eastern cultures remained in obscure ancient languages which only a dwindling priesthood could understand, Jews in Egypt's Alexandria translated the first five books, the Pentateuch, from Hebrew into Greek in the third century BC. Even this much of scripture was an effort of translation on an unparalleled scale in the previous history of sacred texts: a century later, there was a story that the ruler of Egypt, King Ptolemy II, had personally commissioned the translation for his royal library in Alexandria. The story is only a legend, although it has found some eminent believers. Seventy translators were said to have worked on the project which is nowadays known as the Septuagint, or LXX (from the Latin word, or number, for seventy). By 100 BC Greek translations had been made of most of the Old Testament books, although Ecclesiastes may have had to wait until the Christian era.

Only a few extracts from a few of the old scrolls were read in the synagogues, but translation was to give these writings an international future to which the first Gentile Christians were grateful heirs. If Jews could translate into Greek, they could also begin to write in Greek as a first language: from the third century BC onwards we know of such authors by personal names, Demetrius, Eupolemus and so forth. These named authors remind us of an important contrast with the older Hebrew writings which would have struck any Gentile who came across their translations. In Greek, authors of a prose narrative or history usually named themselves at the start of it (unless they were continuing somebody else's work). Contemporaries knew who they were; they attacked them personally; their history or story was subjective and affected an individual's reputation. In Hebrew, everything which we have inferred about biblical narratives has had to be inferred about unknown authors: we read the 'book of Genesis' or the 'book of Kings', not a book by a Simeon or a Nathaniel.

Many literary critics welcome anonymity because it helps us to forget the author and concentrate on the text. Already in 1925 E. M. Forster was writing that 'all literature tends towards the condition of anonymity ... It wants not to be signed. It is always tugging in that direction, saying, "I, not my author, exist really ..." "Temporary forgetfulness" of the author's name and our own, this momentary and mutual anonymity is sure evidence of good stuff.' Nowadays, several types of biblical criticism are more than temporarily forgetful. Structuralist critics are concerned with the text and its reading, not the author and his purpose in writing. Form critics ask what type, or setting, best describes a part of the biblical text. They are interested in its genre, not its author: is it a victory-hymn, perhaps, or a public lament or a family tree? The anonymity of so much scripture has fitted neatly with many modern critical ways of reading it.

E. M. Forster, however, wisely distinguished works of fiction from works of information. If we are being asked to believe something or accept an account of the past, it is very foolish to ignore the author: how does he (or she) know? Anonymous narrative can easily lull us into accepting it, as if it is 'the' story, not somebody's story. It took years of intense biblical scholarship (until 1943) before anyone realized that the seven books from Joshua to the end of Kings were essentially written by one person, or perhaps one person with like-minded collaborators.

Probably, one person also wrote the four books which are our Chronicles, Ezra and Nehemiah, although this theory is under renewed attack. If we all began by knowing that such a high proportion of Hebrew narrative was essentially the work of two main authors, we would view its authority rather differently.

In the Greek world, personal authorship was widespread; so, too, was false authorship, whereby authors pretended to be somebody else. Did this practice dawn on the Jews through Greek contact in the age after Alexander and cause them to look back on their older writings in a new light? We are the practice's heirs: nowadays we read 'proverbs of Solomon', 'visions of Daniel' or 'psalms of David', although Solomon, Daniel and David did not write a word of them. The problem continues into Christian scripture with some of the letters ascribed to Paul and even the Gospel 'according to Matthew'.

Named authorship, however, is very much older than the Greeks. Long before they wrote anything, we know the names of writers in the ancient cultures of Egypt and Babylonia; one of the world's earliest named authors is a woman, Enheduana, if she is correctly credited with the temple hymns in Sumerian (*c.* 2350–2300 BC). Writers included both scribes and authors, and, if we distinguish them, a clear pattern emerges. Books of narrative named no author and were anonymous, whether they were Egyptian tales, Babylonian chronicles, Assyrian annals or Hebrew texts like our books of Kings. In Babylonia, as early as 1700 BC, we know the named writer of one version of the famous Flood story, but he was its scribe, or copyist, not the original author of the narrative; the same is true of other names which were attached as scribes' signatures to other Babylonian mythical stories in later centuries. Scribes might have contributed something to a traditional story which they were copying, but they were not seen as its authors. Conversely, books of wisdom, laws, proverbs, dreams or prophecies cited an author or personal source. This distinction is firm and long-lasting among Near Eastern writers. In the eighth century BC a library in Babylonia listed its books by their authors if they were books of wisdom and so forth or by their opening sentences if they were narratives.

Among the Jews, texts were regarded in exactly this way. Narratives were anonymous but the narrative books of the Pentateuch were known by their opening words (the names in modern Christian Bibles, Genesis,

Exodus and so forth, are the names given to them when they were turned into Greek). Conversely, names were given, or found, for books which were books of wisdom or were thought to be prophecies. We read the books of Hosea or Amos, although these texts were probably compiled by their followers after the prophet's death. Before *c.* 200 BC (when the books were translated) authors had also been found for the book of Proverbs. Originally, they will have circulated in ones or twos: people then ascribed them to wise King Solomon, or Agur and Lemuel, well-meant guesses which greatly enhanced their authority. From the distant past, named songs had survived, the Song of Deborah or the book of Jashar, which was possibly an entire book of Hebrew songs. There were also the many psalms, some of which dated back to the early days of monarchy: some of the oldest were ascribed to David (probably wrongly), an author who gained more and more of them as time passed.

Not until *c.* 200 BC is a Hebrew author known to us by name in a surviving text: Jesus ben Sirach, author of our Bibles' Ecclesiasticus. In naming himself, he was not following the Greeks' example: his book was a book of wisdom for which a personal name had always been appropriate. Conversely, when authors wrote the two narratives which we know as 1 and 2 Maccabees, they did not put their names to them even though one of them was abbreviating a named Greek historian's book. In Hebrew, narratives were still anonymous: we do not know who wrote the book of Esther or the book of Judith. It is easy to miss this distinction because of an apparent exception: Moses was seen as the author (supposedly) of the five books from Genesis onwards. In fact, these books are not a narrative. They are books of law and their narratives were read as prophecies. With hindsight, therefore, they needed a prophetic author's name: surely Moses, the greatest of all prophets, had written them, foreseeing the bits which occurred after his death? We can find something similar in Josephus, although at first sight it seems truly amazing: Josephus believed that the books of Samuel and Kings had all been written by the prophet Samuel: he, too, had had to foresee most of them because he had died very early in their story. To Josephus, these books were not merely histories, as they are to us: they were prophetic and so they needed a named author. Who better than Samuel, the greatest prophet of the age? Such false authorship had a long life: it was not until the seventeenth century that Moses's authorship was refuted by the English philosopher Thomas Hobbes. Until then, it had distorted the texts' authority.

For many hundreds of years, therefore, eastern narratives were issued anonymously, whereas books of prophecy, wisdom or poetry were not. The convention must have had a cause, apart from tradition. Anonymity might seem safer, a way of airing 'things not to our comfort'. In Judaea power often lay with priests and kings, and unwelcome scrolls (like Jeremiah's) could end up on the fire. The most dangerous books, however, were prophecies: according to the book of the law, the punishment for false prophecy was death. Prophecies, none the less, circulated under the prophets' own names, although no names or false names would have been much less risky. The cause of the practice must lie elsewhere. Evidently, it lay in an author's abiding aim for his work: success.

Most of the biblical books of narrative covered such a long span of events (from Joshua to the Exile or Eden to the Exodus) that they could not possibly be passed off as the record of one important eyewitness. Long after the event, the narrator's authority might seem dubious if it was widely publicized to his contemporaries. Anonymity raised its credit. A nameless narrative seemed like 'the' story and could not be attacked for personal bias or ignorance: anonymous authors escape their own errors or lies. If somebody read their nameless book years later and thought that it was truly prophetic, they might ascribe it to someone as great as Samuel: so much the better.

Prophecies, wisdom and visions, however, were personal by their very form, and so they directly raised the questions, 'Who has foreseen this?' and 'Why does he think that he knows?' Their very nature was subjective, and a text stood a better chance of being credited if it hinted at its author. It stood an even better chance if its author pretended to be somebody else. The passionate beliefs of the man next door are only his beliefs; his prophecies are only guesses; it is hard for neighbours and acquaintances to accept that he speaks with authority, that a man (much less a woman) who is not always right about everyday life is suddenly the messenger of God. Lesser people's opinions, let alone their visions or predictions, seem vastly more significant if they appear under greater men's names. At the heart of Hebrew scripture lies just such a text. When unknown authors compiled the core of our Deuteronomy, probably *c.* 700–660 BC, they passed off its laws and exhortations as if they were the words of Moses, speaking as the prophet of God. A lifetime later, in 622/1, this 'book of the law of the Lord' was rediscovered and taken at face value.

A greater name conferred greater authority, but the best mergers, as always, were those which raised the value of both parties. Here, prophecies were beautifully obliging. Earlier prophets could be given much later prophecies which expanded the text of their work: the most elaborate additions were those made to Isaiah, who had lived in the late eighth century BC. The second half of his book now includes the prophecies of an unknown author (Second Isaiah) who had written nearly two centuries after Isaiah's death. This unnamed prophet was merged with Isaiah and gained the full weight of his existing visions and reputation; Isaiah, meanwhile, gained the credit of foreseeing and addressing the Persian king Cyrus, so far beyond his lifetime. The merger was artful and deliberate. The Song of Songs also profited, but here the two parties were unequal. The likeliest origin for this book is a collection of secular love poetry which later readers tried to present as a religious, not an erotic, text. To support their new reading, they ascribed the book to King Solomon, perhaps during the third century BC. At a similar date another Jew composed the thoughtful text which we know as Ecclesiastes. Here, he himself implied that he had ruled in Jerusalem (he had not) and hinted that he was Solomon. Again, the hint lent authority to his work.

These great names of the past were not chosen because a canon of scripture had closed in their era, obliging authors to choose ancient, canonical names, but because they carried a much greater weight. Nowadays, authors and publishers try to pick friendly reviewers; in the later stages of scripture, authors picked suitable identities instead. In each case the aim was similar: success for the book. In antiquity there was no title-page or law of copyright and no easy way of telling an old text from a new one. It was not that the 'timelessness of Hebrew thought meant that centuries could be telescoped and generations spanned' or that 'the close bonds between God's people and their ancestors made their ideas interchangeable' (in the Gospels the crowds do wonder if John the Baptist is Elijah returning, but the Baptist knows full well that he is not). Perhaps authors identified closely with their false namesakes and wrote things which they 'ought' to have written, but the fact remains that they wrote unreservedly under false names. In modern literature, authors have sometimes written under pseudonyms for the amusement of their readers or for the irony of giving wise views to a humbler person. Jewish authors chose the names of superiors, not inferiors, and always found these superiors in the distant past.

The result, quite literally, was a forger's paradise. Visions of the heavens and a future world were passed off on mysterious figures mentioned in the ancient texts (like Enoch who 'walked with God' in Genesis 5:22); Solomon acquired a new store of wisdom, and David gained dozens of musical psalms. In 167 BC the Jews in Judaea underwent the great event of their war with King Antiochus, a successor of Alexander, who attempted to persecute them and impose Greek ways on their religion and culture. Near the end of the struggle, in 164 BC, an unknown author fathered a great prophecy of past history on the legendary person of Daniel, which culminated in a prophecy for the author's own times. These prophecies were then circulated, the first surviving resistance literature in the world, and were combined with an older series of stories about Daniel's exploits. When events confirmed the drift, if not the detail, of their main prophecy, their fame was assured.

False authorship did influence the way in which texts were seen. Sometimes it confirmed their credit (Daniel or the Song of Songs); sometimes it conformed to it (the law of Moses or particular psalms of David). The fair name of Daniel, however, was also put to something new: 'And many of them that sleep in the dust of the earth shall awake, some to everlasting life, and some to shame and everlasting contempt. And they that be wise shall shine as the brightness of the firmament; and they that turn many to righteousness as the stars for ever and ever' (Daniel 12:2–3). Previously, there were Jews who had believed in a new age to be brought about by God: some also thought of a shadowy afterlife of uncertain scope. In the 160s the belief hardened. During the Jews' great war of resistance, martyrs were dying valiantly, but surely they were not dying for ever? Our Bible's first clear account of a bodily resurrection and eternal life for saints and sinners is in a text as late as the 160s BC. It was impelled by a historical crisis and, in order to impose itself, was palmed off on someone who never wrote it.

I I

Not only were the persecutions from 167 to 164 BC a failure: they led to Jewish victories under the leadership of the Maccabees and an era of independence for the Jewish people. Victories bring their own tensions, and this age was also a watershed which saw fundamental changes in Jewish religious life. In the wake of victory, the relation between power-politics and religious piety posed itself acutely and led to important splits between various groups. Out of them emerged the Pharisees and the sect, probably the Essenes, whom we know from scrolls found near the Dead Sea. The Essenes, especially, are known to have had their own understanding of ancient texts on which they wrote commentaries, adjusting them to their own view of history.

No central authority existed to enforce uniformity or orthodoxy; these differing groups emerged beside all the different synagogues, each with texts of ancient scrolls in translation. It is important to remember the problems in defining what exactly Hebrew scripture was thought to say. Our earliest full copy of the Hebrew scriptures nowadays is a manuscript known as the Leningrad Manuscript, which was written in AD 1009. The form of its Hebrew text can be traced further back, to groups of Jewish scholars who were working in the eighth and ninth centuries AD, especially in Palestine. They are known as the Masoretes (*masorah* is the Hebrew word for tradition), and it is to their efforts that we owe the traditional text of the Old Testament. Until recently their Hebrew text stood like a road block across all attempts to trace scripture's route through the fourteen hundred years or more since its earlier parts were written. Apart from a few scriptural inscriptions on early objects and monuments, some of which seemed surprisingly free, there were only some uncertain side-roads round this block in our knowledge. The Greek translations of Hebrew scripture went back in part to the third century BC: where they differed from the later text, were they mistaken or were they using an earlier version of it, no less valid than the Masoretes'? The Pentateuch also survived in manuscripts among the break-away group of Samaritans who had parted from the Jews during the centuries after Alexander the Great. Where their texts differed, were they peculiar to their sect or were they, too, witnesses to an earlier alternative?

The obvious way to answer these questions was to find some early Hebrew texts of scripture surviving among the debris of the world. The search for them has a long history. During the mid eighteenth century biblical scholars in England conceived the idea that purer, unaltered texts of the Hebrew scripture might still survive among Jewish groups who were reported to be living in China as far-away descendants of a lost tribe of Israel. The mirage of these Bibles in China lived on from one Christian adventurer to another until 1851, when China's Jews and their scripture were finally visited: they were owners of nothing older than the well-known Masoretic text.

When travelling failed, archaeology took over. A single piece of papyrus, the Nash Papyrus (dating to the first century BC) was found in Egypt and published in 1903. It was thought at first to be a bit of an early Deuteronomy whose Hebrew wording diverged from the later familiar text: however, it is probably not a scriptural text at all. Since 1947 it has been eclipsed by finds of exceptional importance, the hoards of texts written on papyrus and on animal skins which have been recovered from caves near the ruined site of Qumran, just south of Jericho and near the western shore of the Dead Sea. Against all expectations, we now have the evidence of 175 manuscript copies of a book known in our Old Testament which range in date from *c.* 225 BC to AD 50: only four of them are more or less complete. They are not the only texts found at Qumran, but they include bits of every one of our biblical books except Esther. Their study and publication have been painfully slow, and after more than forty years there are still scrolls which are known only from reports: there is, however, no doubt that these bits of text take us back to a point about a thousand years before the Masoretes' Hebrew text on which subsequent Jewish and Christian Bibles have been based. In the 1950s and 1960s papyri from further caves to the south of Qumran (in Wadi Murabba'at and in Nahal Hever) and from the rock-fortress of Masada emerged to join the Dead Sea texts; they included a very few bits of further texts of scripture. Those from Masada must date to various points before AD 73; those from the caves to varying dates before 132, the year of a major Jewish revolt against Roman rule. Those found in the Wadi Murabba'at caves almost certainly belong between 40 and 132.

Already in the 1750s the great Hebrew scholar Benjamin Kennicott was aware of the gaps between our texts and their originals: 'What was inspired by God was committed to the care of men and we must acknowledge that we have had this Treasure in earthen vessels.' Since 1947, the new finds have alerted us to the Treasure's textual drama and have opened up three particular avenues in study of its vessels' earth: the history of Hebrew and its spelling, the variety in the texts of scripture and the potential value of the early translations into Greek. Now that we have these earlier Hebrew texts, we can look more critically on the ways in which the later Masoretes and their sources assumed that Hebrew words were to be spelt or given vowels: previously Hebrew had been written with consonants only, like speedwriting. Thanks to recent finds, it has become a little easier to correct some of the editors' assumptions. More drastically, we can see how their text is only one late and arbitrary line, surviving from an earlier uncontrolled variety.

This variety would not have been obvious without the finds from Qumran. The other three sites were much less prolific (bits of only eight scriptural texts turned up there), and so far as reports of them imply, none of their texts would have challenged the old view, that the Masoretes' late Hebrew text was the age-old, traditional version. Every one of their scrolls is said to point in its direction, either matching it or at least matching its line of development ('proto-Masoretic'). If this description is right (study of them is not yet complete), they would seem to suggest that our traditional Hebrew Bible was already the accepted form of the text in the lifetimes of Jesus and Paul (bits of Exodus, Leviticus, Deuteronomy, Psalms and Ezekiel have been found at Masada and must all be earlier than the famous siege of the site's occupants in 73; some of the texts in the caves elsewhere may also have been copied before 70). These finds, however, are very few and very fragmented.

It is this comforting belief which the vastly greater finds at Qumran have destroyed. Many of the texts found there do also belong to the line of development on which the Masoretic text eventually drew. Others do not, reminding us what a variety was possible. Even from reports and publications so far, there is a version of the book of Jeremiah which is an eighth shorter than our Bible's, a text of Samuel which is not so very close to the text from which our Bible's Samuel is translated, variants in the text of Job, a doctored text of Ecclesiastes, two differing Isaiahs and many other complexities. We might expect that the holiest books, the first five of scripture, would show much less variation, because they were the law, and were publicly read and recited. They vary less than some but not insignificantly: we have quite a variety of readings for bits of Deuteronomy, a text of Leviticus whose differences resemble no known tradition and an intriguing cluster of readings in a copy of Exodus. It is very important to realize that in most cases these variants are not the silly mistakes of people who were copying the same type of text which we have used since the ninth century A D. They belong in independent streams of development.

Sometimes, we can see one type of text reacting on another, as a scribe tried to adjust to a variant reading or as he used elements of a variant text which we know independently. The movement of the scribes' corrections is not all one way, let alone in the ultimate direction of our Bible's Masoretic text. At Qumran it is noticeable how one piece of Deuteronomy which is quite close to our eventual Masoretic text was copied in *c.* 150 B C but was then recopied on a later scroll, probably in the first century B C, with corrections which took its wording in a totally different direction, closer to the Greek translations of it. If we had only the very few texts from Masada and elsewhere, we might have believed that the eventual Masoretic text of scripture was already dominant before 70. At Qumran the much bigger sample suggests the opposite: there was a great range of texts available, only some of which bore a close relation to the Masoretes' eventual tradition. It is not obvious that they were private copies, and therefore less accurate, or that their variety owed anything to the beliefs of individual groups or sects. In the time of Jesus, scriptures were not standardized, and there was no reason to believe that the text familiar to us would dominate, drive out the others and be venerated as holy scripture.

In short, textual diversity reigned. The diversity is particularly tantalizing, because it bears on the value of the Greek translations of our Old Testament. As they began to be written in the third century B C, might not their surviving texts be witnesses to yet another batch of variant Hebrew texts, as old as anything known at Qumran? The Greek translators were far from perfect, although one wing of Jewish and early Christian opinion eventually defended them by stating that they had all been inspired by God. They were working in Egypt, where Hebrew was not widely spoken. They had no Hebrew grammars, because none existed. Their Hebrew texts were written in a Hebrew script with consonants but no fully expressed vowels, a system which could lead to ambiguity in places where no living tradition of recitation or interpretation preserved the words' sense. Inevitably, they misunderstood and mistranslated from time to time. They also had their pet words and little touches, so that the translation of individual books into Greek varies quite widely. So does the skill of the separate translators who can be identified in any one text: an erratic book of Isaiah is among the worst. Their theology and choice of words often looked outwards to the Greek world and sometimes, therefore, away from the Hebrew. It is not even clear exactly what the first translators wrote. Their translations were revised by fellow Jews, and again by Christians, from the first century BC to the early fourth century AD. These revisions tended to take the Greek ever further from its earliest Hebrew base, and they underlie most of the Greek which we now have.

In the 1940s an acute study of the variant Greek form of the book of Kings did argue that it must have rested on a Hebrew text which was different from the one behind our Bible. The finds at Qumran have greatly raised the Greek translators' credit, because some of the Qumran texts overlap in places, with readings which are known only in the Greek scriptures. We can no longer blame every deviation on the Greek translators' and revisers' own invention: they may simply have been using a valid Hebrew text which was rather earlier and different from ours. Only one text from Qumran, a scroll of Jeremiah, coincides so closely with a Greek translation that we can think of it as almost identical with the translators' own Hebrew original: even one such coincidence is very significant. Its implications have been supported by study of the ancients' own views on translation. 'Literal' word-for-word translation was thought proper by Greek and Roman critics for texts with a precise and practical content, secular laws and so forth. When the translators set to work, parts of scripture might have struck them as literary texts, deserving a free translation, but most of it, as holy writ, would have deserved a word-for-word approach, especially the books of law and prophecy.

The finds at Qumran and these ancient ideas of translation raise the value of the Greek scriptures to a degree which has yet to be defined. Among many examples, a few can convey what is at stake. We do not have rival texts which are totally different, giving completely different persons and events for books like Exodus or Joshua or Kings. Instead, we have some basic disagreements in length, wording, arrangement and that backbone of all history, chronology. The Greek translations give different spans of time for events in Genesis and Exodus (here, the difference is probably their own invention) and different lengths of reign for the kings in Kings and Samuel (here, they are probably right and the Masoretes' Hebrew is wrong). Anyone listening nowadays to books like Samuel or Jeremiah in a church or synagogue service is quite likely to be listening to one arbitrary version, padded out with later material. It may even be that the divergent telling of the events of the books of Samuel, which is to be found in our books of Chronicles, was based on a better Hebrew text of Samuel.

Some of the texts at Qumran overlap with another textual by-way: the text of the first five books, from Genesis to Deuteronomy, which was used by the Samaritans. Here, too, some (but not all) of the Samaritans' wording and arrangement finds support from separate Hebrew manuscripts: one text, in particular, of Exodus points back to a basic form of the text which the Samaritans then altered to suit their sect's interest. Until all the Dead Sea scrolls are published, the details of all these overlaps cannot be sorted out, but there are general views which are already secure. No central religious belief is affected: God is still mentioned with covenants, promises, laws and the Lord's Anointed. The casualties, rather, are faith in unerring scripture and unwary idealization of our Bible as a literary or canonical whole. My comparison with sacking is apt here: the authors themselves did not issue their texts in differing versions (except, perhaps, Ben Sira, whose Ecclesiasticus survives in different forms), but other people padded their originals with later material. Instead of an early definitive canon, we have textual diversity as far back as we can see: the Masoretes' well-meant editing at the end of the line is not very weighty authority. For some scholars, however, and for many Christians and practising Jews, the late Masoretic text has such a weight of familiarity in their reading and services that it outweighs anything else, whether in Greek or early fragments. In fact, these other texts are alternatives, with a respectable weight of their own. The multiple texts from Qumran have been divided optimistically into differing regions – one type from Egypt, one from Palestine, one from

Babylon – and they have even been connected to the known revisions of the Greek scripture, as if each revision tried to conform to a different Hebrew 'regional' text. These views impose tidiness where none existed. There is no reason to isolate Egypt's text of scripture so neatly from Palestine's or both from the Jews' in Babylonia. The fragments are too complex to be assigned to one or other type.

In reply, it is sometimes argued that the text of the Old Testament is no more insecure than the text of Homer's Greek poems, which classical scholars still print in a single agreed version and use and enjoy without further ado. The comparison may seem apt. Like Homer's poems, the early parts of scripture go back to an uncertain date, at least as far as the eighth century BC. Unlike the scriptures, Homer's poems were memorized and recited, and nothing is reported about a written text until some centuries after the likeliest date of their composition. If anything, this difference may seem to increase the chances of the poems' corruption. When we have early papyrus texts of the Homeric poems, between *c*. 300 and 150 BC, they do not overlap exactly with the texts as we now read them. After *c*. 150 BC, however, perhaps after a scholarly programme of revision, the papyrus versions do come back into line and conform to the Homer which we print from the earliest complete manuscripts. So, too, did Jewish scholars revise their scriptures and bring them into a line from which the eventual Masoretic text became fixed. This type of text was written out for posterity by Masoretic Hebrew scholars who inserted the vowel marks which had started to be used to fill out Hebrew's consonantal script (vowel marks had begun to be used in Syriac and were being imitated both in Hebrew and Arabic at a similar date). Sometimes, they guessed the wrong vowels and ruined the sense or rhythm.

However, the Homeric analogy is not as close as it seems. Before *c*. 150 BC the papyri show a Homer which has been padded with later, superfluous additions. They do not show two or more divergent texts which are independent of each other, like the Jeremiahs, Samuels, Jobs or Joshuas revealed by the Qumran finds and the Greek translations. There was one and the same basic Homer, whereas by *c*. 300 BC there was not one and the same basic text of a Hebrew scripture. It is worth wondering why. It is not only that Greek words were written complete with vowels, whereas Hebrew texts omitted them and only wrote the consonants: this difference caused some of the variations but not many of them. Unlike the scriptures, the Homeric poems were composed in an intricate metre which limited possible changes; they were also recited publicly throughout their history, whereas we know nothing about regular public readings of the biblical texts until long after their origins. Hebrew scripture's diverse texts thus pose problems of a different order to the padding-out of Homer. Extreme views are still taken of the sanctity of the Bible's text as we print it, but the papyri of the Old Testament suggest a different perspective. We have scriptures in plenty, more than most readers realize, but the original scripture has been lost and the search for it peters out *c*. 200 BC in an irreconcilable range of types of text.

III

Between *c*. 250 and the time of Jesus, textual diversity was compounded by another habit: close reading. Close reading was different from literacy, the ability to write or read or to do both: it required study and a wish to find answers in a text. For centuries, the Jews had had no schools or higher education: significantly, proverbs had flourished, the symptom of societies where 'limited education imposes the traditional and conventional expression of opinion, wisdom and sentiment' (they flourished, too, in the semi-literate setting of northern England in the 1930s; in Roman literature, they were used to depict the semi-literate society of Trimalchio and his dinner-guests, both wonderfully vulgar and uneducated). We should not be misled by the existence of written law. A class of scribes had emerged, not teachers but people who could cope with the growing need for written contracts, documents and the everyday negotiation of points of legal detail which were too time-consuming for an active Temple priesthood. By most people the words of the holy law were still heard but not seen. Like the written instructions to assemble a modern gadget, the law was a general body of knowledge which was passed on through practice and example: the text was there for reference but was not acted out line by line. Essentials could be obeyed, if necessary, without study or reading: one modern scholar of scripture has aptly reminded us of Jo in Dickens's novel *Bleak House*, who is 'completely illiterate with a very low IQ ... but persevered through a short life without committing a crime'. Many Jews did much the same.

None the less, as synagogues spread back into the promised land, more people would hear rather more of their ancient texts being read. Only short extracts were read from particular passages, but afterwards a visitor might discuss what the texts suggested. We know most about this pattern of service from evidence of the earliest Christian period. In the early to mid first century an inscription tells us of a synagogue in Jerusalem which had been founded for the 'reading of the law and the teaching of the precepts'. In Christian scripture we are told how Jesus and Paul each stood up in a synagogue and surprised their audience by the comments they made after a lesson from scripture had been read aloud.

Although the Temple and its cult were the centre of religious life, there was growing scope for enthusiasts and keen believers to ponder bits of written text for themselves. Perhaps such study took place in synagogues, although we are poorly informed about their uses; texts, education and literary culture were highly valued in the surrounding world of the Greeks, and the same values became more prominent among educated Jews. For Ben Sira (*c.* 200) wisdom is no longer a body of traditional proverbs and sayings: wisdom is the 'book of the covenant of the most high God, the law which Moses commanded'. Close, personal study of it was now becoming desirable, although 'only a visionary could imagine children studying the law and then only in the messianic age' (Jubilees 23:26, which is probably not earlier than the 170s BC). We are far from the Koranic schools of modern Islam where children learn to read and write their holy text, but we are faced with a society where keen individuals would now study and read. In the book of Daniel, chapter 9, Daniel (*c.* 164 BC) is said to have begun one of his visions by 'understanding from the books' what the Lord had said to Jeremiah. Keen readers might even have their own copy of a scriptural text: we need only think of the Ethiopian eunuch, reading a bit of the book of Isaiah when he met Philip the Christian on a long journey.

Once keen readers begin to study, they begin to interpret, affecting the meaning of old texts. Among the Jews, in the century or so before Jesus, these readers played havoc with authors' meanings. They took their texts word by word and read them for the oddest senses; they over-interpreted the words, ignoring their context and general gist. They assumed that words of the prophets which had been general statements, not specific forecasts, must contain exact predictions which were still to come true: these predictions could be found in individual verses or in combinations of texts from different places. Our best contemporary evidence for this torturing of sense and meaning lies in the group (probably Essenes) whom we know from the finds of scrolls near the Dead Sea: their commentaries on scripture were false from start to finish. Nobody put critical, historical questions to the texts which they had inherited, and, as a result, they raped them.

They also avoided the fundamental question: how much, if anything, was true? In this period, philosophy was a respected part of public inquiry and education in the Greek-speaking cities where many Jews now lived. Even the most religious types of philosophy raised basic questions (does God exist? why is justice a virtue?). Although questioners then wrote theology to answer them, philosophy still made people think critically. As a result, in the first century BC 'in Athens and Rome, thinking about religion usually made people less religious'; among Jews, however, 'the more you thought about religion, the more religious you became'. The major reason for this difference was the Jews' possession of scripture. They set the agenda for thought, absorbed it and were never questioned critically.

A fabulous jungle of story, interpretation and prediction thus arose round the tangle of old, composite texts: none of it was true, and by the time of Jesus nobody read the scriptures correctly because nobody knew what they were. They muddled them with Moses's or Samuel's authorship; they distorted their meaning; and, however interesting it is to see what they found or how they did it, the fact remains that almost all of this finding was completely false.

It was compounded by respect for the texts themselves as sacred objects. In many of them, scribes had copied a very important four-letter word, YHWH, the name of God. As Jews made more contact with the Gentile Hellenistic world, this four-letter word became something which was better kept secret; otherwise, God's mighty name might be used in Gentile spells or magic. To name a god was also to imply that his power could be defined and limited. In the centuries after Alexander, therefore, Yahweh went ex-directory; most of the newly written texts of this period did not use his four-letter name but called him by something else. The name still stood, however, in the older texts which had been composed before this era; its presence was now thought to be very holy indeed, and it gave a scroll exceptional sanctity.

The effects of this belief can be seen in a famous custom and a famous discussion: when Jews needed to dispose of an old or unwanted scroll which contained the holy four-letter word, they did not tear it up or throw it away. They put it in a jar and buried it (texts were often put in jars to keep them safe in Near Eastern societies). Some of the holy manuscripts near the Dead Sea were found in jars, and the practice persisted: 'it certainly looks as if this institution of a morgue for sacred or unwanted manuscripts was taken over from Judaism by the early Church'. The idea that the Jews had scrolls which were physically holy became known to Gentiles too. When the Roman emperor Augustus gave a ruling on the privileges of Jews in particular cities in Asia, he and his advisers equated the theft of a Jewish scripture with the theft of a sacred object.

Sacred scrolls were to be handled only with extreme care; we have evidence of discussions between Jewish teachers, or rabbis, on the question of which texts did or did not have this quality. Its evidence has often been pressed in the wrong way. Rabbis of the later first century AD are said to have discussed whether the Song of Songs or Ecclesiastes 'defile the hands' of anyone who touches them: whole theories about the fixing of a Jewish canon of scripture have been built on this evidence alone. These discussions by Jewish experts have been thought to have occurred at a formal council, a council which met at Jamnia in the 80s AD after the disastrous war against Rome had cost the Jews their Temple in Jerusalem. In the wake of it, on this view, their leading scholars gathered to decide on a Jewish canon of holy scripture; they had to argue whether the Song and Ecclesiastes should be in or out.

These theories have had a long life, but they have rightly been discredited. There was no known council at Jamnia; the experts' discussions are not said to have been part of a council or synod; they were not concerned with a canon or whether the Song of Songs was holy scripture. Rather, the participants took for granted that the Song or Ecclesiastes were extremely special texts; what bothered them was whether particular texts made a person unclean if he touched them. The problem arose from a simple difficulty. Neither the Song nor Ecclesiastes contained the holy four-letter word; they referred to God differently.

The book of Esther did not even mention God at all: the effects of handling it, too, were later discussed.

So far from defining a canon, experts were discussing an awkward problem for textual handlers. If a specially admired text did not have the four-letter name, was it none the less so special that like others with the four-letter version, it obliged you to wash and cleanse yourself when you set a finger on it? These discussions rumbled on for centuries (the question was genuinely hard to decide), but the participants were not discussing which texts were holy scripture and which were not.

The conclusion has thrown a new light on the history of Jewish scripture: there is no known record of a council in the 80s which decided which books to include. Without it, one response is to emphasize freedom from any definition at all: Jews had their ancient scrolls of the law, the prophets, the psalms and otherwise, a wide religious literature without any clear boundaries. So far from having a canon of scripture, Jews in the first century (including Jesus) had all sorts of texts with religious value, although the books of Moses were a special group.

This relaxed answer cannot be quite right. When the experts discussed the problem of texts and dirty hands, they did not discuss texts like Ecclesiasticus whose author (Ben Sira) also avoided the four-letter word; they discussed the Song and Ecclesiastes (and, later, Esther) because these texts were more special (like others) and ought to be handled respectfully even if they lacked God's name. How, when and by whom had they already been agreed to be special? Here, we have only one bit of evidence, some remarks by Josephus in the early 90s A D.

In them, Josephus contrasted Jewish scripture with the many conflicting texts of the Greeks: Jews, he wrote, do not have myriads of inconsistent books but 'only twenty-two which are justly accredited and contain the record of all time'. He did not name them, but he referred to the five books of law, thirteen books of history to the time of Artaxerxes (all written, he believed, by prophets) and four 'books of hymns to God and precepts for human conduct' (psalms, proverbs and presumably the Song and Ecclesiastes). He also knows of other books outside this twenty-two, but they are inferior, even if they are history books (they were not written by prophets).

Here, Josephus is scoring a point against Greek writers, but the number is not his invention for this purpose alone. There are twenty-two letters in the Hebrew alphabet: somebody before the 90s had had the bright idea that the number of special Jewish texts corresponded to the number of Hebrew letters. Twenty-two is also the number which the Christian Jerome discovered, three centuries later, from Jewish informants. By then, alternative numbers were also being suggested: twenty-five, according to a Christian who asked informants in Palestine in the 170s, or twenty-four, according to the Syriac text of the Jewish work, Fourth Ezra: this book was written before A D 100, but our Syriac text of it was copied much later; our Latin text of it omits the mention of twenty-four altogether.

Twenty-two, the earliest attested number, was presumably known to Josephus from his time in Judaea before 70: perhaps it was current in Jesus's lifetime. Like the discussions on texts and hands, twenty-two assumed that one group of religious texts was more special than others. It did not specify exactly which texts they were (what about Esther? was Ecclesiastes a separate book?), but its alphabetic principle was rather clever: perhaps it arose among one particular group (the Pharisees are an obvious possibility). It was not an official canon (it might be a well-known idea, but nobody had to accept it); it was not fixed for all time; it did not deny religious value to texts outside it. It was, however, a sign that some texts were more special and that outside the five law books, there was not just a textual free for all.

Anyone was free to ignore it, and even the Pharisees (who perhaps invented it) did not believe that twenty-two texts were the sole sources of authority. The law books, from Genesis to Deuteronomy, were often obscure or contradictory, and so a body of tradition had grown up beside them. It was particularly important to Pharisees and is usually considered to have been a range of teaching and interpretation which was passed on orally. After the fall of the Temple in 70, such teaching and oral interpretation characterized the rabbis and was eventually collected into a book, the Mishnah (*c*. 200 A D), where it is still studied as authoritative. Pharisees, however, were not rabbis before their time: their tradition may have been practical, about details of behaviour, rather than a body of oral commentary and law.

The Pharisees were only one group, Sadducees were another. Sadducees have often been identified with the leading Jewish families who provided the high priests of the Temple under Roman rule, but this view, too, has been challenged. Of the many high priests in this period, only one is said to have been a Sadducee; so far from being Jerusalem's upper class, Sadducees, too, may have been a group defined by a particular view. The Christian author of Acts and Josephus give rather different accounts of their beliefs, but I accept that Acts' author was a contemporary who had visited Jerusalem and that his account cannot be dismissed. Sadducees accepted only the written law, a rather different attitude to those who accepted that twenty-two books were special. The main point, surely, was that they denied any authority to the practical traditions of conduct which Pharisees accepted. According to Acts' author, they also denied the existence of angels and a resurrection. Both these beliefs were late arrivals in texts outside the main law. Probably, a Sadducee did not reject the psalms and the prophets altogether, but was wary about any bits of these books which went beyond the theology of the law or Pentateuch.

The most significant fact is that these groups could still disagree: neither saw the other as heretics, and both groups could co-exist and even co-operate, like British members of Parliament, despite social and doctrinal differences. Twenty-two was an attractive number for the special texts of scripture, but nobody had decreed it, and even the Pharisees did not think that a list of books was the total sum of religious authority.

Nowadays, Jews often regard their scripture as a threesome: the law, the prophets (which include the anonymous books of narrative) and the writings (texts like Job or the Song). This triple division has been traced right back to words of Ben Sira's grandson in the preface to his translation (*c.* 110 BC) of his grandfather's Ecclesiasticus, but it is not the only interpretation of what he says (by 'writings' he may mean something less specific), and anyway the division was not standard practice. In the New Testament we hear of the 'law and the prophets' or the 'law, prophets and psalms'. Among the Dead Sea scrolls, the books of law, prophecy and psalms are the only books which receive a written commentary. Others, it seems, were less special to their readers.

In the time of Jesus, therefore, there was a notion that an inner group of texts was special: those which named God were particularly sacred; the books of the law were the most special of all, but there were others too, the prophets, of course, and at least another four or five (psalms, proverbs and so forth). There was a theory that the special texts numbered twenty-two, marvellously linked to the letters of the alphabet, but there was no idea of a canon which had closed, let alone of a fixed Bible for every Jew's use. There was still scope for disagreement, and before 70 nobody had tried to enforce an 'authorized version' of religious writings. Within the scrolls, even, the wording of texts could vary widely; some people had short versions, some long, and there was probably diversity even among texts used by any one of the various religious parties. Least of all did people agree on what the texts were trying to say. Their inheritance from long years of history lived on in splendid discord. Meanwhile, prominent families filled the high priesthood and did their best to co-operate with the Roman rulers of the moment. On a Friday in March 36, they contrived the execution of a Jew whose followers were to change the way in which the scrolls were read.

6
Jesus and the Scriptures

Jesus grew up among people who had texts but no Bible, and whose predicament is still familiar. The authority of their main texts, the books of the law, was unquestioned, but what exactly did they and all the others mean? There were laws which contradicted each other and did not cover obvious problems; there were apparent contradictions in the narratives, and there were masses of prophecies whose original reference had long passed or been forgotten. The texts themselves had been copied in different forms, and their language was no longer everyone's daily speech. Hebrew was still a living language, perhaps especially among the educated, but most people used Aramaic and when they listened to the Hebrew texts, they might be glad of an Aramaic paraphrase.

In Jesus's lifetime people clearly expected that a great figure from their past would return: Elijah, perhaps, or Moses, or even (according to Jesus, at Luke 11:31) the Queen of Sheba. Suppose that King Solomon had come back instead: he would never have credited it. Here were his descendants, venerating texts which he was supposed to have written and wondering whether or not they polluted people's hands: he had never composed a word of them. One of them said that he had 'uttered three thousand proverbs and his songs were a thousand and five': it was amazing to be thought so clever. There were even people who thought that he had written the Song of Songs: it would have looked to him like a collection of straightforward love poetry (his Egyptian wife had known plenty of bits like it). Why ever had people fallen for this book of the law in which Moses seemed to speak: why had they dreamed up a covenant with God or a future life? He and his friends had managed very well without any of them. They had never believed for one moment that Moses had left a long text of laws or had entered into a pact at the insistence of Number One. It was good to see that people remembered all the horses, the Temple and the women, but they grossly exaggerated the numbers. The bits about the Queen of Sheba also sounded intriguing, even if they failed to specify her gifts and hard questions: in real life, he had never had such a visitor. True, he had sacrificed on the high places, but some of the most conspicuous altars to foreign gods and goddesses had been the idea of his girls. He himself had never imagined that all other gods should be chased off the hills round Jerusalem or that Yahweh was the only one. Nor, in his view, had Yahweh: he had been quite amenable for years on end, and a large, single kingdom had persisted. Look at Israel nowadays: the north had disappeared completely, there was no king and the Romans controlled Judaea. What on earth was the point of this jungle of subsequent writings? Jerusalem still had a priesthood, the Temple was bigger and better than ever, and the calendar of festivals and sacrifices was vastly richer. He himself had thought that a meat offering in the morning and a grain offering at night were quite enough, except in emergencies or on special occasions. Nowadays the priests burned meat twice a day, received sin offerings, guilt offerings and had pulled off a coup by insisting on their tithes, first-fruits and Temple tax. There must be something annoying Yahweh: did he, perhaps, want honours for his consorts? Was he angry that his name had gone ex-directory and that he himself was being worshipped alone?

To Solomon, it might have seemed a jungle, but the scriptures had not survived and retained respect simply because they were old and believed to be holy objects. They told of the national past and explained why the people had suffered and then been rewarded. They assured even their casual hearers that God loved his people, that he cared for goodness in his Creation, that there was hope in adversity and one day, a great future. People read them in the light of their new predicament, but under Roman rule this message remained relevant and powerful. The laws made the Jews special, and a special people can retain a special hope. The laws also had a special virtue: they told people what to do and were thought to tell them what would happen, but they did not exhaust these subjects. They were obscure and often contradictory, and as a result they could accommodate life's changes and improvements. They set a framework which exercised the curious, but left room for people to find what they wanted. The jungle had gaps and holes: it gave much more freedom than readers of Matthew's Gospel or Paul's epistles might suppose.

Enthusiasts loved to argue what the gaps meant. What exactly could people do on the Sabbath? Suppose they wished to tie or untie knots in a bit of rope: could they do one, both or neither? Could they really go no further than two thousand cubits from home? Washing was another problem: it took away impurity, but were all types of water equally cleansing? Jerusalem water was not recycled like London's water, but its sources varied: what about the purity of rainwater or water from melted snow? There were problems everywhere, with women, marriages and better gardening. The Pentateuch told stories of marriage with foreign women, and the law book prohibited marriage only with a few of the neighbouring tribes: what about other Gentile beauties, Greek girls or Phoenicians with widely spaced eyes and expansive smiles? In the early first century BC we first find a text, a poem by the Jew Theodotus, which assumes that legal marriage between a Jew and a foreigner requires the non-Jewish partner to convert. The poet gives this view to Jacob while retelling the story of the rape of Dinah, but the words of the law books had nowhere been so specific. Like life itself, the Promised Land had proved even more exciting than God's original promise. It was not just a place of olives, figs and grapes, milk and honey and sour old pomegranates. The vines had been turned into wine, the olives into olive oil, and Gentiles now marketed wonderful brands of both: there were walnuts by the Lake of Galilee, date palms, spices and foreign fruits. The law had never addressed these temptations. At the Feast of Tabernacles, it merely told people to bring the 'fruit of goodly trees' (Leviticus 23:40): which trees were goodly? By the 90s BC lemons were an approved answer, as we happen to know from Josephus, who tells how the festival's crowds threw their lemons at a wicked high priest. It was wonderful news for the greengrocers, as lemons were a foreign crop: it would have been good news, too, for any priests who organized the trade.

The origins of the legal jungle, meanwhile, had been forgotten. The people who have been described as 'obsessed with history' had not a single historian among them with a critical idea of evidence: critical historical study is a tender plant which roots in very few cultures, and it was not suited by the soil of Jesus's Judaea. God, people assumed, had delivered these ancient texts to people as great as Moses and Solomon. Even Josephus, who wrote history, took it for granted that they were all true. There were prophecies in 'approximate language' about a Suffering Servant or a king who would 'come triumphant, humble and riding on an ass'. To whom did these ancient sayings refer? There were other significant latecomers, added long after Sinai or the reign of David: the most explicit (passed off on Daniel) had introduced the idea of a bodily resurrection, with varying rewards and punishments, as late as the 160s. There were ancient prophecies of a future king, the 'stem of Jesse', chosen by the Lord: many of the most explicit texts about him had been invented under foreign domination during the years of exile in Babylon. Ideas of this future super-star had multiplied freely, and by the mid first century BC we have texts which imagine him as a single Messiah, the Lord's Anointed. During the ups and downs of the Jewish people since the 160s BC, the promise of this Messiah had taken on a new prominence in what people found in their texts.

Instead of Solomon, people encountered Jesus: 'Behold,' he was believed to have said, 'something greater than Solomon is here.' In the Gospels, Jesus accepts the textual jungle's legacy. At Matthew 19:4 the Gospeller makes him quote editorial words by the author of Genesis as if they are words of God himself. At John 10:35 he is said to answer his opponents, 'the written word cannot be broken' after referring to a text in our Psalm 82 (calling it 'your law'). At Luke 24:44 he is said to tell his disciples after his death that 'all things must be fulfilled, which were written in the law of Moses, and in the prophets, and in the psalms, concerning me'. We do not know which texts he (or the Gospeller) would have numbered among the prophets and the psalms, or whether he agreed with those Jews who listed a special twenty-two. At Luke 11:51 he is said to have referred to the murder of prophets from 'the blood of Abel unto the blood of Zechariah'; Abel is the first to die in Genesis, and Zechariah is the last prophet who is named as being killed in our 2 Chronicles. It is not, however, clear that Jesus (or perhaps the Gospeller) was thinking of the entire block of narrative from Genesis to 2 Chronicles in its present order: he might have been thinking of a tradition about Zechariah known to him outside it. At John 7:38 he is said to have proclaimed on the last day of Tabernacles, 'He that believeth on me, as the scripture hath said, out of his belly shall flow rivers of living water.' Nothing in our Hebrew scripture actually says this (Zechariah 14:8 is only approximate). Perhaps he had other 'scripture' in mind. The Gospel did not think that this odd reference troubled his hearers. Far from it: 'Many of the people therefore, when they heard this saying, said, Of a truth this is the Prophet.'

Like other Jews, Jesus observed the food rules and the Sabbath: he regarded the scrolls of the law as of supreme authority, but we do not know which texts, exactly, he would have listed as authoritative beside them or even that he thought of a fixed list, let alone an exclusive one. There is, however, a significant emphasis which every Gospel shares: nowhere is Jesus remembered as beginning from a difficult text, starting with a snippet of scripture and then trying to tease out what its author meant. Even at Mark 12:35 he is said to have begun by asking, 'How say the scribes that Christ is the son of David?' and only then does he bring a text from the psalms to support his existing opinion that they are wrong (Matthew 22:41–6 turns it into part of a dialogue). This silence is significant because in later dialogues, Jews and Christians are described as locked in combat over little bits of text: in the Gospels this later style of argument has not been read back into Jesus's methods. Instead, we encounter a master of the art of using 'set books'. He controls them, and when he adduces them he is not swamped by them. Like his opponents, he knows how to join two different bits together and how to pit text against text to repel an argument. He can turn a verse of Genesis against Moses on the law of divorce (Mark 10:4 ff.); he can confound the conservative Sadducees by an argument from Exodus 3:6 which proves the Resurrection in a truly rabbinic fashion (at Mark 12:26). Perhaps his followers invented the 'proof', for it is a very feeble argument which does not prove anything of the sort: it is, however, not so very different from a line of argument credited later to Gamaliel, a Jewish near-contemporary. We must allow for later Christian elaboration of the Gospel 'proofs', but the four Gospels do not confront us with a simple Galilaean who knows only the deeds of a few great persons in scripture. We might expect that Jesus, like his contemporaries, would sometimes interpret bits of old scripture through distorting traditions, fashionable at the time. The case for such parallels is often argued, in six

118

examples especially, of which the disputed John 8:7 with Numbers 5:30 is the most cogent. However, we know little, if anything, of contemporary distortions, and none of the examples is proven. On present evidence it is Jesus himself who has the views which he then quotes scripture to support. He sees John the Baptist as an important forerunner, a prophet whom (in Matthew 11:10) he connects with 'my messenger' in Malachi 3:1 (perhaps the connection really was made by Jesus, whence Mark 1:2: Malachi, of course, had no idea of it). He acts on scriptural prophecies (the donkey, surely, on Palm Sunday): he knows the texts well enough, after forty years, perhaps, in their contemplation.

His hearers' reactions are familiar to anyone who has lived in the shadow of great contradictory classics, 'set books' which are none the less authorities. Most of the experts were shocked: here was a man, not one of themselves, who was teaching with authority and citing the texts to support his own line. He had not subordinated himself to the evidence. There were experts who wrestled with these writings, men who could quote one use of a word to illuminate another in a different book, who took them steadily line by line and cut each word carefully from its context, who proved the Resurrection from ancient texts which had had no idea of it. Here was a man to whom these arts were secondary. They listened with disbelief, much as great professors of classical set texts would listen nowadays if somebody took their contradictory texts about early Greece and claimed to explain them all as references to global warming. In those days, too, there were many more people than the experts who believed that their set texts were true; nobody, however, seemed able to square them all and agree on the details. Here was a man whose teaching drew texts after it, like bits of metal to a magnet. Jesus told them and showed them what the jungle meant and then added more besides. Much of it he added in parables, a form which was as old as the first known Hebrew prophets. Among the rabbis, we find that parables tend to begin from a biblical text: in the Gospels Jesus never begins a parable from quoted scripture, although once, a parable ends with it (Mark 12:10, where the 'stone which the builders rejected' rounds off the Wicked Husbandmen; at the beginning, in Mark 12:1, echoes of Isaiah 5 are implicit, not explicit). These parables gave people new narratives and story-like comparisons which challenged them to change their perspective. Although the challenge, at first, was too much for them, Jesus founded Christianity on a splendid disregard for textual passages for comment.

He also founded it without any word that it needed more scripture of its own. Nothing in the Gospels suggests that Jesus anticipated a written New Testament. Nowhere is he said to have asked or expected that his teaching should be written down. The first Christians were people of faith, not textual fundamentalists: to hear Peter or Paul was to hear a man with a conviction, not a Bible, and a new message which old texts were quoted to back up. We can take this message back to within four years of Jesus's death through the personal testimony of Paul: he 'received', he tells the Christians in Corinth, that 'Christ died for our sins in accordance with the scripture, that he was buried, that he was raised on the third day in accordance with the scripture', and that he then appeared to Peter and then to others in a sequence which does not match the stories of the appearances in our Gospels. Paul had also 'received from the Lord' that Jesus had broken bread and taken the cup at the Last Supper and said that the bread was his 'body which is given for you' and the cup was the 'blood of a new covenant'. His followers were to maintain these rites in his memory, although the fourth Gospel, claiming to be the work of a privileged eyewitness, did not report this behaviour at the Supper in question.

Presumably, Paul received these teachings from Apostles in Jerusalem whom he met three years after his conversion (Galatians 1:18): if the Crucifixion is dated to 36, his conversion followed within a year of it, bringing these teachings ever nearer Jesus's death. The first Christians who instructed him were Jews who were also Christians: they observed the law, visited the Temple and differed from their fellow Jews only in the belief that the Messiah had come and had risen from the dead. The high priest and some of the other Jews (including Paul) were quick to persecute them for this belief, although the Apostles were able to survive and lie low in Jerusalem: I accept that, in outline, Acts 1–12 is true to the facts, here. Not until Paul's first missionary journey, and its aftermath, did the Christians break with a Jewish identity and accept Gentiles as equals. It was then clear that a Christian was not a Jew who happened to be a Christian, much as some Jews were Sadducees, Pharisees or Essenes. They were Christians, either Jewish Christians or Gentile Christians according to their birth. The change was momentous, and once again it affected diet and men's private parts. The old code of holiness was unravelled. Christians were now free to eat any kind of food, whether it swarmed, flew or had hoofs. Above all, males no longer had to be circumcised, a decision of great symbolic importance. Like much else in Christian history, it affected the two genders differently: the leaders were all male, whereas many of the new Christian converts were females to whom the decision will have seemed decidedly less urgent.

Their movement had arisen from the reports by eyewitnesses of an empty tomb; the reports caused Jesus's followers to realize what he had meant, and now meant to them. It was an odd outcome, which nobody had predicted. The Messiah turned out to be a victim of Roman injustice who had died on a Cross, changing nothing in the power-politics of his day. He caused hopes of a new kingdom, expectations of the end of the world, and no doubt a flood of expressive titles and imagery, beginning in the very week after Easter. If we try to write a history of this way of speech from our New Testament authors, we are building up a neat historical sequence of titles from wholly insufficient sources. Who knows what James or Mary Magdalen said in praise of Jesus as early as Easter Monday? It was no time for precision or theological rigour.

How, indeed, could it have been so? In some sense, it was believed that Number One had sent Jesus as his son; that the wrongful death of a man of Nazareth had been on behalf of other people's sins; that his body was commemorated by eating bread and that his death, the start of a new covenant, was remembered by drinking wine from a cup; that the outpourings of unintelligible language and the new sense of release which occurred among his first followers were not emotional excesses but gifts of a Holy Spirit. Facts were embellished with all manner of interpretations. The horrible death of Jesus was a manifestation of glory, according to one of his own disciples who witnessed it. According to Paul, who never knew him, Jesus had been 'in the form of God', did not cling to equality with God, 'emptied' himself, took on the form of a servant, humbled himself among men, died and was highly exalted by God again above everyone else. Jesus's own family and contemporaries in Nazareth could be forgiven for failing to perceive it at the time; meanwhile, those who believed in him had received another gift from on high, the Holy Spirit. Theology regained a wonderful complexity.

Number One, the God of Abraham and David, had become Only One, the God of Ezra or the author of Daniel. Now, he had broken his solitude with the release of Numbers Two and Three. The truth of their relationships could breed subtle argument for centuries, but the Fond Abuser had not lost his ancient habits. He had had a son, but he sent him to be reviled and crucified; within sixty years of this mission's conclusion, John the Christian saw on a Sunday that the ancient Father was about to exterminate a high proportion of the human race.

Most of this mosaic of interpretation can be traced to themes in Hebrew texts, although its personal subject was new and the mosaic itself was unprecedented. Early in the process Paul had been told that key parts of it had happened 'according to the scripture'. If scripture could be stretched to refer to Roman domination or forgiveness for adultery, it could also be quarried for a death 'for our sins' or a resurrection 'on the third day'. In fact, they had meant no such thing, any more than they had agreed on a life after death or the sanctity of scrolls with God's four-letter name. Like their Jewish contemporaries, Christian Jews caused textual havoc in order to find old backing for new, important beliefs. With supreme confidence, they relabelled their textual inheritance: Jesus's death had begun their 'new covenant', and within twenty years of it Paul was telling Gentile Christians that the Jews, in their books of Moses, were reading the 'old covenant'. Jews' religious writings were no longer the lifeblood of a living religion: they were a preparation, the 'Old Testament'.

This relabelling encouraged people to plunder them with ever less regard for context and accepted reference. In early Christian writings, we can watch the plundering gather momentum. In the New Testament, the books of Genesis and Isaiah are easily the favourite quarries. Nobody happens to quote from Esther or Ecclesiastes or the Song of Songs. It was not that these books were uncanonical or thought to be inferior; rather, Christian allusions took a while to be invented for them. It also happens to be true that only one New Testament book quotes a text which is known to lie outside the likely list of the Jews' twenty-two, and even the book of Revelation does not cast its quotations very wide. The exception is the Epistle of Jude, which quotes from the book of Enoch and the Assumption of Moses. However, this restraint is probably accidental rather than a matter of canon and principle. It might look less solid if we knew more about some curious texts: at Corinthians 2:9 'it is written' for Paul that what 'eye hath not seen, nor ear heard', but it is nowhere written in our scriptures for us (James 4:5 is also a problem).

From *c.* 100 to 250 the Christians' range of proof-texts widened without question. Christian authors paid no attention to any list of twenty-two; they quoted freely from any old Jewish text which could be given a Christian point for a verse or two. Some of their books confront us with snowstorms of such quotations, but they are usually not books which are instinctively Jewish in their religious outlook: they are not the writings of Jewish Christianity so much as of Christians who are plundering old Jewish texts. It was probably such Christian usage and plundering which left us our first specific list of an Old Testament: it includes several books of the Apocrypha, Judith, Tobit, the Maccabean books, Ben Sira and the memorable Wisdom of Solomon. This list was not drawn up by Jews: it was the list of Greek-speaking Christians in Alexandria for whom the list of an Old Testament was important. When they quoted from old Jewish texts, Jews could reply that some of these texts had no particular authority: this retort would make a Christian wish to know which texts did count. The question seemed to be best answered by the old idea of a twenty-two (or four, or seven, depending now on how the books were grouped and counted). Christians who looked into the question found various answers, but it was a question which they themselves had made into an issue. It was particularly important for our Christian Bible's history that Jerome, its famous translator into Latin, made careful inquiries among Jewish contemporaries and was told about the narrow list of twenty-two: 'what chiefly moved him was the embarrassment he felt at having to argue with Jews on the basis of books which they rejected'. These differences had previously made the Christian 'Old Testament' fuzzy at the edges; according to Jerome, the first great Christian council, at Nicaea (in 325), had accepted the book of Judith, although he (and we) have not. These differences surfaced again in the sixteenth century when the Reformation made the definition of scripture an urgent issue for many Protestant Christians when arguing against Catholics. They still show up in the classifying of 'extra books', Ben Sira, Wisdom and so forth, as the 'Apocrypha' in our Bibles.

As for the Christians' own New Testament, the earliest of its texts were letters, not Gospels. The letter gained a new importance because the first Christians combined missionary preaching and an absent apostolic leadership with no agreed structure of local command. When Paul happened to write a letter to his converts in Galatia (*c.* 49/50), he had no idea that he was writing the earliest Christian text which would survive for us, some fifteen years, perhaps, before any of our Gospels existed. Notoriously, Paul's surviving letters are not particularly concerned to quote Jesus's exact sayings at every opportunity: their concern is with Jesus as the risen Christ, although Paul's oral teaching, now lost to us, may have had a different focus. Even when Jesus's deeds and sayings began to be written down, they were not at once idealized as holy books of scripture; oral traditions of Jesus's words were still valued highly, often more highly than a text. We can infer one result from the preface of our third Gospel. The author used our Gospel of Mark but also referred to 'many' previous attempts at writing a narrative of Jesus: in my view, he wrote *c.* 65–9, although others put him after 70. These 'many' other narratives have not survived. Nor have all the letters of Paul; he himself refers to some which are lost to us (the letter written 'with many tears' at 2 Corinthians 2:4).

It is extremely difficult to be sure when a surviving author first quotes from one of our Gospels. We first know the fourth (John's) from a scrap of it on papyrus, datable *c.* 125 by its handwriting. A Gospel by Mark is first known from a reference to its author's name, *c.* 125–40, not from a quotation of our Gospel's text; a phrase now in Matthew's is quoted in the same context (without naming the author) by the major figure, Ignatius (*c.* 110), and possibly by the unknown author of an epistle of Barnabas (probably writing in Alexandria but unfortunately at an unknown date: the usual *c.* 100 is a compromise between 80 and 130). Some people think Matthew's Gospel is used in an anonymous letter from Rome to Corinth (First Clement, *c.* 93), but the allusion is inexact and might be to a general collection of Jesus's sayings which is now lost. The third Gospel (Luke's) raises an attractive difficulty. Our First Epistle to Timothy states that the scripture says, 'Thou shalt not muzzle the ox', a direct quotation from Deuteronomy, 'and the labourer deserves his hire'. The 'and' appears to connect this second quotation to 'what is written': its quotation is only known to us as a saying by Jesus at Luke 10:27. Is the author already alluding to this Gospel or is he quoting some other written source of Jesus's words which is now lost? In the first verse, the author of the letter says that he is 'Paul, an apostle of Christ Jesus'. How, then, could Paul quote from a Gospel which is universally thought to have been composed after his death? Until at least *c.* 120 (possibly *c.* 135–40) no surviving text connects any Gospel with an author's name: the Christian letter-writers, however, were more forthright about their identities. Can we always trust them? 'Behold, I make all things new', but the main aim of authors endured: success.

7

Pseudonymous Christians

In our Bibles these problems of naming are less immediately evident. Unlike the Hebrew scriptures, the Christian scriptures were all composed in Greek and greet us with an impressive array of authors: there are Gospels by two Apostles (Matthew and John), letters from Paul, Peter and James, and three letters and a revelation which are also ascribed to a John. The exception is the Epistle to the Hebrews, which was first preserved as a letter without its author's name and probably without a title or destination. Some Christians respected it because they thought it was by Paul; others realized very early that it could not be, because its style was so different; there was even a view that it was anonymous because it had been written by a woman, Priscilla.

Are these authors' names the true ones? Many of them depend on the titles to the text but not on words in the text itself. Of the Gospels, only the fourth refers to an author ('the disciple whom Jesus loved') in its own text: the reference is in the epilogue which was added later by another hand (John 21:20–24), and its scope is disputed. As for the epistles, those ascribed to Paul or Peter name their authors in the opening verses, whereas 1 John names nobody and 2 and 3 John name only a tantalizing 'elder'.

The title 'Gospel According to . . .' is known from fragments of Gospel texts on papyrus which date to *c*. 180–200. A gap of one hundred and twenty years still yawns between these fragments and the Gospels' composition; so far, arguments have failed to bridge it. Our earliest evidence is still a quotation from Papias, bishop of Hierapolis, whose original book does not survive. Writing probably between *c*. 120 and *c*. 138, he remarked that Mark 'was the interpreter of Peter and wrote down carefully what he remembered of what had been said or done by the Lord, but not in the right order'. This view was not Papias's own, but was quoted as the view of John the Elder, who is elsewhere identified as a disciple of the Lord. This John, if correctly reported, takes the tradition of Mark's authorship back before Papias's own date, perhaps as far as *c.* 90: it is extremely important evidence. Papias also wrote that 'Matthew composed the sayings in Hebrew and each one translated them as he could'. No elder is cited for this separate opinion, which is wonderfully uncertain in its reference.

Was this 'elder' right about Mark? The Gospel begins with the words 'Gospel of Jesus Christ' and although it is in Greek, its style is way beneath the conventions of educated writers. The author is highly likely to have followed the old Near Eastern rule and left his narrative anonymous: what mattered was Jesus Christ and his Gospel. If so, the name Mark is based on tradition or guesswork. Either people knew that Peter himself had written nothing and so they attached the Gospel to a person close to him in order to dignify it (at Acts 12:12 Peter goes to the house of John Mark's mother; possibly, too, the so-called First Epistle of Peter 5:3 misled them). Or they were correct: we cannot know, and the author's own text did not tell them.

As for Matthew, Papias's words reveal that he believed Matthew to have written first ('each one' of the others then translated him). Almost all modern scholarship is united against this widespread early Christian belief. It is highly likely that Matthew followed Mark and used him instead. Beyond that mistake, Papias appears to make another: no Hebrew original is known or evident for our Matthew's Gospel (the case has been argued, but not sustained). Perhaps Papias was referring to a separate text, a Semitic collection of Jesus's sayings which was being ascribed to Matthew (*c.* 120–135) and was not our surviving Gospel: if so, our Matthew's Gospel was still anonymous *c.* 125 and was credited to him later by Christian readers who wished to fix its author. When an early work, the Teaching of the Apostles, quotes a bit of it (probably *c.* 100–110), it cites it as 'the Gospel', not as Matthew's Gospel.

We know that Papias was most concerned with Jesus's reported sayings, not with written texts. He described how he valued them and inquired about them from Christian visitors: plainly, he did not think they were confined to four little Gospels. In my view, he wished to explain how the Gospellers had acquired their 'sayings of Jesus' and why they differed: his answer was that Matthew had compiled a book in Hebrew (or Aramaic) and that each Gospeller had then translated it differently. Either Papias knew about a Gospel of Matthew and misdescribed it because he had not bothered to read it very closely, or he invented the idea of an original Hebrew source and ascribed it to Matthew, thus leaving open the possibility that 'Matthew' had written a separate Gospel in Greek.

I prefer this latter view for two reasons. First, it helps us with a tantalizing piece of evidence which, typically, is not clear-cut. Before *c.* 160 a Christian, Basilides, wrote a commentary in twenty-four books 'on the Gospel': maddeningly, it has not survived, and we do not know if this big work is the same as one which later authors described as the Gospel of Basilides. Several authors imply a date for him in the 130s, and perhaps this book appeared so soon: Basilides is said to have claimed that it rested on the authority of the Apostle Matthias, and, according to his own followers, on the Glaucias who was supposedly Peter's interpreter. We do not know which tradition came first, but it is more likely that Basilides and his followers were answering other Christians' claims to have an apostolic text by Matthew and another, our Mark, by Peter's interpreter. If the claim about Matthias goes back to Basilides himself and his book was composed in the 130s, a 'Gospel of Matthew' would already have been known by that name.

Secondly, the detective work to support Matthew as the author required some close deductions from the Gospel. It is Matthew's text alone which defines Matthew as a tax-collector and substitutes Matthew's name for Mark's Levi. The author stands out for his habit of specifying large sums of money in the parables: would early readers have connected this habit to Matthew's financial career? Perhaps they would, but the authors of false epistles or acts did not need to go to such lengths to deceive their readers. If this Gospel was compiled after Mark's (perhaps as the last of the four) the author himself might have realized that it needed a contemporary's name in order to succeed. By choosing a minor Apostle, he could excel beliefs about the authority of Mark (Peter's interpreter) or the third Gospel (by Paul's companion). He also sheltered himself from people who still knew that the major Apostles had written nothing.

Beyond these doubts, there is one certainty: Matthew's Gospel was not written by an eyewitness disciple. It depends heavily on Mark (except in the view of the very few who argue, unconvincingly, that Matthew was the first to write); it includes none of the independent witnessing or memoirs which a close disciple would have contributed. Either some early Christians wrongly, but cleverly, deduced its author (in my view, they had to do so before *c.* 125, in time for Papias and Basilides) or the author saved them the bother by claiming a false authority himself.

As for the other Gospels, Luke is first named for us *c.* 180 (by Irenaeus) and John *c.* 140–50 (by the heretical Heracleon). The fourth Gospel, John, refers obliquely to the 'beloved disciple' or 'other disciple' at various points in its story: it then attracted an epilogue (chapter 21) by a separate author who assumed that this 'beloved disciple' had written the final chapter and thus, by implication, the entire work. Again, it is evident that this Gospel had not named its author in its own title; instead, people deduced that the beloved disciple was John (the Gospel does not name a John otherwise). As for Luke's Gospel, its companion volume, Acts, breaks intermittently into the first person plural during Paul's journeys, and, despite attempts by scholars to deny the obvious, it stands out as the work of a companion of Paul. The two books were written in a more educated Greek style and addressed to an eminent Gentile, Theophilus. Perhaps, then, they ignored Near Eastern convention and did name Luke in their title or perhaps (like a letter) they merely called themselves 'To Theophilus'.

The four Gospels thus present us with two texts (Mark and John) which began life anonymously, one (Matthew) which may perhaps have begun under a false name and another (Luke) which perhaps named its true author; alternatively (many think more probably), all four appeared without an author's name. Mark's authorship was an early tradition which might be correct; John's may very well be right (the beloved disciple was, I believe, the author), and so long as the third Gospel is credited to a companion of Paul, it is not too important whether we call him Luke or not; Matthew's, however, is wrong, and perhaps a deliberate deceit. 'The suggestion of deliberate pseudonymity on the part of the evangelist need not cause qualms,' a great scholar of this Gospel's origin has tried to reassure us; 'the ancient feelings and conventions about the practice were different from ours.' The truth is exactly the opposite, as Paul's experience shows.

When a Christian issued fake 'Acts of Paul and Thecla' in the second century, he was promptly deposed by bishops, although he pleaded that he had been acting 'out of love of Paul'. As for the epistles, the problem of false names and forgery was acute. Already, in the Second Epistle to the Thessalonians, Paul had to warn his audience against the possibility of fake letters with which some Christians were trying to mislead their fellow Christians about the end of the world. Several modern scholars have repaid the compliment by arguing that this Second Epistle is itself a fake, falsely adorned with a greeting from Paul. That view is not convincing, but this awareness that early pseudo-Pauline letters existed is not misplaced. It may even show up in Paul's own practice. We know that Paul used a scribe to write down some of his letters (the letter to the Romans includes the name of the scribe, 'I, Tertius', and his personal greeting 'in the Lord'), but sometimes they end with a greeting written in Paul's own hand. 'See with what large letters I have written to you with my own hand,' he wrote at the end to the Galatians. Probably, he referred only to the final part of the epistle, acknowledging that earlier sections had been dictated. The letters were written large, not because 'writing was not an easy thing to Paul's workman's hand': he was much too educated and from too prominent a family to have such difficulty with a pen. More probably, they were large so that most of their Galatian audience could read them or see them when pointed out, a skill which would not have been natural to some of the humbler Christians, especially among the women. The big letters helped to authenticate the epistle as Paul's own.

When we have other collections of early Christian letters, we have certain evidence of fakes among them. The important letters of Ignatius, bishop of Antioch (*c.* 110), attracted fake companions which supported the partisan theology of a later age and were not sifted out from the genuine collection until 1646, more than a thousand years after their invention. The letters of Cyprian, bishop of Carthage (*c.* 250), reveal that Christian contemporaries had been faking letters in Cyprian's name quite freely and sending them to other Churches in order to discredit him. In the 170s we have the instructive protest of one Dionysius, bishop of Corinth: Christians were changing and faking his own letters, he said, just as (he knew) they had changed the Gospels.

For these reasons alone, scholars would be right to ask if the epistles which claim to come from Paul are really composed by Paul himself: some pseudo-Paul may have been much too successful for too long. There are three tests which could expose him: his sense of history, his style and his doctrine. They are supported by a fourth, which is less conclusive, the views of early Christian critics and the dates at which each letter is first known to have existed. Doubts still attend Paul's Philippians, Philemon, Colossians and Ephesians in ascending order of magnitude, although in my view, no cogent case can be made against the first three of them, and even Ephesians' broader brush-strokes of style and thought are not quite as self-evidently 'not Paul's' as the overwhelming majority of scholars now accept. The tests can best be applied where they take a firm hold, on two groups of letters which find very few modern defenders: the pastoral letters to Timothy and the two letters ascribed to Peter. The arguments are detailed, and here they can only be condensed, to bring out some of the ways in which they work.

Nobody in the early Church is known to have doubted the pastoral letters, but each of them raises historical problems, and both of them are suspected for their style and content. The Second Epistle to Timothy purports to be written by Paul at Rome in the final phase of his life. If genuine, it would be Paul's last surviving words addressed to the Timothy who had joined him in Asia on the second missionary journey (his mother was a Jewess, but his father had been a Greek: Paul circumcised him). One verse, at the end, is historically incorrect. From Rome, Paul tells Timothy that he has left Trophimus 'sick at Miletus': however, we know from Acts that when Paul left Miletus, Trophimus accompanied him to Jerusalem, where his presence played a crucial role in Paul's arrest (Acts 21:29, referring to this visit), and, after leaving Jerusalem, Paul never went to Miletus again. These facts are not in serious doubt, because this entire section of Acts is based on the first-person version of a participant. To save 2 Timothy, some Christian scholars have suggested that Paul escaped his first imprisonment in Rome (the one with which Acts ends), returned to Asia, left Trophimus in Miletus and was again arrested and imprisoned a second time. This fantastic theory lacks any support and is refuted by Acts 20:25. There, Paul is made to say to the assembled Christians of Ephesus and Miletus that he is going up to Jerusalem, that persecution is predicted for him and that 'ye all . . . shall see my face no more' (Acts 20:25). The author

131

of Acts, his companion to Rome, knew that Paul never returned to Asia after this visit.

One resort has been to split the Second Epistle to Timothy into fragments and assume that a piece which causes problems has been inserted by a later editor who knew that it had been written by Paul, but did not know where it belonged in Paul's career. This explanation has at times been taken too far; up to four such genuine fragments have been suggested, as if many little bits of Paul's letters floated freely without their surroundings. However, this theory may help with the problem of Trophimus. The reference to him stands at the end of 2 Timothy after the final Amen. Perhaps this postscript was added from an earlier letter by Paul, perhaps even from the First Epistle to Timothy, where it would have suited the author's idea of its context. If so, the concluding mention of Trophimus does not prove the entire letter a fake.

It does, however, arouse suspicions which the letter's setting strengthens. We know from the Epistle to Philemon that Timothy had been in Rome with Paul during his imprisonment. The Second Epistle to him makes no reference to conditions at Rome, their time in Paul's prison or any details of their recently shared life. The epistle implies that Paul has made his first defence alone, without friends, and is now awaiting the final trials of his life; when he reminds Timothy of their time together, he remarks on persecutions and ideals which Timothy has 'followed closely', but specifies events in three cities long ago on the first missionary journey. We know from Acts that Timothy joined Paul only when that journey was finished. As a letter to a recent companion, it has an odd remoteness.

The setting of the First Epistle, too, is suspicious. It purports to belong at a time when Paul has gone into Macedonia, but Timothy has stayed in Asia to teach true doctrine in Ephesus. This time can only be the journey of Acts 20:1–3, where Paul goes from Asia to Macedonia and spends three months in Greece before he returns. At 20:4 Timothy is with Paul on his return journey through Macedonia; he is also a co-sender of Paul's Second Epistle to the Corinthians which belongs, beyond reasonable doubt, on Paul's journey into Macedonia from Asia. If Timothy stayed to teach in Ephesus, it can only have been for a very short while, yet 1 Timothy is unaware of these possible changes. At surprising length, it tells Timothy what he must have known, repeating how Paul had told him to act in Ephesus. At 3:14 it assumes that Timothy will stay in Asia until Paul returns; plans can change rapidly, but, like the Second Epistle, the First reads as if it is written at Timothy, not to him. If so, an author (not Paul) has picked on Timothy as a close companion of Paul who is known to have stayed on in the Greek East. He has used him as a likely recipient of advice on Christian doctrine and conduct of a type which Paul ought to have sent to posterity.

The odd relation between setting and content is confirmed by the letters' teaching. They are concerned with dangerous heresy (so, too, was the genuine Paul), but they read as if they are looking over their shoulder at a new generation of enemies. Above all, they are concerned with the qualities of a single leader (*episcopos*, or bishop) who is to lead his Church; there is no hint of a single leadership in the communities addressed by Paul's letters or described in the eyewitness sections of Acts. Bishops were a post-apostolic invention, perhaps when Christian 'elders' could no longer agree among themselves. Here, too, Timothy is the peg for important post-Pauline advice.

Can we separate these letters from the others on grounds of their style? It is style, above all, which damns the two letters of Peter. Their Greek has a degree of education which is enormously improbable for Peter, the Galilaean fisherman. It is not that Peter will have known no Greek at all: he travelled to Rome, had contact with Gentile Christians and had a Greek second name (Cephas); his home town Bethsaida ('Place of Fishes') was reorganized by the ruler of Galilee and given new settlers and a Greek name (Julias, probably 4/3 BC): for all we know, the wife whom he took with him during his Christian travels ('on expenses', as Paul complained) may have been a Greek-speaker. However, a modest grasp of Greek (perhaps in the new Julias-Bethsaida) is quite different from the level of educated Greek prose in these two letters (it is much higher than the style of texts ascribed to John, and the John, anyway, need not be the Galilaean son of Zebedee). Many of the early Christians suspected Peter's Second Epistle (style apart, it refers to Paul's letters as if they are already a much studied collection, yet Peter is believed to have died in Rome in 64 soon after Paul). The First Epistle assumes that Christians in Asia are being persecuted by pagans, not Jews, which is also highly unlikely before 64: it is not the view of the author of Acts, whom I accept as a contemporary witness, a travelling companion of

Paul. We cannot pin down these letters' vocabulary to any particular date between 50 and 120 (despite attempts, our knowledge of Greek prose is too slender), but their style and aspects of their setting disqualify them from Peter's pen. Attempts to ascribe them to his secretary do not remove the basic problems.

Stylistically, the letters to Timothy are less obtrusive. The style of an author is usually analysed in one of two ways: by its infrequent words and usages or by those words and uses which are so frequent that they are not the result of a deliberate literary choice. Infrequent words have been used to isolate a work from its author's other writings or even to date it, by reference to the words' first appearance in the wider body of their language and literature. Common words and constructions have a different relevance. They allow us to compare authors' 'characteristic use of the words they share with all other writers' or to compare such uses between an author's attributed writings. Here, the little details of style have been thought to betray most, like the little details of a painting, the fingernails or earlobes of a portrait which have been considered to be strong evidence of its authorship since the theories of Giovanni Morelli in the 1880s.

Both types of test have been applied to Paul's and Peter's epistles, and they confirm points which already strike casual readers. The letters to Timothy are notable for their much greater use of adjectives, and rather complex adjectives at that. Once again, we cannot date these words' first use (we have no comparable Greek prose of this period), but we can contrast them with the vocabulary of Paul's other letters (the context, however, of the various letters was different). As for the small characteristic frequencies, they, too, have been calculated, even down to the length of the words or sentences in each work. This type of study by measurement ('stylometry') was invented in 1851 specifically in order to study the Pauline letters. In the last twenty years, these and other types of frequency have attracted new attention because of the mechanical aid of computers. Computers have not invented a new test for forgery; they have merely allowed old tests to be applied more thoroughly and quickly (they now have their own survey, *Bits, Bytes and Biblical Studies*).

There has not, however, been agreement as to what such tests should be. Simple stylometry has sometimes been applied superficially to aspects of a text which are not likely to be the result of conscious or unconscious patterns: the length of words, the average length of sentences, the number of uses of 'and' in a text, the length of each sentence's last word. Early studies of this type declared all the Pauline letters to be bogus, except an inner circle of four, a conclusion which carried no weight, except with its computer. The sentences of the Pauline letters (on their usual dating) did grow longer as the years passed, but this greater length does not entail that somebody other than an older Paul had written them. The method has now been refined to give more weight to grammar and syntax, the ways in which words and the moods and tenses of verbs are used. The most recent array of tests (ninety-nine in all) are not all significant (they include the total number of verbs or the number of nouns in the plural), but the outcome is different. Whereas all but four of the letters had been damned by computer stylometry, twelve, including the pastorals, have now been bunched as a similar group, of which none obtrudes unduly on the strength of these tests alone. The odd one is the Epistle to Titus.

However, we have not found a scientific answer to the old problem. All twelve epistles may seem relatively similar as a group, but if we ask which letters stand furthest from the genuine core of the main four, the pastorals still stand away on the outer fringe. As the latest study honestly points out, no test can guarantee authorship: in writing, there is no such thing as a stylistic fingerprint: at most there is a signature, for style, like a signature, can be voluntarily varied by an author and impressively copied by a forger. Here the computer's tests run up against a fact which is central to the Pauline problem. The language and phrasing of Ephesians overlap very closely with the other surviving letters which are rightly ascribed to Paul: Ephesians draws so closely on Colossians that it seems to have that epistle's text by its author's side. Such a strong stamp of Paul might seem to support Ephesians' authenticity, but the stamp is so strong that it may point the other way. Our few surviving epistles account for Ephesians' usages and yet, except to an imitator, these epistles were not the only letters which Paul wrote; almost identical phrases and words from Colossians recur in quantity in nearly half of Ephesians' verses, but they are used in subtly differing senses, as if an imitator has culled them and twisted them to his own thought. Ephesians is not so much Pauline as super-Pauline, to the point where the imitation seems conscious and is not a single author's own pattern. Here, computer tests break down. They can rightly separate a work from a closely defined group whose members are near to each other in date and content (Paul's epistles are not quite so close); they can also show that a text deviates excessively. They cannot prove that one work rightly belongs with others: conscious imitation will always deceive them, and Ephesians is probably just such a deception.

It is certainly wrongly titled. Like Hebrews, its text was probably preserved at first without its present title. Only one of the early manuscript traditions gives its modern name, but it is untrue to the letter's content: the text assumes that the author has not visited the community which he addresses, whereas Paul spent several years in Ephesus. The super-Pauline style and the letter's notorious problems of thought (not least on the relation of Jews and Christians) suggest that the work is not Paul's but a follower's.

The two letters of Peter are damned by their style and by their references to Paul's collected letters and pagan persecution; the two Epistles to Timothy are set suspiciously apart by style and are damned by their content and setting (the single bishop; Timothy's lack of knowledge and his awkward whereabouts). Their authors were very bold in their deceit. 'Peter, apostle of Christ', 'Paul, apostle of Christ Jesus', they call themselves. Perhaps they were writing what they thought Peter or Paul 'ought' to have written, but none the less they lied to their public. If 1 Timothy is a second-century work, it may well have had the third Gospel in mind when it quotes the text on the 'labourer's hire'. It also gives Paul an emphatic text against the ordination of women: 'I suffer not a woman to teach, nor to usurp authority over the man, but to be in silence' (1 Timothy 2:12).

2 Timothy contains the text which fundamentalists have often idealized: 'All scripture is given by inspiration of God, and is profitable for doctrine, for reproof, for corrections' (2 Timothy 3:16). The translation is arguable, as is the text's authority. It is a pleasant measure of the complexities in the Bible's truth: the text which has been misused to support a literal view of the entire Bible's inspiration is itself the work of an author who had lied about his identity.

8

Adding and Subtracting

The final words of our Bibles are well aware of their Christian contemporaries' artfulness. They threaten it with an awful curse: if anyone adds to the author's book of Revelation, 'God will add to him the plagues described in this book'; if anyone cuts anything out, 'God will take away his share in the tree of life and in the holy city'. So far as we know, the curse deterred intruders. The difficulty is to be certain; additions and subtractions are matters of textual history, and, once again, we prejudge them at our peril.

The rise of Christianity took place against a flurry of textual editing which, in part, it encouraged: Gentile religions had seen nothing like it. After the ruin of the Temple in 70 AD, Jewish scholars probably began to straighten out the textual diversity of their old Hebrew scripture: eventually, the type of text prevailed on which most of our Old Testaments are based, the Masoretic Hebrew. We do not know, as yet, when this point was reached, but arguably, not until after 200. The Greek translations of Hebrew scripture also had to be tightened up. Christians had begun to quote from them to support or create their own traditions, and Jews were pained by their use of Greek which betrayed the original Hebrew. From the later first century, Christians worked on the Greek texts, tending to translate them more literally.

Like the Jewish community, the early Church also grew to include some important textual scholars. The most famous is Origen in the early to mid third century; a deeply touching proof of his influence can still be read in one of the earliest surviving book-texts of scripture, the Codex Sinaiticus, which is now in the British Museum. At the end of its book of Esther, we have the note of a Christian corrector who was working in the seventh century; he refers to his use of an 'exceedingly ancient copy' of the text from 1 Kings to the end of Esther which went back to the work of a great admirer of Origen. He and a fellow Christian had worked on this text while in prison, awaiting martyrdom in *c.* 307, and in their cells they had consulted a great treasure, Origen's own corrected copy of his scripture. These two martyr-scholars had been editors in prison, like the heroic William Tyndale, another prison-scholar who was strangled and burned in 1536 for translating scripture into English.

Within two centuries of Jesus, some of the Christians were aware of the need for textual scholarship: how soundly based are the early Christian texts which we now read in our New Testament?

Unlike the Hebrew scriptures, the Christian scriptures are known nowadays in a few book-texts which are relatively close to the time of their composition. The earliest 'New Testaments' are parts of two book-texts of the early fourth century, the Codex Sinaiticus just mentioned, and the Codex Vaticanus which is now in Rome. Both books were copied on to vellum, but the Sinaiticus was never properly finished and was very poorly copied by one of the three scribes who worked on it. We can go back much earlier because from the later first century onwards there are Christian authors who quoted verses known in our Gospels and epistles; like Hebrew scripture, texts of the New Testament have also turned up excitingly on early scraps of papyrus, most of which date to the third century, although the earliest is a fragment of John's Gospel (now in Manchester) dated *c.* 125.

These early books and the even earlier quotations have enabled modern scholars to isolate different avenues in the course of the New Testament text. One type of text is particularly evident and is known as the 'Byzantine', because it prevailed in the Greek East from the seventh century onwards. It was already dominant in the earlier codices and became the sole received text of the Greek scriptures for many centuries. When the English translators produced their fine King James Bible in 1611, they used this Byzantine Greek text without question. Unfortunately, they were mistaken. Individual scholars began to contest the Byzantine text's sole use in the later seventeenth century, and since 1881 its supremacy has been universally rejected. Three earlier types of Greek text were gradually identified beside it, and their readings are often preferable. At first they were explained as the differing texts of different regions of the Christian world. Since then, their number and identity have undergone changes to and fro, and the theory of their local origins has had to be abandoned. At least two types are now universally recognized beside the Byzantine: the so-called 'Western' and 'Alexandrian' texts whose form goes back to *c*. 200 and perhaps slightly earlier.

Once again, papyri have taken the story further back. No early papyrus contains any complete book of Christian scripture, but their fragments do allow us to peer behind the Byzantine, Western and Alexandrian avenues. So far, we have eighty-eight fragments which are datable before 300, although the number whose handwriting can be firmly dated before *c*. 180 is extremely small. However, they do give us some contact with Christian texts within a hundred years of their composition. This evidence is much earlier than the evidence for the Old Testament, and is often contrasted triumphantly with the evidence for various Greek and Latin classics. Whereas our knowledge of Catullus's love poems goes back to one Latin manuscript some fifteen hundred years after their composition, the New Testament can be followed to within two lifetimes of Paul and its other authors. Partly as a result, there is great reluctance to correct any single word in Christian scripture to anything which is the free conjecture of a modern editor. Such reluctance can be defended on scholarly grounds, but it is also sometimes stated as a matter of religious fact. None of the small errors and tiny differences of wording in the texts, it is also said, affects any major item of Christian belief.

This optimism may be misplaced. We have two early papyri which overlap across seventy verses of John's Gospel, and even if the plain errors of their copyists are excluded, they differ at no less than seventy small places. Unlike Catullus's love-poems or Juvenal's satires, the Christian scriptures were a battlefield for textual alteration and rewriting in the first hundred years of their life. In the 140s an important Christian, Marcion, troubled many of his fellow Christians by producing a 'Gospel' which abbreviated Luke's so as to suit his own theology (he omitted the Nativity in the first two chapters, for reasons of theology, however, not history). He edited ten letters of Paul, changing and omitting bits which he did not like and also omitted the Epistles to Timothy and Titus. This enterprise played havoc with the written text. So did the efforts of another extreme Christian, Tatian, who blended all

139

four Gospels into one during the 170s and changed the text to support his extreme hostility to sex. Tatian's 'Harmony' was widely accepted in the Christian East and made a serious impact on Christianity in the Syriac language for many centuries.

If Christian texts were being changed and edited to this degree, even a gap of a century between an original and its first survival on a papyrus is a long and potentially dangerous time. We simply do not know what may have happened to the authors' words at important places: it is not too hypercritical to suspend judgement and keep an open mind. Like almost any texts, the New Testament's confront us with little instances of variant wording (whether to read 'and' or 'but'). These problems are not too significant, except for anyone who may still wish to claim that everything in the Bible is unerring, because it is God's word. However, the differences do also concern more interesting questions: whether, for instance, Jesus is openly called 'God' in the New Testament (at 1 Timothy 3:16 most Bibles tell us 'God was manifest in the flesh', but the earlier and better text says 'he', not 'God'; at Titus 2:13, Romans 5:1 and 1 John 5:7–8 there are similar textual problems). There are also problems with some very familiar friends: the 'lilies of the field' in the Sermon on the Mount, the text of the Acts of the Apostles, forgiveness for adultery and the story of the Resurrection.

In the Sermon on the Mount, Matthew's Gospel gives Jesus a saying which the beautiful English translation of 1611 renders as follows: 'Consider the lilies of the field, how they grow; they toil not, neither do they spin. And yet I say unto you, that even Solomon in all his glory was not arrayed like one of these.' All surviving manuscripts of Matthew's Gospel agree on the Greek from which this English is translated. Lovely though its words are, they do not translate the original text.

In 1938 the scholar T. C. Skeat was examining the text of the fourth century Codex Sinaiticus, the early vellum book which had just been bought with great shrewdness by the British Museum from the Russian government. By ultra-violet light, he found a different set of Greek letters for the opening clause of the verse: they had been erased from the manuscript and replaced with the well-known text. By cross-reference to the various wordings for the verse in Luke's Gospel, he was able to isolate and explain a double error in the text's tradition, uphold the short wording which he had found in the newly bought codex and delight professional textual critics with a classic example of their art. The original text had run: 'Consider the lilies of the field: they neither card nor spin.' The King James translators have beguiled us with the wrong version; there was no growing, no toiling, in what the author wrote. Strictly, there were no 'lilies', because they are a very free translation of the Greek; however, the botanists' favourite candidate for the flower in question (a Sternbergia) would spoil the flow of the saying.

In another case, an author himself may have compounded the uncertainty. In music and drama, we have become used to the idea that an artist may leave two or more versions of a particular work, Shakespeare's *King Lear*, perhaps, or Bruckner's symphonies. In those cases, the search for the sole original is the search for a mistaken ideal. Bible translations seldom give adequate notice, but we also have two versions of the Acts of the Apostles, one of which is about a tenth longer than the other.

The shorter, usual text is based on one of the main Greek lines, the Alexandrian, whereas the longer alternative is best represented in a book-text, Codex Bezae, of fifth to sixth century date which contains the Gospels and Acts in Greek and Latin. Its extra wordings and variant readings are sometimes reflected in early Christian quotations or in early papyrus fragments of Acts' text. Some of them plainly go back into the earlier second century. Although their text is usually known as the Western text, its use was never restricted to the Western Churches.

The view that the author composed both versions was reaffirmed in the late nineteenth century, but has since been rejected by most of the major modern commentaries. Against it, they cite sharp contradictions between one or two of the variant readings and then state their objection to the idea that any of them originate from the same person. These objections are not cogent. Authors can change their minds quite drastically, and anyway the variant readings are not all of equal status. Their main source, Codex Bezae, was itself copied quite late, and its text has some later insertions in its earlier core. This core is hard to define exactly, but it certainly exists. In the past decade, purely textual criticism of the differences has broadened once again into literary and stylistic criticism too. When comparison is possible, the style of the extra material is now argued to match the distinctive style of the rest of Acts, as known in its other text, the Alexandrian line. Even those who oppose the idea of two originals have to invoke a very early Christian reviser who was busy in the wake of the author in the early second century A D and was very well acquainted with his thought and language. Many of the small additions are hard to explain as later padding. Style, together with their very existence, supports the older view that Acts' author revised his own text, issuing two versions in his lifetime. It is still the most attractive answer to an open question.

If it is correct, the longer of the two versions is probably the later, because it is easier to see why its changes were added than why they should have been taken out (although even this view is disputed). The author, it seems, touched up certain passages to emphasize hostility of, and to, the Jews; he added emphasis on the directing role of the Holy Spirit; he even added another instance of a sudden first-person plural, implying that he himself was present quite early at Christian events in Antioch. Jewish enmity, the Holy Spirit, the sudden uses of 'we': these touches are also present in the shorter version, but the author, on this view, increased them in his second edition. He added a few details to journeys and plans, for instance, how Paul did not preach in Thessaly. Individuals are given a clearer identity: Timothy's mother, a Jewess, turns out to have been a widow; the sons of Sceva who practise exorcism in Ephesus appear to be sons of a pagan priest, not a puzzling high priest among the Jews. By a tiny change, the 'leading women' who hear Paul at Thessalonica become 'wives of the leading men', a point which is not always given due weight in modern studies of early Christianity's appeal for women of high and independent status. If the author of Acts wrote two versions, which is the 'unerring' word?

Revision is also visible in one of the Gospels. At John 14:31, during the Last Discourse at the Last Supper, Jesus says, 'Arise, let us go hence.' However, three more long chapters of monologue follow before he goes out with his disciples. We all know the guest at dinner who says to his partner, 'We must be going,' and talks for another half hour, but he surely does not belong at this farewell meal. The word 'arise' has been explained, desperately, as an 'invitation to spiritual, not physical movement'. The likelihood is that chapters 15–17 have been added into a plan which was originally much tighter and briefer. Here, we are confronted not with two alternative versions, but with an unrevised insertion which is probably the author's own.

At John 8:1–11, however, we are faced with a famous addition which is not the author's. In our Bibles nowadays, we read Jesus's moving defence of the adulterous woman who was about to be stoned for her sins: 'He that is without sin among you, let him first cast a stone at her'; 'Neither do I condemn thee: go, and sin no more'. The episode is missing from the surviving fourth-century codices which underpin the rest of the New Testament text; it is not known in an early papyrus or any quotation by an early Christian author, although the subject was relevant to so much which they discussed. Its style is universally held to differ from the rest of the fourth Gospel, and in its present place it interrupts the flow of the text. By *c.* 400 Jerome was aware that it stood in many Greek and Latin manuscripts of the Gospel, although its credentials were doubtful. The story itself may be old; perhaps it is the one which was known to Papias in the early second century from a spurious 'Gospel According to the Hebrews'.

The verses have struck many readers as more Christian than much in Christian scripture, but an editor has plainly inserted them, and textual critics now agree that they are not the Gospel's own. Whereas most early Christian leaders took a very strong line on sexual sin, this scene showed Christian forgiveness in action. It crept in for ethical and doctrinal reasons.

There is a thin and difficult line between a saying (perhaps largely authentic) which Christians inserted into an existing Gospel and those sayings which a Gospeller ascribed implausibly to Jesus himself. In the history of the text, the insertions are the changes which concern us: if this one scene intruded, admittedly rather clumsily, what else might have been added more artfully during the hundred or so dark years in which we know almost nothing of the text's history? What, too, might have been cut out? The question confronts us, notoriously, at the ending of Mark's Gospel, the earliest of the four.

The earliest texts of this Gospel all end at 16:8, omitting the appearances of Jesus which validate the Resurrection in the other Gospels' story. After seeing the angel in the tomb and hearing that Jesus has risen from the dead, the women 'fled from the sepulchre ... neither said they any thing to any man; for they were afraid'. As Luke's and Matthew's Gospels seem to acknowledge, the earliest versions of Mark broke off at this point. It is a remarkable ending, and on one valiant view, it is an original statement of 'human inadequacy, lack of understanding and weakness in the presence of supreme divine action'. An abrupt enigmatic ending also appeals to modern literary tastes: literary critics have now written book after book in recent defence of its subtlety, part of the growing respect for the artistry of the Gospel's author.

Among ancient texts, there are other famous problems over endings, of which the best known is Homer's *Odyssey*. People wonder if its last book and a half are original or if they have been added on to a stopping-point which was known to two good Alexandrian scholars (before 170 BC); they believed the poem ended when Odysseus and Penelope went to bed together. The ending of Mark rests on different evidence: the earliest texts, not the views of early critics. There is also a much simpler doubt. It is unparalleled that a coherent narrative should be left hanging on the weak Greek word at verse 8 which means 'for'. It is also incredible, despite modern literary attempts at appreciation, that the first Gospel should stop so abruptly without showing Jesus risen from the dead.

The sinister view, that the original ending was cut out because it said something awkward, is not compelling: the rest of Mark's Gospel is too straightforward. The obvious explanation is that the last part of the text was lost from a very early copy, perhaps the author's own text. This loss was an accident, and certainly does not affect the Christian tradition that Jesus was seen after his Resurrection: that belief had been attested years earlier by Paul (1 Corinthians 15:4). It does, however, affect our views of how our earliest Gospel was valued when it first appeared: so far from being sacrosanct, it was treated rather carelessly and allowed to lose its final section.

Verses 9–20 which now round off the Gospel are plainly a pastiche by some later hand (the same is by no means certain for the lines which end the *Odyssey*). Here, too, there is a gain in their loss. For these are the verses which make Jesus tell the Apostles that believers 'shall take up serpents and if they drink any deadly thing, it shall not hurt them'. Christians, therefore, could handle what no prudent Jew would touch: not only did their texts of scripture 'defile the hands', but snakes, even, would not bite them. In 1909 these verses so impressed an American Baptist, George Hensley, that he began to handle snakes and pass them to his neighbours at Christian meetings. Eventually he died of snakebite, but not until the age of seventy-five; his practice persists among the snake-handling Churches of God in Carolina and parts of the American South. Their supreme test of the Christian spirit rests on very weak foundations, words which somebody added to the Gospel's ending as if Jesus himself had spoken them.

9

From Scrolls to Books

I

These textual uncertainties belong in a wider context; so long as there were Christians who had heard the Apostles or even Jesus himself, there was no overriding concern to turn Christianity into a faith with its own set books. Some of Paul's epistles were lost; so were some early narratives of Jesus (to judge from Luke 1:1); an early copy of Mark's Gospel, perhaps the original copy, lost its final verses. Books, however, became a Christian characteristic by the later second century. Whereas Jews continued to copy their holy texts on to impressive scrolls of parchment or other solid materials, the earliest surviving papyrus fragments of Christian Gospels and Christian copies of Hebrew scriptures are all in the form of little books, or codices. Christians have even been seen as initiators of the change from scroll to book which gradually spread to non-Christian writings and has influenced the business of reading ever since. Our sample of early Christian papyri, however, is tiny and confined to Egypt: its dating is still disputed. Probably, Christians in the second century merely allied themselves with the change to the book, or codex, which was then beginning around them. The significant point, however, is their break with Jewish practice, and its causes are keenly disputed. Ease of reference, from text to text and line to line, was perhaps a motive, but not necessarily. Some of the early Christian book-texts contained one text only in which cross-reference was easy; rolls continued to serve for official records during the Middle Ages: they, too, needed to be consulted and looked up. Perhaps the Christians simply wished to make a break with the venerable scrolls of the Jews and their synagogues and turned to the existing form of the books of papyrus instead, scruffy books for use whose workaday appearance is quite different from a treasured Jewish scroll written in an elegant script.

The change may have begun with copies of the Gospels and then spread to texts of the Old Testament books which Christians wished to use. Its origin is consistent with the Christians' less reverential attitude to the written word. Nobody argued that a Christian book was so holy that it would defile the hands: when early Christians quoted words which we know in our Gospels, they often mixed up sayings from separate Gospels and quoted them as if they were one. This habit (attested since the 90s) is symptomatic: they were concerned with 'words of Jesus', whether written or oral, but not with separate and individual holy texts. Like most Christian laymen ever since, early Christians assumed that the supreme value of the Gospels was that they reported Jesus's words. They, too, did not give much thought to the fact that the Gospellers had shaped them, or sometimes invented them, to suit their individual views of him.

We can see some of the results in a long letter which was sent from Rome's Christians to Corinth in the mid 90s, the so-called First Clement: the name is given only in the work's title, which was added before *c.* 150. This anonymous letter twice refers directly to 'words of the Lord Jesus', but neither reference is an exact quotation of a saying found in any one of our Gospels. The author is also unaware of any written New Testament and restrained in his use of scripture. He urged Corinth to consult its epistle from the 'blessed apostle Paul' and apparently alluded elsewhere to other Pauline epistles, as if he already knew them in a collection. He certainly knew our Epistle to the Hebrews, though not its anonymous author. However, when he mentioned Paul's Romans 1:29, he continued with a quotation from Psalm 50, introduced by the phrase 'For scripture says ...' It seems that Paul's epistles were not quite the same as scripture in his mind: it is striking that he quoted clusters of sayings from Jesus only twice, whereas he referred over a hundred times to verses in Hebrew scripture. Christianity, for this author, is certainly not yet a 'religion of the book' with its own closed body of texts.

It became one gradually, but we should beware of using our hindsight. By *c.* 100 at the latest our four Gospels existed, but they were not the only ones to be written. During the second century we know of ten or more others, including a Gospel of Thomas, a Gospel of Peter, a Gospel of the Hebrews and a Gospel of Truth. Some of them are now better known from papyri, found in Egypt, which have turned out to contain bits of their texts, not always in their original language. Further surprises are still possible, but our knowledge of these extra Gospels has grown fascinatingly in the past century.

One brisk reaction is to dismiss them all as secondary inventions which add nothing of historical value to the four Gospels now in our Bibles. They are a mixed bunch, some of which are collections of sayings without a narrative, some of which give a narrative, but perhaps not a narrative of the same scope as our four. The Gospel of Peter has a narrative of Jesus's Passion, Burial and Resurrection, but it inserts a vivid appearance of Jesus while being resurrected, seen by the Roman soldiers at the tomb. Its story is steeped in allusions to Hebrew scripture, but it is patently an elaboration of the Passion narrative in the main four: it has filled the gap which they had left by omitting to describe the Resurrection itself.

Not every such Gospel is as blatant as the Gospel of Peter, and here we have two tantalizing candidates. One of them is a Gospel of unknown identity, four fragments of which were published in 1935 from a papyrus found in Egypt. The papyrus was written in Greek not later than the mid second century, and possibly as early as 120, while the text itself could well have been composed even earlier: an early Christian had jotted it down as a copy for private reading. The other is a collection of sayings which led an earlier, varied life before surfacing in the Coptic language in a papyrus of early to mid fourth-century date. It is known as the Gospel of Thomas, a title which is first attested in a Christian author, writing *c.* 200–230, although his idea of its contents does not match ours.

These two types of alternative Gospel are rather different in form. The Unknown Gospel, published in 1935, was evidently a narrative and probably included a full Passion story. In the few Greek fragments we read how Jesus argued about his authority with lawyers and the people; how he escaped when people wished to stone him and when the rulers tried to arrest him; how he healed a leper who expressly says that he had caught leprosy by travelling with lepers and eating with them at an inn; how he brushed aside a question about rendering to kings what pertains to their rule; how he stood by the Jordan, stretched out his right hand and worked a miracle which sounds botanically very welcome (the text is fragmentary, but something 'sent forth fruit'). Except for the miracle, most of these fragments are close to verses in our synoptic Gospels and to sayings in the fourth Gospel, but the author's style and arrangement is different. Is he using an oral tradition of sayings which the four Gospellers have used too or did he depend on their written texts, adding a few bits of tradition of his own? The first modern editors of the papyri even suggested that the fourth Gospeller had used this unknown work as one of his sources: one of its sayings is almost identical with our John 5:39. The Unknown Gospel is not widely known, but, in my view, it drew on the texts of our main four, rephrased and rearranged what it selected from them, and added bits which were known as stories in other oral traditions. It is largely secondary but not entirely.

It may yet turn out to be earlier than anyone admits: a new papyrus could change everything. Even now, its importance lies not so much in its alternative contents as in its very existence. Those who date it after our biblical four must accept that those four did not rule out alternative narratives: the Unknown Gospel belonged to an individual Christian who still wanted it for his own reading. It does not seem partisan or any odder than bits of our biblical four. In the early second century the four had not established dominance.

Unlike the Unknown Gospel, the Gospel of Thomas is not a narrative. It existed in several forms, but our fullest text is a papyrus found at Nag Hammadi in Egypt which gives 114 sayings of Jesus in Coptic, one after another. Since their identification in the 1950s, a minority of scholars have wondered if some of the sayings might not be more authentic than similar words of Jesus which are now in our biblical four. Perhaps Jesus might have said, 'Become passers-by' (Saying 42): perhaps not. Perhaps he said, 'Love your brother like your soul' (Saying 25). It would be pleasant if Saying 95 was more authentic than the similar verses in our third Gospel: 'If you have money, do not lend it at interest but give it to one from whom you will not get it back.' It would be fascinating if Jesus had explicitly spoken against the life's work of bankers. It would also be fascinating if Saying 114 was indeed Jesus's own, and not the invention of an early Christian solitary. 'Simon Peter said to them, "Let Mary leave us, for women are not worthy of life." Jesus said, "I myself shall lead her in order to make her male so that she too may become a living spirit resembling you males. For every woman who will make herself male will enter the kingdom of heaven."'

The question of authenticity leads, in my view, in another direction. Some of the material in the fully fledged Gospel of Thomas goes back to the mid second century, probably earlier still: it takes us into the milieu of sayings which Papias and others knew besides all or some of our biblical Gospels, *c*. 120. Like those Gospels, the Gospel of Thomas is shaped round particular themes: seeking and finding knowledge, the god-like potential in each Christian, the solitary life, an opposition to sex and femininity. These themes are more blatant than those of our four Gospels, and their Jesus has lost contact with his historical, Jewish setting. However, the Gospellers, too, selected, arranged and phrased many words which they give to Jesus himself. Overlaps between their words and words now in Thomas or the Unknown Gospel remind us that such sayings would pass to and fro in different forms: it is not that one is authentic, the other not. None is authentic, or Jesus's exact words. They express what Jesus meant to early Christians, whether a synoptic author, an unknown Christian or the author of other Thomas sayings. It is rather unlikely that Jesus ever said that females needed to make themselves male, and perhaps the Apostles were never so blatantly sexist as Thomas's Simon Peter. But early Christianity was quick to involve them explicitly in problems with which its Churches still live.

II

Not until the early 170s do we happen to know of a Christian who assumed that four, our four Gospels, were special: it was then that Tatian harmonized the four into a special book. Before him, in the 140s, we know of Marcion, who thought that only one Gospel sufficed, our third, and even then he had to cut offensive bits out of it to make it satisfactory. Meanwhile alternative Gospels had continued to appear, the Gospel of Truth and many others.

It is often supposed that heresy first caused our four to be defined as authoritative, in order to see off Marcion and the authors of Gospels five to twenty. Perhaps these alternatives heightened respect for the four, but they are most unlikely to have created it: the Thomas Gospel is only sayings, not narrative; it takes an eccentric modern scholar to consider the Gospel of Peter's narratives from Passion to Resurrection to be somehow more authentic: it is fuller but not more authoritative. The differences are rather obvious. As for the fragments of the Unknown Gospel, in my view, they draw on our four, although they add to them. The dependence is itself a mark of respect, while the author is not alone in reading other material too. At the turn of the century, the Christian intellectual Clement of Alexandria still cited the Gospel of the Egyptians and interpreted a saying of Jesus from it, although he knew very well that it was not one of the four. Around 200 the bishop of Antioch found that the Gospel of Peter was highly esteemed in a church in Cilicia: if it was harmless, he was prepared to let it be read, but when he found that it was heretical (it denied Jesus's suffering), he wished it to be withdrawn. Even so, he admitted that large parts of it conformed to correct belief.

As for the rest of our New Testament, a collection of Paul's epistles existed, perhaps by the 90s, certainly by *c.* 120; First Clement may know it; 2 Peter certainly does. Perhaps it already included the two Epistles to Timothy with their false author. Elsewhere, Christian readers were not so credulous and continued to contest the genuine authorship of Peter's letters (especially 2 Peter), some of John's and especially Revelation. Their arguments were often acute and remind us that since the rise of literary scholarship, authors with false identities no longer had everything their own way. It is sometimes claimed that the Church and the New Testament grew up together, but the relationship, like that of most brothers and sisters, remained decidedly ragged at the edges.

Not until the fourth century do Christian authors list exactly the books which we now accept as the Christian Bible and imply that they are an exclusive list. In the Greek-speaking Churches, Athanasius, the great bishop of Alexandria, sent a letter to his Churches in the year 367 in which he cited the twenty-seven books of our New Testament: he described them as the sole 'fountains of salvation' to which 'let no one add, let nothing be taken away'. In the Latin West, a similar list had hardened by the mid fourth century, and it is usual to appeal to Augustine's exposition and two councils in North Africa (in 393 and 397) which endorsed our list. However, it is also evident that disagreement persisted, especially among thinking Greek-speakers: councils in the East continued to rule on approved lists of scripture, while not always agreeing in their results. In the 370s no bishop had a sharper nose for heresy than Epiphanius, a bishop on Cyprus, but he still classed the suggestive Wisdom of Solomon at the end of his list of New Testament books (perhaps he shared the view that it had been written by Philo, a Jewish contemporary of Paul). Even in the West the combined weight of Augustine and the various local councils did not extinguish the need to reiterate and reassert. Among the many Christians who lived elsewhere, the idea of a clear canon would have seemed odd. In the East the Syrian Orthodox Church still recognizes only twenty-two of our twenty-seven New Testament books for reading in church: their early members also favoured a fake Third Epistle of Paul to the Corinthians. Belief in this text duly passed to the Armenian Church, from whose language the fake letter was translated into English by Lord Byron. The Ethiopian Church, meanwhile, continued to show evidence of two canons, one of which is broad enough to include an extra eight books in the Old Testament, like Clement or a book of the Covenant in two parts.

These variant lists and local complexities could be multiplied, but they confirm two simple points. No central authority ever fixed a New Testament for all the early Christian Churches, any more than a central authority fixed a Jewish canon earlier for the Hebrew scripture. Exclusive lists of New Testament books emerged rather late in the day when people sat down and started to look back at them: for three hundred years Christianity had coped without them, and even afterwards not every Christian acknowledged one and the same list. The Old Testament books were even more contestable: the historic figure of twenty-two, known in Judaea before 70, took on a new importance, not least when Christians began by quoting from a wider range of books and their Jewish hearers complained at their weak authority.

Obviously, it is implausible to cite the early Christians' agreement on their scripture as a proof, or result, of guidance by their Holy Spirit. Even an atheist can see the difference between one of the turgid or most sectarian alternative Gospels and one of the recognized four: as for the others, even early Christians who respected our four could quote sayings from some of the other Gospels too. As for the rest of the New

Testament, it was never agreed definitively, unless the entire Syriac, Ethiopic and Greek Orthodox Churches are disqualified from a share in the Holy Spirit, along with the bulk of those Christians who wrote in Greek throughout the first seven centuries of Church history and made such subtle contributions to Christian theology.

When we read the entire New Testament, we are reading a list of books which some of the Christians' bishops approved and asserted more than three hundred years after Jesus's death. The list of Old Testament books was never so clear-cut, and its edges remained a matter of Christian argument. Three centuries are a very long time: do these late listings really create a unity with such an authority that it directs our understanding? As they stand, they bring a greater risk of increasing our misunderstanding. Their authors' names and individual books compress the rich history of the Old Testament's jungle: its text in our standard Bibles is only the Hebrew text which groups of well-meaning scholars finalized in the seventh and eighth centuries A D. It was not the only sort of text, and when they showed vowels for every vowel sound, their guesses at the vowels were not always right.

As for the New Testament, it, too, runs the risk of being compressed. Matthew's Gospel was not by Matthew; the Epistles to Timothy, Titus and the Hebrews were not by Paul; the Epistles of Peter were not by Peter, and serious doubts surround the Epistles of James and of Jude. The various Johns may or may not be the same person, the Apostle or neither, but there is one certainty about the third of John's letters: its presence in our holy scripture would have appalled the Christian leader of a community to which its author had written. This leader had refused to receive the author or his 'beloved brethren', and if anyone tried to receive them, he 'cast them out of the church'. This Christian leader presumably claimed the Holy Spirit, but he excluded the people behind the very letters which we have now included in holy writ.

This compression matters because it obscures important historical truth. Outside the New Testament, the effect of false identities is unmistakable. In the period *c.* 400–600 'aggressive forgeries' added false letters to the collections of almost every early Christian letter-writer. These fake texts of theology helped to enlist the great authorities of the past on this or that side of a contemporary schism or unorthodoxy. An expert in Church history has aptly concluded:

Under such circumstances the preservation of any authentic texts seems almost miraculous. The needs of dogmatic theology were undisturbed by much historical sense. [By *c.* 600] they had resulted in a distortion of the historical materials on which theology was supposedly built. The absence of any understanding of historical development allowed genuine and false documents to be so thoroughly mixed that they would not be disentangled for more than a millennium.

A critical history of Christian thought could not possibly begin to have been written until after 1500 because of forgeries by Christians themselves.

The same danger besets the New Testament. If we take its authors, titles and the idea of a decisive canon at face value, it seems as if holy scripture ends with the Apostles and their contemporaries, and that a full blueprint for Christian belief and practice was laid down by Jesus's own sayings and his Apostles' inspired texts. In fact, many central items emerged over time: so did some of the Gospels' sayings. That historical fact is highly relevant to Christian self-awareness. Christianity had four Gospels, not one text, and a wide historical range of authors in the rest of its canon. Like the Hebrew scripture, it had incoherence built into it. The grouping of these texts into a Bible did not make them sink their differences, and it did not create an authority which overrides their previous nature. In the late fourth century, an elderly pagan wrote a fine letter to St Augustine in which he commended him to the pagan gods; they were worshipped worldwide, he remarked, in 'concordant discord'. A similar discord still sounds in the Christian Bible. The authors, after all, were only human.

10
Original Scripture?

In such a marvellous tangle, there is no coherence which is enough to support a theory of biblical truth. After a thousand years or more we ended up with a Bible and a canon but not with a single 'work'. The idea that this canon, as we now have it, must be the starting-point for our understanding is singularly feeble. There are communities, the Churches, who have come to accept canonical books and read them in particular ways: in their tradition, they have authority. But their tradition does not overwhelm every other attempt at reading them: readers are not prisoners of all previous readers. By lumping these texts together, there is quite a high chance that a community will misread them. Those misreadings may be remarkably interesting (the idea, for instance, that Isaiah prophesied Jesus's birth), but they are not therefore true. Lumping texts together and reading one in the light of another does not destroy what the texts previously were or what they meant: it adds another way of reading them which may, quite often, be wrong. At times it may even be a confidence trick.

Even within individual books, what we now read in the Bible is the result of padding and reinterpretation. This process shows up in much of Hebrew scripture, not just in the books of prophets but in the books of narrative and wisdom. Like the book of Jeremiah, the books of Samuel existed in several early texts, some of which were shorter than others. The books of Job and Ecclesiastes have both been edited and padded, so that neither of them now makes coherent sense: we all think we know more or less what they are about, but they are not completely intelligible, not least because later editors and revisers have stuck in speeches or comments which undercut the original authors' view. It is not that these insertions have given us a new, intelligible Job or

Ecclesiastes: they have made the texts hard to understand. Literary critics or strict fundamentalists may want to enthuse over the padding, but it is still padding, stuck into earlier books. There is no magic or 'subjective foreunderstanding' or historians' hocus-pocus (as literary critics have sometimes called it) in seeing this material for what it is. Historians are diagnosing what we have, not straining imaginatively for some purer, early condition. Their diagnosis uses method and evidence.

Its results may be negative in important ways. In the Old Testament, especially, historians have helped us to realize that we cannot hope to recover the first, the 'original' text: it is in others, especially non-historians, that the urge to reconstruct it is still extremely strong. The most recent international committee on the text of the Old Testament defined its task by identifying five thousand important places where a Hebrew word was so puzzling that it might need to be corrected. It is not just that such corrections raise difficult questions of method (can we really compare Hebrew words with other Semitic words, Arabic for instance, and deduce a new, unattested sense?). It is that there is a deeper problem: the starting-point, the late Masoretic Hebrew text, already excludes many earlier alternatives. It is only one arbitrary version, hallowed by use, not history. As for the New Testament, in 1966 the United Bible Societies issued a Greek text for students and translators which they, too, described as standard. Their committee considered that there were two thousand places where alternative readings of any significance survived in good manuscripts and then chose between them. It is not just that by 1975 their Greek text had had to be revised twice because no revision has yet proved free from error and improvement. The very aim, a standard version, is misleading and unrealistic. From the variety which we have, any standard involves loss: it does not, and cannot, give us exactly what Paul or the Evangelists originally wrote.

Historians, therefore, are not straining for the flawless original: their unauthorized versions, rather, see a gain, not a loss, in this textual jungle. It affects the status of all the revised or standard versions which are modern translators' aims. It is one thing to change the Lutheran Bible's German or the English of the King James version because we are now certain that a Hebrew or Greek word had a different meaning. It is quite another to change it with the aim of drawing closer to the original scripture. For the original text of the Old Testament is lost to us, and the Greek texts of the New Testament do not take us beyond small variants and alternatives a hundred years or more after the Gospels' likely date of composition. 'Literary authenticity' is a misplaced ideal for Old Testament translations, and in my view, it is misplaced for the New Testament too. Where the original and the authentic texts are lost to us, the ideal of scriptural authenticity has been attractively proposed in their place. There are scriptures but no exact scripture within the range of our surviving knowledge: each group of readers, then, should be free to use the particular form of scripture which is historically rooted in its own traditions of liturgy, prayer, hymns and surrounding language. In English, the Authorized Version has a special place which ought, even now, to be unshakeable; in Greek, the Septuagint; in the synagogues, the Masoretic Hebrew, which is linked to centuries of recitation and liturgical use. We cannot work back to the original: one consequence is that the best-loved translations have more authority than some of their modern critics realize.

As for the canon, it is not so much like a padded room as a room with contents of different dates to which we have agreed not to add or take away. Do the contents therefore add up to a new whole, an interior with a style of its own? No doubt they do, but the objects in such a room do not lose their individual natures. Chairs are still chairs, card-tables still card-tables, even if we now use them for writing or for flowers: texts, moreover, have a meaning and are not dumb objects. Original meanings and right and wrong interpretations are not standards by which other arts are widely appreciated nowadays. People like to restage operas in new periods and costumes; attempts to revive the music of Bach or his predecessors as originally performed are dismissed as a vain ideal, as much of an interpretation as any other; paintings are often exhibited in new relationships, as if the placing of one beside another changes the nature of both. Interpretation is part of the arts, so why should we worry if our interpretation is new or personal? As in art or music, why not be free in reading too: are not historians trying, like Samson's Philistines, to tie us down?

Texts, however, use words for meaning in order to communicate. A biblical text may have had several authors, all of whom are unknown, but these authors still had purposes, even cross-purposes, which guide (but do not exhaust) what they meant. Music has no reference and so it is more malleable, but paintings, too, can refer to subjects and by them they must be understood. If we place a landscape of poplars and willows by Corot beside the golden distance of a classical landscape by Claude Lorraine, we may indeed change the ways in which we look at each of them. A contrast alters appreciation. But it does not alter meaning: Claude's Castle is still enchanted; Cupid still visits Psyche inside it. So, too, with a text: we may read it beside other much later companions; we may read it in their light or with the faith of a later age. If so, we will probably misunderstand it. Despite its place in the Bible, the Song of Songs is still a collection of erotic poetry. Despite the New Testament, Isaiah's Immanuel is still the child to be born from a young woman in the eighth century BC, not a future virgin birth.

PART THREE

11
Ideas of History

Our Bible was born from a long and intriguing history of slowly growing scripture, various types of text and various beliefs, most of them wrong, about the authorship of its individual parts. No other book has had such a history, but there is nothing in that history to make it a book whose contents are true. The canon grew up late with hindsight: it gave some of the Churches our Bible, but it did not give a new coherence to contradictory statements. If we pick and choose between the contradictory statements, we can end up with fewer statements which do, in principle, cohere: to be true, however, they must also correspond to the facts. In the next chapters I will take this answer to Pilate's sceptical question and see if particular parts of scripture conform to it.

Historians are at home with the question of correspondence but they are the first to realize that it is not simple. The biblical books range from psalms to terrifying visions: which parts, if any, can be read and studied as histories? Correspondence is a neat idea, but how do we know the facts to which bits of the Bible might correspond? Facts are not external objects which we can pick up like fossils and match to a section of scripture: it is we who select them and put them into words.

It would be odd to ask if many of the words of a psalm correspond to historical fact. The Lord might well be the psalmist's shepherd, his 'tabernacles' might well be 'amiable' and his judgements might indeed be 'more to be desired than gold, yea, than much fine gold', but historians cannot contribute to the subject. Correspondence, rather, is a question for the many books of narrative. 2 Samuel 16:22 tells us that 'they spread Absalom a tent upon the top of the house'; and Absalom went in unto his father's concubines in the sight of 'all Israel'; and John

161

11 says that Jesus 'cried with a loud voice, Lazarus, come forth. And he that was dead came forth, bound hand and foot with grave clothes: and his face was bound about with a napkin.' Either these things happened or they did not. The events were public, unambiguous and witnessed. 'All Israel' is said to have watched while Absalom went tirelessly into a tentful of ten concubines, and 'many of the Jews' are said to have 'seen what Jesus did, and believed'. If the event happened, this bit of the Bible is true; if not, it is false.

We must, however, hesitate before we brandish facts in the narrative's face: what if this part of Samuel or the Gospel or most of these two books is story, not history, for which the question of fact is as irrelevant as for incidents in *The Golden Legend* or Tolstoy's *War and Peace*? There are theologians who describe biblical narrative as story, literary critics who call it historicized fiction or prose fiction, and historical commentators who agree with many fundamentalists and call it history. These labels need to be sorted out, because the question of truth is not equally relevant to all of them; it is relevant to a history, but not to a story or a historicized fiction. They also relate to popular views of the Bible's people, the Israelites, and the Bible's own relation to God. 'The Israelites,' it has been suggested, 'were more obsessed with history than any other nation that has ever existed.' The Bible has even been valued as the record of 'God's revelation in history', a record which made the Jews' religion unique among its surrounding cultures. History, here, is a reassuring word which seems to make the Bible's authority more solid.

Much depends on how we define it. We can be strict and confine history to writings about the past which have a critical method, weigh up their evidence and try to write the truth. We might even exclude authors who introduce gods as the main explanation of events because gods, in principle, can explain anything. This definition would be very strict: it would rule out most writers about the past in the Middle Ages and quite a few writers in our own times who do not state a method in weighing or choosing their evidence (many biographers, especially, are naïve about what they tell). We should perhaps reserve the definition for good history, while allowing room for history which is not so good or even very bad. We merely need to exclude myth or heroic poetry or the amiable art of storytelling. If an author is trying to record the past, perhaps he ranks as a historian. To my mind he also needs to try to make sense of its interconnections and, in general, try to tell the truth. The interconnections will involve him in dating events, however simply. Dating, or chronology, has been considered to be as important for history as exact measurement has been for physics. People may give dates wrongly or very rarely; they may distort them or try to give them a significant order or deeper meaning. If so, they are very bad historians, but if they are totally indifferent to true sequences of time, they are not historians at all.

At a distance of two thousand years or more, it might seem impossible to decide what an author was trying to do and irrelevant to apply our modern ideas of truth and falsehood. I disagree. The Israelites had no theory of truth, but it is patronizing to assume that pre-philosophic people could not concern themselves with evidence or whether something was true or false. The Israelites had a strong tradition of laws, law courts and judging. It is they, not the philosophic Greeks, who have left us the world's first reference to the cross-examination of witnesses in a trial: it survives in the story of Susanna and the Elders (of uncertain date, perhaps *c.* 200 BC). Sometimes, a suit at law was pressed to give a grievance a public airing, and sometimes (as nowadays) it was settled by compromise. But truth and evidence could also come into it. As for the idea of a historian, none of the early cultures, whether Egyptian, Babylonian or even early Greek, had such a word, but their authors could write history perfectly well before anyone came up with the word to pigeon-hole them. The Greek author Thucydides is a superb historian by any standards, but he did not give himself a tidy label. The product preceded the profession.

Authors' aims are not obscure simply because they are ancient. Sometimes, ancient authors set them out for us, but usually we have to infer them from what they write; the aims of modern authors, especially poets, are usually a matter of inference, too. However, it helps to form our inferences if we compare ancient writings in several related cultures and widen our ideas of what authors might attempt. Biblical narrative has two types of neighbour: the Greeks, whose language eventually became the New Testament's, and the various cultures of the Near East, Assyrian, Babylonian or Egyptian, which impinged on Israel in the earlier period.

The Near Eastern cultures were well aware of the interest and use of writings about the past. During the age of David and Solomon, scribes in Assyria were recording the campaigns of Assyrian kings in the first person (the royal annals which have been found in their palaces); there were records of their buildings, lists of their kings, texts which reconstructed the geography of remote predecessors' kingdoms (for the honour of a contemporary king) and even a text which interrelated the kings of Assyria and Babylon, and blamed the Babylonians for persistent breaches of the treaties which governed their boundaries. We have only a tiny sample of these texts and may yet discover much more behind or beyond them. There are also traces of Assyrian chronicles which were written in the third person year by year, and which may perhaps have been the source for the inscribed royal annals. Between the time of Ahab and Jeremiah, scribes in Assyria produced a very varied literature by recording, imagining and distorting past events; natural journalists of Near Eastern affairs, they quickly understood its uses.

In Egypt an undergrowth of tales and romances had long flourished, as it still does. Here, too, records of the past were centred on the ruler and were frequently inscribed: they, too, concerned his public deeds and the approval of the gods, although they were less concerned about truth and even less about change. In Babylonia, especially during the seventh and sixth centuries BC, the past was a lively subject for those who were literate. It was recorded in the diary records of astronomers, the books which were concerned with omens and predictions from them, and also in a long and remarkable continuous chronicle. This Babylonian chronicle is a most significant rediscovery of recent scholarship. We are now aware of a long sequence of texts which listed major events and dated them year by year, beginning in 747 BC and running on past 539 BC (the coming of the Persians) and beyond Alexander the Great. In Babylonia, too, there were king lists and imaginative attempts to reconstruct chronicles of a vastly older past, way back before 2000 BC. These reconstructions of remote eras are unlike the contemporary chronicles, and need to be borne in mind when we try to assess the nature of the Bible's Genesis or Numbers. There were also books which explained events by a simple theme which was usually religious (the observance, or neglect, of a god and his festival). One very interesting text, the Chronicle of Esarhaddon (written after the 660s BC), used the information in, or behind, the year-by-year chronicle but doctored it heavily to throw the best possible light on Esarhaddon and explain away a grim period of Babylonian history. This enterprise is not so dissimilar to aspects of the Bible's own books of Kings.

Like the authors of Hebrew scripture, writers in these cultures were concerned with lists, precise dates and the remote past. They dated events by the years of a king's reign (their calendars and methods of counting them were varied and rather complicated); the Babylonian chroniclers even gave dates which tried to synchronize events between different kingdoms (Assyrian, Babylonian and Elamite). There is a close similarity here to the style of dating in the biblical books of Kings. There is also a similarity of explanation. Babylonian authors could explain a reign or era in terms of the neglect of one of their gods (one of these texts, the Weidner Chronicle, is probably as old as *c.* 1100 BC); years later, biblical authors were certainly not unique in explaining events of history by transgressions against Yahweh. Nor were they unique in their methods or their anonymity. These Near Eastern texts observe the firm rule of all narratives in the area, including the Bible: they do not name their authors. None of them shows self-awareness about its methods or open criticism about the use of evidence: neither does Hebrew narrative. There are, however, considerable differences, as any Israelite would have realized if he had penetrated a library, found the Babylonian chronicle and managed to translate it.

Near Eastern authors centred their writings upon kings (the Babylonians, but not the Assyrians, divided them into dynasties). Sometimes they transferred the texts or deeds of one ruler and credited them to another, but they never suggested that monarchy might cease to govern their world. Although the Babylonian chronicle seems factual, it contains brief lists of events which give no explanation in terms of human motives: it is still arguable that it was written only to assist the science of omens. By contrast, biblical narrative is so much richer, longer and more carefully motivated than anything known from these cultures. It is aware of change, from an era without kings to a temporary monarchy, and on to days when a king might be restored. Although it, too, looks forward to the future, it has no connection with omens or astrology. It is importantly connected with prophecies, and for a long while its books were read by Jews as prophetic, in the broad sense of the word. Packed with speeches, far more so than any other Near Eastern text, it is also alive with explanations, human predicaments and the driving themes of interpretation and promise. It brings us back to the question of Israel's uniqueness. One reaction is to suspect that the Hebrew narratives are much like the narratives of surrounding Near Eastern cultures, and that they also could have had scriptures if they had selected and pieced some texts together. On our present evidence, the Israelite authors of narrative were not unique in Near Eastern history, but although there are similarities, the differences are greater. Perhaps one or two of the Babylonian writers of the seventh and sixth centuries BC do qualify as historians, because they were trying to record, reconstruct and explain the past truthfully; a case has been argued for the Editor of the chronicle. But at present there is a gulf between their brief and very monotonous writings and the great narrative from Joshua to 2 Kings which was being constructed by exiled Jews in the Babylonians' own country.

If we then look westwards, not eastwards, these biblical narratives were followed by the first Greek historians. The Bible's narratives were unknown in classical antiquity. The Roman Cicero believed (like some modern classicists) that the father of history was Herodotus, active *c.* 460–420 BC. His claim to be a historian is indisputable, but he reminds us that an early work of history could cover quite a range of what we would now consider to be sins. He reported conversations which he could not know: sometimes a god or a necessary destiny explains the course of the story; dreams and visions motivate big decisions; he had a pious trust and interest in the prophecies of seers and oracles; his speakers are often warners; and important people in his narrative regularly come to grief when pride or ambition carries them too far. None the less, Herodotus was certainly a historian, greater than the sum of his errors or the imagined details which are fictions to us but were not to him. He introduces us to an important distinction between imagination and falsification. In my view, he never distorted his evidence deliberately or made up an entire incident, knowing it to be misleading. He did, however, imagine: he was 'inventive', as later classical historians knew the term, helping the truth along, animating what he knew, and sometimes telling how it must have been.

Biblical narrative shares these features, but it is not disqualified as history on the strength of them: they do not disqualify Herodotus.

However, Herodotus had a different idea of his task. His histories were 'his' version, and, unlike biblical narratives, he wrote so that he himself could read them aloud in public: prose words and personal speech were still closely related in his world. Unlike any Hebrew author, he tells us his name and his purpose: to preserve great deeds and tell how a great war came about. Remembering was also an important aspect of the Hebrew book of the law, but it had a different reference: it lay in its command to remember God's help for his people. This remembering was to be kept up orally within families, and fathers were to pass on the story to their sons: the story acquired its own life, but it was not based on any one person's written, researched version. Here, a wide gulf of method and self-awareness distinguishes Herodotus. His history is a memorial based on personal inquiry, on interviewing, travelling, looking and listening across thousands of miles and many separate cultures (although he knew no oriental languages). To find out, he walked, watched and talked. This inquiry is *historie* in Greek. It is personal because he commented on his findings and their credibility or causes more than a thousand times in his nine books. He did not believe everything which he reported. For Herodotus, discovery was never separable from appreciation.

The Hebrew narratives are quite different from this enterprise. They are anonymous and conceal the fact that they are subjective, the fact which Herodotus proclaimed in his first sentence. Subjectivity is central to our modern awareness of what history is. Nowadays, we realize that history may tell us about its author as well as about the events to which it refers. We can suggest that 'history begins with a personal question' or even that 'all history is contemporary history': these suggestions are heirs to Herodotus's way of writing. The Hebrew authors, by contrast, show no sign of travel, interview or research outside other people's books and well-known stories: they did not distinguish the 'duty of reporting from the legitimacy of believing'. The main biblical narrative runs continuously from the Creation to the Exile without any no-go areas or reservations about its evidence. By contrast, Herodotus did not claim to know the continuous history of the world. He could conceive of an immensely ancient past, more than twenty thousand years away from his own lifetime when the physical world looked different (the biblical story implies a total span from Creation to Christ of only four thousand years). In this longer perspective, Herodotus noted people who are the 'first of whom we know'; most of them cluster round the mid sixth century BC, about a hundred years before his time of writing. Sometimes, he reasoned from evidence to a theory about the remote past (his word for this evidence, *tekmerion*, became as fashionable to Greek thinkers of the classical age as 'structure' has become to modern historians). Implicitly, he drew a line between stories and knowledge, even if he did not always draw it where we would like.

Five hundred years or more after the events, biblical authors wrote about what Gideon or Samson did, without any explicit awareness of the problems of truth and inaccurate tradition. They directed their stories by the running theme of obedience, or disobedience, to God's orders: Herodotus had no directing theology of history, and when the gods are mentioned in his work, they usually accompany a complex web of human aims and motives. They tend to answer the question 'Why him, or her, in particular?', not 'Why did the events of an entire reign or era occur in this way?' Herodotus, a true Greek, was often cautious about citing a god as an explanation; only one working lifetime later, this caution blossomed in his great successor, the Athenian Thucydides (active *c*. 435–398).

Like Herodotus, Thucydides distinguished between the remote past when inference and caution were appropriate: he would have wondered about the logistics of the Exodus and would not have been fobbed off by bread from heaven. He prefaced his contemporary narrative with an admirable statement of his method and research: unbiblical as ever, he took exactness and realism as his guiding lights. He wrote in the hope, since justified, that his history would be useful to future generations (but only in so far as human nature might perhaps stay constant): it would help our choices and decisions in the face of political crisis. Unlike the authors of the Bible, Thucydides never addressed the future directly through prophecies or implied typology. He gave a new role to three of history's protagonists: speeches, dating and the gods.

Biblical authors invented speeches for their human participants, as did Herodotus; they give us dialogues some of which (especially those of kings) are like short conversations in Herodotus's book. From Moses to Stephen, they also give us something else: longer speeches which are single, which address us like sermons and often tend to prophesy. 'The thundering voice of Elijah deafens us to the answer of Jezebel. We hear the Maccabees, but not their foes.' Herodotus was not so one-sided, but the sharpest contrast is with Thucydides. He faced the need for accuracy in speeches which he reported and, unlike the Hebrew Bible, he aimed to 'keep as close as possible to what was actually said'. Often, he gives us pairs of speeches which bring out the wider issues in a great decision. These decisions were too complex for a single sermon (except for his political hero, Pericles, whose speeches are never answered back).

Herodotus and Thucydides composed narratives which covered a long stretch of time. The biblical books, too, are teeming with dates, genealogies and lengths of time, people's life spans, kings' reigns or a few bigger calculations, the time in Egypt or the time from the Exodus to the first Temple. Chronology was very important to them. In Herodotus, there are some precise lengths of reign for Eastern kings, but dates are much rarer, and often we have to do our own clever sums: once only he gives us a date by the year of a magistrate in Athens. Thucydides had quite a different outlook. He thought carefully about the problem: he criticized others' solutions; he saw the difficulties of local calendars; he was concerned with exactness and accuracy and had a word for them; he used his own system of numbering years. Like a scientist, he cared about exact measurement.

So, at first sight, did some of the biblical authors, but they never explained their methods of counting; the reign of a king could be reckoned in several different ways, and calendar years began at different points in different places. There are acute difficulties in squaring all the dates for kings which they give us (errors in copying their text are only one problem). Above all, their bigger numbers look suspiciously systematic: '430 years' in Egypt; '480 years' from the Exodus to the first Temple; '430 years' again from the Temple to its destruction; '50 years' from its destruction to the beginning of the second Temple, making '480 years' from the first to the second Temples. Similar number patterns can be detected in Genesis, from Creation to the birth of Abraham, Abraham to the Exodus and so forth. Some of these bigger pattern numbers sit at odds with the shorter numbers for reigns and so forth which are given within their span. Evidently, they were imposed on the narrative not for reasons of accuracy but for system, prophecy and significance. Herodotus, let alone Thucydides, never abused numbers and dates for ulterior or hidden meanings.

Greek authors' ideas of motives and causes are also free from hidden systems and meanings. Their long narratives are a tangle of human motives and natural causes: political, geographical and even, sometimes, economic. Herodotus did have a view that people who are too good or too successful are inevitably brought low: his speakers express various views, that 'man's life is a circle' or that the gods are 'jealous and a cause of disturbance', but he was not writing with a grand, commanding theology of history. In the Bible, human motives interrelate in much shorter spans of action, and the long view is guided by the moods of God, which the authors claimed to know. By one of the great leaps of human understanding Thucydides left Herodotus's supernatural explanations behind him and made his histories quite unlike biblical narrative: he removed the gods from historical explanation; gods explain everything and therefore nothing. Naturally, it was a leap which biblical authors never contemplated.

With these two Greeks, we are faced with qualities which still make up good history: the contrast helps us to appreciate the Bible's narratives. Like the Deuteronomist, author of the books from Joshua to Kings, Herodotus and Thucydides both wrote in exile from their home cities. In their different ways, none of the three was merely amassing information about the past. Rather, they put questions to it: 'Why did Greeks and Persians fight?', 'Why were the Jews deported to Babylon?', 'Why did Athens and Sparta go to war?'. All of them were impelled to write, explain and record by a great event: the Exile to Babylonia, the Greeks' defeat of the Persians' invasions, the 'greatest war' between Sparta and Athens. Their backgrounds, however, were quite different. Herodotus and Thucydides were heirs to the questioning and intellectual interests of two great ages of theory, one in Ionia and the other in classical Athens. Among the Jews, a priest or a courtier or an antiquarian in exile was not part of a culture of intellectual thought. He also had no political experience, apart from the intrigues of a closed society. In the Greek cities, however, political change was frequent and affected all citizens. Political debate was open and often democratic; the supreme realism and rational judgement of Thucydides owed much to his own experience of political arguments and decisions. In the Greeks' world of separate little 'cities', an individual in exile could uncover conflicting stories from other individuals by his own research and questioning. There was no single 'Greek version'. Neither Herodotus nor Thucydides wrote as a priest or found their information in a single reservoir of priestly tradition. Kings or despots impinged on their evidence, but their own hopes for monarchy did not distort their story.

This contrast in method and culture relates to a fundamental contrast in evidence. Neither of the two Greek authors was the heir to authoritative written sources. Almost all of their evidence survived orally, apart from the implications of a few inscriptions (when Herodotus first cited an inscription, he noted, more wary than we moderns, that it was a fake). Nowadays, the oral histories of pre- or semi-literate cultures are more often studied by anthropologists than by historians, but we have become much more aware of their variety and flexibility, their chances of accuracy and their length of life. A community may pass on a relatively fixed story of its origins (a new colony abroad, perhaps) and a family may preserve a long line of ancestors: I have heard Eskimos tell of their ancestors in a chain through eleven generations; their deeds, however, may vary according to the times in which they are retold. By word of mouth, traditions can live and develop without any basis in fact ('Prester John', in the medieval world), but the length of life for accurate detail is less predictable. Big events or notorious actions of a king may sometimes be handed down in simple outline across several centuries. Within families, distant turning-points can also survive, while aristocrats, especially, can be very retentive of their long-past glories. In most oral cultures the detailed memory of events peters out about two generations from the teller's own time; grandfathers tend to be names, much as they are to us in our own culture of oral family history, which is passed on beside a receding habit of reading and a growing tidal wave of print. Memories of a grandfather's early life can go back about a hundred years from the time of telling (obviously, this span varies between families and individuals; historians may hit on long-lived or exceptional informants). Beyond that point, an oral tradition's information narrows drastically, before bulging out into a dense range of myths and stories about founding fathers, early heroes and ancestral people who began the group's existence. This pattern of information has been neatly compared with an hour-glass, narrow in the middle and broader at either end.

This same pattern of remembered detail is gratifyingly visible in

Herodotus, who used orally preserved evidence: it ties up with the rarity of precisely numbered dates in so much of his narrative (oral traditions tend to arrange people in generations or by 'befores' and 'afters'; they tend not to synchronize events in different places or to preserve numbered years). At first we have a similar impression in the Bible. The early reaches of narrative tell us much about founding fathers and the great event of the Exodus (like the Greeks' great event, the Trojan War). The information is arranged by genealogy and successive generations: after the Conquest, the narrative keeps up a very tenuous continuity through the age of the Judges, but then (in many critics' views) comes into detailed history with the reign of David (where some of its scholars have argued for an informed early written memoir underlying our biblical books). The difference then shows, both in the careful numbering of kings' reigns and particular years, and also in the amount of detail as we approach the main author's own memory span of two generations, the 'grandfather principle'. In Herodotus, the story becomes very much fuller from that point onwards, mentioning most of the people who are 'the first of whom we know', about a hundred years before Herodotus's own age. However, in 1–2 Kings detail and density do not suddenly develop when we reach *c.* 650 BC, at the limit of the author's likely grandfather span (the main author of this narrative wrote in the Exile, probably *c.* 550 BC). More of the details are accurate where we can check them against outside evidence, but there is no Herodotean change of quantity; indeed, the details are much scarcer from *c.* 610–560 BC. The reason points us to a second, more basic distinction.

The ultimate authors of the story from Joshua to the Exile wrote in the sixth century BC and did not rely on their own verbal inquiries; for the most part they interwove or drew on other people's books and it was from them that they found their detailed dates for kings' reigns. In the fourth century BC the anonymous Chronicler did the same, using earlier writings for his story from 1 Chronicles to (probably) the end of Nehemiah. Their degree of knowledge did not depend on the natural bulges of human memory: it depended on writings which seemed authoritative. The authors inherited a written tradition which they were more concerned to combine than to question.

Here, we risk forgetting that any accurate tradition, whether written or remembered, only begins from a person who witnessed the event.

Herodotus and especially Thucydides sought out witnesses, among whom they themselves were sometimes included. Personal witness or reminiscence is a primary source, whether it is written down or told; contemporaries are not necessarily primary sources, and even our written statistics or documents are accurate only if a primary witness (the person who counted or described) underlies them. If a personal story is retold within or between generations, it ceases to be a primary source. It becomes an oral tradition, which is secondary for the events to which it refers. The same distinction applies if it is rewritten.

For the question of historical truth, the line between primary witness and secondary source or tradition is more fundamental than the line between oral and written. In the Hebrew Old Testament it is clear that no book is primary in this strong sense. The authors have selected from older books, helped them along with their own additions and given them their own interpretations. Only one, Nehemiah, is agreed to have a primary source behind part of it. In the Christian New Testament, too, many critics end by denying that any of the narrative's authors was primary, although in my view there are two exceptions.

This contrast between the Hebrew books of narrative and the first Greek historians helps to correct an ancient and a modern view of their difference. In the 90s AD the Jew Josephus who knew the Greek authors praised the Hebrew scripture's superior merits as history. It was in this context that he referred to the twenty-two books which gave a written history 'of all time' from Creation to King Artaxerxes (465–424 BC). They did not contradict each other, and they had been written by inspired prophets (from Moses onwards) and preserved by priests whose purity of descent (like the purity of the text) was carefully maintained. The Greeks, by contrast, wrote for fame and gain. Their books on their early history were written long after the event and contradicted each other freely. Josephus was interestingly mistaken. He was wrong about these 'prophetic' authors (most of the twenty-two were written long after the events which they describe); he was wrong about the priests' unbroken descent; he was seriously wrong about the text's integrity. Above all, he did not stop to wonder if this single version, which struck him as so harmonious, was a sign of insufficient critical sense. Among the Greeks, Herodotus reported conflicting stories and perhaps as a result, remained aware of the limits of knowledge; Biblical authors told one story which was much less solidly grounded than Josephus believed (it was not primary) and which never faced the problems of method which were raised for inquirers by conflicting oral sources.

There are, however, modern anthropologists who have argued that a critical attitude to history can develop only when records begin to be written down. Oral traditions of the past (they believe) will adjust themselves into harmony with the present, whereas written records cannot be rewritten so substantially. The narratives of the Bible and the first Greek historians suggest exactly the opposite. Herodotus and Thucydides found many local and individual traditions about the past which differed widely and had not all been adjusted to the present. Tireless interviewers, they were admirably aware of a line between knowledge and story, and they both tended to be wary and write the history of the recent past. Among the Jews, the biblical authors inherited old and anonymous books about very remote times, but their existence was a barrier to critical method and doubt; they wrote unreservedly about events where there was no primary knowledge. Good history, with a method, was born not from this type of work but from personal interview and inquiry. If Herodotus had known an old and anonymous book of remote oriental history, he would certainly have been amazed by it. It is a nice question whether he would have doubted it; as an 'inquirer', he had had enough experience of humans and their stories to take it with a large pinch of salt.

12

The First Historians

Like its participants, history can cover a multitude of vices, and in the ancient world it should not be defined too narrowly. Critical Greek inquiry led to good history writing, while the Babylonians kept a chronicle whose claim to be history is more arguable. The claim is not even appropriate for other early writings about the past. Texts about the wonderful glories of King Sargon or one of the Pharaohs, a thousand years after their lifetimes, were not histories at all. They were stories told without evidence.

We now need to place the biblical narratives in terms of these alternatives: otherwise we may start to hunt for history where it was never intended. This placing involves two separate questions. Was the author trying to write a true and interconnected account of the past, even if he failed? If so, he deserves to be called a historian. Did he base it on primary evidence so that he might be telling us the truth? If so, his work is historically accurate. The two questions are separate. A historian may quite often write something which is not history, because it is wrong; none the less, his work may be historically fascinating, because it tells us how he and others saw things at the time of writing. No doubt, if one of the Hebrew prophets or the twelve disciples could return and read bits of this book (or many others about themselves) they would be quick to see the difference between these two questions.

Biblical narratives fall into five compartments, from Genesis to the Christians' Gospels and the Acts. I will characterize them in very general terms, bypassing hundreds of details and the many arguments about their early and later editions and insertions by like-minded editors. Those readers who are inclined to accept that much of the biblical narrative is true need to face two simple issues. Is this or that bit of it to be labelled history at all? Did its author have any worthwhile evidence?

The first compartment runs from Genesis to the end of Numbers, from the Creation to the arrival on the edge of the Promised Land. These five books rest on earlier written sources which have been woven into our present text. Since the later nineteenth century, four separate sources have been diagnosed, and although their dates, nature and number have been vigorously disputed, the old view, that a foursome underlies the Pentateuch, still holds the field. The most recent attempts to overthrow it have merely strengthened the argument by their failure. It should not surprise anyone that an old text has been patched together from several much older texts: historians of the Greek and Roman worlds live happily with this reality in their sources, while the lazy art of 'book-making' was freely admitted and practised by medieval writers. In the Bible the four earlier sources were combined by a fifth person, an unknown author who must have worked on them at some point between *c.* 520 and 400 BC, in my view, nearer to 400 BC. As he interwove these sources, he tried to save their contents and have the best of several worlds (and Creations). He was a natural subeditor who belongs on a project to produce an encyclopedia: he was not, in my view, a historian, but I think he would be amazed if somebody told him that nothing in his amalgamated book was true. He assumed that his authorities had all got it right.

Its chances of being historically true were minimal because none of those sources was written from primary evidence or within centuries, perhaps a millennium, of what they tried to describe. How could an oral tradition have preserved true details across such a gap? At most, it might remember a great event or new departure: like the Greeks' Trojan War, the Israelites' Exodus from Egypt was just such an event which its heirs assumed to be true. Perhaps it was indeed a historical memory: we cannot know, but I find it hard to believe that no Israelites ever came out of Egypt under the guidance of their special god, Yahweh, although the Exodus was perhaps not the migration of an entire people. As for the 'giants on earth', the Tower of Babel or the exploits of Jacob or Abraham, there is no good reason to believe any of them: the most detailed story in Genesis is the story of Joseph, a marvellous tale, woven from two separate sources, neither of which needs to rest on any historical truth (the accurate touches of Egyptian colour are few and not fixed to any one period: attempts to date them way back in the era from *c.* 1900 to 1800 B C have not succeeded).

The latest of the four underlying sources is the priestly author (P). Attempts to deny that P was more than an editor or to date him before the Exile have so far failed, and I have already shared the older view that he wrote a text of his own, no earlier than *c.* 540 B C and probably when the Exile in Babylon had just ended (*c.* 530–500). What we can infer about his work makes it seem a jungle of lists and rules (almost none of the Genesis stories are his), but even this core has a unity. He began with the sabbatical Creation, the promise to Noah, a story of the Flood and the all-important covenant of God with Abraham, which is described in Genesis 17. This covenant was to last for ever: nothing would break it, and so there was no need to describe a second covenant to Moses made many years later at Sinai. After the Exodus and the Wandering, what concerned P at Sinai was not a covenant but the bringing of the people under God's domination and the building of a tent-like tabernacle with its own priesthood. This tabernacle and priesthood looked forward to the eventual Temple and priesthood in the promised land: for P, a true priest, they were Sinai's great events. It is possible that his book stopped without any narrative of the Conquest itself: instead, it included the laws of holiness and purity (including diet) which are in our book of Leviticus. Perhaps the author was content to leave the Promised Land beckoning before his readers: he had shown how the people could make themselves holy and fit for God. In an era of exile and return to Judaea, the implications of this message were clear enough.

It is arguable whether such a selective and forward-looking account of the past deserves to be called a history: the author is more interested in the present and future than in the past for its own sake. His interests have even been upheld as models for our own late industrial age. P's story of Creation, the Bible's first, is vegetarian; its 'dominion' for man over the animals can be retranslated as 'shepherding'; meat-eating is a later concession to sinfulness. P is not just priestly, but pacifist, never describing wars or conquests, at least, on one view, of his lost text's full extent. A peace-loving, lentil-eating P may be a possible voice for our future, but what we know of his writings has a note which must make historians uneasy. Dates and spans of years are scattered through the text but their numbers of years have been neatly explained round pivotal events like the birth of Abraham, the ages before and after the Temple, before and after the Flood and so forth. An era of four thousand years in all has been detected: Abraham's first year stands in 1600; the first Temple begins midway through the remainder of the era, in the year 2800. Perhaps P's antiquarian lore and his urge to explain and interpret do just rank him as a historian, but the decision is not easy.

The other best-attested source is the text I have called the 'southern version', accepting that it was written in Judah before *c*. 722 BC (it is unaffected by the fall of Israel or the political actions after *c*. 722 of such neighbours as the Edomites). The author calls Number One 'Yahweh', and so he is widely known as the Yahwist (J): he is the source of the story of the Garden of Eden. The most optimistic datings of his work extend to *c*. 950 BC, but even then, more than three hundred years would have passed since supposed dates for the Exodus, let alone for the doings of Jacob or Abraham. These narratives were composed from unwritten stories whose status as true history is non-existent. J's stories run on with Moses, Sinai and the years in the wilderness, but, like P's, J's stopping point is highly disputed: did he finish with the words of the heathen Balaam, blessing Israel at the end of Numbers and looking forward to the future? Or did he go on to tell about the conquest of the Promised Land, so that bits of his version confront us in the book of Joshua? I incline to the second view, although the book of Joshua, I believe, is the separate work of a very different editor-bookmaker.

What we know of J begins with Creation (our Adam and Eve) and certainly continues through the doings of the patriarchs, and one version of the story of Joseph, to Moses, the Exodus, the encounter with God at Sinai and so forth. What we can discern of his work is highly attractive: it is a narrative of some of the Bible's best short stories, sparsely told with word-plays, puns and ironic uses of speech and cross-reference. Unlike P, J had not the slightest interest in priestly rules and rituals, nor did he put emphasis on a covenant of God with Israel: J moved in an earlier uncluttered world before the prophets, priests and Deuteronomists complicated life.

The impetus to write such a narrative is as unclear as its scope and contents. J has been seen as reacting to other authors; the older, shadowy northern version was probably known to him, but it is unlikely that he wrote only to correct it. It is a modern fantasy that J was a woman, or a courtier perhaps, under Solomon, a long-suffering scribe – why not? – who resented Bathsheba and David's adultery, and thus made Eve the cause of man's Fall. We have no idea, any more than we know his politics. Hints of a political bias have been seen in his version, as if it attacked the division of Israel under wicked King Rehoboam and admired, by implication, the older united age of David. No such bias is evident: J's one likely reference to the future is more general, a promise of blessing by God.

What we do know is that his stories helped to explain how this or that came about; he did not think he was telling myths (which were untrue) and I doubt if he thought of his information as stories which he could replace with other stories if we did not like them. The earlier stories explained universal facts of life for all humans: Creation, perhaps, or the origin of languages (Babel). The later stories explained the origins of Israel's tribes (they had been named after their ancestors, Benjamin and so forth) or facts about Israel's neighbours (the story of Esau, Jacob and the 'mess of pottage' concerns Edom and Israel; others concern the Ishmaelites or Ammon and Moab). There were also the stories of the Exodus, the Wandering and the Conquest: Numbers 21 gives details of the Israelites' wars and refers to an ancient song and a 'book of the wars of the Lord' (21:14; perhaps we are spiritually better off without it). It reminds us that the Yahwist had the wits to use ancient songs, too, as sources: we have a boastful, bloody little bit of song in Genesis 4:23, another bit in Jacob's blessings in Genesis 27 and perhaps some other scraps in other blessings and curses, especially in the book of Numbers. The attempt to support a story about past events from ancient 'poetry' is quite sophisticated: Greek authors, too, were later drawn to it. None of these poems, however, is a primary source for what they narrate, but at least they are earlier than J's own time of writing.

We could wander through this maze of stories for several chapters, noticing its change of tone from the primeval stories to the tales of the patriarchs (Genesis 12 onwards) and some of the events on the Israelites' long march in Numbers. There is, however, one particularly curious chapter, Genesis 14. Here, a list of foreign kings with sonorous names march against other kings (including the king of Sodom) in a setting of place-names and precise lengths of time. It used to be thought that the foreign kings' names could be identified with kings who are known in

Near Eastern texts of the early second millennium B C, that the chapter therefore gave a date for Abraham (he joined in the fighting) and that J was using a very old campaign record, preserved from the remote past. None of these beliefs has survived scrutiny: King Amraphel is not the great Hammurapi of Babylon; the style of the story does not suggest an original campaign history, let alone a foreign source; Abraham has been tacked on to the exploits of the kings as an after-thought. Their datings, therefore, would not prove his date, or even his existence: the sonorous kings are now being seen as a late story themselves, perhaps no earlier than the tenth to ninth century B C.

None of J's other stories is likely to be true, but I am still more inclined to class him as a potential historian than not: he created his long narrative from various sources and traditions, and he assumed (I believe) that he was telling how things had once been. The stories which he recounted show a recurrent concern. They tell us the origins of this or that, not just the origins of language or horticultural labour, but why Israel is superior to Edom, why Bethel is called Bethel, or why there are wells at the place called Beersheba. This type of 'just-so' story is widespread in other cultures. For many centuries, it played a conspicuous part in the writings of Greek historians, poets and travellers, and it even underlay some of the Greeks' own myths, near contemporaries of J's stories. A just-so story (or 'aetiology') will sometimes emerge when an author adds his own passing comment into an independent story. We all tend to do this: 'And that is why children began to sing "Ring-a-ring of Roses",' we might say, after describing the history of the Great Plague in London. However, the search for an 'origin' can also inspire an entire story. Why is the landscape round the Dead Sea so scorched and burnt? (Surely God punished Sodom for its sins . . . What sins? . . . Something awful . . . Maybe they tried to rape a visiting angel . . .) Why is Bethel called 'Beth-el' ('house of God')? (Because Jacob dreamed there about Jacob's Ladder . . .) Behind the just-so story we reach back to pure human curiosity and the wonderful tales which it could devise on long afternoons in order to explain what it saw around it. It explained names on the map, odd features in the landscape, and even other people's customs: at Genesis 47:26, it is probably J who wrote that it was because of Joseph that the Pharaoh began to levy a 'fifth part' off his subjects' produce, a payment which lived on in Egypt in the author's own day.

Perhaps it did (unfortunately, we have no evidence), but it was only J's patriotic guess that the tax had begun with a Jew and arisen in an awful time of famine.

Just-so stories are not history, but they come from a curiosity which might well grow into it. They wish to explain facts in the present by events in the past; they have a sense that things were different once and that now we are heirs to relics from a different age. Here J was much more restrained than P; he did not read back all sorts of social and ritual practices from his own times under the kings into a remote antiquity (Genesis 25:23, however, does predict 'two nations'; compare, too, Genesis 27:29 and 27:39). He kept the distant past at arm's length, and he was not tied up in theological knots. Theological motives have, of course, been ascribed to him by theologians: a concern for the election of Israel or the covenant (those ideas took shape, however, after J's time) or a conviction that 'the law was mediated in history' (J was not too interested in law). I believe that he wrote, on the whole, to tell us both how it had come to be and how (God willing) it would be. He used stories to show how foreign languages arose, how Israel's neighbours originated, how Israel came out of Egypt and so forth. We can also see him looking forward: in Genesis 12:1–4 God promises Abraham a land, that his descendants will be blessed and that 'all the families of the earth shall bless themselves [or "be blessed"]' in Abraham too. Here, J looks optimistically forward with a blessing which is not conditional: it implies that one day Israel, Abraham's descendants, will be blessed throughout the world.

From an author of the mid eighth century (or earlier) this faith in a worldwide future for Israel is extremely touching. However, the same combination of explaining facts in the present and looking hopefully forward despite them reappears in the narrative's next compartment. From the book of Deuteronomy to 2 Kings, we begin a second stretch, one whose underlying unity was decisively shown by Martin Noth in 1943. It is his elegant theory which presented us with a single author, writing the bulk of these books in the age of exile during the mid sixth century BC (the Deuteronomist, or D). Since then some scholars have argued that the work appeared in two stages: an earlier one (under Josiah in the 620s) and a later (after 560 BC). I have already rejected this theory of two editions, preferring to think of one later author in exile, using material from earlier pre-exilic sources. Even so, this D was not a lone figure: he shared the outlook of a particular group, those Jews who held fast to the book of the law, which had been found in the Temple in 622/1. His achievement is truly heroic: nothing like this composition is known in the previous literature of the world.

It is not that D necessarily wrote the truth. He did, however, have particular gifts which can still stir historians who respond to scale and vision. He used a variety of written sources between which he changed from one period to the next; he struggled to give a chronology in precise lengths of years; he kept up a running theme which explained the past, and, against all odds, he cast a hopeful look at the future. Again and again he returned to the fact that Israel would one day be driven from the land; this emphasis helps us to infer that he wrote outside it, among the exiles in Babylonia, for whom this fact was all too true. Babylonian authors, his near-contemporaries, explained their country's history by the neglect or observance of cults and festivals of particular gods. D was not unduly interested in the small details of cult in God's Temple; instead, he saw misfortune as the result of disobedience to the words of God's law.

He was fascinated, therefore, by prophets of the past, especially in the northern kingdom, and the fulfilment of what they 'must' have said. In his writing, Samuel, Nathan or Ahijah all preached a message which was contained in the book of the law: they warned, too truly, of the dire consequences of breaking it. Even Moses and Joshua, D believed, had foreseen that obedience in Israel was a historical non-starter. With this emphasis his work could well have become nothing more than a history of how 'they told you so'. It is something finer, because its perspective became longer and deeper in a way which touches us too.

In exile, D looked none the less to the future. If God's people could turn to him again, repentance might assure them of something good from God. 'If any of thine be driven out unto the outmost parts of heaven, from thence will the Lord thy God gather thee' (Deuteronomy 30:4). Like-minded editors have worked over D's original text, and so we must be wary of these hints of a brighter future: the editors may have added most of them. In our Bibles, however, the books of Kings (D's territory) end with a mention of the release and honour of the captive king, Jehoiachin, by the Babylonians. This great event of the year 562/1 proved to be a false dawn, but there may be a hint of D's own hope in the episode with which he appears to have ended his narrative.

With one eye on past sins and another on future hope, D was a natural and fervent speech-writer. For the first time, long speeches reinforced the themes of a historical narrative, and, like the later historians of Greece, D knew how to place them at climactic points in his story. Naturally, they are his own invention: nobody knew what, if anything, had once been said. We hear from Moses or Joshua, about to die; we are addressed on the eve of the conquest of the land or the start of the monarchy: the author himself addresses us when the northern kingdom falls in *c*. 722. Crowds gather round D's speakers who rise (like the author) to the occasion: beyond the story, they address us too, like speeches in the script of an epic film. In the true biblical manner, there is no pairing. Each of the speeches goes without an answer: D is the first known author of sermons.

Characteristically, he began his work with a long speech which he ascribed to Moses as he waited beyond the Jordan, outside the Promised Land. Then, he inserted his revered authority, the ancient 'book of the law of the Lord' which had followed its supporters into exile: the text had been refound in the Temple in 622/1, but since then bits had been updated and added. Moses followed it up with one final rousing speech; in our Bibles a later hand has added a further song and blessing. Our book of Deuteronomy was thus compiled, and the narrative could sweep forwards from Joshua through the Judges to the Kings and the great event of the Exile.

With Deuteronomy before him, a late unknown bookmaker could patch together the Pentateuch, or first five books of our Bible. At work (I believe) in the fifth century BC, he stitched together four very different threads, J (*c*. 750 BC or earlier), a few bits of E (perhaps earlier still), D (*c*. 550–540 BC) and P (*c*. 530–500). They are a foursome for anyone's imagination, with different strengths and weaknesses: I picture them, sometimes, in a corporate venture, P as the stickler for detail and small print, the natural company lawyer; D as the eloquent author of circulars, the natural head of marketing with an explanation of why things go wrong; E, a shadowy non-executive presence; and old J, the thoughtful, punning chairman, wondering how things came to be there but convinced, no the less, that his group had a great worldwide future. There are no women in my pentateuchal boardroom, but inevitably its four voices contradict one another: the chances of straightforward history from such voices, so far removed from the events, were minimal.

With the book of Joshua, D's narrative gathers momentum, leaving the secondary bookmaker behind it: from now on, D is on his own, but we can catch obvious traces of older sources used by him within his narrative. After chapter 12 he draws piecemeal on lists of peoples and cities which are connected with Israel's occupation of the land. These lists were not primary sources and were written at least three (perhaps seven) centuries later than any of the settlements which they aim to describe: they sit rather awkwardly with some of Joshua's other exploits. In chapter 10 he also quotes from a book of Jashar for Joshua's doings at Gibeon where 'the sun stood still' (this book is mentioned only in the Masoretic Hebrew text, not in the earlier independent Greek translation but I do not think the reference is therefore a mistaken guess). From references elsewhere, we can see that the book of Jashar was a book of songs composed no earlier than the age of David: the song about Gibeon was perhaps a late invention, nowhere near the heat of a historical moment. D (or perhaps his source) took the song's words too literally, as if a poetic flourish had really happened and the sun really did stop in the sky. Perhaps D himself thought it almost incredible, and so, just for once, he appealed to his ancient source and named it, as if to support the story.

It is conspicuous that once again many of the stories in Joshua's first thirteen chapters are just-so stories which attach to facts of society or the landscape. Perhaps D was using J's book as the source for them: I suspect that he was, because the themes are so similar, but the case is highly disputed. In this stretch of narrative the just-so stories are particularly interested in rocks in the landscape. They explain to the reader why twelve prominent stones still stood in the middle of the Jordan, why the city of Ai was a heap of stones, why big boulders stood by a particular cave (they were blocking the corpses of five royal enemies of Israel whom Joshua had hanged and thrown inside it). These stories are, literally, based on rock: they owe to it their fanciful origins. It is hard to believe that D first wrote them down in the Exile from stories which had survived in hearsay, far away from their landscape. I suspect that he took them from J and that is why they disappear from his narrative when he changes sources for its later course.

None of these sources is primary, except possibly the Song of Gibeon, yet there are archaeologists who still struggle to rescue their truth. To round off the story of Joshua, the text gives him two speeches, delivered as death approaches (Joshua 23 and 24). Both address 'all Israel' and have been prized as historical sources: might they not reflect a 'Festival of the Covenant' at which early Israel annually renewed her covenant with God? This festival has even been upheld as the source which preserved the book's early stories: they were recited yearly during its celebrations, at Shechem.

This vivid theory rests on no evidence outside the speeches themselves and is wonderfully wide of the mark. There was no such festival, no early covenant; we are not tuning in to historical echoes of the tenth century BC. The two speeches are riddled with themes which concerned the Deuteronomist and like-minded editors after him. They invented them. In Joshua's dying days, they made him tell the Israelites what they believed to be the meaning of life. In the first speech, Joshua bids them to observe 'all that is written in the book of Moses', to worship Yahweh alone and not to marry foreign women. After a brief mention of God's past favours, he warns them not to break the covenant with the Lord their God. The second, longer speech is set at Shechem and is even more forceful. Joshua warns the tribes that they 'cannot serve the Lord'; they are sure to go astray. At the end he writes his words in the 'book of the law of God' and sets up a huge stone in God's sanctuary (probably at Shechem) as a witness against the people. The stone, too, had heard God's words, but unlike the people of Israel it would never deviate: earlier, Joshua had written the law of Moses on Mount Ebal, also on stones, and read it, curses and all, to Israel, including the 'women, and the little ones'.

These scenes are admirable inventions of their authors after 560 BC. It is unlikely that D, the original author, wrote both speeches, and, in my view, it is the first which is the later addition, written by someone who shared the deuteronomic outlook but wished to emphasize the wickedness of foreign marriage; this theme had not been developed so strongly in the original book of the law. The second one, therefore, is probably

D's own, and appropriately it looks forward to the history of growing infidelity which he intends to trace through Judges to the end of Kings; its themes suit a date in the time of the Exile when he himself was writing. His picture has the power of a master-artist. Here is Joshua writing down Moses's law book (which did not exist until about six centuries later) and reminding the people of God's past favours: he urges them to hold fast to God's commands. As predicted, the people did the opposite: they turned to gods beyond the river, a chilling rebuke to Jews of the author's own lifetime who were living 'beyond the river' in Babylon. All the while the great stone still glowered at Shechem, a witness that it was Israel, not God's word, which had gone astray. For once, D does not tell us that the very stone was still visible. Perhaps he knew a rock near Shechem: more probably he had taken the idea of it from other significant stones in his sources. At this crowning moment in his story, he added one last menhir to the heap.

The resulting book of Joshua arouses strong passions: like its God's relation to his people, either you hate it or love it. To my mind, it is the intersection of two great composers: J, who turned just-so stories into narrative, and D, the Jew in Exile, who worked from multiple sources and preached the book of the law. Its killings are beastly, and its speeches and stories are quite untrue, but it is an eloquent historian's masterpiece.

The book of Judges, which follows it, affects us like an intermediate movement in a symphony of simpler themes. In the Greek translation, the ending of Joshua is longer, and a good case has been made for this ending being earlier and closer to the original: the first two chapters of Judges may also be a later addition, and if so D's book may have moved straight on to Judges 3. The text which follows has less of a unity than Joshua, but here, too, the author worked from ancient songs and stories. In chapter 5 he quotes the famous Song of Deborah, which is plainly very old (probably the oldest in the Bible) and may well be a primary source, composed for the victory over Sisera *c*. 1100 BC. Its context has been filled out, and in chapter 4 the story of Deborah and Sisera is told all over again in a prose narrative. This chapter is probably D's own version: it connects the old battle of the song with a battle (probably a separate one) against King Jabin, and it also lays a much greater stress on Deborah as a true prophet. She predicts the great deed of a woman, and, sure enough, Jael fulfils her words by killing Sisera in her tent. This prediction is not the concern of the song which then follows.

Faulty connections between a source and an event and a strong concern to show how a prophet was proved right are features which recur in D's work. In the rest of Judges we move from one individual to another, from the well-told tale of the death of Ehud to the doings of a Gideon or Samson. There are critics who believe that these stories, too, derive from a written source which was perhaps compiled in Jerusalem under King Hezekiah (*c.* 715–687 BC): here, we simply cannot know. What we do know, however, is that these stories read like oral tales of great deeds: Jephthah makes a fateful vow (he has to sacrifice his daughter); Gideon tests his troops; Samson poses riddles, suffers from an unreliable wife and assaults the Philistines' crops by setting light to pairs of foxes and launching them into their fields (he cannot have used this vile tactic: two foxes, if tied together and ignited, would panic and pull in opposite directions).

It makes little difference whether our author inherited these traditions in a book or compiled them from popular hearsay as late as 550 BC; at best, original reminiscence had faded here into secondary oral traditions. At a distance of at least four hundred years, they may have preserved a few names of real heroes, but they have wildly invented their exploits. None the less, D used them as if they were history and imposed a pattern, not so much by speeches as by his own connecting refrain. Again and again, we read that the people did evil, God gave them to oppressors for a specified time and then the process began again. D arranged his stories with precise lengths of time, but many of his figures are based on 'forty years'. 'Forty years' is the conventional number for one generation: probably, the original stories were told in terms of generations (the usual time chart for oral stories), and our author tried to convert them to numbers.

We progress to the books of Samuel and the books of Kings, which are also D's constructions from varied texts: they take us from the age of judges to the age of kings, beginning with Saul, David and Solomon. The books of Samuel, especially, are a textual scholar's paradise, because they existed in several early versions of which our late Hebrew manuscripts give only one. They also have their share of legend. In the opening scenes the choosing of Saul, then David, is based in part on popular tales, no more true than any other legend of a 'once and future

King'. For historians the most enticing question is raised during David's reign, from 2 Samuel 9 to Solomon's accession (1 Kings 2, omitting 2 Samuel 20).

This section of the royal narrative is unlike any other. It contains no miracles but is full of intrigues and devious tricks: women are prominent in the action. It reports the private dialogues of persons of high rank; it tells an interconnected story, from the wars against Ammon to the affair of David and Bathsheba, the deaths of two of David's sons and the manoeuvres to succeed to his throne. Its style is wonderfully restrained (the death of Ahithophel), but its story is woven from different points of view (the news of Absalom's death); it is also full of pathos in the face of death (David's response to the sickness and death of Bathsheba's first son or to the loss of Absalom, his favourite). Parts of it are neatly interconnected, and there is a constant human interest of sin and error, ignorance and forgiveness, loyalty and betrayal, and the knowledge, underneath, that an action has been profoundly wrong.

During these twenty years or so of David's reign, the main focus is on events at court among David's friends and enemies. As a result, D's source for these chapters has been described as a court history, the work of a near-contemporary with access to court secrets: was the author Nathan the prophet, perhaps, or Abiathar the priest or even (why not?) Bathsheba herself? The scope, nature and date of this source are naturally strongly contested (we have to infer them), but there is no mistaking its difference of tone: its picture of King David is not unduly flattering (he commits adultery with Bathsheba and kills off her husband, Uriah). On the strength of it, this source has been classed as an 'anti-history' and dated late during the Exile in reaction to others' idealizing of David, the head of the royal 'messianic' line. Yet there is no trace anywhere else of such 'anti-history'; the later our sources, the more they idealize David the king. Rather, the work's detail, tone and focus point to a text which was written much earlier: how else did the author know so much court detail and geography, tell it relatively straight?

I share the general view that behind these chapters lies an early history which was composed from court sources. If it shows some of the wisdom which is found in the book of Proverbs, it is because that wisdom was traditional and itself a part of the author's own culture. The text is quite unlike the fictional stories of courtiers which are known in

Egyptian literature: it is also unclear whether or not it has any political purpose. Solomon does finally emerge as David's heir, but if the author (Nathan?) wished merely to confirm Solomon's legitimacy, there were better and more blatant ways to do it: Near Eastern authors were not exactly reticent if they wished to drive home a particular bias. The text, therefore, was not an official history to support Solomon's kingship: it was, I suspect, a court narrative, which was based somehow on primary knowledge of its personalities. It was written either in Solomon's kingship or later, on the strength of a detailed, earlier memoir.

Long before Herodotus, therefore, we must reckon with the world's first historian, who told a tale of court politics and family warring. Like Herodotus, he had a moral instinct: he liked to note how the loyal supporter received a reward, while the cruel captain met his just deserts. He used dialogue and speeches of winning rhetoric (the scene with the woman from Tekoah is a particular masterpiece of speech: she flatters David, but he sees straight through her words, knowing that Joab has put her up to them). The stories interconnect neatly, and, like Herodotus, their author was drawn to the significant short scene or personal gesture. Unlike Herodotus, however, he told his story anonymously without any critical doubts about its sources.

God is present, but there are no sermons, and there is no explicit plan behind every event. This restraint has caused acute problems for theological readers. Wishing to find God in every biblical event, there are those who argue that the text marks a new religious world-view. Gone are J's old stories of miracles and encounters with angels. Now 'all the threads are in God's hands'; he is present even in profane affairs, in the struggles of the royal family, not just in the mighty deeds of judges and heroes. In this change (it is said) lies an 'age of enlightenment', which affected the author's world-view at Solomon's court.

The text, however, resists such misreading. At the other extreme, a great historian of ancient Greece and the Near East, Eduard Meyer, considered that it is 'a purely secular work ... any kind of religious colouring, every thought of supernatural intervention is wholly excluded'. He even claimed it as 'the prevailing irony of all human history, that these thoroughly secular texts are regarded both by Judaism and Christianity as holy scripture'. He, too, exaggerated. God is indeed present: just as Nathan the prophet predicts, it is God who punishes

David for his murder of Uriah (David's sons die); when Solomon is born, we suddenly hear that God loves him; it is God who contrives that Absalom will be misled by false counsel; God is present in the many prayers and blessings and in the advice of the woman of Tekoah. We are certainly not reading a 'secular' source. It does, however, have no single theology of history by which each act unfolds: here, its outlook is strikingly similar to bits of Herodotus's story. For Herodotus too a particular error or coincidence or 'just reward' sometimes happens 'necessarily', as the gods ordain (compare Absalom's rejection of good advice). When Herodotus's gods intrude, they too intrude for individuals, explaining why this person, in particular, is so treated at this particular time (compare God's sudden love for Solomon). Like Nathan's prophecy, an oracle in Herodotus's Greek world might foretell disaster in return for some injustice (Herodotus believed in the truth of oracles): unlike prophets, however, oracles were ambiguous or of uncertain reference. In Herodotus, people misunderstand prophecy; in the Bible, they ignore its explicit message.

The court narrative is neither purely secular nor proof of a new theology: it is an ancient reminder of what might have been, a historian in Israel who referred to God sparingly, who wrote before any idea of a covenant or priestly books of lore, and before any books of the law of Moses gave a running sermon to authors on the past. For these few chapters, we catch the echo of such a historian, but the heir who saved this echo then takes over. D does not follow his source's lead: he ignores it and swamps him. With D, indeed, a new world-view interposes, but it kills the biblical voice which is nearest to Herodotus, the Greek world's father of history.

13

From David to Paul

I

As soon as the books of Kings sweep on beyond David's Court History, they appear to ignore what its author had described. David becomes the ideal king, the king to whom God has promised a lasting line of kings, with the one condition (required by later history) that he would suspend the promise if his successors misbehaved. Unlike the Court History, D writes with an eye on the future, looking to the hope of a revival in great David's royal line. 'And it shall be, if thou wilt hearken unto all that I command thee, and wilt walk in my ways, and do that is right in my sight, to keep my statutes and my commandments, as David my servant did' (I Kings 11:38): D makes God say these words to Solomon. What statutes are they, what commandments? David had coveted another man's wife, seduced her, lied and arranged her husband's murder; his dying words included specific orders to pay off old debts by killing two legacies from his reign and bringing 'his grey head down with blood to Sheol'.

Ideals, therefore, buried facts, the first historian's facts: from the reign of Jeroboam onwards (*c.* 932–587 BC) D's narrative does not so much bury the facts as select them and distort them. For there are facts behind it, at least as D himself implied: he referred to the 'books of chronicles of the kings of Israel' and of the 'kings of Judah'. He noted them in a way which impresses us with a sense of completeness and his own authority: 'the rest' of a ruler's acts, are they not in the books of chronicles, as if 'the' entire story survives, he himself has given us what matters and 'the rest' is available elsewhere? If these books tell us 'the rest' of a ruler's deeds, we can probably infer that our author drew some of the deeds in his own stories from the same source too (I assume that these references are not a lie, invented to impress us: at Esther 10:2, a much later book, a similar reference is bogus).

What, then, were these books of chronicles? They have been seen as secondary sources which were composed as a narrative from earlier royal records: they have even been downdated to the time of the Exile, on the mistaken grounds that no monarchy before the Babylonians' in that period kept such 'chronicles' and that 'the Babylonians' discovery of the "antiquarian chronicle" in the sixth century was the impulse to the "chronicles of Israel and Judah"'. Neither argument is convincing. We know too little of earlier Assyrian texts, but there are fragments which probably derive already at this date from third-person chronicles, while their first-person royal inscriptions listed the king's wars, booty and buildings (just like the Bible's books of Kings) and probably rested on separate royal chronicles, now lost to us. It is also possible that the kings of Tyre had kept annals, although we have only a hint of them in a Greek version, known to Josephus, which might be a well-meant invention.

In my view, the Hebrew books of chronicles were exactly what the author of Kings believed: genuine records of the king's public deeds and major events, copies of which had survived the catastrophes of 722 and 587 and were available to an inquiring Jew in the years of Exile. Probably, these 'chronicles' were primary records or at the very least based directly on such primary material. The biblical references to them show that they referred not only to royal building works and new cities, to deeds of might and war, but also to conspiracies and revolts. These contents are entirely credible, from what we know of royal annals or chronicles in other Near Eastern monarchies.

From Jeroboam onwards, therefore, written sources of primary importance are a framework for the biblical narrative. D used them in various ways. He picked some of his facts from them (these chronicles are the likeliest sources for details of the treasures and building-works in the Temple of Solomon: temple affairs are prominent in the Babylonian chronicles too). D also drew from them his opening details about each king: 'Manasseh was twelve years old when he began to reign, and he reigned fifty and five years in Jerusalem. And his mother's name was Hephzibah' (2 Kings 21:1). These introductions are differently worded, and only the ones about the southern kingdom, Judah, name the king's mother. These differences suggest that there were indeed two separate works involved, one chronicle about Israel, the other about Judah. D then rounded off the story of each reign with an allusion to these chronicles for 'the rest of the acts' of the king in question.

There is also the vital matter of time and dating. The books of Kings give lengths of reign, ages at accession and occasionally the year of the reign when something significant happened; they also refer sideways at a few points to events, kings and regnal years in the other kingdom of the two. From these numbers, historians still calculate their chronologies for Israelite history, but their efforts are beset by problems: the numbers vary between the Hebrew, Greek and Samaritan texts for any one king's reign; interrelations of the Judah kings and Israel kings do not readily match the reign lengths which are given in each individual kingdom: there may be a schematic pattern influencing the few numbers of bigger extent which are scattered variously in our Hebrew and Greek texts.

There are various ways of minimizing these problems. The numbers in our Hebrew text may have been miscopied here and there; the Greek numbers may be more accurate; there may have been co-regents when two kings ruled together in one kingdom (the text itself does not state this, but scholars invoke it in order to square the numbers). There is also uncertainty about the ways in which the lengths of reign were reckoned. Did the fraction of a year count to a king if he died before the year's end? Was it credited to his successor too? Were years counted inclusively? When did the calendar's New Year begin, and did that point change during the centuries under discussion? What type of calendar was it, lunar, solar or lunisolar, and how much did it err over a period of years? On answers to these questions our idea of the kings' dates depends. Answers are not easy, and the most recent study opts for a lunisolar calendar, whose New Year fell in autumn; Judah then changed to the Babylonian calendar whose New Year began in spring (the change probably happened under Josiah); then Judah (arguably) changed to postdating, so that a king's first year ran from the New Year following his accession. Previously, both kingdoms had used 'inclusive antedating'. That answers can be inferred at all depends on an important fact about D: he must have inherited these reign lengths from the older books of chronicles (hence the variations in their reckoning, because the chronicles' practice changed as time passed); he did not alter or invent the numbers himself. When he made a cross-reference between events in Judah and events in Israel, those dates, too, probably derived from the chronicle books. As their kings came into frequent contact, references to each other's reigns in the official chronicles would be quite likely.

At one level, then, this bit of the Bible is based on primary dates, but at another level, there are severe difficulties. The total numbers appear to have been fudged to fit a symbolic chronology. At I Kings 6 we confront an important grand total: 480 years are said to have passed from the Exodus to the foundation of the first Temple. This date has been credited to D and used as a key sign of his authorship of everything from the Exodus up to this point.

A new problem, however, has emerged. If the individual reigns of the kings who follow are added up, from the first Temple to the Exile, they come to 430; a further 50 years run from the Exile to the origins of the second Temple; once again, a total of 480, centred on the Temple. These totals are almost certainly too neat to be a coincidence: somebody has fiddled the lengths so that the two totals coincide.

This scheme cannot be D's own: he wrote during the Exile, before the final 50 years had finished; the first 480 from Exodus to the Temple conflicts with the individual totals given in his work from Judges to Samuel (430 in all). We have already suspected a priestly hand behind these schemes: the total at 1 Kings 6 falls in D's general stretch of narrative but is likely to be P's insertion. If D himself had a grand scheme in mind, it may perhaps emerge from figures in the Greek text of the era of his Kings: 480 years from King David to the Exile, matching 450 years from the settlement of Canaan to Eli (in the Hebrew text of his Judges to Samuel) and a further 30 for Samuel's lifetime. Once again the numbers balance around 480, from the Conquest to the Exile: D, perhaps, worked with this general pattern, while preserving the separate reign-lengths in his sources, the books of royal chronicles.

The important point here is that grand number-patterns have no place in good history: they make a point about the past, while fudging the truth of it. Elsewhere D was not so secretive about his fudging: if he had a point of view, he imposed it flagrantly on what he found in his sources. He wrote in exile by using books, not personal archaeology; he did not go to the trouble of verifying what he read by looking for inscriptions or surviving grave monuments. He was not an antiquarian: he turned what he read into what he was determined to say.

Between the reign of David and the two chronicles, one for Judah, one for Israel, he faced a gap: the reign of Solomon. Here, he refers us to a 'book of the acts of Solomon' for 'all that he did, and his wisdom' (1 Kings 11:41). His version of the reign has some splendidly fictitious sermons and some lavish stories of wisdom and women which do not look at all like entries in a royal chronicle. By the time D wrote, stories about Solomon must have multiplied, and it was probably impossible to set the record straight. Some of the stories have entered his narratives (the two women and the baby; probably, the Queen of Sheba). However, there are also a few verses of mundane fact (I Kings 4 or 9:15 ff.), while details of the building of the Temple and the palace could have featured in a royal chronicle. Whether or not the 'book of the acts of Solomon . . . and his wisdom' was such a source, it does seem here that bits of a primary record are scattered through D's version. Either this 'book of Solomon' used a primary source or it was such a primary source itself: once again, D has filled it out with later legends and his own moralizing.

It would be naïve in the extreme to take the narrative of Kings as a true or comprehensive history. It admits that it is selective (the 'rest of the deeds', if you want, are listed elsewhere), and the polemic is obvious: it judges each reign by its non-observance of the deuteronomic law. It is, however, wonderfully bad history which is partly built on better history (the David source), and always a witness to a valiant author's point of view. D began with old songs and just-so stories of origin: he ended with primary books of the deeds of the kings. Throughout, he was driven by his view of the past and future, a historian whom we can understand without ever needing to believe.

He is followed by a lesser author, the Chronicler, whose distortions were even greater and whose use of sources more erratic. His compartment takes us from the two books of Chronicles to the books of Ezra and Nehemiah (Ezra and Nehemiah are detached from it by some modern scholars, but their arguments are not convincing). Here, too, an author was aiming to give a compelling account of the past which brings out a wider truth. His method, however, puts us on our guard.

Essentially, the two books of Chronicles reuse passages from D's books of Samuel and Kings. They know the books of Samuel in a Hebrew text which often diverges from the one used by our Bible (finds of manuscripts of the book of Samuel near the Dead Sea have thrown new light on this). Yet textual problems do not account for the Chronicler's treatment of David. David, now, is the ideal king: the entire story of the Court History is left out because the Chronicler disliked it. It spoilt his image.

In 1896 a careful critic concluded:

. . . no fact of Old Testament criticism is more firmly established than this, that the Chronicler as a historian is thoroughly untrustworthy. He distorts facts deliberately and habitually: invents chapter after chapter with the greatest freedom and what is most dangerous of all, his history is not written for its own sake, but in the interests of an extremely one-sided theory.

The Chronicler was not quite so inventive, but subsequent study has done little to tone this judgement down. A close examination of 2 Chronicles 10–36 as history recently concluded that only eight and a half verses certainly (and six verses probably) were based on any historical fact independent of our Kings' narrative (2 Chronicles 11:5–10; 2 Chronicles 26:6, 10; 32:30 and 11:22–3 with 21:1–4): even these verses might be reduced if we found a fuller, early text of the books of Kings (it might contain them, too). Possibly, the Chronicler did consult the older books of chronicles and picked up a few royal deeds which our books of Kings had omitted; if so, his research was very haphazard. We are referred to books like the 'book of Iddo the seer' or 'Shemiah the prophet' for the 'rest of the acts' of rulers (the word 'of' in the titles may mean 'about'). Some critics suspect that he was showing off here, and trying to persuade us by naming fictitious sources, but perhaps he really did have these texts beside his copy of Kings and had kept a few facts from them.

When did this splendid liar write and who was he? Plainly, he wrote long after the return from the Exile: once, he mentioned a Persian coin (a daric of Darius), and he looked back on Isaiah and the early prophets as authoritative books. If (as I accept) his work included the books of Ezra and Nehemiah, it ended with the Jews' great favours from the Persian kings. There was no hint that these favours might change or be interrupted: it is easier, then, to suppose that he wrote in the fourth century BC under a Persian Empire which seemed likely to last, before the 330s, therefore, and its conquest by Alexander the Great. His emphasis on one Israel also fits such a date, before the split with the Samaritans which led to their separate temple to Yahweh in the north. In the books of Chronicles he was extremely favourable to the Levites in the priesthood: he ended with Nehemiah, noting how he restored the Levites to high honour. Perhaps the Chronicler was a Levite himself, writing in Jerusalem *c.* 350 BC.

Nobody can dispute his Chronicles' very strong bias. He idealized David and Hezekiah; he gave an unusually big role to King Jehoshaphat; amazingly, he ignored the separate existence and fall of the northern kingdom of Israel altogether. Such is his tone that his work has even been considered as a sermon which was composed by a Levite for preaching to the people. Certainly, its bias can best be related to the author's own time, when Jews were back with their Temple in their homeland. He began his book with long genealogies which ran back to Jacob and Israel; in keeping with the drift of much of his narrative, they present the continuity of the people in their one land, just as it had been united by King Hezekiah. Here, with a vengeance, was defiance of the facts. The transgressions of the past, he implied, had been paid off and the right course was to look in due humility to a unified future.

Here and there, the author used bits of old information which were ignored in Kings. His work is patently secondary, with a strong historical bias, a pleasant gift for fictitious monologues and little value as historical truth. The enterprise, however, was the enterprise of a historian, even if we can rarely trust him further than we can throw him.

I share the widespread view that the narratives of Ezra and Nehemiah are also the Chronicler's heavily edited arrangement of older evidence. This evidence is uniquely valuable. It includes official Persian documents, most of which are genuine. Above all, parts of Nehemiah are based on Nehemiah's personal memoir which he composed later than the 430s BC. At last, a primary participant is telling us his version of events in his own person, a very sharp break with previous biblical narratives and their anonymous tradition. The change is best explained by his new predicament: Nehemiah was a reformer whose actions had been very contentious. The source of Ezra's narrative is more dubious, although some believe that a memoir by Ezra underlies it too. The editing of both books is chaotic, and their relative datings are still insoluble, but they are the only books in the Old Testament which do quote excellent primary sources, although they themselves are secondary. This material makes them one of the happiest of hunting-grounds for historians.

From the most historical we pass on to the final Hebrew compartment which is largely made up of the most fictional: the stories of Jonah, Ruth, Daniel and Esther have no true basis in the events to which they refer. The book of Jonah was probably written *c.* 450–300 BC (the Book of Tobit alludes to it); Ruth's date is uncertain but probably after 450 BC (in *c.* 433–424, Nehemiah had attacked marriages to foreigners in Jerusalem: none the less, the author of Ruth is not bothered that Ruth is a foreign woman who married honourably into Israel). The book of Daniel is the one certainty: it was composed partly from older stories about Daniel which had circulated between *c.* 280 and 180 BC, and partly from prophecies between 167 and 164 BC. The book itself must be slightly later than 164.

The book of Esther is less easily placed. Unlike Ruth, Esther is a Jewess (by adoption) who marries out to a Gentile, the Persian king: her intercessions then save the Jews from ruin (one of the courtiers, the wicked Haman, has deceived the king into an edict against the Jews and their property). The book is a fiction with a Persian setting: it presupposes the world of the Diaspora after 300 BC (each Jewish community takes its own decisions); it does not mention the Holy Land, the Temple, the cult or even (explicitly) God. Some scholars would date it after the 160s and the great persecution of the Jewish cult and way of life by the Gentile king Antiochus, though the story does not reflect any of these awful events. The threat is to the Jewish people, not their cult, law or Temple. It has a personal cause: Haman feels that he has been slighted by the Jew Mordecai; the king agrees in ignorance, and the story ends without any hatred for him; the King is foolish but not malicious. After the 160s an author would less readily imagine persecution as an accident and neither the law nor Jewish practice as at risk. The persecuting King, Ahasuerus, is merely ignorant; Esther, a Jewess, becomes his queen without any worry over her own Jewish observances.

I would date the book, therefore, between *c.* 280 and 180 BC. The simplest theory is that its author was a Jew living in the region of Susa, the old palace-centre of the Persian kings (he has local knowledge of its festival, Esther 9:26–8, and parades his 'knowledge' of old Persian customs). He has a coherent literary art and weaves together the themes of older court tales, prefacing them with a fine little story of feminine disobedience (it leads to a royal edict ordering women throughout the Persian Empire to obey their menfolk). The main aim of his story was to promote and dignify the origins of a popular festival, Purim, which (then, as now) was being celebrated by Jews around him. He attached it to a story of the Jews' escape from accidental persecution: Purim, he said, marked the days of the two counter-edicts which had been obtained by Esther and Mordecai. He mixed touches of accurate Persian colour, perhaps known in tales round Susa, with his own inaccurate fictions. None of these events happened, but he wished to imply that they had. His literary style reinforces the royal Persian setting: deceitfully, he referred at the end to the 'book of the chronicles of the kings of Media and Persia', as if his story attached to them. On matters Persian, he protests too much.

His vivid story became popular, as did Purim. Other Jews then had the idea of writing letters and a history to promote observance of a festival: we have one for Encaenia, written from Jerusalem in the 120s BC. Perhaps in imitation, the book of Esther was translated in Jerusalem from Hebrew into Greek in 78/7 BC (by then, an element of racial animosity intruded); in turn, it was sent (like the Encaenia letter) to Jews in Egypt in order to publicize its festival. Later in the century, probably under Augustus (after 31 BC), an author in Egypt imagined another tale of abortive royal persecution (our 3 Maccabees) in order to explain the origins of a festival observed by Jews in Egypt; probably, he had the book of Esther as a model for this enterprise.

Biblical narrative, therefore, ends as it began, with a just-so story to explain a custom's origins; in Genesis we learn the origins of hard labour, in Esther, the origins of a popular festival. If we want a historical pendant to Hebrew scripture, we can find it not in these fictions but in the first and second books of the Maccabees, although Christian Bibles print them among their Apocrypha. They were written at least thirty, perhaps as many as sixty, years after the momentous events of war and persecution during the 160s BC which they narrate. 1 Maccabees is a Greek translation of a lost Hebrew original (written *c.* 130–110 BC) whose narrative is sometimes incoherent; 2 Maccabees (after

124 BC) is based on an epitome of an earlier Greek work, now lost, to which have been added prefatory letters in order to justify the rightful celebration of the Encaenia festival. Unlike Esther, it has an exact grasp of the court titles and style of its historical setting, to a degree matched only by the primary source in Nehemiah. Although neither Maccabean book is primary, 2 Maccabees abbreviates a Greek contemporary writer and is the most historical narrative to have bordered on Hebrew scripture. It is heavily interpreted in theological terms; it is not told in chronological order and is not a balanced account of events; it quotes several official letters, although one (2 Maccabees 9:19–27) is a fake.

II

From the well-meant tales of origins in Genesis and Joshua, we have come down through at least six centuries to works where primary sources begin to be diagnosed. It is tempting to explain the birth of history as a natural result of this progression, from stories of origin (the great rocks in Joshua) through stories about great heroes (Gideon and his fleece; Samson and his foxes) to primary stories about political events (the Court History of David's succession). The progression, however, has not been universal in human societies, many of which have told stories of origins or stories about heroes without going on to write history: the gap between a gift for storytelling and a causal, written reconstruction of the past remains very wide.

In Israel, authors did cross this gap: they used early stories in such a reconstruction, with their God playing a central role: theologians, therefore, have credited Him with the birth of historical writing and linked it, famously, to 'unique religious faith', as if the Israelites 'came to a historical way of thinking, and thus to historical writing, by way of belief in the sovereignty of God in history'. However, theology was not a primary cause of historical writing: it soon throttled the child it was supposed to have fathered. Such writing owed much more to the impulse of two great events, the Exodus and Conquest, and the Exile of 587 BC. These events left Jews with an interest in how their tribes had first come to settle and with an urgent need to explain why history had happened so disastrously, and where it might lead them next. In constructing an answer, they turned to written records in which mention of God had played a much smaller part: a Court History from David to Solomon and the books of chronicles of later kings. It was monarchy, not theology, which first caused these books to be written.

As for the Israelites' 'unique obsession with history', it needs to be carefully qualified. What is so striking is their composition of a continuous story, which runs from Creation to the fifth century BC; among the Greeks, by contrast, historical traditions passed into a dark age around 800 BC before picking up, four centuries further back, with tales of the Trojan War. The Israelite story avoided such a gap, even in its staccato age of the judges. It was a selective story (the 'rest of the deeds', if you really want them), and it ran into a blank wall at the opposite end of the tunnel: it broke off with events around Nehemiah, resumed briefly for the Maccabees, but, to judge from their surviving literature, 'in the second and third centuries AD the Jews stopped writing history for more than a thousand years'. Of course the past continued to matter to them, but history writing was not their response to it.

To our eyes, they had not written accurate history so often as mistaken history, story rather than fact. Yet it did have an overwhelming effect: it banished independent myths and presented the Israelites with a legacy to which future storytelling attached itself. Whereas the Greeks had a teeming mythology followed by a gap, then a warring cacophony of histories, the Jews had their universal story which inspired a host of other stories but no known independent mythology outside it. Their scriptures took over and, not for the last time in their history, induced an easy amnesia among their heirs.

Perhaps we should not compare the Jewish writings with the best of the Greeks, who had minds like quicksilver, but should look instead to the Romans, who were also wrapped in the lead of a traditional society, respectful to custom and seniority. Like the Jews, the Romans left very little trace of any early mythology outside their tapestry of early history: the factual sources of this history were not royal chronicles but annals which were kept yearly by their priests. The stories which we now read, from Romulus to King Servius, were written up by later authors who are widely suspected of free invention to fill in the gaps: like the early history of Israel, the early history of Rome emerged 'not as an objective critical reconstruction: rather it was an ideological construct, designed to control, to justify and to inspire'. The works of the Chronicler or the

Deuteronomist fit this description rather well, but there are important differences, too. The Roman tradition was not a tradition with a strongly religious purpose, either priestly or prophetic: much of it was based on the histories of competing families. We know it best from the long literary version of Livy, who was writing in the late first century BC: he was a thoroughly secondary source, but, unlike the secondary biblical writers, he himself expressed doubts about the certainty or truth of much which he wrote about the early past. Most of the Roman tradition was the invention of authors in the second or first centuries BC, but their invention was different from the Deuteronomist's or even the Chronicler's work. These two biblical authors interpreted old sources very heavily, though without (in my view) inventing large parts of the story of their own accord. They wrote with historical aims, narrating the past and explaining 'how' and 'why'; their evidence was often inadequate, and their view of the truth distorted it. On a relaxed definition, they were historians but not very good ones: they might, none the less, have been serving the very purpose in which they believed. For, as the writer Samuel Butler reminded his Victorian readers, 'though God cannot alter the past, historians can; it is perhaps because they can be useful to Him in this respect that He tolerates their existence'.

III

The final biblical compartment is Christian, the books of the New Testament. Here the problem of tradition confronts us across a much shorter gap, but its narratives, so far as they are history, still have the historian's divine usefulness. They have selected a tiny proportion of Jesus's life (three years out of perhaps forty or more: the narrative time of the incidents in the fourth Gospel covers barely two and a half months). They have interpreted events against types and prophecies in Hebrew scripture: have they, perhaps, distorted their Messiah, his kingdom and the grounds for his arrest because they wrote for a sensitive Gentile readership?

These questions will return in due course, but here we need only remember that the Gospels were written about thirty to fifty years after Jesus's death. They stood much closer to the possibility of genuine reminiscence than any book in the Old Testament (except Nehemiah):

the author of Mark, the first, probably had an earlier written source, now lost to us, which was even closer to Jesus's lifetime and to which he could refer. The interrelationships of the four Gospels remain a challenge which could sustain an entire scholarly lifetime, but their historical labelling is a simpler matter. They are historical works, in intention, because they aim to give the true actions and sayings of a historical person during phases of his biography; they are distinct from historical romance, because their authors believe that they are telling the truth. They have a religious aim (the fourth is written 'so that we may believe and have eternal life'), but their status as 'good news' Gospels does not override their historical aspiration: if Jesus does not do what they describe, meet the people whom they mention or do the basic actions which they interpret, then they are false. Even here, they may be trying to bring out some truth about Jesus's purpose or significance, but none the less they are doing so through historical falsehood.

The Gospels also tell us what Jesus and others said. Here, they could claim a bit more latitude, as they could be giving us the general drift of things, not an exact record, thirty years on, of every turn of speech. Invention, in the classical sense, might be at work: helping the truth along, bringing out what the participants meant. There are some fine distinctions, however. We might be reading something which Jesus did say (in the same context or another), something which catches the main point of what he said, something which brings out what he meant to the author or something ascribed to him (unhistorically) by Christian tradition between his lifetime and the Gospels' dates. All these levels of truth may exist in a Gospel's totality of sayings, but the last two are historically the most awkward. If we trust the author, either of the Gospel or of the early tradition, then even a non-saying may be historically illuminating about the primary Jesus: this was what a primary source, perhaps even a close one, thought that he meant. But how do we distinguish between what Jesus did mean, what an early close acquaintance thought that he meant and what later Christians claimed that he had said?

A straightforward acceptance of everything as Jesus's historical words is simply wrong: sayings vary between the Gospels, and there is no exact agreement. Quite often we confront not what Jesus said or meant, but what he meant to the authors or to the sources which they accepted. We confront this variety, even if we cannot draw firm lines to define each group in it.

There will certainly be posthumous invention in bits of it all, but the historical status of each bit varies with its place in the chain of invention.

Of the four Gospels, those ascribed to Mark, Matthew and Luke share a common core of information but do not see it from the same point of view. Luke's tells us that its author was not a primary source, but that 'many' had already written about Jesus before him. He used the Gospel of Mark, as did Matthew, who was more respectful of the order of Mark's narrative. Matthew's and Luke's Gospels also share non-Marcan material, probably from a common source, rather than from Luke's use of Matthew: it is widely believed to have been a written work and thus available to two different authors at different times. This written source is the famous source of modern Gospel scholarship whose existence continues to be challenged by critics, although the case for it still seems stronger than the case against. The finer points of its nature, or non-existence, do not affect a wider fact: neither Luke's nor Matthew's Gospel rests on the author's primary witness, and it is unlikely that Mark's does either (it is only one theory among many that the young man who ran away naked when Jesus was arrested in Gethsemane at Mark 14:52 is the author's allusion to himself).

These three Gospels drew on oral traditions of Jesus's life and sayings, some of which went back to the reminiscences of those who had known him: two of their authors, Luke and Matthew, had not known him at all, and probably, the third, Mark, had not either. A small core of what Jesus actually said has probably survived the chain of reminiscence: the problem is how to detect it. As a start, we might pick out agreed material and leave on one side, as historically vulnerable, anything which addressed the early Christians' own later concerns: this is not, of course, to say that Jesus might not have been prophetic about details of the fall of Jerusalem in 70, or Christian persecution, but historians cannot responsibly accept this material as true foresight. The pressures to invent it later were too great. As for sayings which are not agreed or which conform to each Gospel's distinctive drift, they are probably signs not of what Jesus said but of what he meant to the author. As the three synoptic authors are not primary and had never known Jesus closely, this material (whose scope is unclear at the edges) is evidence for his posthumous impact, for early Christian points of view, not the historical Jesus's own teaching.

Many readers and scholars would find the fourth Gospel (John's) most easy to classify: they treat it almost entirely as unhistorical, viewed simply as a record. It interprets its story very heavily, and it clashes head-on with the routes, words, dates and encounters of the other three. However, I believe that it is historically the most valuable. It gives us a hint of its ultimate author: its final verses are a postscript, added by a later writer who stated his belief that the Gospel's final chapter ('these things': a limited reference) was based on the written legacy of the 'disciple whom Jesus loved'. We cannot date this postscript, but we do know that the final chapter was added on to the rest of the Gospel after the beloved disciple had died. Presumably the addition was made because all the preceding Gospel was already considered to be the work of this same beloved disciple too. In the prologue the author claimed to have been an eyewitness: 'we beheld his glory' (1:14). In context, this glory must relate to Jesus's earthly life.

When the Gospel first appeared, it would almost certainly have observed the rule of Near Eastern narrative: an anonymous presentation (the title, 'According to John', cannot be argued back with any cogency to years before 120, at the earliest). Yet the text gives passing references to one character in a most unusual way: its mentions of the 'other disciple' and the 'disciple whom Jesus loved' at the Last Supper or the high priest's house or the Crucifixion or the empty tomb have often been read as hints of the author's true identity. I cannot think of any parallel in Greek to these knowing references to an unnamed participant: early in the text's life, the editor who added the final chapter to the Gospel assumed that they were references to the Gospel's author himself. When early Christians do express an opinion on this Gospel, they all agree with this view: I believe that they are right, and that their reading is the one valid explanation of this odd group of allusions. If so, the fourth Gospel rests on an excellent primary source: a disciple who was very close to Jesus, who reclined beside him at the Last Supper, who saw into the empty tomb.

Our only other clues are the style and viewpoint of the Gospel itself: are they consistent with such an origin? Here, at least, we can make progress by avoiding proven dead-ends. One is that this Gospel is unduly Hellenized to the point where a modestly educated Jew could not have written it: here literary study of its style and vocabulary is decisive. The author managed only a few of the connecting words which give good Greek such force; he let in homely words and phrases; he liked repetition and parallel clauses, and his use of them was not at all stylish in a Greek way. However, his writing was not naïve and crude. Like Luke, he knew the Greek translations of scripture, and almost all of his vocabulary can be found in their texts. It is not necessarily that he was echoing them at every turn: many of their shared words are common words in Greek, and sometimes the Gospel uses them in quite a different sense. The overlap is significant, but only if we contrast it with the low overlap between the Gospel and the pagan Greek religious writings with which scholars have sometimes compared him (calling his the 'Hellenic Gospel').

Rather, the fourth Gospeller was steeped in Jewish texts and piety, a dimension which has grown with our improving knowledge of both. He need not have been a member of the sect, but we have come to know of intriguing parallels between some of his distinctive phrases (the 'sons of light'; the 'water of life'; 'doing the truth') and phrases used by the Jewish group whom we now know from the Dead Sea scrolls. At no point did he draw on Greek thought or Greek literary style, although he wrote in Greek himself. His understanding of Jewish practices also suggests an informed Jewish milieu. He knew that big water-pots of stone were used for baths of purification, that Tabernacles and Encaenia were major festivals in Jerusalem, that circumcision was not to be done on the Sabbath. His account of Jesus's arrest was circumstantial; he knew details of the high priests; unlike the other Gospellers, he assumed that Jesus went to and fro to festivals in Jerusalem during the year (we can see from Josephus that such pilgrimages, even from Galilee, were nothing unusual). He gave small details of place, time and distance: the pool of Siloam; the twelve hours in the Jewish day; the distance from Bethany to Jerusalem. He puzzled his readers with his 'pool' in Jerusalem and its 'five porticoes', until the pool of Bethesda with its two basins, pillars on four sides and a fifth in between was found by archaeologists. Sometimes we cannot prove or disprove him: we have no cogent evidence for or against his assumption that Jews, including priests, would not enter Pilate's residence (a Gentile headquarters) for fear of pollution on the eve of Passover. Until he is disproved, I am content to assume that his assumption here was correct. On our present knowledge, nothing which he said of Jerusalem, Jewish practice or Jewish groups, however detached or hostile he may be, presupposes a date after 70 when the Temple cult ended and Jewish piety changed decisively in the wake of the war against Rome.

However well informed, he evidently wrote outside Judaea for an audience who were not practising Jews. He explained his non-Greek words; he looked back, therefore, on the Jews as a separate group; his Jesus even tells Pilate that he has been 'delivered to the Jews' (18:36, but he himself was one). At the Last Supper he tells his disciples, 'as I said unto the Jews' (13:33), although he is addressing Jews in the room. Whereas the guileless Nathaniel is a 'true Israelite', Jesus's followers will be cast out of the synagogues by people who 'hate' them. A split with the Jewish communities lies behind this Gospel, but it has been wrongly connected with a formal cursing of Christians, agreed, perhaps, at some Council of Jamnia in the 80s: the evidence of such a cursing is not cogent, and the Council is not attested. For a context we need look no further than Acts, the work (I will argue) of Paul's companion, where such a split happens very early indeed. Paul himself (a 'Pharisee of the Pharisees') is said to have begged letters from the high priest in order to round up anyone of the 'Christian Way' in Damascus's synagogues and send them, bound, to Jerusalem (9:1–2). Less than a year had passed since the Crucifixion, and, even if the details have been exaggerated, the author, Paul's companion, believed in such a split so soon. Like the beloved disciple, the author of Acts also looked on the Jews as a separate group in the cities outside Judaea.

What we have, then, is a Gospel which knows exact details of Jewish life and piety before 70 but which looks back from outside on the Jews as a separate, hostile group (although salvation is 'of them' at 4:22, in the sense of their truly offered worship to God). Its Greek style, language and allusions are consistent with a Greek-speaking Jew; it also assumes an audience outside Judaea. These facts are consistent (but not exclusively so) with a beloved disciple who has left Judaea for the Gentiles, even with one of the Johns (writing, possibly, at Ephesus or in Asia Minor): they reinforce the belief of the author of the postscript, the apparent belief of the author of the epilogue (chapter 21), and the odd, oblique references to the disciple in the Gospel itself.

The disciple's name and identity are even more open to dispute. Was he some unknown John or was he some other member of the Twelve who was none the less as important as Peter and the first to enter Jesus's tomb (20:8)? Or was he the famous 'John, the son of Zebedee' whose name is never mentioned in the fourth Gospel? One of Jesus's 'sons of thunder', he was a Galilaean, stitching nets in his boat (John 1:19): could such a person really have been known to the high priest's household (John 18:15) and written such a book in Greek? If we do have the text of John, son of Zebedee, we would have another profound reversal in human character. Peter, who denied Christ, became a leading Apostle, although he was less than a rock in his early attitude to those Gentile Christians who ignored the law (Galatians 2:11). Paul, who hunted out Christians and had them bound, became Christ's Apostle, and was whipped and killed for his sake. John the 'son of thunder', who wanted to see a Samaritan village burned and to sit at Jesus's side in glory, would have to have written the Gospel whose supreme commandment is to 'love one another'. Those changes, however, were what Christianity involved.

Those who find it incredible can appeal to the possibility of another John among the disciples; this John could perhaps tie up with the elder who wrote the three epistles and with 'John the Elder' who was known to Christian tradition, also as a disciple, by *c.* 125–40. I prefer to identify the author as the 'beloved' or 'other' disciple but to reserve judgement about his name. John, son of Zebedee, was a Galilaean fisherman; Mark 10:39 appears to hint already at this John's martyrdom, and unless its words are truly prophetic here, we face the problem that the author of the fourth Gospel does seem to have lived on to take account of Mark's text (among several hints, John 6:25–59 on the Bread of Heaven perhaps corrects and amplifies Mark 8:14 ff.).

Nameless or not, a primary source was still the author: marvellous vistas open for those who accept this. His Jesus speaks, travels and acts in ways which both differ from the Jesus of the other three Gospels and conflict directly with their framework: do we simply believe the beloved disciple and reject them? Primary witnesses, too, can select, reinterpret, invent and rearrange: does this Gospel's art affect its historical truth? We will return in detail to these questions, but one point, at least, is certain. Of all the biblical books, the fourth Gospel is the most explicit about an eyewitness's evidence: at the Crucifixion, 'blood and water' are said to have flowed from Jesus's side, and 'he that saw it bare record, and his record is true: and he knoweth that he saith true' (19:35). Many have inferred that this witness is the author himself, the beloved disciple who was at the Cross, but the inference here is not very compelling. It is, however, an explicit citation of a primary source, by an author who, in my view, is primary himself.

The final book of narrative is the Acts of the Apostles, which is the beguiling sequel to Luke's Gospel, its companion volume. In chapter 16 the main line of the Greek text breaks suddenly into the first person plural and uses it intermittently for the rest of the story; at 11:28 the variant Western line of the text (which, as we saw, may be the author's own 'second edition') had already used a 'we' at Antioch before the first missionary journey began. The obvious conclusion is that the author was incidentally referring to his own presence. Many critics still dispute this awkward fact, partly because they think the author's theology is late (there is nothing conclusive, here) and above all because they believe that his book clashes with the writings of Paul. I do not find these clashes insuperable: some are felt to be factual (I share the view, however, that the council in Acts 15 derives from the events told by Paul more accurately in Galatians 2:1–9); some are intellectual (Acts does not contain all the theology of Paul's letters); some suggest a different context (Paul's letters appear to address Gentile Christians, but Acts tells how Paul began by preaching with some success in the Jews' synagogues, often in the cities to which he later sent letters). We must not over-estimate the companion's closeness; Acts' author could well have made mistakes about Paul's early career or about periods when they were apart; Acts does insist on the Jews' hostility in most cities, including Thessalonica and Corinth to which Paul writes; successes in the synagogues may have been very few, so that the majority in Acts' churches, just as in Paul's letters, were Gentiles or Gentile 'god-fearers' who previously attended synagogues. As for Paul's theology, the surviving epistles are only a small part of his opinions, his 'all things to all men', and are directed to existing Christians, not to possible converts, like most of Acts' speeches. A travelling companion could well have missed the theology we now have in them (Acts' author did not use the letters as a source); pupils, even, see masters very differently (Socrates taught both Plato and Xenophon, but their books about him are remarkably different). We are left, I believe, with a fascinating question.

In Acts we have a companion's portrait of Paul, including speeches for him, which we can put beside Paul's own letters: they do not overlap very much. In the fourth Gospel we have a companion's portrait of Jesus, which also includes long speeches; we have nothing by Jesus himself as a control, but should we conclude that this companion, too, has misrepresented his subject's thought? The difference, I think, is in their closeness to their subject and their intelligence: in the fourth Gospel we have the beloved disciple, not an intermittent companion, not the bland, well-meaning, humane author of Luke–Acts, who was a smoother of difficulties, not a perceiver of burning potential.

Those who divide Acts' author from Paul's company have produced no other valid explanation of the first-person plurals which he used at odd moments in describing Paul's career. They fit very well with the author's varying knowledge of detail and fluctuating range of information: they show him to have been an eyewitness. I regard it as certain, therefore, that he knew Paul and followed parts of his journey. He stayed with him in Jerusalem; he spent time in Caesarea, where he lodged with an early member of the Seven, Philip, who had four prophetic daughters, all virgins (Acts 21:8–9). It must have been quite an evening. He had no written sources, but in Acts he himself was a primary source for a part of the story. He wrote the rest of Acts from what individuals told him and he himself had witnessed, as did Herodotus and Thucydides; in my view, he wrote finally in Rome, where he could still talk to other companions of Paul, people like Aristarchus (a source for Acts 19:23 ff.; cf. Acts 27:2, 17:1–15) or perhaps Aquila and Priscilla (whence Acts 18). From Philip he could already have heard about the Ethiopian eunuch (Philip met him), or Stephen and the Seven (Philip was probably one), or the conversion of the Gentile Cornelius in Caesarea (Philip's residence); from the prophet Agabus, whom he met at 21:10, could come knowledge of Agabus's earlier prophecy in 11:28. By contrast, the early chapters on Pentecost, the healing miracles and the killing of Ananias and Sappheira are not true history; they reflect the author's attempts to make historical sense of the highly coloured stories which Christians in Antioch, Caesarea or Jerusalem had told him about the community's early years. As we have seen with the Nativity, myth-making began early. Despite it, his narrative has a particular value: the first part is a web of early Christians' stories, the second is based on an account of events by participants, including himself. He also brought out their wider significance by the speeches which he placed in his narrative. Often he had no sources and no first-hand knowledge of what people had said, but he gave them appropriate words (although he was not above a historical blunder: at Acts 5:36 the speaker, Gamaliel, is made to allude to events which occurred after his own death).

From the Bible's first narrative to Acts, its last, we have traced a long progression. In or before the eighth century BC an unknown Yahwist in Judah had written and arranged stories which explained the origins of what people knew and saw around them; in the fifties and sixties AD the author of Acts was blending his own memories with the memories of important Christian acquaintances, engaged in personal research as a Herodotus or Thucydides had known it. On grounds of style and form, too, he has been classed as a 'Hellenistic historian' and compared with these great Greek predecessors.

There remain, however, significant differences. Not once did the author of Acts doubt the stories of the recent past which he had worked together from hearsay. It is not just that his chronology is pleasantly erratic in some of his earlier chapters: in what he tells, there is none of what Thucydides assures us to have been 'stringent testing'. When he breaks into a speech, he is also aptly biblical. A generation of modern scholarship has pointed to this use of speeches and compared it with classical Greek historians. Yet here, too, the author deployed a different art. In the biblical manner, his speakers address us in sermons or in self-defence: only one class of person speaks at any length, Christians to whom there is no reply. There are no paired speeches and answers, and only two exceptions to the all-Christian rule: Gamaliel the Jew speaks once and so does a hired orator, Tertullus, who was required to argue in court before a Roman governor. However, Gamaliel's speech is highly favourable to the Christians, while Tertullus falters after a few sentences and is obliterated by Paul's long reply.

Like a classical historian, the author of Acts selects and steers his story by his own interpretation. We see Christianity through others' misunderstandings; we hear, three times over, of the total innocence of Paul. He is guided, however, by knowledge of an unseen presence: the 'plan of God'. Thucydides, king of Greek historians, would have winced.

14
Digging and Travelling

From Genesis to Acts, we now have more of a feel for the narrative, whether its authors, or their probable sources, have a claim to be writers of history, where the few patches of primary information may lie, how the entire sweep from Adam to Paul varies greatly in its concern, or approximation, to fact. We have also found that guessing an author, let alone an anonymous author and his sources, is a delicate art where convictions have often outrun truth. Not everybody accepts that the Deuteronomist wrote so much or that a disciple wrote our fourth Gospel. I am satisfied that they did. I now wish to make the hunt for facts more precise by setting bits of biblical narrative against evidence which we know outside it and seeing whether the two correspond. I will use three such sources of evidence: digging and travelling; written evidence outside the Bible; and the evidence of the future, as known to historians nowadays but not to biblical authors at the time. Where such evidence conflicts with the Bible, we may be helped to decide which (or neither) to believe, if we remember how this patch of biblical narrative struck us as history, good, bad or secondary.

We will have to proceed by samples only, and at times the arguments have to be rather detailed: at this level, small details count. I will begin with digging and travelling, although the details of archaeological dating and discovery are often too technical to be more than summarized here. Digging and travelling have their own immediacy, none the less, to which non-specialists (like myself, here) can readily succumb.

Biblical tours have a very long history: seeing, maybe, is believing, but believing also ensures that there is plenty to see. Within a hundred years of the Crucifixion, there were already Christians who were venerating a particular cave at Bethlehem as the cave of Jesus's Nativity, although the Gospels never mentioned a cave and the birth at Bethlehem was a legend, not a historical fact. By the mid third century the writings of the great Christian scholar Origen were a companion guide to the great scriptural sights. Origen had done the circuit of the Old Testament, visiting places like the Tomb of the Patriarchs at Hebron or the wells which Abraham was said to have dug at Ascalon; he thought that they were dug 'in an extraordinary style compared with other wells'. Naturally, Christian places also caught his attention as he went 'in search of the traces of Jesus, the disciples and the prophets'. He even proposed to relocate the Gadarene swine because he had visited the very place where they had careered over the cliff. It was being shown to visitors beside the Sea of Galilee.

At the time of Origen's visit, Christianity was a persecuted religion in the Roman Empire, yet there were people in Galilee willing to show visitors the very spot where their texts alleged that a herd of pigs had stampeded miraculously over a cliff. Christianity had been quick to find its local guides, artful campfollowers whom it has benefited ever since. In 324 the Holy Land gained a new protector. It came under the rule of Constantine, the first Roman Emperor to adopt the Christian faith: the supposed site of the pigs' stampede eventually acquired a monastery and a big church. Before then, we can follow the sights which were open to all comers through the itinerary of a Christian pilgrim, one of those marvellous survivals among texts from the ancient world.

In the year 333 this unknown pilgrim left his home in Bordeaux and travelled across the Alps, through Asia Minor and down into Palestine, a journey of three and a half thousand miles which must have taken about six months on roads of varying discomfort. The enterprise is a tribute to the open horizons of Constantine's new empire, and the pilgrim's written itinerary leaves no doubt that it was all worth while. Neither Moses nor Joshua had ever seen the Promised Land through such enhanced eyes. The pilgrim believed he had visited Job's very own country farmhouse; in Jericho he was shown the house of Rahab the harlot; he saw the mountain which Abraham had climbed with Isaac (it was 1,300 steps to the top); the site of the rape of Dinah; and the well where Christ had talked with the woman of Samaria: Jacob had dug it and planted it with plane trees which were still growing happily. Nowadays, we marvel at the olive trees in Jerusalem which are older than the Christian faith, but this pilgrim found a different link between botany and the biblical past. At Mamre, he saw the very tree by which Abraham had entertained Yahweh and his two angels; by the road to Jerusalem stood the sycamore which Zacchaeus had climbed to see Jesus. Jerusalem was the climax of the journey. On the ancient site of the Temple, he saw the blood of Zachariah on the marble 'so that you would say it had been shed that very day'. He even saw the stone 'which had been set at naught of the builders, but which is become the head of the corner'. The centrepiece had just been unearthed. The Emperor Constantine had ordered an excavation to remove a pagan temple of Venus which was believed to obscure the tomb of Christ. Several tombs were discovered, but one had been chosen as Christ's, on unspecified evidence, 'surpassing all astonishment', in Constantine's opinion. The mood of the times was strongly in its favour: 'The surprise would have been even greater,' its most recent historian has concluded, 'if nothing had been found.'

Back went the pilgrim on the long land-route to southern France, brimming over with stories and evidence for his neighbours in Bordeaux: within two decades the sights had multiplied behind him. Pieces of wood from the Cross itself were believed to be circulating from Jerusalem as far afield as North Africa, encouraging the legend, which no history supports, that the Cross and its two neighbours had been found by Constantine's mother Helena and that its nails had been sent to adorn the bridle of the emperor's horse. By the 390s an enterprising nun added the ultimate sprig to the store of sacred botany. She had seen the very Burning Bush from which God had spoken to Moses: it had been cut back hard, she wrote, but 'it was still sending out shoots' on Mount Sinai.

From the start, biblical travel did not broaden the mind: like a modern cruise, it confirmed the beliefs which minds brought to it. Truth, like beauty, lay in the eyes of the observers, and the sense of place ushered in a false dawn of explanation. Nowhere did it break more clearly than in the widely bought *Vie de Jésus*, which has been endlessly reprinted since its publication in 1863. Its author, the great French scholar Ernest Renan, visited Palestine for twenty-four idyllic days in the spring of 1861, accompanied by two female disciples, his wife and sister. 'The striking agreement of the texts and the places, the marvellous harmony of the Gospel Ideal with the countryside which served as its frame were for me a revelation. I had before my eyes a fifth Gospel, tattered but still legible.'

In Galilee, during spring, Renan saw only a simple beauty. The mountains had a harmony, and the peasantry led a 'contented and easily satisfied life' which 'spiritualized itself in ethereal dreams', while the tone of the place extended to the animals, 'small and gentle creatures', tortoises, even, with 'mild eyes' like extras in a cartoon film. This setting, he felt, had profoundly affected the young Jesus: it explained the 'delightful pastoral' which local stories ascribed to his early life. The desert, by contrast, was suited to the 'austere John the Baptist', while the 'parched appearance of nature in the neighbourhood of Jerusalem must have added to the dislike Jesus had for it'. Renan opposed the gentle Galilaean to the harsh, complex world of Jerusalem, a contrast which he derived from the tattered Gospel of the Landscape. 'The East,' meanwhile, was surging with 'passion and credulity': together, they 'create imposture', and so Renan decided that Jesus, late in his career, had been obliged to work his miracles merely to satisfy the Eastern crowds. The sense of landscape directed this recasting of the Gospels, and, in turn, it helped to sell it. Renan was a Breton by origin, sensitive to the natural world: a new pilgrim, from Brittany not Bordeaux, had found his fifth Gospel in the place-names, roads and landscape of the Holy Land.

The impact of fifth Gospels is still with us: surely seeing helps believing, and Holy Land travel deepens our vision of the Bible's story? In his *Spiritual Exercises*, Ignatius of Loyola urged the value of picturing the scene for a deeper contemplation of scripture: 'Picture to yourself in imagination the road from Bethlehem in its length and breadth . . . Is it level or through valleys or over hillsides? Study the place of the Nativity . . . Is the cave spacious or cramped, low or high? How is it furnished?' Spiritually, perhaps, the exercise might be helpful, but it is irrelevant to historical truth: there was no cave in the Gospels, and Jesus was not born in Bethlehem. None the less, in the late twentieth century, modern visitors to the Holy Land are still convinced that the local sights are helping them to picture biblical stories. Camels and Bedouin suggest the tented life of biblical times; the Dead Sea is still scorched and salty; Galilee bursts into flower in springtime; and Jerusalem can still be a nightmare. The picture, however, can be severely misleading: in biblical times, nobody is known to have worn the cloth head-dress, or *kaffiyeh*, which has become the hallmark of biblical films.

When Renan visited Palestine, he was taking a holiday from a year's research in Phoenicia, where his remarkable studies of graves and surface ruins are still fundamental to the area's history. However, the antiquities of the Holy Land left next to no mark on the *Vie de Jésus*, and, although Renan used his knowledge of place-names to relocate points in the story, he never suggested that the sites could be better understood if they were excavated. It was an odd omission, because twenty years earlier, the discovery of the palaces of the Assyrian kings had already astonished the biblical public. It was corrected in 1865, two years after Renan's book, when a Palestine Exploration Fund was set up independently in London. Its president was to be the Archbishop of York, and it disavowed controversy while aiming at 'biblical illustration': its first excavations were in the heart of ancient Jerusalem, conducted by a military officer who overapplied his skills of military mining. In 1870 a similar group, though shorter lived, was founded in New York, the Palestine Exploration Society, which was aimed not only at 'illustration' of the Bible but also at 'defence'.

Seeing and travelling were now being joined by a third dimension: digging. However, the exponents of science and systematic study were still charmingly unaware of what to dig. The main sites in Palestine had grown layer by layer into mounds, or tells, which rose above the ground on the debris of successive cities. Visitors believed that these mounds were the bases for ancient towns or buildings which had unfortunately disappeared from their summit. Not until 1890 was the nature of such a mound in Israel demonstrated by Flinders Petrie's masterly excavations at Tell el-Hesi: like our book of Deuteronomy, a tell turned out to have grown up by stages, in each of which diggers (like textual critics) could find a separate phase of life. A new age had begun, but its systematic study did not exclude scriptural optimism. If anything, it increased it. The faith of Renan or the Bordeaux pilgrim now extended below ground as well as above it. Excavation was biblical archaeology, liable to confirm what the scriptures said. The Burning Bush, maybe, had succumbed to old age, but who was to say what the spade might not find in the years when Egypt and Nineveh, Troy and King Agamemnon's death-mask, amazed their excavators' public?

It was not in Palestine but in Iraq that biblical archaeology first became worldwide news. In 1854 J. E. Taylor, the British consul at Basra, investigated Tell al-Muqayyar (the Mound of Pitch) in southern Iraq, about ten miles west of the River Euphrates. The mound was a man-made ziggurat, or terraced construction for religious worship: in the highest surviving terrace he found cylinders of baked clay whose inscriptions proved that in the mid sixth century B C, the king of Babylon had had this terrace restored. As so often, clay cylinders had been deposited in the foundations of royal building-work: they referred to the site as Ur. In 1922 a young graduate of New College, Oxford, Leonard Woolley, returned to the mound to direct a joint expedition which was financed by the British Museum and the University of Pennsylvania. Between 1926 and 1928 he found an amazing series of royal graves, dating back to *c.* 2500 B C. Back to the daylight came temples and walls, the huge staged tower, or ziggurat, whose top had been restored *c.* 550 B C, and an area of houses, squares and narrow alleys which dated from *c.* 2000 B C. The excavators gave homely London and Oxford names to the street plan (Broad Street; Carfax; Paternoster Row), but Woolley was also the son of a clergyman, brought up on the Bible's text. The city, he believed, was the ancient Ur of the Chaldees; the houses belonged to the age of Abraham; Abraham, said one verse in Genesis, had left Ur of the Chaldees to go on his travels, and Woolley, therefore, believed he had found the very quarter in which Abraham had grown up.

In Jesus's lifetime, Abraham's second home had been on show near Damascus: 'Even now the name of Abraham is famous in the region,' we are told by a man of Damascus, Nicolaos the historian, who was secretary to Herod the Great, 'and people point to a village called "the house of Abraham".' In the 1920s news of Abraham's new Mesopotamian address caught the imagination of the Western press: magazines carried drawings of 'A House from the Lifetime of Abraham', and Woolley warmed to his theme. Abraham was no wanderer among cattle, camels and women of the tents. 'We must radically alter our view of the Hebrew patriarch when we see that his earlier years were passed in such sophisticated surroundings. He was the citizen of a great city,' living among two- or three-storeyed houses where merchants and educated schoolboys looked out across Broad Street. Their middle-class homes belonged in a society which was 'highly individualistic, enjoying a great measure of personal liberty, materialistic and moneymaking, hard-working and most appreciative of comfort'. One grave of the royal cemetery revealed a model goat, rampant on one side of a golden tree: it caused Woolley's mind to make a symptomatic leap, from the cemetery at Tell al-Muqayyar to the 'ram in the thicket' which was mentioned by Genesis when Abraham prepared to sacrifice Isaac. In spring 1929 Woolley dug deeper beneath the cemetery and found a layer of 'clean clay, uniform throughout, the texture of which showed that it had been laid there by water'. Over eight feet deep, it 'could only have been the result of a flood'. Woolley believed that he had found a 'real deluge' to which the biblical and Mesopotamian 'stories of the Flood alike go back'.

The city's grave goods were an amazing discovery, but neither Abraham's birthplace nor the Flood, let alone the ram in the thicket, has survived the test of time. Historians no longer believe the stories of Abraham as if they are history: like Aeneas or Heracles, Abraham is a figure of legend. The Bible is divided on his place of origin; Ur of the Chaldees is only one candidate (ignored in the Greek translations of Genesis). The 'ram in the thicket' was a charming fancy, and as for the Flood, other excavations soon found similar deposits at widely differing levels and dates in southern Mesopotamia. Since 1929 Woolley's Flood has subsided and become more and more local, not an area of '40,000 square miles': there is no reason to trace the Mesopotamian and Hebrew stories back to any one flood in particular; the Hebrew fiction is most likely to have developed from the Mesopotamians' legends. The stories are fictions, not history.

Woolley's discoveries remain on a justified pinnacle in archaeology, but his interpretations are a cautionary tale. Not only did they spread a belief, repeated many times since, that proofs of the Bible might emerge at any moment from the ground, but they assumed in the simplest terms that the Bible's narrative was all historical (Woolley never asked if any of it was primary) and that 'dumb objects', without any text or inscription, could confirm a written narrative. Heroic excavations continued in his wake, but the mirage of contemporary, scientific evidence still hung round scriptural study. It peaked, perhaps, in the post-war years. On one side, the foundation of Israel brought a people back into the Holy Land with the strongest commitment to mapping and naming its sites and excavating its past: archaeological objects were even seen as the 'gifts of the ancestors', and their pursuit found strong political allies. On the other side, there were theologians who wished to uphold Israel's God as the 'God of events' who had acted in history and was evident, still, in its material relics. A strong alliance grew up between archaeology and defence of the Bible as history: it passed naturally to fundamentalists for whom archaeology promised immediacy and 'scientific' evidence.

There were archaeologists, historical critics and theologians who were much more cautious, but the new science of archaeology continued to spread Woolley thoughts worldwide. Not all experts held them, though almost all the public were willing to be fed them; newspapers had an eye on the post-Woolley scoop, and encouraged the stories which would work as news. In 1956 a German journalist, Werner Keller, demonstrated the strength of the public's belief in the link between scripture, digging and travelling. His book, *The Bible as History*, first appeared under the title *The Bible is Indeed Correct*, with the subtitle 'Archaeology Confirms the Book of Books'. Keller was wary of Woolley and noncommittal about the long-running fantasy that people had found bits of Noah's legendary ark (in 1955 fragments of wood from Mount Ararat had been solemnly misdated to 4000 BC by a forestry institute in Madrid). After this brief exercise, scepticism was put to one side, and Keller offered a grand tour through the landscape and recent 'discoveries' from Genesis to the Dead Sea scrolls. His book became a school text, was translated into twenty-four languages and sold over ten million copies within twenty years.

Neither the style of the book nor its illustrations had been unduly attractive, but the oddest fact about its success was that, on careful reading, nothing emerged directly from archaeological evidence which confirmed anything significant about the Book of Books. The hills by the Dead Sea are salty and windswept, and the erosion of the pillars of salt on their cliffs may explain the just-so story that Lot's wife had become one of them: it does not prove that the Bible's story is true. The familiar hand of cards was being played once again, ranging from Phoenicia to Babylon, but never descending to relevant texts in Hebrew, for the simple reason that none had been discovered. Severe problems of chronology, storytelling and historicity were skated over, as if the Bible's text could identify the archaeological evidence, which in turn was supposed to be confirming the Bible's text in its latest Masoretic form.

By the 1970s biblical archaeology was more widely mistrusted. The biblical story still helped to fix the names of ancient sites and lent a romance which encouraged funds to be given for digging: it inspired many of the excavators and made their finds (or non-finds) of wider interest. Its sites and objects were direct, immediate evidence, but in order to be significant, they needed personal interpretation and rigorous dating: there was no great likelihood that bits of pottery or house plans would tell anything of any significance to readers of complex biblical stories. However, there was always the possibility of a buried archive, a written mass of legible texts which could speak to the Bible from its own time. The odds were very slim, but in 1976 they seemed to have come up at an obscure mound in Syria. At Tell Mardikh, a mound fifty feet high and about forty miles south of Aleppo, an Italian archaeologist, still in his mid twenties, hit on a dream of a discovery: he found eighteen hundred intact clay tablets and fragments of another sixteen thousand or so, ten thousand of which were very small.

The tablets were assigned to an Italian epigraphist who began the difficult task of decipherment. The script was Mesopotamian, and the texts were largely intelligible from a knowledge of Sumerian: cuneiform signs were used throughout, but at times they rendered what appeared to be a local language (Eblaite?) into a Sumerian vocabulary. Tell Mardikh had turned out to be ancient Ebla, and its tablets were interpreted with dramatic results. Syllables like 'Yahweh' were detected in the formation of personal names; five cities appeared to be named in sequence, exactly the five 'cities of the plain' in the old and vexed chapter 14 of the Book of Genesis; sign-words for Sodom and Gomorrah sprang up from the ancient clay; there was even a name like Abraham's ancestor, Ebrum. News broke to the press of a long lost kingdom of Ebla whose contacts, as seen in the tablets' place-names, stretched far and wide through the known world. Here were cities known to Abraham and links (of a sort) with the age of the patriarchs which had therefore shown up to be vastly earlier than all but the most hardened optimists had ever credited. On 5 November 1976 optimism reached its peak in the Quadrangle Club of the University of Chicago. Fresh from his revelations, the texts' Italian decoder met a well-known biblical archaeologist over breakfast. 'It was an astounding moment,' he later told his public: the name of Birsha, king of Gomorrah in Genesis, seemed to be attested in an Ebla tablet of the third millennium B C.

From 1978 to 1981 books of biblical archaeology found fresh heart and a new second chapter; the press spread the news that Abraham had a historical context. The sequel, however, was not so widely broadcast. The king of Gomorrah did not survive a rereading of his tablet; two of the five cities quickly went the same way (all five had never been attested on the same tablet); Sodom, Gomorrah and the others turned out to be a misinterpretation. Like the pet-names for Yahweh, Abraham's ancestor receded as a scholarly mirage; the tablets were intelligible only in so far as they coincided with Sumerian (about a quarter of their texts did not); as for Ebla's fabulous contacts and wide horizons, they dwindled fascinatingly on closer study. Many of the tablets gave lists of words or place-names, but they were present in the Ebla archive only because they were a standard writing exercise for scribes at this interface with the Sumerian way of writing. Like place-names in a child's first reading book, they said nothing about local trade routes. The famous list of place-names turned out to have an exact pair further east: it had been found without any popular fuss at Abu Jalabikh, south-east of Babylon. Ebla, therefore, has shrunk to a site with some interesting jewellery and the usual anonymities of archaeology; enthusiasts will ponder a 'Tomb of the Lord of the Goats' which dates from *c.* 1750 B C. It is one early site among others in which scribes' exercise tablets have been discovered, but it happens to be further west and better stocked with remains. Neither the site nor the archive throws any light whatsoever on anything in the Bible's text.

'Those who work on the tablets from Ebla are now doing their best to put all this hullabaloo behind them and to look upon Ebla as a Syrian city producing material relevant to the culture and history of Bronze Age Syria.' Theologically, historically and archaeologically, the main tide has turned against rock-hard biblical excavation. Objects do not become hard facts of history unless we, the observers, interpret them: like the Bordeaux pilgrim, it is we who animate the silent finds which confront us. With the help of the Bible, we may animate them wrongly, turn a story into pseudo-history or forget the problems of the text of scripture itself. There are many, therefore, who disclaim the very idea of biblical archaeology and opt for 'Syro-Palestinian excavation' instead. They wish to dissociate object and text, and propose to interpret both as two types of evidence on different planes. Here, it is worth comparing the standing of Homeric archaeology in the adjoining Aegean world. Crude proofs of Homer's accuracy from objects found here and there in any one period have caused archaeologists to rebel against the very title and classify it as 'Aegean archaeology from the late Bronze to early Iron Age'. However, this 'Aegean archaeology' does bear directly on our continuing attempts to place and date the Homeric poems: it helps us not by uncovering the scene of the poem, Troy, or by claiming to find bits of Agamemnon's kingdom, but simply by showing how the material objects combined in Homer's poems are an impossible combination, mixing metals or burials or houses of widely separate dates. The Homeric world cannot ever be excavated, but parts of it can be, and have been untangled in a way which bears directly on our understanding of its nature and invention.

The Homeric experience is relevant to biblical archaeology: excavation cannot prove a narrative, but it may help us to judge how and when that narrative arose. Among all the hullabaloo from Ur to Ebla, we risk forgetting that the failure to prove does not entail the inability to disprove: like Homeric archaeology, excavation can help us to establish a negative. It is here, paradoxically, that biblical archaeology is still valid and relevant to truth. It remains, then, to see where, if anywhere, digging bears on the Bible in this helpful way.

II

Archaeologists are most helpful to historians when they find a written text on an object, whether a wall, a dish or a bit of papyrus. Any one such discovery could change our understanding of whole stretches of the biblical story: in the past eighty years the gains here have been enormous, although indirect. Thanks to archaeologists, we have texts of Babylonian and Canaanite stories of Creation, gods and mythology: the Hebrew Bible no longer confronts us as a text without neighbours. From finds in and around Israel, we have no text of such relevance, but we do have dozens of lesser finds which give a clearer idea of the development of the Hebrew script. They give us scattered evidence of writing and bear directly on the question of early Hebrew literacy in Israel. From the age of David and Solomon, *c.* 980–920 BC, we have no royal inscriptions and no solid external evidence for the widespread court culture of literacy or 'enlightenment' which critics of the sources of Samuel and Kings have sometimes assumed. Written records were probably kept, at least for the 'acts of Solomon', and somehow the early court historian knew and wrote a detailed story of events and places in David's career. But as yet archaeological finds cannot help us. The evidence of inscribed potsherds is evidence beginning in the ninth and increasing from the eighth century onwards, and even then it is not direct evidence for widespread Hebrew literacy which could serve most people's needs. It is joined by the evidence of seals and in the eighth century by stamped clay sealings from archives and private documents. This evidence, too, is of limited scope. In the Near East people still own a stamp or a seal with their name on it, although they cannot write themselves; finds of seals, therefore, do not prove that the owners were literate; simple writing does not prove that the same people ever wrote at length, still less that they read as a habit; reading and writing are separate skills which exist independently.

I will reserve the question of written texts for the next chapter. Here, I will pay more attention to the staple diet of 'dirt archaeology', sites and objects which carry no written words. If we wish to relate them to external history, we need to be sure of two preliminaries: their dating and the questions which they are capable of answering.

In the biblical era, the dating of the various layers of a site is an extremely delicate question which continues to alter. Often it depends on sequences of dates for the durable objects found in it, especially the bits of pottery; they relate, in turn, to the phases of other sites where similar objects may have been found beside written material. The framework needs a linchpin, and in the second and early first millennium BC, it can be found in the dates for Egypt's Pharaohs. Ultimately, they are based on astronomical reckonings, and so they allow us to equate them with a numbered year. From these (more or less) fixed points, we can then fit in our knowledge of the maximum number of years for which each Pharaoh ruled (contemporary buildings, documents and inscriptions give us these figures: we can also watch out for a jubilee year in a reign, usually the thirtieth, and compare the lengths of reign given by an antiquarian Egyptian priest, Manetho, who was writing in Greek in the third century BC). The resulting sequence is not completely secure (the correct understanding of the astronomical dates is still disputed), but the area of serious doubt is not usually considered to be more than twenty to thirty years in the main biblical era (*c.* 1400–700 BC).

At sites in biblical lands and at key points in biblical narrative, we often have a trail which radiates out to a solid dating by one of Egypt's kings. There are, however, other sequences of objects whose dates are not so secure. Whether dated or not, there are limits to what they can tell us: dumb objects have to be interpreted, and, although 'the spade cannot lie', this merit has been well ascribed to the fact that it cannot speak. In its most direct form, archaeology charts the development of the dumb objects themselves. It classifies artefacts and shows the process of change in 'material culture', the adoption of different metals (first bronze, then iron), various types of funerary practice (cremation or burial) or changes in the style of history's durable rubbish, the bits of pottery. Surveys on the ground and from the air may show something of an area's pattern of settlement, which can sometimes be arranged in phases and studied for its changes. Surveys of its places of settlement, whether villages or bigger cities, can show something about their changes too: one settlement replaces another, and sometimes there are signs of destruction or burning which may help to explain the process.

Dumb archaeology, therefore, is most likely to bear on a literary text when the text refers to a distinct phase of settlement on a particular site or when the text describes changes in material culture or the nature of a particular object or building at a particular time. The Old Testament contains central texts of this type, of which the most famous are the texts about the Israelite entry into Canaan after the Exodus. It is here, not in views about Abraham's origin, that archaeology's dumb evidence can be brought significantly into play.

The latter half of the book of Numbers and the whole of the book of Joshua describe the Israelites' entry into Canaan. The text describes a series of memorable conquests: Heshbon, city of Sihon king of the Amorites, was taken and occupied by the Israelites (Numbers 21:25); Dibon is implied to have suffered a similar fate (Numbers 21:30 and

32:3); Joshua made the walls of Jericho tumble (Joshua 6:20), whereupon the Israelites slaughtered every man, woman and child except the household of Rahab, a friendly harlot; the people and city of Ai came to the same wretched end (Joshua 8:28); the people of Gibeon artfully saved their skins (Joshua 9:26); Lachish was 'put to the edge of the sword, and all the souls that were therein' (Joshua 10:32); Dabir was similarly treated, and it was all extremely pious: Joshua 'destroyed all that breathed, as the Lord God of Israel commanded' (10:40). Hazor was then taken, slaughtered and burned, together with the cities of its allied kings. These conquests culminate in a great score-card of violence (Joshua 12) which takes the Israelites on a pious slaughter far and wide.

The victories are said to have been total, but only Hazor explicitly is said to have been burned. It was probably a later reader who inserted 11:13, to explain why burning was not mentioned everywhere: 'cities that stood on mounds' were left unburned. The original author had probably assumed it everywhere as part of the general slaughter. With or without burning, there was absolute desolation, and archaeologists ought to be able to find signs of it.

During the past fifty years, they have excavated mounds which are identified with these conquered cities. Some of the identifications are certain, others are highly probable, and perhaps only Dabir is low as a possibility in the list. The results have attracted much less publicity than the first reports from Ur or Ebla, perhaps because they have grown cumulatively, perhaps because they cast serious doubt on the claims of the Bible to be straightforward history at this point.

When should this point be dated? Here, we need texts to give us a fixed sequence, but we do not yet have the right texts for the job. At 1 Kings 6:1 we are told that 480 years had passed between the Exodus and the fourth year of King Solomon. The date is schematic (twelve generations of forty years), and, as we have seen, it balances the Israelites' length of time in Egypt (430 years at Exodus 12:40). If we took it literally, it would put the exploits of Joshua back at *c*. 1420–1400 BC: it is not, however, a correct figure. Without it, the only fixed point is an inscribed text from Egypt which celebrates events under the Pharaoh Merneptah. It refers to a plundering of Canaan, a defeat of Askelon, a capture of Gezer and the annihilation of Yaro'am, a town which lay just to the south of Lake Galilee. Then come the vital words: 'Israel is laid waste and his seed is not.' Merneptah's reign belongs in the late thirteenth century BC (*c.* 1224–1214 BC, on the likeliest dating). By *c.* 1220, therefore (the text belongs in his fifth year), Israel certainly existed in Canaan: any Israelite conquest or Exodus must have belonged at an earlier date. The Pharaoh's text is still the earliest known reference to Israel in our surviving evidence, and it uses the hieroglyphic sign for a people, not a place. It also uses a distinctive gender: place-names in Egyptian texts are feminine, but Israel, here, is masculine. Careful readers of Israel's laws and early stories will not wish to quarrel with the Pharaoh's sexist decision.

Before *c.* 1225 BC, therefore, perhaps as much as two centuries before, we need to look for evidence of burning and desolation at sites in the Promised Land. Here two major interruptions confront archaeologists: one is the change from the middle to late Bronze Age and the other from the late Bronze Age to the early Iron Age. The former involved the destruction of several walled settlements, among which were Jericho, Hazor and Gibeon. These signs have sometimes tempted partisans of Joshua, but they face insuperable problems. There is no knowing whether these various destructions were the work of invaders, let alone the same invaders (or Israelites). There is also an acute problem of dating. In Palestine the change from middle to late Bronze Age coincides with the conspicuous presence of a particular type of pottery (Cypriote Bichrome Ware) in the relevant levels of a site. This pottery dates back to the sixteenth century BC (one way of dating it rests firmly on textual evidence which has been found at Alalakh, a nearby site in Syria). The change from middle to late Bronze Age is therefore earlier than any date for Joshua which is implied by the biblical narrative, not just in its schematic numbering of time. We would need to assume that a century or more had fallen out of its narrative's sequence if we link Joshua with events *c.* 1500 BC. A rearguard action is still continuing, but attempts to connect Joshua with this bit of archaeology create many more problems than they solve.

These attempts have only re-entered the arena because the other age of change poses such uncomfortable problems. At site after site, the cities and walls which Joshua is said to have stormed are faced by firm negatives. In the 1930s re-examination of the site at Jericho appeared to suggest 'clear traces of a tremendous fire', a collapsed inner circle of walling and a destruction of the city around 1400 BC. Others promptly downdated the event to 1200 BC, but they were too trusting. On further inspection, the wall receded a thousand years, to a point (*c.* 2350 BC) which was very far from the reach of Joshua. The top of Jericho's mound might have been more relevant, but it had slipped away with the passage of time: even so, it left none of the evidence of a great wall or city which ought, then, to have survived among the debris lower down the slope or at the foot of the site. When dug and redug, Jericho has offered no more to biblicists than a few of its older tombs which were found to have been reused *c.* 1400–1300 BC; one little building, datable *c.* 1320 BC, was found beside the mound, but it contained only a jug, a small clay oven and a few bits of pottery, leaving the excavators to remark that it might be 'part of the kitchen of a Canaanite woman who may have dropped the juglet beside the oven and fled at the sound of Joshua's men'. There may have been a fair-sized village at Jericho by *c.* 1320 BC, but there was nothing like a city or an impregnable wall. After 1300 the place was not settled at all: on the usual dating of the Exodus and Conquest (*c.* 1250–1230 BC), the Israelites would not even have needed to blow a trumpet to take the site by storm.

At Ai, a first excavation up to 1935 was repeated up to 1972, but neither did anything to help Joshua's credit. The excavators found an early town which was destroyed in about 2350 BC. Thereafter, there was not a trace of settlement on the site, nothing whatsoever to frustrate the invading Israelites, let alone to cause them to try a second time and reduce a city to a heap of stones and blood. On either dating for Joshua, a settlement at Ai simply did not exist. During the eleventh century BC a few farmers did start a small village on the site, but their efforts are too late and too paltry to fit the biblical story. Attempts to deny that the excavated site (et-Tell) is indeed the site of Ai have met with no success.

At Gibeon, the Bible tells a remarkable tale. 'Gibeon was a great city, as one of the royal cities, and because it was greater than Ai, and all the men thereof were mighty' (Joshua 10:2). When five kings attacked it because it had befriended Joshua, Joshua and the Lord 'slew them with a great slaughter at Gibeon', while the sun 'stood still' upon Gibeon to lengthen the day of vengeance. The site of Gibeon has been identified beyond all doubt, but when it was first excavated, the archaeologists concluded that no settlement whatsoever had existed in the late Bronze

Age, the preferred dating for Joshua's arrival. Later the pattern altered, but only very slightly. A few pieces of pottery from the period were found in seven tombs, but these seven were older tombs, reused since their origin in the middle Bronze Age; they were a tiny part of a large and old cemetery, the rest of which was not reused and which numbered fifty-five tombs in all. Whoever reused these seven tombs had hardly made a major mark on the site. The visitors might belong 'to temporary camps in the vicinity, but there can be no doubt,' their excavator concluded, 'on the basis of the best evidence available that there was no city of any importance at the time of Joshua.'

At Hazor, seat of King Jabin, the Israelites 'smote all the souls that were therein with the edge of the sword, utterly destroying them: there was not any left to breathe: and he [Joshua] burnt Hazor with fire' (Joshua 11:10). Here archaeology seemed at first to be more suggestive. At the end of the late Bronze Age, the site was indeed ravaged. The big lower city was abandoned and the upper city was left uninhabited until some simple, temporary settlement began later. The key to dating this destruction lies in pottery of Mycenaean Greek type which was found in the relevant level on the site. The sequences of this widely known pottery continue to be meticulously studied, and we have hard evidence of its association with named and dated objects from the reigns of Egyptian Pharaohs. When Hazor was first excavated, the pottery was placed *c.* 1230 BC, making Joshua a possibility. However, the dating was mistaken, and specialists in Mycenaean Greece have continued to argue it downwards to *c.* 1200–1190 BC. That date is too late for any Israelite arrival; Pharaoh Merneptah knew 'Israel' by *c.* 1220.

Until quite recently, biblical optimists also had hopes of Lachish. 'The Lord delivered Lachish into the hand of Israel, which took it on the second day, and smote it with the edge of the sword' (Joshua 10:32). The site was certainly ruined at the end of the late Bronze Age, but after years of archaeological argument, a fortunate find in 1973 dated the ruin conclusively to a point in or just after the reign of the Egyptian Pharaoh Rameses III (*c.* 1194–1163). Once again, the ruin is too late for Israel's arrival, according to Merneptah. The same problems recur at several other sites in Palestine which are named in the books of Joshua and Judges: either they show no signs of walled, urban settlement at the preferred date for Joshua or they show no signs of a single wave of common destruction.

The last resort is to challenge the archaeology. Perhaps more digging would find new evidence; perhaps the digging has been in the wrong place; perhaps 'site-shift is the obvious answer'. These evasions are not convincing: too many sites imply too complex a story, and it is highly unlikely that most of the place-names are wrongly identified or that controlled samples through each of the various levels on a site have missed settlements of the scale and strength which the Bible presupposes. It is better not to contest the evidence but to accept that it is helping us to read the Bible correctly. The book of Joshua tells a powerful tale of conquest, supported by a God who showed no respect for most of the Holy Land's existing inhabitants. Even now, the tale has not lost its power, but it is not history and it never was.

Here, archaeology pleasantly supports historical criticism. Most of the battles over site-slippage and middle Bronze Age datings have been waged in the interests of an unsubtle view of the biblical text. The book of Joshua which our Bibles translate and archaeologists defend is based on the late Masoretic Hebrew text. Not only do we have an earlier Greek translation which omits and includes some subtly different phrases, but there is a fragmentary Hebrew text of Joshua, found among the Dead Sea scrolls, which is still unpublished and which is said to overlap exactly with neither our Greek nor the Masoretic Hebrew. Plainly, there were early versions of the book, and the Masoretic version behind our Bibles is not the only authority.

We have also seen that the book was the late composition of the unknown Deuteronomist, who had an eye at this point for just-so stories and was in no sense a primary source. The relationship between this sort of text and any ancient object is likely to be more subtle than most archaeologists assume. At 5:2 the Lord tells Joshua to 'make thee sharp knives and circumcise again the people of Israel'. The Hebrew, but not the Greek, text adds 'a second time': the Israelite children had dodged the operation, the author, or a later reader, explains for us, during all the years of wandering in the wilderness. Mass male agony was inflicted by order of Joshua; the people stayed in camp until they were healed; the scene of the surgery was named Gilgal: the meaning of the place-name was explained by this great occasion of male mutilation, a story which it helped to inspire. However, it did also attach to evidence, as we can see if we look at the Greek text of the end of the book, which is longer than the Hebrew's. When Joshua died, the Greek tells us, the very flint knives which had done the deed were buried in his grave at Timnath-serah and remained there 'unto this day'. Here, archaeology is helpful: 'the discovery in 1870 of Stone Age artefacts at Timnath-serah, the burial-place of Moses's successor, gives us a clue to the origins of this tale'. Flint tools, it seems, from the Stone Age past had continued to turn up near Joshua's legendary grave. They amazed their discoverers, who came up with a theory: what else could this primitive cutlery be if not the very knives with which Joshua had turned his male contemporaries into proper Jews? Like modern archaeologists, some of the Israelites had found stone objects on a hillside and had reasoned from dumb evidence to a biblical story. Their thinking was worthy of Woolley himself, but our archaeology, centuries later, has allowed us to see how their just-so story arose. It does not prove the Bible, but it helps us to understand it; it also supports a detail which only the Greek translation gives us, suggesting that here it does indeed go back to an early Hebrew version of the text.

Having made this negative point, archaeology now suggests something positive, although it cannot be explained finally. While the costs of digging a single major site were rising ever higher, the validity of the exercise began to be questioned. Why should one or two cities be studied in isolation, ignoring the network of settlements which once covered their surrounding territory? Since 1960 excavation has given way to field surveys which amass the evidence for small settlements, so far as they can be traced by teams of field-workers who note debris on or near the surface of the soil. The method is not new in the Near East. It was brilliantly applied across the Jordan in the 1930s, while awareness of the relation between city and territory goes back to the 1890s and once again to Flinders Petrie, who applied it skilfully in Egypt.

Surveys are very slow work, but certain areas in ancient Israelite history have now been surveyed thoroughly enough for a change in the pattern of their settlement to be evident. In later chapters of Joshua (16–17) and in Judges 1:27 ff. we have details of the lands which were allotted to the tribes of Manasseh and Ephraim, and occupied by them: surveys here have found very little sign of scattered rural settlements before the early Iron Age begins *c.* 1180–1150 BC. Then, quite suddenly, over a hundred such settlements turn up in the landscape: furthermore, they are settlements of a distinctive type. They are unwalled; their houses form an outer ring, or enclosure, round the site; their houses tend to be stone-built, using stone pillars in a space of three or four rooms. Their inhabitants grew crops and also kept livestock which could be sheltered in the centre of some of their villages, protected by the houses' 'corral'. Whatever their origin, these villages show an important change in the region's pattern of residence which must have been relevant to Israelite history in this period.

Is it the missing evidence of the Israelites' own arrival with Joshua? Unfortunately, it is not. Dated after 1200 BC, it is certainly too late for masculine Israel's first appearance in history (Merneptah's victory text). Might it, however, relate to a second phase? When these settlements were first discovered, many archaeologists argued that particular features proved an Israelite presence: they could be identified by a particular type of collared storage jar and the practical habit of digging water cisterns and plastering their interiors to allow them to store water. They introduced a new house plan of up to four rooms, not a two up, two down, but four on the ground floor in a rectangular design. They also tended to use pillars in the interior. The new practical Israelites, with their jars, plastering and house plan, moved in on Canaan (it seemed) and started a new village life.

Their trail no longer seems so conspicuous. At this period, Israelites were only one pressure group among the Philistines and many others: the Promised Land contained a mosaic of peoples, Hivites, Peruzzites and so forth, whom the Bible rehearses for us, then leaves us to forget. The jars, plastering and house plans might be theirs too. Surveys of regions across the Jordan are beginning to turn up similar evidence to the surveys in Israel, although Israelites after the Exodus are not said to have settled them decisively. Once again, what had seemed uniquely Israelite turns out to be something which was merely found first: Israel had been more intently studied and explored, throwing it into unnatural isolation. The settlements of its early Iron Age are part of a bigger pattern which is too broad for any one people.

Until we can tell the debris of an Israelite from the debris of a non-Israelite, we can only note that this new evidence of settlement fits rather well with patterns implied in the book of Judges: Ephraim and Manasseh appear to be settled first; Canaanites seem to persist in the latter much more than the former; in Ephraim, the new settlers have left a distinctive material culture and appear to centre on Shiloh. From those areas, the pattern gradually moves south into the open areas of Judah. At present, it is attractive to guess that the Egyptians' influence in Canaan diminished *c*. 1170–1150 BC. The Philistines gained in power in the wake of them; other peoples (perhaps primarily the Israelites) settled the new villages, although at many places these settlements were not long lasting. Few of them survived beyond 1050–1000 BC or grew into walled towns in the succeeding age of David and Solomon.

This evidence is consistent with Judges 1, but it does not prove it: its dumb objects do not come stamped with an Israelite trademark. It does, however, revise our ideas of the age of settlement. By proving a negative point, it disarms Joshua and turns his bloodstained stories peacefully out to grass; it may even cool down their impact on biblical readers, although it has emerged too late for several would-be Joshuas (Oliver Cromwell, above all, who took Joshua as his model in his lethal campaign against Ireland's Catholics). The evidence implies, but does not prove, a longer period of co-existence between the future villagers and the culture of Canaan in the late Bronze Age (during late thirteenth century BC). Then, there followed a period of new settlement; perhaps the Israelites had previously been semi-nomadic. If so, there was not so much a conquest as an infiltration, perhaps by various tribes who had co-existed with the town culture before settling into four-roomed houses of their own. Meanwhile, none of the major phases of destruction at an early Canaanite site can be confidently ascribed to Israel or her warring Yahweh.

The identities or causes of these various destructions are not known from their dumb evidence; perhaps the Canaanite cities fought and destroyed each other. We certainly cannot take fighting entirely out of early Israelite history (the blood-curdling Song of Deborah is evidence enough of it in Judges 5), but archaeology alone cannot confirm it. Nor are we in a position to erect a better political story in place of the Bible's own. We cannot justify the latest of these myths, that Canaan was torn apart by social revolution and one small group of migrants fled south in Egypt; then, they returned to rally their oppressed brethren and preach 'liberation theology' in the Promised Land: the returning groups then gave them an 'Israelite' identity among their former Canaanite kinsmen.

This myth ignores the biblical narrative entirely. These new theories are no more proven, or suggested, by archaeology than are any of the sackings, burnings and grand circumcisions by Joshua. Archaeology can disprove a myth of settlement, but it cannot support an entirely new myth against an old one.

15
Fifth Gospels

I

After the great questions of Exodus and Conquest, biblical archaeology does not lose momentum. Dozens of sites, objects, levels in a mound and bits of pottery have been mobilized to put scripture in context or support what the Bible says. The skill and energy of these excavations are admirable, with the ever-present possibility of the find of a new text which will change our understanding. With the help of such archaeology, the biblical story has begun to find more of a context, but for the purposes of its truth, context matters less than direct contact. Here, progress is more arguable.

From the age of David to the later episodes of the main biblical narrative (*c.* 398 BC), archaeology within Palestine has confirmed a handful of biblical verses. When 1 Kings 16:23–4 tells us that Omri, king of Israel, reigned first at Tirzah, then at Samaria, we can match this statement exactly to the archaeology of the two sites: Tirzah was deserted, whereas Samaria started to flourish with the same surviving type of pottery, which then developed further at Samaria (but not at Tirzah). At 2 Kings 20:20 and 2 Chronicles 32 King Hezekiah is said to have made a pool and a channel, and brought water into Jerusalem (probably *c.* 710–701 BC). Archaeologists have found the Siloam Tunnel cut into the rock beneath the ancient city. At Lachish, they have found a siege ramp which was almost certainly built by Sennacherib during his siege in 701 BC; in Jerusalem they have evidence of the sack of the city by the Babylonians in 587 BC, especially on the eastern ridge of Ophel. But the historical evidence for Sennacherib's and Nebuchadnezzar's campaigns was never in doubt.

What is less obvious at first reading is that we have almost nothing else which overlaps with biblical narrative: one change of palace, a tunnel and two sieges are not exactly the living heart of biblical truth. The reason, of course, is that there is hardly likely to be a significant overlap between the evidence of a complicated narrative and dumb objects found on sites which are extremely hard to date. Pitfalls continue to multiply. Until very recently, bits of ivory-carving from Samaria used to be described as 'Ahab's ivories', and the ground plan of a temple in the city of Arad used to be compared with the plan of Solomon's Temple in Jerusalem, to which it was believed to be a near contemporary. The Arad shrine was said to illustrate the biblical text on Solomon's building in 1 Kings 6–7 (although its details fitted uneasily), and the bits of ivory, a popular book illustration, were cited for 1 Kings 22:39. However, the ivories have now descended from Ahab to the later eighth century (when Amos 6:4 knows of ivory beds in the north), and the Arad temple has been downdated drastically, to long after Solomon. This downdating is a constant threat because the dating of objects and levels in Palestine *c.* 1100–700 BC is more than usually precarious. So much depends on the changing sequence of pottery styles, with a major dispute over the pottery from the earliest level at Samaria. Does it date to Omri's move to this site *c.* 880 BC? It so, it throws out one line of chronology by fifty years. Or do we save the chronologies by assuming that the site of Samaria was not a virgin site when Omri bought it (although the Bible does not say so)?

None the less, sites and place-names have their own immediacy, the effect of a 'fifth Gospel': it is fun to stand once again on the fortified site of Beersheba, visit ancient Jericho or call on the Philistines at Askelon, Ashdod and (probably) Ekron. It is very much harder to picture the scene. From these sites, the view is often impressive, but excavations in Jerusalem have had to centre on sections of disputed walling, while the remains of biblical cities might suggest to a casual visitor from Greece or Egypt the words which an eminent classical scholar bestowed on the findings at Troy: 'a network of unworthy lodgings spreads to right and left ... gloomy little bungalows, thin-walled, partly walled, barely furnished ... an offence to the eye and an injury to pride'.

What, then, of the fabled reign of Solomon, where the Bible tells us such a story of buildings and horses, women, wisdom and song?

Archaeologists cannot recapture song and wisdom, and even the royal team of seven hundred wives, princesses, and three hundred concubines has eluded excavation, short of some undiscovered harem or a mass grave. Archaeology would be particularly precious here because of our uncertainty about whether the 'book of the acts of Solomon' was indeed a royal primary source and about how much of the biblical narrative goes back to its authority. There is also a question of Solomon's prestige and setting: was there really a fabulous realm of gold and exotic trade, from Ophir to Sheba and north Syria, or is the archaeology significantly against it?

Solomonic building does have some visible support: at Megiddo, Hazor and Gezer there have been shrewd arguments for identifying particular gateways with the age of Solomon, and although the gateways' style is no longer unique to Solomon's period or kingdom, the arguments still hold (1 Kings 9:15–27 connects building at precisely these three sites with Solomon's use of forced labour; unfortunately, archaeology cannot tell us about the workmen's status). In Jerusalem the south-east edge of Solomon's Temple platform has been cleverly inferred among the later walling on the site; at Megiddo the search for Solomonic building turned into something wider.

In the 1930s long buildings at Megiddo were identified with Solomon's time and explained by his biblical interests. 'The archaeologists' astonishment,' Werner Keller assures us, 'grew with every new structure that came to light.' Near the end of ten years' slow digging on the site, its two archaeologists believed that they had unearthed nothing less than Solomon's stables. 'Guy counted single stalls for at least 450 chariots and sheds for 150 chariots.' Neither the date nor the purpose survived for very long. The buildings were soon downdated to the century after Solomon: the very existence of purpose-built royal stables was dismissed as 'anachronistic'; there was even less belief that the excavators had found the horses' mangers. However, earlier kings in the Near East, from Egypt to Assyria, certainly did have special stables; we know of them from texts. One of the buildings is now thought to stand above an earlier one from the time of Solomon. If the breeds of horse were as small in Solomon's age as horse-skeletons suggest that they were elsewhere in Asia, horse-experts are still able to accommodate at Megiddo at least ten loose boxes round a central court with a cistern for water;

there is a cobbled floor for healthy hoofs and holes for the horses' halters. Even the mangers are back in favour, shallow mangers, admittedly, but not of an impossible size or depth for an Iron Age horse.

Mangers are not exactly a major issue in the biblical narrative except in the Bethlehem story. What, though, of Solomon's fabled riches? In 1974 the archaeologist James Pritchard posed the dilemma: the so-called cities of Megiddo, Gezer and Hazor, and Jerusalem itself were in reality 'more like villages. Megiddo's area is reckoned at about thirteen acres; Gezer's at about twenty-seven; Hazor's at about thirty. Within were relatively small public buildings and poorly constructed dwellings with clay floors. The objects reveal a material culture which, even by the standards of the ancient Near East, could not be judged sophisticated or luxurious ... The "magnificence" of the age of Solomon is parochial and decidedly lacklustre, but the first book of Kings implies exactly the opposite.'

An archaeologist is claiming too much for his subject here: excavators cannot hope for a full recovery of precious or perishable goods from a site. Solomon is said to have acquired large quantities of gold, to have started joint ventures at sea with King Hiram of Tyre, to have made silver as common in Jerusalem as stones and to have dealt in horses, ivory, apes and peacocks. These luxuries' chances of survival are extremely slim, not least because fine metals would be looted or melted down: further north, in Asia Minor, the kingdoms of Croesus or Midas have also left no stronger evidence of their famous gold. We can argue, rather, about the sources of these goods, the pattern of trade and the objects' destination.

According to 1 Kings 9:26, Solomon built a fleet on the Red Sea at Ezion-geber; King Hiram sent Tyrian seamen to help it, and together they brought masses of gold 'from Ophir'. In the 1950s a remarkable potsherd was found at Tell Qasile in what is now a suburb of Tel Aviv. Without its inscription it would have meant nothing, but it said, '[G] old [of] Ophir. To Beth-Horon – 30 sh[ekels]' (the thirty was written in the Phoenician style, which was used also in Tyre and Sidon). The date of the text is uncertain, but it is probably at least two centuries later than Solomon: gold, it proves, did eventually come from Ophir (*c.* 725 BC) and was traded as far as the sea coast of Palestine.

Where, then, was Ezion-geber? Archaeologists are probably right to

site it on 'Coral Island' just south of Aqabah in the Red Sea, where
Egypt's Pharaohs had probably once had a port: Ophir, then, might
be modern Somalia across the Red Sea in Africa. A joint venture from
this port to the African gold mines would not be implausible. What,
though, did the sailors export in exchange? In the Bible, King Solomon
has no mines himself, but archaeologists have kindly supplied them for
him. Their first strike, just north of Aqabah, turned Solomon into the
'great copper-king' and Ezion-geber into the 'Pittsburgh of Palestine'; it
then emerged that the site, Tell al-Kheleifeh, had nothing to do with
copper mines and was not worked seriously until long after Solomon's
death. The second strike, in the Timna Valley north of Aqabah, found
deposits of copper, mining camps and evidence of their use in biblical
times until *c.* 1150 BC. Radiocarbon dating implies that work continued
at the site from the tenth to the seventh centuries BC, but its margin of
error is wide and the evidence extremely thin.

In the Bible, Solomon's only copper comes from the north and is a
legacy from his father, David: nothing connects his gold with the copper
trade except moderns' concern to find his exports and our fondness for
the legend of Solomon's mines. His fleet, perhaps, raided Ophir and
business might have been one-sided: profiteering off long-distance trading in metals, spices and rare goods does have a long later history on the
routes from Red Sea ports into Syria and the north. In the tenth century
BC, moreover, camel transport began to develop beside the slower,
more limited donkey: perhaps Solomon was more of a raider and a
caravan organizer than an exporter of industrial slag. At 1 Kings 10: 27–
8 we may even see the other end of his dealing and peddling: the Greek
and Hebrew texts of the verses vary, but none the less they throw
unique light on biblical horse-dealing. Solomon's horse-traders are said
to buy horses in Kue and chariots and horses in Egypt. The price is
given in shekels (a high price but not without ancient parallels) and the
'kings of the Hittites and the Aramaeans' also acquire horses 'by sea' (in
Greek) or 'through them' (in Hebrew). Kue (in the Greek text) is the
region of Cilicia, round Tarsus and southern Asia Minor; it was famous
for horses (one Greek tradition places the mythical winged horse Pegasus
there), and in the age of Solomon it had its own rulers and contacts with
Phoenicia. Both texts of the verses in 1 Kings specify Egypt, whose
chariots were famous, but perhaps we should read Musri instead, an

even greater centre of horse-breeding in central Asia Minor (ancient Cappadocia). It may be that this trade in horses is vividly and accurately remembered here: Solomon's dealers, perhaps, swapped rare metals for chariots in Egypt and southern Asia and then sold chariots on to the Asian and Syrian kinglets because they had artfully bought more stock in the south than they needed themselves. A chariot trade would make political and geographical sense in the later tenth century and would suit the idea of Solomon as a dealer (even a car-dealer), not miner and producer.

In 1 Kings 10:14 ff. Solomon's gold comes to a climax in the five hundred shields of gold which he is said to have put in his palace, the 'House of the Forest of Lebanon'. He spattered gold all over his throne; he drank only from gold vessels (silver, by then, was too common), and he smothered Yahweh's Temple and its inner sanctuary with gold and gold chains; if he had had running water for his bath, no doubt he would have had golden bath-taps. None of this extravagance has survived for archaeologists, but it is not so curious beside the temple culture of neighbouring kingdoms. The earlier Pharaohs in Egypt are known to have dedicated tons of gold in their temples: at Karnak, Tutmosis III's Temple of the Sacred Boat is believed to have been sheeted with gold, fixed to the slits which survive in its stone pillars. Nearer Solomon's time, the precise records of the Assyrian kings detail some remarkable hauls of gold which were brought back by the ton from temples which they sacked: the figures are minutely detailed, and the early versions may go back to scribes who accompanied the campaign. In one case the texts and carved reliefs describe how the Assyrian king Sargon sacked a temple on his borders which was decorated with gold shields. The story of Solomon's shield-work is at least not fantastic. We risk underestimating the huge weight of gold and silver which was immobilized by ancient kingdoms and given dutifully to the gods, those constant brakes on inflation and the money supply. In Egypt and Assyria we should think not of stone and timber cathedrals on the Western Christian model but rather of the golden temples of the Hindus and Buddhists which are visible nowadays from India to Thailand. From Assyrian records and carved reliefs, we know of at least one temple on Assyria's borders which had been decorated with gold shields. King Sargon looted them, along with another ton of the precious metal.

A golden temple is not incredible, but comparisons cannot make it true in Jerusalem. Here, contemporary texts have been cleverly brought into play. After Solomon's death, Shishak, Pharaoh of Egypt, is said to have approached Jerusalem and taken away these shields of gold from Solomon's son (perhaps they were used to bribe the Pharaoh to go north). The traditional view is that Shishak is the Egyptian Pharaoh Sheshonk; it is, I believe, correct. It can be shown that Sheshonk's son, Osorkon, claimed to have made enormous dedications of gold and precious metals in Egypt's temples although the figures have been calculated from one detailed text carved during his reign. The gold alone totals 205 tons, vastly more than the gifts of his father or his successors. Was he dedicating his father's loot from Jerusalem? Did Solomon's gold plating end up, perhaps, in the temples of Egypt?

Texts, monuments and clever inferences appear to support what the Bible tells us, but the result is very fragile. Sheshonk's campaign towards Jerusalem may not have fallen near the end of his reign; we only know that it fell before his twenty-first year on the throne. It is odd, then, that he dedicated little, according to his texts, while his son later claimed to dedicate much more. The figures for Osorkon's gifts may be hugely exaggerated by the one text which gives them (royal publicity often lies, then and now). Even if they are roughly correct, Osorkon may have had a gold strike of his own, like Solomon, perhaps, in nearby Ophir. There are too many uncertainties for anything in scripture to be confirmed by the results.

The problem recurs neatly in the second episode of Jewish temple-building. In the mid sixth century BC, Cyrus, King of Persia, is said to have issued an edict in favour of the Jews, their return to Jerusalem and their rebuilding of the ruined Temple's site. The book of Ezra (6:3 ff.) purports to give the wording of King Cyrus's decree, including the measurements and materials which the new Temple was to use: it was to have 'three rows of great stones, and a row of new timber'. The passage has recently impressed an archaeologist of the old Persian palaces, who acutely observed that buildings on three courses of stone are characteristic of Persian palace architecture in the reign of Cyrus. The style can be seen in Cyrus's palaces at Pasargadae, far away in the Persian heartland, but the 'use of such costly, multicourse stone socles was abandoned in Iran after Cyrus's reign'. Does archaeology, therefore, prove that the decree is authentic? Again, it need only imply that it was composed with accurate knowledge, but a simpler comparison lies nearer to hand. Solomon's original Temple stood on 'three rows of hewed stone' (1 Kings 6:36) and conformed to the exact measurements which Cyrus's decree is said to have specified (1 Kings 6:2 with Ezra 6:3). Either the Jews who petitioned Cyrus had asked for just such a Temple, and his scribes (as elsewhere) copied the wording of their request into the royal permission, or the details are a literary echo of the old Temple, which was known to an author who invented all or part of Cyrus's edict. The idea that Persian archaeology could prove its truth is extremely appealing, but it is not cogent. The letter's historicity is best approached through comparable texts, not dumb objects, and it is from those sources that its authenticity has best been argued.

'Solomon loved many foreign women . . .': six nationalities at least, which Number One was later said to have forbidden to Israelite husbands: valiantly, he 'clung to these in love'. It is fun to imagine their talk of trade routes from Tarsus to Somalia, the horse-dealing and chariot-touting, the monkey-catching and gold-bagging (1 Kings 10: 14–22). Archaeology can help our imaginations here, by not proving a negative and by allowing a pattern of speculation. For in Solomon's case, the argument from silence works differently from its relevance to the sites of Joshua's conquests. Its silence does not disprove the tales of a trade in luxuries: gold and luxuries (unlike ruined cities) are highly unlikely to survive. It does not disprove the possible splendour of this era, for the silence which surrounds Solomon is one which extends across most of his Near Eastern neighbours too. In the 'dark age' of the tenth century, it does not refute what the Bible implies. The numbers no doubt are inflated; the tales of wisdom are only stories, but behind the verses on buildings, trade routes and objects in the Temple, there may well be a primary royal book of acts, worked over, perhaps, in a secondary book which the Deuteronomist then used for the reign.

Can archaeology, finally, say something about the religious practices and beliefs which went on inside the buildings? Pre-historians, who have no texts, are only too aware of the problems: when is a room or building a shrine, not a store-room or private house? Statues, precious objects, animal bones and so forth may suggest religious worship, but they are very far from proving it. The Bible, again, provides texts, but it is not immediately clear what dumb archaeology can add to them.

One approach has been through the imagery of the Old Testament's poems, proverbs and psalms. Their range of metaphors and similes suggests that the authors may have pictured God and his relationship to man and the world in terms which owed their precision to art and pictorial imagery. As Israel has produced no art of its own, sources for the psalmists' imagination have been sought in the sculpture and imagery of neighbouring Near Eastern religions. Just as Canaanite texts from the site of Ras Shamra have helped us to understand a word or turn of phrase in Hebrew psalms, might not the art of Mesopotamia, Egypt or Syria explain images which the biblical poets had in mind?

The dangers in these attempts are greater than the merits. Without an accompanying text or inscription, we can only be partially sure what a scene in a Near Eastern sculpture is supposed to mean. Even the inscriptions themselves may be misleading: in Near Eastern art, there is no neat overlap between the name of a divinity which is inscribed on an object and the scene which the inscription accompanies. The name may refer to one god, while the scene illustrates another, a problem which studies of Greek or Roman art seldom have to confront. There is a risk, too, that vague similarities between text and object will be pressed too hard, as if everything in the book of Psalms which concerns God's relation to trees or plants derives from some common Near Eastern tradition in art of vegetation-gods or trees of life. The Hebrew psalms stand too far apart from Egyptian hymns and religious imagery for such derivations, and it is doubtful whether comparisons between their texts and art have yet shown influential contact between the two.

To archaeologists, practice may be more relevant than symbolism, but there are even greater problems in knowing from a dumb object what practice must have been. When we find pig bones on Israelite sites, or the skeleton of a pig at Hazor *c.* 730, or figurines of nude women, bulls or horses in some quantity in Jerusalem, what exactly are we to infer from the discoveries? The eating of pigs was prohibited in the dietary laws of the book of Leviticus, and so the Jewish excavator of Hazor judged the find of the Hazor pig skeleton to be due to a conquering Assyrian: it was the meal of a Gentile 'celebrating his triumph' when taking the city, because it 'could not' be the food of a Jew. The food laws, however, were written down much later, and in the eighth century we cannot know that they applied to everyone in theory, let alone in practice. As for the figurines, are they statuettes of goddesses, storm gods or sun gods: without inscriptions, how can we know how people regarded and used them?

Further south, in the Negev, recent finds of dumb and written evidence have widened our sense of the possible. At Kuntillet Ajrud, excavations have recently revealed a rectangular building of stone with towers at each corner and a courtyard in its centre. It is not obviously a shrine or temple, but on fragments of its wall plaster, visitors invoked their gods and wrote graffiti during the building's active life in the ninth and eighth centuries BC. Some of the Hebrew inscriptions invoke a blessing by Yahweh and by his *asherah*, the wooden image of a goddess, a female consort for Yahweh himself. At first sight the idea that Yahweh was worshipped with a female partner by Hebrew-speakers seems unexpected, but evidence of similar worship had already been known from an inscribed pillar of the later eighth century (found in a cave near Lachish) and from papyri which were left by a colony of Jews at Elephantine in Egypt during the fifth century BC. Scripture, after all, contains a long polemic from its Deuteronomist against the worship of wooden *asherim* from the reign of Ahab onwards: Yahweh alone, we have argued, was the view of only one group in Israel. If Solomon could partner hundreds of foreign women, why could not God have a female beside him from time to time? In this out of the way site, archaeology confirms that Yahweh, too, had a mistress. But to see it, we needed a written inscription: by itself, the building and its dumb objects would never have proved this enticing point.

II

When we come to the New Testament, we are within reach of primary sources. The texts tell us about people in a historical setting which we know independently: we do not face the problem of a Solomon or Joshua, and we need not wonder whether Jesus of Nazareth lived and could have visited the places which the Gospels name. However, the texts interpret actions in terms of other scriptural texts, and theology is central to what we now read. Non-textual archaeology has little relevance to the truth of such writings, except to confirm that small details of their setting are at least plausible. Most of what it illustrates should never be seriously doubted, anyway.

None the less, bits of palace walling, town plans, coins and tombs continue to be assembled to illustrate the Christian books. It is implied that 'exciting new finds' deepen our knowledge, not just of stonework, house plans or material culture (where they actually might deepen it), but also of Jesus and the Gospels' meaning or their place within Judaism. Just as texts from Babylonian and Canaanite sources have given Hebrew Scripture the neighbours and contexts which they lacked in the nineteenth century, so the New Testament has gained not proof but neighbours and contexts from continuing discoveries.

Many of them bear on the disputed role of Greek language and culture in Galilee, Judaea and Jerusalem between the conquests of Alexander and the age of Jesus. Here, finds of dumb objects and sites do sometimes tell us about the cultural preferences of particular groups in at least one part of their lives. At King Herod's court the Greek style was prominent, and the archaeology of its main sites has enlarged our grasp of it: there were race-courses, theatres and at the winter palace in Jericho we even have the flowerpots of Herod's sunken gardens, made locally but in a style which matches flowerpots from Pompeii and the Greek world. Objects can imply social customs, but the acid test of Hellenization is language, and texts continue to feed disputes on the role of Greek in Jesus's Jerusalem, if not in Galilee itself. For Greek inscriptions are continuing to be found on stone bone-boxes, or ossuaries, in which people were buried in Jerusalem and its neighbourhood: they date from *c.* 100 BC to AD 130 (in 1988, 228 such inscriptions were known, 71 of which have writing in the Greek script only and a further 16 in Greek as one of two scripts).

Should we, therefore, change the usual view that Greek was not widely current in the age of Jesus among Jews born in Judaea? The case for such a change has been vigorously argued, but the evidence before 70 is still remarkably thin for most places, outside a likely proportion of the upper classes. The ossuary burials with Greek inscriptions included visitors, pilgrims and migrants to Jerusalem from known Greek cities abroad: they do not prove very much. The most interesting find before 70 is the tomb of the Goliath family in Jericho. Sited near the hippodrome, it contained 32 inscriptions (17 in Greek) and the burials of 28 people with Greek names who were connected to this prominent family linked with the Jerusalem priesthood. However, Greek style in a family of this high status does not prove anything about Greek's wider social role. On the crucial question of language, we must certainly allow for Greek-speaking visitors in Jerusalem, for Greek-speakers in high society and for people who could use a few words to service their needs. However, nothing yet found makes it likely that Jesus himself spoke fluent Greek or that any such accomplishment was widespread among most Jews who knew him locally.

Apart from questions of language and culture, there is ample scope for fifth Gospels and their sense of place. In Jerusalem the siting of the Antonia fortress so close to the Temple helps us to picture Acts' scene of Paul's arrest. It is fun, too, to follow him on his missionary journeys, to stand in the ruins of Philippi or in the theatre at Ephesus (although it has been rebuilt since his visit). In the Holy Land we can even track down John the Baptist in the newly excavated fortress of Machaira, where he was kept in prison until Herodias asked for his head during dinner. (At Mark 6:21–4, Herodias's daughter goes out from the male guests to find her mother: the excavators found two adjoining rooms and on the strength of this episode, identified them as dining-rooms and suggested that their find showed that guests at the birthday dinner had indeed been segregated into different chambers for the two sexes.)

'Master, see what manner of stones and what buildings are here!' the disciples are made to say to Jesus at Mark 13:1, when they see the newly built Temple in Herod's Jerusalem: we can share a little of their wonder when we look at the masonry of Herod's Temple-platform and the huge stone, recently reckoned to be 415 tons in weight, which stood in its west retaining wall. However, many of the Gospel's landmarks are not known for certain. Despite local guides and traditions, we still cannot be sure of the site of Emmaus or Gethsemane or the house of Caiaphas, the high priest in Jerusalem. The palace in which Pilate interviewed Jesus was almost certainly the former palace of Herod which the Roman prefects had taken over. If so, it lay to the west of the Temple and has an important implication: we know the route which has been followed by pilgrims since the Middle Ages as the Stations of the Cross, but they have been going in exactly the opposite direction to the one which Jesus is most likely to have followed.

Fifth Gospels illustrate where they do not mislead: objects and places can also bear on our view of the four Gospels' nature. They do not prove them, but we need to remember Joshua: they might disprove some of the details, challenging a claim that they rested on primary knowledge. These details would not be main elements of Christian belief (they are beyond all excavation), but they could well be details of place and setting. Thanks to the recent reconstruction of an ancient trireme, we understand at last what the author of Acts meant when the crew of the ship 'undergirded' it in the storm off Crete (Acts 27:17). They must have run a double length of rope from stern to bow inside the hull and drawn it tight to stop the boat from bending under the force of the waves: the manoeuvre was the right one to make, suiting the view that the author was himself an eyewitness on board the ship.

The fourth Gospel is the most specific and has the most to lose, but its grasp of detail is continuing to be shown to be plausible. At John 5:2–9 we read of the pool in Jerusalem by the sheep market which had five porticoes and was probably called Bethesda: excavators in the 1950s found a double pool in the right place and explained the oddity of the five porticoes (there were two pools with two porticoes on either side and one in the space between them). At John 19:13 Pilate sits on his judgement seat at the place called 'the Pavement' (or *Gabbatha* in Aramaic): if his 'praetorium' is identified with Herod's more westerly palace, this detail fits well. Gabbatha refers to the height of this commanding site, 'up there' in the west, and the Pavement is a cobbled area outside the palaces. Thousands of tourists inspect it in the wrong place, at the 'lithostrotos', which has the marks of a game traditionally ascribed to the Roman soldiers. This piece of paving is certainly later than Jesus's lifetime; like the so-called Ecce Homo arch, it probably dates to the reign of Hadrian in the 130s. The soldiers who are said to have cast lots for Jesus's clothing were not playing dice on this bit of stonework.

The fourth Gospel, therefore, has bits of local knowledge which go back to a source before the destruction of the Temple in 70. They do not prove that the source was the author himself: a few correct details of setting can also occur in historical novels. It is, however, important that they do not disprove this view. At a more positive level, they can illustrate a detail but cannot confirm a story. What, then, of the central story, the matter of Jesus's death?

If death has its Gospel, it also has its archaeology. Tombs, burials and

246

grave goods are deposits which make up the majority of all dumb evidence, and in Judaea, between the mid first century BC and AD 70 we can follow an intriguing change of custom. People's bones were laid in solid stone ossuaries, or bone-boxes: either the flesh was stripped off or the bodies were dug from their first graves when the flesh had rotted naturally (in dry climates it would sometimes have to be stripped). Probably, the aim was to commemorate the dead more permanently: bone-boxes were inscribed with the names of the dead people inside. Perhaps, too, there was a new concern for purity, although belief in a personal resurrection is a more arguable motive: why, then, disturb people's bones from their first grave? During Jesus's lifetime, these bone-boxes were certainly one type of burial, although not an unduly cheap one: they may, however, be an older practice than their survivals in stone suggest. A bone-box of wood has been found in a tomb at Nahal David in the Judaean desert: wood, perhaps, was the earlier material, in use before 100 BC, though elsewhere it has rotted and we no longer find its evidence.

The first Christians will have known these bone-boxes, but they did not use them for their Lord. A burial and a conventional tomb of stone are described at the climax of Christian scripture, and there was no known plan to rehouse Jesus's bones later: has archaeology coincided with any of the biblical details? Modern Jerusalem offers its visitors two possible sites for Jesus's tomb. The first, the Holy Sepulchre, was uncovered by excavations for the Emperor Constantine and his advisers in the year 326; they were guided by a tradition that the tomb lay under a subsequent temple of Venus. This temple had been built in the reign of Hadrian, when the city was given a new pagan identity after the final Jewish war in 135. The siting of the pagan temple need not have been a deliberate blow to Christianity, but there might still be truth in the later Christian tradition: a site under a pagan temple was perhaps an odd site to invent for Jesus's grave on no oral evidence at all. When Constantine's excavators dug it, they found ancient tombs and, near the presumed tomb of Christ, a big rock projecting high above the surrounding strata. This rock has now been refound by recent archaeology: the area had plainly been used for the quarrying of white stone, and the projecting rock has even been identified with the very site of Golgotha. It does seem that Christians in the fourth century made this same identification;

there were also claims that the very stone which had rolled away at the Resurrection had been found among the excavators' debris. There is no certainty that they were right: from an early date they were wrong about Bethlehem, and we do not know if Constantine's excavators chose the right tomb among several found on the site. Golgotha, therefore, has not been convincingly located: the Church of the Holy Sepulchre goes back to Christian tradition but not necessarily to historical truth.

What we do know is that the rival tomb, the Garden Tomb, has not a shred of historical evidence in its favour, despite the relative peace and charm of the modern site. It was picked out by Claude Conder, one of the first archaeologists to work for the Palestine Exploration Fund, and achieved renown when its claims were supported by General Gordon on a visit to Jerusalem in 1885. Gordon convinced himself, for a series of tortuous biblical reasons, that the site of Golgotha ('the place of a skull') lay on the nearby cliff, outside Jerusalem's wall. More recently, guides have begun to show visitors how the shape of a skull is visible in this cliff-face beside caves with names like Jeremiah's Grotto. Even since 1885 the cliff-face has changed its shape: the skull pattern is the result of modern quarrying and was not the reason for Gordon's decision. The Garden Tomb is not near the known site of Calvary, it has no early Christian connection with cult, and its association with Jesus is a pleasant fiction of the past hundred years.

The sites, therefore, still elude us, but what about the manner of Jesus's death? Here, archaeology re-entered the argument in 1968, when a remarkable set of bones was found at Giv'at Ha-Mavtar in north-east Jerusalem. They had been laid in an ossuary in a grave which dated to the first century, before the year 70. One group of bones belonged to a little child; among the others were found the bones of a man whose feet were still held by a huge nail and a strip of wood: he had been cruci-fied.

In some haste the bones were subjected to medical study. An inscription on the ossuary named the man as Yehohanon, and doctors reconstituted him as twenty-four to twenty-eight years old and about five foot seven in height. In the excitement of the moment, the shape of his bones suggested a very handsome face and a body of 'gracious, almost feminine allure'. His shin bones were believed to have been smashed by a hard blow, perhaps from a hammer (the Jews suggest the same method to Pilate in John 19:31); scratch marks were reported on the lower armbones, suggesting a nail in that position (the fourth Gospel implies a different treatment for Jesus: the disciples and doubting Thomas look at Jesus's hands, not his lower arms). Both feet were thought to have been pierced by the same nail: sketches, therefore, showed Yehohanon on his cross with his legs bent, arms and feet nailed, and a little seat under his buttocks (this seat, or sedile, is attested in several Roman descriptions of crucifixion).

Bone study is an important addition to the archaeologist's armoury, but on every significant point these medical studies have now been refuted by a second examination. The shins were not broken; the arm bones were not pierced; the feet were not fixed by the same long nail; Yehohanon was probably crucified without a seat and with one foot on either side of his cross's central post (the puzzling inscription on his ossuary has been translated as the man 'who died with his knees apart'). Above all, none of the fixed points of his death overlaps with any of the Gospels' (his arms were probably tied to his cross). The discovery of his bones did lead to a useful reiteration of the role of suffocation in deaths by crucifixion (this role is known from the evidence of Nazi and Japanese war camps where crucifixion was recently practised). The weight of the body pulls down on the arms, while the pinning of the feet prevents the victim from moving; as the legs weaken, such a strain is put on the torso that the lungs are torn short of air. In the fourth Gospel Jesus was found to have died sooner than the thieves on either side of him: probably, he had suffocated. The thieves' legs were then smashed to hasten their death before Passover: the idea was that they would lose their support and suffocate more quickly.

So far from illustrating the Gospel, this find of bones has merely shown us that techniques of crucifixion varied. It is central to the Gospels' stories that Jesus's hands were pierced, whereas Yehohanon's were probably not. According to the fourth Gospel, Jesus's body was then taken from the Cross by Joseph of Arimathea; Nicodemus brought an enormous quantity of spices (myrrh and aloes: the aloes have now been explained as the True Aloe, native to the Yemen, and traded or transplanted widely from its home; the aloes of Psalm 45:8 were eaglewood). The body was bound in linen cloths and another cloth, or napkin (John 20:7), was put on Jesus's head. Spices were used too, and the binding and spicing were in keeping with the burial customs of the Jews. The point is not stated, but this preparation must have included the customary washing.

It is here that the texts on Jesus's death come into contact with its most notorious relic. Since the 1350s remarkable claims have been made for a big piece of woven cloth, over fourteen feet long, now known as the 'Shroud of Turin': it has continued to appeal to enthusiasts as a burial robe of the period, perhaps the very burial robe of Christ.

In 1988 small pieces of the cloth were subjected to radiocarbon dating and were confirmed to be of a fourteenth-century date. Radiocarbon tests can err by a margin of a century or so but not by as much as a millennium and a half: the Turin Shroud's fate is widely agreed to have been settled by science. The remarkable fact is that 'science' was not intellectually necessary: historically, the evidence was already overwhelming that the Shroud was a late fake. When it was first produced, at Lirey near Troyes, the bishop of Troyes inquired carefully into its origins and reported that he could find no evidence of its antiquity. Instead, he had even found (so he said) the very person who admitted faking it. Two other inquiries by Christian authorities supported him during the first thirty years of the Shroud's historical life. The 'Shroud' is a medieval fake, and the image on its cloth, which has faded with time, was artfully imprinted by a craftsman who used chemical compounds available to him. His technique has been simulated since, and traces of his pigments have been found on threads of the cloth. There were no ancient blood stains, no 'scorching', no mysteries about a 'negative image'. The Shroud shows the image of a naked body, crowned, possibly with thorns: the hands are folded across its private parts, a pose which has no ancient parallel but which agrees with images of the crucified Jesus in fashion among painters of the fourteenth century. The cloth first appeared in the church which the family of de Charny founded at Lirey and inaugurated in 1356. At the time there was a lively contemporary market for cloths, burial shrouds and so-called veronicas ('true images') which could be connected with Jesus Christ; an unknown forger produced the boldest of them all in central France.

So far from confirming the details of the Gospels, the curious fact was that the Shroud contradicted them. Its supporters, often unwittingly, argued that it was evidence of Jesus's death, but, in doing so, they refuted the only evidence for that event, the Gospels, especially the fourth (which appealed firmly to an eyewitness at the Cross, John 19:35). The 'disciple whom he loved', arguably its author, had entered the tomb and seen linen cloths and the napkin for Jesus's head: he had not seen a single shroud of herringbone weave dating from the 1350s. Jesus's body, he tells us, had been washed and spiced with Nicodemus's gifts, but the image of the Shroud, bloodstained and untended, presupposed that John 19:39 ff. did not know what it was talking about. Attempts to connect it with an earlier cloth or kerchief which had become famous at the Syrian Christian town of Edessa were also historically false. The Edessa Cloth was said to have been imprinted with an image of Jesus's face, but our historical evidence requires that its origins go back no further than the 560s. It was a cloth, not a shroud, and its discovery at Edessa has been plausibly linked to a partisan battle between the city's Christian factions in the mid sixth century A D. Reports that pollen in the weave of the Shroud belonged with plants specific to the areas round Jerusalem and Edessa were also misplaced. They contradicted botanical knowledge and were not adequately checked or presented.

The Shroud itself remains a fascinating relic of the high Middle Ages, but it is not irrelevant to my unauthorized version. Historical criticism has always been able to refute the claims made for the Shroud, but first its supporters tried to obscure them by science (the negative image, the pollen count and so forth) and were then refuted by scientific technique (the radiocarbon dating). Science, not history, has widely been felt to be the decisive factor: 'Why doth this generation seek after a sign?' (Mark 8:12). It had a sign already, not in a fake bit of cloth but in the text of the Gospel whose author alone appealed to a witness and implied, in my view, that he himself was the primary source. Here, the fifth Gospel of places and dumb objects returns to the fourth Gospel of written evidence, the move which we must follow next.

16
Concurrent Heathens

The dumb evidence of digging and travelling relates obliquely, if at all, to the truth of the biblical narrative. Written evidence is much more powerful: it allows us to compare dates and events, and to set one story against another. It may survive as a narrative, perhaps as a piece of history which has come down to us after many centuries of copying in a manuscript of the text of a Greek or Latin author; it may be an oriental text which survives on its original papyrus or clay-cylinder. It may not even be a narrative at all: it may be a datable inscription which survives on a stone or a coin or a seal stone; it may be a contemporary letter on a piece of papyrus or an everyday contract, perhaps with its date and witnesses, on its original clay tablet. By pure chance, its contents may bear directly on some fixed point in a biblical book, a date, perhaps, or a person's whereabouts. These golden moments, when chance survivals overlap with a story which is known to us but not to them, are extremely exciting.

The same standards apply to heathen evidence as to biblical. Is it based on a primary source? Is it biased, ambiguous or simply wrong? Relevant evidence is extremely scarce; what, if anything, does silence imply? In the early parts of the Bible's story, biblical persons have yet to be identified correctly in any external source. There have been many attempts, and some confident claims, but as yet there is no good reason to identify Moses or Joseph with any known person or period in ancient Egyptian records; Abraham's actions are not better understood through the clay tablets of the ancient kingdom of Mari; even the curious list of warring kings in that recurrent battleground, Genesis 14, is no longer agreed to name historical rulers. Amraphel is not King Hammurapi of Babylon; Tudal is not one of the Hittites' kings called Tudkhaliash. These old theories are linguistically unproven and chronologically inconsistent; nothing found in the tablets at Ebla has any bearing on their truth.

The names of places are better attested, but we still do not know if biblical stories happened at the places in question. In Egypt, the Israelites are said to have laboured as builders at two of the Pharaoh's cities, Pithom and Raamses (Exodus 1:11): the places are attested in Egyptian evidence, and we know that one of the Pharaohs who built there was Rameses II (*c.* 1300–1280 BC, early in his reign). We do not know that the biblical story belongs in his era or that the mention of these cities is historical: they could also occur in a historical novel.

It is not only that we have no evidence outside the Bible for Moses, Joshua or any of the judges: we have none for David or Solomon either. The first external contact falls in the later tenth century BC. At 1 Kings 11:40, during the reign of Solomon, the future king of Israel, Jeroboam, flees 'into Egypt, under Shishak king of Egypt'; at 1 Kings 14:25–6 the Pharaoh Shishak then invades Judah in the 'fifth year of king Rehoboam [Solomon's son]'. Traditionally, Shishak is identified with the Pharaoh Sheshonk I, who is known from Egyptian monuments: we still have a piece of the large inscribed stone which he set up to mark his conquests at Megiddo, way to the north-west of Jerusalem. Back in Egypt, we also have an illustrated text of his campaign which was carved for a royal monument at Karnak in his twenty-first year. The text is not complete, but it proves that Sheshonk invaded Palestine and claimed to have conquered more than a hundred and fifty places. There are, however, problems. Jerusalem is not mentioned, and many of the hundred and fifty places lie in the north in areas near to Jeroboam, the Pharaoh's former refugee. Pharaohs were as fickle as anyone, and perhaps we should infer that Shishak set out against Jeroboam's enemies in Judah, was bribed with the promise of gold from the Temple's treasures, and changed his plans, going north against Jeroboam instead.

Shishak's activities are not of undue religious significance, but they do bring the Bible and heathen evidence together, suggesting that here they overlap. For biblical dating they are extremely important: Sheshonk's campaign brings the biblical story into contact with Egyptian chronology, a cornerstone of modern dates for the books of Kings. It is not, however, a solid rock: we do not know when Sheshonk began to reign; the margin of guesswork is more than twenty years; the date of the Palestine adventure is known only to belong at some point before his twenty-first year: the precise overlap with the 'fifth year' of Rehoboam at 1 Kings 14:25 may be a biblical error. We have the impression of contact with confirmed fact, but no way of being exact about the contact.

In 1967 Shishak was joined by an extraordinary find which might seem, at first, to have confirmed a vastly older biblical person. During excavations of a building at Deir Alla in the Jordan Valley, it was recognized that fragments of white wall plaster carried inscribed texts. The inscriptions are not complete, and although their language is broadly intelligible, its exact classification is still disputed; perhaps it is Ammonite. After skilful restoration, they were found to name 'Balaam' and 'Balaam, son of Beor'. Balaam, son of Beor is well known from Numbers 22–4, where he is asked to curse the invading Israelites. He is warned by God that the Israelite people are blessed, but despite this he goes up to the heathen king Balak; an angel threatens his donkey ('Balaam's ass') and blocks his path; he ends by blessing the Israelites instead of cursing them. Balaam is a visionary prophet, a heathen, but in touch with God. In the new inscriptions from Deir Alla, he emerges in a similar role, announcing his vision of a council of heathen gods.

This remarkable find might seem to extend the Bible's historicity back into the thirteenth century BC, the age of Balaam, perhaps even earlier. It is not, however, so simple. The inscription was not written before the mid eighth century BC and possibly as late as 600 BC; the book of Numbers derives the story of Balaam from the Elohist's northern version which was probably written in the ninth/eighth centuries BC; the inscription proves only that Balaam's fame was long-lived in the old region of the Ammonites (perhaps in the Bible, too, Balaam came from Ammon; the Greek text of Numbers implies that he did; he may have been the same Balaam as the one who is later said to have been killed by the Israelites at Joshua 13:22). This one text is much too late to prove that Balaam really existed: like the Greeks' Orpheus, he may have been a mythical seer. It merely proves that his name was famous outside Israel at least five hundred years after his biblical context. Perhaps this fame is the reason why the northern version told this story about him. Old Balaam was a revered authority: how better to glorify Israel than to put her praises into the mouth of her enemies' admired prophet?

Shishak's invasion, therefore, is still the first event in the Bible to which external primary evidence relates. It is not the last. Across the next nine centuries, from Ahab in Kings to the events in Acts, I will now use a sample of heathen evidence from five of the Bible's surrounding literate cultures: Assyrian, Babylonian, Persian, Roman and Greek. This sample could be multiplied but it is chosen to bear on the biblical narrative at its strongest points, where primary sources (I have argued) lie behind it. With its help, we can strike up a dialogue with the Deuteronomist and his use of the 'book of the chronicles of the kings of Israel and of Judah'; we can try to place Nehemiah and Ezra, and we can test the narrative of the Gospels and the testimony of two special Christian sources, the beloved disciple and a frequent companion of Paul. 'If on the Book itself we cast our view,' wrote the poet John Dryden, 'Concurrent heathens prove the story true.' The relationship is not so monotonous: it can set our imaginations free.

II

Based in Mesopotamia, the kings of Assyria were to harass and dominate much of the Near East in the ninth to seventh centuries BC. They destroyed the northern kingdom of Israel in *c.* 722 BC, failed to capture Jerusalem in 701 and overlapped with many famous events in 2 Kings and the books of the prophets. Finally, their own capital at Nineveh was sacked in 612 BC, an event which is bloodily approved by the Bible's brief book of Nahum but omitted by the author of Kings, because it was beyond the horizon of his history.

The inscribed monuments of an Assyrian king give the earliest fixed date and reference to any Israelite known in the Bible: 853 BC, long after the era of David, let alone of Moses, Joshua and Gideon. In that year (probably the summer of 853) the Assyrian king Shalmaneser III fought against an alliance of twelve Near Eastern kings whose armies are listed in some detail in his royal inscriptions. Among them was King Ahab of Israel, who brought no fewer than ten thousand infantry and two thousand chariots, the mainstay of the allied forces. Characteristically, the Assyrian inscriptions claim a victory, but Shalmaneser fought against similar allied armies in three more years, 849, 848 and 845, until he finally broke through to Damascus in 842/1. The great battle in which Ahab fought had kept Assyrian troops out of the Near East for twelve years, and he and his Israelite successors may well have joined the allies in their next three confrontations.

In the Bible we know of Ahab through the work of the Deuter-onomist, who was writing the books of Kings *c.* 550–540 BC. He had various sources before him, stories which involved prophets, especially Elijah and Elisha, and the 'book of the chronicles of the kings of Israel'. These chronicles, we have inferred, were primary sources: they described Ahab's 'ivory palace and all the cities which he built' and 'all that Ahab did'. They must have included his glorious role at the huge battle of Qarqar: D, however, omitted the entire exploit.

He omitted it because it did not suit his case: Ahab, he believed, was wicked: he married Jezebel, a foreign queen from Sidon; he worshipped Baal; he set up wooden idols shaped like trees and he had no truck with Yahweh alone: 'Ahab did more to provoke the Lord to anger than all the kings of Israel who were before him.' The trouble was that the chronicles, the primary source, had nothing which reflected badly on Ahab the promiscuous worshipper. He had built fine cities and palaces, and won a spectacular victory against Assyria, followed, perhaps, by others in the next eight years. If Assyria had won, Yahweh's prospects would have been very much poorer: D suppressed these triumphs and built up another Ahab from other evidence.

Here, the most promising sources were the stories of the prophets: tales of Elijah's extremism show up the wickedness of Ahab and his court. Yet there is another difficulty. These stories say that Elijah prophesies to Ahab that dogs will lick his blood because he has seized Naboth's vineyard; Ahab has allowed its poor owner to be put to death, behaving almost as wickedly as the glorious David. When and where will this blood-licking happen? It is most awkward. According to the book of the chronicles, Ahab dies and sleeps 'with his fathers', a phrase which is usually understood to mean a peaceful end.

Ever resourceful, D found his answer in a second batch of prophetic stories which were attached to unspecified wars with Syria. In the Greek translation of Kings, Ahab is not an unqualified monster. When he hears that Jezebel has killed off Naboth, he mourns the poor man before taking control of his vineyard. He weeps, as if to repent. In return, God agrees to withhold his punishment and visit it on his son (compare our 1 Kings 21:29). Ahab, however, goes wrong again. In a war against Syria, the captives have all been vowed to God, but Ahab commits the ultimate sin of showing humanity: he spares the king of Syria. An unnamed prophet then announces that Ahab must die for this act of mercy, and in the next war with Syria, Ahab is duly slain. Someone draws 'a bow at a venture'; Ahab is hit and bleeds freely into his chariot; he dies from the bow wound, and when the chariot is washed 'by the pool of Samaria', the dogs at last have a lick. At 1 Kings 22:38 we are even told that harlots join in the fun: they wash themselves in Ahab's blood.

In our Hebrew Bible, Ahab does not weep over Naboth; the scene with the vineyard divides up two Syrian wars, so that the neater (to my mind, older) order of the Greek text is lost. None the less, we can see through D's art. In one story, Elijah is said to have foretold blood-licking, but the king dies peacefully: to save Elijah's credit, God is said to have forgiven Ahab and stored up vengeance for his sons. In another story, an unnamed prophet curses an unspecified king of Israel during a war with an unspecified Syrian king (several Ben Hadads ruled successively in Syria). In a second war, this unnamed prophet is proved right: the king is shot by a clever bowman. Why not identify this unnamed king with Ahab, spin out the arrow wound, allow the blood to drip on the chariot and let the dogs (with a few harlots) prove Elijah's original prophecy right? In the history of Israel, D believed that, throughout, the prophets had foretold the truth.

The Assyrian inscriptions imply something less drastic. In 853 Ahab and Syria fought on the same side against Assyria, and presumably they stood together against the Assyrians' failed attempts of the next eight years. It is highly unlikely that they fought three wars between themselves in this brief period: Assyria was their common enemy. It is also unlikely that Ahab was fighting to recover Ramoth-gilead: in 2 Kings 8–10 Israel still owns the place, losing it only after 842/1 under another king. For these and other reasons, I share the old critical view that D took two later wars with Syria and promoted them up to the time of Ahab. His sources specified a Ben Hadad as king in Syria (there were several) and an unnamed king of Israel and Judah. It is even possible that the wars in fact belonged where he later retold them: if so (this is uncertain), the victory occurred under King Jehoash at 2 Kings 13:17–24 (who won it at Aphek, the site of 'Ahab's' victory) and the defeat under King Joram at 2 Kings 8:25 (Joram, too, was helped by a king of Judah: like Ahab he fought at Ramoth-gilead and like Ahab he was seriously wounded by an archer while fighting).

The Bible's account of King Ahab is extremely bad history, both in what it includes and what it leaves out. It is, however, a marvellous narrative: Ahab's greatest victory is suppressed, the dogs get their dinner, Elijah is proved right, and even the harlots have a field-day. The history, however, does not improve: it continues at the same low level in the matter of Ahab's successors.

In 2 Kings we read of a revolt by Moab after Ahab's death: Ahab's son, the new king Ahaziah, clashes with an intransigent Elijah; Ahaziah dies; Elijah is translated to heaven; King Joram rules in Israel and King Jehoshaphat rules in Judah; together, they mount a campaign against rebellious Moab which involves Elisha the prophet and ends unsatisfactorily. There are some memorable scenes on the way: Elisha calls for a minstrel to play, 'and the hand of the Lord came upon him' (a rare insight into the connection of music and inspiration); the Moabites mistake red pools of water in the middle distance for their enemies' blood and presume that Israel, Edom and Judah have massacred each other (a reasonable guess); the king of Moab takes his eldest son and 'offers him for a burnt offering' on his city wall. However, we happen to have an amazing survival, a non-biblical text about this war from the other side.

In summer 1868 a large thick stone of black basalt was shown to the missionary Frederick Klein by one tribe of the Bedouin in Jordan. It was inscribed with ancient lettering, news of which led to a keen rivalry among the Western powers with consulates in the country. Eventually, a rival faction of the local Bedouin cracked the stone into fragments (they believed that it must contain treasure or some precious holy power) and dispersed them among their followers. Only a rough copy of the text had already been taken and the fragments were never reassembled in full. About two thirds of the stone came into French hands and eventually reached the Louvre in 1873: by then it was known to bear a text of the deeds of King Mesha of Moab, the person who is mentioned in 2 Kings 3 as the payer of a hundred thousand lambs and a hundred thousand rams as tribute to King Ahab and who leads the revolt against Israelite rule. Reports of this extraordinary find and its decipherment fascinated the European press in 1870; they presented it as proof that the biblical story was historical.

According to the text on the black stone, Moab had been subjected by King Omri (Ahab's father) and by Omri's son for half his reign, making forty years of subjection in all. In 2 Kings, however, Moab revolts only after Ahab's death, and on no possible chronology do Omri and half his son's reign add up to forty years. We should probably not give any weight to such a round number as forty or believe that the Moabites' counting of time or kinship was exact (Omri's son should probably be his grandson, one of Ahab's children). None the less, the text involves the biblical story in some very serious problems.

According to the Bible, Elisha foresaw a crushing victory, and the Israelites turned back only when King Mesha burnt his eldest son: there was 'great indignation against Israel', and so they departed. According to King Mesha, the Moabites scored a series of victories and captured Israelite army-bases in precisely named places which the Bible ignores. Perhaps these victories were part of Mesha's counter-attack, but his text mentions no defeats and no human sacrifice, and these bases may well be the first successes of a highly successful rebellion. Even if we allow for Moabite bias, these are not the actions of a nearly defeated king. Elisha's prophecy, passed down in a story, is thus challenged by the enemy's own record of success: reports of war have long been a minefield in the Near East. So have their results. According to the Bible, 'indignation against Israel' caused their army to withdraw, although it is not quite clear whether this was the wrath of Yahweh or, more probably, that of the Moabites' own god, Chemosh. According to King Mesha, it was the 'anger of Chemosh' which had subjected Moab to Israel in the first place. On both sides ill-tempered gods were thought to be active: Hebrew scriptures are not the only Near Eastern texts to explain history by the anger of a god.

There is another deeper problem: which kings were involved and when? At 2 Kings 3:1 the invasion of Moab is a joint action by Joram of Israel and Jehoshaphat of Judah, but at 2 Kings 1:17 Joram is said to have begun to reign only when Jehoshaphat was dead (the Greek text of Kings agrees). One or other date must be wrong: it may even be that both are mistaken. At 2 Kings 1:1 Moab's revolt is placed under Joram's predecessor, Ahaziah, whose short reign was associated with Elijah, as D knew from prophetic stories. The Moabite war, he also knew, was associated with Elisha. As he believed that Elisha succeeded Elijah, he had to assume that the war began after Ahaziah's reign, not during it (when Jehoshaphat certainly ruled in Judah). The stories of it had survived, perhaps, without naming the kings involved: once again, D may have ascribed a war to the wrong rulers (it occurred under Ahaziah).

At least this error was an attempt at consistency, but others were once again wilful. According to King Mesha, both Omri and Ahab had subjected Moab for many years. The subjection was a very impressive extension of Israelite power into what is now Jordan, where it crushed an old national enemy: the chronicles of these kings must have mentioned it, but once again D left it out. In our scriptures, King Omri is merely the wicked friend of strange gods and false cults who built a new capital at Samaria (the action which causes such serious problems for biblical chronologies based on styles of pottery). In contrast, Assyrian inscriptions regard Omri as a landmark long after his death, perhaps because they had confronted him personally: they describe his successors as of the 'house', or family, of Omri, as if he had indeed had a fame which D obscures.

The evil that men do lives after them, and so does the evil of historians who wish only to see them punished for their sins. In the Bible, Omri's dynasty finally reaped its reward at the hands of usurping Jehu: he killed all Ahab's surviving family (over seventy people) and had Jezebel pitched to her death from a window in one of the most vivid biblical scenes of action and reported speech. 'Who is on my side? who? And there looked out to him two or three eunuchs. And he said, Throw her down' (2 Kings 9:32–3).

Who, then, was the greater sinner? In the Bible, Jehu is best known for driving furiously, but in contemporary Assyrian art and inscriptions, he can be seen from another angle: not driving but grovelling. He is shown crawling abjectly on the ground before the Assyrian king Shalmaneser in a famous Assyrian sculpted relief which is now in the British Museum. The scene is the only known artistic representation of a

Hebrew Old Testament king by a contemporary: its accompanying inscription describes the gifts which Jehu offered with his surrender. Just as scripture says nothing about Ahab's Assyrian involvement, so it omits all reference to Jehu's submission to an international power. Yet the submission must have been a turning-point in international affairs. Until Jehu changed sides, it was presumably with Israel's continuing help that the allied kings kept Assyria at bay. Immediately afterwards, in 842/1, the Assyrians overthrew the old alliance: scripture upholds Jehu as the long-predicted scourge of wicked Omri's dynasty, but in fact he was a miserable turncoat on the international stage. Once again, Assyrian evidence fixes the date for us: 843 for Jehu's surrender, a date which neatly refutes both the Greek and the Hebrew chronologies for the reigns of Ahab and his sons.

From Omri to Jehu, over fifty years, D picked and chose, distorted the timing and imposed his own bias: from Ahab's death to Jehu's glory, his narrative is highly untrustworthy. These errors are all the more telling because he had the royal chronicles of the Kings' reigns, primary sources which could have given him a framework of royal deeds. He also had the Elijah stories, with their tales of crimes as black as the murder of Naboth. Perhaps they exaggerated. Elijah too had his impossible side, and it must have been hard to live with such a prophet, who was always spoiling Jezebel's fun. There may, indeed, be another biblical source for her character. Among the psalms, the forty-fifth is the song for a royal wedding, between a young king and his bride 'in gold of Ophir'. His 'royal sceptre is a sceptre of equity'; he loves righteousness and hates wickedness. As for her, she is 'decked in her chamber with gold-woven robes'. She is a princess whom Tyre will honour: Psalm 45, to be sung 'according to Lilies', may be the old wedding-hymn for Ahab, composed for the righteous king of Israel when he married Jezebel, his royal Phoenician bride. She did, indeed, have distinguished relations: from evidence known to Josephus, we can work out that Dido, queen of Carthage, was Jezebel's great niece. It is fortunate that D never knew Virgil's *Aeneid*. Dido loved the visiting Roman Aeneas, then killed herself when her love was betrayed. Virgil made the story into a poem of the deepest pathos: D would have relished it as one more proof of God's vengeance on Ahab and his house.

III

The books of Kings have been described as 'a monumental achievement simply considered as a factual history of the Jewish kingdoms', but external evidence from Assyria and Moab proves that for the reigns and events of the ninth century this description is quite untrue. As its story advances, however, the players change: Assyrian power was broken in the years down to 612 BC, and the kings in Babylon emerged to contest its legacy. Year by year some of their actions are known from the long series of clay tablets whose texts have recently been recognized as a continuous Babylonian chronicle, from 747 BC to the death of Alexander and beyond. It is not so dishonest as to suppress every Babylonian setback or so short-sighted as to see every event in terms of honours for a god or festival (other Babylonian texts are turned in these directions). It is a secondary text, but its yearly information was probably extracted from primary records which Babylonian astronomers had kept as diaries for their own needs. Its sources, then, are reliable, although it has no critical method.

A statement, then, in this chronicle has a solid standing as fact. Once again, it allows us to enter into dialogue with D. During this period, after the fall of the northern kingdom, his main literary sources were the chronicles of the kings of Judah in the south; he supplemented these with popular knowledge of these great events, about fifty years back in his readers' memories (within the grandfather span). In 1956 a clay tablet which describes events from 605 to 595 BC was discovered in the British Museum and published with other parts of the Babylonian chronicle. It overlaps excitingly with the stories of 2 Kings 23–5, the prelude to the fall of Jerusalem and the beginning of the Exile which played such a part in the history of Hebrew scripture. For the first time Jerusalem's impending ruin could be seen through the writings of Nebuchadnezzar's Babylon.

Unlike the Assyrian records of Ahab, this Babylonian text confirms and amplifies scripture's hints of international politics. At 2 Kings 23:29 'Pharaoh Necho king of Egypt' went up against the king of Assyria to the River Euphrates; King Josiah of Judah (finder of the book of the law in 622) went up to meet him, in order to stop him, and was killed at Megiddo. In the Babylonian chronicle a 'large Egyptian army' did indeed cross the Euphrates in the year 609, and a king of Assyria is mentioned: the death of Josiah belongs, then, in 609; the Egyptian army pressed on eastwards, failed in a siege (the chronicle, again) and returned past Judah a few months later. According to 2 Kings 23:31, Josiah's successor was deposed after a mere three months, again by the Egyptian Pharaoh Necho. This event and its timing fit well with Necho's return journey, which can be inferred from the Babylonian record.

The next great event is the battle of Carchemish, which was fought against the Egyptians by the Babylonian regent Nebuchadnezzar. Jeremiah 46:2 refers to this major Babylonian victory (although it implies that Nebuchadnezzar was already the Babylonian king): the chronicle dates it firmly in summer 605. At the time, the king of Judah was Jehoiakim: at 2 Kings 24:1 he became the servant of Babylon for three years when Nebuchadnezzar 'came up' against him. This surrender fits neatly with the chronicle for 604, a year after the Babylonian victory at Carchemish. In that year we find Nebuchadnezzar receiving 'all the kings of Hattu [Syria] and their heavy tribute' and capturing a city in Syria or Palestine. Jeremiah 36:9 tells how a communal fast was proclaimed throughout Judah in November 604: it fits beautifully as a terrified appeal to God on news of Nebuchadnezzar's march west to the area, at a time when King Jehoiakim had not yet surrendered. During winter 604 surrender followed.

'Three years' at 2 Kings 24 lead on to 601, when the chronicle tells how Nebuchadnezzar marched down against a reinforced Egypt in order to fight 'an open battle in which they smote each other and defeated each other heavily'. The Babylonians returned to lick their wounds for the following year, and it is in this setting of renewed Egyptian success that Jehoiakim, king of Judah, revolted from Babylon. After a year's delay, the Babylonians returned in 599 B C, according to their chronicle, and 'went off to the desert and plundered the possessions, animals and gods of the Arabs', presumably in south and central Syria. 2 Kings 24:2 connects a Babylonian raid with tribal attacks by Aramaeans, Moabites and Ammonites, each of which is easily fitted to the Babylonian chronicle's picture (perhaps it was now that the king of Babylon smote the king of Hazor, as the contemporary Jeremiah predicted, 49:28–33).

Late in the year 598, Jehoiakim, king of Judah, died: his son Jehoiachin succeeded him, and the armies of Babylon once more came against Jerusalem. At 2 Kings 24:10 the Masoretic Hebrew text says that Nebuchadnezzar's servants began the siege of Jerusalem, whereas the Greek translations say it was Nebuchadnezzar himself. Probably, the deputies began it, and Nebuchadnezzar joined later, just as we find in the chronicle, where he 'encamped against the City of Judah', and on a specified day, which we translate as 15/16 March 597, he captured the city and seized the king. He appointed a king of his own choice and, taking heavy tribute, brought it into Babylon. The framework of 2 Kings' narrative fits comfortably. Nebuchadnezzar had probably appointed his own king, Zedekiah, before the city actually fell, and he certainly transported Temple treasures and the ex-king Jehoiachin back to his capital. Separate Babylonian texts survive from Babylon's southern palace which show that Nebuchadnezzar granted rations of oil and food to Jehoiachin 'King of the Judaeans' between 592 and 569, while his five sons also benefited in the care of a Babylonian delegate, a man with what is probably a Jewish name. According to 2 Kings 25:29, in 561 BC the exiled Jehoiachin was eventually honoured by Nebuchadnezzar's son and promoted from prison to eat the king's bread. This type of honour is well-attested at the Babylonian court, although there is no way as yet of confirming this biblical coda in Babylonian evidence.

From 609 to 598 details in the biblical narrative fit well with what the Babylonians' texts imply: on one side, we have the Babylonians' chronicle, and on the other, quite separately, a narrative by D which is based on a chronicle of the kings of Judah. There are, however, two difficulties. According to the Babylonian chronicle, Jerusalem was captured and the king seized in Nebuchadnezzar's seventh year, but 2 Kings 24:12 puts the event in Nebuchadnezzar's eighth year. The city did fall near the end of a Babylonian calendar year, but the dates do not agree: probably, the biblical authors were unclear when Nebuchadnezzar had first ceased being a regent and become a king. The second awkwardness lies in the Bible itself. According to Jeremiah 52:28–30 (possibly, an addition to the contemporary Jeremiah's own work), 3,023 people went into exile after the defeat; according to 2 Kings 24:16, there were 8,000 (7,000 men of might and 1,000 craftsmen), while 2 Kings 24:14 opts for 10,000. Despite endless attempts to square the dates and the numbers, it seems that the book of Kings has muddled the year and exaggerated the exiles. Even where the Bible is supported by outside evidence, the authors are capable of basic error.

After 595 BC surviving fragments of the Babylonian chronicle cease, but we know that Egyptian power revived under a new king, and it is clear, and painfully memorable, from Jeremiah's prophecies that the choice between Egypt and Babylon continued to exercise the Jews under Nebuchadnezzar's client-king in Jerusalem. Fatefully, the king Zedekiah veered to the Egyptians' side and violated the oath by his own god, Yahweh, which the Babylonians had exacted from him. In 587 BC (here too, Jeremiah 52:12 is more likely to be right than 2 Kings 25:8 about the exact year of Nebuchadnezzar's reign) Nebuchadnezzar returned, took the city of Jerusalem and tried and punished the rebel Zedekiah. He had his disobedient subject blinded, and a month after the city's capture ordered the deportation of prominent Jews and the destruction of the city and Temple.

No Babylonian narrative overlaps with these events, but we may have some slight contemporary evidence from recent archaeology. Scattered finds of seals at sites in modern Israel have included several which bear names known in the biblical story: the name on one such seal matches the name of the Jew whom the Babylonians appointed as their official in Judah. We even have seals with the same name as that borne by Jeremiah's own secretary, Baruch, and the royal official, Jerahmeel, who burnt the scroll of warning which Jeremiah sent up to the king. It is very tempting to believe that they are relics of these famous biblical people. It is also tempting to believe that we have evidence of ex-king Jehoiachin in various finds of jar-handles made at sites in Judah. They show that jars were stamped with 'Eliakim, assistant of Jehoiachin'. In the Exile, Jehoiachin was still called king: possibly, these jars came from estates which had been ordered to supply wine to Babylonian troops after 587 BC.

Without the Bible, none of this evidence would give us any idea that Jerusalem had been captured for a second time or that a huge invasion had taken place. Support for it, however, has been sought in a group of twenty-one potsherds inscribed with letters in Hebrew which were found during excavations at Lachish in the 1930s. Only three of them had legible texts of any length, and their placing is uncertain. A subordinate seems to be writing to his superior: both of their names are based on Yahweh, a figure whom the subordinate also mentions. The whereabouts of the sender and recipient are uncertain, but the letters do refer to fire-signals, troops moving south from Palestine to Egypt and princes who are working against the king; there may also be a reference to a prophet with a certain Tobiah (the translation is not certain). Some spectacular guesses have connected these texts with the Babylonians' invasion and events in the book of Jeremiah. No such biblical connection has been proved, and as evidence for scripture these letters on potsherds turn out to be useless.

In Jerusalem itself, archaeologists have argued for various signs of the city's destruction in 587, especially along the city's then eastern wall. The siege itself is not in doubt, although the Bible as yet is the one source for it: the problem, again, is the scale of the sequel. According to Jeremiah 52:28–30, 832 people went east into exile in 587, followed five years later by another 745; the Babylonians certainly did not resettle the site with colonists of their own. According to 2 Kings 25:11–12, however, the exiles amounted to the 'rest of the people', apart from the poorest of the land. D, it seems, has exaggerated again, as if the exiles in his own lifetime were the centre of the Jewish nation: 1,577 exiles are not exactly the ending of an entire people. A few of them, but no total number, show up in independent Babylonian evidence: several years later, on a Babylonian tablet, we find a gardener in Babylon who almost certainly has a Jewish name. Some of the exiles, drawn from the better classes of Judah's kingdom, settled down to a life in their captors' flowerbeds, like other prisoners of war since.

While the exiles regretted their lost estates and the ruin of their city and Temple, Babylonian texts remind us of something different: there had been two sides to the argument. Like the Jews, the Babylonian kings fought wars in the company of their god: if they won, it was because their god had assisted them, and the war was therefore both just and pleasing to him. In the Lebanon, Nebuchadnezzar's scribes have left us inscriptions cut into the rocks which refer to his earlier campaigning. Nebuchadnezzar, they said, had sent troops to 'recover the forest of the god Marduk' and his victory 'allowed the people to lie down safely' (like flocks) and not to be 'frightened by anyone'. Like most kings who ruled in Mesopotamia, Nebuchadnezzar wrote of his special relationship with the god for, and with whom, he conquered: 'you fathered me and entrusted me with rule over all peoples ... lead them to love your exalted lordship'. More than most kings, however, he stressed his concern for 'justice' in his inscriptions. Judah, after all, had offered him tribute and then rebelled; the client-king whom he had chosen had sworn oaths of loyalty by his own god Yahweh, but had rapidly perjured himself and turned to the Egyptians. Had King Zedekiah continued to submit, there would have been no siege and no destruction of Jerusalem, no Exile, and perhaps very much less scripture. Justice (as Israel's prophets agreed) was due to anyone who sinned against God.

In the age of Omri and Ahab, heathen evidence exposes gross distortions in the biblical story and alerts us to the scale of its falsehood. In the last years of Judah, it matches small details of the biblical story but helps us to balance its interpretation and pick between its datings. The period was still within oral memory of D's readers, and there was less scope, therefore, for liberty with the facts. Explanation was another matter. In D's view, it was not Nebuchadnezzar or the god Marduk who had stirred up armies against the king of Judah: it was Yahweh who was punishing the king for past religious sins. The last two kings of Judah would have been surprised by this argument: they had taken regnal names which meant 'Yahweh will fulfil his word' and 'righteousness of Yahweh'. D, however, claimed that fulfilment and righteousness had come in 587's ghastly disaster. It was a punishment for the sins of the previous king Manasseh who had set up wooden idols and altars for foreign gods, consulted familiar spirits and wizards, and rivalled the awful 'wickedness' of Ahab (2 Kings 21–24:3).

On either side, in Babylon and Judaea, a righteous god was believed to have caused the events. In Babylon, Marduk was thought to have been punishing a flagrant case of perjury and political betrayal by a Jewish vassal. In Judaea, Yahweh was thought to have taken revenge for the religious sins of a king which were more than fifty years old. Of the two explanations, the Babylonians' was nearer the truth than the Bible's. Both sides justified what happened, but it is the god of the losers, not the victors, who still has historical heirs.

IV

Not much later, in the mid sixth century, the kingdoms of the Near East began to fall to a Persian king and his armies, players of no previous significance in the dramas of oriental history. In 539 BC Babylon fell to

King Cyrus, and the Jews in exile came under Persian rule which was to last for just over two hundred years.

The experience has left a direct impression on biblical narrative and books of prophecy. The first points of contact run from 539 to *c.* 519, the years of the Jews' return from exile and their attempts to rebuild the Temple in Jerusalem. The later chapters of the book of Isaiah are the work of a prophet (not Isaiah) who hailed Cyrus as the Lord's anointed; the book of Ezra purports to quote something of the highest significance, Cyrus's edict, permitting the Jews to go home; it then refers to episodes in their efforts to rebuild. The book of Ezra is the late composition of an author in the fourth century BC who is generally, and in my view rightly, thought to be the Chronicler, author of the books of Chronicles and our book of Nehemiah. Events and persons in this same phase of rebuilding are also known through primary sources, our books of the prophecies of two contemporaries, Haggai and Zechariah.

We then face a gap of at least sixty years until the adventures of the namesakes of two biblical books, Ezra and Nehemiah. With the usual talent of a biblical editor, the Chronicler has muddled his sources and put bits of Nehemiah's story into his book of Ezra (Nehemiah 8 and probably 9; I would add Nehemiah 7:5 to the end of the chapter). One document which belongs in Nehemiah's career has been misplaced in Ezra's (Ezra 4:6–23 which belongs, in my view, with the events of Nehemiah 6). The dating and sequence of the two reformers are still highly disputed: the Chronicler's dates are ambiguous and possibly wrong, and he may well have been wrong to put Ezra first of the two. These muddles have been imposed on a great rarity, Nehemiah's own memoirs, a primary narrative source. There may perhaps be such a memoir behind bits of Ezra too.

The work of these two reformers is highly significant in our understanding of the history of scripture and the law. Both of them come down from the court of King Artaxerxes, either the first or second of the three Persian kings with that name. This royal setting recurs in the late book of Esther, a vivid story of justice and injustice at the court of a King Ahasuerus. The book was composed long after the Persian era (probably *c.* 200–180 BC), but here and there it has realistic details: the name of one incidental Persian (Parsandata, Esther 9:7) has recently been confirmed as a possible name by its discovery on a Persian seal. The book is a fictional story, but its author parades its Persian colour by learned asides and his own literary manner. The book of Daniel also exploited a connection with King Darius, and there is Persian colour in the apocryphal stories of Tobias.

We have no 'Persian version' or chronicle to set beside the Bible's Persian contents, but we do have a fascinating array of evidence both inside and outside the great Persian Empire which continues to grow through new discoveries and to bear on details in the stories.

Private contracts from Babylonia, preserved on clay, show us other Jews under Persian rule; from the Persians' own palaces, we now have many documents which license rations and travel grants for workers and important persons; as yet, we have none of the other royal records which the Persian kings maintained, but we do have some of the royal texts which were issued for public inscription and circulation; in Babylonia we have a few clay cylinders which narrate actions of a few of the kings. We also have the histories which visiting Greeks wrote of Persian affairs, especially the histories of Herodotus, who talked to bilingual contemporaries, travelled as far east as Babylon, and arguably knew one or two Persian official texts in a Greek translation. Inside the empire, we have some original letters and documents which were written to or from Persian governors on behalf of one important prince; they are preserved on papyrus, leather and parchment. We also have invaluable documents from another group of Jews who had their own temple of Yahweh and lived up the Nile at the first Cataract (by modern Assuan) in a Persian garrison in Egypt. Yet another set of letters, which is still unpublished, overlaps with the name of a key enemy of Nehemiah, while a remarkable group of inscribed seals and clay sealings from documents found in Judaea was published only twelve years ago and contains names which sometimes match those in the books of Ezra and Nehemiah: the name of a maidservant (or concubine) of a self-styled high official matches the name of the daughter of the famous Zerubbabel who led the Jews' rebuilding of their Temple. The dating of these seals, however, is disputed, like the dates of Ezra and Nehemiah themselves. We also have a small silver coin whose inscription has recently been read as referring to the name of a priest in the books of Ezra and Nehemiah. It belongs to the fourth century BC, but this new evidence is also not straightforward.

The Persian presence in scripture begins with the praises of Second Isaiah, the unknown prophet whose work has been added on to Isaiah's sayings and who hails Cyrus as the Lord's Anointed, bringer of a new world order. These prophecies were probably composed shortly after Cyrus's conquest of Babylon, not before it, and possibly preceded his decision to favour the Jewish exiles. They catch the hopeful mood of an observer, some of whose language makes an interesting match for phrases known in contemporary Babylonian texts about Cyrus's kingship.

In the book of Ezra we meet something even more remarkable: two quotations, as if from Cyrus's own edict, allowing the Jewish exiles to return from Babylon and to rebuild their Temple in Jerusalem. They are to bring back their sacred vessels and offer lavish sacrifices to their god and pray for the Persian king and his sons. This decision was one of the most momentous in the entire history of Judaism, but to many critics the likelihood that its wording had survived without invention seemed very slim, because the Bible quotes two different versions of it, one in Hebrew at Ezra 1:1 and the other in Aramaic at Ezra 6:3–5. However, the two texts have been brilliantly explained as parts of a historical practice which reinforces their claim to be genuine. The Hebrew is the text of the edict which royal heralds proclaimed widely in the Jews' own language: this oral publication is known elsewhere and naturally occurred in the recipients' own language (compare Esther 3:12). The Aramaic version was a memorandum of the king's decision which was made for his palace records. Like previous oriental rulers, Persian kings kept written records of their rulings, and Aramaic was the standard language which the royal secretaries used between themselves: Persians were illiterate.

The double texts, in two languages, point to a genuine practice which forgers were most unlikely to imitate. In the book of Esther we have fictitious royal edicts, but they are not quoted in this double form. Nor is their language so neatly matched by the language of our other original Persian documents. In the book of Ezra, King Cyrus calls Yahweh the 'God of Heaven', the name which is used by later Persian officials in their letters. He associates his own vast kingdom with Yahweh's favour, just as he associates a deity of Ur with his rule in a contemporary Babylonian text; he returns Yahweh's people and cult objects, just as he returned peoples and gods (presumably statues) to their various former abodes in Babylonia and eastwards over the Tigris. These independent actions are known from the famous text of the Cyrus Cylinder, an inscribed record on clay which was found at Babylon in 1879 and amplified by further discoveries in 1972. The text is neither so unprecedented nor so universal in scope as some of its readers have believed, and it certainly does not prove that Cyrus favoured the Jews. It does, however, fit the theme of the two biblical letters very well. According to the Cylinder, Cyrus favoured some of the displaced gods and worshippers in Babylonia: in just this spirit, the Bible shows him favouring Yahweh and his displaced Jews.

The two languages of the Ezra documents, the two types of their texts, their details and their general content have been given such a comparative setting that it is hard now to reject their essence as a fiction or forgery. Their date and sequence are questions of greater complexity. According to the first verses of the book of Ezra, Cyrus's proclamation occurred in 'the first year of Cyrus, king of Persia', 539/8 BC. It is not clear that this date was given in the surviving text of his edict, and perhaps it should not be allowed too great an authority: a later author might have ascribed the king's deed without any proof to his first year of rule. The sequel is also obscure. King Cyrus sent back Sheshbazzar, a Jew whose name is probably Babylonian, honouring the sun god, but down in Jerusalem it is unclear what progress he made with building the Temple during Cyrus's reign. The Jews' neighbours resented their return, and perhaps, too, there were fellow Jews who needed persuading about Sheshbazzar and his mission. Those Jews who had never been exiled from Judah would not be unduly pleased to see exiles returning, among them, perhaps, those families who had owned most of the land. Perhaps, too, there were Jews who resented the rebuilders for trusting so much in the help of a foreign king.

The book of Ezra jumps confusingly through this interval to the 'second year of the reign of Darius', the next Persian king but one who succeeded Cyrus. Sheshbazzar has vanished, and we now learn of the leadership of one Zerubbabel in Jerusalem and the incitements of 'Haggai the prophet and Zechariah the son of Iddo' which impelled the Jews to set to and build their Temple in earnest. Here, we can turn to primary sources, the books of Haggai and Zechariah themselves. After

Cyrus's death 'in the second year of Darius', the prophet Haggai is told by God to tell Zerubbabel, leader of the Jews in Judaea, that he will shake the heavens and the earth, and honour Zerubbabel as king. Like Sheshbazzar, Zerubbabel is a Jew with a Babylonian name, but he is a very important person: the grandson, no less, of Jehoiachin, king of Judaea, who had been exiled and maintained by Nebuchadnezzar in Babylon. Prophecies of upheaval and a new kingship were most dramatic to this particular person at this moment, but their dating has long been a puzzle. On the usual reckoning, the Babylonians' season of spring is the best-known 'New Year' for a king's reign, but it would date Haggai's prophecy to a time when Darius was firmly established on his throne and predictions of a local royal upheaval would be wildly eccentric.

The puzzle has now been sorted out by applying another system of reckoning. A king's years could also be reckoned from the time of his accession and could be credited with the short reign of a previous usurper. Darius claimed to have defeated just such a predecessor: if we reckon by this system, Haggai's prophecies fit beautifully into October and December 521 BC. At this time we know from the official royal inscription of Darius himself that large areas of the Persians' conquests had been shaken by revolt: in autumn 521 Babylon rebelled for a second time. An Armenian stood forward there as a new King Nebuchadnezzar IV and was only defeated on November 27. Haggai's first messianic prophecy belongs neatly in this context: there was a new king in Babylon, so why not a new king in Judaea? The second prophecy, a mere three weeks later, either assumes that the revolts will continue, or is already aware of another upheaval which was to preoccupy Darius in the next year around Susa itself.

This understanding of Darius's years in the books of the prophets allows a further, suggestive connection. Zerubbabel, the new rebuilder of the Temple, turns out to have reached Jerusalem between 23 July and 21 August 522, a time when Darius was not yet fighting for power and when Persian affairs were being controlled by a previous usurper at court. The Jews, it seems, took shrewd advantage of this interlude in the Persian monarchy to reassert their position and go ahead with their rebuilding. We can understand, better than ever, why hostile neighbours tried to stop the rebuilding in Jerusalem by writing to Darius, and why the Jews then insisted that their action had Cyrus's approval. Darius had not permitted the building himself, but the new Jewish leaders could not justly cite the support of the Persian usurper in whose time they had taken the new initiative. Instead, they cited the precedent of Cyrus.

In October 521 Babylon was in revolt under a new Nebuchadnezzar and Haggai was hailing a new king from Judah's old royal dynasty. His candidate, the royal prince Zerubbabel, was laying the new Temple's foundation, but by late November Babylon's latest Nebuchadnezzar had been captured and impaled. The prophet Haggai continued to speak of God choosing Zerubbabel, overthrowing the thrones of kings and breaking the great king's power, but he was too optimistic. Darius survived unbroken, and by February 520 Zechariah the prophet was announcing a very different vision. He had seen a horseman on a red horse, among myrtle-trees and other horsemen, and learned that they were envoys reporting a different message: 'all the earth sitteth still, and is at rest' (Zechariah 1:11). Peace had replaced the expectations of chaos. Darius had indeed established himself as king, and so far from finding a new David, Jews as far away as Egypt ended up with a copy of King Darius's narrative of his victories over his rivals. It was translated into Aramaic, a version which has recently been reconstructed more fully.

The Bible thus throws a powerful but intermittent light on the crucial years from Cyrus to the early reign of Darius. It is an era for any historian's imagination, but the book of Ezra muddles it through its author's poor arrangement of his few sources. After quoting from Cyrus's edict, the text leaves the years between Cyrus and Darius in obscurity, along with the feats of the first rebuilders; in my view, Ezra 4:5 is its author's mistaken connection and 4:6–23 are misplaced, belonging originally among the sources for Nehemiah. At Ezra 4:24 we return to the late 520s and to details which we can match with external fact. At 5:3 the Persians' 'governor beyond the River' becomes involved in the dispute between the Jewish rebuilders and their neighbours. 'Beyond the River' is the Persian administration's well-attested name for the region west of the River Euphrates (it included Syria, although there are problems in defining its extent at any one time: probably its scope varied under different rulers). The governor, Tattenai, whom the Bible names, can be matched with one Taat[anu] who is independently attested as governor 'beyond the River' in a Babylonian text dated to 502. This overlap seems solid, but it would be even more gratifying if we did not know of a different governor of 'Babylon and beyond the River' who was active in the relevant earlier period of Darius's reign. Perhaps Tattenai was one of his subordinates.

If we stand back from the problems of dating and continuity, the book of Ezra does give us documents from the Persian king and his governors, an impression of very skilled petitioning by the Jews and their neighbours, a scene of Temple building in a Persian province with royal approval, and local resentment of a new group of activists. Comparisons can make events plausible, not certain, but we can compare these themes with a famous letter in Greek which was sent at an unknown date by King Darius to his governor in Asia Minor. It survives in a much later copy inscribed on stone, but is rightly considered authentic. In it, Darius protects the local priests of the Greek god Apollo: presumably, they had appealed against the governor's abuse of them, perhaps because they had uprooted his carefully planted fruit-trees and used them for the tree-bearing cult with which they worshipped their god. Here, too, King Darius was respecting a foreign god whose spokesmen, like Yahweh's Isaiah, had favoured Cyrus: Apollo, he said, had spoken the 'entire truth' to 'his ancestors', presumably Cyrus himself. From the side of the Persians' subjects, we also have a fascinating petition, a copy of which survives on its original papyrus. It comes from the Jewish community who had settled in a garrison post up the Nile in Egypt: their leaders sent it to the Persians' governor of Judaea and the sons of the satrap of neighbouring Samaria. The petition begs for a letter of support for the rebuilding of their own little temple to Yahweh which they had been maintaining, without the slightest mention in scripture, on their Nile island. The local Egyptians had destroyed it, not least because they hated the Jews' habit of sacrificing animals, and so the Jews were writing to important Persians and stressing the temple's great antiquity and the favours they would ask of their God in return for Persian support. This plea for rebuilding a local temple of Yahweh belongs in 408 BC, but it is a mirror image of processes which are described at a more senior level in Ezra 5:3–6:15. However, what no letter or edited narrative can tell us is just what happened in Jerusalem between *c.* 538 and 522/1. The book of Ezra's documents bear on important history here, but the book is in no way a history itself.

V

After this sequence of bright light and shadow, the biblical narrative sinks into darkness for at least seventy years. However, we now have the external evidence of private contemporary sources which suggest a shift of real importance in Jewish opinion outside Judaea. Between *c.* 530 and 460 contemporary business contracts survive on clay tablets from Nippur in Babylonia and they or their accompanying seals contain many Jewish names among their signatories. In the 470s a sharp increase has been detected in Jewish names which are formed round Yahweh, rather than round Babylonian divinities: even Zerubbabel had had a Babylonian name. In this period fathers with Babylonian names can be seen to have changed and to have begun to give Jewish religious names to their children. Both Ezra and Nehemiah were outsiders who came down to Judaea from the Persian court; both are said to have acted to encourage piety and prevent foreign marriages among the Jews. If their missions from Babylonia and the East belong no earlier than the 450s and 440s, they can themselves be related to this new 'Yahweh generation' which is visible outside Judaea in Babylonian documents. This external evidence would give a suggestive context for the visitors' extreme piety and their disgust at the laxity of fellow Jews in the old homeland.

However, the dating, sequence and purpose of Ezra's and Nehemiah's missions are among the most disputed problems of all history in the Bible, so much so that the two Jews' very existence has been questioned. Here, at least, we can set themes in each book against what we know of life under Persian rule and then argue for their authenticity. The Chronicler puts Ezra first, so we can begin with what he tells us. It is often very vivid. We can picture Ezra as he sets out from the Persian court with a large treasure but without an armed escort. His mission is legal reform, his destination Judaea. At a river on his route, the Bible tells us, he waited and fasted in order to seek God's help; inside Jerusalem, he stood on a pulpit of wood and read aloud the book of the law of Moses to the assembled men and women; assistants explained what he read and 'all the people wept, when they heard the words of the law'. This great scene is a cardinal point in our ideas of scripture's history: it is the first hint that a Pentateuch, the first five books of our Bible, had at last been stitched together by its bookmaker, using the earlier sources of J, E, D and P. Three months later, Ezra is said to have summoned the people and condemned their marriages to foreign wives: the crowd listened 'trembling because of this matter, and for the great rain'. Ezra's concern for the racial purity of the Jewish people went beyond the letter of the books of law he had read out.

Details in this book do coincide with external evidence about Persian methods of rule. Ezra is said to have been sent with lavish presents and huge offerings from King Artaxerxes and the 'seven counsellors' to the Temple of God in Jerusalem; his followers were to be granted very large rations of silver, wheat, wine and oil by 'all the treasurers beyond the river'. Official letters which grant specified rations to royal envoys and approved personnel are now well attested in original documents surviving in the bureaucratic languages of the Persian Empire: they are worded in a familiar style as part of an elaborate system. Ezra was approved by his royal letter as 'the priest, a scribe of the law of the God of heaven', the name for the Jews' Yahweh in other Persian documents. The seven counsellors fit neatly with the seven privileged families in Iran who are known to Greek sources and are linked with the special helpers who are mentioned by Darius in his official text of his accession.

As seen through the eyes of a Persian treasurer, this mission would have seemed like nothing more than another official permission which had been granted from a Persian king to a special envoy and which agreed gifts for yet another foreign god. There was, however, something more: the king agreed that Ezra's law was to be the law for all the Jewish people 'beyond the river' (7:25, where some manuscripts wrongly imply it was to be a law for 'all people', not all Jews). This important licence would obviously mark a crucial moment in the status and future of the scrolls of Hebrew law and scripture, but it might seem highly unlikely that a Persian king should have bothered with Jewish minutiae. It is not implausible at all. From documents of the Jewish garrison in Egypt, once again, we know that the question of festival observances by local Jews in the season of Passover went up through a hierarchy of important Persians to a later king, Darius II himself. One of the Persian princes at that time, Arsames, had a secretary with a Jewish name (who could draft but not write), while there was another important Jew at court who could advise King Darius II on Jewish affairs (compare Nehemiah 11:24). As for endorsing the Jewish law for Jews, King Darius I had taken a parallel step when he had asked for Egyptian laws to be collected soon after his accession, presumably so that his governors could apply them in cases between Egyptians under their rule.

Once again comparisons make the narrative plausible, but they do not confirm that it happened, let alone when. The book of Ezra does indeed break into the first person, as if Ezra's own memoirs underlie it, but as yet we have no external story with which to confirm what it tells us. It sounds good, yet we cannot be absolutely sure. In Nehemiah's story, however, the details and setting of the mission are even richer. He intercedes with the Persian king for his ruined city of Jerusalem while serving at a royal dinner. When he arrives, he helps us envisage the sad ruin of Jerusalem's walls and his perils as he arranges their rebuilding. He returns for a second visit, and we find that he, too, reformed Jewish misbehaviour. He abolished the debts of poor Jews to the rich: he shook out the lap of his robe as a symbolic warning. He restored tithes for the Levites; he upheld the Sabbath: all foreign traders were expelled from Jerusalem. He, too, took action against Jews who had married foreign women. More impassioned than Ezra, he tells us that 'I cursed them, and smote certain of them, and plucked off their hair.'

Nehemiah strikes us as a fervent champion of justice, sustained by a strict idea of his city and its law. Where he touches on Persian affairs, his story also conforms to independent detail. He intercedes with the king while serving as the royal cupbearer at dinner: the job of royal cupbearer is familar in royal legends, and we also know of another important cupbearer at the Persian court who is a non-Persian, in Herodotus's Greek histories. Nehemiah notes explicitly that the queen was present at the dinner: it was worth noting, because Greek sources remark that usually she did not attend the heavy drinking. He receives letters of commission, including one for the keepers of the king's forests to grant him timber: in Egypt under Persian rule, we have an official letter which shows the extraordinary degree of bureaucracy required to approve and release materials, including timber, for a single Nile boat. Like other known bearers of Persian royal travel documents, Nehemiah is given an escort. In Jerusalem he then finds that the poor are mortgaged to the hilt in order to pay the king's tribute, which is only too credible. He appears to be the king's 'governor': we know this same Aramaic title from seals of the Persian period found in Judaea and from letters of the Jews in Egypt under Persian rule, although the exact hierarchy is uncertain. He claims credit that he did not levy the usual 'bread of the governor' or buy up land, but that he did hold officially supplied dinners for a hundred and fifty important people. The tribute, the official bread, a labyrinthine system of rations and dinner allowances and the acquisition of lands in the provinces are all well-attested Persian practices in oriental and Greek evidence.

When the book of Nehemiah gives us details of Persian rule, they fit admirably with our best control on it, our knowledge of the Persian Empire from its own contemporary documents. When it quotes letters, they are of the right type with the right feel to them. In my view, the letter inserted at Ezra 4:7 is another such letter from Nehemiah's source, and here, too, its official titles can be explained through Persian documents. The Bible's mysterious 'Dinaites' in its sonorous verse 4:9 mean 'judges' in Aramaic, and the 'Apharsathchites' are either under-governors or envoys. There is, of course, a ready explanation for all this exact detail and documentary quotation: the book of Nehemiah breaks frequently into the first person and is based, just as it claims, on the written memoir of Nehemiah himself.

This underlying primary source, unique in the Hebrew Bible, is of the highest interest in the history of world literature: it is the memoir of a reforming public figure which he wrote as a justification in later life. Nehemiah was not being paid vast sums to write it, nor are his memoirs the world's first example of this very long-lived genre. In Greece, a century and a half earlier, the great Athenian law-giver Solon had composed and issued poetry in defence of his political achievements in the year 594 BC. In Egypt, too, we have the long inscription of a high-ranking scribe and man of affairs, a lifetime after Solon, who set out his achievements *c.* 518 BC, appealing to the gods to remember them and assist his fame: he had changed sides and supported the Persian king. Nehemiah's memoirs, as we now discern them, were longer and more personal than the Egyptian's account of himself. They also had a different audience to Solon's poetry. Whereas Solon addressed his fellow citizens and invoked the gods as witnesses of what he had achieved for them, Nehemiah addressed his God, asking him to remember the good which he had done.

Nothing in the books of Ezra or Nehemiah conflicts impossibly with what we know of Persian government and personnel. In the book of Esther, by contrast, we have a historical fiction whose Persian details are very vivid, but at one point we can catch them out. The author wrote long after the ending of Persian rule and arguably lived in Susa, a former palace-city of the Persians. Among his rich details of the king and his concubines and banquets, he imagines that at the old Persian court, Haman the Jews' enemy was promoted second in rank after the king 'above all the princes' (3:1–2). The highest known rank for a non-royal courtier was the 'chiliarch' who had military duties and commanded cavalry. Haman, however, is seen solely as a court official: the author has pictured his role here in terms of the different royal bureaucracy of his own later age.

The book of Esther can illustrate a Persian custom which we know independently: it cannot prove one for which it is our only authority. The books of Ezra or Nehemiah are authorities in their own right, but the historical questions still remain. Who came first and when did they come down? In our Bible the Chronicler has put Ezra first, but Ezra's book refers to a populous city (10:1), whereas Nehemiah's memoir has a moving account of the ruined and thinly peopled state of Jerusalem. Ezra refers to a 'wall' for Jerusalem, whereas it is Nehemiah who is said to have rebuilt the city's wall. Ezra is supposed to have read the law of Moses to the Jews and been very strict about mixed marriage, but Nehemiah also needs to reform abuses in Jerusalem and to deal with mixed marriages. Above all, his memoirs never mention Ezra or his work or imply the existence of either; the two incidental mentions of Ezra at 12:26 and 12:36 are rightly dismissed as later insertions into older lists of names. Nehemiah refers to Eliashib as an important Temple priest, whereas Ezra (10:6) refers to a son of Eliashib, Johanan, in a similar role. Some of these problems can be evaded, but the easiest answer is that the Chronicler has carried out a biblical act of editing: he has muddled his two main sources and wrongly put Ezra before Nehemiah.

This answer solves the old problems and involves no new ones: when, though, did Nehemiah and Ezra do their work? Ezra is said to have come down in the 'seventh year of King Artaxerxes': there were three Persian kings called Artaxerxes, any one of whom could place Ezra's mission in 458 (the traditional date), 398 or 352. The only other clue may lie in Ezra's important priest, Johanan. In the Aramaic papyri, surviving from the Jewish colony in Egypt, we know that a Johanan was high priest in 407. On a small silver coin of Judaea, issued in the fourth century, the battered Hebrew letters have recently been read as 'Yohanan the Priest', presumably the most important priest of the time. The coin cannot be dated to a particular decade, despite hopeful claims to the contrary: on a comparison of styles with other silver coins, it is probably dated no earlier than 380 BC. Johanan is a common name, and the coin's inscription may have been misread, because the coin is badly damaged. Strictly on present evidence, what we can infer puts Ezra in the fourth century BC: 398, not 352, as the latter date is so close to the Chronicler's likely time of writing that his muddle would become incredible.

As for Nehemiah, his two missions belonged in the twentieth and thirty-second year of a King Artaxerxes: the only possibilities are 445 or 384. One of his main enemies was Sanballat the Samaritan, but new discoveries have multiplied the probabilities. We now have two finds of papyri which refer to an important Sanballat: one was high priest a generation before 410, the other a generation before 354.

We also need to consider the priests. Nehemiah's high priest was Eliashib, who bears the same name as the father of Ezra's Johanan: it may be right to assume that the two Eliashibs are one and the same man, and that Nehemiah therefore preceded Ezra. If so, the acute problems of his silence, Ezra's 'wall' and so forth are easily solved by reversing the biblical order. Nehemiah came down in 445 or 384; if Ezra followed him, he came in 398 or 352. I prefer 445 for Nehemiah, then Ezra in 398, largely because these dates leave more time for their editor (probably the Chronicler, writing not before *c.* 350 BC) to muddle up the truth.

On a wider view, this dating has interesting implications. Our first knowledge that a complete law of Moses existed is the reference to Ezra reading it out: assuming that it is our Pentateuch, we have to downdate the first attestation of the first five books of our Bible from 458 to the fourth century B C. Nehemiah, too, opens broader horizons. If his wall-building mission fell in 445 B C, it fitted into a web of Persian problems with their western provinces. Shortly before, the Greek cities on the western coast of Asia had been conceded by the Persian king in an agreement with the Athenians, Greece's ruling power (although the existence of this agreement, too, still finds its doubters): on one view, these cities' walls had been dismantled as a result. In Egypt, however, the 450s had seen a serious revolt from Persia, and so it would have made sense to send Nehemiah in the 440s to strengthen and wall Jerusalem, which was still in the Persian king's domain. At this date Nehemiah becomes the king's agent in an era of far-reaching changes, involving the king, the Egyptians, the building and breaching of walls and the Athens of Pericles.

In the early fourth century another such context can be found for Nehemiah. Although the Persian king had regained the Greek cities in Asia (it is only a minority view that he then unwalled them), in the late 380s Egypt was in revolt once more and shows signs of having exported the trouble up the coast to Phoenicia. Once again, Nehemiah becomes an agent of major Persian provincial policies, but the setting for his walling is more one of Egyptian than Greek disturbances.

What we have, then, are two texts, both of which claim a personal basis for their narrative; one quotes plausible Persian letters, the other quotes its hero's own memoirs. The intervening narrative is heavily interpreted in a theological style (the return of the Jews is told with touches of the colour of a second Exodus); the biblical author has muddled his sources' contents and, in my view, the sequence of the two heroes: those who prefer their facts straight may anyway suspect the honesty of a public figure's memoirs, even if they appeal to God. For those reasons, we cannot say that these books 'correspond to the facts', and indeed their theological views are beyond such verification. However, they do contain documents and details which no historian of the Persian Empire can afford to neglect, while the snatches of Nehemiah's memoirs are personal and historical in a way which is entirely human. There is nothing else like them in the entire Old Testament narrative, even if we are not now certain exactly when they belong.

17
Jesus on Trial

In the New Testament the relation between the narrative of scripture and history takes on a new complexity. The narrative was written much closer to the events which it describes; it is composed in Greek and one part, the Acts of the Apostles, can be aptly compared with Greek ways of writing history; the Gospels are four separate books which can be compared with each other; more is known about their social and political framework, the years of Roman rule in the Greek-speaking cities and Jewish communities than we will ever know about the times of Ahab or Nehemiah.

Our knowledge is still growing, bringing new uncertainties with it. In Acts we sometimes meet people called 'those who fear' or 'worship God', among whom the Christians' preaching finds a sympathetic hearing. 'God-fearers' turn up in a few later inscriptions in Greek, usually in a Jewish context, but we now have a much longer inscription, recently found at the Greek city of Aphrodisias in modern Turkey where it related to the affairs of the Jewish synagogue. It lists fifty-four god-fearers by names which show that the majority were Gentiles of varied occupations, and it supports the old view, that Acts' god-fearers were Gentiles who sympathized with the Jewish faith but did not convert and obey all the Jewish laws. Christian preachers offered such people an attractive new Israel with its Messiah and fewer rules: the new inscription, however, dates from *c.* 200, perhaps later, and, although it is suggestive, it cannot prove what a god-fearer meant nearly two centuries earlier in Acts.

There are also continuing finds of texts on bits of papyrus: a newly published group of papyrus documents from caves in Judaea has added an interesting postscript to the context of Jesus's teaching on sex and marriage to Jews in the Gospels. Among the letters, several relate to the business of a Jewish woman in the 120s who was one of her husband's two wives. After the splendid polygamy of the patriarchal age in the Bible, multiple wives are usually limited to a few exceptions in the highest Jewish society. This woman's bigamous husband was relatively well-off, as was she herself, but she did not belong to the very highest class. Bigamy, it seems, was not confined to a few members of the beau monde.

Besides papyri and inscriptions, we have the historical writings of a contemporary Jew, Josephus. Younger than Paul by a generation, he lived none the less in Judaea before the great catastrophe of 70 when the Temple was ruined and groups like the Pharisees or Sadducees disappeared from history. He wrote between the 70s and the mid 90s, and, although he refers to John the Baptist, his books never comment on Jesus's career: the one passage which appears to do so is agreed to be a Christian addition. Josephus's memories are not perfect, but they are much closer to the Judaea of Jesus's time than are the many texts which were composed much later by Jewish scholars or rabbis. Sometimes they look back to Judaea before 70, but they are not primary sources and often idealize or distort what they tell us.

The Gospels, too, are not straightforward histories, but they do relate significant events and sayings from the single life of a historical Jesus: they are biographical, in this sense, with a strong religious purpose. They are not so distorted by a date or setting outside Judaea that they show us Jesus only in settings with which a Gentile townsman would have been familiar. The absence of slavery and the allusions to the 'high and mighty' (*megistanes*) in Mark's Gospel suggest a credible social pattern in Galilee, one supported by Josephus's writings; in the Gospels, Jesus never enters the two new Greek cities which had been recently founded in Galilee, although this type of city and its social structure were to be the setting for most of Christianity after his death; people like Mark's Syrophoenician woman, a Greek by race (7:26), light up the cultural complexity of an entire era. At a different level, whether true or not, the anecdotes about 'rendering unto Caesar' are of primary importance for understanding provincials' awareness of their emperor and the degree to which subjects of Rome were assumed to take any notice of the types and images stamped on their coinage.

At this level, episodes in the Gospel are rightly valued as evidence by historians of Roman provincial life. Historians of Jesus and Judaism have a more awkward task. After his death, Christians and Jews came into conflict. Their arguments have not necessarily been read back into the Gospels, but the existence of such conflicts has influenced the way in which Jesus's own disputes are told to us. The fourth Gospel, famously, looks back on the Jews as a hostile group, almost as if Jesus was not one of them. In Mark's Gospel some of the disputes have been felt to have extraordinarily unrealistic settings: 'Pharisees did not organize themselves into groups to spend their Sabbaths in Galilaean cornfields in the hope of catching someone transgressing (Mark 2:23 ff.), nor is it credible that scribes and Pharisees made a special trip to Galilee from Jerusalem to inspect Jesus's disciples' hands (Mark 7:1).'

Above all, there is the problem that we have four Gospels, not one. Their routes for his movements differ irreconcilably, and when they give us his sayings and dialogue, here, too, their wording and context do not often agree. Narrow readings of every word in the Gospels as a history of what Jesus said have given way before the insight that the four authors shaped their material in different ways. Like their shaping, this material is sometimes evidence only for what his Christian heirs believed him to have said and done. It is quite clear from the hesitations of the Apostles in the first chapters of Acts that there was a firm tradition that Jesus had not ordered a mission to the Gentiles. Fitfully, like sparks from a central fire, such a mission took place, and then, in reflection of its new blaze, we find the Jesus of the Gospels credited with sayings which urge the Apostles to go to the Gentiles in specific terms (Matthew 26:17; 28:19; Luke 24:47). The later experience of the community has here shaped the sayings ascribed to Jesus. This instance is certain, and elsewhere the question is where to draw this line between what was actually said and what was later believed to have been said.

Faced with this line, theologians have sometimes written as if we can know the 'Christ of faith', whereas the 'Jesus of history' is lost, or even rather unimportant. Not only Christians, however, read the Gospels, and those who do not accept the 'Christ of faith' are still confronted with four accounts which are attached to a person of history, Jesus of

Nazareth, who lived, taught and died, and was believed to have related himself to the idea of a Messiah and a God who was already known. This historical Jesus is directly relevant to the future 'Christ of faith'; God was not believed to have raised just any old person from the tomb. What, then, can historians know about him?

The secure minimum lies in actions which were publicly recognized and on which all Gospels agree. We know that Jesus regarded the Twelve as a special group among his disciples (Paul, in 1 Corinthians 15:5 shows that the significance of this number was known very early indeed; John 20:24 acknowledges it); characteristically, we do not know who the Twelve were, because their names differ in the various lists. The number twelve, however, was known to be significant, whoever belonged to it, and thus it was maintained immediately after Jesus's death (Acts 1:15–26). We also know that this person with a Twelve spoke in some sense about a kingdom of God (John's Gospel says the least about it, but it is stated to Nicodemus already at John 3:5); the inscription on the Cross, a public fact, labelled him as king of the Jews. We know that he came into conflict with some of the Jews, that he was arrested though his close followers were not, that he was put to death by the Roman punishment of crucifixion (the Roman authorities, therefore, were involved). Even these minimal certainties exclude several interpretations, that Jesus was only a miracle worker (why the talk of a kingdom?), that his was 'the eminently credible personality' of a devout Galilean holy man (why the Twelve? Twelve, surely, for the Twelve tribes of a new Israel; a new community was never the concern of any known 'Galilaean holy man').

There are two main ways forward from the secure minimum. We can compare the four Gospels' accounts and give particular credit to facts or sayings on which agreement is most significant: one interesting test is also to look for agreements between the Gospels which are otherwise the least closely related, John and Luke, for instance, or even John and Matthew. Another method is to compare the 'secure minimum' with our knowledge of other 'criminals' who confronted Romans in Judaea before the war of 68–70. We know about them from the histories of Josephus, and although he never mentioned Jesus's arrest or death, we can ask what Jesus must have done to be so different from these trouble-makers as to deserve the injustice of a Roman crucifixion. Josephus's histories show us that in the 40s, Roman soldiers (not Jews or their priests) went out to arrest a charismatic Jew called Theudas who had drawn crowds by his promise to divide the River Jordan: after a military exercise, the Romans took him and put him to death. Roman troops also attacked and slaughtered an Egyptian prophet and many of his followers who were believed to be planning a forced entry into Jerusalem: Josephus says in one book that the followers numbered 30,000, in another that 400 were killed and 200 taken prisoner, while Paul in Acts 21 refers to 4,000 followers, probably of the same character. Up in Galilee, during Jesus's lifetime, it was left to Herod Antipas, a client king, to arrest and kill John the Baptist: in Josephus's view, John was arrested as a preacher of repentance and baptism (his Herod Antipas reasons that 'it would be much better to strike first'; 'eloquence which had so great an effect might lead people to revolt'). Finally, thirty years after the Crucifixion, another Jew called Jesus, a 'simple rustic', went through Jerusalem at the Feast of Tabernacles in the year 62, crying 'a voice from the east, a voice from the west, a voice from the four winds; a voice against Jerusalem and the sanctuary, a voice against all the people'. Some of the leading citizens took him in anger and flogged him: when he went on lamenting, the Jewish authorities brought him before the Roman governor. There, he answered every question with the same words of lament, whereupon the governor released him and the man continued lamenting for another seven years.

It was also at a Feast of Tabernacles, according to John's Gospel, that another Jesus, a 'rustic', no doubt, to the likes of Josephus, cried aloud on the final day: 'If anyone thirsts, let him come to me and drink . . .' The shouts of religious pilgrims must have been common at Tabernacles, a time of tub-thumping. Just like his later namesake, our Jesus is said to have been threatened with arrest by the Jewish authorities: he escaped on this occasion, but eventually at a Passover he caused the authorities to bring him to the Roman governor. Unlike his namesake, he was then put to death. He was, therefore, something more than a prophet of doom against the Temple and the nation. He was not a revolutionary prophet like the unnamed Egyptian, nor was he a political Messiah like Theudas, the parter of the Jordan; Roman troops went out to attack them, but they did not attack Jesus and his followers. Like John the Baptist, Jesus was best arrested quickly for fear that his religious message might provoke trouble. Unlike John the Baptist, however, he did not provoke Herod Antipas to arrest him up in Galilee: his hour came in Jerusalem, and unlike the Baptist, he was killed after events which involved Jewish authorities, the Roman governor and a Roman penalty. People's reactions are not necessarily consistent across thirty years, but there does seem to be a pattern here.

In his captors' eyes, Jesus was less than a rebel but more than a preacher of doom and repentance. He was something more, because he talked of a new kingdom of God, and the Romans could not give that talk the benefit of doubt. He was also something more because of his impact. The Baptist, too, preached repentance and drew popular support, but only Jesus was believed by his followers to have risen from the dead.

These followers have left us with four accounts of him which take us far beyond mere patterns and secure minimums: they devote the greatest proportion of their story to when, how and why Jesus was arrested, questioned and put to death. Part, but not all of it, makes contact with external evidence, Greek, Roman and Jewish. The degree of that contact and the nature of the evidence have turned the trial of Jesus into a scholarly battleground where progress is still being made. Its battles are waged on questions of historical accuracy, but they are also concerned with the issue of guilt. One deeply felt charge against Jews in Christian societies has been their apparent responsibility for Jesus's death. Have the Gospels exaggerated their role and can external evidence correct them? If Jews were responsible, why was Jesus killed by a Roman punishment?

The four Gospels do agree on a framework of events. It runs as follows: Jesus is arrested though his companions are not; he is questioned by the high priest; he is taken to Pontius Pilate and questioned again; at some point he is scourged; Barabbas is released instead of him, and he is dispatched by Pilate to be crucified. Most of this framework is made up of publicly witnessed events: the questioning by Pilate did end with a scene between Pilate and the crowd which implied that Pilate and Jesus had met. As for the high priest, Peter is said, surely correctly, to have waited in the high priest's house: at John 18:15 'another disciple' who was known to the high priest is said to have entered with him. It is an old belief, and in my view a correct one, that this disciple is the source of our fourth Gospel.

The framework, therefore, could rest on primary sources, but at once it opens wider horizons. What exactly happened in the intervening hours: who said what in private and when? Even an eye-witness could be confused by all the comings and goings in the night, and our first three Gospels were not written by witnesses (the 'young man' at Mark 14:51 is not, in my view, the Gospel's author and, anyway, he ran off). The Gospels do not hesitate to tell us, but one conventional tactic is to match their details to external evidence, especially to Jewish and Roman evidence for the legal procedures of a trial. I will begin with this same tactic, although it requires us to pick details out of each Gospel: I will go on to argue that it conceals a deeper problem, the Gospellers themselves.

The main Jewish evidence lies in texts which were written by later rabbis and date from *c.* A D 200 onwards; it is particularly cited for its views on the offence of blasphemy and meetings of the Jewish Sanhedrin, or council. Blasphemy, their texts imply, is a capital offence if it concerns the worship of idols or the 'naming of God's name'; neither of these offences fits exactly with Jesus's blasphemy as proclaimed by the high priest to his fellow hearers at Mark 14:64. Here, Jesus is merely said to have assented to the suggestion that he was the Messiah, 'Son of the Blessed', and to have referred impersonally to the coming of the 'Son of man', alluding here to the mysterious figure who is known from the book of Daniel. Neither of these remarks profaned God's name. The Sanhedrin is also highly problematic. In the synoptic Gospels a 'council of Jews' ('Sanhedrin') interrogates Jesus and, at Mark 14:64 it 'adjudges' him worthy of death: all three synoptic Gospels place this hearing during the Festival of Passover, and Mark and Matthew place it at night. However, the rabbinic treatise on the Sanhedrin (written *c.* 200) states that its meetings could not be held on a Sabbath or any festival day, let alone by night, and that a sentence of conviction to death could be finalized only on the day after trial.

These discrepancies have been combined with external sources on the character of Pontius Pilate. The educated Jew Philo, a Greek-speaking contemporary in Alexandria, quoted a letter of the Jewish king Agrippa I, a very well-placed source, which describes Pilate as 'harsh, unbending and stubborn', while Josephus's histories record several attempts by Pilate to provoke or cow his Jewish subjects. Coins issued in Judaea during Pilate's governorship also suit this picture: they are the first coins during Roman rule to show objects used in pagan religious cult, an affront to Jewish feelings. On the strongest interpretation, the Jewish evidence is said to refute the charge of blasphemy in Mark's Gospel (what was blasphemous about mentioning the 'Son of man' or the Messiah?) and to overturn the idea of a trial and condemnation by the Sanhedrin at night (such a meeting was impossible), while external sources refute the Gospels' image of a feeble Pilate who would merely give in to a Jewish crowd. The next step is to claim that Christians distorted the truth in order to blame the Jewish Sanhedrin for an act which was due to the Roman Pilate's own harshness. The punishment, after all, was a Roman punishment, and a crucial hint of the Romans' true part in it has been discerned at John 18:3. Unlike the other Gospels, John here implies that the group who went out to arrest Jesus in Gethsemane was a 'band' of soldiers (he uses the Greek word for a Roman cohort). They were led by an officer whose title is the Greek word generally used for a Roman tribune.

Much has been built on this alternative evidence, but its weaknesses are greater than its strengths. The most interesting point is internal to the Gospels, not external to the rabbis: the mention of Roman soldiers in John. However, John might be wrong (the others disagree); even if he is right, Roman soldiers could have been called out by the Jewish authorities if they claimed a dangerous emergency (we will return to the logic of this). The other points are not cogent. Harsh Pilate may have had an off day: contemporary papyrus records of Roman trials or Christian accounts of martyrdoms describe several governors who give in to the clamours of a crowd. Mark's 'blasphemy' must be read in context: the Greek word need only mean 'insolence', not specific 'insolence to God'. Above all, Mark is presenting the hearing as a shambles. The accusers cannot agree; Jesus remains magnificently silent; when the high priest declares blasphemy and tears his clothes, it suits the flow of the Gospel if he is overstepping the truth and jumping to an arguable conclusion. As for the meeting of the Sanhedrin, it can be argued that no formal 'Sanhedrin' was involved, only 'a' council ('a' *synhedrion* in Greek) which the high priest had gathered quickly to assist him. An off-the-cuff council is not a stated meeting of Judaea's formal council (at 14:55 Mark did write of 'the chief priests and all the council', but perhaps his language is too formal for the reality). Whatever the council's status, its night-time meeting need be envisaged only as a hearing, not a formal trial. At Mark 14:64 Bibles translate the Greek as 'they all condemned him to be guilty of death'. It may be less formal: 'they adjudged him worthy of the death penalty', leaving 'condemnation' to another time and place.

It is, then, far from clear that Mark's Gospel means a full condemnation or that he is right if he is imagining a formal Sanhedrin council in this case. Historians have even begun to argue that no such formal Sanhedrin endured in Judaea throughout its rule by Herod and his Roman successors: in my view, its existence in the Christian era is proved by Acts (5:27; 5:34 and especially 21:30 ff., in a 'we' part of the book, based on the author's primary knowledge). This extreme view, therefore, is wrong, but we do not need it in order to avoid a conflict between the Gospels and the rabbinic Sanhedrin texts. Despite Mark 14:55, no formal Sanhedrin need have been involved in Jesus's case: the rabbis' views on the Sanhedrin were anyway written long after the real thing had ceased to exist (it ended with the Jewish war against Rome in 68). The rabbinic authors have imagined details of this glorious council of the distant past and idealized its conduct: strictly, they refer to it as a court (*Beth din*) and hardly use the word 'Sanhedrin' at all. Its members, all seventy-one, were supposed to have sat in a semi-circle in which the young ones would vote first on a serious charge so as not to be overawed by their elders. These texts and others do not describe the workings of a historical court.

More cogent evidence lies in texts on Roman justice and local government. Most of it derives from the period up to *c.* AD 200, but it survives in historical narratives, not texts of wishful thinking: we even have official papyrus records of hearings before Roman governors whose powers and duties were the subject of texts by legal writers and are preserved in the later collections of Roman law. Between the dates of the Gospels and the dates of this evidence (up to *c.* AD 230), not too much had changed in governors' ways of keeping the peace.

It is about thirty years now since the Gospels' Passion narratives were last considered in detail by a specialist in Roman law: he was impressed by their grasp of the 'legal and administrative background and its technicalities'. The 'technicalities' are a mixed bunch, ranging from the times of day to the procedure of sentencing. In all four Gospels, Pilate is approached early in the morning: the routines of other known Roman dignitaries suggest that they did attend to their business early and that they relaxed from the sixth hour (noon), when John's Gospel states that Pilate brought his hearing to an end. John's and Matthew's Gospels mention the judgement seat of Pilate, using an exact technical term, *bema*; accusers are present at the hearing, as Roman procedure usually insisted; Pilate is reluctant to condemn, and his repeated putting of the question to his prisoner is held to conform to the practice of governors in later Christian trials when they put the question of guilt (it is said) three times. In Luke's Gospel, Pilate even sends Jesus, a man from Galilee, to be interrogated by Herod Antipas, the ruler of Galilee who happened to be in Jerusalem. The later texts of Roman lawyers mention a man's right to trial by his 'place of domicile', not the 'place of crime': Pilate, it is suggested, was working by this legal rule.

In Mark's and Matthew's Gospels, Jesus is heavily scourged before being crucified, but in Luke's he is threatened with only a beating as a preliminary to release. The Gospels' two words for these two types of beating are exactly chosen and their difference is supported in Roman law. One refers to the heavy beating which was administered before a death sentence, while the other refers to a cautionary beating which was also recognized as a legal option. During his time with Pilate, Jesus is dressed in a purple robe and a crown of thorns, and mocked by his captors: such cruelty can be connected to a prophetic text (the 'Suffering Servant'), but it is all too credible, and we can compare a scene described by the Jew Philo in Alexandria in summer A D 38, when a simpleton was dressed up in a blanket, a papyrus crown and sceptre, and was saluted and treated as king by some Greeks who wished to mock the true king of the Jews, Agrippa. Finally, Jesus's clothes are said to have been taken by the soldiers who cast lots for them. John's Gospel cites an apt verse from Psalm 22, but we also know from a legal ruling by the Emperor Hadrian (*c.* 120) that the seizure of a condemned man's 'old clothes', and the definition of this 'old clothing', were matters which needed official attention. The emperor allowed a criminal's clothing, pocket money and trinkets to be taken off him by his attendants. According to a later view, the provincial governor ought to take them himself and spend their value on the expenses of his own job, on paper, perhaps, for the office or presents for visiting barbarians.

These contacts with the outside world are reassuring; they remind us that the connection of an event with an old prophecy does not entail that the event itself never happened. However, they might be literary realism, not reality. On closer inspection, most of the 'technicalities' are not so impressive as they once seemed. The morning routines of Romans could vary like anyone else's; Luke is perhaps thinking of a delegation, or 'remission', to Antipas, but he is not thinking of anything so formal as a right of trial by domicile, let alone by origin, and there are very strong grounds for suspecting the historical truth of the story (as we will see). As for the three-fold questioning of Christians by Roman governors, it is attested in two other hearings (the Christians before Pliny the Younger and the martyr Polycarp in the 150s), but it is not a procedural rule.

The most discussed technicality has been the power of the Jews, or their Sanhedrin, to put a man to death under Roman rule: even if a formal Sanhedrin was not involved, could Jesus's execution have been managed so as to keep the entire business out of Roman administration? In John's Gospel the Jews do tell Pilate: 'It is not lawful for us to put any man to death' (18:31). The scope of this remark is still argued: did they mean that it was unlawful at any time or merely unlawful at Passover? If we leave it aside, the best we can do is to infer the position from other examples and the evidence from other Roman provinces. At Acts 7:57–8 Stephen, the first Christian martyr, appears to have been lynched, not formally condemned: in the Temple court, an inscription warned Gentiles that they, too, risked lynching if they went further inside it; lynching, though, is not the same as capital power, and although no decisive legal statement survives from Roman Judaea itself, the argument from other Roman provinces is overwhelmingly against the death penalty's free exercise. Only in a few highly privileged cities and in a literary novel of highly uncertain historical content (*The Golden Ass*) do we know of communities under Roman rule which appear to have been legally able to impose a sentence of death. Otherwise, capital sentencing was firmly vested in the Roman governor, although it could perhaps be delegated to such subordinates as he chose to name (the legal evidence on this point is unclear). Jerusalem was a most unreliable and delicate community, where Roman governors had even taken charge of the ceremonial robes of the high priest since their direct rule had begun in A D 6. Control of the high priest's dress was an important matter, and if the Romans intruded this far, they would surely have controlled his capital jurisdiction too, just as they controlled this power almost everywhere else in the empire.

The Roman punishment, therefore, does not imply that Jews had played no major part: legally, they could not kill Jesus as 'King of the Jews', and so Jesus's enemies had to persuade the Roman governor. All four Gospels show Pilate questioning the prisoner and reaching a conclusion, a pattern which matches the inquisitorial jurisdiction which a Roman governor exercised in this period. Beyond that, the extreme arguments fail. Jewish texts do not refute the Gospels' story of the process. Roman texts do not prove that they are riddled with correct technicalities. There is a question, however, which goes even deeper: do the Gospels themselves agree on the way in which it happened?

II

In 1899 the great Roman historian Theodor Mommsen could still describe the Gospels' stories of Jesus's arrest as 'agreeing together and conforming on their essential points to historical truth'. In 1935 a brilliant study of their detail, by Elias Bickerman, isolated the nature of their differences and matched each alternative with aspects of official police and judicial procedure which are known elsewhere in Roman historical sources and papyrus records. Each narrative, it emerged, had been shaped by its author's own coherent line of presentation. This masterly study of the Gospel evidence has still not been fully absorbed by many subsequent writers on the subject, some of whom have ignored its existence.

The Gospels' disagreements begin at the most basic level: they do not even agree about the day on which things happened. The synoptic Gospels believe that the Last Supper took place on the day of Passover, whereas the fourth Gospel (whose beloved disciple is said to have been present) puts the Supper on the day before. He fixes the trial and Crucifixion on the day of preparation and keeps Passover as the sequel: this dating is important for the entire course of his meeting between Pilate, Jesus and the Jews. The synoptic Gospels agree that the Crucifixion fell on a day of preparation, but they appear to think that this preparation was the day before an ordinary Sabbath, not before Passover, which was already over. There were theological advantages in either dating: the synoptics made the Last Supper into a Passover meal; the fourth Gospel made the eve of Passover the day of the death of Jesus, the 'Lamb of God' (as the Baptist called him at 1:36). In my view, the fourth Gospel is correct (it rests on a primary source), and the first Christians wrongly equated their first Lord's Supper with a Passover.

This conflict should put us on our guard: the exact day of Jesus's Crucifixion was a basic fact, but the Gospels do not agree on it. This disagreement extends to smaller details within the main framework: the significant point here is that they belong with very different ideas of Jesus's trial and arrest. To bring out the differences, I will take them one by one.

In Mark (and Matthew, who probably used him), Jesus is arrested by a group of unspecified status which is organized by the high priest. He refers to this band as if they were a home guard sent out to catch a bandit by the local authority of a city. He is brought to the high priest and accused by witnesses before the 'chief priests and all the council'. The witnesses cannot agree; Jesus tells the high priest that he is the Messiah and that the Son of man will soon be seen coming in clouds of glory; the high priest exclaims at this blasphemy, and the meeting 'adjudges him fit to die'. A second meeting in the morning holds a consultation (doubtless as to how to have him killed) and concludes by handing him over to Pilate. Jesus arrives bound; Pilate asks him, 'Art thou the King of the Jews?'; Jesus evades, whereupon the chief priests accuse him 'insistently' (or 'of many things', a less likely translation). But Jesus says nothing, like a man with the right to silence.

At this point the crowd intervenes. Pilate has a custom of releasing a prisoner at Passover, and the crowd presses him to act on it. He asks if they want their so-called king, but the chief priests have stirred up the crowd to ask for Barabbas. Pilate asks what to do with their king, whereupon they call for his death. He obliges them and first has Jesus scourged.

In Mark's view, the initiative is entirely the Jews'. The high priest hastily cites blasphemy and rends his own clothing: the entire council adjudges Jesus guilty; when Pilate begins his questioning by asking without prompting if Jesus is king of the Jews, we should infer that the

Jews have brought their prisoner complete with a formal statement of his offence. This procedure has various parallels, and in papyrus records we find it in action: the receiving Roman governor, like Pilate, plunges straight into the charge with his first question to the prisoner. When Jesus evades it, the burden is thrown back on the high priests, who repeat the accusation: Pilate is left with the unconfirmed findings and charge of the Jews, and a prisoner who refuses to speak. There happens to be no other evidence for the custom of a release of prisoners at Passover, but Mark is insistent that Pilate gave in on this point to Jewish agitation. In Mark there is no formal judgement by Pilate and no reported sentence. Pilate knows that the Jews have delivered Jesus 'for envy', but to keep the peace he simply lets them have their way with their so-called king. On a strict reading, it is not a formal trial at all.

There are arguable points of translation, how to take the words for 'blasphemy' and 'condemnation' in the Jewish hearing, but Mark's angle is clear. The Jewish authorities decide that Jesus should die, and so they pass him on to Pilate under a simple political charge ('King of the Jews'). When Jesus stays silent, Pilate hesitates and only hands him over after orchestrated protests from a Jewish crowd. The story is human and intelligible, and it can be matched (except for the Passover privilege) with Roman governors' behaviour in trials elsewhere in the empire.

Luke's account is subtly different. Jesus is arrested by the Temple police; he is taken to the high priest's house, but there is no night-time meeting of any council. Only at a morning meeting does a council ask him questions: first, is he Christ; second, is he the son of God? The whole company then brings him to Pilate, where they start to accuse him openly, evidently because they have not arrived with a formal charge or a report of their own prior finding (they have held no such session to establish it). Pilate can find no fault; the Jewish accusers elaborate; Pilate sends Jesus to Antipas, who is pleased to meet him; Antipas, too, finds no fault; Pilate decides to flog Jesus and release him, but the Jews then shout at him to crucify Jesus and release Barabbas. Pilate judges in favour of their charge and hands over Jesus to their will.

Historians have preferred Luke's account, because it is smoother and easier: that was precisely its author's intention, and we cannot conclude that it is therefore true. Unlike Acts, his Gospel was not based on primary evidence: Luke knew Mark's written version, and his own has two tendencies. Characteristically, it smoothes out Mark's. When the Jews question Jesus, they ask him if he is son of God, easing the logic and translation of the blasphemy in Mark's account: there is no night-time council but only one meeting, held in the morning. There is no curious Passover custom, but there is ever more insistence on Pilate's intention to set Jesus free. As a result, the procedure has a revealing shape: it resembles the trials of Christians which Luke's second volume, Acts, goes on to describe after Jesus's death. Sometimes Luke knew participants in these conflicts, while he himself was a man of the Gentile cities, aware of Romans' procedure in a hearing outside Jerusalem. Like the Jews in Acts' trials, his Jewish council meeting does not adjudge Jesus formally: the Jews merely believe that they have a case and then go directly to Pilate, where they act as accusers. No witnesses, therefore, appear in Luke's story before a prior Jewish hearing; significantly, the Jews bring no formal summary of their charge from which Pilate can plunge straight into his questioning. It is all quite different to Mark's idea.

The next step is that Pilate remits Jesus to Antipas, because Antipas rules Galilee (which was outside direct Roman rule), not because Jesus could benefit from some general right of trial by domicile under Roman law. No other Gospel refers to Antipas here; did Luke invent the entire scene? Among the early Christians in Antioch, he could have met Manaen (Acts 13:1), who had been brought up with the young Antipas: would Manaen, perhaps, have heard the story from his friend? It is much more likely that the story arose from a text of scripture than from a well-placed source: at Acts 4:26 Luke's Gospel quotes Psalm 2, 'the kings of the earth stood up . . . against his anointed'. Which kings were they, if not Antipas? The story sits awkwardly with all the other Gospels, but it would have appealed to Luke not just because it fulfilled the psalm, but because it emphasized a greater truth: that Jesus was wholly guiltless and freely declared to be so. Only Luke's story tells us of the Roman soldier below the Cross who declares, 'Truly, this man was *dikaios*.' Here, this Greek word does not mean the 'just one', or Messiah: it means 'innocent'. In Luke's story, Pilate's judgement is contradicted by his own disbelief, the disbelief of Herod Antipas and the words of one of his own soldiers.

Luke's account is coherent, but it is not at all the same as Mark's. As for Matthew's, it essentially repeats Mark's, with elaborations (Judas's suicide; the high priest's questions) and further proofs of Jesus's innocence (Pilate's wife knows that Jesus is innocent and has realized it in a dream; Pilate washes his hands of the whole affair): the proofs, once again, are brought in to bring out the central truth: Jesus was guiltless.

In the fourth Gospel events take a very different course. Not only is the day of Passover still in the future, but Jesus is never questioned at all before a council of Jews. He is taken first to the house of the high priest's father-in-law, Annas, where he is questioned only about his disciples and his teaching. His self-professed titles or status are not discussed. From there, he goes on to the house of Caiaphas, the high priest, and from there, to Pilate's residence. Pilate asks the Jews what accusation they are bringing, and the Jews reply that they would not have brought Jesus unless he was a 'wrongdoer'; Pilate tells them to take him, then, and try him by Jewish law, but the Jews say that 'it is not lawful' for them to put a man to death. Pilate, it seems, had not expected that Jesus's offence was so grave: he had been hoping that the Jews themselves could sort out the evil doer whom they had arrested. The Jews' reply has been interpreted in two different ways. Following Augustine, many Catholic Christian teachers relate the illegality to the approach of Passover. At such a festival, how could the Jews put a man to death and not be unclean for its celebration? The Gospeller has just told us that the Jews refused to enter Pilate's residence for this very reason, their fear of pollution before Passover: does not the one refusal explain the other? Pilate, however, has also told them to try Jesus according to their law and their reply, 'it is not lawful,' seems to pick up his suggestion. As written, their answer reads like an unqualified impossibility: it is 'not lawful' at all, before Passover or on any other day. If so, their reply fits the drift of our other evidence for the capital powers of Rome's subjects: like other communities, the Jews had lost the right to inflict the death penalty.

In sharp contrast to the other Gospels' stories, the fourth Gospel leaves the Jewish contingent to wait outside Pilate's residence while Pilate questions Jesus inside, going to and fro between the prisoner and his accusers. The Jews cannot enter for fear of becoming unclean. In private, therefore, Pilate asks Jesus if he is King of the Jews; the dialogue develops memorably into the dialogue on truth. Pilate goes out to tell the Jews that he can find no guilt, but in view of their custom of asking him for a prisoner at Passover, would they like to take their King of the Jews away? They call for Barabbas; Jesus is scourged, crowned and mocked and then brought out, being declared innocent ('Behold, I bring him forth to you . . .'). The Jews shout for crucifixion, and Pilate tells them to take him and do it themselves (legally, they could not): to stave off this ironic suggestion, they tell him that Jesus is the son of God. Pilate is then afraid; he questions Jesus again, and on his return the Jews subtly warn him that if he releases this king, he will not be Caesar's friend. Only now does Pilate come out and go to his official seat of judgement. Here, the story specifies the place, the day, the hour: it describes how Pilate presents the prisoner ('Behold your King'); the Jews clamour for a crucifixion, and Pilate concurs, handing over Jesus 'unto them', the Jews. The words 'unto them' underline this Gospel's view of the authors and villains of the piece.

In Matthew's Gospel (but not Mark's), Pilate's judgement seat is mentioned; Luke's also thinks of a formal verdict (23:24); the fourth Gospel's careful marking of the seat, the time and the place show that John, too, was thinking of a formal judgement by a governor who was sitting in authority: it quotes the title on the Cross and specifies that this official statement was written in three languages. Plainly, it is telling us the result of a formal trial. However, it is a Roman trial, because the fourth Gospel knows of no trial before a Jewish council, no preliminary hearing, accusation or judgement. These remarkable differences have been decisively explained by a difference in the earlier drift of this Gospel's story. In Mark, Jesus's entry on Palm Sunday draws a crowd, but is not followed by explicit opposition from the Temple authorities. Rather, it is Jesus's action in the Temple which brings the Jewish leaders' fears to a head: after it, they are afraid to allow Jesus to go on teaching, but they are also afraid of the crowds who are gathering for Passover. In the fourth Gospel, however, the high priest and Pharisees send minions to arrest Jesus at a much earlier point, after his teaching at the Feast of Tabernacles (John 7:32). Again, after the raising of Lazarus, the high priest Caiaphas is said to have remarked that it was 'expedient for us, that one man should die for the people'. Jesus, meanwhile, disappears into the wilderness; the chief priests and Pharisees had 'given a commandment, that, if any man knew where he were, he should show it, that they might take him' (11:57).

This order has been beautifully explained by the outlawing, or proscribing, of wanted criminals which local authorities practised elsewhere in cities and towns of the Roman Empire. Criminals' names were posted, and Roman subjects would be encouraged to denounce them, as we can see from the first-hand papyri on this topic which survive in Roman Egypt. This proscription is fundamental to the shape of the later part of the fourth Gospel. After the first order for arrest at Tabernacles, Jesus still returns to teach in the Temple; the second order, which follows the raising of Lazarus, has more impact. Jesus walks 'no more openly among the Jews'; as a wanted man, he withdraws to the wilderness: the authorities wonder whether he will dare to come to Jerusalem for the Passover, but when he does, they are not brave enough to arrest him, because he now commands such a following. Jesus leaves Bethany and withdraws to the garden 'over the brook Cedron': significantly, there is no prior discussion of betrayal between Judas Iscariot and the high priest, as in Mark; on the fourth Gospel's showing, Judas would already have known from the outlawing that Jesus was a wanted man. Judas also knows the place of hiding: the 'outlaw' has used it often in the past (John 18:2). It is not, then, surprising that this Gospel's language implies that Roman soldiers, a 'cohort' and a 'tribune' were present at the arrest. Jesus was an outlaw, so the author assumed that the Jewish authorities would have called on Roman police-troops to come out on urgent business and help them make a long-decreed arrest. Once they have taken their man, there is no need for the Jewish authorities to question him in council and establish his guilt (Mark's Gospel has to make them use outside witnesses at this point). Their wanted notice presupposes that this guilt exists. Instead, the high priest asks Jesus about his disciples and doctrine before passing him on to Pilate. There is one highly significant disagreement. In Mark and Luke, the Jewish authorities do not bind Jesus until after his hearing. In the fourth Gospel he is bound from the very moment of his arrest. The reason is simple: in this Gospel, his criminal status had already been guaranteed by the outstanding notice for his arrest, first issued in 7:30 and intensified at 11:57.

This Gospel's narrative is not Mark's or Luke's: it is differently shaped and dated, but we cannot say that it is false. Indeed, it fits very neatly with the evidence for policing and arrest in other provincial communities under Roman rule. It is, then, possible, as it attests, that the authorities did indeed outlaw Jesus and that his accusers did scare Pilate into a formal trial by warning that he was not behaving like a 'friend of Caesar' (the phrase is attested elsewhere; governors were always very wary that their subjects might denounce them to their own emperor; King Agrippa mentions Pilate's fear of denunciation in a near-contemporary letter). It is easy, too, to surrender to the deeply moving course of events, questions, generalized answers and comments which the author gathered into his story. Yet this Gospel's story is not the only one. It is also entirely possible, as Mark implies, that a meeting of Jewish authorities did first adjudge Jesus to be guilty, not perhaps as a formal Sanhedrin, but as a 'council' summoned by the high priest which then went to Pilate with a prepared charge. Luke, even, might be right that this council met only once in the morning and then went straight to Pilate to lay accusations immediately. Historically, all these procedures are possible. The trouble is that they cannot all be right: each of them contradicts the others.

The synoptic Gospels have been said to give us a 'photograph taken from slightly different angles', whereas the fourth Gospel is 'a free portrait by a painter who worked with a markedly individual style'. The versions of the trial belie this view of them. There are no synoptic photographs of the same subject: there are three separate paintings, worked in three different ways from a broadly similar framework. It may be tempting to base bits of this framework on contemporaries' own primary knowledge, on Peter and the other disciple who waited in the high priest's house, on Manaen, perhaps, who knew details about Antipas, or on Joseph of Arimathea, a friend of Jesus and later, of the Christians who belonged to the Jews' council and might have attended their meeting. Even if true, these primary sources do not take us very far. It is not only that eyewitnesses might have mistaken what was happening by night or in a crisis: could Peter and the beloved disciple have been certain of the exact status of all the Jews who were coming and going at night through the high priest's house? The greater problem is that as soon as we press the primary framework too closely, even the synoptic part of it divides over matters of importance. Did the Jews meet by night and again by morning, or only in the morning? Was Antipas involved or not? Even if there is a primary base for the framework behind them (the arrest; a time with the Jews; Pilate; crucifixion), it has been heavily interpreted in its context and manner of telling. 'Pilate realized,' says Mark's Gospel, 'that it was out of envy that the chief priest had delivered Jesus up.' How did anyone know what Pilate realized?

As for the fourth Gospel, it is not necessarily a 'free portrait': I accept, and will later support, the traditional view that its author was the beloved disciple, a well-placed primary source. If so, any primary base for the framework in the other three becomes even less solid: on matters of date, procedure and timing, this framework is being challenged by an author who ultimately depended not on eyewitnesses but on his own witness and knowledge. His is not a free portrait, but a portrait from life, also highly interpreted: some of its detail may be photographically accurate, and it derives from the author's own camera.

In the narrative of Nehemiah, the external evidence of its setting, the Persian Empire, could back up some of the detail and support the story's claim to be resting on Nehemiah's own memoirs. In the broadest terms, the events of the Jewish Return and rebuilding of the Temple and walls fit into the context of other known Persian edicts and decisions (though the dates can still be disputed). The narratives of Jesus's trial have exposed a more difficult relationship. We have three main lines of narrative, each of which is internally coherent and corresponds with external evidence, but which contradicts the other. From the early Church to modern historians of Jesus's trial, these accounts have been harmonized by taking some details from one source, others from the others. Harmony is a misguided method: if we want the truth, we have to choose one of the three paintings, or none.

Those who accept that the fourth Gospel derives from the beloved disciple accept that it derives from a primary source. Should we not then accept him and reject the other three? The problem, naturally, is how much even a primary source could have known and told, years later, without reshaping. In my view, he was primary: he knew the date; he stood in the high priest's house and had a better idea of who came and went, and from which house to another, than any of the others. On observable details and accessible matters of fact, I will give him higher authority than the others' stories, which are at best second- or third-hand. What, though, of the fourth Gospel's all-knowing style and strong interpretation: he had a coherent procedure in mind (I suspect it is true), but did he really know exactly when or why or whether the Jewish authorities outlawed his Master? Perhaps this detail was accessible to him, but did he also know what Jesus and the high priest said, or what Pilate, Jesus and the Jews said in private? Even if he did, he shaped it, 'invented' it in the classical sense, to bring out Truth, 'how it ultimately (not actually) was'. The portrait painter soon takes over from anything which his memory may have photographed.

If the Gospels do not agree on how, can they at least tell us why, why Jesus was arrested and artfully sent to his death? All of them date Jewish hostility early, but they do not agree exactly about who was involved (Mark thinks first of Pharisees and Herodians; later, there are disagreements over scribes, elders and so forth). In the three synoptic Gospels the murder plan (or extreme hatred) begins with the healing of the man with the withered arm; in the fourth Gospel, it begins in Jerusalem (not Galilee) with the healing of the cripple on the Sabbath and also (only in this Gospel) because Jesus says God is 'his Father'. In the three synoptics it is the scene in the Temple which brings matters finally to a head, followed by the parable of the Wicked Husbandmen (which the 'outsiders', the Jewish hearers, understand only too well). In the fourth, it is the preaching at Tabernacles which induces the first order for Jesus's arrest and it is the raising of Lazarus from the dead which intensifies it. The other Gospels omit the Lazarus episode alto-gether whereas the fourth puts their critical scene, the actions in the Temple, right at the start of Jesus's ministry and does not connect it with any Jewish hostility. Within the text of the Gospel, there are serious reasons for suspecting some dislocations: has the scene with Lazarus been inserted where every other Gospel has the scene in the Temple? If so, the Temple scene was promoted to the beginning, neutralized and explained in terms of Jesus's Resurrection.

Was it really the public teaching at Tabernacles, let alone the raising of Lazarus, which prompted the Jews to outlaw Jesus? It seems hard to believe that there was not more to it: a saying, at least, against the Temple and fears, perhaps, of this new kingdom which crossed the boundary between the political and the religious spheres and put at risk the Sadducees' entire compromise with Rome. Yet these explanations are not the fourth Gospel's. If, then, it is right about the outlawing and the arrest, the absence of a Jewish trial and the date, it is not entirely reliable about the origins of the hostility and the cause of the order. Perhaps we should not be surprised: did the disciples really know what the authorities were thinking? The order for arrest was one thing, its motives another: one Gospel seems cogent in its idea of the order and arrest, the others rather more plausible on the causes of the trouble. Can we, then, credit the fourth Gospel's framework of action and formalities, yet refuse to credit its causation and origins? Or do we have three separate portraits, not one of which is historically accurate? My inclination is to follow the fourth's framework but reject its motivation, the one being primary, the other of the author's shaping. Others would suspend judgement: at their climax, on either view, the Gospels do not give us one single Gospel truth.

I I I

There are four Gospels, but there is one Acts of the Apostles, our only narrative of the earliest Christianity from 36, the Crucifixion, to *c.* 60, Paul's detention in Rome. Here, too, we encounter a primary source, the author himself (in the sections marked by intermittent 'we'), and elsewhere, the memoirs and oral traditions which he met, like a Herodotus, on his travels, largely in Paul's company.

The new date of 36 for the Crucifixion adds momentum to the narrative. I accept (what many dispute) that at Galatians (2:1 ff.) Paul referred to the events behind Acts 15 (the Council of Jerusalem) and omitted the more trivial encounter with the Apostles which he had in Jerusalem at Acts 11. 'Fourteen years,' he wrote, had then passed since he first saw the light on the road to Damascus. Counting the years inclusively, they would run neatly from a conversion in 36/7 to spring 49. The second missionary journey followed promptly, bringing Paul to Corinth in winter 49/50 (this date, our next fixed point, depends on a recently published Greek inscription which mentions Gallio but which needs a bit of guesswork and is not absolutely cast-iron).

The scheme is tight, but it fits and has suggestive results. The events of Acts 1–9, from the Ascension through Stephen's martyrdom to Paul's conversion, are much more compressed in time than readers might now imagine. The author gave no hint of a chronology, but in my view the main events are more plausible if they moved fast. The Apostles waited at first in the Temple surrounds, wondering if Jesus would somehow 'restore' a new one; they clashed with the high priests; they won converts, only too plausibly, among groups of Greek-speaking foreigners in Jerusalem, some of whom would be pilgrims, glad to hear that they had coincided with the new Messiah. These successes caused Stephen's arrest and martyrdom, so that some of the Christians scattered; Paul, that 'Pharisee of the Pharisees', set out northwards to arrest any Christians as far north as Damascus, unearthing them through the synagogues; he had powers to tie them up, man or woman, and bring them to Jerusalem (Acts 9:1). The breach therefore, between church and synagogue began very early: in the view of Acts' author, Paul's future companion, it began within less than a year of Jesus's death.

This early dating helps with two famous difficulties. In Damascus, after his conversion, Paul was at risk to King Aretas (or so he wrote, 2 Corinthians 11:32) and was let down from the city walls in a basket (Acts 9:25 agrees about the basket but omits Aretas). King Aretas ruled from Petra, and his daughter was at the heart of the row with Herod Antipas: he had divorced her. In 36/7 it is entirely credible to find Aretas's agents active so far north in Damascus: Aretas had won a great victory over Herod Antipas in the wake of the divorce scandal and had overrun bits of the tetrarchy of Philip, Herod's brother, who had died in 33/4. Not until early 37 did Antipas manage to mobilize Roman support against the Petran king and defeat him: Paul's dangers in Damascus fit beautifully into the interval, while Aretas's troops could still make the most of their northern gains.

According to Paul himself (but not Acts), he then withdrew into Arabia, probably Aretas's own lands around Petra, for three years (37–9, inclusively). Not long afterwards, Acts 10:1 tells us of the first Gentile convert, Cornelius, who 'feared God with all his household', the 'centurion of the Italic band'. The recently found inscription at Aphrodisias has supported the old view that Cornelius was a Gentile sympathizer, 'of good report among all the nation of the Jews' (10:22), who attended the synagogue but had not gone as far as the pain of being circumcised. The 'Italic' band is now a soluble problem. In *c.* 39–41 Caesarea was still under direct Roman rule, and the presence of Roman troops in the chief city residence of the governor is only to be expected.

Looser chronologies, which begin from a Crucifixion in 30 or 33, have made heavy weather of Cornelius: they have put him after 41, when the province returned briefly to the Jewish client-king Agrippa and an 'Italic cohort' of Roman troops is much harder to explain. It is not surprising, on my view, that the author knew this fact: he had stayed in Caesarea, not least with Philip and his seven virgin-daughters, and the Christians there would have known the origins of their first, famous Gentile.

On any chronology, but particularly on mine, we then run into a fascinating gap: Paul withdrew to his home town Tarsus and did not re-emerge for several years, on my view not until 44, at the earliest. He returned to prominence when Agabus (whom the author met, Acts 21:10) prophesied worldwide famine to the Christians in Antioch: they sent a collection, perhaps with Paul, to Jerusalem. From the evidence of contemporary Egyptian papyri and other literary sources, this famine left its mark from A D 45 to 46. If Agabus was a notable prophet, he would not have spoken much after spring 45, responding to the prospect of a serious crop failure in Egypt. At about the time of Agabus's warning, Acts' author described the worm-ridden death of blasphemous King Herod Agrippa: Agrippa died in spring or early summer 44, suggesting that Agabus spoke during that year.

Paul, then, confronts us with a large gap in his early Christian years. Obsessed with his journeys and letters, we readily forget it: there he sat, the persecutor turned Christian, living in Tarsus for at least five years after his emergence from Arabia. Eight or nine years had passed since the 'blinding light', but the future Apostle to the Gentiles made no known missionary moves outside his home city and did not involve the Apostles in a Gentile crisis. Did he, perhaps, expect a rapid end to the world, like those who had known Jesus well and whom he had briefly met in Jerusalem?

In *c.* 45 the Christians sent famine aid to the brethren in Jerusalem, and according to Acts, Paul went with it: perhaps the author was wrong about Paul's movements here (he does not use a first person 'we' for this mission), or perhaps Paul ignored the episode at Galatians 2:1. From then on, we are guided by the 'fourteen years' from his conversion in 36 to his meeting with the Apostles (Galatians 2:1 ff.) and then by his arrival in Corinth in 49/50. The first of his missionary journeys thus belongs in 47 or 48, but we cannot know the immediate reason for this new departure. As a first move, Paul set off to Cyprus with Barnabas (a man of the island) and won over the Roman governor, Sergius Paulus, the most conspicuous of his successes in high society. From Cyprus, he made an astonishing leap: he returned north-west to the mainland, sailing across to Perge, where one of his followers left him: from there he struck hundreds of miles inland to Pisidian Antioch, a newish Roman colony which had a synagogue but no obvious attraction for two Christian preachers who were warily testing the new Gentile world.

In Acts' narrative, decisive turns in the missionary journeys are usually accompanied and urged by the Holy Spirit, but this remarkable detour into pure Gentile territory is left without any comment. However, we have a prominent public inscription from Pisidian Antioch which honours a Sergius Paulus, almost certainly the governor of Cyprus's son. One of his descendants, probably his granddaughter, then married a powerful man of the city and attained the great distinction of the Roman Senate in the early 70s, presumably with her family's help. In Asia the local influence of Sergii Pauli is also linked with their known ownership of a great estate near by in central Anatolia. It is quite likely that all or most of these connections go back to the lifetime of Paul's own Sergius Paulus, who was converted while governing Cyprus. If so, they give us the link which Acts omits: Paul went from Cyprus to Pisidian Antioch, of all remote places, because Sergius Paulus, his new convert, directed him to the very region where members of his family had land and power. The author of the Acts never used 'we' in his account of this first missionary journey and ascribed its course, if at all, to the Holy Spirit. No doubt the sense of the Spirit was strong, but so were Roman family networks: Christianity entered the Gentile world of Roman Asia on advice from the highest Roman society. The connection is crucial, but it was ignored by the author, whom so many have hailed as the first true Christian historian.

In spring 49, fourteen years from the blinding light, Paul confronted the Christians in Jerusalem with the Gentile question (Acts 15). Up to this point, Acts' narrative has been fascinating but decidedly mixed. Perhaps the author had been present in Antioch (the Western Text uses a 'we' at 11:26, which is perhaps the author's own second edition), but he had not known the earliest events personally, and he was not on the first missionary journey (Paul could have told him bits of it later). His subsequent visit to Caesarea brought him the chance of meeting Agabus and Philip: he noted their stories, the famine, the Ethiopian eunuch, the names of the Seven (Philip had been one), the conversion of Cornelius and the doings of Stephen (Philip's co-worker). Beyond that, he had traditions and highly coloured stories (some of which he could have met during his late months with Paul in Jerusalem). He stitched them into a simple view of the early Christian community: linked by pious generalization, they have no firm idea of time or sequence and no critical sense of evidence. The gift of tongues at Pentecost is only a story, contradicted by John 20:22 (where Jesus himself gives the disciples the Holy Spirit at Easter); the sudden death of Ananias for withholding property is a cautionary tale; the author's informants said remarkably little about the earliest Christians (James, John and the rest are shadows).

From Acts 16 onwards, the author's own memories enliven events. It is not that he was now above mistakes: he was slightly wrong about the proper civic description of Philippi, although he had visited it; his understanding of the geography of Jerusalem's outskirts and surrounds was also hazy. These small errors are familiar in travellers who are not primarily scholars taking notes (and sometimes, even then). He had a clear grasp, however, of the route from Caesarea to Jerusalem and the relation of the Temple to the Antonia fortress: both areas, significantly, are covered in his 'we' sections. So, too, is Paul's momentous sea journey to Rome where the places, persons and incidents are the author's own first-hand memories. Naturally, he had no hesitation about miracles en route; when Paul shakes off a snake, barbarians hail him as a god; an angel appears to the Apostle in a storm; a theological allusion to the Church has been seen in Acts 27:35, where Paul takes bread and gives thanks to God, using the verb for 'eucharist', and all in the ship were 'two hundred three score and sixteen souls'. However, this ship is perhaps not a lasting metaphor for the Church, as it is promptly lightened of its cargo and smashed to bits by the winds.

Throughout the author enlivens his narrative with single speeches and venial misunderstandings. They bring the setting to life and put possible responses to Christianity before us. We see how the new faith is misunderstood by so many outsiders, by money-minded pagans or simple rustics in Lystra: we learn what Christianity meant to many different hearers, whether Gentile 'god-fearers' in synagogues, Jews in council, simpler pagans in Galatia or the educated class of Athens's highest council (the Areopagus) and Roman governors in Caesarea. The book thus shows faith from so many angles, with the unquestioned assumption that its contents are true and that its preachers, Jesus and Paul, though condemned by Romans, are totally innocent. This assumption well suited the book's addressee, 'most excellent Theophilus', a socially eminent Gentile.

This emphasis is clear in the book's most famous point of contact with non-biblical fact: the trial of Paul. On his return to Jerusalem, Paul's Jewish enemies accuse the Apostle of introducing a Gentile into the inner Temple, an offence which we know independently to have been grounds for immediate lynching without Roman permission. The Roman garrison saves him; Paul alarms the centurion by revealing that he is a Roman citizen, a status which then affects his legal treatment. By it, he is legally exempt from casual flogging; two years later, before the governor, Festus, he picks up the charges which his Jewish accusers have now expanded against him (he is now said to be acting against Caesar) and appeals to Caesar. Here, Luke's Gospel uses the correct Greek word for the Roman citizen's right of *provocatio*, which was originally an appeal to the tribunes of the particular year, but which by now (even outside Rome) had become an appeal to the emperor, the holder of a tribune's power. Paul appeals at this late stage in his arrest because the charge has now grown into one on which he thinks he can gain by appealing to a higher authority. The scene fits exactly with the rights of a Roman citizen in the first century A D; it is all the more interesting, therefore, that Paul elsewhere has allowed himself to be beaten by the magistrates of a Roman colony (Acts 16:23: 'they had laid many stripes upon them') without mentioning his rights as a Roman citizen until after the event (16:37). 'I bought this citizenship for a large sum,' a Roman centurion himself tells Paul in the fortress at Jerusalem (22:28), implying that he had bought it from the Emperor Claudius and his advisers. So far from devaluing Roman citizenship, as enemies alleged, Claudius's freedmen evidently charged a high rate for it: when a Roman citizen chose to make use of his privilege, it was a priceless protection against arbitrary officials in the empire.

Although this legal setting is exact, the presentation of Paul's arrest is concerned with a higher truth. The council of Pharisees and Sadducees argue fiercely over theology and are feared likely to tear Paul to pieces (23:10): the Roman officer writes to his governor, emphasizing (in a private letter) that Paul does not deserve to be arrested; the governor, Felix, hears Paul and visits him privately, but when Paul tells him of 'righteousness, temperance, and the judgement to come', the venal Felix begs him to stop; then, a new Roman governor, Festus, sends Paul to be heard by the king of the Jews, Agrippa, saying once again that 'he had committed nothing worthy of death'; Agrippa concludes, after a fine speech, that 'this man might have been set at liberty, if he had not appealed unto Caesar'. It is the last word on the subject in Acts, although Paul was executed later in Rome. Like the trial of Jesus in its previous volume, Acts' trial of Paul is concerned to emphasize the truth of its prisoner's innocence at every literary turn. That innocence may be historical, the source a primary witness, but the method goes way beyond history to a subtle apology in form and detail.

18
Back to the Future

I

Through this sample, we have seen that biblical narrative does not necessarily correspond to what happened: the past is only one of its dimensions. It looks ahead to what will happen, promising, prophesying and inspiring hope in ways which still help readers to endure. The Gospels are not just a battlefield of tax decrees, birthplaces and the procedures of trials and arrests: they say much more about the future and challenge the present by their views of it. In Hebrew scripture, too, the narrative books often have the future as a running theme. It is present in the Deuteronomist's tour de force, both in the prophecies which mark important turns in the narrative and in the general interpretation which drives it. It is also present in the promises in Genesis and the recurring example of the Exodus. In the Greek world, Thucydides and his heirs believed that their records of the past, its events and decisions, might help readers to decide and to act if a similar circumstance ever arose (it might not); histories were also written and read as sources of moral examples. In the Bible, authors spoke frequently for God on the topic of future events; they addressed the future directly; they told us what he said, both to long-dead persons or non-persons, and to themselves.

The spokesmen in their own persons are the male prophets whose sayings we still read, from Amos (c. 760 BC) to John on Patmos in a year (I will argue) in the mid 90s, as Christian tradition believed. Those prophets whose words survive (or are said to survive) are only a sample from a much larger cast: not only were there prophets of Baal in the ninth century BC, there were court prophets, individual prophets, women

311

(Huldah, who vouched for the newly found book of the law) and alternative Jeremiahs whose words were probably just as impassioned but who never made it to posterity. Prophets were not peculiar to Yahweh, let alone to Israel: they are amply attested for all sorts of gods at other royal courts across the Near East. Nor was there anything peculiar about their techniques or the style of their heavenly contact. They responded at times to the effects of music (Elisha at 2 Kings 3:15); they might fall into a trance which in turn would pass to others (Moses and the seventy elders, at Numbers 11:25); they fasted, a practice which became ever more attested (Daniel 9:3); they saw symbolic visions by night and day; they had the sense of talking with angels and listening to their words (in heaven, John understands the strange sights which he sees by the voices and song which he hears); they did not, on the whole, repeat dreams. There are parallels for every one of these styles and procedures, although we have to pick and choose them from evidence in ancient Greece or Arabia or modern Africa. The Hebrew prophets were also conscious of compulsion, the necessity of speaking, whether or not they wished: prophecy was a force, or burden, and encounters with God and his angels were extremely alarming.

In the very years from 760 to 750, when Amos struck a new note in Israelite prophecy, the great oracular shrines of the Greek world were also becoming established. In Greece the prophets at oracular sites like Delphi are almost all unknown to us: after a careful preparation and ritual, the gods were believed to speak through them, causing sounds and words which were interpreted as oracles in the god's own person. Among the Greeks one model of prophecy was the invasion of a man or woman by a god: he took full possession of their inner being and suspended their normal faculties. In Israel, however, prophets were enhanced rather than suspended: they announced the word of God in their own persons ('Hear the word of the Lord . . .'); their God communicated with them, rather than banishing their own identity and speaking through them; sometimes, like Isaiah, prophets were connected with the Temple and the cult, but even then we know their names and hear their personal voices. In Greece, personality was often effaced.

Biblical prophets did not only speak what they saw or received from their god: they communicated their message by symbolic actions and names. In the service of the Lord, Hosea even involved his marriage with his message: he married a promiscuous woman at the Lord's bidding, seeing in their relationship a symbol of Israel's own infidelity. When she was unfaithful, the analogy deepened: he continued to love her, as God loved errant Israel, and left us the most poignant prose-poetry of a loving husband, continually hurt and rebuffed by the object of his love. The symbolism even extended to the names of his children: the family took on the contours of the prophet's own message, an errant wife, a first son (called first, 'God scatters' and then 'God sows') and a daughter ('Not-pitied', then 'Pitied') and a second son ('Not my people', then 'My people'). It must have been quite a family for its neighbours, with all these infidelities and the children whose curious names kept being changed. Nobody who followed the drama could miss the religious message.

As speech did not suffice, a Hebrew prophet might call for attention by going naked and barefoot, by wearing a yoke or conspicuously smashing pottery. In Babylon, Ezekiel, a home-owner on the city's 'Grand Canal', suddenly knocked a hole through the wall of his house, took his luggage and carried it out by nightfall: by decamping so abruptly, he was acting out the defeat and Exile of Jerusalem. For deeds could speak louder than words, as they still speak for the seers of Arab Bedouin. 'We are dealing here with something more than symbols or emblems: there is a drive towards total identification of the individual with the nation, even to the point of taking a whole group's sins into one's own body.' It extended to the most painful of moments. Once, the 'word of the Lord' told Ezekiel, 'Son of man, behold, I shall take away from thee the desire of thine eyes with a stroke.' His wife, his heart's desire, then died at nightfall, but, just as God ordered, Ezekiel came before the people in the morning: he was eating no bread and showing no sign of his grief. The people were amazed, and so Ezekiel explained God's message: just as God had killed his wife, so God would profane his sanctuary, the 'desire of their eyes', their own sons and daughters in Jerusalem would fall by the sword. Like Ezekiel, they should neither mourn nor shed tears at their loss, for they would pine away for their iniquities. 'Thus Ezekiel is unto you a sign . . . and when this cometh, ye shall know that I am the Lord God.'

On the morning after his wife's death, this man stood before his hearers, neither crying nor weakening, in order to tell them that his

313

plight was a symbol of the much worse plight awaiting them. The intensity of those who bore these horrible burdens, thinking that they were from God, still touches us chillingly and directly. We are also touched by what they saw. From Amos to John's Apocalypse, prophets saw signs and symbols (the Valley of Dry Bones; the Seething Cauldron; the Four Horsemen), and their interpretations have lodged them in our minds. They also had visions of heaven, carefully dated and placed; generations of mystics and visionaries, both within Judaism and outside it, have been inspired by a vision in the 730s BC and by another, seen on Babylon's Grand Canal, in 593. In the first, Isaiah saw into the court of heaven (one of the seraphim seemed to touch his lips with a burning coal). In the second, Ezekiel saw the heavenly chariot and God in his glory: when God showed him a scroll, written on the front and back, Ezekiel responded in his vision by eating it. His message, therefore, was thoroughly digested, 'and it was in my mouth as honey for sweetness'. Many centuries later, when John ate a scroll 'in the Spirit on the Lord's day', its taste was much less pleasant: it seemed to be bitter, affected, no doubt, by its harsher contents.

Nowadays, prophets confront us as voices against the current who are speaking against their own generation, whether in Jerusalem during the 730s or in Babylon during the Exile. It is easy, therefore, to imagine them as outsiders, particularly because of the style in which they often write. They have a poetic manner; their sayings exploit familiar forms of speech, the lament or funeral dirge, the language of the law suit or legal indictment, the proverb or parable. To heirs of Romantic visionary poetry, such voices imply individuals who are speaking in isolation and are set against their world. There is also the force of what they denounce. They say much about justice and selfish oppression: they become, then, social or political radicals to their modern admirers, who see them as allies and heroes in modern struggles against colonial rule or the violent birth of a just society in South America.

These ways of imagining the prophets are misleading. Poetic speakers were not Romantic loners, the Blakes or Shelleys of their day. In many ancient societies, poets could have a public moral role, in early Greece or Arabia no less than in the Israel of Deborah or Amos. So far from being marginal figures, some of the prophets had close connections with the priesthood (Isaiah, Jeremiah and Ezekiel, especially): Isaiah's vision and calling occurred in the Temple, and the course of the Temple's morning service has been persuasively detected in the imagery of John's Apocalypse. At times, prophets did speak strongly against self-satisfied trust in the Temple cult, but they were not enemies of the entire system. Nor were they the social or political radicals which modern admirers have made of them. Prophets might speak out against individual kings, but they did not speak for popular rule or persistently oppose monarchy itself. Already in Hosea (3:5) we find an idealized image of David, not the David of the Court History who planned lies and adultery as badly as anyone who disgusted Hosea among his own contemporaries. Prophets have almost nothing to say of a political system or government, while their social and ethical views are more truly seen as traditional than as new and radical. Although they speak nobly for justice and against oppression of the poor, they are not speaking for social redistribution or for new values, unknown to contemporaries. Rather, their ethics have traditional roots in the laws which we can attribute to a period before their lifetime: in Israel, law and prophecy should not be romantically opposed. Prophets also knew the traditional wisdom of families' upbringing, which is embedded for us in the later collections of old proverbs: here, too, prophets addressed hearers 'who had lost touch with the roots of their own traditional culture'. They also assumed a natural law, applicable both inside and outside Israel. This assumption helps us to see a coherence in the failings which are denounced by Isaiah, not merely oppression, drunkenness, pride, luxury and injustice, but also idolatry and the seeking of foreign alliances, putting other peoples before trust in God alone. Human self-assertion underlies all these sins which are exercised against the natural order of God and his creation. 'The keynote is order, a proper submission to one's assigned place in the scheme of things . . . the avoidance of any action that would challenge the supremacy of God or seek to subvert the order he has established.' Like the prophets' audience, we are in the presence here of values common to other Near Eastern societies, a hatred of arrogance and excessive self-assertion of man before the gods. The message was more effective for striking a traditional chord. It went with a sense of poetic justice that the man who amassed houses would be left with them in desolation, that the owner who built up vast estates would end with a wretched harvest off an even bigger area. These values and their views of traditional order were not a revolutionary's creed.

We still respond to many of these values, and we also respond to those who speak out against the tide. It is easy, then, to see prophets solely in such terms as 'morally sensitive laymen', as patron saints of social reform or even of theologies of liberation. Some of their home truths, we feel, are still our truths in an instant burst of recognition. Yet their ethics are only one part of the prophets' message: they also saw beyond events to the future, and here they raise a straightforward question. Did their vision of it correspond to what happened: bluntly, were they right?

This question does not exhaust the value or interest of prophetic writings, and it may seem simple-minded. Some of their modern admirers have very little to say about it, except that predictions were not an important part of the prophets' job: they spoke out, telling forth, not foretelling. Even if it may not always be the right question for the prophets themselves, for their followers and heirs it is inarguably relevant. Prediction and fulfilment were extremely important for the people who filled out the prophetic texts which we now read: with hindsight, they added true 'forecasts'. They also read the older texts as if they had still to come true. This habit passed to the first Christians who frequently wrote as if the old prophets' words had suddenly come true in Christian events. Foretelling was seen as a bond between the past and the Christian present: even now, there are people who see it as the main bond between the Old and New Testaments.

There is also a belief that what was said then might yet be fulfilled in our own modern times. Even if a prophecy has proved right once in the past, might it not be proved right again, in Libya, perhaps, or in Middle Eastern politics, in a nuclear holocaust or up in Central Asia in the parched and poisoned landscape which has recently replaced the old Aral Sea: 'the sky is covered by a salty curtain, the sun becomes crimson and disappears in the salt dust. Not one tree grows on the land. The livestock are perishing. The people are falling sick and dying . . .'? Is this desolation, perhaps, the future to which the prophets spoke? The belief that prophets predicted the future has increased the volume of the writings which now pass under their names; it profoundly coloured the Christian Bible; it still surfaces in ways of looking at our own times. It is, however, a belief to which historians can make a decisive contribution.

I I

'Hear the voice of the Bard!/Who present, past, and future sees' (William Blake). A prophet can prophesy one of two futures: good or bad. When we read the good prophecies in Hebrew scripture, we tend to suspend questions of their truth. Wolves have yet to lie down with lambs: children cannot put their hands on cockatrice dens, but the vision that one day they will is a vision of a better tomorrow where poetic licence is forgivable. Prophecies of evil are less comfortable, especially when they run red with anger and vengeance; yet here, too, there may be a moral vision behind them, of justice, perhaps, for the weak, or the punishment of greed and pride. It can strike us as true, whatever the fate of the people whom it addressed. Good or bad, the details of this future take second place to the values with which they were seen, whether hope or optimism, belief in peace, universal rewards for all nations or a moral diagnosis of the faults of a human community.

The prophets, however, claimed to speak the word of God and the visions which God brought to them: their words were often specific, and their views on the future were more than a broad moral outburst. There are times when God's word seems extremely apt. In Genesis, God promised a host of descendants to Abraham, and up they sprang in history, as Israel grew, then scattered through the world and multiplied. In the Exile, the Deuteronomist looked forward to the hope of a possible good from God: within thirty years of his text, Israel was restored to her land. Amos, Hosea and Micah had all warned the northern kingdom of Israel that it was heading for total ruin, and, sure enough, in the 720s the Assyrians destroyed the place totally. In Jerusalem, Isaiah preached not pacifism but a policy of non-alignment in the face of Sennacherib's Assyrian army: in 701 BC the huge Assyrian army departed from the walls of Jerusalem without capturing the city. In the 590s and 580s Jeremiah insisted that the Babylonians were too strong for Judaea and that the Egyptians were not a reliable counter-weight; the Babylonians invaded, the Egyptian forces melted away, and, as predicted, the city of Jerusalem was wrecked. Jeremiah also said that a future hope remained with the exiles who were already in Babylon: about fifty years later, Cyrus allowed these exiles' descendants to return to Judaea. Meanwhile, in exile, Ezekiel saw a valley of dry bones which would one day live; he also envisioned the ideal outline of a future Temple. The dry bones of exiled Israel did live and come home and a new Temple was finally built.

Foresight seems all the more impressive when later, anonymous authors added 'prophecies' after the event: prophecies attached to Isaiah (*c*. 740–700 BC) predicted the coming of Cyrus in the 530s BC. Our book of Isaiah combines the words of at least two, possibly three, prophets who were separated by about two hundred years. The people who added and combined these sayings were concerned that their prophets should be seen to have predicted events correctly at long range. The book of Zechariah was particularly successful. What we now read in his name derives from at least two different prophets, the second of whom begins in chapter 9: this second part was written much later, possibly even later than the conquests of Alexander the Great in the 330s BC (a reference to the deeds of the great young man is often suspected in 9:3–6 but, reluctantly, I suspend judgement). In this late section, chapters 9 to 11 were to be one of the Christians' happiest hunting grounds for proofs and prophecies of Jesus's last days (the donkey on Palm Sunday; the Shepherd whose sheep scatter; the piercing of Jesus's side; the thirty pieces of silver). Presumably, they thought that these sayings were Zechariah's own, delivered in the sixth century BC (or even the seventh: Matthew 23:35). In fact, they are much later and are so detached from any one context that we cannot date them closely or give them an agreed place of origin.

We can detect these artful changes, not merely by being sceptical: we can also consider the state of the text and the tone of the edited whole. Problems of the original Hebrew text are often acute in prophetic writings, nowhere more so than in our book of Jeremiah. It survives in a Greek translation which is considerably shorter and differently arranged from the Masoretic Hebrew text: it probably reflects an earlier and purer version of this tantalizing book. It allows us to check the Masoretic version, from which most Bibles translate, and watch out for later padding. Apparent predictions have multiplied as the bulk of the book has grown: in chapter 27 Jeremiah speaks out on those highly disputed objects, the furnishings of the Jerusalem Temple, and begins by rebuking those prophets who say that they will return to the city after their removal in 597 BC. The Greek text stops with this realistic reproach, but the later Hebrew text has used hindsight and makes the prophet foresee these objects' future movements, from Babylon back to Jerusalem where (supposedly) they returned in the much later age of Ezra. Such padding is all too prophetic.

The very form and shape of a prophetic book are also misleading. They present us with words out of context, selected from a much wider whole which is lost to us: this lack of setting conceals what the prophet himself may have meant and invites us to look for long-range prophecies. Here, editors had a particular power. The hard core of Jeremiah's sayings were arranged into a book with an obvious message to the exiles in Babylon after 587, and its editors added yet more prose and narrative which shows that they shared the Deuteronomist's point of view. There are even those who wonder if like-minded Deuteronomists may have edited our books of Amos, Hosea and others who spoke in northern Israel. As we now read them, they appear to address Judah in the south: perhaps, editors changed their original focus.

Editors, up-daters and deceitful inserters have thus increased our impression of long-range forecasts. What about the prophets themselves? Have their editors distorted their priorities: when they spoke out forcefully, were they forecasting the future or were they warning their hearers and trying to avert it? Why, indeed, should the 'word of the Lord' be inflexible: if people responded to a warning and circumstances changed, might not the future be avoided? Did prophets 'tell forth', but not foretell: was an accurate forecast a sign that their mission had failed?

The very nature of the Hebrew language has been thought to favour 'forthtelling'. Its verbs do not have future tenses, and so a general statement ('the Lord punishes ...') might be mistaken for a future prophecy ('the Lord will punish ...'). Translators, perhaps, make the prophets seem more prophetic than they meant to be. At Joel 2:1 we usually read 'the Day of the Lord is coming, it is near', but the first words might also mean 'it has come' or 'it comes', and the second bit may have been added to save Joel's credit if it did: wonderfully slippery, it could mean 'it is near, or it has come, or it is coming or it is approaching ...' What better language for a prophet's purpose?

It was not, however, a language in which nothing specific could ever be said about the future. Hebrew verbs do not have English tenses, but it is untrue that Hebrews, therefore, had a hazy idea of the line between future and past. Context almost always made it clear, as prophets and their hearers knew. Hebrew verbs express actions as complete or incomplete: in a prophetic saying, verbs like 'die' or 'return' had an obvious future meaning when used in the incomplete form. If a prophet wished to predict, his Hebrew would not stop him.

We also need to think why prophets from Amos onwards began to speak and why their words were remembered from the 760s, whereas Nathan or Samuel were remembered only in stories. If their sole purpose was to denounce, 'tell forth' and perhaps initiate change, they must have begun to forthtell because they were particularly distressed by Israelite sins and misconduct. Promiscuous worship obviously bothered some of them: Hosea, especially, spoke out against worship of other gods beside Yahweh: it was he who created the vicious threesome, idolatry, adultery and the jealousy of a cuckolded God. Such worship, however, was not new or on the increase, while its other sins seem rather run of the mill: the rich were being harsh to the poor; there was a steady stream of adultery; pampered women, the 'kine of Bashan', were growing fat and selfish in an Israelite bull market. Was it all so different from the way that people had behaved in the days of Ahab or even wise old Solomon? Then, too, the charioteers must have been a hard-living bunch, and the horse-dealers cannot have been morally much better. Perhaps there were more opportunities in the mid eighth century for the rich to be yet more grasping, but was it really a society with such a new sickness that the mere sight of it would make a prophet 'tell forth'?

The 'telling forth' was extremely bleak. We know of many earlier prophets through the stories in Samuel and Kings where the Deuteronomist has woven them together: the main difference between the words of an Elijah and an Amos or Hosea is chillingly simple. Prophets in the books of historical narrative direct their predictions against individuals and families, usually the royals. Amos, Hosea and their heirs direct them against the entire people: because of the sins of a few fat cats, adulterers and Baal-fanciers, the entire people of Israel (they say) are going to be annihilated. 'Thus saith the Lord . . .': cosy ideas of a special relationship, choice by God or the hope of making up for it all by killing and burning animals in a temple were disastrously misguided.

The punishment is indiscriminate and utterly awful beside the quality of most poor Israelites' lives: was the punishment, therefore, the prophets' starting point? By emphasizing their moral messages and reading them as ethical voices, do we perhaps misunderstand their mission? Suppose they began with a 'word of the Lord' that Israel's ruin was imminent, with an awful conviction from God that a crash was coming: might not the ethical warnings, the diagnoses of sin, be secondary, an attempt to explain why God should suddenly wish to act in this dreadful way? In the books of the eighth-century prophets, there is condemnation but seldom an exhortation to change. Amos, Hosea or Micah have very few suggestions of how things might yet be different, and where their books mention repentance, the idea may have been inserted by a later editor or included as part of the punishment itself: 'perhaps we have not perceived the full and terrible impact of classical judgement prophecy until we realize that a subtle part of the judgement lay in the temporary inefficacy of the repentance to which the people were nevertheless called'.

This new emphasis has even been connected with the forms of prophetic speech. When prophets denounce their contemporaries they tend to 'tell forth' their words on their own authority. When they speak of imminent judgement, they qualify their words by 'Thus saith the Lord'. Surely the Lord's word is the most important part here, a sign of their priorities: if so, the future came to them first and they felt obliged to speak what they foresaw; the moral denunciations, the 'telling forth' and diagnoses of sin grew from a conviction about the future and tried to explain what the Lord was about to do. If the explanations were rather tenuous, the Lord was the Lord and who could justify his whims? The brows of the early prophets were morally furrowed, but on this understanding of their logic, they spoke in the manner of blackbearded men with placards, predicting bleakly 'Ruin is Nigh'.

Seen in this light, the prophets of the eighth century were primarily concerned with the future: the emphasis on repentance developed later, in Jeremiah, where it is only one of several themes, and especially after the Exile, when prophets began to look to hopes of a new start. It was taken up by the Deuteronomist, writing his great history in exile, and imposed by like-minded editors on other prophetic books, especially on Jeremiah's, which we now read in an edited form. If we describe the first prophets as moral preachers, we miss their main inspiration, the future which they foresaw.

This way of reading them changes many Christians' expectations, but it is not the whole story. 'Thus saith the Lord' does not always precede a beastly prediction or a warning; as we now read them, the prophets are sometimes uncertain, as God's will, perhaps, was uncertain too; they do call for repentance sometimes, even Amos, in verses which are not demonstrably a later addition. Reconstructions of a prophet's logic can also become too tidy. Perhaps the predictions of total ruin so far exceed the sins because of a simple prophetic necessity, the need to be heard. Elijahs and Nathans had come and gone: there were dozens of other good prophets and how was a 'herdsman, and a gatherer of sycamore fruit' like Amos to be widely recognized? The exaggerations need not have been conscious or artful: we all know the pundit who predicts a crash on minimal evidence and thus wins a hearing, even a following, although his inference is wildly implausible.

None the less, convictions about the future were extremely important, perhaps not all-important but arguably more important than the calls for moral reform which modern readers pick up first. In Jeremiah's lifetime, we read of Jeremiah's constant struggle against other committed prophets who were urging an opposite course of action. The struggle, we have to believe, was one between truth and falsehood, not between two types of interim statement which might induce moral changes of heart. Falsehood, not misplaced warning, was a mark of a false prophet (Deuteronomy 18:16 ff.), although people were probably not so unsubtle as to think that false prophets never spoke bits of the truth occasionally.

It is not, then, misplaced to ask nowadays if prophets foretold the future and foretold it correctly. One aspect of it is obvious, except to posterity. When prophets predicted imminent ruin, they must have predicted it to their own contemporaries: there was no point in Isaiah addressing a future six centuries beyond him before an audience who would by then be long dead. The primary meaning lies within a lifespan: who really cares about the sin of felling rain-forests if the world will only begin to warm in six hundred years' time? Something in God's Creation will probably have turned up to change the remote prediction. When prophets give a general view of a new age of wrath or peace, their time scale may be vaguer and more long term. When they are specific, about enemies from the north or west or total ruin for Israel or the fall of Jerusalem, they are not predicting events in the 1990s but precise events which their own hearers could anticipate.

Our chances of finding prophecies which have turned out to be false might seem very slim: editors are likely to have omitted them or rephrased them; their wording may have been forgotten; they may have been turned into open-ended generalities. None the less, there are examples, and I will pick from three groups: specific prophecies of an individual's fate, predictions of the outcome of great political events and specific predictions of a brilliant future. In the books of Kings many prophets predict the fate of an important person or place, but the Deuteronomist, their ultimate author, is much too artful to allow these prophecies not to come true. In the prophets' own books, there seems to be more of a conflict. At Amos 7:11 Amos is said to be predicting that King Jeroboam will die by the sword; at Hosea 1:4 Hosea is told how to name his own son in order to publicize the Lord's intention, that 'yet a little while' and God will punish the house of Jehu and end the 'kingship of the house of Israel'. At Jeremiah 22:19 Jehoiakim, king of Judah, will be 'buried with the burial of an ass, drawn and cast forth beyond the gates of Jerusalem'. Jehoiakim was the king who threw Jeremiah's scroll of prophecies on to a fire: at 36:30 (copied faithfully, we are told, by Jeremiah's scribe Baruch) his 'dead body shall be cast out in the day to the heat, and in the night to the frost'.

It is a delicate question whether any of these prophecies proved true. According to 2 Kings 14:23 King Jeroboam 'slept with his fathers' after a long reign of forty-one years: it is a hostile priest, however, who reports what Amos had 'said' against the king (7:10 ff.), whereas words ascribed to Amos himself only predict death for the 'house of Jeroboam' with the sword (Jeroboam's son was indeed assassinated and the dynasty came to an end). Perhaps the priest misrepresented what Amos announced: alternatively, the priest's version is correct, and Amos's editors have saved his face (changing the king to the 'house of the king'). At Hosea 1:4 Hosea is perhaps right about the house of Jehu ('yet a little while' involved a delay of about ten to fifteen years) but not right about the 'kingship'. The death of the last of Jehu's house did not end kingship in the north: it lasted for yet another twenty-odd years. It is not even clear that Hosea's words refer only to kingship in the north: on one view, they refer to kingship in 'all Israel', Judah and Jerusalem included, which lasted for more than a hundred and fifty years. As for Jehoiakim the book burner, he has 'slept with his fathers' too, according to 2 Kings 24:6. Nothing is said about a violent death or an outcast's burial, and traditionally, 'sleeping with the fathers' is understood as a peaceful end. If so, the editors of Jeremiah allowed an amazingly false prophecy to be repeated twice over without removing it. Although the peaceful implications of 'sleeping' have recently been questioned, it is still the case that nothing is written elsewhere of Jehoiakim's death which matches Jeremiah's prophecy, although a harsher end for him would probably have suited the book of Kings' outlook. It is likely that here too the 'word of the Lord' was wrong. Elsewhere, when it appears to be right about the wretched end of a Pharaoh or a Babylonian king, the reason is simple: its prophecy was written after the event.

In political affairs, the future was hardly less complex. Whom exactly did Amos imagine as the devourers of the kingdom of Israel? In the 720s the Assyrians fulfilled his prediction, but when he spoke in the 760s to 750s, a revival of Assyrian power would have been a very eccentric guess: he may have meant the Aramaeans (dispute continues, here). Isaiah's predictions raise even more tantalizing problems. In 701 King Sennacherib's army withdrew from before the walls of Jerusalem, a fact which we also know from his official Assyrian version. In 2 Kings we have two stories of the retreat: at 18:13–16 King Hezekiah submits to the Assyrian king and pays him the necessary tribute; in 2 Kings 19, after a long prophecy ascribed to Isaiah, an 'angel of the Lord' slays 'an hundred fourscore and five thousand' Assyrians, and their army then slinks home defeated. Sennacherib's death follows, although we happen to know that he did not die until twenty years after this campaign.

In the book of Isaiah, the prophet plainly denounces King Hezekiah's attempts to strike up an alliance with Egypt against Assyria between 705 and 701: these sayings belong exactly in a historical context. There are also oracles against the pride of the Assyrians and their own future ruin (10:5 ff.; 14:24; 17:12; 29:28; 31:5). It is natural to run the two themes together and assume that Isaiah denounced his king's search for foreign alliances, and that he continued to denounce Assyria too, and assert that their ruin would also come about (it did, but about a century later). However, there is a much stronger case for separating the two themes: when Isaiah attacks Judah's searching for foreign aid, he speaks as if Judah's fate is already sealed, and Yahweh will come up against her like a ravening lion (31:4 ff.). The future ruin of the Assyrians is either a separate theme, prophesied on a later occasion, or a theme which has been added to Isaiah's work. In the prophet's own view, an invading army would ravage a faithless Jerusalem, a vision of doom as bleak as any in Amos. On another occasion, Isaiah may also have spoken of Assyria's imminent ruin, but if so, he was wrong on both counts. So far from being ruined, Hezekiah and Jerusalem surrendered and cleverly bought their survival; as for the Assyrians, they returned home richer and survived for almost a century, much of it at the peak of their power. The discrepancy bothered Isaiah's heirs, and in 2 Kings 19, we can read their alternative version: here, Isaiah predicts Assyria's ruin (not Judah's) in 701, and an angel of the Lord miraculously carries out a massacre in order to prove his prophet right.

The incident remains a major textual battlefield, but other prophecies are more clear-cut. In Isaiah 20 we read how Isaiah walked naked and barefoot for three whole years to emphasize his prophecy of an imminent conquest of Egypt: it had been given, we are told, at the Lord's command. In Jeremiah 43 we find the prophet Jeremiah in Egypt after Jerusalem's ruin in 587 BC; he is picking up big stones and piling them up on the pavement of a 'house of Pharaoh' in the Egyptian frontier town of Tahpanhes to symbolize (on the word of the Lord) that King Nebuchadnezzar of Babylon would reign over Egypt and 'set his throne upon these stones that I have hid'. Total disaster is also foreseen for all Jews in Egypt (Jeremiah 44): it is not with them that hopes remain.

The naked walking and the stone-piling both turned out to be misplaced. There is no evidence of any conquest of Egypt in Isaiah's lifetime, and although Nebuchadnezzar is known to have fought the Pharaoh in 568/7, there is no evidence that he set up his throne or established his rule in the land. Far away up the Nile, one group of Jews continued, despite Jeremiah, to serve and pay worship to Yahweh: we meet them in their papyri as late as *c.* 410 BC, where they are actively petitioning others for help and have not been wiped out, despite several setbacks. They had a tradition of religious services in their independent temple and the engaging habit of worshipping Yahweh with other gods.

Defeats and deaths were hazardous guesses, but blessings, surely, were a safer bet: if phrased more generally, they could live on beguilingly for many years. Prophets, however, were prone to human over-excitement: in chapter 9 Isaiah hails the new prince of peace for ever and ever ('unto us a child is born'), but whether he meant Hezekiah or a royal baby, his hopes for eternity were extravagant (the 'child' did not last: the long-range Christian reading of the passage is misplaced). In the 520s we have seen how both Zechariah and Haggai heaped royal hopes and praises on leaders of the Temple's rebuilding in Jerusalem during a turbulent period at the Persian court: 'I will shake the heavens and the earth', the Lord seems to tell Haggai in 2:21, but peace soon returned to the Persian Empire and Zerubbabel disappeared from history; he was not the Anointed, and Zechariah then saw a vision which cancelled the prospects of a few months before. Misplaced optimism was only too easy in this momentous era: in the 530s it confronts us, above all, in an unknown prophet, who has been passed off by editors as if he were Isaiah.

At Isaiah 45:1 ff. this unknown Jewish observer hails the Persian king Cyrus as the Lord's Anointed. He was speaking from Babylonia, evidently after Babylon's capture: the city had not been destroyed or burned, contrary to various prophecies against it which occur in our book of Jeremiah. Cyrus turned out to be the king who permitted the Jews to return to Jerusalem – perhaps this very prophet's praises impressed and influenced Cyrus's advisers – but neither the Return nor its initiator lived up to expectations. During Cyrus's reign, little progress, if any, was made with the Temple's rebuilding; there was no new golden age and the new Anointed came to a hideous end of his own making. The Greek historian Herodotus claimed to know many different stories of Cyrus's death, but pointedly, he tells the version in which the king is berated by a queen of the barbaric Scyths. Far away beyond the River Oxus, Cyrus invades the Central Asian steppes, only to be told that he is thoroughly aggressive and 'insatiate of blood'. The Scyths then kill him in the ensuing battle and their queen fills a wine-skin with human blood; she seeks out Cyrus's corpse and stuffs the head of the 'Lord's Anointed' into the wine-skin to take the revenge which this man of war deserves.

Prophets, in short, did prophesy, foretelling specific events throughout the ups and downs of at least two hundred and fifty years. Events, however, were elusive, and the prophecies' foresight is no more impressive or accurate than a moderately able foreign journalist's. We may admire their moral visions of truth, and we respect, above all, their predicaments, at such risk to kings and enemies and even, as Jeremiah realized, to people who would not, and by nature could not, change under threat of disaster. But we should also respect the ordinary Israelite. In the prophetic books and stories, we catch glimpses of other competing prophets, the Micaiahs and Hanoniahs whom our prophets oppose. Like uncertain investors, plain men of the world were beset with conflicting advice. It was all meant sincerely enough, and the word of the Lord was claimed by both sides; those who outlived Amos or remembered Isaiah in 701 were old enough to know that human predictions from the Lord simply did not come true. Why, then, should they heed one rather than the other? Predictions, like insiders' circulars, were always seductive, but in simple terms of performance against the future's index, there was a very clear case for leaving Isaiah or Haggai, Jeremiah or even Amos at the mercy of their own convictions.

Prophets, however, were more fortunate in their friends and editors than in the exact course of the future. When we read them nowadays, most of the rivals have been eliminated; contexts have been dropped or altered; hindsight has been brought to bear and failures bypassed by various routes. If a predicted disaster did not happen, was it, perhaps, that people had heeded and repented before God? At 3:12 Micah predicts that 'Zion for your sake be plowed as a field, and Jerusalem shall become heaps': by *c.* 600 BC nothing of the sort had happened, but we can see from Jeremiah 26:18 ff. that people explained the failure by claiming that King Hezekiah had repented of his sins and staved off the prediction. Traditionally, Hezekiah was said to have been so virtuous that he ought to have had nothing much worth repenting of: of all the eighth-century prophets', Micah's original sayings had probably been the bleakest announcements of woe and incontrovertible doom. Repentance was invoked to save their credit.

If the worst had not happened, might not people have become better: if the best had not happened, must they not have become worse or omitted an important condition, rebuilding the Temple, for instance? Even if people were much the same as usual, what about God? In one poignant outburst even Jeremiah stated the belief that God had deceived him and made him tell nothing but lies: the Christian thinker Origen used these verses to support the view that there were beneficial lies which intelligent Christians should maintain before their simpler brethren. If God's word was not a deceit, might it not be genuine vacillation? In Eden, after all, God had threatened death and promptly gone back on the warning: why could not God repent of some beastly purpose and behave like any fair-minded liberal (Amos 7:4–6 states an example of it as a fact; Ezekiel 26 predicts very clearly that Nebuchadnezzar will take and destroy Tyre, but by 29:18 the 'word of the Lord' has changed its tune and God is said to be giving his army Egypt in return for their awful labours in vain at Tyre itself). Complications were endless. When prophets spoke, who should change first: God, whose word they believed they were preaching, or the hearers, who might, then, prove the prophets to be false? It was awkward enough for the hearers, but for the prophets themselves, it risked being self-defeating, at least until admiring people recast their sayings and turned them into scrolls for a new generation.

III

In the centuries before the Exile, probably before 300 BC, the conflict between true prophecy and repentance, God's knowledge and God's mercy, impelled an unknown author to a minor masterpiece on the dilemmas of a prophet's calling. At 2 Kings 14:25 (in the mid eighth century) a prophet, Jonah, is said to have predicted Israel's rule over a large and reluctant fraction of the entire Near East. Nothing more is known of him until he was given a story of his own.

Its main lines are simple. God tells Jonah to go down to Nineveh and 'cry against it' because of its wickedness: Jonah refuses and catches a boat to Tarshish in the opposite direction. The storm rises up; the sailors panic; Jonah reveals his sin against God; he allows himself to be pitched overboard; the storm abates; the sailors praise Jonah's God and a sea-monster swallows the drowning Jonah and saves him. Not until the Middle Ages was the monster identified as a whale (the Greek of Matthew 12:40 is not specific); in the 1960s, 'near the oil rigs of Mosul, the pious visitor could still admire the remains of Jonah's whale in a mosque bearing Jonah's name'.

Already, the story has a wide horizon. The men of Nineveh are Gentiles, yet God wishes to punish their wickedness: like the early prophets, the author had realized that there were universal laws of behaviour, that a natural justice extended outside Israel, and that God and his envoys were not only concerned with breaches of the Jewish law. As for Jonah's disobedience, we learn that he has run away, knowing 'that thou art a gracious God, and merciful, slow to anger, and of great kindness, and repentest thee of the evil'. It was not that Nineveh was dangerous, although it was extraordinarily big, three days' journey in breadth, like London during office hours. It was that God had a soft heart. What if the Ninevites were to change their habits? Why go east and cry instant doom in a crowded traffic jam if God, and the hearers, might change their minds and prove the prophet wrong? Jonah refuses to play the Amos or Hosea and be made to look foolish by the sequel: Nineveh was Nineveh ('Israel's most barbaric and savage enemies, comparable,' to one scholar, 'with the technicians who ran the gas-chambers of Auschwitz'): why go and warn them, if God might go back on his word as a result, saving the enemy and discrediting his own envoy? Signs of liberal rot had already begun to show in Eden: God had threatened Adam with the death-penalty, but as soon as it was due he had cancelled it. Why run the risk of being employed to let a liberal God off his own essential wetness?

The sailors, decent men, are Gentiles, but they end by worshipping Jonah's God. They try to spare their passenger; they beg pardon from God; they jettison him only when they have no other resort; Jonah himself is willing to die because he does not wish these decent Gentiles to die because of his naughtiness.

The Lord, however, scoops him into the sea-monster, and after a typically biblical interlude, in which Jonah is given a long hymn of thanks out of context, and tells him again to go down to Nineveh: this time, Jonah obeys. He cries, 'Yet forty days, and Nineveh shall be overthrown': Micah or Amos had never been bleaker, but unlike Israel, the Ninevites listen: they 'believed God'. They begin to fast: they put on sackcloth 'from the greatest of them even to the least of them'. When their king and his nobles hear, they order even greater amends: every 'beast, herd and flock' is to fast and wear sackcloth, sweat rugs, perhaps, for the cattle and ashen little jackets for Assyrian cats. 'And God saw their works, that they turned from their evil way; and God repented of the evil, that he said he would do unto them; and he did it not.' We might well wonder nowadays if God is indeed omniscient: if so, does he know all along that Nineveh will save itself? Neither Jonah nor the author sees the story in these terms: Nineveh (they imply) might not listen and the place might have to be destroyed: there is genuine uncertainty for God too. Either way, Jonah will still be the loser. By repenting, the Ninevites refute his prophecy; but if they do not repent, then his mission is pointless (why send him, if Nineveh is never going to listen anyway and will thus be destroyed none the less?).

The author (and Jonah) saw the prophets' paradox: 'the only true prophet is an ineffectual one, one whose warnings fail to materialize. All good prophets are false prophets, undoing their own utterances in the very act of producing them.' Jonah, therefore, is angry and asks God to take his life: the Lord questions him ('Doest thou well to be angry . . . ?'); Jonah sits to the east of the city and broods, waiting to see 'what would become of the city': would Nineveh, perhaps, sin again or would God change his mind, perhaps when he saw that his prophet was so cross? It was not so much that Nineveh, that 'barbaric and savage enemy', had been allowed to save itself. It was, rather, that Jonah had been publicly shamed and made to look a fool. 'So, too, might anger take the sweet-natured head of Save the Earth, having warned that millions will shortly perish owing to the greenhouse effect on the planet.'

When the Gentile sailors are in danger of dying, Jonah agrees to die for them, but when Gentile Nineveh escapes death by repentance, Jonah sits and scowls. In reply, God sends a rapidly climbing plant to shade his prophet: he then sends a worm to kill it. Jonah is angry, because he misses the shade: God (who has now shown that he can be destructive) reproaches him for pitying a mere plant while not pitying 'six score thousand persons' in Nineveh who 'cannot discern between their right hand and their left hand; and also much cattle'. Jonah who had pitied the Gentile sailors, is now shown that he should pity a city where 'creaturely ignorance' tells in its Gentiles' favour. The story maintains its universal sweep, from storms to seas, wind and sun, subfusc animals in sackcloth, to two groups of Gentiles and a worm-eaten plant. Traditionally, the plant has been seen as a gourd, but the Hebrew word is uncertain. When Latin biblical translators changed it to ivy, Augustine knew of congregations in north Africa who rioted until the gourd was brought back to the text. Ivy would not have liked Nineveh: when Alexander the Great tried planting it near by, it died from heat, not heavenly maggots.

With its many paradoxes, the story lays bare the prophets' predicament. Why be an Amos and preach disaster or a Jeremiah whom God might be deceiving anyway? In his mercy, God was greater than all of them, but a prophet had to surrender his own self-respect so that God might be wonderfully liberal and go back on his prophesied word. It was not much of a vocation. People harassed these prophets and tore up their scrolls: they mocked, disbelieved and hated them in their own countries: prophets spoke out against the tide, and it was believed that they had suffered, perhaps even died, for the sake of what they said. To crown it all, God might then go and prove them wrong. There must be another way, to anyone who thought like Jonah's inventor. In the Bible's book of Daniel we can unravel such a way, the artful alternative of 'the only book of the Bible of which the origin and purpose can be known with certainty'.

The book has the familiar ingredients of a biblical success story: its hero probably never existed; he was credited with visions he never saw and actions he never did; the book itself arose from two separate sources, cunningly joined into one, while its dates and kings are incorrect and its setting is a fiction, posing as history. Daniel himself is a puzzling figure. In the book of Ezekiel he is suddenly mentioned as a very wise person who is aware of secrets in the future and who is to be one of only three survivors (with Noah and Job) of God's wrath at human sin (Ezekiel 14:4; 28:3). His name means 'God has judged' and seems to refer to a legendary sage with whom Jewish hearers were familiar. The name Danel (but not Daniel) has been found in tablets from the Canaanite site of Ras Shamra which were written way back in the second millennium BC, but Jewish sources knew a separate Danel who was supposedly a son of the legendary Enoch. The name Danel in the tablets does not prove that a real Daniel had lived in the historical past.

Like Jonah, Daniel became a peg for subsequent stories. The ones which we now have all place him at the court of the Babylonian king Nebuchadnezzar, where he was said to have been deported in the early sixth century BC. In our book of Daniel 1–6 we read how Daniel insists on vegetarian food at court; how Nebuchadnezzar dreams of an image of four metals with feet of clay; how Daniel refuses to bow down to the king's golden idol at the sound of music and is thrown into the Fiery Furnace. Nebuchadnezzar also dreams of an over-tall tree (and learns that he will eat grass like a beast of the field). At Belshazzar's feast, a hand writes mysteriously on the palace wall and Daniel explains it; later, Daniel refuses not to pray to his God as usual and is thrown into the Lion's Den.

These six stories survive in two different languages (Hebrew for the first one, Aramaic thereafter) and are only a selection from a wider group of Daniel tales: we also find him in the story of Susanna and the Elders (now in the Apocrypha of English Bibles), and in Bel and the Dragon, and no doubt we could have found him in many more. Probably, some of these stories had led an earlier, separate life: twice they call Daniel by the second name of Belteshazzar, a Babylonian name which perhaps was the name of the stories' original hero. Some of their details, too, have probably been updated: the number of metals in the king's dream image (originally there would have been three, not four); the reference of the writing at the feast (to kings, at first, not kingdoms); the king to whom the dream of the tree applied (Nabonidus, perhaps, as the last king of Babylon, not Nebuchadnezzar, the Jews' deadly enemy). As we now read these recycled stories, they have no true connection with Nebuchadnezzar's history. They date from the third century BC, as certain details show us. Nebuchadnezzar's music is played on instruments with Greek, not Hebrew, names (including the first known use of the word *symphonia*, source of our symphony). The marriage of iron and clay in the king's dream-image almost certainly refers to a notorious marriage in the 240s BC between the kings of Egypt and Syria who were successors of Alexander the Great.

These stories, then, were improving fictions which would gladden a good Jew's heart in the third century's age of foreign monarchies and widespread contact with the Gentile courts. At the time their Aramaic language was understood from Antioch to the River Oxus, from Jerusalem to the Punjab: in their cosmopolitan style, the stories told how Daniel, a Jew in exile, rose ever higher up the ladder of an oriental court, onward and upward despite lying courtiers, foolish monarchs and punishments which the kings themselves regretted later. Daniel succeeded by his own skill, piety and essential goodness, a talented yuppie who always observed the code: he was a happy example for Jews in this world of Gentile kings. Daniel ate no heathen food, but his face beamed brightly on his vegetarian diet. He bowed to no idols, and he prayed as and when he wished. His God was the greatest who outclassed all others and, like Jonah's, earned Gentile respect: God even drew praises from a chastened Nebuchadnezzar.

It was not Daniel's business to prophesy spontaneously so much as to interpret on demand: when asked, he coped with two royal dreams and with heavenly writing on the wall. Their interpretations involved him in specific views of the future, and here there were some influential hints. 'Over against the candlestick upon the plaster of the wall of the king's palace,' a hand wrote four words at Belshazzar's feast: *'mene, mene, tekel, upharsin.'* In Semitic script the hand would have written these words like speedwriting, as consonants without any letters for vowels: their natural meanings were weights and measures (two minas, a shekel and two parts: perhaps in an earlier story they had referred to four Babylonian kings). Daniel, however, interpreted only three of the words, not four, and understood the last word's consonants (prs) as *peres*, not as *parsin*. His free choice of reading and his word-by-word decoding played havoc with the natural sense. The message became 'Thou art weighed in the balances, and art found wanting', a much more immediate threat to a king.

Belshazzar's feast is a landmark in the history of constructive misreading: by similar methods texts were to be deciphered word by word in subsequent Jewish and Christian groups and reread for prophetic meanings which they never had. The dream of the king's colossal image (clay and four metals) was also influential. Daniel interpreted the metals as four successive kingdoms (the equation of metals with kingdoms or empires was probably a Greek idea by origin): they were followed, however, by a fifth kingdom which would 'break in pieces all others' and itself 'never be destroyed'. This promise of a future 'fifth monarchy' was a new and exciting idea which could be updated to fit all manner of historical change: it lived on, therefore, as a challenge to current kingdoms, whether French or even English (in the brief Civil War of 1649). Daniel's author believed that the fifth monarchy would be a future kingdom of the Jews and their God. This little hint of eternal rule was artfully presented. It was ascribed to old Daniel, back in the Babylonian Age: his other predictions were already known to be correct (at the author's time of writing, four kingdoms, or empires, had indeed come or gone). If Daniel was right about so much, who was to say that he was not also right about this future kingdom of the Jews?

There was a lesson here for budding prophets. Instead of running the risks of a Jonah, why not stay on the sidelines and pass off your prophecy as somebody else's ancient text? Why not preface it with 'prophecies' which had already come true in order to support your own? This method was safer and more impressive (age lent great credibility): there were no nasty puzzles about God's word and God's possible wetness or about proving to be true only if your words to Nineveh fell on deaf ears. A lifetime or so later, this answer to Jonah's dilemma confronts us in the remainder of the Daniel book.

First, the meaning of the image in Daniel 3 had to prove to be false. Instead of collapsing feebly, the era of 'iron and clay' (the era of the successors to Alexander the Great) turned out to be harsh and vindictive; Daniel had been wrong about the present and also turned out to be wrong about the eternal fifth monarchy of the future. In 168/7 the Greek-speaking successor-king, Antiochus IV, marched south and was frustrated on a venture in Egypt: on his return, he began to persecute the Jews in Jerusalem. He forced them to behave like Greeks, to abandon their law and cult, and to allow the altar in their Temple to be defiled by heathen gods. Now, if ever, was a time for renewed prophecy, yet who would be a Jonah when the fate of the nation hung in the balance? Artfully, an unknown author decided to be Daniel instead. First, he composed a prophetic vision in Aramaic which cleverly picked up the language and themes of the old story of Daniel and the image of the four metals. Then, he added three further visions which (he said) were Daniel's own, revealed or explained by angels from heaven.

The Daniel stories had been told anonymously because they were narratives; these new utterances, being visions, were told personally as if by Daniel himself. In the first of them (our chapter 7) Daniel sees four monstrous beasts (four successive kingdoms in Asia), the last of which (Alexander's heirs) is sprouting an eleventh horn (King Antiochus IV). This eleven-horned beast is slain by a deeply significant figure, the 'Ancient of Days', the first passage in scripture which envisages God as old and white-haired. He is joined by 'one like the Son of man' who seems to be an angelic figure: he comes on clouds, receives eternal dominion and one day will exalt the 'saints of the most High' (who are angels, elsewhere, in Hebrew scripture): they in turn will exalt the Jews, the people in their care.

According to this vision, God will kill Antiochus IV, the persecuting monster, and deliver the Jews to eternal dominion after they have suffered for 'three times and a half'. Conspicuously, this vision does not state that Antiochus will end the cult of God in Jerusalem's Temple. The cult, we know, was abolished at the altar in December 167 BC, and as the author did not mention this fact, presumably he wrote before it had happened. In 168 BC, therefore, when the troubles began, he had looked ahead to 'three years and a half' of suffering (half a sabbatical period): afterwards, Antiochus (he thought) would die in mid 164 and the Jews would triumph.

In mid 164, however, Antiochus was alive and well and persecution was still raging on. What, exactly, were the 'three times and a half': were they three and a half years or more? Patently, more visions were needed from Daniel, and in 8–12 we can still read the results. Daniel 'ate no pleasant bread neither came flesh nor wine' in his mouth; he learns that Antiochus will overthrow the cult in the Temple and last for 2,300 days. The cult ceased late in December 167, and on this view, six more years would follow before the 'beast' was dead. Hunger, therefore, had increased the visionary time-scale.

Reading, however, then shortened it: in chapter 9 Daniel is said to begin by reading the old prophecy of Jeremiah that Jerusalem would lie desolate for seventy years. The angel Gabriel explains the timing: 'half a week' remains, or 'three and a half years' from the ending of the Temple cult: here, persecution has been shortened from 161 to the middle of 163 BC.

The author gave a fine impression of the terrors of a vision and the effects of fasting for too long: perhaps his own experiences were behind the ones which he ascribed to Daniel. Certainly, they impinged on the final chapters (10–12). From another mighty angel, Daniel here learns a very specific sweep of history which had already occurred since the death of Alexander the Great. Hindsight improved its apparent foresight, but the author then risked some future details. King Antiochus would be rebuffed by Rome (this had already happened in Egypt): he would return, however, to conquer Egypt and would then turn east and north on diverting news. Finally, he would encamp in Syria where Michael, Israel's angel, would defeat him spectacularly. A time of awful trouble would follow, 'such as never was'; then, many of those who had died would awake. The unrighteous would be shamed for ever, but the righteous would shine like the stars in eternal life. There would be no mistaking the two groups: sinners and eternal glow-worms, their names were already written in a heavenly book.

The author put a time limit to this extremely turbulent future: from the ending of the Temple cult to the Last Judgement there would be 1,290 days (in a postscript, a later author extended the number to 1,335). They ran, therefore, from December 167 to spring 163: the author, presumably, was writing in early 164 (perhaps when the first prophecy of 'three times and a half' was looking too optimistic). Undeterred, he foresaw mayhem with Michael, victory, appalling suffering and then the rewards for those in the virtuous columns of God's heavenly book.

Reassuringly, his foresight (unlike his hindsight) was extremely poor. He ignored the new element of Roman power which would certainly have intervened again and prevented Antiochus from ever conquering Egypt in the 160s. He gave only the vaguest hint of the Jews' own increasing resistance, led by the heroic Maccabees, which would eventually save their traditional way of life. Blind to power-politics, he was also wrong about the timing, place and manner of Antiochus's end. Antiochus did not die in spring 165; he did not come into conflict with the angel Michael: he caught a sickness, like many since, on a journey to territories in central Iran. The book was right, however, about one cardinal fact: against all odds, Antiochus did die suddenly, and the persecution ceased.

Daniel's four visions of history (the first in Aramaic, the rest in Hebrew) were then connected together and attached to the six older stories of Daniel in Babylon (the first in Hebrew, the others in Aramaic). According to the author, Daniel had sealed up all these visions in a book during the sixth century BC: without the constraints of a title-page or copyright, he himself then issued what he had faked and pieced together. Soon after December 163 BC he launched the first known book of resistance literature, a fiction and fake in one.

Unlike Jonah's simple prophecy, this complex series of visions was written, not spoken, and was issued under a false name. It revealed the course of a turbulent future and led up to a final climax: in this sense, it was apocalyptic. It was not, however, so very different from the scope of older Hebrew prophecies: apocalyptic writing is a natural heir to the final predictions of an Ezekiel or Zechariah or even 'first Isaiah's' chapters on total destruction. Apocalyptic writing was more detailed and more literary (the newer prophets could ponder the older ones' texts); it was also much more explicit. The most obvious difference was merely that it was written, not uttered, and that it hid itself under old and false names: apocalyptic writings solved Jonah's dilemma.

Daniel's apocalyptic text was beautifully peppered with obscurities: 'seventy weeks', 'a time, two times and a half', 'one like the Son of man', and the new age of pious, eternal glow-worms. All these references could be recycled by anyone whom the main prophecy impressed. Two hundred years later, Christians were still recycling it: they claimed that Daniel, that ancient figure, had predicted their Christ and his Resurrection: the 'seventy weeks' of one of the prophecies were cleverly interpreted to give a date (the birth of Jesus) under Herod the Great. In the later third century (*c.* 270–300) a sharp-eyed pagan critic, Porphyry, remarked that Daniel's accurate knowledge stopped abruptly in 167 BC: the book, then, must have been faked at that moment because after 167, it was wrong. Nobody believed him, neither Jews nor Christians, and under a Christian Empire the book in which he had argued the truth was burned. In its absence people continued to believe that Daniel was a genuine prophet and that the 'seventy weeks' looked forward to Christ. Not until 1672 was the truth rediscovered and not until the nineteenth century was it accepted as basic knowledge by scholars.

Long before then, the predictions of its unknown author had rebounded on his people. 'Art thou the Christ, the Son of the Blessed?', the high priest is said to have asked Jesus in Mark's Gospel. 'And Jesus said, I am,' according to the Gospel, 'and ye shall see the Son of Man sitting on the right hand of power and coming in the clouds of heaven.' It was enough, said the Gospel, for the high priest's patience. He 'rent his clothes and saith, What need we any further witnesses?' The Gospel, perhaps even Jesus, took the imagery of Daniel's vision as open and yet to be fulfilled. The heroes of the Jewish resistance, meanwhile, lay dead, not resurrected, in their graves.

19

The Old in the New

I

Among the early Christians, scripture seemed to have come wonderfully true: correspondence could be found everywhere; texts and events confirmed each other; and biblical truth was thought to blossom. Soon after his conversion, Paul learned from the Apostles in Jerusalem that 'Christ died for our sins according to the scriptures; And that he was buried, and that he rose again the third day according to the scriptures' (1 Corinthians 15: 3–4). Less than a year had passed since the Crucifixion, but old scripture already seemed to confirm what was thought to have happened. In Luke's Gospel, Jesus himself is said to have taught his disciples the texts which had now come true: he taught them (so the Gospel claims) when he met them after his Resurrection. During Jesus's last days, even statements as obscure as those in Second Zechariah (9–14) appeared to have come true in a rush. Biblical commentaries were never easier to write: the author of Acts, Paul's companion, made Paul tell King Agrippa that he is 'saying none other things than those which the prophets and Moses did say should come'.

New movements like to claim inevitability and to attach their events to what has gone before. In Matthew's and John's Gospels, things are said to have happened 'that the scripture might be fulfilled': they range from Jesus's decision to use parables to the driving of a spear into his side on the Cross. What, though, was the nature of this fulfilment? Perhaps the Hebrew prophets should pronounce on it: if they had heard the Christian scripture, they would have been amazed, perhaps even indignant. Here were people who claimed that Isaiah, addressing King Ahaz in the later eighth century BC, had predicted the birth of Jesus

338

(Immanuel), when all he had meant was the birth of a royal prince in the later eighth century BC. They ignored the surrounding context and forced the meaning of the words. In Hebrew, Isaiah's word for the child's mother meant 'young woman', not virgin: when a translator later turned it into Greek, his Greek word, at a pinch, could have the same double meaning. Christians, however, began to read it one-sidedly as a prophecy of Jesus's virgin birth. They were doubly misguided: it did not concern Jesus nor did it concern a virgin.

The end of the story had no more been foretold than the beginning. According to Luke 24, Jesus had taught that it was written that the Christ should suffer, and on the third day rise from the dead. Where, exactly, was it so written? Key texts about suffering could be found in the book of Isaiah, where they derived from an unnamed prophet in the later sixth century BC. It was, admittedly, not obvious whom he meant when he wrote so movingly about his Suffering Servant; almost certainly he meant Israel, but perhaps he left other possibilities open. The situation, therefore, might seem to have been left somewhat vacant, but the prophet certainly did not imagine that a single Messiah (the Christ) would fill it: Messiahs did not suffer, let alone die on crosses. As for rising 'on the third day', Messiahs were not forecast to rise either. The one remotely similar allusion was in the book of Hosea (6:2): in the mid eighth century he had said of Yahweh that 'on the third day he will raise us up, and we shall live in his sight'. The text did not refer to individuals or empty tombs, and Hosea would have considered such a reading to be rubbish. He would have been thankful to turn to more recent Christian commentators: 'The people, the "we", are the subject: they are not portrayed as dead. Rather, they are sorely wounded and Yahweh is expected to revive them by restoring their vitality and so saving them from death. There is no notion of a . . . resurrection.' The text, in short, had no Christian implications.

When Christians quoted those old prophecies, they used Greek translations which were untrue to the Hebrew originals: they ran separate bits of a text into one; they twisted the sense and reference of the nouns (Paul, at Galatians 3:8, is a spectacular example); they mistook the speakers and the uses of personal pronouns (John 19:37 or Matthew 27:9); they thought that David or Isaiah had written what they never wrote (Acts 2 or Acts 8:26); they muddled Jeremiah with Zechariah

(Matthew 27:9); they reread the literal sense and found a non-existent allegory (Paul, to the Galatians at 4:21–3). There are vintage errors in the famous speech which Acts' author gives to Peter at Pentecost: Peter tortures bits of Psalms 16 and 132, mistakes their meaning and context, and quotes them in a poor Greek translation, although Greek was not the historical Peter's mother tongue and most of his supposed audience would not have understood a word of it.

Among all these proof-texts and old prophecies, the clamour of fundamentalists and the talk of new keys to Old Testaments, it is hard to hear the Hebrew prophets on their own terms. What, in fact, had they predicted about Jesus Christ or Christianity? The answer is extremely simple: they had predicted nothing. There were no such long-range forecasts, and 'accord' and 'fulfilment' were not of this type. Convinced that they were, Christians were much too quick to find evidence of them. The texts, in turn, took on their own impetus, and there were occasions when they created Christian events in Christian tradition. The events were then supposed to have fulfilled the very texts which had created them. This fact is often denied, because of its implications: it is, admittedly, rare but the Nativity at Bethlehem is a clear instance; elsewhere, it may account for details, like Judas's 'thirty pieces of silver', deduced from the text of Zechariah; it would, however, be naïve to think that every Gospel detail which overlaps with a bit of Hebrew scripture is therefore a Christian invention.

In terms of truth, there is a plain answer to this scriptural snowstorm: it is not true, and the proportion of truth to statement in the Christian scriptures would be higher if it were taken out. Matthew's and John's Gospels and the Acts of the Apostles would be particular losers, but the heart of Christianity would not be lost without it. Christians did not begin to quote these scriptures because they had begun with a series of puzzles in the Old Testament, experienced their time with Jesus and then returned to the texts, feeling able to understand them. They began with a faith in their new Christ, his Resurrection and his promises: Jesus's career and the reports of his empty tomb created their faith and then caused them to look back and quarry the old scripture. When most people did not believe them, they found a further confirmation: the old prophets (they said) had predicted this disbelief, in words against their own companions. What had happened had to happen, and disbelief was part of it: psychologically, this circle of self-reinforcing prophecy was very comforting.

Christians were not alone in these arts. Among their Jewish contemporaries, texts were raped and sense tortured in almost all the same ways: we can watch them in scrolls found near the Dead Sea, where the commentaries on scripture have the New Testament's tricks of the trade. We can even compare misinterpretations: the words of Isaiah 40:3, 'Prepare ye the way of the Lord', are applied to John the Baptist by Christians and to the study of Moses's law by one of the scrolls (the prophet had referred to neither). In the scrolls, however, we do not find the phrase 'that the scripture might be fulfilled': the groups who wrote them tended to look forwards, on their own scheme of history, whereas Christians also looked back, to what had happened or was happening around them as a result. For Christians, 'fulfilment' had its full force. It was not a filling-out of a past prophecy but its realization for the first time.

Errors do not cease to be errors because everyone at the same time is committing them: does this abuse of scripture matter? Jesus in the Gospels and Paul in his letters tend to cite old scripture to support a point which they wish to make anyway: they use it as an illustration, not as a starting-point (although Jesus at Luke 4:21 amazes the synagogue in Nazareth by reading a lesson from Isaiah and telling them, without explanation, that 'This day is this scripture fulfilled in your ears'). The argument from prophecy is strongest in the Gospellers' own comments, not in what Jesus or Paul say. In practice, however, Paul may have been less restrained. His surviving letters are all to existing Christians, but the author of Acts, his companion, wrote how Paul would speak to newer audiences, arguing for three weeks 'out of the scripture, opening and alleging, that Christ must needs have suffered, and risen again from the dead'. One abiding aim was to win converts by these proofs: in Acts 8:26 ff., we read how Philip won over an Ethiopian eunuch by expounding the text of Isaiah on the Suffering Servant. The eunuch had been reading it while he travelled, but Philip explained (incorrectly) that Isaiah was here referring to Jesus Christ. In the Gentile world, arguments from prophecy continued to be an important road to conversion. Old oracles and predictions were widely respected, and several people cite the Hebrew prophecies as a reason why they turned to Christ.

If a false argument converted people to a harmless cause, perhaps we should not be too bothered. For modern Christians, the cause still stands without these false arguments to support it. We should, however, be bothered if they make us mistake the Hebrew Bible, as if the New Testament could ever explain what the Old Testament meant. The relationship is rather different: Hebrew scriptures were relevant to the New Testament, but not as prophecy to proof. In the Hebrew texts there were no expectant forecasts, words pregnant with long-range Christian meaning; but was there, perhaps, a deeper level running between events, not bits of text?

In Paul's letters there are hints of such a relation between past and present persons and events. He cited the figure of Adam as an anticipation of Christ; the Israelites' years in the wilderness, he explained, were written as a 'type' and serve as our 'examples: and they are written for our admonition, upon whom the ends of the world are come' (1 Corinthians 10:6–11). Was the past, then, a 'type' for the Christian present and should Christian readers follow Paul's lead? When the fourth Gospel tells us how Jesus's tomb lay in a garden and how Mary Magdalen saw him and mistook him for the gardener, should we not read this text in the shadow of Genesis, where Eden was the garden, Adam the gardener, death the penalty and woman the agent of the Fall? A Tree, even, assisted the Fall, whereas the Tree of the Cross brought salvation; in this new Garden, the new Adam reverses the Fall, restores woman and conquers Death. Although the story is to be taken literally, can it not be read deeply, too? At the Gospel's beginning, we could weave similar patterns round the story of Jesus's baptism: the Trinity, perhaps, can be seen here in outline, with the Dove resembling Noah's Dove and bringing a second release, from evil, not the Flood. 'The spiritual meaning *is* the literal meaning . . . in what Jesus was and did, we have not a symbol of something else but that to which all the symbols refer.'

It is fun to embellish a text and play scriptural cat's-cradle round it, but this festoon of wool has nothing to do with truth. It is not that the Bible is somehow unique in its power to pile symbol on symbol, or that it is a book like no other book because the shadow of one half lies deeply over the other: the same symbolic games can be played with other bodies of writing, both within an author's work (Virgil's poetry) or between authors (the canon, perhaps, of children's authors). Even in the Bible the foreshadowing is highly selective: bits of a story may seem symbolic, but other bits seem quite irrelevant (Noah or the Flood or the dry land are not exactly relevant to Jesus's baptism in the River Jordan). As poets or lovers of scripture, we may like to put passages side by side: 'just as Noah's dove', so did the Dove descend at the Jordan. But if we then claim that one event prefigured or looked forward to the other, we have left poetry and similes behind: in search of the pregnant forecast, we have joined in the business of raping the Hebrew text.

Rape, indeed, has been justified by claims that the Hebrew scriptures always needed a child: they have been seen as 'inconclusive', a 'history of failure' or even as a headless torso, waiting for the master who would round them off. These Christian readings are stupendously patronizing. The 'Old Testament' is a Christian invention: Christians rearranged its books and put the prophets last in the sequence; only Christians end the Old Testament with the prophet Malachi: 'Behold, I will send you Elijah the prophet before the coming of the great and dreadful day of the Lord' (Malachi 4:5), so that the New then begins with the new Elijah, John the Baptist, as if the Old leads into the New, a 'rise toward the end, not a decline from the beginning'. Among the Jews, however, there were scrolls, not an inconclusive book: so far from documenting failure, these scrolls threw a kaleidoscopic light on a history of great survival. Common sense would have made lesser men give up Yahweh years ago for something stronger, but in defiance of the facts groups of believers in Israel had held on to this faith and won through.

The connection is not one of head to torso or of a new David to struggling, half-cut figures who are wrestling to find meaning, like figures in Michelangelo's unfinished marble. The early Christians made the connection the wrong way round and in the wrong place. The New did not fulfil the Old: rather, without the Old, the events and conflicts of Jesus's lifetime could never have happened. It was not only that the Old Testament told of the same God and formed the views of Jesus's opponents: it formed the cast of Jesus's mind, his self-understanding and his aims. It did not necessarily confine him, but it did relate to many of his ideas: a new kingdom or a heavenly Father or the sense of an imminent crisis. He was not the 'simple Galilaean', unaware of all the textual meanings which the Gospellers (based, in part, on Galilaeans, too) lavished on his actions and sayings.

As Jesus must have known, the prophets had expressed themselves in deeds as well as words: could not his own actions be based on a prophecy and imply (without explicit statement) that its meaning was being fulfilled? Perhaps such an allusion underlay his symbolic actions in the Temple; critics still dispute the point, but it surely impelled his decision to ride to Jerusalem, a publicly witnessed event, on the 'foal of an ass'. Behind the act lay the prophecy of Second Zechariah: 'Behold, thy King cometh unto thee . . . lowly, and riding upon an ass' (it was left to an evangelist to miss the rhythm of the text and add an extra animal to fulfil it, a colt as well as a donkey: Matthew 21:7).

In those actions there was none of the hesitation of Jonah: the time was coming. The Jesus of the fourth Gospel is certain that he knows the Father, and that the Father will not suddenly change his will: unlike Jonah, the Jesus of the Gospels is never allowed to think that he might be being used. Within days the authorities had taken him, beaten him, crowned him with thorns and arranged the most agonizing death. With hindsight, his heirs interpreted many of this Passion's details as fulfilments of yet more psalms and prophecies, especially those in Second Zechariah. Yet we cannot limit the motivating role of prophecy to events which Jesus himself initiated. It may also have confirmed him in what he suffered.

By the first century AD there were particular reasons why it might. In Hebrew scripture we do not know how the namesakes of any of the prophetic books met their deaths. By Jesus's time, however, it was widely assumed that they had died because their fellow Jews had killed them. Stories began to be told of Isaiah's awful martyrdom or Jeremiah's horrible end: in Matthew 23:37 a slight error has involved the prophet Zechariah in a similar fate. 'O Jerusalem, Jerusalem, thou that killest the prophets, and stonest them which are sent unto thee': perhaps, when the agonies started, this prophetic image confirmed Jesus in his own endurance. 'Which of the prophets,' the martyr Stephen then says at Acts 7:52, 'have not your fathers persecuted?' By the first century, the old scriptures were viewed in the light of intervening tradition. Then, the deaths of Jesus and Stephen made that tradition seem even more prophetic.

Besides fulfilling older scripture, Christians added predictions of their own. The Holy Spirit fell on individuals who were highly respected as prophets in their Churches: Paul himself had visionary experiences taking him 'up to the third heaven' (2 Corinthians 12:2). Like their Hebrew forebears, these prophets could tell forth and call for repentance or a moral change. But they also foretold, raising the plain question of truth.

The author of Acts twice referred to such a prophet, Agabus, whom he himself must have met in Caesarea (21:11). On that occasion, Agabus bound his own hands and feet with Paul's girdle and announced that the Jews in Jerusalem would bind its owner thus and hand him over to the Gentiles. He gave the prophecy as the Holy Spirit's, but it was not too extreme a guess for anyone who knew the mood in Jerusalem: it was soon proved right. Earlier, at 11:28, Agabus had stood up and foretold by the Spirit that there would be a great famine over all the world. Historians would nowadays prefer to call the famine a food crisis and limit it to some of Rome's eastern provinces, but essentially the author and Agabus were right again: and it 'came to pass in the days of Claudius Caesar'. How bold a guess had it been?

In autumn and early winter 45 we know from papyri in Egypt that the price of grain had soared: in 45/46 we know from Josephus of a severe famine in Jerusalem which the visiting queen Helena then tried to alleviate by buying food from Cyprus and Egypt (probably at Passover 46). On one occasion the Nile is known to have risen abnormally high during the reign of Claudius, way beyond the point with which Egyptian farmers could cope: perhaps the rise occurred in autumn 44; the crops failed in 45 and hence prices were so high that autumn. A shortage in Egypt had severe effects elsewhere in the Near East and could lead to a crisis around Jerusalem in the following spring as part of a chain of disasters. In Acts, Agabus's prophecy occurred at about the time of King Agrippa's death (in late spring/early summer 44): Acts' dating is not precise, and probably we should postpone Agabus's forecast until later in 44 or early 45. By then, the dreadful news of the Nile's abnormal flood would have been a current rumour: the Holy Spirit put the fears into words and 'forecast' a famine on the back of a known Nile disaster: it was only wrong if it extended the crisis dramatically to 'all the world'. Alive to the gossip, Agabus had prophesied accurately: people agreed that his Spirit was holy, and the Christians duly sent gifts of aid to their brethren in Jerusalem.

Agabus, therefore, has an unblemished record, nowhere surpassed in scripture: two prophecies, twice on target. In the Gospels, Christian tradition had been less accurate. Their ideas of the End of the World are varied and endlessly disputed, whether the kingdom was among them or (a likelier translation) 'within their power', whether the End was more than the end of the social order or the eventual fall of Jerusalem. It is, however, certain that some believed that the Apostles would not 'taste of death' until it came (Matthew 16:28); its imminence unsettled Paul's Thessalonians, while the failure of the End to precede the death of the beloved disciple caused a further chapter to be added to his Gospel (John 21). Those who had predicted it in the plainest terms were wrong.

No picture of the End is more vivid than John's in the revelation seen on Patmos 'in the Spirit on the Lord's day'. Its sights and sounds, its numbers and colours, its sweeping imagery of horror and perfection have continued to haunt religious and artistic imaginations from Pierre in Tolstoy's *War and Peace* to D. H. Lawrence, who responded strongly to its Apocalypse. Its literal reading and symbolism run through William Golding's recent novel *Darkness Visible*. Its central figure, the disfigured child Matty, emerges through the fire of a London bombing. Badly burned, he holds fast to his subsequent study of the Bible: on 6 June 1966 (6/6/66: the number of the Beast, in John's vision) 'many people,' he writes in his journal, 'will know the carnal and earthly pleasures of being alive this day and not brought to judgement. No one but I have felt the dreadful sorrow of not being in heaven with all judgement done.'

In John's brilliant mental video, the imagery owes much to the prophets' previous experience. Unlike the author of Daniel, John did not acknowledge his pondering of old books, but his debt to them is evident, especially to Daniel, Zechariah and Ezekiel: the first eight chapters work through Ezekiel's imagery almost in sequence. John's heaven, too, may owe some of its contours to remembered details from his past: they have been cleverly related to a likely pattern of morning service in the old Temple at Jerusalem. John transposed the incense, the song, the sacrificial Lamb and so forth to the heavenly Temple which had outlasted the Earthly Temple: the old Temple service's praises for God as Creator, his law (compare John's scroll) and the redemption of the Exodus are blended in the new song heard in John's heaven.

More immediate inspirations depend on the date of this astonishing torrent of imagery and sound. There are specific signs of a date before 70, perhaps in 69: in chapter 11 John's words imply that the Temple in Jerusalem is still standing but known to be about to fall (the great war with Rome began in 66 and the Temple fell in 70). In 17:10, 'five kings' who have fallen are significant; perhaps they are the five Roman emperors, from Nero to Vespasian, four of whom ruled in 69. However, John has probably worked these earlier facts into a vision which was seen and composed at a later date. In the year 69 no Jew could seriously have expected the Temple to be about to fall, despite the war with Rome, and even after its eventual destruction there was no reason to think at first that its ruin was final. The hint of this catastrophe implies hindsight, the 90s, not the late 60s: like Daniel's visions, which John knew in detail, the text has used hindsight to enhance the impression of foresight. A later date also suits one of its central themes, Christian martyrdom and the shedding of persecuted Christians' blood: Christian martyrs are seen in triumph, dressed in white, beside the throne of God, while the letters to the Seven Churches concern Christians' compromises with pagan worship and their falling away from strict Christian loyalties. When were these concerns so urgent?

In Rome, Christians were persecuted by the Emperor Nero, who made them scapegoats for the city's great fire in the year 64. Perhaps persecution then spread by example to the provinces because Roman governors had Nero's precedent for treating Christians as criminals. However, we know of no such cases occurring so early: in later Christian tradition, John's vision was placed in the 90s, precisely in the year 95. The point has often been missed, but it is at exactly this date that we have good evidence of Christians' persecution. We know from the histories of a pagan senator (Bruttius, as quoted by the Christian Eusebius) that many Christians were persecuted in the year 95: Bruttius's exact words do not survive, but the drift of his evidence is clear enough. In Christian tradition the reigning Emperor Domitian was soon remembered as a persecutor: it is probably to his reign in the 90s that we should refer the pseudonymous Christian letter, First Clement, whose opening sentences also imply a persecution in Rome.

Nero or Domitian: can we be more decisive? In chapter 6 John sees his famous vision of the Four Horsemen (based on Zechariah's imagery before him): the first two horsemen cause conquest and war, but the third, on a black horse, carries a balance and proclaims a food crisis ('a measure of wheat for a penny, and three measures of barley for a penny'). In 92/3 we have an inscribed copy of an edict from the Roman governor of Asia Minor in which he sets a maximum price for wheat at a time of acute shortage round Pisidian Antioch (where Paul had preached in Acts 13): the horseman's price is eight times higher than the governor's, although his ratio of barley prices to wheat prices is rather more generous. Food crises were frequent between regions, and the horseman's cry of famine is only one of partial famine ('see thou hurt not the oil and wine' he continues), but it would fit very well with the crisis attested inland in Asia during Domitian's reign.

'Behold a pale horse . . .': the next horseman then brings pestilence, a hazard which can also be diagnosed in Asia during the early 90s. According to the Roman historian Dio, in the year 90 (and perhaps for a while afterwards) there were people who 'made it their business to smear needles with poison and prick anyone they wished . . . many people died unnoticed. This did not only happen at Rome but also in practically the whole world.' These pin-pricks recur as a popular story at another time of plague in the Roman Empire: it is particularly suggestive to picture John's Revelation against a worldwide background of plague and poison pen-work.

Neither of these links with the 90s is conclusive, but the pale horse is followed by the opening of the fifth seal and the cry for vengeance of those who have been slain as martyrs: in 95 we know martyrdom had been a prominent fact. The sequence of the seals thus fits powerfully with a date of 95 for the entire vision: at that time John's Christian audience would have included people in Asia who had first endured a food crisis, then a plague and then the trauma of martyrdom. As in the book of Daniel, true history lent weight to the final prophecy. In it, the sixth seal releases a shattering earthquake. Perhaps here, too, there was a topical reference, because earthquakes in Asia were a common hazard: then, the human authorities are thrown into panic and the world is left waiting for the seventh seal, the End. If the preceding seals all referred to recent happenings, who were the readers of the vision to dispute the final prophecy?

When the seventh seal is opened, the horrors build up in a brilliant sequence towards the Last Days, the millennium and the eventual descent of the New Jerusalem. After half an hour's silence, seven trumpets start to usher in atrocious sufferings for non-Christians: in chapter 11 the fall of Jerusalem features as their setting, and after the fall of Satan and a cosmic struggle, we encounter the famous imagery of the Beasts. One is to reign for 'three times and a half', while another, his agent, appears to enforce worship of the first beast's image and work wonders as a false prophet (19:20: the 'image of the beast' is itself made to talk). The number of the first Beast ('666') probably equates with the letters of the name of Nero, but the name here might be symbolic. For in this patch of swirling horror, we are not so much seeing past history as historical details transformed by a potent visionary. The image, however, and the false prophet have been plausibly connected with specific facts of the 90s: at that time a colossal statue of the Emperor Domitian was set up in the heart of the city of Ephesus, where it towered, up to twenty-five feet high, as the focal point of the province of Asia's cult of the Roman emperor. Statues of pagan gods were widely credited with powers to work wonders and speak oracles (Christians did not doubt these powers: they merely ascribed them to demons): perhaps the false prophet stood for the pagan priest who served such a cult image. 'All those who would not worship it' were to be put to death: in the wake of the stories of the book of Daniel, this huge image of a ruler could symbolize the pressure on Christians to conform to pagan worship; perhaps the new ruler's cult did indeed make life more difficult for Christian minorities. John's picture, however, is not specific, and other details float round it. When he emphasizes the mark of the Beast on its worshippers' foreheads, he is echoing the practice of tattooing the hands and foreheads of pagan worshippers of particular gods; on present knowledge, it is not attested for participants in the cult of any Roman emperor. According to John, only those with the mark of the beast will be allowed to buy and sell. Exemptions from taxes did often benefit the crowds who attended a major pagan festival in a province: perhaps this detail has inspired John's imagery, combined with the tattooing which was practised on troupes of gladiators (gladiatorial fights were privileged shows, given by priests of the Imperial cult in a province: they occurred with the cult of Domitian at Ephesus).

Unlike the author who revived Daniel, John did not give his audience a sweep of exact political history. Instead he left a vision in which snatches of the 90s can be situated, whereas snatches of the 60s are rarer: on either dating, echoes of reality have blended into something with complex, prophetic roots. None of these roots takes us outside the Hebrew books which we now accept as scriptural: John did not look beyond the recognized twenty-two.

Like the visions of these Hebrew prophets, John's awesome vision is sometimes read metaphorically, as an image of the ending of corrupt rule and oppressive social order in the world. Its imagery takes us over, beyond any single historical context, while such vivid expressions as the slaying of the Beast have been traced back to roots in themes of Hebrew myths, not history: 'It is misleading to say that the monster *is* Rome . . . Rome is only its latest embodiment.' To the author, this longer perspective might have seemed irrelevant: Rome was very much the cause of what he wrote. To us, his words can open out on a longer and broader canvas. If we go further and claim that Rome was for him the latest, but not therefore the last, we are jumping beyond his prophecy: it was not what he meant.

In what sense, though, did he prophesy: did he 'tell forth', not predicting but envisioning what might happen in order to bring his hearers to avert it by a change of heart? He has been read in this way, so that the truth of his book does not depend on the historical sequel. Repentance, however, was not at all his purpose: the majority of his human contemporaries, he believed, were utterly doomed to atrocious suffering: it would be poured on them by angels of the Christian God and represented a just revenge. He was more concerned with steadfastness. Those Christians who stood fast and, if necessary, died in the act were assured of the new Jerusalem; but whatever other people did, God was going to round off the earth in phases: only after his punishments would any surviving nations come to him in worship. First, Babylon (or Rome) would fall; Satan would be cast into the pit; seven bowls of God's wrath would be ladled on to non-Christians and Christian backsliders. These visions were not conditional: they saw behind earthly power to its heavenly reality and purported to tell what was sure to come. They exalted Christians who stood firm, but even if many more Christians were to join them, the phases of the End would still strike the rest of humanity. One of the seven angels, after all, had assured John of the message. 'These sayings,' he told him, 'are faithful and true: and the Lord God of the holy prophets sent his angel to shew unto his servants the things which must shortly be done. Behold, I come quickly.'

The angel, or his appearance, was mistaken: mercifully, John's vision was false. The End did not begin and history has continued to add to its human horrors. Yet the text still speaks to us through its imagery of debased worldly power and heavenly perfection. It did not correspond to the facts, but the facts, it reminds us, were not everything.

PART FOUR

20

The Bible as Story

So far, we have followed the slow, incoherent growth of the scriptures and their texts; we have cut down to size the claims for the 'text as we have it' or the biblical canon as keys to their meaning; we have marked out the likeliest areas of primary information (the last half of 2 Samuel; the books of Kings; bits of Nehemiah; the fourth Gospel and the Acts), and we have set samples from these parts and others against evidence outside them, in Gentile texts, below and above ground and in the known course of the future. The results refute anyone who might wish to argue that long stretches of biblical narrative are true because they correspond in detail to the facts. Beyond a minimal framework, even the primary sources interpret and elaborate events in a fascinating range of ways. Elsewhere, biblical authors can be shown to have failed to describe what happened; they disagree between themselves; they address the future, but even with the help of friends and editors, their details are no more accurate than those of a weather-forecaster who is not speaking the 'word of the Lord'.

At one level, the Bible may contain all these errors and inventions, but there is still something more to it than their sum: one response to these conclusions, therefore, is to ask, 'so what?' It implies that historians' findings are all old hat, the results of a pedantry which was popular a hundred years ago but which has no surprises for modern readers. The problems in Luke's Nativity story or Mark's trial of Jesus are not exactly new. The groundwork was laid by scholars in the nineteenth century, and, despite it, the Bible is alive and well.

The Bible is indeed alive, but these particular problems are still not common currency among many of its readers: old truths bear repetition. They also refute certain ways of reading the text. It is not just that they refute strict fundamentalism. They disprove the notion (widely taught and preached in the 1950s and 1960s) that the people of Israel were unique because they alone had a God who was active in history and was known through events. It is not merely that many other ancient peoples, whether Greeks, Hittites or the people of Moab, had gods who were active (they thought) in historical events. Many of the events, we now see, in which this biblical god was supposed to have acted, were non-events, except, perhaps, in their authors' minds. Nor is the Bible a special book because 'types' bind its two halves uniquely together. The Bible, on this view, has something more solid than the deeper meanings or allegories which other texts may have beneath their words or stories: it has 'types' which are 'events', not allegories, and which foreshadow future events (the Dove at Noah's Ark, perhaps, as a type of the Dove at Jesus's baptism). We have already seen through the claim that these types are genuine intimations of anything in the future, but there is another problem too. Most of these types are no different from allegories in any other book or story. They are not events because they never happened.

Scripture, then, is not an event-course, but it is still a body of writings which can come home to people, or find them, whether or not it is factually true. We all have our mental images of the Bible at work in this way, but two particular settings loom large in mine. One is the English parsonage at Haworth in north Yorkshire, home to the Brontës and the literary genius of the three sisters, Charlotte, Emily and Anne. The house happens to be Georgian, and, like the biblical text, its inner style has been padded by pious but unfaithful hands. The sitting-room, however, is much as Father Brontë knew it. Prints of Belshazzar's feast and biblical scenes hang on the walls and copies of paintings by the visionary artist John Martin. A Bible lies open on the table, and here Revd Patrick Brontë would sit, a survivor, like Jacob, of his family's tragedies. In early youth, two of his daughters died from a fatal infection, caught at a Christian school for clergymen's children. When his only son, Branwell, died in his thirties, Patrick Brontë could not be comforted, Charlotte's letters tell us, but mourned him with the biblical cry 'Absalom, my son, Absalom.' Branwell's death led to the deaths of

Anne and Emily after their brief sojourn, as Patrick Brontë saw it, in this world: Charlotte then followed to an early grave. During these years of tragedy, Patrick Brontë would withdraw and sit by himself 'like an extinct volcano' in his sitting-room off the main hall. Here, the Bible was his companion, and we still have his copy of the Hebrew prophets. Into it he had inserted texts on damnation from the New Testament: hell and eternal punishment were important themes in his view of the world.

From Yorkshire in the 1860s, my mental image moves to Monte Gargano, the rough spur on the eastern side of Italy's boot-shaped peninsula. In August 1930 the Bible came home to one of the farm-workers in the village of San Nicandro, a man with a recognized gift as a storyteller and speaker. Donato Maurizio was moved by a vision which impelled him to the opening chapters of Genesis: 'I took the Bible and opened it at the early part and with a great amazement I *saw* the Creation and how the Everlasting existed before the earth was created and how he created every single thing. And afterwards, a light was lit in my heart.' In 1930 this Italian village was converted to Number One, the ancient God of Abraham, Isaac and the patriarchs: a growing audience of villagers followed suit; they wrote to the synagogue in Rome, asking to be circumcised; the rabbi obliged, but when they were introduced to the Talmud and rabbinic writings, they viewed them with 'disgust'. They had converted not to Judaism, but to the religion of Israel with only the Pentateuch behind it. They had once known Christian teachings, but now they were uninterested in Christ: Donato and his fellow converts had been found by the Creation and the Sabbath, the idea of a chosen people and a God of justice. They put the Star of David on their donkeys' bridles and persisted in their faith, a village of Jewish converts on the edges of Fascist Italy. At the end of the war, British soldiers visited them and told them of the Holy Land: they visited the new state of Israel, but, like true Jews of the Diaspora, they were repelled by its rampant Zionism. When their historian, Elena Cassin, visited them in Italy, she remarked that 'the converts' unquestioning acceptance of the ancient biblical stories must be unique in the history of Judaism . . . The Pentateuch was still very much alive. Its stories seemed to them quite simple and natural, the sort of adventures which they themselves, or their friends and relations, might very well have had.' In Genesis 38 the widowed Tamar disguises herself as a harlot, seduces Judah, her father-in-law, and then sends him proof that her baby, fathered in ignorance, is his. Whenever the story was read in San Nicandro, 'all the men and women present understood the episode perfectly. Tamar's stratagem did not shock them in the least: they took it for granted that what a woman desires above everything else is to have children.'

At the time Patrick Brontë would have assumed that the Bible was the word of God, and when Donato saw the Creation, he might, perhaps, have thought of it as God's revelation. However, these homecomings did not depend on mistaken ideas of the Bible's nature: scripture also put words to feelings; it offered hope and comfort; it seemed to make sense of life (of earthly life, only, in Gargano: the villagers' chosen books of Hebrew scripture had no idea of a life after death). Different parts of it had come home in different ways: in Yorkshire, the psalms and the prophets' theology; in Italy, the Pentateuch's stories and the account of the Creation of the world.

Questions of factual truth bear differently on these two types of text. With few exceptions, they do not bring us very near to the power of texts like the psalms. Only a few of them review past events: Psalm 104 is the most explicit, a great call to remember God's wonderful works (from the covenant with Abraham through Joseph and Moses to the Exodus). It becomes harder to sing it wholeheartedly when we realize that none of these works had actually happened, and that the psalmist is rehearsing stories without knowing it (Psalms 77 or 105 are others with this false dimension). Yet there are more general hymns of praise too (not only in the psalms: Paul has left one of the best, in his great praise of love, or 'charity', in 1 Corinthians 13); and throughout the Bible there are prayers for people's hour of need (the Hebrew books of narrative have almost a hundred of them, for David, Jonah, Nehemiah and many others). Like the great speeches on evil and understanding in the book of Job, they can still engage us, even if their surrounding story is untrue. There was never a 'man in the land of Uz, whose name was Job' who would rise early in the morning and burn offerings to God for each one of his sons in case they had 'sinned, and cursed God in their hearts': none the less, we can respond to the speeches which follow, on the place of wisdom or the lot of man, 'born unto trouble, as the sparks fly upward'.

These great addresses have particular forces which work in their favour. Often, they have a poetic form and a poetic use of language, although the exact distinction between prose and poetry in Hebrew is still highly disputed. They are also heard or sung in religious worship. Here, the setting is solemn, the extracts are selected, and old memories are present; one occasion recalls others, earlier in life. In less powerful contexts, some of these songs' attitudes might repel us: the psalmists are prone to whinging and self-pity; there are some beastly cries for vengeance against their personal enemies; Psalm 137 even wants God to dash children against stones. There are also bits which speak for a mood, or way of asking, with which we can identify. For this impact, we might look beyond Patrick Brontë to generations of political prisoners, from the early Christian martyrs, singing psalms in the mines on the very borders of Egypt, to Jews in the Nazi prison-camps or modern victims of terrorism, kept sane by the psalms during solitary confinement. We can also think of Augustine who turned first to the psalms when he was being brought to Christianity (those 'sounds of devotion . . . against the swelling pride of the human race'). As a young convert, 'I was burning to recite them through all the world'; then, when his mother, Monica, died, it was the psalter, again, which Augustine's friend took up, 'and began to sing and all of us in the household answered him, "I will sing of mercy and judgement to thee Lord"' (Psalm 101).

What, though, of the villagers of San Nicandro? Those who share their faith would probably not worry that they had been brought to it by mistaken beliefs: if God moves in mysterious ways, he might as well work through error. In the Bible itself, the Ethiopian eunuch is won to faith by Philip's false explanation of a prophecy which was wrongly ascribed to Isaiah. Yet if somebody had explained to Donato and his hearers that Creation did not happen in that way, and that the narratives in Genesis were not history, would they really have succumbed so strongly? They believed what they heard: would they have believed it if they had been told first that they were being read a story?

Story, however, is the conclusion which most biblical scholars, and the samples of my unauthorized version, assert for most of the narrative. Where, then, is its truth? At one persistent level, the Bible shows us what authors in Israel and its self-styled heir, the Church, believed about God (even if he himself is a bit of story too). They assume a knowledge of this God, and even if their stories are wonderfully false, most of them are told with a faith that God was at work in them: one book, Esther, does not mention him, but the story strongly presupposes his presence. In scripture this God is not revealing himself: human authors are creating him, as he is supposed to have created them, 'after their own image'.

At this level there is truth in the theology: across eight centuries or so, the Bible shows us what people in Israel believed of their God. The narrative, however, is much more than the sum total of its allusions to God and his son: those who believe in neither do not read it with nothing but disbelief, interspersed with horror and regret. It may not be historical, but there is still a power in much of it. Is it the power of a story, then, not history? Is it literature, even, or is it a mixture of all three? Does this power, perhaps, lie in its humanity rather than its divinity, humanity in the broadest sense, bad as well as good? Each of these ways of reading it relates differently to the question of truth: I will take them in turn, beginning (like Genesis) with story.

II

Much has been made of the presence of history in Hebrew scripture, but the Jewish faith is not dependent on whether its contents happened or not. The entire narrative might be a story, but there could still be a God for the people of Israel, the ultimate Creator and so forth; the scriptures would merely show us that authors had shared this faith for centuries and had involved it in dozens of stories. Only at the heart of Christianity does faith need historical truth: either Jesus rose from the dead or he did not. If he did not, Christianity is untrue. On the available evidence, historians cannot decide the matter: in my view, there is a primary source, the 'beloved disciple', who later claimed to have seen burial clothes in the empty tomb, but was his claim correct and did he draw the right conclusion? Historians can show that other people in antiquity continued to believe that they saw close friends or relations after their death, in visions, dreams and so forth. There were also stories that great figures of the past had been taken up to heaven. Perhaps this familiar pattern of response and the intensity of previous experience caused the Christians' conviction that Jesus was alive, after all, and had been witnessed. If so, historians must also accept that the conviction was so strong that its immediate witnesses not only passed it to hundreds of other people: they ended by dying because of it.

In the rest of scripture, stories might even have advantages over straight history. E. M. Forster, the novelist, believed that 'in fictions, we can know people perfectly and we find here a compensation for their dimness in life. In this direction, fiction is truer than history because it goes beyond the evidence and each of us knows from his own experiences that there is something beyond the evidence.' The Bible is not unduly concerned with characterization, but its stories do seem to have a particular power: we need think only of the book of Jonah, written as a story yet still pointing us to profound and subtle truths. We can also think of ourselves. We are expelled from our Edens and sacrifice our happiness to the ambitions of our intellects. All of us flee our Egypts, and some of us receive our revelation, and trek through our deserts to a promised land which only our children or our children's children may enjoy. Like the children of Israel, they then complain when they have it. There is something universal here, we all feel.

Unlike the facts of history, stories can also be enlarged, improved and multiplied without telling lies. Our Bibles are a hive of such industry, as people imagined and filled in gaps which the text had left. It was not dishonest, not like the giving of prophecies to people of a much earlier date or updating predictions after the event. Sometimes the main story inspired more stories: what had happened to minor characters on one of its branch lines, the Asenath, perhaps, whom Joseph married in Egypt? Sometimes the main text left unsaid the things which people wanted to know: these gaps led to an entire body of writings which took their cue from biblical stories, the Midrash of Jewish writers. This process is still alive in our own literature: in his recent novel, *God Knows*, Joseph Heller has given us a brilliant elaboration of David's Court History in 2 Samuel, its women, its tribulations and the ups and downs with God. The process is also still visible in our Bible's Hebrew text. At Genesis 18:16 God sends his angels to punish Sodom: surely Abraham must have realized and tried to plead with him (so a story of this pleading, at Genesis 18:23, was invented and added). At Genesis 12:17 Abraham concealed his wife as his sister in a foreign country, and God was very angry with a Gentile who wooed her in ignorance: surely God was not always so harsh to innocent mistakes (Genesis 18:17 ff.; 20 and 26

361

probably grew out of gaps and problems in the older story). Bits of the Bible thus grew in answer to earlier bits, and inspired a mass of connected stories, like the script of a weekly serial which passes from author to author, while retaining the same setting and characters. Seen in this light, even such modern fictions as the coming of Joseph of Arimathea to Glastonbury or *The Holy Blood and Holy Grail* have antecedents in the Bible itself.

This storytelling was encouraged by a recurrent feature of Biblical narrative. Very often, especially in the early Hebrew books, the narrators are extremely laconic, saying the minimum. The story of Abraham and Isaac in Genesis 22 is a famous example: when God gives Abraham his command, he uses words of three-fold beastliness ('take ... go ... burn'), but he gives no reason (he merely refers to Isaac's value, 'Take now thy son, thine only son Isaac, whom thou lovest'). Abraham, too, says nothing: he rises up early in the morning and never explains his purpose. Isaac asks a pertinent question ('where is the lamb for a burnt offering?'), and Abraham answers with spare irony ('My son, God will provide himself a lamb': ambiguity has even been seen in the words 'my son', which both address Isaac and answer, all too truly, the boy's question). Then, the two of them trudge on, the son lugging the wood with which his father plans to burn him. The narrator merely repeats the sentence: 'they went both of them together'.

Through reticence, the story has become the most ghastly walk in literature: its sparseness has even been ascribed to the author's monotheism, the faith in one God who directs the narrative and gives it a deeper background. Theology, however, is not the cause of it: people with many gods can write in this way too. From Homer to the great historian Thucydides, pagan Greek authors have commanded this same reticence: 'noble restraint allowed the event to speak for itself'. Later Jews found this reticence too much for them, monotheism or not. When Josephus retold the story, he tried to fill in the gaps: he brought the pathos before us in long speeches between father and son at the altar. Generations of Jewish readers have explored the story's blanks: why ever did Abraham's wife Sarah agree? What did she say when Abraham took the boy Isaac away: had Abraham, perhaps, told a white lie? Possible lies were infinite, but one view was that Abraham told her that he must now take Isaac away to school: the patriarch Shem had opened a good one up in the mountains. Dropping an innocent son at a boarding school might seem an apt concealment for murder. Other readers, however, worked out by cross-reference that at the time Isaac was thirty-seven years old.

Once pointed out, this reticence emerges as a recurring feature of so much biblical narrative. When Jacob, expecting Rachel, marries the wrong one of Laban's two daughters, we hear only the wonderful comment, 'And it came to pass, that in the morning, behold, it was Leah.' Reticence heightens the Bible's many tales of terror: Abraham silently prepares to burn Isaac; an abominable Levite in the book of Judges lends his concubine to 'sons of Belial' who abuse her 'all the night until the morning', when he finds her dropped on his doorstep. 'And he said unto her, Up, and let us be going. But none answered.'

Reticence is an important impulse to yet more stories. Like the honeycombed framework of a prefabricated building, this biblical style leaves its public to fill in the gaps which yawn between its girders. The framework of the story is marvellously controlled (on their walk, the words of father and son say it all by saying so little); there is irony, exact cross-reference ('God will provide') and the statement, nothing more, that Abraham walked for so long, until the third day. So far from dominating us or remorselessly excluding alternatives, this scripture leaves room in which we can breathe and speculate. It provokes our art by the limits of its own telling: what it tells us may not be rich in insight, but it can produce insight while we ponder what it has left unsaid.

In the Bible, therefore, stories invite us to expand them by their own limits and their oddness some of which results from textual confusion or editors' rewriting or the merging of conflicting versions. It is open to us to expand them, but as stories they can expand our ideas of ourselves too. Unlike facts, stories can continue to grow with their readers and their societies; they are, therefore, a particularly apt focus to which groups of people can relate. Spaniards invented an ideal El Cid; Romans took on Aeneas. Different Spaniards and Romans related differently to them, but the Jews were particularly close to their story because they believed it (the Exodus) and had spun it across such a length of time. In turn, other peoples could identify with its branch lines. Like Greek myths, biblical stories have given new peoples or practices origins and affected the ways in which they (and others) regarded their identity.

In the Bible itself, the book of Esther is a fine example. This fictional story was pieced together from a framework of familiar tales of kings, queens and courtiers: its author combined male chauvinism, suspense and a bloody finale into a single tale which then became a popular hit. Not a word of it was true, but it purported to explain the origins of a festival of celebration and merriment, Purim, which is still observed with gusto in the Jewish year. Its days marked the Jewish people's deliverance from a wicked courtier's attempt to have them annihilated and to confiscate their goods: they were saved by two counter-edicts, one obtained by the court Jew, Mordecai, the other by his adopted daughter, Esther, who had become the Persian queen. The two days of these edicts, the author suggested, were the two days on which Purim should be celebrated. This story of drama and romance had some of the irony, but none of the reticence, of the tale of Abraham and Isaac: its plot and its realistic details (the interior decor at royal parties; the scents and oils for royal Persian concubines) encouraged readers to take it as reality (it also appealed, deceitfully, to chronicles of the kings of Media and Persia). The story and its festival, Purim, both caught on. In the Christian era, in the year 409, we find Christian Roman emperors having to legislate to prevent Jews from provoking anti-Christian insults and trouble on the days of Purim by identifying the story's wicked courtier Haman with Jesus and the gallows on which he was hanged with the Christian Cross. The story had acquired yet more momentum: the Christians themselves had already given Haman this Christian significance in their own writings, yet it was all untrue, the invention of a Jew who was possibly writing near Susa between *c.* 250 and 170 B C.

Biblical stories have enlivened people as well as festivals. In the seventeenth century, Holland's Calvinist society identified powerfully with the biblical image of a people saved from God's Flood, an idea which suited their own predicament among the floods and hazards of the low countries. In South Africa, the Afrikaners regarded their great trek as an Exodus: they even believed they had found the Nile and Moses's bulrushes, and named a town to mark the spot. In Ethiopia, by contrast, the dynasty of kings became related to the Queen of Sheba: then, this origin was combined with ideas of the Messiah, the persecution of the Jews and the subjugation of black people (the true Jews) to whites, the web of ideas which created Rastafarianism in the 1930s. As the Bible told such a long story, it was possible to reach back behind it and be new while claiming to be old. Here, the greatest founder has been Abraham. In the earliest surviving Christian text, Paul wrote to people in Galatia (the hinterland of Asia Minor, now modern Turkey), telling them that they are 'children of Abraham' and that Moses, who came later, is irrelevant to them. Many of them will not have known this ancestry before. But six centuries later it extended its branches southwards to Mecca and reached a man in his forties, that spiritually fertile decade: Muhammad, too, made the link with the faith of Abraham, forerunner of his own new faith, the future Islam.

None of these effects, however, does anything to make a story true. If we change ground and label all the biblical narratives as stories, we may well feel easier in their company and look around for their positive interest. But we are using 'story' or 'fiction' to cover two different things. The books of Job or Jonah or Ruth or Esther were stories or fictions by design: the authors made them up. To us, the biblical story of the Nativity is a fiction because we can see that it is untrue: it was not a fiction to the third Gospeller who believed, wrongly, that the story happened. By relabelling it, we have accepted, rightly, that the author got it wrong.

Historians are not so pedestrian that they cannot see how truth can be found even in an unintended fiction. A story may be wonderful evidence for what the narrator and his audience believed and assumed: it may help to hold their view of reality together. The beliefs may concern a god or an independent Satan (a late arrival on the biblical scene): they may be odd until we unravel them, like the curious story of Jacob in Genesis 30 who strips the bark off fresh twigs, puts them in the water trough of his sheep and is somehow thought to have made them conceive speckled lambs as a result (it is not even that he had any speckled rams to father them: Laban had taken the speckled rams away). For centuries, scholars could still understand this story, as we have recently been reminded: it turned on the widespread belief that a mother's conception was influenced by whatever she looked at during sexual intercourse. In the water troughs, the stripped twigs looked dark and mottled; Jacob's ewes gazed on them and conceived mottled 'Jacob's flock', just as horse-breeders believed that a mare would conceive a fine foal if she saw her handsome stallion in a mirror while being mounted (in 1726 a woman amazed London society by claiming that she had given birth to rabbits after looking at a rabbit, but it emerged that she was wrong). Behind Genesis 30, which is story, not history, lies a widespread belief about conception and the facts of life. As late as 1950 there were commentators who claimed that it was true (which is another story and also a part of history). It was left to Augustine to wonder why the ewes did not conceive twigs.

Stories may also point us to a social practice from which they arise: a pattern of marriage between close kin lies behind our story of Ruth. They might even take us down deeper structures in a people's mentality: the case has often been argued for myths told orally as a living part of a pre-literate society: there have been attempts to prove it for written stories in early bits of scripture, but so far they are not convincing. It is particularly interesting when a story overlaps with stories known in many other cultures: it forces us to ask why this particular type arises. Moses in the bulrushes is a neat example. Moses was to be a great leader of the future, and so this once and future hero must be set outside a normal family and then return to rule his people. Stories of the exposure of a once and future ruler are very widely known in other societies, from India (Chandragupta) through Persia (Cyrus) to Greece (the first tyrants), Rome (Romulus) and England (King Arthur). Behind Moses's infancy, we can find a bit of history about a way in which peoples have often thought. It is not, however, history itself. There were no baskets, no bathing maidens, no bulrushes and perhaps no Moses either. If we label these books as stories, their truth retreats to a tapestry of other people's firmly held views.

I I I

Such a tapestry is not trivial: it can touch on themes of intimate religious experience. One way with stories is to compare them, breaking them down into sequences of actions, 'moves', even, like moves in a pattern or game. Biblical narratives have been studied by structuralist critics who wish to explain the meanings which we now find in them by relating them to structures of literary expression. The structures of narratives are sometimes deduced from the folk-tales of other literatures, especially Russian tales (largely because Russian folk-tales have been collected and broken down in this way). In the Hebrew scripture, David's slaying of Goliath has been compared with the sequence of moves in a romantic epic; Jacob's wrestling with the angel at the River Jabbok until the break of day has been compared with the moves in a tale of 'sender, helper and opponent' which it subtly reverses: God, the sender, turns out to be the opponent too. The famous structuralist critic Roland Barthes even called this reversal 'audacious' and claimed that it was otherwise typical of stories of blackmail! Alternatively, stories have been broken down round opposing themes (male and female in the Eden story; nature and culture in the story of Jephthah who accidentally vows to kill his virgin-daughter and causes her to run wild on the mountains; intermarriage with foreigners in the tale of the rape of Dinah).

The familiar problem with these readings is that they force varied stories into a straitjacket in order to compare them mechanically with a story somewhere else. The less familiar problem is that they tend to start from the 'text as we have it', irrespective of its authors, editors and complex history. As a result, some of the structuralists' most detailed studies fall wonderfully foul of the nature of the biblical text. For, like the story of David and Goliath, the story which they analyse may be a patchwork of separate, conflicting versions which do not follow any one series of moves. Like Jacob and the angel, the oddity and paradox may be nothing more 'audacious' than an editor's change in an older story which no longer seemed tolerable to him. Despite Barthes's dances round the text, these verses of Genesis are merely a story in which Jacob, originally, encountered a local river-spirit who was guarding the river's ford. This spirit had to slink away at daybreak, like the ghost in *Hamlet* or a minor divinity in the pagan world: later editors did not like this demon, who was independent of Yahweh, and so they altered it to God or his angel, spoiling the flow of the story. As its best commentator reminds us, 'all the profound theological consequences drawn from Jacob's supposed encounter with God have no basis in the text'.

As yet, no structuralist reading of scripture has established anything which was not well known before: however, the value in comparing stories is not therefore diminished. Rather than looking outside scripture, to Russian tales or South American myths, I wish to follow one type of story through the Bible itself, from Genesis to Acts. It shows how one type of experience was expressed within broadly similar conventions, until those who wished to imagine it would describe their story in those terms and even (although this is harder to know) be inclined to interpret a hope, an expectation or a sense of sudden 'otherness' in terms of this literary tradition. If so, story itself may have enhanced belief. The belief is extremely important: it involves an encounter with God or a heavenly being, from Abraham to Jesus's Resurrection.

Throughout the Bible, people hear voices from heaven or see visions in which they hear divine words: in Hebrew scripture, if they are Gentiles, God speaks to them too, but only in dreams. The authors have to envisage this contact and make it real to us: they express it in scenes which we can compare, looking for patterns which may recur and help them (and their audience) to imagine these lively moments in the story.

Yet encounters can also be closer than words and visions. People meet divine beings, and once again we can compare the episodes and see how a pattern develops through the scriptures. In the oldest stories, great figures of the nation might even encounter God himself. At Mamre, beneath the oak-tree, it seems from our Bible's text that the Lord himself calls on Abraham at his tent: two others came with him, angels who would later go down to Sodom. At first Abraham mistakes them for strangers. He arranges water with which they can wash their feet; he tells his wife Sarah to make cakes (angel cakes, no doubt: 'small round ashen cakes baked on hot stones', according to modern experts); he brings milk and a special calf. Remarkably, the angels eat, although later angels never taste humans' food: the angel cakes prove tempting. One of the three, perhaps Yahweh himself, predicts a son for old Sarah in a year's time. It is not stated openly that Abraham recognizes his visitor. Only when two of the strangers go on down to Sodom does Abraham plead with the third, God himself. This scene has been added to an encounter which had originally been less explicit.

When visiting Abraham, God takes on a human form. The meeting is exceptional and is never exactly repeated, not even for Moses in Hebrew texts. When Moses first meets God, the setting is a fire, a voice and a burning bush (Moses is afraid to look); the next meeting is on Mount Sinai, where two separate stories stand in the narrative. In the one which stands second in our Bibles, Moses and Aaron go up the mountain with two companions and seventy elders and see the God of Israel: beneath his feet, they look 'on a paved work of sapphire stone, as it were the body of heaven in his clearness'. This full vision of God and heaven in its blue purity is probably the oldest of the Sinai stories. In the later version (probably) of the Yahwist, J, the encounter becomes less direct. The people of Israel have to prepare themselves dutifully, before God will so much as speak through the thunder and the earthquake: for three days they 'had not to go near a woman'. Even then, Yahweh is only heard, not seen: he does not expose himself to his chaste visitors, and instead they see only clouds and fire. Afterwards, God continues to appear at the Tabernacle outside the Israelites' camp, but the people see only a cloudy pillar. With Moses alone, God speaks face to face, as a man speaketh unto his friend, (Exodus 33:7–11). Yet even this much soon seemed too direct: in the following verses, Moses is allowed to see only God's back (33:23) as he passes by. The sight of God's face would be death to him.

As direct contact with God receded, the two old scenes of it, at Mamre's oak and Sinai's mountain, fascinated their many heirs. Who were the three who had come so curiously to Abraham and was God known at once among them? Christian authors, naturally, saw their Holy Trinity, visiting man on earth. On Sinai, the awe of a divine division, the 'paved work of sapphire', the privileged contact, face to face, like a friend, influenced two thousand years of spirituality, from the vision of Hebrew prophets and mystics to the hopes of Christian saints in their desert and cell.

In the patriarchal age, therefore, God might appear in person to exceptional people; by others, he might be heard but not seen. He was elusive, though, whenever people were sinful: in order to see clouds and hear him, all Israel had to be chaste. This connection of sinlessness and God's presence was also important in the Temple cult. There, the priests atoned for human sins and there, in the Holy of Holies, God's presence might be felt in fire, smoke and trembling, but not directly, face to face. Sometimes a psalmist expresses a hope, or strong desire, for seeing the Lord's face but only once does a psalm refer to a past experience (Psalm 63:3, to be translated as 'Thus I saw you in the sanctuary, beholding your power and glory'). Even so, this 'face' and 'seeing' may be broader than a person-to-person meeting, an experience, perhaps, of light and presence. Only to the prophets, at Isaiah 6 and Ezekiel 1, does a more direct vision of God occur. In each case it belongs in a Temple setting and is described through imagery of fire, light, enthronement and so forth. It is granted to exceptional people in an awesome type of appearance.

Otherwise, there was the possibility of meeting a visiting angel. In the patriarchal age angels were seen quite openly, not just by Jacob ('And when Jacob saw them, he said, This is God's host', Genesis 32:2), but by the slave-girl Hagar, driven from her jealous Sarah's household. In a scene of exceptional influence, the messenger of God meets her: he tells her to go back home and submit to her mistress (liberation theology is not to the taste of angels). 'Behold . . . you are with child . . .'; she is given the name of the child, a reason for God's action ('the Lord has given heed') and the child's future ('He shall be a wild ass of a man . . .'). Then, enigmatically, she greets her visitor as God: she has met him face to face, but she survives.

In Sodom, by contrast, disguises are in order: it is a city of sin, and when the heavenly Two go down to it, they go as humans, all too desirable humans to the naughty Sodomites, but human, too, to the virtuous Lot, who greets them as strangers, unawares. Again they eat, but this time their food is unleavened bread. These angelic visits (without the eating) are to be the pattern of the post-patriarchal age when encounters with God are no longer open, except for Moses and a very few of the prophets. When Joshua meets an angel, sword in hand, he mistakes him for a man of war, seeing only the human form: 'Art thou for us, or for our adversaries?' On learning the truth, he then falls and worships as a servant, not a friend. In the book of Numbers, it is Balaam's ass, but not the heathen Balaam, who first sees the angel blocking the road. In Judges, two exquisite stories explore the mould in which these scenes were now imagined: Gideon, and Samson's parents.

Unknowingly, Gideon (like Joshua) encounters an angel in human form who promises him that he will save Israel and slaughter the Midianites. Gideon doubts his words ('my family is poor in Manasseh', Judges 6:15); he asks for a sign (is it really an angel?), and when he brings his visitor hospitality, 'under the oak' in Ophrah, the angel does not eat it; instead, he causes the cakes and raw meat to burn (the idea is of a consuming fire). The angel then departs from view; Gideon is deeply afraid ('I have seen an angel of the Lord face to face'); the Lord answers reassuringly ('Peace be unto thee; fear not: thou shalt not die'). Like Jacob on his journeys, Gideon builds an altar to mark the very spot (the author of Judges thought that he could still see it). The promises, the doubts and the hospitality precede the sign and the departure; there is fear, then reassurance, then a cult to mark the place. This pattern is a precise sequence of literary description whose parts recur in many attempts to envisage such a scene in subsequent scripture.

A few chapters later in Judges, Samson's parents replay it with touching variations. Samson's mother meets an angel who promises her (like Abraham's Sarah) a special son; she does not recognize her visitor, and she remains in honourable, Mediterranean anonymity, the 'wife of Manoah'. She tells her husband, and we learn that she still believes the angel to be a human prophet, a man of God ('his countenance was like the countenance of an angel'): he had not revealed his name. Manoah prays for a return visit from this 'man of God': the angel duly visits his wife as she sits in a field. She fetches Manoah; they talk; he shows that he is still unaware, because he offers the angel bread and meat (since Sodom, angels have gone off their food: no, says the angel, 'thou must offer it to the Lord'). The angel refuses to give his name, and when Manoah offers the meat to the Lord, he departs from view. 'Then Manoah knew . . .'; he is afraid: 'We shall surely die, because we have seen God.' But it is his wife now who reassures him: the Lord has received their offering, and so he cannot wish to kill them.

These visits are still exceptional moments, under oak-trees or in cornfields, promising babies or victories to biblical people with great futures. They would not happen to you or me, but as time passed, this possibility, too, began to be aired quite freely. In the book of Tobit (*c.* 350 BC) an angel attends an ordinary man and his son who are living out their story without any great future in the Persian Empire, east of Judaea. Young Tobias receives a helper whom he believes to be a man: he is even told the names of his family and ancestors. Together they travel on their mission, but when Tobias tries to pay him for his services, the angel reveals himself. 'I am Raphael, one of the seven holy angels.' Tobias and his father are afraid, but he tells them, 'Fear not,' and departs for ever. He also has never eaten: he has only seemed to do so, he explains, by causing an illusory dream of the scene. Angels now have names, but not appetites: sometimes they tell mortals to write their story in a book, but the same pattern still fills ideas of their presence: disguise and revelation, dieting and no drinking, then departure and mortal fear.

To the West, without any contact or borrowing, these close encounters had a natural pair in the contemporary Greek world. Greek gods, too, were heard as well as seen, through visions, dreams and heavenly voices: in Homer's poems, too, there lived the awareness that once, in the distant past, gods had appeared directly to the great and good, to the Phaeacians in the *Odyssey* whose land was as favoured as Mamre. Since then, like angels in Sodom, gods would visit the world in disguises: the wicked cannot see them and even the good, the heroes, mistake them for mortals. In Greece, too, they reveal themselves: occasionally, they drink, but usually they abstain from mortal dinners, like angels in the age after Abraham. When they reveal themselves, sometimes by a word, sometimes by a sign, they bring fear; they depart; cults begin from brief encounters, and an altar, like Gideon's, marks the very spot.

There is a similarity, too, between Greece and Israel at times of worship. In some of the psalms, the authors wrote as if God were present and about to be seen in high moments of cult in his Temple: the same expectation lived for centuries in pagan Greek hymns. Like the authors of Judges or Tobit, Homer and his heirs knew a usual pattern of these scenes and developed them for literary effect. There are, however, differences. In Israel, Yahweh was not depicted in art and his form was too awesome to be seen: among the Greeks, great art and sculpture helped to define the forms of the gods and bring them more readily into mortals' dreams. In the Greek world, there was no belief that those who saw God would surely die; divine strangers were less shy about revealing their names; their words were not always prophetic: they did not promise children so much as father them; in Greek myth, a woman who lies with a god becomes pregnant every time.

From Sicily to Israel, there was a similar potential, sustained by hymns and stories: you never knew when meeting a stranger or seeing a distant form on the hills. Similar beliefs were clothed and enhanced in remarkably similar literary forms. The authors of the New Testament were these patterns' direct heirs, but, although they wrote in Greek, they drew on the scriptural, not pagan Greek, sources. They needed to tell us of an Annunciation, a Transfiguration and their risen Lord: to do so, they expressed these convictions in the ancient biblical forms. In Matthew, the birth of the child is promised in dreams, but in Luke it occurs as a visitation, closely matching the old biblical encounters, scenes which Christian storytellers knew. 'Fear not, Mary . . .', no more than Gideon or Tobias; God has his reasons; you will have a son; you will give him this name; his future will be as follows – the pattern is exactly the pattern of the angel's words in Genesis to Hagar the slave-girl. At the empty tomb, Matthew's Gospel tells of the great earthquake and a terrifying angel who says to the women, 'Fear not . . .' In Luke's, however, the women see two angels and fall (like Joshua) before them in servility. On the road to Emmaus, like Lot or Tobias, disciples meet a visiting stranger, Jesus in disguise; in Jerusalem, they see him again, and he greets them in peace, but 'they were terrified' until he reassures them. In the fourth Gospel, Jesus appears like a gardener or a stranger by the lake; here, too, there is disguise, but in John there is no fear, except a 'fear of the Jews' among the disciples in their upper room. Significantly, in both Luke and John, Jesus is seen to eat: he is not yet the resurrected being and he still has human qualities, raised from death.

In the apostolic age, there is still the expectation of 'angels unawares', but actual sightings by daylight dwindle away. Twice Acts describes the experience of Paul on the road to Damascus, but neither version specifies that he sees the risen Christ in person: rather, he hears a voice. When angels communicate, they appear at one remove in visions or dreams: once, by night, an angel does come in person to guide Peter from prison, but even then it seems to Peter as if the experience is all a dream. Direct encounters are becoming an expectation, no longer realized in life: the serving girl Rhoda thinks she is seeing Peter's angel, but it is Peter himself; in the rural towns of the Roman Empire, Gentiles are quick, but wrong, to see visiting gods when Paul or a companion amazes them with miracles. Through these Christian narratives in Acts, the two worlds, Gentile and scriptural, collide again and remind us of their similar notions of the presence of a god.

When we hear or read these scenes, we need to remember that they came to their hearers with the familiarity of a way of telling, repeated across a thousand years. Nobody knew what Gideon or Samson's parents or (probably) Mary had experienced, but a precise, literary pattern allowed authors to put a story of it into words. It was not so much a fiction as a way of expressing 'how it must have been', and we need to be sensitive to its sequences and small variations. It persisted for centuries in two cultures, and with its help we can correct one way of looking at Israel's view of God. For there had been no change from a pan-sacral age in Israel in which the divine was encountered anywhere, in miracles or close encounters; there was no change to a later age of enlightenment in which God's hand in events was constant but unseen. Instead, the pan-sacral sense of presence persisted from Genesis to Acts, wherever the form of the story was likely to evoke it, in scenes of Nativity or human adventure, for births or deaths or beyond the grave. In it all, we are not studying mere words, but words which helped to fix, and perhaps even encourage, a sense of religious otherness and supernatural presence. From Gideon by the oak-trees to the disciples in their upper room, people were said to have been 'terrified and affrighted', but 'Peace be unto thee; fear not: thou shalt not die.' The last encounter was told, and perhaps experienced, with echoes of the older stories: it acquired its own momentum and impelled historical change.

21
'Divine Letters'

If we label most of the Bible as story, we accept that much of it is not true, but we do not put it out of historians' reach: we change the questions and interests which they pursue in it. It becomes a book whose authors have invented or made mistakes but who share, none the less, religious beliefs which many people share too. Historians will not look for truth in every event or detail, but they will still try to infer truths – about the beliefs, outlooks and assumptions of the biblical authors and their audience.

Historians, however, are a minority, vastly outnumbered by people who would simply prefer to read. Why not read the Bible as literature and leave historians to fuss about the dates of Jeroboam or the weird beliefs about conception in a chapter of Genesis? Might there not be truth at this level too, whatever the factual status of the narrative or the mentality of its authors?

In the past thirty years responses to the 'Bible as literature' have become a tidal wave in writings about holy writ. They are not a new approach. In the centuries after Alexander, when Jews encountered Greek literature, they already asked literary questions about their own texts: what, for instance, was the nature of Hebrew poetry?

Josephus claimed that Moses and David had both used the hexameter for particular songs in scripture, an impossible belief which early Christians inherited. Even Jerome, who knew Hebrew, believed that Job broke into hexameters in the second half of the book. These beliefs belonged with growing praises for scripture as literature. At first early Christians contrasted 'literature' and 'scripture', both of which were

Latin words: literature was heathen, the pagan classics which were taught in schools. Then scripture began to be seen as 'divine letters', a possible education in its own right. The problem was that its style seemed so rough and barbarous to educated ears. Was it, perhaps, the divine style of God? Or was it better rewritten? By the year 330, soon after the conversion of the first Christian emperor, a well-born Spaniard, Juvencus, rendered the Gospels into Latin hexameters. He claimed to be adding poetic sweetness to their contents.

These questions of biblical style did not fade away: from the later seventeenth century onwards, people took the opposite course and admired a rough grandeur in the Bible's unkempt sublimity. In the past thirty years literary critics have again upheld it for roughness and abruptness, but this time for a different reason. Changes in modern literary taste have brought new interests to bear; critics look for gaps and 'creative contradictions', odd directions in narrative, 'voices of incomplete fulfilment' and hidden significance in episodes which seem to interrupt the flow. A new age of literary theory has also found scope for its practice in short biblical scenes: they confront us as texts without authors' names, not works which raise questions of authors' intentions or personal histories. Structuralists try to explain the meanings which we already perceive; deconstructionists undercut the idea of any one meaning or external reference; theorists of reader-response ask which readers a text is presupposing (the Jewish hearers, addressed by Jews in the Gospel; the Gospel's first Christian readers; you and I, here and now); each group will probably find a different meaning in what they read. A text's meaning thus becomes open and varied, its form less straightforward. In modern novels we no longer assume that a text must move in a single, connected direction: why, then, should the old biblical narratives? 'A generation which has experienced *Ulysses* and *The Waste Land* should be able to do this more easily than one whose idea of a book and a unity was a novel by Balzac or George Eliot.'

One result of these new readings has been some spectacular implausibility. The book of Judges is thought to test our sense of irony by the stories which it strings one after another; the text of 2 Samuel (but not, surely, the author) is believed to leave open the possibility (or 'gap') that Uriah the Hittite knows as well as King David that the king has seduced his wife by the time of their first interview in the text.

Above all, neglect of the text's origins has led to the weirdest claims on its behalf. The 'text of Ecclesiastes as we have it' is thought to be challenging us by a subtle use of contradictions: its editors, merely, have stuck in their own modifications to an original which they felt to be too shocking. Their alterations have made bits of it incomprehensible. Even the book of Esther, a robust '*roman à thèse*', has been upheld for its use of gaps and false turnings. Here, the original text has been wrongly reduced by a chapter and a half, so that the book can be made more palatable without its final scenes of massacre: 'It would be a delightful irony, and one fully worthy of the Jewish sense of humour, if the resolution of the conflict between the two royal edicts had been left up in the air: a stalemate is perhaps in the end the best one can hope for and it is certainly infinitely preferable to a defeat.' Esther's author would be appalled: the shortening betrays his aim and his literary style.

Textual muddles have even been misread as signs of some ancient purposeful technique. In 1 Samuel 16 and 17 we have two contradictory stories of young David's rise to King Saul's notice. In one, he is already one of Saul's companions when Goliath challenges Israel; in the other, he arrives in the middle of the challenge, the youngest son, fresh from his father's flocks. The first story is coherent in itself; the second has more of a fairy-tale feel to it (it is good, however, on the elder brother's attitude to the youngest in the family). The contradictions have long been evident, and the entire story of Goliath's slaying is probably legend; elsewhere in the Bible (2 Samuel 21:19), it is ascribed to Elhanan, not even to David. However, the contradictions have found a critic to appreciate them: apparently, they are an 'easily recognizable sophisticated but well known and in all periods very common literary device of suspense narrative'; the conflicting stories about David have been put side by side because this is the 'characteristic biblical method for incorporating multiple perspective'. This 'method' works not through a 'fusion of views in a single utterance but a montage of viewpoints arranged in sequence'. The Bible's Iron Age narrative thus anticipates the art which nowadays we know from films.

In fact, this montage is the result of a typically biblical act of creation: two variant stories have been run into one by an editor, although they contradict each other. There is no particular art in this muddle, only a wish to preserve both stories at once. We can demonstrate their existence by referring to the Greek translation of the book (parts of it have now been matched by an early Hebrew text among the Dead Sea scrolls). The Greek translator of these chapters was not abridging a longer Hebrew version: he was using a separate Hebrew text which had only one of the two conflicting stories. We do not know if this text was the earliest, or original, Hebrew, but we do know that our Bibles have translated a conflation of two separate tales. They are not the subtle montage of an Iron Age narrator: they are the patched-up salvage of an editor, rather late in the day.

The Bible does not cease to be literature because there are modern critics misrepresenting it: in Hebrew scripture the problems of the text and its editing merely need to be taken more seriously. 'Literature', however, has been attacked more fundamentally: it is said to be the wrong label altogether. There are theologians who think that it degrades scripture and misses its religious content; there are literary critics, too, who think that it implies a sophistication and artifice which the Bible lacks. A literary reading, however, need be only one among others, religious readings included, while parts of the Bible do have undeniable art. From the puns and intricate word-play of J to the realistic detail of the author of Esther, biblical narrative has its own careful tricks. It is surprisingly strong in irony, from Abraham's answers to Isaac on their walk ('God will provide'), through the twists and turns in the story of Joseph, to the expectations of wicked Haman in the book of Esther at least five centuries later (he is hanged on the very gallows which he has built for Mordecai the Jew). Its language can be wonderfully rich and open, as its translators recognized long before the rise of literary criticism. It adopts various literary forms and plays with them, a lament, perhaps, or a wedding-song or a hymn of victory: it can echo the language of a law suit or the rhythms of antiphonal song (in Homer, too, the Muses sing antiphonally, although we no longer have their words; the early Christians kept the antiphonal habit, as we know from the pagan Pliny, their inquisitor, *c.* 110). In the most modern idiom, biblical writings are 'intertextual': they deepen their meaning by referring back to other texts in their number. This cross-reference is not confined to the New Testament. After being told as a story, a great theme like the Exodus recurs as a reason for biblical laws (Leviticus 25:42), as a proof-text of God's help (1 Kings 8:51 or Amos 3:1), an analogy underlying the entire return from the Exile in the book of Ezra, or a source of hope for future 'signs and wonders' (Ecclesiasticus 36:6). The Exodus also underlies the stories of Jesus's temptation in the wilderness or the fourth Gospel's feeding of the five thousand; it is the source of an allegory in Paul's epistles or a contrast between Jesus and Joshua, his namesake, in Hebrews 3–4. We have to read closely in order to pick it up. It also relates to broader literary themes, the importance of the desert or of wandering, which its authors played on, just as their heirs in Western literature have played on them too.

There is a considerable subtlety of speech and narrative. We tend to think of narrative as the natural way of writing, but it is a literary form, like any other (it now has its own theorists, or 'narratologists'). In the Bible the authors are all-knowing: they tell us what was said or felt (even by God) and exactly what was done. This stance is their own convention, but we need to be aware of it if we are not to surrender too quickly to the truth of what they relate. We also need to be alert to their angle of vision. The book of Ruth has the best-constructed plot of any long biblical narrative, but even here the author may have left significant gaps on purpose (did he make Boaz deliberately fail to tell the unnamed kinsman which of the two widows he would be expected to marry, Ruth, not Naomi? Did Boaz himself feel unsure what exactly had passed between himself and Ruth when she lay beside him at night? Might she, even, be pregnant?). The narrative leaves significant details unsaid in order to engage us by its art.

We are also guided by differing viewpoints through which the author allows us to watch an action. At 2 Kings 6:25 there is a great famine in Samaria, caused by a Syrian invasion; the king of Israel passes by on the wall and reacts to the pleas of a woman who has boiled and eaten her son, but has been tricked by her neighbour; he rends his clothes; 'he passed by upon the wall, and the people looked, and, behold, he had sackcloth within upon his flesh'. Through the onlookers' eyes, we suddenly see that the king, too, is imploring God: in the sequel we hear him blame the kingdom's troubles on Elisha, the man of God, but we know that the king is wrong, a sinner against the Lord. The Bible leaves us to pick up the connections in what it has shown us from the people's viewpoint. The king is doing penance, we see with them, but we know from the story's framework that the penance is unavailing.

Similar subtleties show up in speech, not just in unanswered questions (a biblical favourite) but in the great arts of persuading and requesting. At 2 Samuel 14 we have a superb animation of narrative by speech which derives, in my view, from that oldest and most Herodotean source, the Court History of David. The 'woman of Tekoa' leaves almost no worthwhile trick to be found by later rhetoric. She grieves; she tells her little story; she implores; she flatters the king. Then she speaks her purpose, turning the story back against David himself; then she moralizes beautifully and swiftly returns to her personal woe; again, she flatters ('my lord is wise, according to the wisdom of an angel of God') and implores. Yet we know she is lying throughout (the iron-hard Joab has told her what to say), and King David knows it too. But he takes the one point which she makes against himself. There are literary critics who have floundered and even concluded that although the Bible is literary, it is not literature. What could be more sophisticated than the woman of Tekoa, except for the man who invented her? For non-critics, literature is a broad enough field to include such marvellous texts.

Literary readings are rather ridiculous if they pick on biblical laws or genealogies or the instructions for making a tabernacle in the book of Leviticus: bits of the Bible may be literary, but we need not struggle to show that everything in it is. In the right places, however, a literary approach may well bring out why the text has such power. Long before theories of literature, readers could pick up its art. In 1713 the English man of letters Richard Steele composed two fine letters to the *Guardian*. In the first (on 9 May) he gave his response to his reading of King David's lament for Saul and Jonathan. David, he remarked, grieves for Saul, his enemy, 'without any allusion to the difficulties whence he was extricated' by Saul's fortunate death: without Saul, David could now become king. But when David turns to lament Jonathan, the sublimity ceases; not able to mention his generous friendship, he 'sinks into a fondness that . . . turns only upon their familiar converse: "thy love to me was wonderful, passing the love of women".' Saul's 'merit' causes David to neglect his own newly gained worldly power and its grandeur, but his praise for Jonathan is expressed in terms of 'how much they both loved, not how much Jonathan deserved'. In this great lament, literary style reinforces our instant impression of human insight.

In his second letter, from Oxford on 16 June, Steele contrasted two types of description, one in Homer and Virgil, the other in the book of Job. Both concern that 'generous beast', the horse. In the classical poets (he argued) the horse, galloping free, is painted only in its outward 'figure, lineaments and motions'. In Job the author 'makes all the beauties to flow from an inward principle in the creature he describes'. He dwells on the force of its neck, not just on its mane: 'there is a peculiar beauty in the horse "not believing he hears the sound of the trumpet": that is, he cannot believe it for joy, but when he is sure of it and is "amongst the trumpets, he saith, Ha, Ha: he neighs, he rejoices"'. Steele linked this inner force with the inspiration of the biblical author who was here (he believed) giving the words of God. We might rather think of the idea of Creation which links God with the animal's temper, a mystery (absent from Virgil) to which Job's author was referring his hearers.

In each of these letters, a literary reader helps us to see something true about the Bible: how an author varies his laments for a king and a friend, how another author chooses to see the power of a horse (we could make a similar point about the view of animals in some of the psalms: our 'fellow pensioners' before God, as C. S. Lewis once expressed it). These truths, however, concern unknown authors and their ways of writing: they do not concern the truth (or fiction) of what their stories are telling us as if it happened.

II

In the Hebrew scriptures we can live more easily with the label of story and a level of truth which lies with the authors' own ways of telling things, not with the events themselves. We infer that in Israel there were people who believed this or that, including various things about God (once, even, that he tried to kill Moses, Exodus 4:24): by reading carefully, we can find various truths, some of them rather profound, about the ways in which they wrote their stories up. The Hebrew Bible, then, becomes true evidence for how certain Hebrews saw things (the things themselves, like their God, may none the less be false).

In the Christian scriptures this label and level are not so comfortable. Most readers of the Bible are not too concerned that God did not say what the authors of Genesis imagined when telling the stories of Eden or Abraham: they have given him words which their faith, or story line, required. Yet many Christians still take the reported sayings of Jesus on trust. They are a framework for their beliefs, even for their ideals of how to behave. Events and actions can be slightly more flexible: Christians can live with a story or two, a transfiguration, perhaps, or a few miracles, or even (as if we knew all along) the entire Nativity. But even here, story cannot extend its tentacles too far. Christians will want to depend, ultimately, on historical fact, on a Crucifixion and a Resurrection, based on the same Apostles' evidence which also claimed that somebody walked on water or blasted a fig-tree to death.

In the Gospels, therefore, literary readings encounter once again the question of historical truth; for this reason, I will concentrate on one of them, the fourth Gospel, in particular to bring out what reading the Bible as literature can help us to recognize. Like Steele's letters on Job or David, one branch of literary study has helped to bring out the power and originality in some of the Gospel sayings. At times, they use repetition to drive home their point: 'judge not, and ye shall not be judged: condemn not, and ye shall not be condemned' (Luke 6:37; contrast Matthew 7:1–2). They like to set up sharp contrasts between two halves of a balanced saying: 'For whosoever will save his life shall lose it; but whosoever will lose his life for my sake, the same shall save it' (compare 'Consider the lilies of the field' or 'Lay not up for yourselves treasure on earth'). Sometimes the second half of a saying reverses the drift of the first: 'Ye have heard that it was said by them of old time, Thou shalt not commit adultery: But I say unto you . . .' Other sayings give us several examples and then round them off with the general idea which lies behind them: 'Whosoever shall smite thee on thy right cheek . . . if any man sue thee at the law . . . whosoever shall compel thee to go a mile . . .' It is for us to extend the series to similar moments in our own life, holding fast to the conclusion: 'Give to him that asketh thee . . .'

These distinctive styles of speech raise the question of their possible origin with one person: are we hearing Jesus himself or do they derive from Christian tradition or individual Gospellers? The question has been posed and decisively answered for the most distinctive sayings, the Gospels' parables which many would wish to uphold as Jesus's very own words. However, parables take distinctive forms in each of the three Gospels, not only the parables which are individual to a Gospel but the parables which they share in common. In Mark, parables tend to be stories based on nature, like the parables which are spoken by prophets in the Old Testament: they are set in the little world of the village, without any vast sums of money or extravagance; they are not stories of paradoxical conduct: they are parables about the kingdom, some of which allow an allegorical reading (the Sower; the Fig-tree). Matthew's parables, by contrast, have much grander settings ('when it comes to money, Matthew moves among the millionaires'); they contrast good and bad, wise and foolish (the Builders on sand and on rock; the Just and Unjust Stewards); they tell of highly paradoxical behaviour (the labourers who start work in the vineyard at the eleventh hour receive the same wage as those who started early; the merchant sells everything to buy one pearl of great price). In Luke's parables there are contrasts too, but whereas Matthew's pairs of contrasted figures are stock caricatures, 'in Luke all is alive ... his parables have names in them ... we see into their persons' hearts'; they require us to realize 'how much the more' will God do this, or should we do that; they emphasize a simple moral about faith or alms or repentance. Unlike Mark and Matthew, Luke avoided allegory. His Gospel's parable of the sower omits several points of potential meaning in Mark's, because 'his eye is on the story' (he added incidental detail) 'and the meaning can take care of itself'.

It is particularly interesting that each Gospel's parables are shaped in ways which match that Gospel's own teaching: 'Matthew's parables emphasize Matthaean doctrines of Hell and Angels which hardly occur in Mark'; Luke's parables soften the stress on hell but 'feature Lucan doctrines like Prayer, Faithfulness and the danger of money'. In each case the Gospellers have shaped what they may (or may not) have received as a core. Like the stories of Jesus's trial, the main parables confront us in separate, coherent forms: none of them, therefore, can be taken as Jesus's exact words.

Here, literary study has had a direct relevance to biblical truth, but there is a further complication: the parables, the Sermon on the Mount and the ethical sayings are found in some, or all, of the three synoptic Gospels, but we have a fourth Gospel which strikes a different note. Its Jesus speaks in long monologues; he is entirely open about his status as

383

the Son whose Father is God; there is the commandment to 'love one another', but no words on marriage or the relations between the sexes, and no special emphasis on the poor and the sinners; the word 'Apostle' is never used, and only twice does the Gospel refer to a kingdom. On one recent Christian view, if the fourth Gospel had not been included in the Bible and confronted us now for the first time, it would strike us as 'exceedingly strange and rather heretical'. Yet we have seen the coherence, even the cogency, of the author's account of Jesus's arrest and trial, and I have argued that the entire Gospel is derived from a primary source, the beloved disciple who may or may not be John. There is a debt, here, to be paid off: is this Gospel the nearest to historical truth? If we read it for its literary art, we may see this question more clearly.

III

As a literary work, the fourth Gospel has conflicting qualities. It is more than a third longer than Mark's, but it uses only three-quarters as many words. Its themes recur and lend it unity: Glory, Light, Eternal Life, Truth and so forth. It has even been credited with 'hieratic monotony', the repetitive style of a priestly writer. Yet it also moves with sudden bumps from scene to scene; at 14:31 Jesus says, 'Arise, let us go hence,' but he talks on for three long chapters of soliloquy before picking up the action. Chapters 5 and 6 are also a challenge which would run more smoothly if their sequence were changed round. There are respectable reasons, too, for questioning the coherence of the raising of Lazarus (peculiar to this Gospel) with its surrounding context (11:47 could pick up directly from 10:42). In the other three Gospels, sayings against the Temple occupy its place, but in the fourth, these sayings stand defiantly at the start of Jesus's career: they are carefully explained not as sayings about the Temple building, but as sayings about Jesus's own body and death.

Some of this Gospel's abrupt turns might be explained if its text had had a turbulent early history. We have no good reason to suppose so (there are no variant texts of it like the texts of David and Goliath) and no grounds for invoking a later editor: the style and vocabulary of the Gospel are remarkably uniform, and detailed studies have shown that nothing stands out in it as another author's work. Might, then, the

384

unevenness go back to the author himself? Certainly, the beloved disciple had had time to consider and rewrite, to add chapters like 15 and 16 and (perhaps) promote 2:13–23. He had followed Jesus, but he probably wrote in the wake of Mark's Gospel; if so, he was no longer young when he composed the last parts of his work. Age, even, has been seen as the explanation, as if the Gospel were written by a heroic witness who worked on it piecemeal for years, who taught a school of pupils, reacted to their comments, slowly revised it and finally 'changed his custom of writing when he became older and needed a secretary . . . How may we expect to understand (and criticize) the strange work of an early Christian charismatic teacher who has been occupying himself for years with the same subject?' Like the head of an early Christian department, this ideal hero died before his professorial book was finally to his liking.

This battling professor-Elder is a pleasant patron saint for his modern critics, but he is only one guess among dozens, made to explain the conflict of an uneven structure and a narrowly focused style. This conflict does not mean that the author was without literary art: his telling of a scene was not at the mercy of a new secretary's shorthand. Among many examples, one of the best known is his Last Supper, where art and historical witness coincide. For, if the author was the beloved disciple, he had a privileged seat, reclining beside Jesus, and yet his account is quite different from those of the other Gospels. Its artful shaping at once raises difficult questions of fact and truth.

To the synoptic Gospels, the meal was a Passover, whereas this Gospel puts it on the previous day; the discussion is different (there are no words from Jesus about the future rite of Bread and Wine, although the existence of such words was passed on to Paul by the early Christians before any of our Gospels had been written). Bread, instead, is the token with which Jesus marks out the traitor, Judas; as he leaves, the disciples wonder, is he going out to give something to the poor? (Shortly before, at Bethany, Judas had protested at Mary's anointing of Jesus, saying that the cost should be given to the poor: he wanted to steal the money, according to one of the Gospeller's personal comments.) Up to this point the Gospeller has not specified the hour or place of the Supper, saying nothing about an upper room. Only now, as Judas leaves the room in Satan's power, does he interpose the time: he 'went immediately out: and it was night'.

Into the night goes the man of Darkness in order to betray the Light of the world, who has warned us 'night is coming' (9:4). Like the authors of Genesis or Kings, like so much in Homer's poetry, this author knew the power of dramatic reticence. Just as Homer said nothing of Achilles's tent until the plot of his final book required it, so the author delayed the mention of night until it enhanced the course of events. Here, however, we are also drawn to read the scene symbolically. The night, suggested Origen, the great early Christian scholar, was a symbol of the darkness in Judas's own soul. There is nothing so resonant in the reticence of Homer or Kings.

The author's control did not falter after this exit. Words of Jesus mark the occasion: 'Now is the Son of man glorified, and God is glorified in him.' In the night, there is glory, and soon God will glorify this son of man too. 'Glory' runs like a key word through the Gospel, going beyond its one climactic mention in Mark (by James and John at 10:37). In the fourth Gospel Jesus comes down from glory with his father, dies the most awful death but is 'raised up' by it and 'glorified', in the touching view of his beloved follower. Here, the tenses of the verbs are significant: aorist for the glory which is fulfilled in the hour of betrayal, future for glory which will continue through the Crucifixion and its sequel. It is all such a contrast with Luke's Last Supper; there, Jesus talks of a new kingdom, and it emerges, through the disciples' misunderstanding, that it is not to be a kingdom of swords or fighting. In the fourth Gospel, however, Jesus gives them not a kingdom but a new commandment: unlike the kingdom, it cannot be misunderstood politically. It is the commandment to love one another. 'Ye shall seek me: and as I said unto the Jews,' (yet they are Jews too) 'Whither I go, ye cannot come.' Peter then asks him, 'Lord, whither goest thou?' and 'Why cannot I follow thee now? I will lay down my life for thy sake.' In Luke's Gospel Jesus begins by addressing Peter and warning him that Satan wants him, while in the fourth Gospel the irony is held back. It is Jesus, we know, who will die on behalf of Peter: only in the Gospel's last chapter, added later, do we catch a hint that Peter will also die as a martyr. Jesus ends with an ironic contrast: 'Wilt thou lay down thy life for my sake? Verily, verily, I say unto thee, the cock shall not crow, till thou hast denied me thrice.'

The irony is sharper, and Judas's exit is more dramatic (though it is not surprising: Jesus has known his betrayer's identity all the time); the running theme of 'glory' is drawn tightly together; love, not the kingdom, is the lasting message. Perhaps here, too, something too open to worldly misunderstanding has been pushed from the centre of this Gospel's story (in this Gospel the 'kingdom' is only mentioned once to Nicodemus, at 3:5, and once in answer to Pilate's explicit question, at 18:36). If the beloved disciple is the author, he witnessed this Supper, but he has told it with singular art. The scene is linked to his own interpretation of what Jesus's mission meant (the theology of glory, and so forth): it also has the reticence, irony and use of question and answer which we have picked up, perhaps like the Gospeller himself, from the Hebrew scriptures' style.

In such a text, how far can we press our search for its deeper meanings? The early Christians faced this hard question as they pondered the Gospel's very first sign, the wedding feast in Cana, where Jesus turns the water into wine. The story is certainly not an allegory: it purports to tell us what happened. However, a close reading can also find about thirty connections between its words, the rest of the Gospel and Christian meanings. If all of them are valid, this story is a highly stylized piece of art. Are Jesus's hard words at Cana to his mother ('mine hour is not yet come') a veiled allusion to the messianic hour of the 'true Vine' and the hour of the Christian eucharist which will dawn after his death? Is it only a life-like, ironic detail when the butler tells the bridegroom that contrary to normal practice, the best wine is being brought out last? Is it not, perhaps, an allegory: did not Christ finally bring the best wine, as opposed to the water in the Jewish water pots which were used for purification under the old law? The miracle may seem a trivial one, worked just for the fun of it at a party in a well-off household (there were servants present): yet would this context alone have sufficed to preserve it? Like wine, perhaps, the wedding feast could be a symbol of joy, the joy brought by Christ to his companions. At none of these points are we helped by the author: should we therefore over-interpret him? Or did he leave the meaning open, telling the story because it was the first known to him but choosing to tell it in this way, not because he knew what Jesus had said at the time to others, but because this artful presentation, 'how it must have been', had many other connections which its readers were free to make?

If we allow this degree of art and shaping, the results of literary study are already pushing historical truth to one side. The dialogue between art and fact underlies all written history, however dull, but it is much more intense in a Gospel which is written with hindsight, to present religious Truth. Yet we also know that explicit truth mattered centrally to the author's purpose. Twenty-five times he used the word 'truth', not always for higher theology: his book insists on 'testimony' and twice it cites its primary authorities, uniquely among biblical texts. John the Baptist testifies to Jesus in his own words (the other Gospels prefer to use narrative here), and at the Cross the eyewitness of the blood and water from Jesus's side is said to have 'saw it bare record, and his record is true: and he knoweth that he saith true, that ye might believe' (many readers deduce that this witness is the author himself, but the reference is not necessary). If we read for hidden meanings and dense symbolism, we are missing this direct dimension of truth and witness. For once, we know a biblical author's purpose because he wrote it himself: 'that ye might believe Jesus is the Christ, the Son of God; and that believing ye might have life through his name'.

It is not that deep symbolism and a wide range of meanings are inconsistent with this aim, but they cannot be the main aim, for then, only the subtlest critics would ever believe fully and 'have life'. Those who study only the literary form risk missing the element of fact and witness: they are impressed by apparent patterns: 'Jesus goes three times to Galilee; three Passovers are mentioned and three other Jewish feasts. John the Baptist appears three times as witness: Jesus speaks three times from the Cross and there are three Resurrection appearances.' The author's familiarity with the 'liturgical practices of Jewish worship' is implied to lie behind these markers of time, so that reality recedes before his fiction. 'The subtleties of construction, the more or less occult relationship of parts that we admire in favoured novels, owe a largely unconscious debt to ancient liturgical practice. This is part of one's justification for calling John a proto-novelist.' But the festivals are partly there because Jesus went to them, like so many pilgrims in Josephus's histories. They were three because they ran from AD 34 to 36. Recurrent threesomes do not, by themselves, add meaning: for that, we would need a further reference, to the old view, perhaps, that the 'three and a half years' of this Gospel's story allude to the 'time, two times and a half' of the famous prophecy in the Book of Daniel.

Such a reference could co-exist with historical fact, but would the author himself have been so cryptic? For once, we can read a biblical text in terms of its intended readers, for these, too, the author made plain. He was addressing Christians or potential Christians ('that ye might believe'). Many scholars infer that he wrote for his own small community, but the inference relies too heavily on the postscript to the last chapter. This section is not the Gospeller's own work, but a later author's: 'we know that his testimony is true', it says, but this author need not be a pupil or disciple addressing the author's own community. Altogether, people think too easily of the author as a teacher (the First Epistle, ascribed to John, steers us in that direction). The 'we' of the postscript might only be a Christian audience who are being addressed by a reader of the Gospel in a less formal setting. The Gospel itself makes almost no use of the language of a community. Its Jesus meets individuals, Nicodemus or the Samaritan woman: in chapter 6 the eucharist of Bread and Wine is almost certainly presupposed, but it is not laid down for a community's future at the Last Supper. Jesus, rather, makes a show of foot-washing, as a servant and master in one: it is this personal gesture which he commands to his followers (far into the Middle Ages, washing the feet of the poor remained an individual Christian's good work).

The Gospel's intended audience, therefore, need only be individual Christians, not a small community with its own hidden codes and meanings. The book, then, must speak to each of us 'that we might believe'; to this end, the author used the historian's great privilege: hindsight. Sometimes, perhaps, his hindsight went back to something which Jesus himself asserted, but always it was the author who selected the emphasis. Throughout, he looked back with hindsight on the Jews, looking in on them from outside Judaea; with Christian hindsight, he wrote how Jesus himself summed up famous themes in Jewish piety and scripture. For Jesus's battle, in this Gospel, is not with the Jewish law: instead, he is the coping-stone of Jewish beliefs. The Gospeller selected, arranged and presented his material so that we, in the new Christian age, could grasp this crucial relationship.

Seven times in the fourth Gospel Jesus tells Jewish hearers 'I am . . .', and each time, his claim makes sense against a context of Jewish hopes for Israel. 'I am the true Vine . . .': like Jesus, Israel had been called the

Vine (Isaiah 5:7 ff.; Ezekiel 15), an image which also looked forward to the messianic age. Israel, too, was the living Resurrection (Ezekiel 39, the vision of the 'dry bones'), the psalmists spoke of a Light to lighten the Gentiles and agreed with the prophets that the Lord was their Shepherd: during the Exodus, Israel had lived on bread from heaven and a stream of water. Bread and Living Water, Light and Life, the Resurrection, the 'true Vine': these are the Gospel's metaphors for Jesus. He is also the Door, the Way and the Truth. The claims place him in relation to Hebrew scriptures (he is the true Bread, the true Vine), just as other sayings show how he sums up Jewish practice. For, Jesus's body, the Gospel tells us, is the new Temple; Jesus is the new Manna, the new Water at the Feast of Tabernacles (where water had an important role), the new Lamb (1:36, according to John the Baptist) and, by implication, the new Lamb for Passover, the sequel to his death. The story and the sayings thus place Jesus and the Christians in relation to the piety of the Jews who stand against them both.

Perhaps Jesus did use some, or all, of these images, although the other Gospels do not pick them up in this way. However, he did not use only these words at exactly those moments, and we have to allow for a unity and a theme which the author's own hindsight and understanding have imposed. Its imagery is not 'more or less occult', as literary critics have suggested, as if only a critic's deep divination can reveal it in the text or only a cohesive Christian sect could grasp it. Yet it is remarkably insistent and narrowly focused, particularly when applied to miracles. In Galilee, the first sign is the miracle of wine and water; the second is one of life; the third is bread; and the last (in the postscript) a miracle of the Christian symbol, the fish. No narrative in Hebrew scripture, let alone in the pagan Greek world, had been so densely woven round a web of coherent themes. Light and Darkness, Wine and Water, Truth, Bread, Eternal Life return again and again in what is said and done. Either we see or (like 'sons of darkness') we do not: these themes have special meaning for the Gospel's individual hearers because they live in a new Christian context. With hindsight, they have deeper insight: it is this gap which the author so strikingly exploits to bring home Truth.

In part, he exploits it through quotations from the Hebrew scriptures. What happened (they show us) had to happen, and at first sight we might think that Jesus himself made all these connections. In the text he is made to cite scripture to support his foresight of his own betrayal (13:18), his arrest and his death (15:25). He is also said to have told the disciples to 'Search the scriptures' in order to understand him: are the scriptural connections in this Gospel, then, his own, uttered in his lifetime, or are they results of the author's (and others') searches? There are some difficult lines to draw here, but sometimes the author's own hindsight is evident. On the Cross, Jesus, 'knowing that all things were now accomplished, that the scripture might be fulfilled, saith, I thirst'. What fulfilled the scripture: these particular words or the ending of 'all'? We cannot rule out this wider claim, but on either view it is the author who ascribed this wish to fulfil scripture to Jesus's inner intentions: at such a moment, how could he have known?

When Jesus speaks and acts against the Temple, it is through scripture that the disciples are said to have realized his meaning, but the realization only came later (2:22 ff.): here, hindsight is evident, and the particular scripture is not even cited, as if the Gospel's audience would have known it. At 12:37 ff. the author gave one of his own 'notes and comments', a statement in his person which, in this case, uses scripture to guide his Gospel's truth. With a double quotation from Isaiah he rounded off his account of Jesus's miraculous signs. One quotation is from the great prophecy of the Suffering Servant, the other from Isaiah's heavenly vision in which (in the Greek translation) Isaiah sees the glory of God in heaven. The two prophecies are set in the Gospel just before Jesus's last Passover and tie up two of the author's own interpretations, that glory was to be revealed in the suffering of Jesus's death. It is a consistent interpretation: when some of the Gentiles approach Jesus in Jerusalem, he responds by saying, 'The hour is come, that the Son of man should be glorified' (12:23). This hour and glory begin to be realized at his betrayal (13:31): then, the Gentile mission follows but only after the glory of his death. Through scriptural allusions, we are being guided to surrender to this interpretation.

By such intertextuality, the author deepened meaning and forestalled doubt. For it is he who fixed the balance of knowledge. Jesus is said to know, and the scriptures know; the author knows and we know too, with the promised gift of the Holy Spirit. The author was conscious of the sequence of history: at the time, people misunderstood, but now we have hindsight and the Spirit to help us. The 'hard sayings' on Bread and Wine are not puzzling to Christians who now know the eucharist: the Gospel's readers, unlike its participants, know the paradox of Eternal Life and the meaning of a Christian flock with its Shepherd. From the prologue onwards, we have a narrator who foresaw the end in the beginning: together, we know, and so he could open a gap between appearance and reality to bring out truth.

In Luke's Gospel, too, the misunderstandings of people in the text help to bring out true belief. It is the author who chose to present facts and beliefs in this way, but in the fourth Gospel the misunderstandings go deeper and are a cue for partial instruction. Peter, who wonders why he cannot follow 'whither thou goest', is told that he will not die now but will deny his master first; Nicodemus cannot grasp the truth of spiritual rebirth, but if he cannot grasp even this much, what will he say 'if I tell you of heavenly things'? We do not learn the truth only through answers to other men's errors. We have the sense that there is so much more which Jesus could have told, that he has the authority of a total view which covers all in heaven and earth. In the face of it, misunderstandings are left hanging in their utterers' own unanswered questions. The Jews are made to ask innocently, 'Whither will he go where we cannot find him? To the dispersed among the Gentiles and teach them?'; Pilate asks, 'What is truth?' Neither question is picked up, but Christian readers know their answers.

Jesus, by contrast, is credited with a foreknowledge which extends beyond mere events. He knows his disciples even before they come up to him; before his first miracle, he knows that he has an appointed hour and that it has not come; he knows the tangled private life of a Samaritan woman before she even tells him; he knows that he must work a miracle with the loaves and fishes, and when he asks Philip where to buy bread, it is only 'in order to prove him'. He knows that he must die, that there are Jews who cannot believe him, that Judas will betray him, that God is thereby glorified. When many people believe in his miracles, he remains apart from them, not needing them 'because he knew what was in man'. Perhaps it was really like that and Jesus, like the great spiritual fathers of Christian life, left others feeling that he knew them better than they knew themselves. But the Gospeller claims to know as if he had stood where he could never stand, in Jesus's own mind. He sets it all before us, drawing us through the first six chapters.

If Jesus knew so much which was true, should we not simply believe the rest of it, like the Samaritans who believed after one woman's report of him (4:39)? Must he not also have known when he said that he would rise on the third day, that he was son of the Father in heaven, that the hour of judgement was coming (but has it, yet?)? We must aspire to be his friends, not servants (15:15), but this friendship is also a surrender: 'ye are my friends, if ye do whatsoever I command you'.

Here, too, we are in the hands of a powerful selector who has shaped what he tells us. His Jesus knows, and we know, sharing a knowledge with the author which is hidden from people in the text. This uneven balance of foresight and hindsight opens the door to irony, just as in the Hebrew scriptures, from Abraham to Esther. It is not a sceptical irony, contrived against those who believe that they know what cannot be known. It is an inclusive irony which includes us, the community of 'knowers', and reinforces our knowledge through others' innocence or incapacity for faith. It is sharpest, naturally, against the Jews, although even they are said to be split. In his omniscience, the author could even tell us what they said among themselves: 'Never man spake like this man'. The divisions and uncertainties isolated those of them who remained in error.

To see, we learn with hindsight, is not necessarily to believe, any more than to hear Jesus was to understand. In this Gospel (unlike Mark's), Jesus is not reluctant to work miracles, signs by which the crowds will believe that his name has supernatural power or that he is a new prophet or even the Messiah. We look on with hindsight, while the 'man which was blind from his birth' benefits from a sign and is drawn gradually by leading questions – twice from the Jews, then from Jesus himself – to recognize that Jesus is the 'Son of God'. Others think that they see when they are denied insight; belief, we are shown, is unpredictable even when confronted with Truth. It is not that we must therefore work hard and long on the text of this Truth before us: we are thought to have the Spirit and we do have a greater knowledge of events, so that the truth is no longer obscure. It was different during Jesus's mission between AD 34 and 36. In a complex play on the ideas of sight and insight, Jesus tells the Pharisees at the end of the healing of the man born blind: 'For judgement I am come into this world, that they which see not might see; and that they which see might be made blind.' The man born blind now sees and 'sees' the Truth, but the Pharisees, 'who say, We see,' are blinded through their sin.

In the Greek tragedies of Sophocles nearly five centuries earlier, this same contrast of sight and insight, vision and understanding, had already been exploited on the stage. Blinded Ajax could not see the goddess Athena and was blind to the madness of his ways. The spectators knew, as the Gospel's readers also knew, and, like the Gospel, the drama developed in irony. In the tragedy, however, those who failed to see were not damned. They were not being asked for faith or chosen by someone who expounded truth. The Gospeller, however, was not exploring this same drama of knowledge and responsibility because of any literary example in Greek literature. Once again, the theme could be found in the Hebrew scriptures where the relation of knowledge, sin and forgiveness is such a major presence in the stories, from Abraham to the book of Job. In the fourth Gospel it had a further twist: those who are blind are sons of the Devil (the Jews at 8:44; Judas at 6:70).

Belief, however, was not automatic, the only possible response at the time. For some while, not even the disciples fully believed (we are told), and even then their insight lags behind our hindsight. Knowledge comes in a spiral of repetition and misunderstanding, until, at the Last Supper, Jesus at last speaks no longer in parables but explains to his chosen friends the claim which Christian readers have already grasped. The disciples succumb: 'Now are we sure that thou knowest all things, and needest not that any man should ask thee: by this we believe that thou camest forth from God.' But Jesus also knows what is in man, and so by a prompt and poignant irony, 'Do ye now believe? Behold, the hour cometh, yea, is now come, that ye shall be scattered, every man to his own, and shall leave me alone . . .'

Among the early Christians, miracles have sometimes been emphasized as the primary sources of conversion to the faith. The fourth Gospel had already presented a subtler perspective. There are, indeed, those who see or hear, and believe, but they tend to believe only in the surface, seeing Jesus as a new prophet or a conventional Messiah. To understand, they must usually pass through a spiral of question and discourse, and even then they lack the hindsight which events and the Spirit have given us. At the time of the events, however, it was very much harder to believe: what were people to think when Jesus spoke so persistently of a missing person, this Father from whom he knew the Truth but of whom nothing was seen or known directly? The one sign from him was a clap of thunder which divided its hearers: 'The people therefore, that stood by, and heard it, said that it thundered: others said, An angel spake to him' (12:29). In the narratives from Genesis to Kings, authors had written freely of what God was supposed to have said or done; nobody is known to have opposed them, but when a living teacher or prophet claimed to know the same, the normal give and take of argument broke down. 'The Pharisees, therefore, said unto him, Thou bearest record of thyself; thy record is not true. Jesus answered and said unto them . . . It is also written in your law, that the testimony of two men is true: for I am not alone, but I and the Father that sent me.'

There is no arguing with this 'penetrating monomania'. Again and again, from the Jews to Pilate, Jesus does not answer a question directly. He talks beyond it, at us as much as to them, master of the 'transcending non-answer' which makes better sense to our hindsight than ever to his questioners' limited vision. But the transposition works on us too: if Jesus, it seems, knew so much, who are we to doubt that he knew the truth of this Father also? Artfully, the speaker anticipates doubt and promptly excludes it: 'In my Father's house are many mansions: if it were not so, I would have told you.' 'If it were not so . . .'; we almost forget to wonder.

Perhaps these great themes were, in essence, Jesus's own: the beloved disciple did hear him and know him. They cannot, however, be exactly his, for a simple, literary reason: when John the Baptist or Nicodemus speak, they address us in recognizably the same style as the Gospel's own. As the author himself tells us (20:30), he has selected what he includes: by revealing his art, literary readings of the Gospel bear directly on views of its truth.

As a primary source, its author, I believe, gives us the most accurate framework of times, places and persons: we have met them repeatedly, from the three Passovers during the ministry (34–6, I have argued) to the recurrent visits to Jerusalem's festivals and the procedure of Jesus's arrest and trial. As a primary source the author should be preferred at this level at almost every point where he conflicts with the other three Gospels. The exception would be a point where he might have had strong reasons for rearranging the true order; there is one likely candidate here, Jesus's sayings against the Temple. It is an old and attractive view that at first they stood where we find them in the other three Gospels, but that the raising of Lazarus then intruded (unique to the fourth Gospel) and the sayings were promoted to the start of Jesus's career; they were also toned down and redirected, away from the Temple building to Jesus's own person. There was an obvious motive for this change (a saying against the Temple was notorious, a cause of Jesus's arrest). The Gospeller, perhaps, promoted them, rephrased them and thus coped with the major obstacle first: apologists will recognize his motives and art. The case, however, is far from proven, a suspicion, nothing more.

The rest of his framework, I believe, is true, but even a witness does not guarantee the events he describes within it. Jesus went early to Cana or twice to Bethany, but he did not therefore turn water into wine or raise a man from the dead. Like anyone else, a primary source can over-interpret, misunderstand or embroider the truth with the passage of time. He is selecting the events which he tells, and selection can guide us as powerfully as rearrangement. His particular arts, the hindsight, the irony, the narrowly focused themes, are directing throughout what he tells: in the sayings and speeches they are dominant. Some of them, perhaps, Jesus did utter, but not exactly in this sequence or order: an inventive use of speech had been natural for the authors of Hebrew scripture and even a beloved disciple's memory could not hope for more than a general gist. Rather, the author lets Jesus say what the author 'knew' he meant: that knowledge grew with time and long reflection and mixed memory with virtuous invention. But it also began from close personal acquaintance. In the other three Gospels we read the secondary traditions which reached authors who never knew their subject personally. In the fourth we have the portrait, developed with hindsight, of a man who knew him and (so he felt) was loved by him.

Years had passed since the day in March 36 when he had entered and seen the empty tomb. Other Gospels had appeared and given a different emphasis, while in the Light of the Spirit he himself felt that he had come to know the Truth. At the Supper which he had attended, he placed the most poignant of all biblical beliefs: was it Jesus's own or was it the later comfort of those, like the author, who had been his personal friends? The world, Jesus says, will be rejoicing at his absence, whereas the disciples will know sorrow, though their 'sorrow will turn into joy', just as a woman knows sorrow in the pain of childbirth but forgets it when her child is delivered 'for joy that a child is born into the world': 'So you have sorrow now, but I will see you again and your hearts will rejoice, and no one will take your joy from you.'

While the author wrote, there were Christians who believed that he himself would survive until Jesus returned (they are attested by John 21:22–3). To judge from the saying he has given to Jesus, it was a belief which the author, too, shared. Yet soon after Jesus's death, the sorrow took a particular turn: Christians began to be persecuted, at first among their fellow Jews. The Gospel already looks forward to this phase: 'They shall put you out of the synagogues: yea, the time cometh, that whosoever killeth you shall think that he doeth God service' (16:2). Perhaps Jesus really was so prophetic, even before his own arrest and death, but it seems unlikely; at first his followers were left unscathed. Probably, the saying grew up in the wake of Christian experience.

In the epistles ascribed to John, we reach a second phase which the Gospel does not discuss precisely. The First Epistle, especially, implies a pressure on Christians to conform not to Jewish but pagan Gentile worship: 'Little children,' the letter concludes, 'keep yourselves from idols' (1 John 5:21). Compromise with idols was a natural response in times of Gentile persecution: in this setting, too, we can understand the author of the letter's further anxiety, that fellow Christians were minimizing the reality of Jesus's own sufferings, as if they had been more apparent than real. There is more here than the doctrinal battles of an old man, fought against pupils who had strayed from Truth and Light, and 'were influenced by "new ideas" from outside which they mixed one-sidedly with provocative theses from their teacher'. This denial that Jesus really suffered belonged with a view that Christians, also, could compromise rather than suffer as martyrs.

The authorship of these letters is endlessly disputed, but I see no reason to exclude the Gospeller himself as the author of the first of the three: it is written by someone who is in close sympathy with many of the Gospeller's ideas. If so, we can see where the 'sorrow and travail' had led in his lifetime: in the Gospel he restrained his hindsight to Christian sufferings in the synagogues, their first phase, but in the epistle he addresses pagan persecution, a fact from the 60s onwards. 'So you have sorrow now, but I will see you again and your hearts will rejoice': the sorrows increased, but the beloved disciple did not live to see his master again.

22
Human Truth

___

I

If we read biblical narrative as a story, we abandon its historical truth. If we read it as literature, we will often find literary art in it, but this art takes us further from truth which corresponds to fact: the fourth Gospel is an author's strong interpretation, not an exact memoir. What, though, about the contents? They may be historically mistaken; they may be a fiction; but can they not seem true to us, in the way that other great scenes in stories and fictions seem true too, Hector's farewell to his wife, perhaps, in Homer's *Iliad* or Prince Andrei's rather different farewell to his wife in Tolstoy's *War and Peace*? The biblical stories are usually religious, but we do not need to believe in their God in order to be drawn into them in this way. When they show us people who are living and responding to their God's presence, we can be engaged by a sense of how it would have been, for somebody who did think that God was sometimes unjust (as Abraham tells him before Sodom) or that God really did send his Son who rose from the dead and was witnessed (the story of the women in the Garden). Those who do believe in this God will also accept that the authors of the stories were pointing in the right direction, even where the stories themselves are untrue.

What we find here is not straight truth but this sense of 'how it would have been': this sense depends, in turn, on statements we think to be true about other people, that the plotters against a younger brother (Joseph) will be haunted by a sense of guilt, that an important man's servant may try to cheat him (Gehazi) and so forth. There is nothing divine or mystical in the scriptures' nature which causes this impact, nor is it unique to them. The scriptures are not a divine mirror but a human labyrinth of authors, persons and predicaments. We respond to them because of a movement on our part, not on theirs: recognition, not revelation.

Recognition does not require historical truth, and so it reopens doors which parts of this book may seem to have shut. In the Bible we recognize a human awareness in what scores of anonymous authors have written (including their human ideas of a god). This level of recognition is not at all the same as reverence for the Bible as a handbook for life, a role for which its detail is not well suited. The Gospels are not often specific on detailed points of conduct, and as a handbook they would be very patchy indeed. Those who want such details have to look back to the Hebrew books of law, but here, too, they face problems. If they are Christians, it is not obvious why details in these old books should continue to have such authority for them. Whether Christians or non-Christians, they have to pick and choose between the books' details or else appeal to broad principles in order to bend the texts to circumstances which they never envisaged, popular capitalism, perhaps, or even feminism. It is not only that the many different texts in scripture give conflicting points of view on anything from an after-life to polygamy or the value of riches. One and the same book of law can contain texts on charity for the poor, sanctions for the death penalty, public stoning, slavery or outright genocide (Deuteronomy 7:1 ff.; 20:16–18). Many of these commands are no longer any sort of guide to decent living: how, then, can we pick out bits which are still tolerable to our moral sense and claim that they have an external authority because they are biblical, while denying that other biblical bits which stand beside them are to be taken as authoritative?

As for the four Gospels, the idea that they usually give us Jesus's exact words in their exact context is a popular mirage: there are too many disagreements. Most of their ethics is given by implicit principles, not detailed rules of conduct, and even when we do find details many Christians would nowadays go against them. At Mark 10:10 ff. we can be sure that we have the earliest surviving form of a saying on conduct, Jesus's categorical words against divorce (in Luke and Matthew the words have been toned down). Many Christians, however, would consider the words not binding because they were spoken for their time, not ours. The argument is not that they were tailored to the standards of a different society: divorce was as accepted a practice in Jesus's Jewish society as it is in most of the modern West. The argument, rather, is that the words were spoken in expectation of an imminent end of the world.

We also live in complex political societies, but the Bible is not a helpful guide to details of political life. In Hebrew scripture, kingship is a concession to human sinfulness, allowed by God to his people although they ought not to need it. Democracy, revolution or political liberation trace back to ancient Greece, but they are not biblical notions: even the Exodus was not so much a liberation as the rescue of a servant-people by their real master, God. In the New Testament, kingdoms are temporary unless they are 'not of this world': meanwhile, Christians should 'render unto Caesar' and 'submit to the powers that be', whose earthly representatives are the necessary agents of God's wrath. As for slavery, it is a persistent fact of life among God's people: Christian slaves should abide in their social position, according to Paul, and 'serve the more'. A slave's obedience to his master was a religious duty: 'this Biblical morality was one of the great handicaps that the emancipation movement in the United States had to overcome'. As an opponent of abolition said in 1857, 'Slavery is of God.'

When we recognize 'how it would have been', we are not, therefore, reading 'how it must be' for us now, as for people then: we can recognize something without approving it. Recognition is not a name for self-centred readings, tuned only to the comfortable views with which we begin. We set out with beliefs, but we can all imagine others which are different: we can also recognize what is not part of our own personalities or something which is, but is not what we often admit. Unlike the texts of other religions, so much of the Bible is a narrative: it confronts us, therefore, with scores of people who are not so much characters as persons in settings and predicaments. The Gospels' parables are masters of this potential, whether in the extreme predicaments of Matthew's individuals or the moral tales in Luke: both draw us in and turn us round by their use of persons and narratives. In Hebrew scripture, too, we are drawn in by the private lives and public predicaments of scores of individuals, from the polygamous homes of the patriarchs to the adultery of King David or the endurance of the prophet Hosea with his unfaithful wife. Beside the big names, there are minor persons everywhere whose presence is so enlarging. They say little, do little, but this reticence provokes our imaginations: they also provoke our sympathy. For we too are minor persons, readers, merely, of these great stories, or minor participants and onlookers in the great collective events of our own times. Like Zacchaeus, we may climb a sycamore for a better view of events; we look on, wondering, while David claims Michal to be his wife, and 'her husband went with her along weeping behind her to Bahurim. Then said Abner unto him, Go, return. And he returned.'

II

In the Bible, therefore, we recognize human truth even when the stories themselves are untrue. Among readers and hearers, the sense of nearness and closeness to a text will vary according to who the recognizers are: I doubt, however, if biblical people, authors or stories will ever vanish beyond the horizons of shared humanity. Not that its humanity is always a comfortable companion, especially for half the human race. Women may look for alternative voices nowadays in the scriptures, but biblical women do not have the role, scope or range which most Jewish or Christian women would nowadays recognize in their lives. Childbearing and infidelity are the two actions which most often bring women to the centre of the story, but only if the child in question is to be a significant son. We meet Deborah, who was both a prophet and a mother in Israel back in the eleventh century BC, but for a parallel to her deed of valour (the slaying of Sisera in her tent) we have to look ahead to Judith, a figure of fiction (*c.* 130–100 BC). We meet resourceful harlots (Rahab or the first of the two harlots who was judged by Solomon) and widows who are close to God (Hebrew laws of inheritance were stricter to widows than the known laws of other early Near Eastern societies, although they also urge particular charity to them). Often wives are women of ingenuity (Rachel or Delilah or Abigail or the Shunammite woman) and can be adept at playing the game of inheritance which men have defined (Sarah or Tamar or Naomi). They are not, however, in authority: there were no female priests in the Temple, no women in Jesus's Twelve, and when we do find texts on women's capacity for Christian leadership, they are all of them negative. 'There is neither Jew nor Greek, there is neither bond nor free, there is neither male nor female: for ye are all one in Christ Jesus' (Paul to the Galatians, 3:28), but unity does not entail equality. There is an awareness that women may be resourceful, but there is not the sense that they are inscrutable and that there may even be pleasure in this aspect of their characters. The Bible, here, stands in sharp contrast to Homer's *Odyssey* which has this sense of inscrutability for its gallery of female personalities.

There are limitations, too, in biblical stories of war and foreign prophets, and again we can contrast them with Greek literature. In Deuteronomy, genocide is a pious action, approved for Israel against some of her neighbours. It is not that this fight would be a holy war, waged to win Gentiles to God. Rather, God will fight with Israel in the fray: 'It was Yahweh who fought for Israel, not Israel who fought for its God.' Genocide was never a part of pagan Greek piety, although Greek armies did believe that protecting gods would fight by their side. In Greek literature, war did not kill the possibility of sympathy for a foreign enemy (seven years after the Greeks' great war against Persia, the dramatist Aeschylus could imagine the Persians' defeat as seen through the eyes of Persians at home with their women). Even the heroic Greek poetry of prowess was a poetry centrally concerned with death, the common leveller of either party. As for foreigners, Homer's Trojans are in many respects like the Greeks themselves; the death of their hero Hector is central to the pathos of the entire *Iliad*.

In the Hebrew scriptures the ancient Song of Deborah (like Aeschylus's Greek drama) pictures the impact of defeat on an enemy's royal women: the singers imagine the dead Sisera's mother, framed by that frequent biblical setting, a window, yet the song is a gloat over her predicament: 'So let all thine enemies perish, O Lord.' The song is a victory ode, whereas Aeschylus's play is a tragic drama: the contrast is between two types of literature, not between the views of every single Jew and Greek, but the fact remains that in the Hebrew scriptures nobody takes the viewpoint which Aeschylus explores. There is a similar contrast in the way in which the exploits of great King David are presented. They are told as a combination of personal tragedies (Absalom, Jonathan; Bathsheba's son) and bouts of glorious slaughtering against Israel's neighbouring tribes. In Homer's *Iliad*, this same combination of personal loss and battle-fury interrelate in the person of Achilles: finally, the aged Trojan, Priam, comes to Achilles, his own son's killer, and together they transcend the violence by dwelling on their shared human sadness. In the Bible David's grief and David's slaughtering are not connected in this way: his enemies are the Lord's enemies, and in battle the Lord is with him, assuring victory against people who are not his own.

What we recognize in these biblical stories, therefore, is not what we necessarily respect, yet there are themes running through them which also draw us in. It would be supremely pedantic to go through the biblical books, pointing to human probabilities which people can recognize or perhaps endorse: the role of shame, perhaps, in Deuteronomy's book of the law of the Lord, in the books of Kings and in the third Gospel (the Bible is not all about guilt, any more than Western cultures are cultures where shame is not prominent: we feel guilt for our own thoughts and actions, but we feel shame at other people's, besides shame at what they think of us). There is also the running theme of hope and promise, from God's ancient promise of greatness to Abraham's descendants to the newer promises of the kingdom and the world to come, made some eight centuries later in the Christian scriptures. I wish, however, to follow something no less pervasive which plays on a truth about humans and their predicament: the place of error and wrongdoing, excuse and forgiveness, sin and conscience. It, too, rests on the level we have reached, where human recognition comes home to us and a story strikes us as 'how it would have been', not necessarily true (although it may be) or therefore compelling our agreement.

The Bible, it has been well observed, is not concerned with what is accidental, the random chances of nature, the fortuitous losses of goods or limbs. In the Old Testament there is only one accidental death: the baby which the prostitute before Solomon has smothered in her sleep; its death is incidental to the story of the king's judgement. Even a sickness is a punishment from God or the cue for deliberate acts of healing, carried out by men of God. For although God is not the active cause of everything, he is an ever-present agent and the world is his Creation. It is he who sends plagues or floods or enemies; he is the ultimate author of famine, and it is to him that its sufferers must appeal for relief. The Bible has no idea of the human, economic causes which are now known to make a food crisis into a famine. If we followed the biblical diagnosis and nothing else, we would never find preventions for these human disasters.

It is not because of God alone that accidents are kept out of the biblical narratives: its stories are about humans' relationships as partners with God and with one another. The broken wheel on a chariot may round off a story with pathos or drama, but it diminishes the human predicament by closing it beyond control. In the Bible, humans bring about their own catastrophes, giving scope for a powerful exploration of error and sin.

At its simplest level, people may be trapped by the unforeseen power of words: a vow, perhaps, or a blessing, a promise or a contract. To utter such words is to commit oneself to action or even to bring something about: societies with a keen sense of law or custom cannot help confronting the problem of words which bring about something which their performer never foresaw. He may genuinely have been imprudent, like Jephthah who vowed to sacrifice whatever he first met on his return from victory: he met his virgin daughter. One party may be tricked by another, especially if he is dealing with Jacob, the Artful Dodger of the biblical world. All over the world, tricks make powerful stories, and in Genesis we meet plenty of them: how Jacob deceived Esau over his birthright or Isaac over his blessing, how Jacob outwitted Laban over his speckled sheep or how Laban turned the tables on Jacob by marrying him off to Leah, the unexpected daughter. In many of their contexts, words which have been said cannot be undone: once Isaac has blessed Jacob, he cannot unbless him; once Jacob has married Leah, he cannot unmarry her. Agents, therefore, must live with the unforeseen consequence of what they have said.

It is a small step from stories in which words bind unforeseeably to those which turn on a detail in what, precisely, was said. For the author and audience, there is pleasure in a tale of clever evasion. When Laban comes to hunt for the family's idols which Rachel has stolen, he and Jacob agree 'whoever is found' to have them must hand them over. Jacob does not yet know that his wife Rachel has them, and Rachel avoids being 'found' by pleading in her tent that she has her monthly period and cannot get up (she is sitting, in fact, on the stolen goods). By a trick, she evades the letter of the bargain: she is not actually 'found' in possession. This gap between reality and implication has been thought to be important, too, to the story of the book of Ruth: on one modern reading, Ruth leaves Boaz uncertain what passed between them while he slept; Boaz's words leave the kinsman uncertain which widow he must marry if he acts on his family responsibility and redeems Naomi's field.

There are also cases of rough justice, harsh but true to the letter and not therefore unjust. At a vulnerable moment, King David promises not to kill the obstreperous Shimei who has cursed him publicly, but although he stands by his promise, it is not binding on the next king, his son Solomon. Solomon, therefore, is told to kill Shimei: he warns Shimei that if he goes out beyond fixed limits around Jerusalem, he will be put to death. Some of Shimei's slaves run away, and, like any other master, Shimei goes out to retrieve them: he passes the limits, and, exactly as specified, he is killed. Solomon, here, obeys the letter and Shimei errs in breaking it, but we cannot help reflecting on the spirit of the event. It is not a crying injustice (Shimei had been lucky to be spared for so long), but the precision of the bargain enhances the force of it.

In these and other narratives, law and storytelling are intertwined. There is no absolute divide between the minds which worked out the biblical case-laws in the various texts of law, and the minds which devised and appreciated these stories in the books of narrative. At their simplest level, law and the form of words set up an unforeseen circumstance and animate our human interest. At a deeper level they can be exploited in ways which come home to us, for pathos, for suspense, for 'poetic justice' (a favourite, too, of the prophets) and especially for irony (in a small masterpiece of ignorance, Uriah is made to carry, unknowingly, the letter from David which orders his own death: there is irony, too, in many of the turns in the tale of Joseph and his brothers). 'Little did they know . . .': here, formal casuistry is being developed for human impact. A similar use of knowledge and ignorance, foresight and hindsight, shows up in the art of the beloved disciple and his Gospel: here, too, his way of telling owes a strong debt to his Jewish culture.

The next step is to pass beyond forms and raise moral questions. Is ignorance an excuse? Does error ever diminish responsibility? Can we be forgiven for what we did not know? At times Hebrew law reads like a crude and blunt instrument: it refers to retaliation; it has a very limited concern with chains of consequence; it prescribes ordeals (the test of the water and dust which a woman had to drink publicly when suspected of adultery). In context, however, it is not all so savage; retaliation did confine revenge by limiting it to the person who had done wrong (other societies allowed a victim to take reprisals against any object or person who stood in a similar relationship to the wrongdoer). There were also the limits of practicality which restricted what could be enforced but not what storytellers could think and feel. 'We must rid ourselves of the notion, still widespread, that the "primitives" were blind to the shortcomings of ritualism. They were not: only, given a loose and precarious organization of society they could not but assign it a huge role.' In stories we find the human awareness which laws and prescriptions could not accommodate.

Circumstances, for one thing, can complicate an apparent wrongdoing. In Genesis 38 Judah's daughter-in-law, Tamar, is left to confront widowhood because none of her surviving brothers-in-law will do their duty, marry her and father the children to perpetuate their brother's line: when one brother-in-law remains, her father-in-law Judah fails to give him to her (he is afraid of the consequences because God has punished the previous husband). Tamar, therefore, dresses as a prostitute, encounters her father-in-law Judah on his travels and seduces him. Judah acts in ignorance and gives her a pledge that he will send her the agreed fee (a young kid); she disappears and three months or so later he is told that his daughter-in-law has played the harlot and is pregnant. 'Bring her out,' he orders, with the true authority of the patriarch, 'and let her be burned.' Tamar shows him the pledge; he realizes that the child is his, that she has gained a well-merited heir by trickery, and that he ought to have lived up to his position and given her the last of the brothers-in-law in marriage. 'She is more righteous than I,' he concludes: the prehistory of the case has overridden the rule that a daughter who dares to play the prostitute shall be burned. Right emerges from an apparent wrong, as it never could under a law which looked to actions, not motives.

Here, Tamar is blameless for acting knowingly to correct an injustice: what, though, of wrongdoings which themselves are committed in ignorance? This delicate question confronts us at once in the early patriarchal stories. Three times in Genesis, as we have seen, patriarchs who are in foreign countries pass off their wives as their sisters in order to keep themselves safe; they are afraid that they will be killed for the women's sake if they admit the truth of their relationship. The first story, probably the oldest, is plain and blunt (Genesis 12). Abraham says

Sarah is his sister in Egypt; the Pharaoh takes her into his household; he showers Abraham with favours because of her; Sarah, presumably, commits rampant adultery; Abraham, perhaps, enjoys the presents as a compliant brother-husband (typically, he passes no comment). The Lord then afflicts Pharaoh and his house with plagues because of Pharaoh's behaviour: the Pharaoh could not possibly have known his own mistake, but none the less he turns Abraham and Sarah out of the house.

This matter-of-fact story soon worried those who were aware of it. In Genesis 26:6 Isaac plays the same sister-trick with Rebecca in the Philistine land of Gerar: the king looks out once again from that favourite biblical vantage-point, a window, and sees brother and 'sister' fondling each other; he draws the right conclusion and reprimands them for their deceit. Somebody, he warns them, might have been caught up by their pretence, and so he orders that the married couple should not be infringed. Here, the story is entirely proper: there is no adultery and no punishment for the ignorant Gentile from God. The teeth of the older episode have been tactfully drawn.

The third story is more penetrating. Abraham plays the same trick with Sarah in the land of Gerar: the king, Abimelech, takes her, assuming that she is a sister, not a wife. However, in a dream God tells him bluntly, 'Behold, you are a dead man.' Abimelech has not laid a finger on the girl, and so he argues back: he has been acting innocently and how could he possibly have known that the woman was already married? God backs down: if Abimelech will give back Sarah, he can live. Because he is God, he is allowed to save face: he always knew, he tells us, that Abimelech was good and honest, and that was why he had stopped him 'sinning against me'. The implication is that if Abimelech had gone any further with Sarah, God would have punished him dreadfully because adultery is such a sin against heaven.

Here, ignorance is admitted as an excuse for guilt: God himself has to climb down before it, and so he lets Abimelech off. It is, however, important that the ignorance is genuine and combined with innocence: God and Abimelech agree that integrity of heart is an important ingredient which affects the rights of the case. In human law, ignorance was a difficult plea to accommodate: if it was accepted, surely anyone would plead it in the hope of acquittal? Hebrew laws, therefore, tend not to allow for its scope, but we can see from biblical narrative that people were not blind or archaic about the issues. Between God and man, a story explores the question which human judges could not admit.

In one particular story the exploration has a depth and intricacy which has sustained generations of artists, readers and dramatists. 'In the land of Uz' lived Job, the righteous man whom Satan, God's agent, provoked God to test. Job was extremely righteous, Satan granted, but largely because he had prospered in return: very well, said God, take away his worldly goods and see if he curses me. Job lost his flocks, his servants and all his sons and daughters, but 'the Lord gave,' said Job, 'and the Lord hath taken away; blessed be the name of the Lord'. Afflict Job himself, said Satan, and then you will see the truth: 'all that a man hath he will give for his life'. So Job was struck with sores and boils: he took a potsherd with which to scrape them and sat wretchedly in dust and ashes. His wife (significantly) weakened and told him to curse God and die. But Job refused.

Ignorance, therefore, is built into the story: Job has no idea of its framework, God's callous bet with Satan. Unlike Abimelech, he will not be excused by ignorance: the bet concerns his righteousness, and if he weakens, however forgivably, a plea of ignorance will not preserve his virtue. In our present book of Job the afflictions are only the prelude: Job is visited by three of his close companions, whose wisdom he himself has shared for many years. For seven days and seven nights, they sit on the ground in a memorable silence, like mourners of the dead. Then, the speeches begin.

It is impossible to understand the speeches totally because of the usual biblical obstacles: bits of their Hebrew are obscure to us, their order and length have been altered by later editors and one entire speech (the 'angry young man' Elihu's, at chapters 34 and 38) and bits of others have been inserted. The book is not a unity because people who found the original speeches unsatisfactory (or shocking) added or corrected views in its text. None the less, the world has never been short of books, plays and scholarship with a view of what (most of) the book of Job is about. It is not that some new, significant meaning emerged by accident from the various authors' changes and rearrangements. Rather, no one view does justice to all the contents of the present book. Its broad themes are clear, but a general view depends on which of the themes it isolates.

Job is often admired for a classic statement of the problem of evil: why do the righteous suffer while the ungodly flourish? We cannot date the book more closely than '*c.* 600–200 BC' (a usual guess, which I favour, is *c.* 400–300), but by then the problem of evil had been freely explored in Near Eastern literature; many of the psalmists had aired it already, and Job's first audience would not have found it so very surprising. The more startling fact is that we (but not Job) know the problem's immediate answer from the book's first chapters: Job is suffering because God and Satan have had a bet. Will Job in his ignorance curse God or not? He begins by cursing the day of his birth; he laments, he complains, he calls on God to appear. He does not, however, abandon the Cosmic Gambler: he meets his suffering by upholding God's awful omnipotence and challenging him to explain why he bothers with such a wretched, feeble thing as man. Throughout, Job is entirely realistic about life and death: there is only this life, to which death will be the finish. Without allusion, he complains before God, but it is against the words of his friends that he rebels most strongly. Each friend misunderstands his predicament: Job lives in ignorance of the bet between God and Satan, but the friends are both ignorant and in error. They also do not know it.

The burden of their speeches is that God always punishes the wicked; no man can hope to be entirely sinless, and if Job is being punished, it must be because of something he has done. Those who repent and call on God are forgiven, whereas Job is railing against his plight. The morality of the friends is secure and traditional, a world in which sinners suffer and hardness of heart is punished, but where those who humble themselves before God will be forgiven and comforted. It has no room for heavenly betting or inscrutable wisdom: it does not make sense of Job's plight, and he knows it.

When young Elihu speaks, we hear the clear-cut morality of a later author who had evidently found the original text too oblique. The speech sits oddly in its context, but its main theme heightens the irony of what we now read. The friends have called Job righteous in his own eyes, while assuming that he is not righteous in God's. Elihu is more blunt: Job's errors are his own rebelliousness, which he has voiced in his speeches, and his crass ignorance before the ways of God. Ignorance, indeed, is present in the case but not as Elihu believes.

As if Elihu has never spoken, God now speaks from the whirlwind, silencing Job's complaint. The original text has resumed its direction, but it takes an audacious turn. The Cosmic Gambler says nothing of his wager or the immediate reasons for Job's testing. Instead, he tells the human piece on his table to look at the power and incomprehensibility of all that his God has made. How can Job question and complain, when he does not understand the world and the seasons, when he has not made the stars or two of earth's awesome monsters, Leviathan and Behemoth? These monsters have the fascination of animal power, the crocodile and (probably) the hippopotamus. They may also be symbols of something more, the powers of evil and disorder in Creation. It is often remarked how Satan seems to vanish after the opening bet in the book. If these animal monsters have a wider symbolic dimension, Satan returns here, in this final theme of God's speech. In the book of Job there is no independent Devil, working for Evil against God's creation. Satan is God's own agent and accuser. Like Leviathan, he is active but under the ultimate power of God.

Job himself has already touched on some of the themes which God develops (the wonder of the world, especially at 9:4–13; its marvels beyond man's understanding, 9:10); God's speech, therefore, is not totally detached from undercurrents in what has been said before. It is, however, an imperious answer, from a Gambler who does not even admit his bet: how can someone question his conduct if he cannot even grasp the self-made rules which govern the rest of his game-park? In reply, Job does not confess sin, as the friends had been urging him in speech after speech. He does not say 'I am vile' (the Authorized Version mistranslates him) but 'I am of small account'.

Already in Hebrew scripture people had aired the human possibility that God may not always act justly and that an element of cosmic sadism may be present, among so much else, in the attributes of Number One. In Genesis, Abimelech had to complain and protest before God responded justly to an error: 'Shall not the Judge of all the earth do right?' asks Abraham of God before Sodom ('doing right' here meant only the sparing of the entire city because of a few just men inside it). In the psalms, too, there are unknown authors who had raised complaints which are close to those in Job (Psalms 1 and 37, especially, with 44, 74 and 79). The justice of God had not gone unquestioned by his prophets either (Jeremiah in 12:1–4 wonders why the 'way of the wicked prospers', while God knows and tests his prophet's heart). Above all, there is the doubting call of the prophet Habakkuk, voiced (perhaps) before Job was composed. In the face of Israel's foes and disasters, Habakkuk asks his basic question: 'Art thou not from everlasting, O Lord?' He withdraws to his watchtower to wait for an answer: like Job, he receives a reply.

The reply of Job's author is not a comfortable one. God does support the voice which has complained so loudly against his actions: it is Job, he says, not his friends, who has 'spoken of me what is right'. What the friends have called wilful ignorance turns out to be right and just. Their knowledge, in turn, is an ignorance for which they are threatened with punishment: they are left to ask Job to pray for them and win their pardon. For if God is a father or husband to Israel, why should he always be just or willing to act on demand? What, too, if this father likes to gamble? It is an unsettling, uncomfortable notion which can still come home to us: it arises directly from modern theories of the universe, our quantum mechanics. 'The theory hardly brings us closer to the secret of the Old One,' wrote Einstein, when first confronting the unpredictabilities which his theory has now forced on us, 'and I am at all events convinced that He does not play dice.' In the book of Job (as in our quantum theory) this is exactly what he does. When he places a bet on his own Creation, he is not betting on a certainty: neither he (nor Job) can know what he may do. Who then are we, his children, to question his motives? The author of Job thinks that he himself knows this much, no more: eventually, God forgives people who suffer faithfully, knowing only that they cannot understand. Others may wonder where knowledge begins here and ignorance ends.

III

Outside the land of Uz, evil is not confined to the world and its tribulations: it lies, too, in our own worst enemies, ourselves. Here, biblical authors have a keen sense of humans' hidden potential which goes beyond errors and excuses to knowledge and the sense of sin. Once again the Christian scriptures have been anticipated by themes in the Hebrew texts.

'The eye,' Greek philosophers had said, 'is the mirror of the soul': in the Bible people see differently, down into secrets of the heart. At 2 Kings 8:6 Hazael comes west to Damascus to meet the prophet Elisha: he is a special envoy of the ailing Ben Hadad, king of Syria. Camel loads of presents accompany him for the 'man of God', a prelude to the question which the king wants answered: 'Shall I recover from this sickness?' Hazael bestows the presents and Elisha replies, 'Go, say to him, "You shall certainly recover"; but the Lord has shown me that he shall certainly die.' It is a curious answer, taken by itself: like a sanctimonious doctor, Elisha appears to be denying his patient the truth. Was he, perhaps, afraid of being blamed if the king died after those gifts of favour? The sequel goes deeper: he fixes his gaze 'and stared at him, until he was ashamed. And the man of God wept.' The text is not explicit, but it is Elisha, surely, who stares at Hazael until Hazael feels shame; it is Elisha who weeps, telling Hazael that he weeps for the damage Hazael will soon do to Israel. Elisha knows, and duly tells Hazael, that Hazael is to be king of Syria: he also knows his man. For Hazael returns to the king and tells him that Elisha has said that he will certainly recover: he knows, however, that his king must die, and, on the very next day, he smothers Ben Hadad in his bed. Elisha is proved right twice over. It is not the sickness which kills Ben Hadad but Hazael, the future king, into whose heart the prophet had seen.

This story must have passed to its ultimate author, the Deuteronomist, as one of many tales about the northern prophets. The moral is not that Elisha caused the king of Syria's murder by an incautious answer, but that the 'man of God' could see with devastating power into the hearts of men. It is the first surviving evidence of the diagnostic power which was a prophetic gift from the Lord, the 'searcher of hearts'. It cut through words and unspoken hopes, and fastened on human nature: from Elisha to the spiritual fathers of the Christian monasteries, it has lived in the wake of scripture for more than two thousand years.

In Elisha's gaze it anticipated human sin and weakness; elsewhere it brought people to recognize a truth which they had sought to suppress. In the intricate tale of Joseph and his brothers, ironic error and misunderstanding go to work on a sense of guilt and lead to confessions of sin: the brothers have tried to kill Joseph; they believe they are rid of him and they do not recognize him in Egypt. However, Joseph makes them bring him Benjamin, his father's beloved son; by a trick he then makes it appear that Benjamin is guilty of theft. The brothers offer to suffer collectively, as if the guilt is theirs; fearing for Benjamin, they see the events as God's judgement on their crime; they confess it, therefore, to Joseph. 'Do you not know,' he tells them, 'that such a man as I can indeed divine?' In fact, he sees their guilt, not because he is an Elisha but because he has been the object of their plan. A false charge of theft has uncovered their guilt: their error (and Joseph's deceit) causes the truth to be confessed. They continue to see God's hand in the events, but we know that the active hand is Joseph's own.

In King David's life, by contrast, one wrong compounded another and the sense of sin became dormant. It was not enough for the king to meet a prophet like Elisha: he needed to be drawn out and to listen and respond. David had arranged Uriah's death and enjoyed adultery with his wife until the old Court History brings Nathan the prophet into his presence. Nathan comes with a parable for the king, the story of the rich man and the poor man's precious lamb: the story fits loosely with David's predicament (on one view, it was an earlier story which had been applied to an evil act by King Saul), but it is enough to loosen David himself. 'As the Lord liveth,' says David on hearing it, 'the man that hath done this thing shall surely die.' 'Thou art the man,' says Nathan: the story reflects back on the hearer who has correctly filled in its moral. It brings the king of Israel to recognize the truth which he is hiding from himself.

In the Hebrew scriptures and their translations there is no word for conscience: the great texts on it are often felt to be Paul's, especially that mine of human truth, his Romans 7. However, the idea of it is present, without the word, in the story of Joseph and the old Court History of David. Each false charge against Joseph's brothers throws them back on their sense of guilt at their 'murder': their consciences are stirred. So, too, when David has defeated his rebellious son Absalom, he holds an audience with the turbulent Shimei, the man who had cursed him before his victory. Shimei does not simply say, 'I sinned, forgive me': he says, 'For your servant knows that I have sinned': not just sin but the uneasy knowledge of it.

Years later, when David has died, his son Solomon sends for Shimei in order to kill him. Wise Solomon repeats the emphasis: 'You know in your own heart all the evil that you did to David my father.' He has inner knowledge, twice over: like the brothers' attempt to murder Joseph, Shimei's cursing of King David had lived on in a biblical conscience. The evil in man, therefore, can suppress evildoing as well as promote it: it is through their sense of human wickedness that biblical authors come home to us here with singular truth. It did not need Christian teaching for this truth to be explored: it runs freely through both Testaments, and through texts which, in date and arrangement, fall between the two. 'Let us crown ourselves with rosebuds before they wither . . . everywhere let us leave signs of enjoyment,' say the wicked speakers in the Wisdom of Solomon, composed by an unknown Jew in or before the first century A D. 'Because this is our portion in life . . . let us oppress the righteous poor . . . let our might be our law of right.' But the righteous are a reproach to them, by the way that they think and by the very fact that they exist. 'Let us lie in wait for the righteous man because he is inconvenient to us . . . he calls himself a child of the Lord . . . the very sight of him is a burden to us and his ways are strange . . . He calls the last end of the righteous happy and boasts that God is his father . . . Let us see if his words are true.' The Jewish author of this text was not a Christian and did not have Christianity in mind, but his sense of human wickedness is uncannily apt for Christian events. 'If the righteous man is God's son, God will help him and deliver him . . . let us test him with insult and torture that we may learn how gentle he is . . . Let us condemn him to a shameful death, for (as he says) he will be protected.'

In the New Testament, likewise, knowledge and ignorance, forgiveness and the evil in men, are essential to the setting in which Jesus is presented: righteousness, in his person, was duly put to death. The particular twist is that the knowledge and insight are now the victim's own. Already in Mark's Gospel (10:27) Jesus knows the wickedness of his petitioners: he knows that one of the Twelve must betray him. In the fourth Gospel he could not trust the crowds in Jerusalem, according to his beloved disciple, 'because he knew what was in man'. In his conversation the art of the parable finds a new and greater exponent than Nathan; although the Jesus of the fourth Gospel tells no parables, like Elisha he sees deep into human hearts, knowing them better than they know themselves. When ignorant mortals put him to death, in one

Gospel (Luke's) he prays for their forgiveness (but not in every manuscript of the text): 'Lord, forgive them, for they know not what they do.' The people in question are probably two-fold, and ignorant in different ways. The Romans 'know not' because they cannot know: like Job or Abimelech, they had not been told. The Jews do not know because their nature stops them (like Jeremiah's hearers) from knowing. Elsewhere in the Gospels this incapacity is reviled as blindness, an inevitable hardness of heart, 'lest they should turn again, and be forgiven' (Mark 4:12). On the Cross, in the third Gospel, incapacity is cited as a plea in a wrongdoer's favour.

From Eden to the Apocalypse, the Bible is a record of human error and wickedness. They are two of the human truths in its stories (from David to Judas Iscariot), and my unauthorized version has traced them in the authors themselves: they, too, err and lay claim to false identities; they are only too human in their views of others, from the psalmists' bitter hatred against their enemies to the divine approvals of genocide or the slaughter of most of humanity in the Revelation of John. There is no comforting progression, from a barbarous God of war to a later and milder God of love: Omega ends in John's Revelation by behaving much as Alpha had begun to behave with the Flood. These ideas of God are human creations, and, like the stories of Creation, they remain contradictory to the end. After Eden, how could human texts be otherwise?

The scriptures are not unerring; they are not the 'word of God'; what we now read is sometimes only one textual version among earlier alternatives; its story may be demonstrably false (Joshua's conquests or Jesus's Nativity); it may ascribe sayings to people which they never said. Throughout, my unauthorized version has tried to reach for what the authors meant, insisting that it can undercut what Churches, literary critics or modernizing readers now claim that the scriptures mean. To Christians, that present meaning may be ascribed to the Holy Spirit, promised (according to the beloved disciple) as a help in seeing what scriptures are saying (John 16:13). Others may wonder if the Spirit is indeed so holy when interpretations have often been so false, saddling us with original sin, the virgin birth, or the belief that bits of the Old Testament predict the New.

Biblical authors and their reference are often remote, but the attempt to reach back to them rests on method, inference and evidence. It does not diminish us, or them, to have a sense of D, his sermons and distortions, or the beloved disciple and his artful hindsight, or even P with his vision of wholeness at the heart of this world. The Bible is teeming with human authors, first authors and later editors, letter-writers and revisers. They are witnesses to ideas of God to which the modern world still has many heirs. Their events and stories are often untrue because they are contradictory or because they do not correspond to facts which we know outside. Yet they show us a truth, that people in Israel or among the first Christians believed this or that to be so. So far from being the word of God, the scriptures confront us as a mirror of fallen man.

That mirror is the setting against which Jesus, too, is presented. Like their fellow men, the Twelve male disciples are acutely capable of ignorance and weakness. Like Job's friends they fail to understand; they wonder if a man's blindness is the result of his parents' sin (John 9:2); they do not grasp the idea of the kingdom; they argue about rank and precedence, who shall have the seats of honour in the new age; they object to the wasteful gift of ointment; in the hour of arrest they fall asleep, then run away. No other religion has texts with such a human foil to its story. In the awful moment of Jesus's arrest, the web of error and foreknowledge, conscience, human weakness and deeply unceremonial weeping closes round one of their number, just as his Lord had predicted. 'Truly, I say to you, this very night, before the cock crows twice, you will deny me three times.' While others scatter, Peter follows, but only at a distance. In circumstantial detail, by the firelight, he denies three times; the cock crows and in all three synoptic Gospels, he 'wept bitterly'. The doings of servants and fishermen lay far below the horizons of dignified classical historians, but in all four Gospels this scene between a servant and a fisherman stands rooted in the Passion narrative. Perhaps, for once, it derived from a primary source, from Peter himself, or perhaps the beloved disciple who was with him in the high priest's house. Between the Gospels, its main details cohere, and the scene may correspond to primary, witnessed fact. At cockcrow, Peter confronts his own error, as it had been foretold by the one who knew 'what was in man'. Human truth coincides here with what may be historical evidence; Peter, therefore, answers Pilate's question with which this unauthorized version began.

22
Notes and Bibliography

———

I have given a brief bibliography, mainly in English, at the head of the notes to chapters or parts of chapters whose main themes are well covered in recent, accessible works. Readers who wish to explore these themes beyond my text will find that these bibliographies set them on their path. Those who want more can best find it either in the individual notes to each chapter's main points or in the excellent guides to current work which summarize the main lines of new books and articles by scholars. The Society for Old Testament Study issues an invaluable book list yearly, with summaries of new books' contents. The Catholic Biblical Association issues Old Testament Abstracts thrice yearly, summarizing new articles, including articles on archaeology: copies are available by subscription from Old Testament Abstracts, the Catholic University of America, Washington, DC, 20064. The same association, with Weston School of Theology, issues New Testament Abstracts, summarizing new articles on New Testament subjects: copies are available by subscription from the same address. The fullest guide to all work on biblical texts and theology is the Elenchus of Biblica, issued by Editrice Pontificio Istituto Biblico in Rome: the 1991 volume covers work published in 1988 and gives full bibliography, but not summaries.

In my notes I have cited only the main secondary works that have helped me most, tending towards the most recent because they give up-to-date further bibliography which I then presuppose.

PART ONE

1 As It Was In The Beginning

I

p. 13   *Discontinuous dialogue*: A. D. Nuttall, *Overheard by God* (1980) 129, with whom, however, I disagree over John 18:33–8.

p. 13   *Augustine*: Homily CXV on John 18:38–9 (*P.L.* 35.1941).

p. 13   *Interpreter*: I disagree with J. N. Sevenster, *Do You Know Greek?* (1968) 26–8: John 12:20 (Sevenster, p.25) supports the view that Jesus was not a Greek-speaker; narrators and historians in antiquity frequently fail to mention interpreters' presence.

p. 14   *Truth theories*: brief survey in S. Blackburn, *Spreading the Word* (1984) ch. 7; for another truth, which I reject, A. J. Welburn, *The Truth of Imagination* (1989), an important book.

p. 14   *Matthew Arnold: Literature and Dogma* (*Works*, vol. VII, Macmillan edn., 1903) 238 and 135.

II

The fullest commentary is now C. Westermann, *Genesis: 1–11* (1984, E.T.), with bibliography which I presuppose. B. W. Anderson, ed., *Creation in the Old Testament* (1984), has some valuable essays; J. Rogerson, *Genesis 1–11* (1990), is a short, helpful survey of the problems and alternative theories. I owe a particular debt to James G. Turner, *One Flesh* (1987), with bibliography.

p. 16   *Second Day*: Origen, *Letter to Africanus* 4; N. R. M. de Lange, *Origen and the Jews* (1976) 124 ff. In general, D. T. Tsumara, *The Earth and the Waters in Genesis 1 and 2* (1989).

p. 16   *1:27 and feminism*: P. Trible, *God and the Rhetoric of Sexuality* (1978) esp. ch. 4.

p. 16   *Galen*: *De Usu Partium* 11.14, with R. Walzer, *Galen on Jews and Christians* (1949) 12.

p. 17   *Creation by word*: S. Morenz, *Religion u. Geschichte des alten Ägypten* (1975) 328 ff., for speech and creation.

p. 17   *'Longinus'*: *On the Sublime* 9.9, with D. A. Russell's edition (1982, rev. edn.) 92 ff. I disagree with him: 9.8 runs so neatly to 9.10; I do not see why an interpolator might not quote Genesis 1 freely; we must allow for the textual diversity of these verses. As for the tense of 'Let there be . . .', *genestho* is attested both as a reading and in quotations in Philo and Eusebius: see the critical apparatus in the *Göttingen Septuaginta*, ed. J. W. Wevers (1974).

p. 17   *Words at 2:4*: B. S. Childs, *Introduction to Old Testament as Scripture* (1979) 145–50, is wrong.

p. 18 *Problems in Eden*: H. N. Wallace, *The Eden Narrative* (1985); N. P. Williams, *The Ideas of the Fall and Original Sin* (1929); J. G. Turner, *One Flesh* (1987), with bibliography: 22 April is discussed on p. 29. Sex, in P. Lindenbaum, *Milton Studies* (1974), and especially in the outstanding study by Peter Brown, *The Body and Society* (1988) 95 ff. and 387.

p. 18 *Serpent*: R. W. L. Moberly, *J.T.S.* (1988) 1–28, important, too, for the main Eden problems. P. Brown, *The Body and Society* (1988) 95.

p. 19 *Adam's helper*: P. Trible, *God ... Sexuality* (1978) reinterprets the 'help-meet'; compare the debates in J. G. Turner, *One Flesh* (1987) ch. 3; Aug., *De Genesis and Litteram* 9.5 (*P.L.* 34.396) on a male garden-helper as preferable (I owe this to A. D. Nuttall).

p. 19 *'At Last, this'*: G. Anderson, *H.T.R.* (1989) 121, with bibliography, esp. 123–9. Jubilees 3:2–5; Josephus, *A.J.* 1.35 also assumes the animals came in mating pairs.

p. 20 *Two Creations*: e.g. Philo, *De Leg. Alleg.* 1.31.

p. 20 *La Peyrère*: R. H. Popkin, *Isaac La Peyrère, 1596–1676, His Life, Work and Influence* (1987).

p. 21 *Two sources*: H. B. Witter, *Jura Israelitarum in Palaestinam* (1711) for the first dissection; see A. Lods, *Jean Astruc et la critique biblique au XVIII siècle* (1924).

p. 21 *Priestly author*: see chs. 4.2 and 12; J. A. Emerton, *J.T.S.* (1988) 381; on the Sabbath, H. J. Kraus, *Worship in Israel* (1966) 87, and E. W. Nicholson, *Preaching to the Exiles* (1970) 124–5. Pre-exilic Sabbaths of course existed: Exodus 20:8–10, 23:12, 24:21, but after 587 the day is more prominent.

p. 21 *Eden's author*: see my ch. 3, pp. 58–9 and 12, pp. 178–81.

p. 22 *Doctrine in Genesis 1*: C. Westermann, *Genesis 1–11* (1984) 80–88.

p. 22 *Creation theory*: I quote C. Westermann, *Creation* (1971) 48.

p. 22 *Myth in Genesis 1–3*: E. R. Leach, *Genesis as Myth* (1969), which is extravagant; J. Barr, *Vet. Test.* (1963) 1; B. W. Anderson and H. Gunkel, in B. W. Anderson, ed., *Creation in the O.T.* (1984) 1 and 25; B. S. Childs, *Myth and Reality in the O.T.* (1960) esp. chs. 1–4; H. Frankfort, ed., *Before Philosophy* (1949); S. Dalley, *Myths from Mesopotamia: Creation, the Flood, Gilgamesh and Others* (1989) is important; also, B. Otzen, H. Gottlieb, K. Jeppsen, *Myths in the O.T.* (1980) chs. 1–2; W. G. Lambert, *J.T.S.* (1965) 285; S. G. F. Brandon, *Creation Legends of the Ancient Near East* (1963) chs. 2–4; Hesiod, in *Theogony* 25–35.

p. 23 *Creation and the Fall in later Scripture*: J. Barr, in *Christian Authority: Essays ... Henry Chadwick*, ed. G. R. Evans (1988) 59.

p. 24 *Ben Sira*: Ecclesiastes 25:33 with E. J. Bickerman, *Jews in the Greek Age* (1988) 198, on women.

p. 24 *Pangs of childbirth*: male commentators (unlike many modern women) are almost unanimous that the pains at 3:16 are childbirth, not also menstruation (C. Westermann, *Genesis 1–11*, 261–2).

p. 25 *St Augustine and original sin*: Romans 5:12, with Ambrosiaster, *Comm. in Rom. 5.12*, and N. Williams, *Ideas of the Fall and Original Sin* (1927) 307–9; 378 ff. 'The fatal legacy was received only too gladly . . .' e.g. Aug., *Sermo* 294.15; *C. is Epp. Pel.* 47; *C. Julianum* 6.75; E. Pagels, *Adam, Eve and the Serpent* (1988) 142 ff.

p. 25 *Voltaire*: *Dictionnaire Philosophique*, s.v. Genesis; James G. Turner, *One Flesh*, 39, n. 2.

p. 25 *Christian art*: H. Maguire, 'Adam and the Animals . . .', Dumbarton Oaks Papers (1987) 363.

p. 26 *Aphrodisiacs*: James G. Turner, *One Flesh*, 156 (Rabbis and the Physiologus); 43–9 (Augustine) and 301–4 (Milton). The Rembrandt etching of 1638 is Turner's apt frontispiece.

p. 26 *Donne*: *The Progress of the Soul*: Metempsychosis (1601) stanza 11.

p. 26 *Modern interests*: D. Jobling, *The Sense of Biblical Narrative* II (1986) 17 and the essays in *Semeia* vol. 18 (1980), for structuralist readings; Mieke Bal, *Poetics Today* 6 (1985) 21–42, arguing (wrongly) that the text of the second Creation at 2:22–3 does not put woman in a subordinate role and that 'in a semiotic sense' the woman was formed first, then the man (p. 27). B. W. Anderson, in his (ed.) *Creation in the Old Testament* (1984) 152, on ecology, with N. Lohfink, in N. Lohfink, ed., *Gewalt und Gewaltlosigkeit im A.T.* (1983), and E. Zenger, *Gottes Bogen in den Wolken* (1983), both on the Priestly author.

p. 26 *Eve's apple*: is Tabernemontana indica.

III

The essential study is still E. Scheurer, *History of the Jewish People* I (1973, rev. edn.) 399–427, as revised by F. G. B. Millar and G. Vermes: inevitably, attempts to escape an awkward truth continue, but although I hope I have covered those published since 1972, none has affected Schuerer's central arguments. On chronology, the key point is developed by N. Kokkinos, in J. Vardaman, E. M. Yamauchi, eds., *Chronos, Kairos, Christos: Studies . . . Jack Finegan* (1989) 133: not all his supporting arguments are strong, but the main point (and AD 36) stands none the less. I presuppose the bibliography in both for what follows.

p. 28 *Quirinius*: Josephus, *Jewish Antiquities* 18.1; cf. 17.355, 18.29, 20.102. For the date of this work, T. Rajak, *Josephus* (1983) 237; compare his *Jewish War* 7.253 with 2.118 and 433 (on its date, Rajak, p. 195). The inscription known as Titulus Tiburtinus is irrelevant to Quirinius: R. Syme, *Roman Papers* III (1984) 869.

p. 29   *Client kings*: D. C. Braund, *Rome and the Friendly King* (1984) for recent discussion; at pp. 36–7, he doubts if kings ever paid tribute to Rome; direct taxation of their subjects, by a Roman census, is not even a possibility.

p. 29   *Worldwide census*: E. Scheurer, *History of the Jewish People* I (1973) 401; T. P. Wiseman, *N.T.S.* (1987) 479–81, suggests a census of all citizens for the new inheritance tax, introduced in 6; the suggestion is unconvincing and it does not affect the Gospel's muddle.

p. 29   *Direct rule in Judaea*: Dio 55.27.6 with E. Schuerer, *History* . . . I (1973) 354–7 and Strabo 16.2.46.

p. 32   *'All' and 'everywhere'*: e.g. Acts 2:5; 11:28.

p. 33   *Antipas and Herodias*: this cardinal point has been disengaged by N. Kokkinos, in J. Vardaman, E. M. Yamauchi, eds., *Chronos, Kairos, Christos* (1989) 133 ff.; the source is Josephus, *A.J.* 18.109 ff., and I agree with Kokkinos's analysis; at 18.113, however, I keep the manuscript reading Gamala and explain it by assuming Aretas invaded the tetrarchy of Philip after Philip's death (hence the exiles from that area who assist Antipas against Aretas at 18.114); a similar view in G. W. Bowersock, *Roman Arabia* (1983) 65 ff., who is, however, unduly agnostic about the dating of Antipas's marriage. Antipas was defeated; if Tac., *Anns.* 6.27 is right, he then appealed to Tiberius, using the Parthian Summit at the river Euphrates (*Anns.* 6.37: AD 35) as his cue for a letter to Rome, currying favour (Jos., *A.J.* 18.104–5). In March 36 Jesus was crucified; in winter 36/7, Aretas is still in control of Damascus (Paul, 2 Corinthians 11:32); Vitellius moves to remove him (*A.J.* 18.120 ff.) at Passover 37, but withdraws, hearing of Tib.'s death (occurred March 37); Bowersock, *Roman Arabia*, pp. 68–9, opts for a later and briefer tenure of Damascus by Aretas.

I square the Crucifixion in March 36 with Paul, Galatians 1–2 (i) by counting the 3 and 14 years of 1.18 and 2.1 inclusively; (ii) by assuming that the 14 are 14 after his conversion, not after 1.18; (iii) by identifying the Council in Acts 15 with Paul's visit in Galatians 2:1; either Paul overlooked Acts 11:30 or the author, not yet his companion, misrepresented his role then.

p. 34   *The Star and the comet*: N. Kokkinos, in *Chronos, Kairos, Christos* (1989) 133 ff., lists arguments for 12 BC, Halley's Comet and the Magi: I am not convinced. D. W. Hughes, *Nature* 26 (1976) 513, argues for a triple conjunction of Saturn and Jupiter in Pisces (7 BC): compare his *Star of Bethlehem Mystery* (1979). I am not at all persuaded; A. J. Sachs, C. B. F. Walker, *Iraq* (1984) 43, refute the alleged relevance of a Babylonian almanac fragment.

p. 35   *The Star prophecy*: on Numbers 24:17, for Bar Kokhba, see E. Schuerer, *History* . . . I (1973) 543–4.

p. 36   *Jesus's age*: Irenaeus, *Adv. Haer.* 2.22.5.

p. 36   *Dates for Christmas*: Christmas, s.v. in *Dictionary of Christian Antiquities* I

(1879) 356 ff. (by R. Sinker) with L. Fendt, *Theologische Literaturzeitung* (1953) 2; H. Frank, *Archiv für die Liturgie Wissenschaft* II (1952) 11.

p. 36   *Infancy narrative as story*: much material in R. E. Brown, *The Birth of the Messiah* (1977), although we disagree on basic points of history.

p. 37   *The Wise Men*: sources and survey by Gertrud Schiller, *Iconography of Christian Art* I (1971, E.T.) 94 ff., on which I mostly depend; in the East, U. Monneret de Villard, *Le Leggende Orientali sui Magi Evangelici* (1952).

p. 37   *Marco Polo*: *Travels*, transl. R. Latham (1958, Penguin) 58–60.

p. 37   *Saveh*: W. Dalrymple, *In Xanadu* (1987) 136–9, although I disagree with his interpretation.

p. 38   *Augustine's youth*: *Sermons* 51.6.

2 The Unerring Word

J. Barr, *Fundamentalism* (1981) and *Escaping from Fundamentalism* (1984) are fundamental to my theme; Louis Jacobs, *God, Torah and Israel: Traditionalism Without Fundamentalism* (1990), sees the problem clearly from within Judaism; R. K. Harrison, *Introduction to the Old Testament* (1970) is an example of a fundamentalist approach; R. Nelson, *The Making and Unmaking of an Evangelical Mind* (1987) studies a fundamentalist's formation; L. Caplan, ed., *Religious Fundamentalism* (1987) takes a worldwide perspective. N. M. S. Cameron, *Biblical Higher Criticism and the Defence of Infallibilism in Nineteenth-century Britain* (1987) surveys one crucial epoch.

On historical criticism, S. Neill, *The Interpretation of the New Testament, 1861–1986* (2nd edn., 1988), is clear and admirable; A. Richardson, *History Sacred and Profane* (1964), is an unconvincing attempt to divide historical criticism of scripture from what 'real' historians should do. On the 'unerring word', W. J. Abraham, *The Divine Inspiration of Holy Scripture* (1981), does his best; compare B. Vawter, *Biblical Inspiration* (1972) and P. J. Achtemeier, *The Inspiration of Scripture* (1980). On allegory, E. J. Tinsley, in A. T. Hanson, ed., *Vindications* (1966), is perceptive about the N. T.; in general, J. Barr, *J.S.O.T.* (1989) 3; a defence is attempted by A. Louth, *Discerning the Mystery* (1983) 96.

p. 39   *An unknown Christian*: I quote Clem. 45.

p. 41   *Origen's allegory*: Origen, Sel. in Ps., *Patrologia Graeca* (ed. Migne) 12.1080.

PART TWO

3 'Hear, O Israel . . .'

I am particularly indebted to the outstanding study by E. W. Nicholson, *God and His People* (1986); on the questions of Yahweh Alone and his early worship, Morton Smith, *Palestinian Parties and Politics that Shaped the Old Testament* (1987, rev. edn.) chs. 1 and 3, are brilliant, provocative statements. Most recently, M. Smith, *The Early History of God* (1990), and Johannes C. de Moor, *The Rise of Yahwism* (1990, E.T.), return to the subject, although I disagree especially with the latter. R. Radford Ruether, *J.S.O.T.* (1982) 54, emphasizes the problems of gender in Patriarchal Religion: compare her *Sexism and God Talk* (1983) for a feminist reaction to them.

I

p. 50   *Four Gospels*: Irenaeus, *Adv. Haer.* 3.11.8; compare *Panegyrici Latini* 8.4.2. on Four Emperors (in 297).

p. 50   *Inspiration*: I quote P. Achtemeier, *The Inspiration of Scripture* (1980) and F. F. Bruce, *The Books and the Parchments* (1984, rev. edn.) 101.

p. 51   *Canonical Criticism*: seminal statements by B. S. Childs, esp. in his *The New Testament as Canon* (1984) and *Old Testament Theology in a Canonical Context* (1985).

p. 52   *A heap of scrolls*: J. Barr, *Holy Scripture* (1983) 57.

II

p. 53   *Exodus 19–34*: E. W. Nicholson, *God and His People* (1986) 121–50.

p. 53   *'Ten' Commandments*: I quote E. Nielsen, *The Ten Commandments in New Perspective* (1956, E.T.) 10; compare pp. 118–44 on problems of dating in the survey in J. J. Stamm, M. E. Andrew, *The Ten Commandments in Recent Research* (1962, E.T.) 22 ff.; L. Perlitt, *Bundestheologie im A.T.* (1969) 90 ff., important.

p. 54   *First Commandment*: J. J. Stamm, M. E. Andrew, *The Ten Commandments* . . . (1962) 79–87.

p. 55   *'Divine names'*: J. H. Tigay, *You Shall Have No Other Gods* (1986), is the source of my numbers; J. D. Fowler, *Theophoric Personal Names in Ancient Hebrew* (1988), covers similar material differently; on it, see J. Barr, *J.T.S.* (1990) 136; J. C. de Moor, *The Rise of Yahwism* (1990) 10–41, criticizes both, reaching yet other conclusions.

p. 55   *Meaning of 'before me'*: J. J. Stamm, M. E. Andrew, *The Ten Commandments in Recent Research* (1962) 79–81.

p. 55   *Yahweh's exclusiveness*: see J. J. Stamm, M. E. Andrew, *The Ten Command-*

ments ... (1962) 80–81. In general, H. P. Mueller, in O. Keel, ed., *Monotheismus im Alten Israel u. seiner Umwelt* (1980) 99.

p. 55   *Exodus: 34:13*: downdating in E. W. Nicholson, *God and His People* (1986) 134–50 with bibliography.

p. 57   *Early prophets and stories*: J. Day, in D. A. Carson and H. G. M. Williamson, eds., *It is Written* (1988) 39.

p. 58   *The Yahwist*: one view in R. Friedman, *Who Wrote the Bible?* (1987) 51–88, with bibliography: I disbelieve Harold Bloom, *The Book of J* (1990); for dating, K. Birge, *Die Zeit des Yahwisten* (1990).

p. 59   *The Elohist*: a view, again, in R. Friedman, *Who Wrote the Bible?* (1987) 51–88.

p. 59   *Yahweh's choosing*: E. W. Nicholson, *Deuteronomy and Tradition* (1967) 56 ff.; 96 ff. (important).

p. 60   *Genesis 15*: E. W. Nicholson, *God and His People* (1986) 46–8, 90, 112; for other views, R. E. Clements, *Abraham and David* (1967) esp. 15–34.

p. 61   *Foreign women*: J. A. Emerton, *V.T.* (1976) 79; Morton Smith, *Palestinian Parties and Politics* . . . (1987, rev. edn.) 12–13.

p. 61   *Hosea and covenant*: E. W. Nicholson, *God and His People* (1986) 179; compare J. Day, *V.T.* (1986) 1, on Psalm 78.

p. 62   *Hosea's imagery*: memorably discussed by Morton Smith, *Palestinian Parties and Politics* . . . (1987, rev. edn.) 32–3; a vigorous feminist view by T. Drorah Setel, in Letty M. Russell, ed., *Feminist Interpretation of the Bible* (1985) 86.

p. 63   *Israel's charioteers*: S. Dalley, *Iraq* (1985) 31. I have inclined to the usual date of 722 for the fall of the northern kingdom, although Jeremy Hughes, *Secrets of the Times* (1990) 207, rightly emphasizes its uncertainty: he prefers late 724–early 723.

III

R. E. Clements, *Deuteronomy* (1989), is a clear, up-to-date survey of the main views and problems whose further bibliography I presuppose. On the text's origins, I am most readily persuaded by E. W. Nicholson, *Deuteronomy and Tradition* (1967) esp. chs. 4 and 5, with his *God and His People* (1966) 112–14. On its ethos and shame-culture, D. Daube, *Orita* 3 (1969) 27, is extremely perceptive. On Yahweh Alone, Morton Smith, *Palestinian Parties and Politics* . . . (1987), rev. edn.) 22, 165 n. 111 and 37 (the 'pious fraud' theory). N. Lohfink, ed., *Das Deuteronomium: Entstehung, Gestalt und Botschaft* (1985), is the most important recent collection of scholarly essays; on the book of the law as scripture, J. Barr, *Holy Scripture* (1983) 6 ff.

I reject the arguments for a pre-exilic edition of the Deuteronomistic History, widely accepted recently in published work (of which B. Halpern, *The First Historians*, 1988, is a forthright example, in the line of teaching descending from

F. M. Cross). For a concise view of its date and place of composition, E. W. Nicholson, *Preaching to the Exiles* (1970) 71–93 and 117 ff.

4 In Defiance of the Facts

On the exilic period, Peter Ackroyd and E. J. Bickerman in *The Cambridge History of Judaism* I, eds. W. D. Davies, L. Finkelstein (1984) 130 and 342; P. R. Ackroyd, *Exile and Restoration* (1968) and *Israel under Babylon and Persia* (1970), cover a wide range of topics; M. Noth, 'The Jerusalem Catastrophe of 587 BC and its Significance for Israel', in his *Laws in the Pentateuch* (1966, E.T.) 260, is clear and provokes further thought. E. W. Nicholson, *Preaching to the Exiles* (1970) 117 ff., is convincing on the date and context of the Deuteronomist's History.

I

p. 71 *Lamentations*: B. Albrektson, *Studies in the Text and Theology of the Book of Lamentations* (1963).

p. 72 *Narrative in Exile*: M. Noth, *The Deuteronomistic History* (1987, E.T.), and my Ch. 12; I quote Morton Smith, *Palestinian Parties . . .* (1971) 36.

p. 73 *Priestly author*: J. A. Emerton, *J.T.S.* (1988) 381, with bibliography, including opposing views; for an early, pre-exilic date for P material, see R. Friedman, *Who Wrote the Bible?* (1987) 161–216, and on 'linguistic' grounds, Z. Zevit, *Z.A.W.* (1982) 481, with A. Hurvitz, *Z.A.W.* 100 (1988, Supplement) 90.

p. 73 *Exiles: Babylon*: E. J. Bickerman in *The Cambridge History of Judaism* I (1984) 342–58: Jewish occupations, pp. 346–8, and I quote p. 348.

p. 74 *Second Isaiah*: Isaiah 44:6 ff. with C. R. North, *The Second Isaiah* (1964) 15–16 and 138 ff.

p. 74–5 *Sabbath and Atonement*: H. J. Kraus, *Worship in Israel* (1966) 86, and Jeremy Hughes, *Secrets of the Times* (1990) 169 n. 26 on pre-exilic Atonement.

p. 75 *'Schools' in Exile*: I disagree with A. Lemaire, *Les Écoles et la formation de la Bible* (1981); L. L. Grabbe, *J.T.S.* (1988) 401, on absence of evidence for synagogues; M. Haran, in J. A. Emerton, ed., *Congress Volume: Jerusalem 1986* (1988, supplement to *V.T.* 40) 81, likewise on 'schools'.

p. 76 *Ezekial*: W. Eichrodt, *Ezekial* (1970, E.T.) 26–48, esp. 38.

p. 76 *Persecution*: J. M. Wilkie, *J.T.S.* (1951) 36 with Isaiah 41:10–16; 51:12 ff.

p. 76 *Israel and the Servant*: I accept M. D. Hooker, *Jesus and the Servant* (1959) 41–53, against other views.

p. 76 *Cyrus and Anointed One*: S. Smith, *Isaiah, Chapters XL–LV* (1944) esp. 49–75; Smith, pp 73–4, denies a specifically messianic reference.

p. 77 *Messiah and Davidic king*: E. Scheurer, *History of the Jewish People* II (1979) 488–554, for survey; R. E. Clements, *J.S.O.T.* (1989) 3.

p. 77   *Restored gods*: A. Kuhrt, *J.S.O.T.* (1983) 90–94, and E. J. Bickerman, *The Cambridge History of Judaism* I (1984) 353.

p. 77   *Restored exiles*: D. R. Jones, 'The Cessation of Sacrifice after the Destruction of the Temple', *J.T.S.* (1963) 12, is, to my mind, decisive; E. J. Bickerman, *Studies in Jewish and Christian History* III (1986) 297, on lack of foreign colonists.

II

On P as a separate source, J. A. Emerton, *J.T.S.* (1988) 381, and E. W. Nicholson, *Irish Biblical Studies* 10 (1988) 192, with whom I agree against opposing scholars. I reject the high datings for P proposed (e.g.) by R. Friedman, *Who Wrote the Bible?* (1987) 161.

On Leviticus 11, the most recent and significant study is by E. Firmage, in J. A. Emerton, ed., *Studies in the Pentateuch* (1990) 177, with bibliography; M. Douglas, *Purity and Danger* (1966) 57 ff., is essential (but see S. J. Tambiah, *Ethnology* 7, 1969, 423) and is refined in her *Implicit Meanings* (1975) 261–74; independently, note also J. Soler, in the *New York Review of Books* (14 June 1979) 24 ff. On the rules for blood, J. Milgrum, *J.B.L.* (1971) 149. I presuppose these studies and differ slightly from each, as also from M. Harris, *The Sacred Cow and the Abominable Pig* (1985), on 'optimal foraging strategies'.

III

P. R. Ackroyd, *The Chronicler in His Age* (1991), is now the most comprehensive account of questions on which I touch.

p. 84   *Male priesthood*: L. J. Archer, *Her Price Is Beyond Rubies* (1990) 85 ff. and in *History Workshop Journal* (1987) 3–7, suggests a broader context.

p. 85   *Ezra and Nehemiah*: see my ch. 16. 4–5; Nehemiah 5 and 13; Ezra 7:25 and Nehemiah 8:2 with H. G. M. Williamson, in D. A. Carson, H. Williamson, eds., *It Is Written* (1988) 29–31.

p. 85   *Pentateuch and Ezra*: for modern views, H. G. M. Williamson, *op. cit.* (1988) 25–6; against (on historical grounds), R. Rendtorff, *Z.A.W.* (1984) 165, and (on general grounds) C. Routman, *O.T.S.* (1981) 91; for, H. G. M. Williamson, 'Ezra–Nehemiah' (*Word Commentary*, 1985) xxxvii–xxxix.

p. 86   *Law and Persian king*: Ezra 7:25–6 with H. C. Ginsburg, *Eretz–Israel* 9 (1969) 49.

pp. 86–7   *Prophecy*: J. Barton, *Oracles of God* (1986) 105–15.

p. 87   *Post-exilic Judaism*: the most perceptive studies are E. J. Bickerman, 'The Historical Foundations of Post-biblical Judaism', in *The Jews*, ed. L. Finkelstein, I (1949) 70–115, and his *Jews in the Greek Age* (1988) 26–33 and 133–305.

p. 87   *Egyptian temple*: B. G. Porten, *Archives from Elephantine* (1968).

p. 87   *Chronicler*: against single authorship, views are listed and advanced by H. G. M. Williamson, *Israel in the Books of Chronicles* (1977) 5–70. Some are already countered by D. Talshir *V.T.* (1988) 165, and U. Kellerman, *Bibl. Notizen* 42 (1988) 49; P. Ackroyd, *Z.A.W.* (1988, Supplement) 189, on more general problems. E. J. Bickerman in *The Jews*, ed. Finkelstein, I.78 ff., is particularly acute on the Chronicler; good survey in H. G. M. Williamson, *Israel in the Books of Chronicles* (1977) esp. 71–83, on genealogies; S. J. de Vries, *J.B.L.* (1988) 619, on Moses, David and the Levites; on sources and prophets, H. G. M. Williamson, in D. A. Carson and H. G. M. Williamson, eds., *It is Written* (1988) 31–5. See further my ch. 13.

p. 88   *Range of writings*: magisterially discussed by the editors of the new edition of E. Scheurer, *History of the Jewish People* III. 1 and 2 (1986). On Job, Jonah, Ecclesiastes, Daniel, E. J. Bickerman, *Four Strange Books of the Bible* (1967), is a masterpiece; on Ecclesiastes and the 'acquisitive society', I quote his pp. 139–67. On Job, I quote Morton Smith, *Palestinian Parties and Politics* (1971) 120.

5   *Authors Anonymous*

I

The main theme of this chapter begins from E. J. Bickerman, *Studies in Jewish and Christian History* III (1986) 196; his *Jews in the Greek Age* (1987) is a masterpiece on the period between Alexander and the Maccabees.

p. 91   *Samaritans*: E. J. Bickerman, *Jews in the Greek Age* (1988) 8–12 and 187; Ben Sira, 50.26, on the 'fools in Shechem'.

p. 91   *Diaspora worship*: Scheurer, *History . . .* III.1 (rev. edn. 1986) 1–176: note esp. the Leontopolis Temple in Egypt, founded in *c.* 160 BC, where sacrifice was offered till the 70s AD: Schuerer, III.1 47–9, 145–7.

p. 91   *Synagogues*: Scheurer, *History . . .* III.1 (1986) 138–49; S. Safari, in M. Avi-Yonah, Z. Boras, eds., *Society and Religion in the Second Temple Period* (1977) 65–98; L. L. Grabbe, *J.T.S.* (1988) 401, for present evidence; I disagree with the earlier datings by (e.g.) Morton Smith, *Palestinian Parties . . .* (1971) 42.

p. 92   *Holy books*: acute remarks by A. D. Nock, *Gnomon* 26 (1954) 420–23; generally, J. Leipoldt, S. Morenz, *Heilige Schriften* (1953).

p. 92   *Septuagint*: eminent believers include E. J. Bickerman, *Studies in Jewish and Christian History* I (1976) 167 ff.

p. 93   *Anonymity*: E. M. Forster, *Anonymity: An Enquiry* (1925) 14, 18, 22; J. Barton, *Reading the Old Testament* (1984) 121–203.

p. 94   *Two authors*: M. Noth, *The Deuteronomistic History* (1981, E.T.) and *The Chronicler's History* (1987, E.T.), with H. G. M. Williamson's introduction (esp. pp. 20 ff.).

p. 94 *Near Eastern authorship*: E. J. Bickerman, 'Faux Littéraires . . .' in his *Studies in Jewish and Christian History* II (1986) 196, is the essential study; for early Babylonian names, see now S. Dalley, *Myths from Mesopotamia* (1989) esp. 3 (Nur Aya, scribe of Atrahasis), 47 (traditional author of Gilgamesh), and esp. 284 and 311–12 (Erra and Ishum, revealed in a dream to their scribe/author: again, he is scribe of Erra's words, not original author). Library list in W. G. Lambert, *J.C.S.* 16 (1962) 59.

pp. 94–5 *Jewish authorship*: Morton Smith, in *Entretiens Foundation Hardt* 18 (1972) 189; rather differently, D. W. Freedman, *A.U.S.S.* 25 (1987) 9; on the psalms' headings, B. S. Childs, *J.S.S.* (1971) 137, with bibliography. I disagree with M. D. Goulder, *The Prayers of David: Psalms 51–72* (1990), an ingenious defence.

p. 95 *Josephus and Samuel*: Jos., *A.J.* 6.66, and J. Barton, *Oracles of God* (1986) 130.

p. 97 *Pseudonymity*: M. Hengel, in *Entretiens Fondation Hardt* 19 (1972) 229; D. S. Russell, *The Old Testament Pseudepigrapha* (1987); D. G. Meade, *Pseudonymity and Canon* (1986); C. Rowland, *The Open Heaven* (1982) 62 ff., 240 ff., with none of whom I altogether agree. On the erotic Song of Songs, I sympathize with M. D. Goulder, *The Song of Fourteen Songs* (1986), and M. V. Fox, *The Song of Songs and the Ancient Egyptian Love Songs* (1985), though their other arguments are not all convincing. On Ecclesiastes, R. N. Whybray's recent commentary (1989). On Daniel, E. J. Bickerman, *Four Strange Books of the Bible* (1967) 51–139, and my ch. 18.

II

The most up-to-date and carefully weighed general survey of the textual problems I discuss is E. Tov, *Journal of Jewish Studies* (1988) 5–37. E. J. Bickerman, *Studies in Jewish and Christian History* I (1976) 167 is extremely perceptive although wrong, I believe, on the connection between Ptolemy II and the LXX.

p. 99 *Hebrew texts*: outline of main versions by F. F. Bruce, *The Books and the Parchments* (1984, 4th edn.) chs. 9–12.

p. 99 *Textual variety*: I presuppose the full bibliography in the most up-to-date survey by E. Tov, 'Hebrew Biblical Manuscripts from the Judaean Desert: Their Contribution to Textual Criticism' in *Journal of Jewish Studies* 38 (1988) 5. J. A. Fitzmyer, *The Dead Sea Scrolls, Major Publications and Tools for Study* (1977, 2nd edn.), and C. Koester, 'A Qumran Bibliography, 1974–1984' in *Biblical Theology Bulletin* 15 (1985) 110, are basic guides.

p. 99 *Septuagint and Samaritan Pentateuch*: broad outline in F. F. Bruce, *The Books and the Parchments* (1984, 4th edn.) chs. 10 and 12; F. M. Cross, *The Ancient Library of Qumran and Modern Biblical Studies* (1980) 172–94.

p. 100   *Chinese Jews*: D. S. Katz, in *E.H.R.* (1990) 893: I owe this to Dr P. H. Williams.

p. 100   *Nash Papyrus*: S. A. Cook, *P.S.B.A.* (1903) 34, and F. C. Burkitt, *J.Q.R.* (1903) 392 and (1904) 559

p. 100   *Qumran*: F. M. Cross and S. Talmon, *Qumran and the History of the Biblical Text* (1975), although Cross's suggestions of regional text-types no longer stands up. E. Ulrich, *C.B.Q.* (1984) 613, for more recent overview.

p. 100   *Other sites*: Masada, in Y. Yadin, *Masada* (1966) 168–89; Wadi Murab-ba'at, in P. Benoit, J. T. Milik, R. de Vaux, eds., *Documents from the Judaean Desert* II (1967) 75–85, 181–205; Nahal Hever: bibliography in J. A. Fitzmyer, *The Dead Sea Scrolls . . . Tools for Study* (1977) 46–7.

p. 101   *Spelling*: E. Qimron, *Hebrew of the Dead Sea Scrolls* (1986); E. Tov, *Textus* (1986) 31; E. Tov, *Journal of Jewish Studies* (1988) 20–27, with bibliography, to which add J. Barr, *The Variable Spellings of the Hebrew Bible* (1989).

p. 101   *Jeremiah*: J. G. Janzen, *Studies in the Text of Jeremiah* (1973); on Samuel, see E. Ulrich, *The Qumran Text of Samuel and Josephus* (1978) with bibliography, and E. Tov, ed., *The Hebrew and Greek Texts of Samuel* (Jerusalem, 1980) 45 ff.; Ecclesiastes, in J. Muilenburg, *B.A.S.O.R.* (1954) 20.

p. 102   *Independent Pentateuchal texts*: P. W. Skehan, *B.A.S.O.R.* (1954) 12; K. A. Matthews, *C.B.Q.* (1986) 171; J. E. Sanderson, *An Exodus Scroll from Qumran . . .* (1986). In general, E. Tov, *H.U.C.A.* (1982) 11; the corrected Deuteronomy, 5 Q Deut., in A. Baillet, J. T. Milik, R. de Vaux, *Discoveries in the Judaean Desert* III (1962) 168.

pp. 102–3 *Septuagint*: E. Schuerer, *History of the Jewish People . . .* III. 1 (1986) 474–504, with bibliography; the articles by S. P. Brock, *Oudtestamentische Studien* (1972) 11 and *Sourozh* 29 (1987) 32, are important, with his *Syriac Perspectives on Late Antiquity* (1984) ch. 3, on biblical translation; E. J. Bickerman, *Studies in Jewish and Christian History* I (1976) 167, is an outstanding study; also H. M. Orlinsky, *H.U.C.A.* (1975) 89.

p. 103   *Book of Kings*: J. D. Shenkel, *Chronology and Recensional Development in the Greek Text of Kings* (1968), for a positive view; a survey in G. H. Jones, ed., *1 and 2 Kings* (New Century Bible, 1984) 2–9.

p. 103   *Qumran and LXX*: E. Tov, ed., *The Hebrew and Greek Texts of Samuel* (Jerusalem, 1980) 45–67. On Jeremiah, E. Tov, in P. M. Bogaert, *Le Livre de Jérémie* (1981) 145, and E. Tov, *Journal of Jewish Studies* (1988) 29 with notes.

p. 104   *LXX's disagreements*: Jeremy Hughes, *Secrets of the Times* (1990) 122–58, on chronology.

p. 104   *Samaritans' Exodus*: J. E. Sanderson, *An Exodus Scroll from Qumran: 4QpaleoExod^m and the Samaritan Tradition* (1986).

pp. 105–6   *Homeric text*: S. L. West, in A Huebeck, S. L. West, J. B. Hainsworth, *A commentary on Homer's 'Odyssey'* I (1988) 33–48.

III

J. Barr, *Holy Scripture* (1983), is particularly clear and incisive on the idea and history of a scriptural canon. On the Pharisees and their supposed oral law, E. P. Sanders, *Jewish Law from Jesus to the Mishnah* (1990) ch. 2, is an important corrective.

p. 106   *Knowledge of law*: E. P. Sanders, *Jesus and Judaism* (1985) 191–4, quoting *Bleak House*; E. J. Bickerman, *Jews in the Greek Age* (1988) ch. 19, esp. p. 170.

p. 106   *Proverbs*: N. Horsfall, *Greece and Rome* (1989) 76–8.

p. 107   *Wisdom and learning*: Ben Sira 24.23, with E. J. Bickerman, *Jews in the Greek Age* (1988) 169–70, which I quote; the 'visionary' is Jubilees 23:26; the synagogue is Theodotus's, in *Corpus Inscript. Judaicarum* II.1404. Compare Philo, *Embassy to Gaius* 156; Josephus, *Against Apion* 2.175.

pp. 107–8   *Textual exegesis*: M. J. Mulder, *Mikra: Text, Translation, Reading and Interpretation of the Hebrew Bible* ... (1988), for recent studies and bibliography.

p. 108   *Philosophy and scripture*: I quote A. Momigliano, *On Pagans, Jews and Christians* (1987) 91.

p. 108   *Yahweh's name*: E. J. Bickerman, *Jews in the Greek Age* (1988) 262-6, and *Studies in Jewish and Christian History* III (1986), 270–81, with bibliography; at Qumran, J. Spiegel, *H.U.C.A.* (1971) 159.

p. 109   *Jars*: C. H. Roberts, *Buried Books in Antiquity* (1963), with bibliography.

p. 109   *Defiling hands*: evidence and an alternative view in M. D. Goodman, *J.T.S.* (1990) 99.

p. 109   *Council at Jamnia*: P. Schaefer, *Judaica* 31 (1975) 54, for its death-knell; compare S. I. Katz, *J.B.L.* (1984) 43; it succeeded the notion of a 'Great Synagogue' under Ezra, on which we see W. Robertson Smith, *The Old Testament in the Jewish Church* (1881) 148–76, esp. 169.

p. 110   *'Jewish canon'*: J. Barr, *Holy Scripture* (1983) 49–74, with J. Barton, *Oracles of God* (1986) 13–95; a more rigid view, which I reject, underlies R. Beckwith, *The Old Testament Canon of the N. T. Church and Its Background in Early Judaism* (1985). Rabbinic evidence is given in S. Z. Leiman, *The Canonization of Hebrew Scripture* ... (1976).

p. 110   *Lists of books*: Josephus, *Against Apion* 1.37–42; Ecclesiasticus, Prologue and 49.10 (the Twelve Prophets); Fourth Ezra 14:37 ff. with E. Scheurer, *History of the Jewish People* ... III.1 (1987, rev. edn.) 304–6, and R. H. Charles, *Old Testament Apocrypha and Pseudepigrapha* I (1913) 624, for the textual problems in the relevant verses.

p. 111   *Alphabet lists*: Jerome, preface to Samuel and Kings (*P.L.* 28.555–7), knows this explanation; J. Barton, *Oracles of God* (1986) 88–9, wonders if the lists were mnemonics, to help children 'reel off the names of the books of the Bible'.

p. 111   *Pharisees and tradition*: E. P. Sanders, *Jewish Law from Jesus to the Mishnah* (1990) ch. 2, is an essential corrective.

p. 111   *Sadducees*: J. Le Moyne, *Les Sadducéens* (1972), corrects the conventional view that high priests were necessarily Sadducees, as M. D. Goodman reminds me.

p. 112   *Threefold division*: Ecclesiasticus, Prologue, with J. Barton, *Oracles of God* (1986) 35–63, 75–82.

6 Jesus and the Scriptures

J. Barr, *Holy Scripture* (1983) 12–22, and *Old and New in Interpretation* (1982, 2nd edn.), are outstandingly clear discussions of the relations between Jesus and the Old Testament, the Old Testament and the New Testament. Among recent works on the historical Jesus, E. P. Sanders, *Jesus and Judaism* (1989), is the essential study: his *Jewish Law from Jesus to the Mishnah* (1990) ch. 1, is now basic on the Synoptic Jesus and the law. On the rise of the earliest theology, Paula Fredriksen, *From Jesus to Christ* (1988), is clear and a stimulus to further thought. B. M. Metzger, *The Canon of the New Testament* (1987), cites a wide range of evidence; F. F. Bruce, *The Canon of Scripture* (1989), is thorough and traditional; R. Longenecker, *Biblical Exegesis in the Apostolic Period* (1975), covers the main ground. E. E. Ellis, *The Old Testament in Early Christianity* (1991) 126 ff. differs helpfully from my views.

p. 114   *Languages*: J. A. Emerton, *J.T.S.* (1973) 1; Schuerer, *History* ... II (1979) 23–8, with bibliography.

p. 116   *Legal Puzzles*: M. D. Goodman, in P. R. Davies, R. T. White, eds., *A Tribute to Geza Vermes* (1990) 227, on Gentile oil; E. J. Bickerman, *Jews in the Greek Age* (1988) 249–50, on Gentile girls; Deuteronomy 7:8, on the land; Leviticus 23:40 on fruits with Josephus, *A.J.* 13.372, a point I owe to T. F. R. G. Braun.

p. 117   *Messiah*: variety is the fact most evident from E. Scheurer, *History* ... II (1979) 488–554; R. E. Clements, *J.S.O.T.* (1989) 3, for a history of (over)interpretation.

pp. 117–19   *Jesus and scripture*: incisively presented by J. Barr, *Holy Scripture* (1983) 12–22; a more 'canonical' approach in (e.g.) E. E. Ellis, *The Old Testament in Early Christianity* (1991) 126 ff; rabbinic patterns of arguments in the Gospels have a big, but generally flimsy, scholarship: D. Daube, *J.T.S.* (1944) 21, *J.T.S.* (1951) 45 (on Mark 12) and E. E. Ellis, *The Old Testament in Early Christianity* (1991) 130, do not alter the point I wish to emphasize, nor does debate over Matthew's Gospel (particularly illuminating in K. Stendhal, *School of St. Matthew*, 1954, and M. D. Goulder, *Midrash and Lection in Matthew*, 1974, esp. 3–70 and 124–36); D. Daube, *Appeasement or Resistance* (1987) 11–31, argues for a Jesus in the Gospels who cites the O.T. in the light of contemporary reinterpretation (John 8:7, his pp. 29–31 is the most cogent of his six examples).

p. 119 *Jesus and the law*: E. P. Sanders, *Jesus and Judaism* (1985) ch. 9, is now the essential starting–point.

p. 119 *Parables*: D. D. Flusser, *Die Rabbinschen Gleichnisse und der Gleichniserzähler Jesu* (1981), on rabbis and parables: at Mark 12:1, there are implicit, but not explicit, echoes of Isaiah 5.

p. 120 *'Old Covenant'*: 2 Corinthians 3:14; on 'testament', F. F. Bruce, *The Books and the Parchments* (1984) 65.

p. 123 *Proof-texts*: J. Barton, *People of the Book?* (1988) esp. 15–16, is of the first importance, against loose definitions of 'Jewish' or 'Judaeo' Christianity, based on the density of Jewish textual citations in an early Christian work.

p. 123 *Alexandrian list*: A. C. Sundberg, *C.B.Q.* (1968) 143; for doubts (which I do not share) J. Barr, *Holy Scripture* (1983) 55.

p. 123 *21 and 24*: Eusebius, *H.E.* 4.26 (Melito, *c.* 170, lists no Esther and strictly twenty-five books, but I expect Ruth was an appendix to Judges in his informants' view, as later for Origen's); Eusebius, *H.E.* 6.25 (22, for Origen); Jerome, Preface to Comm. on Daniel, gives twenty-four 'among the Hebrews'; his Preface to Samuel and Kings (*P.L.* 28.555–7) knows twenty-two or twenty-seven, matching letters of Hebrew alphabet.

p. 123 *Jerome*: I quote J. N. D. Kelly, *Jerome* (1975) 161: see ch. 15 throughout. On Judith, Jerome Preface to Judith (*P.L.* 29.39); on the Apocrypha, F. F. Bruce, *The Books and the Parchments* (1984) ch. 13.

p. 124 *Early Gospel quotations*: the 'John' papyrus: P. Ryl iii. 457 with E. G. Turner, *Typology of the Early Codex* (1977) P 52; 'Mark' (ours?): Papias, in Eusebius, *H.E.* 3.39.15; Matthew 3:15, in Ignatius, *To Smyrna* 1; words of Jesus now in Matthew are combined with others in 1 Clem. 13.1–2 and his Lord's Prayer in *Didache* 8.1–3: in neither case, lacking the context, do I suspect a direct use of our Gospel. As for the Ep. of Barnabas, its date may be nearer the 130s; the possible citations of Matthew (at 4:14, 5:9, 7:3) are not certain; B. M. Metzger, *The Canon of the N.T.* (1987) 57.

7 Pseudonymous Christians

E. P. Sanders and Margaret Davies, *Studying the Synoptic Gospels* (1989), give the best modern introduction to the problems of Synoptic Gospel criticism, although we disagree on the finely balanced question of the reality of

Q. M. Hengel, *Studies in the Gospel of Mark* (1985) 64–84, takes a more optimistic view of the Gospel's titles than I can accept.

p. 126 *Hebrews*: E. J. Bickerman, *Studies in Jewish and Christian History* III (1986) 336; Priscilla, see A. Harnack, *Z.N.T.W.* (1900) 16, though the participle at 11:32 is masculine.

p. 126 *John's epilogue*: I share the views argued by C. H. Roberts, *J.T.S.* (1987) 409, especially that 'these things' (in 21:24: 'tauta') refers only here to the Epilogue of ch. 21, at most.

p. 126 *Gospel titles*: full, but over-optimistic, discussion by M. Hengel, *Studies in the Gospel of Mark* (1985) 64–84: he gives all the known evidence, but I cannot accept his conclusions. On epistles, E. J. Bickerman, *Studies . . .* III (1986) 344–9, is now a basic starting point.

pp. 126–7 *Papias*: Eusebius, *H.E.* 3.39.15; I am not convinced by U. H. J. Körtner, *Papias von Hierapolis* (1983) esp. 88–94, who tries to date Papias *c.* 110; further discussion and bibliography in J. Kürzinger, *Papias von Hierapolis und die Evangelien des N.T.* (1983). On the meaning of the famous sentences, contrast M. Hengel, *Studies in the Gospel of Mark* (1985) 47–50, 69–70, with E. P. Sanders, M. Davies, *Studying the Synoptic Gospels* (1989) 8–16.

p. 127 *Mark and Matthew*: E. P. Sanders, M. Davies. *Studying the Synoptic Gospels* (1989) 151–123, with bibliography.

p. 128 *Basilides*: E. Henneke, W. Schneemelcher, *N. T. Apocrypha* I (1963) 311–46 ff.; B. Metzger, *The Canon of the N.T.* (1987) 78; at Clem., *Strom.* 7, ch. 17, it is, strictly, only his followers (not B. himself) who are said to claim that B. was taught by Peter's Glaucias. At Hippolytus, *Ref. Haer.* 7.8.1, Matthias appears to be B.'s own claim.

p. 128 *Matthew's clues*: Matthew 9:9, against Mark 2:14; on money, J. Jeremias, *The Parables of Jesus* (1954) 210.

p. 129 *Named authors*: Irenaeus, *Adv. Haer.* 3.11.7 (Luke); E. Pagels, *The Johannine Gospel in Gnostic Exegesis* (1973), on Heracleon and John; M. Hengel, *The Johannine Question* (1989) 8–9, puts Ptolemy, another Valentinian, slightly earlier; compare J. A. T. Robinson, *The Priority of John* (1985) 95 n. 250; 280, 346–7; on Luke, Acts, despite (e.g.) E. Haenchen's great work, *The Acts of the Apostles* (1971) 112–24, and the inconclusive arguments of E. P. Sanders, M. Davies, *Studying the Synoptic Gospels* (1989) 16–20, I take 'we' at face value and see no insuperable problem in the consequences. See further my ch. 13.

p. 129 *Pseudonymity*: I quote G. D. Kilpatrick, *The Origins of the Gospel According to St Matthew* (1946) 139.

p. 130 *Paul and fakes*: 2 Thessalonians 3:17; E. Best, *I and II Thessalonians* (1972) 7–13, on authenticity; Galatians 6:11 with H. C. Youtie, *Scriptiunculae* II (1973) 970.

p. 130   *Fake letters*: Cyprian, *Epist.* 9.2, 20; Eusebius, *H.E.* 4.23.12.

p. 131   *Pastoral letters*: I am not alone in rejecting the contrary case, reassembled by J. A. T. Robinson, *Redating the New Testament* (1976) 67–83; I also dissent from P. N. Harrison, *The Problems of the Pastoral Epistles* (1921); the main arguments are documented in C. K. Barrett, *The Pastoral Epistles* (1963) 2–34.

p. 133   *Peter's letters*: again, J. A. T. Robinson, *Relating the New Testament* (1976) 150–99, for bibliography, argument and unconvincing conclusions for an early date. On Bethsaida, E. Schuerer, *History* II (1979) 171–2; on Greek's currency, II 74–80, with bibliography.

p. 134   *Stylometry*: A. Kenny, *A Stylometric Study of the New Testament* (1986) is now basic, with bibliography on the points I raise: pp. 120–21 are suitably cautious. D. L. Mealand, *J.T.S.* (1988) 194–6, reviews the case acutely; earlier studies were by A. Q. Morton, *Paul, the Man and the Myth* (1966); see further, John T. Hughes, *Bits, Bytes and Biblical Studies* (1987).

p. 135   *Ephesians*: C. L. Mitton, *The Epistle to the Ephesians* (1951), still basic on the style; A. van Roon, *The Authenticity of Ephesians* (1974), a major statement of a case which is not convincing; further bibliography in J. A. T. Robinson, *Relating the New Testament* (1976) 62–7; on letter-titles, note E. J. Bickerman, *Studies in Jewish and Christian History* III (1986) 339–40.

p. 136   *'Inspired' scripture*: J. Barr, *Escaping from Fundamentalism* (1984) 1–7, on 2 Timothy 3:16.

8 *Adding and Subtracting*

For different views to mine, see most recently W. L. Petersen, ed., *Gospel Traditions in the Second Century* (1989), esp. F. Wisse 39–54.

p. 137   *Adding to texts*: W. C. van Unnik, *Vigiliae Christianae* (1949) 1.

p. 137   *Revisions of Greek scripture*: E. Scheurer, *History* III.1 (1986) 480–504.

pp. 137–8 *Pamphilus's corrections*: H. J. M. Milne and T. C. Skeat, *Codex Sinaiticus and Codex Alexandrinus* (1963, 2nd edn.).

p. 138   *New Testament text*: B. M. Metzger, *Text of the New Testament* (1968), is a basic source; J. Birdsall, in *The Cambridge History of the Bible* I, ed. P. R. Ackroyd and C. F. Evans (1970) 308–77; K. and B. Aland, *The Text of the New Testament* (1989, E.T., 2nd edn.); G. D. Kilpatrick, *New Testament Textual Criticism* (1990).

p. 139   *Early Christian papyri*: J. van Haelst, *Catalogue des papyrus littéraires juifs et chrétiens* (1976).

p. 139   *Their divergences*: G. D. Kilpatrick, *New Testament Textual Criticism* (1990) 4.

pp. 139–40 *Marcion and Tatian*: B. M. Metzger, *Canon of the N.T.* (1987) 90–99; 114–17.

p. 140   *Textual problems*: J. Barr, *Escaping from Fundamentalism* (1984) 139–47.

p. 140   *Lilies of the field*: T. C. Skeat, *Z.N.W.* 37 (1938) 211; J. E. Powell, *J.T.S.* (1982) 490–92 is quite convincing.

p. 141   *Acts' text*: E. Haenchen, *Acts of the Apostles: A Commentary* (1971) 50–60, arguing (not cogently) that the 'very fact that the texts often contradict each other' excludes two editions by the author himself. The Western Text is discussed and set out in *The Beginnings of Christianity*, eds. Foakes, Jackson and Lake, III (1926) ccxv–ccxlix and 3–255. M. E. Boismard and A. Lamouille, *Texte Occidental des Actes des Apôtres* (1984) I–II, is of major importance (but see *J.T.S.*, 1988, 571–7) and I merely disagree that the Western Text has the earlier 'first thoughts' of the author. On Sceva, see W. A . Strange, *J.T.S.* (1987) 97; women, Acts 17:4 in *Beginnings of Christianity* III (1926) 162–3.

pp. 142–3   *The Adulterous woman*: R. E. Brown, *Gospel According to John (i–xii)*, Anchor Bible (1966) 332–6; D. Lührmann, *Nov. Test.* (1990) 289.

pp. 143–4   *Mark's ending*: N. R. Petersen, *Interpretation* (1980) 157; D. Via, *The Ethics of Mark's Gospel* (1985), and J. L. Magness, *Sense and Absence: Structure and Suspension in the Ending of Mark's Gospel* (1986), are recent literary defences; against, the case summarized in D. E. Nineham, *Commentary on Mark* (1963); compare Roberts–Skeat, *Birth of the Codex* (1983) 56–7.

p. 144   *Odyssey's ending*: S. West, *Proc. Camb. Philol. Soc.* (1989) 113.

pp. 144–5   *Snake handling*: Paul Gillespie, ed., *Foxfire* 7 (1982) 372 ff., which I owe to Eric Christiansen.

9 From Scrolls to Books

B. M. Metzger, *The Canon of the New Testament* (1987), is a mine of information for this chaper too; the Gospel of Thomas is translated in R. M. Grant, *Secret Sayings of Jesus* (1960), or B. Layton, *The Gnostic Scriptures* (1987), or with more schlolarly discussion, in his edition of Nag Hammadi Codex II.2–7, I (1989). For the Unknown Gospel, whose interest is still not exhausted, H. I Bell and T. C. Skeat, *Fragments of an Unknown Gospel* . . . (1935), publish a translation and discussion. I have not appealed to the 'Muratorian Canon' because I do not believe that it is early, let alone an official, orthodox canon: A. C. Sundberg, *H.T.R.* (1973) 1, and G. Hahnemann, *Studia Patristica* (1989) 359, argue for its origin in the fourth century.

I

pp. 146–7   *Scrolls to books*: C. H. Roberts, T. C. Skeat, *The Birth of the Codex* (1983) is classic, but not definitive; J. van Haelst, in A. Blanchard, ed., *Les Débuts du codex* (1989) 13, for the best critique.

p. 147   *First Clement*   1 Clem. 13.2 and 46.7–8 (Jesus's words); 47 (Paul); 17.1, 19.2, 21.9, 27.2, 36.2–5 (Hebrews). At 35.5–6, he quotes Paul, then a psalm.

pp. 147–8   *Pseudo Gospels*: B. M. Metzger, *Canon of the N.T.* (1987) 166–174, with bibliography. M. R. James, *The Apocryphal N.T.* (1924), with E. Hennecke, W. Schneemelcher, *N.T. Apocrypha*, eds. R. and L. Wilson (1963); J. M. Robinson, ed., *Nag Hammadi Library in English* (1977).

p. 148   *Unknown Gospel*: H. I. Bell and T. C. Skeat, *Fragments of an Unknown Gospel . . .* (1935), with H. I. Bell, *H.T.R.* (1949) 53.

p. 149   *Gospel of Thomas*: B. Layton, ed., *Nag Hammadi Codex II.2–7*, I (1989), is now the fullest schlolarly discussion; some fine remarks by H. C. Puech, *En Quête de la Gnose* (1978), on its cryptic theology. Translations have been frequent: among the most recent is M. W. Meyer, *The Secret Teaching of Jesus* (1984) 17–39.

II

p. 151   *Quoted sayings of Jesus*: B. M. Metzger, *Canon of N.T.* (1987) 145–51, on Justin, with A. Wartelle, *St Justin: Apologies* (1987) 49, on Gospel of Peter; Clement, *Strom.* 3.13.93, with Metzger, *Canon* 132–5; Serapion of Antioch, Eusebius, *H.E.* 6.12.3. In general, J. Jeremias, *Unknown Sayings of Jesus* (1964, 2nd edn.).

p. 151   *Athanasius*: B. M. Metzger, *Canon* 210–12 and 312.

p. 151   *Latin West*: B. M. Metzger, *Canon* 229–47.

p. 152   *Epiphanius*: *Panarion* ch. 76.

p. 152   *East Christians*: B. M. Metzger, *Canon* 218–28, with bibliography.

p. 153   *Third John*: Diotrephes, in verses 9–11, is probably the recognized leader of the Church!

p. 153   *Aggressive Forgery*: I quote R. M. Grant, *J.T.S.* (1960) 13, esp. 23.

p. 154   *Emergent authority*: R. E. Brown, *The Critical Meaning of the Bible* (1982).

10 Original Scripture

p. 155   *Texts of Job and Ecclesiastes*: J. H. Eaton, *Job* (1989), for survey, and H. H. Rowley, *The Book of Job* (1983, repr.) 8; I side with G. D. Barton, *Ecclesiastes* (I.C.C. Commentary, 1908) 43–6, on its editing (R. N. Whybray, *Ecclesiastes*, 1989, 17 ff., agrees, but looks for unity first); John Barton, *Reading the Old Testament* (1984) 61–76, esp. 74–6, raises the critics' problems clearly.

p. 156   *Textual puzzles in O.T.*: B. Albrektson, *Oudtestamentliche Studien* (1981) 5, with J. Barr *J.T.S.* (1986) 445–50, on the Preliminary and Interim Report on the Hebrew Old Testament Text Project (3 vols., to 1977); the Jewish Publication Society of America also completed in 1982 a three-volume translation of 'Holy Scripture According to the Masoretic Text'.

p. 156   *Word comparisons*: J. Barr, *Comparative Philology and the Text of the Old Testament* (1968).

p. 156   *United Bible Societies*: *The Greek New Testament* (1966), eds. K. Aland, M. Black. B. M. Metzger, A. Wikgren.

p. 157   *'Scriptural authenticity'*: D. Barthélemy, *Critique textuelle de l'ancien testament* I (1982), Introduction: I owe my knowledge of this to S. P. Brock (see his article in *Sourozh* 29 (1987) 42).

p. 157   *'Original' music*: R. Taruskin, in N. Kenyon, ed., *Authenticity and Early Music* (1988) 211.

PART THREE

11 Ideas of History

J. van Seters, *In Search of History* (1983), is a full work of reference, but its own arguments are often implausible and its definitions arbitrary: the review by Z. Zevit, *B.A.S.O.R.* (1985) 71–83, is important. B. Halpern, *The First Historians* (1988), puts an opposite case, at times to excess. A. K. Grayson, 'Assyria and Babylonia', *Orientalia* (1980) 140–94, is fundamental; G. A. Press, *The Idea of History in Antiquity* (1983), ranges widely. The great connoisseur of this subject was A. Momigliano: I single out his *Studies in Historiography* (1969) chs. 8 (on Herodotus) and 11 (on oral and written sources); *Essays in Ancient and Modern Historiography* (1977) chs. 11 (on change) and 12 (on time); *On Pagans, Jews and Christians* (1987) ch. 1 (biblical and classical studies) and his *Sesto Contributo alla Storia degli Studi Classici del Mondo Antico* II (1980) 33–67 (Greek historiography) and 361 (historians' audiences). T. Rajak, 'The Sense of History in Jewish Intertestamental Writing', *Oudtestament. Stud.* (1986) 124, covers an area I necessarily neglect, from a different starting-point.

p. 162   *Story, history, etc.*: J. Barr, *Scope and Authority of the Bible*, Explorations in Theology 7 (1980) 1–18; R. Alter, *Art of Biblical Narrative* (1981) ch. 2, esp. p. 24 ('prose fiction'); M. Steinberg, *The Poetics of Biblical Narrative* (1985) 24–35; Y. Zakovitch, *Proc. of 8th World Congress of Jewish Studies* (1983) 47; B. O. Long, *V.T.* (1985) 405; B. Halpern, *The First Historians* (1990) 1–34.

p. 162   *Israelites and history*: H. Butterfield, *The Origins of History* (1981) 80.

p. 163   *Truth and evidence*: J. Barr, *Semantics of Biblical Language* (1961) 195–7, on 'true'; D. Daube *R.I.D.A.* (1949) 200–201, on Susanna's trial.

p. 164   *Assyrian records*: J. van Seters, *In Search of History* (1983) ch. 3; with A. K. Grayson, *Orientalia* (1980) 149–71, with bibliography.

p. 164   *Egyptian records*: J. van Seters, *op. cit.* (1983) ch. 5, with bibliography.

pp. 164–5   *Babylonian records*: A. K. Grayson, *Assyrian and Babylonian Chronicles* (1975), and his important survey-article in *Orientalia* (1980) 140–94.

p. 165   *Synchronisms*: A. K. Grayson, *Assyrian and Babylonian Chronicles* (1975) 6 (his category D).

p. 165   *Babylonian chronicles, diaries and omens*: A. K. Grayson, *Orientalia* (1980) 174–5, concluding 'it is at least possible' that we are faced with a 'brief and accurate record of Babylonian history for its own sake'. I am not persuaded by his arguments.

p. 166   *Herodotus*: J. Gould, *Herodotus* (1989), is the best short guide, now, with 'Herodotus and the Invention of History' in *Arethusa* 20 (1987), esp. the reasoned bibliography, and C. Meier, on *The Origins of History in Ancient Greece*.

p. 167   *Prose/speech*: E. J. Bickerman, *Studies in Jewish and Christian History* III (1986) 207.

p. 167   *Subjectivity*: I quote R. G. Collingwood, *The Idea of History* (1946) 9.

p. 168   *Herodotus and 'knowledge'*: B. Shimron, *Eranos* 71 (1973) 45.

pp. 168–9   *Biblical speeches*: I quote E. J. Bickerman, *Studies in Jewish and Christian History* I (1976) 263.

p. 169   *Chronologies*: A. B. Lloyd, *Herodotus Book II* (1979) 171 ff.; A. W. Gomme, *Commentary on Thucydides* I (1945) 1–8.

p. 170   *Herodotus's speakers' 'theology'*: e.g. 1.32 or 1.207 or 9.16.4, among many. In general, R. Lattimore, *C.P.* (1939) 24, on the 'wise adviser'.

p. 170   *Change and history*: A. Momigliano, *Essays in Ancient and Modern Historiography* (1977) 166.

p. 171   *Oral history*: R. Thomas, *Oral Tradition and Written Record in Classical Athens* (1989), esp. 1–100; 123–31, with bibliography of comparative work, which I presuppose, esp. the studies of J. Vansina; his *Oral Tradition as History* (1985) and his paper on memory in *The African Past Speaks*, ed. J. C. Miller (1980) 262, are helpful. M. I. Finley, *Use and Abuse of History* (1975) 11.

p. 173   *Primary sources*: P. A. Brunt, *Fall of the Roman Republic* (1988) 508–10.

p. 173   *Josephus*: C. *Apionem* 1.30–46.

p. 174   *Oral and written tradition*: I think especially of J. Goody and I. Watt in J. Goody, ed., *Literacy in Traditional Societies* (1968) 27, with further thoughts in J. Goody, *The Interface Between the Written and the Oral* (1987). B. Street, *Literacy in Theory and Practice* (1984) is also helpful, esp. pp. 153 ff. on Koranic schooling and its effects.

12 The First Historians

p. 176   *Sources and the Pentateuch*: J. Wellhausen, *Prolegomena to the History of Israel* (1885, E.T.), is still an essential classic; summary of modern theories in

R. E. Friedman, *Who Wrote the Bible?* (1987) 26 ff.; R. N. Whybray, *The Making of the Pentateuch* (1983), does not succeed in overthrowing the 'documentary hypothesis'.

p. 176   The '*natural subeditor*': D. J. A. Clines, *The Theme of the Pentateuch* (1982), for a more optimistic view; R. E. Friedman, *Who Wrote the Bible?* (1987) 218–33, has even persuaded himself that there is a 'high likelihood' the subeditor was Ezra!

p. 177   *P source*: E. W. Nicholson, *Irish Biblical Studies* 10 (1988) 192, on its independence; J. A. Emerton, *J.T.S.* (1988) 381 (with bibliography); Jeremy Hughes, *Secrets of the Times* (1990) 48–54; K. Elliger, *Z.Th.K.* (1952) 121. I disagree with the early dating of (e.g.) R. E. Friedman, *Who Wrote the Bible?* (1987) chs. 9–12, but his account of P's tendencies is clear and helpful. E. Zenger, *Gottes Bogen in den Wolren* (1983), and N. Lohfink, in his (ed.) *Gewalt und Gewaltlosigkeit im A.T.* (1983), see P as a pacifist, friendly to the environment.

pp. 178–9   *J source*: Harold Bloom, *The Book of J* (1990), builds extravagantly on R. Friedman, *Who Wrote the Bible?* (1987) ch. 3, esp. p. 86: the dating, 'irony', sex, political message and 'covenant' of Bloom's J are all unconvincing. K. Berge, *Die Zeit des Jahwisten* (1990), with bibliography for other views.

p. 179   *Genesis 14*: J. A. Emerton, in J. A. Emerton, ed., *Studies in the Pentateuch* (Supplement to *V.T.* 41; 1990) 73, with bibliography.

p. 180   '*Just-so*' *story*: B. S. Childs, *V.T.* (1974) 387, with J. van Seters, *In Search of History* (1983) 24–6, 213–27; G. von Rad, *Problem of the Hexateuch and Other Essays* (1966, E.T.) 168–9.

p. 181   *J and blessing*: H. W. Wolff, *Interpretation* 20 (1966) 131.

p. 182   *The Deuteronomist*: M. Noth, *The Deuteronomistic History* (1981, E.T.), is classic; G. von Rad, *The Problem of the Hexateuch and Other Essays* (1966, E.T.) ch. 9, and esp. E. W. Nicholson, *Preaching to the Exiles* (1970) 72–93 and 117–35. Jeremy Hughes, *Secrets of the Times* (1990) chs. 3–4, on chronology; W. Brueggemann, *Interpretation* 22 (1968) 387, on future; Babylonian Exile, E. W. Nicholson, *Preaching to the Exiles* (1970) 117 ff. I reject the Josianic first edition–exilic second edition, although ably proposed again most recently by R. D. Nelson, *The Double Redaction of the Deuteronomistic History* (1983), and accepted by B. Halpern, *The First Historians* (1988). I also reject the 'history-prophecy-law' strata.

p. 183   *Speeches*: a literary response, now, by R. Polzin, *Moses and the Deuteronomist* (1980).

p. 184   *Joshua 13 ff.: the lists*: J. Gray, *Joshua, Judges, Ruth* (New Century, 1986) 44–51, for optimistic theories and alternatives.

p. 184   '*Book of Jashar*': add 2 Samuel 1:18 and possibly 1 Kings 8:12, with J. Gray, *op. cit.*, 108–9.

p. 184   '*Just-so' in Joshua*: J. Gray, *op. cit.*, s.v. *Aetiological Traditions* (index, p. 408).

p. 185   *Joshua 23 and 24*: E. W. Nicholson, *God and his People* (1986) ch.7; for other views, W. T. Koupmans, *Joshua 24 as Poetic Narrative* (1990); A. Rofé, *Henoch* (1982) 17, for textual problems of the ending.

p. 185   *Foreign marriage*: J. A. Emerton, *V.T.* (1976) 83.

p. 186   *Judges*: B. Halpern, *The First Historians* (1988) ch. 6, with bibliography; above all, the fine commentary of H. Alberto Soggin, *Judges* (1987, 2nd Eng. edn.), with bibliography, and W. Richter, *Die Bearbeitung des Retterbuchs in der deuteronomischen Epoche* (1964).

p. 186   *Song of Deborah*: I follow B. Lindars, *B.J.R.L.* (1982–3) 158; other views in B. Halpern, *H.T.R.* (1983) 379, with bibliography.

p. 187   *Samson's foxes:* O. Margelith, *V.T.* (1985) 224.

p. 187   *Saul and David*: J. van Seters, *In Search of History* (1983) 250–70, with bibliography.

p. 188   *2 Samuel 9 ff.*: G. von Rad, *Problem of the Hexateuch* . . . (1966, E.T.) 176–204, is classic, though not always plausible; R. N. Whybray, *The Succession Narrative* (1968), P. K. McCarter, *Interpretation* 35 (1987) 355, J. W. Flanagan, *J.B.L.* (1972) 172, and J. van Seters, *In Search of History* (1983) 277 (a later dating). All these studies see a purpose, or a genre, in this section: contrast P. R. Ackroyd, 'The Succession Narrative (So-called)', *Interpretation* 35 (1981) 383, G. Keys, *Irish Biblical Studies* (1988) 140, and D. Daube, *Ancient Jewish Law* (1981) 125–6, for sin, error and conscience.

p. 189   '*Age of Enlightenment*': G. von Rad, *The Problem of the Hexateuch* . . . (1966, E.T.) 201–4; contrast E. Meyer, *Geschichte des Altertums* II (1953, 3rd edn.) 285–6, which, like von Rad, I quote.

13 From David to Paul

I

p. 192   *Books of Chronicles*: B. Halpern, *The First Historians* (1988) 213–18, with bibliography; J. Montgomery, *J.B.L.* (1934) 46. 'Secondary' source, G. Garbini, *Henoch 3* (1981) 26–46; 'Exilic', J. van Seters, *In Search of History* (1983) 297; other chronicles, B. Halpern, 216–18; Tyrian annals, Josephus, *C. Apionem* 1.117; *A.J.* 7.144 and G. Garbini, *I Fenici* (1980) 71–86, a sceptical view.

pp. 192–3   *Introductory notices*: S. R. Bin-Nun, *V.T.* (1968) 414.

p. 193   *Time and dating*: my account is based on Jeremy Hughes, *Secrets of the Times* (1990) 55–232, which I prefer to J. Hayes, P. K. Hooker, *A New Chronology for the Kings of Israel and Judah* (1988), although they too deny the 'co-regencies'. Alternative views in E. R. Thiele, *The Mysterious Numbers of the Hebrew Kings* (1983).

p. 193   *Calendars*: I follow Jeremy Hughes, *Secrets of the Times* (1990) 159–82.

p. 194   *The '480' years*: against M. Noth, *The Deuteronomistic History* (1981, E.T.) 18–29, Jeremy Hughes, *Secrets* . . . (1990) 32–7, esp. 33 n. 17 and ch. 3.

p. 195   *The 'Acts of Solomon'*: B. Halpern, *The First Historians* (1988) ch. 7 and 208–12, for the most extreme view of D's original sources.

p. 196   *The Chronicler*: C. C. Torrey, *The Composition and Historical Value of Ezra–Nehemiah* (1896) 52, M. Noth, *The Chronicler's History* (E.T., 1987), and especially the shrewd insights of E. J. Bickerman, in L. Finkelstein, ed., *The Jews* I (1949) 77–82, are my preferred guides; also the commentary of H. G. M. Williamson (1982) and his *Israel in the Book of Chronicles* (1977). On speeches and prayers, M. Throntveit, *When Kings Speak* (1987); the bibliographical review by S. Japhet, *J.S.O.T.* (1985) 83, is valuable, as is her *Ideology of the Book of Chronicles and its Place in Hebrew Thought* (Hebrew, 1977). T. Willi, *Die Chronik als Auslegung* (1972), is a detailed study, also summarizing earlier scholarship.

p. 196   *2 Chronicles 10 ff. as history*: P. Welten, *Geschichte und Geschichtsdarstellung in den Chronikbuchern* (1973).

p. 196   *The 'Daric' coin*: H. G. M. Williamson *Tyndale Bulletin* (1977) 123.

p. 197   *Ezra–Nehemiah*: commentary by H. G. M. Williamson (1982), although we disagree about the Chronicler's role (bibliography in his *1 and 2 Chronicles* 3–17). See also my ch. 15.

p. 198   *Jonah and Daniel*: E. J. Bickerman, *Four Strange Books* . . . (1967) 1–138.

p. 198   *Ruth*: purpose discussed recently by J. Gray, *Joshua, Judges, Ruth* (1986) 368–71, and A. J. Phillips, *J.J.S.* (1986) 1.

p. 198   *Esther*: the outstanding studies are by E. J. Bickerman, *Four Strange Books* . . . (1967) 171–240 and H. Striedl, *Z.A.W.* (1937) 73; D. J. A. Clines, *Ezra, Nehemiah, Esther* (1984), is not always convincing; older articles collected by C. A. Moore, *Studies in the Book of Esther* (1982).

p. 198   *Dating*: before 167 BC, H. Bardtke, *Das Buch Esther* (1963) 252–5, and A. Momigliano, *Alien Wisdom* (1979) 90. I agree, against E. J. Bickerman, *Four Strange Books* . . . (1967) 207, and *Studies in Jewish and Christian History* I (1973) 239.

p. 199   *The Susa connection*: brilliantly exploited by E. J. Bickerman, *Four Strange Books* . . . (1967) 207–9; compare H. Striedl, *Z.A.W.* (1937) 98. On Purim, *Encyclopaedia Judaica* 13, 1390 ff. (very vivid). On the book's purpose, I disagree with W. L. Humphreys, *J.B.L.* (1973) 211 (more apt for Daniel 1–6).

p. 199   *Festival letters*: E. Schuerer, *History of the Jewish People* . . . III.1 (1986) 531–7, on 2 Macc. 1:10–36; on Greek Esther, E. J. Bickerman, *Studies* . . . I (1973) 246–74, for 78/7 date (I accept it); E. Tov, *Textus* 10 (1982) 45 on the text's status; E. Schuerer, *History of Jewish People* . . . III.1 (1986) 537–42, on the (later) 3 Macc. 6:36.

p. 199   *First Maccabees*: E. Schuerer, *History of the Jewish People* . . . III.1 (1986, rev. edn.) 180–85 (survey by G. Vermes).

pp. 199–200   *Second Maccabees*: E. Schuerer, *History* . . . III.1 (1986, rev. edn.) 537–41 (survey by M. D. Goodman) and especially C. Habicht, *H.S.C.P.* (1976) 1, on the documents.

II

p. 200   *Progression of stories*: H. Gunkel, *The Legends of Genesis* (1964, E.T.), is still challenging; subsequent studies surveyed in J. van Seters, *In Search of History* (1983) 209–37.

p. 200   *History and theology*: I quote G. von Rad, *The Problem of the Hexateuch* . . . (1966) 170, part of a magnificently wrong-headed essay.

p. 201   *Greek 'dark age'*: see also J. van Seters, *Z.A.W.* (1988) 1, for a different comparison, in several ways less apposite.

p. 201   *Jewish history-writing*: A. Momigliano, *Studies in Historiography* (1969) 260; Y. H. Yerushalmi, *Zakhor* (1982).

p. 201   *Scriptural amnesia*: W. Witakowski, *The Syriac Chronicle of Ps. Dionysius of Tel Mahre: A Study in the History of Historiography* (1987), for a good example.

p. 201   *Roman early 'history'*: I quote T. J. Cornell, in I. S. Moxon, J. Smart, A. Woodman, eds., *Past Perspectives* (1986) 83; compare T. P. Wiseman, *Roman Studies* (1987) Part III; on Livy, e.g. Preface to 1.6–7; on the scanty Roman myths, J. N. Bremmer, N. M. Horsfall, *Roman Myth and Mythography* (1987); I distinguish Jewish Midrash from mythology.

p. 202   *Samuel Butler*: I quote from *Erewhon Revisited* (1925, Shrewsbury Edition) ch. 14, 132.

III

p. 202   *The Gospels*: E. P. Sanders and Margaret Davies, *Studying the Synoptic Gospels* (1989), is now an excellent starting-point for all I discuss: their bibliographies are presupposed.

p. 203   *Sayings and authenticity*: E. P. Sanders, *Jesus and Judaism* (1985) 8–22 and ch. 4; Craig A. Evans, *Life of Jesus Research: An Annotated Bibliography* (1989) 100–112, for the various criteria on offer. The Gospel of Thomas continues to raise acute comparative problems; B. Layton, ed., *Nag Hammadi Codex II.2–7* (1989), for survey, with H. Koester, *Ancient Christian Gospels* (1990) ch. 2.3.

p. 204   *Synoptic problem*: excellent survey in E. P. Sanders, Margaret Davies, *Studying the Synoptic Gospels* (1989) 52–111, although they differ from me over Q (as does M. Goulder, *Midrash and Lection in Matthew*, 1974).

p. 204   *Synoptic authors*: C. F. Evans, *Saint Luke* (1990); M. Hengel, *Studies in the Gospel of Mark* (1985) 1–31, for the various views (and a confident one of his own); on Matthew, G. Stanton usefully surveys research in *Aufstieg und Niedergang der Romischen Welt*, ed. H. Temporini, W. Haas, Part 2.25.3 (1985); also M. Rese (on Luke) and P. Pokorny (on Mark) in the same volume.

p. 205 *John's Gospel*: fullest commentary by R. E. Brown (1966), in two vols., which I presuppose (without always following) on all I discuss; most recently, D. A. Carson, *The Gospel According to John* (1991) esp. 68–81, on authorship (against the vague 'five stages' of R. E. Brown, xxiv–xxxix); M. Hengel, *The Johannine Question* (1989, E.T.), is characteristically lucid and decisive, but often questionable; B. Lindars, *John* (1990), is the most recent survey-guide in English.

p. 205 *The epilogue*: I agree with C. H. Roberts, *J.T.S.* (1987) 409, on the prepositions' force. It is not necessarily an epilogue addressed to a special 'Johannine community'.

p. 205 *The beloved disciple*: John A. T. Robinson, *The Priority of John* (1989) 106–18, is characteristically clear and imaginative: he cites all the evidence.

pp. 205–6 *Style*: E. Ruckstuhl, *Die Literarische Einheit des Johannesevangeliums* (1987, repr.), is fundamental; I presuppose the further bibliography in M. Hengel, *The Johannine Question* (1989, E.T.) 88–110 and 202–8. Note especially A. J. Festugière, *Observations stylistiques sur L'Évangile de S. Jean* (1974) esp. 28 ff. and 123.

p. 206 *Use of Greek scripture*: G. D. Kilpatrick, in F. L. Cross, ed., *Studies in the Fourth Gospel* (1957) 36–45.

p. 206 *Fourth Gospel and scrolls*: M. Hengel, *Johannine Community* (1989) 111–12, with bibliography, esp. H. Braun, *Qumran und das N.T.* II (1966) 112 ff.

p. 206 *Jewish framework*: M. Hengel, *Johannine Community* (1989) 111, with notes. On the festivals, Josephus, *B.J.* 2.19.1, with F. Millar, in P. R. Davies, R. T. White, eds., *A Tribute to Geza Vermes* (1990) 361–2, 379–80 (important).

p. 207 *'The Jews'*: J. Louis Martyn, *History and Theology in the Fourth Gospel* (1979), is clear-headed, although wrong about Jamnia; M. Hengel, *Johannine Community* (1989) 213 and 215, for further studies; E. Graesser, *N.T.S.* (1964–5) 74 and J. Ashton, *N.T.S.* (1989) 40.

p. 208 *John son of Zebedee*: P. Parker, *J.B.L.* (1962) 35, lists twenty-one arguments against, of varying merit.

p. 208 *John, Mark and the Synoptics*: H. Windisch, *Johannes und die Synoptiker* (1926), and C. K. Barrett, *The Gospel According to St John* (1978, 2nd edn.) 42, with bibliography.

p. 209 *Acts of the Apostles*: the fine commentary of E. Haenchen, *Acts of the Apostles* (1971, E.T.), is basic, although I disagree fundamentally with its 'historical' sections: pp. 81 ff. for sources and 'we'. W. W. Gasque, *A History of the Criticism of the Acts* . . . (1975), for scholarship which I presuppose before forming my view in the text; C. J. Hemer, *The Book of Acts in the Setting of Hellenistic History* (1989), goes in the directions I have long judged correct, but by different routes and arguments: pp. 312–34 survey the 'we' controversy.

p. 209   *Council in Acts 15*: I accept much of M. Dibelius, *Studies in the Acts of the Apostles* (1956, E.T.) 93 ff.; Acts 15 is heavily shaped by the author and does not 'challenge' the primary Galatians 2:1–10. M. Hengel, *Acts and the History of Earliest Christianity* (1979) ch. 10, for an attempted reconstruction.

p. 210   *Paul and Acts*: E. Haenchen, *Acts* . . . (1971) 112 ff., for a check-list of 'difficulties'.

p. 210   *Author as researcher*: I will amplify this elsewhere, but mention J. Wells, *Studies in Herodotus* (1923) 95 (however speculative in places), for the approach to oral informants which (I believe) explains so much in Acts. M. Hengel, *Between Jesus and Paul* (1983) 97, is basic, on the author's geography.

p. 211   *Speeches*: M. Dibelius, *Studies in the Acts* . . . (1956, E.T.) ch. 9, is basic, but too focused on 'the classics', not the Greek scriptures: so, also, E. Pluemacher, 'Lukas als Griechischer Historiker'. Pauly *Realencyclopaedia* . . . Supplement XIV (1974) 235–63, a valuable survey.

p. 211   *'Plan' of God*: Acts 2:28. 4:27, 13:36, 20:27.

14 Digging and Travelling

The best general guide is P. R. S. Moorey, revised edition of K. Kenyon, *The Bible and Recent Archaeology* (1987), to which I am greatly indebted; see also H. D. Lance, *The Old Testament and the Archaeologist* (1983). For quite a different approach, K. A. Kitchen, *The Bible in Its World* (1977).

I

p. 213   *Early pilgrims*: E. D. Hunt, *Holy Land Pilgrimage in the Later Roman Empire* . . . (1982), a brilliant account, with bibliography: pp. 3 ff. (on the Cave), with index, s.v.Bethlehem.

p. 213   *Origen*: *De Princip.* 4.3 (Hebron); *C. Celsum* 4.44 (the wells); Comm. on John 6:40–41 (Gadarene swine).

pp. 213–14   *Bordeaux pilgrim*: *Itinerarium Burdigalense*, ed. P. Geyer, O. Cuntz (Corp. Christ. Lat. 175, 1965, 1) with E. D. Hunt, *Holy Land Pilgrimage* . . . (1982) 55 ff., 82 ff.

p. 214   *Holy Sepulchre*: I quote E. D. Hunt, *Holy Land Pilgrimage* . . . (1982) 8; P. W. L. Walker, *Holy City, Holy Places* (1990) ch. 8, for fuller discussion.

p. 214   *Nails of Cross*: Ambrose, *De Obitu Theodosii*, ed. Fuller (C.S.E.L. 1955) 47.

p. 214   *Burning Bush*: *Itin. Egeriae* 4.6–52, with J. Wilkinson, *Egeria's Travels* (1971), and E. D. Hunt, *Holy Land Pilgrimage* . . . (1982) 86 ff.

pp. 214–15   *Renan*: A. Dupont–Sommer, *E. Renan et ses voyages* (1973, Institut de France) 14 ff., with my quotations from R.'s *Vie de Jésus*.

p. 215   *Ignatius of Loyola*: I quote the Second Contemplation, in the *Spiritual Exercises*, trans. by T. Corbishley (1964) 47 ff.

p. 216   *Palestine Exploration Fund*: Roger Moorey, *Excavation in Palestine* (1981) 20 ff., 110 ff.

p. 217   *Woolley and Ur*: H. V. F. Winstone, *Woolley of Ur* (190) is now the most vivid and useful account, esp. chs. 6–9.

p. 217   *Abraham*: Nicolaos of Damascus, in Josephus *A.J.* 1.159. I quote L. Woolley, *Abraham* (1936) 132, see chs. 3–5. On the legend, T. L. Thompson, *The Historicity of the Patriarchal Narratives* (1974), is fundamental; also J. van Seters, *Abraham in History and Tradition* (1975).

p. 220   *Ebla*: useful survey in L. Vigano, *Biblical Archaeologist* (1984) 6–16, with Paolo Matthiae, in same issue, pp. 19 ff.; contrast D. N. Freedman, *Biblical Archaeologist* (1978) 143, with p. 153 for the Quadrangle Club breakfast; on the 'past hullabaloo', I quote J. D. Muhly, *Biblical Archaeologist* (1984) 29; for scribal name-lists, R. D. Biggs, 'Ebla and Abu Salabikh' in L. Cagni, ed., *La Lingua di Ebla* (1981) 121.

II

p. 223   *Literacy*: A. R. Millard, in J. Aviram, ed., *Biblical Archaeology Today* (1986) 301; also M. Haran, in J. Emerton, ed., *Congress Volume Jerusalem 1986* (1988) 81. The date of the Gezer calendar is uncertain, perhaps no earlier than *c.* 870–850 BC.

pp. 223–4   *Egyptian chronology*: E. F. Wente, C. C. van Siclen, in *Studies in Honor of George R. Hughes* (1976) 217; for a sceptical (and radical) alternative, P. J. James, in *Studies in Ancient Chronology* I (1987) chs. 9–10. I have not followed his suggested revisions in what follows.

pp. 224–5   *Joshua's conquests*: P. R. S. Moorey, rev. edn. K. Kenyon, *The Bible and Recent Archaeology* (1987) 69 ff., for survey of the key evidence; V. Fritz, *Biblical Archaeologist* (1987) 84, is the most careful recent survey with bibliography, which I presuppose; an earlier survey by M. Weippert, *The Settlement of the Israelite Tribes in Palestine* (1971), sets out rival theories; K. L. Younger, *Ancient Conquest Accounts* (1990) 197–265, and K. W. Whitelam, *J.S.O.T.* (1989) 19, for another perspective. Also R. Drews, *J.S.O.T.* (1989) 15, on chariots, iron and late chronology.

p. 225   *Merneptah stele*: J. B. Pritchard, *Ancient Near Eastern Texts relating to the O.T.* (1969, 3rd edn.) 376–8, with notes; more bibliography in the recent study by L. E. Stager, in B. Mazar, Y. Yadin, eds., *Nahman Avigad Volume* (1985) 56, important; also I. Singer, *B.A.S.O.R.* 261 (1988) 1.

p. 226   *Cypriote Bichrome*: P. R. S. Moorey, *J.T.S.* (1980) 112; opposed by J.

Bimson, *Redating the Exodus and Conquest* (1981, 2nd edn.), who is challenged again by (e.g.) B. Halpern, *B. A. Rev.* 13 (1987): Bimson answers in *B. A. Rev.* 14 (1988) 52.

pp. 226–7   *Jericho*: J. R. Bartlett, *Jericho* (1982) 83–107, esp. 107.

p. 228   *Hazor*: V. Fritz, *Biblical Archaeologist* (1987) 88, on the pottery dating. On the Song of Deborah, I follow B. Lindars, *B.J.R.L.* (1982–3) 158.

p. 229   *'Site shift'*: I quote K. A. Kitchen, *The Bible in Its World* (1977) 88.

pp. 229–30   *Joshua and circumcision*: I owe this to E. J. Bickerman, *Jews in the Greek Age* (1988) 179, which I quote; for the textual history of the LXX, H. Orlinsky, *V.T.S.* (1969) 187.

pp. 230–31   *Israelite settlement*: P. R. S. Moorey, rev. edn. K. Kenyon, *The Bible and Recent Archaeology* (1987) 77–84, with bibliography; V. Fritz, *Biblical Archaeologist* (1987) 92–9, likewise, with R. B. Coote and K. W. Whitelam, *The Emergence of Israel in Historical Perspective* (1987).

p. 232   *Israelite revolutionaries*: above all, N. K. Gottwald, *The Tribes of Israel* (1979); a general critique by E. W. Nicholson, in *A Word in Season: Essays . . . W. McKane,* eds., J. D. Martin, P. R. Davies (*J.S.O.T.* Supplement 42, 1986) 3, esp. 11 ff.

15 Fifth Gospels

I

p. 234   *Tirzah*: P. R. S. Moorey, rev. edn. of K. Kenyon, *The Bible and Recent Archaeology* (1987) 127, also 88–9.

p. 234   *Siloam tunnel*: G. E. Wright, *Biblical Archaeology* (1962) 172–4, and J. B. Pritchard, *Ancient Near Eastern Texts . . .* (1969) 321, for the inscription.

p. 234   *Lachish*: D. Ussishkin, *The Conquest of Lachish by Sennacherib* (1982) 25; for alternatives, P. J. James, *Studies in Ancient Chronology* 1 (1987) 60–62.

p. 234   *Jerusalem*: K. Kenyon, *Digging Up Jerusalem* (1974) ch. 9.

p. 235   *Ahab's ivories*: rejected by I. Winter, *Iraq* (1981) 124.

p. 235   *Arad temple*: not Solomonic, acc. to D. Ussishkin, *I.E.J.* (1988) 142.

p. 235   *Troy*: I quote Sir Denis Page.

p. 236   *Solomonic gateways*: P. R. S. Moorey, rev. edn. of K. Kenyon, *The Bible . . .* (1987) 98–104, for summary.

p. 236   *Solomon's stables*: G. I. Davies *P.E.Q.* (1988) 130, for important revision.

p. 237   *'Villages'*: I quote J. B. Pritchard, ed., *Solomon and Sheba* (1974) 35.

p. 237   *Tell Qasile text*: B. Maisler, *J.N.E.S.* (1951) 265.

p. 238   *Ezion-geber*: discussion by A. Flinders, *B.A. Rev.* 15 (1989) 30; P. R. S. Moorey, *op. cit.* (1987) 105–6.

p. 238   *Solomon's mines*: B. Rothenberg, *Timna* (1972); I am unconvinced by J. J. Bimson, *Tyndale Bulletin* (1981) 124.

p. 238 *Solomon's trading*: J. D. Hawkins, *Cambridge Ancient History* III.1 (1982, rev. edn.) 372.

p. 239 *Horse-trading*: J. Gray, *I and II Kings; A Commentary* (1970) 269, a sceptical view.

pp. 239–40 *Solomon's gold*: A. R. Millard, *Vox Evangelica* (1981) 5; A. R. Millard and K. A. Kitchen, *B.A. Rev.* 15 (1989) 20 and 30.

p. 240 *Osorkon's gold*: K. A. Kitchen, in J. A. Emerton, ed., *Congress Volume* 1986 (1988, Supplement to *V.T.*) 117–9, with bibliography.

pp. 240–41 *Cyrus and the Temple*: D. Stronach, in J. Aviram, ed., *Biblical Archaeology Today* (1986) 484; compare his *Pasargadae* (1978) 62.

p. 242 *Psalmists' imagery*: O. Keel, *The Symbolism of the Biblical World* (1978), to be used critically.

p. 242 *Pigs at Hazor*: Y. Yadin, *Hazor* (1979) 181–2.

p. 243 *Kuntillet Ajrud*: Z. Meshel, *Kuntillet Ajrud* (Jerusalem, 1978); B. Otzen, *S.E.A.* 54 (1989) 151; J. Day, *J.B.L.* (1986) 385; D. N. Freedman, *B.A.* (1987) 241; W. G. Dever, *B.A.S.O.R.* 255 (1984) 21; and Z. Zevit, *B.A.S.O.R.* 255 (1984) 39. I disagree with J. Tigay, *I.E.J.* (1990) 218.

II

M. Hengel, *The 'Hellenization' of Judea in the First Century* AD (1989), discusses the evidence clearly, but his inferences are not always convincing; on sites, J. Wilkinson, *Jerusalem as Jesus Knew It* (1988, 2nd edn.), is fundamental with P. R. S. Moorey, rev. ed. of K. M. Kenyon, *The Bible and Archaeology* (1987) 154–83; A. R. Millard, *Discoveries from the Time of Jesus* (1990), is more popular and optimistic.

p. 244 *Herod's lifestyle*: M. Hengel, *The 'Hellenization' of Judea . . .* (1989) 11–12, 35 ff.; J. Yellin, J. Gunneweg, *I.E.J.* (1989) 85, flowerpots; K. L. Geleison, *B.A.I.A.S.* 7 (1987–8) 21, gardens.

p. 244 *Ossuary inscriptions*: L. Y. Rahmani, in M. Hengel, *The 'Hellenization' . . .* (1989) 10 and 66–7.

p. 244 *Goliath family*: R. Hachlili, *B.A.S.O.R.* (1979) 31.

p. 245 *The Baptist and Machaira*: S. Loffreda, *Antonianum* (1983) 112–22.

p. 245 *Temple stonework*: A. F. Rainey, *B.A.S.O.R.* 272 (1988) 69.

p. 246 *Uncertain landmarks*: J. Wilkinson, *Jerusalem as Jesus Knew It* (1988) 162–4 (Emmaus), 127–30 (Gethsemane), 133–6 (House of Caiaphas), 140–45 (Pilate's palace).

p. 246 *Acts' ship*: J. S. Morrison, J. F. Coates, *The Athenian Trireme* (1986) 197–200

p. 246 *Bethesda*: J. Jeremias, *Die Wiederentdeckung von Bethesda* (1949), with J. Wilkinson, *Jerusalem as Jesus Knew It* (1988) 98–104.

p. 247 *Bone-boxes*: E. J. Bickerman, *Jews in the Greek Age* (1988) 273, important;

E. M. Meyers, *J.Q.R.* (1971–2) 95; R. Hachlili, A Killebrew, *P.E.Q.* (1983) 109; L. Y. Rahmani, *P.E.Q.* (1986) 96.

p. 247 *'Tomb of Christ'*: summary in P. W. L. Walker, *Holy City, Holy Places* (1990) ch. 8, with the excellent account by J. Wilkinson, *Jerusalem as Jesus Knew It* (1988); C. Couasnon, *The Church of the Holy Sepulchre in Jerusalem* (1974), an important survey, and V. C. Corbo, *Il Santo Sepulcro di Gerusalemme* (1981), too optimistic; Z. Rubin, in L. I. Levine, ed., *Jerusalem Cathedra* 2 (1982) 79, is usefully sceptical.

p. 248 *Garden Tomb*: J. Wilkinson, *Jerusalem as Jesus Knew It* (1988) 198–9; W. S. McBirine, *The Search for the Authentic Tomb of Jesus* (1979), is unconvincing.

p. 248 *Crucified skeleton*: N. Haas, *I.E.J.* (1970) 38, corrected by J. Zias, E. Sekeles, *I.E.J.* (1985) 22; in general, M. Hengel, *The Cross of the Son of God* (1986).

p. 249 *Aloes*: F. N. Hepper, *P.E.Q.* (1988) 146.

pp. 250–51 *Shroud of Turin*: Joe Nickell, *An Inquest on the Shroud of Turin* (1983) is an acute exposé by a private detective; A. Cameron, *The Sceptic and the Shroud* (1980), on the supposed Edessa link: N. Kokkinos, *Ainigmata* 70 (1981) 32–7, with good bibliography; A. R. Millard, *Discoveries from the Time of Jesus* (1990) 136 ff., on the scientific tests; L. Fossati, *La Santa Sindone, Nuova Luce su Antichi Documenti* (1961), discusses the contemporary texts; Ian Wilson, *Holy Faces, Secret Places* (1991) 14 ff., gives translated extracts (the book is evasive); L. Kuryuluk, *Veronica and Her Cloth* (1991), expands on related 'veronicas'.

16 Concurrent Heathens

J. B. Pritchard, *Ancient Near Eastern Texts Relating to the Old Testament* (1969, rev. edn.), remains a basic source; John R. Bartlett, *The Bible: Faith and Evidence* (1990) chs. 3–8, is a balanced up-to-date guide; J. A. Soggin, *A History of Israel from the Beginning to the Bar Kochba Revolt* (1984), and J. M. Miller, J. H. Hayes, *A History of Ancient Israel and Judah* (1986), are up-to-date histories with a clear sense of evidence; G. Garbini, *History and Ideology in Ancient Israel* (1988), is a stimulating, though generally unsuccessful, attack on many points of accepted historicity.

I

p. 252 *Egypt and Joseph*: S. Israelit Groll, ed., *Pharaonic Egypt: The Bible and Christianity* (1986), for various aspects of the 'overlap'; J. Vergotte, 289 ff., is not convincing in its date for the Joseph story. On Genesis 41:42, note W. Hallo, *Biblical Archaeologist* (1983) 25: he relates the obscure cry of 'Abrek' to an Assyrian status, with obvious consequences for (impossibly) early datings of the Joseph source at this point.

p. 253 *Genesis 14*: J. A. Emerton, in J. A. Emerton, ed., *Studies in the Pentateuch*

(Supplement to *V.T.* 41; 1990) 73 ff., with bibliography: the first section is 'to be dated not earlier than the 7th century and it may be later still'.

pp. 253–4   *'Shishak'*: K. A. Kitchen, *Third Intermediate Period in Egypt* (1977) 72–6, 298–303, with E. F. Wente, *J.N.E.S.* (1976) 275–8; G. Garbini, *History and Ideology in Ancient Israel* (1988) 29 ff., a more radical view. P. J. James, I. J. Thorpe, N. Kokkinos, J. A. Frankish in *Studies in Ancient Chronology* I (1987), have attacked the entire accepted framework of Bronze to Iron Age dating: their work does, at least, bring out the centrality of Egyptian evidence very well; E. F. Winte, C. C. von Siclen in, *Studies in Honor of George R. Hughes* (1976) 217, for an alternative, coherent view.

p. 254   *Deir Alla*: J. A. Hackett, *The Balaam Text from Deir' Alla* (1984).

II

Outline history of the Omrids is in A. Soggin, *A History of Israel* (1984) 203 ff., and J. Maxwell Miller, J. H. Hayes, *A History of Ancient Israel and Judah* (1986) ch. 8; also S. Timm, *Die Dynastie Omri* (1982). The most helpful English commentary is G. H. Jones, *1 and 2 Kings* (1984) in the New Century Bible Commentary series: I presuppose his bibliographies, though not always his conclusions.

p. 255   *Battle of 853 BC*: J. A. Brinkman, *J.C.S.* (1978) 173, for date; a translated text of the Assyrian Monolith Inscription is in J. Maxwell Miller, J. H. Hayes, *A History of Ancient Israel . . .* (1986) 258–9, 261.

p. 256   *Wars of 840s*: M. Elat, *I.E.J.* (1974) 25.

pp. 256–8   *Ahab's death*: 1 Kings 20–22:38, with esp. 1 Kings 21:19. I agree with much of C. F. Whitley, *V.T.* (1952) 137; compare J. M. Miller, *V.T.* (1967) 307, and *Z.A.W.* (1968) 337. See, too Jeremy Hughes, *Secrets of the Times . . .* (1990) 187–8 and his important n. 60. G. H. Jones, *1 and 2 Kings* II (1984) 336 ff., 360 ff., 371, rehearses alternative views.

pp. 256–7   *Greek text's Ahab*: D. W. Gooding, *Z.A.W.* (1964) 269, with whose conclusions I do not altogether agree.

p. 258   *Moabite war*: J. M. Millar, *J.B.L.* (1966) 441.

p. 258   *Mesha's Inscription*: English translation in J. Maxwell Miller, J. H. Hayes, *A History of Ancient Israel . . .* (1986) 283; for its discovery, N. Silberman, *Digging for God and Country* (1982). An extreme view of its conflict with the Bible in G. Garbini, *History and Ideology in Ancient Israel* (1988, E.T.) 33–8.

pp. 259–60   *2 Kings 1–3 and chronology*: clear summaries in Jeremy Hughes, *Secrets of the Times* (1990) 89–93 (the Greek LXX) and 182–90 (rejecting 2 Kings 1:17).

p. 260   *Jehu's submission*: the Black Obelisk text, excerpted in J. Maxwell Miller, J. H. Hayes, *A History of Ancient Israel . . .* (1986) 286.

p. 260   *Jezebel and Psalm 45*: Ahab was proposed by F. Hitzig in 1863; he is the 'only known case of an Israelite king marrying a daughter of Tyre' (W. O. Oesterley, *The Psalms*, 1953, 250) and is preferable, therefore, to other alternatives (Jehu; Jereboam II or Joram and Athaliah), for which see E. B. Briggs, *The Psalms: I.C.C. Commentary* I (1906) 384.

p. 261   *Jezebel and Dido*: this emerges from Josephus, *C. Apionem* 1.123–5 (Jezebel was King Ithobal's daughter).

III

p. 262   *Kings as history*: I quote E. W. Heaton, *The Hebrew Kingdoms* (1968) 63.

p. 262   *Babylonian chronicle*: D. J. Wiseman, *Chronicles of Chaldaean Kings in the British Museum* (1956), is fundamental; A. K. Grayson, *Assyrian and Babylonian Chronicles* (1975) and *Babylonian Historical–Literary Texts* (1975); also his article in *Orientalia* (1980) 140.

pp. 262–4   *The chronicle and biblical narrative, 609–598 BC*: details in D. J. Wiseman, *Nebuchadnezzar and Babylon* (1985) 12–33, with Jeremy Hughes, *Secrets of the Times* (1990) 225–9. They give further bibliography.

p. 264   *Jehoiachin and rations*: D. J. Wiseman, *Nebuchadnezzar . . .* (1985) 81 ff. For the date of his release (in 561 BC, Jeremy Hughes, *Secrets . . .* (1990) 157.

p. 265   *Siege of 587 BC*: I follow Jeremy Hughes, *Secrets . . .* (1990) 229.

p. 265   *Seals of Baruch and others*: N. Avigad, *Biblical Archaeologist* (1979) 114.

p. 265   *Jar-handles*: W. F. Albright, *J.B.L.* (1932) 77 and (1943) 66; Wiseman, *Nebuchadnezzar . . .* (1985) 82.

pp. 265–6   *Lachish potsherds*: ambitiously used by H. Torczyner, *The Lachish Letters* (1938); for translation and bibliography, J. B. Pritchard, *Ancient Near Eastern Texts Relating to the O.T.* (1969) 321–2. The dating and significance are still open questions.

p. 266   *Number of exiles*: 2 Kings 25:11–12; Jeremiah 52:28–30.

p. 266   *Gardener in exile*: E. F. Weidner, in *Mélanges syriens . . . à René Dussand* II (1939) 927; 'Salamyama' the gardener would be Shelemaiah (compare Jeremiah 36:14).

pp. 266–7   *Nebuchadnezzar's inscriptions*: E. J. Bickerman, *Studies in Jewish and Christian History* III (1986) 282, with bibliography; compare D. J. Wiseman, *Nebuchadnezzar . . .* (1985) 98–104, although his attempts to use Daniel 1–6 for history of this period are all misguided.

IV

Of recent commentaries, the fullest is by H. G. M. Williamson (1985) in the Word Biblical series, vol. 16; he has also published a shorter version (1989) as an Old Testament Guide. D. J. A. Clines, *Ezra, Nehemiah, Esther* (1984), is also usefully up to date.

I disagree with Williamson at various historical points, but especially in his view that Ezra belongs in 458, preceding Nehemiah in 445 and that the author of the books is not the Chronicler.

Bibliography on the dating is endless: H. H. Rowley, *The Servant of the Lord and Other Essays* (1965) 137–68 and *Men of God* (1963) 211–76 cover the main issues. Morton Smith, *Palestinian Parties and Politics* (1971), is particularly interesting on Nehemiah's reforms; W. Hinz, *Darius und die Perser* (1976) ch. 6, gives the Rebuilding more of a context; E. J. Bickerman, *Studies in Jewish and Christian History* III (1986) 327, solves the chronological problem of Nehemiah 1:2.

B. B. Porten, *Archives from Elephantine* (1968), and G. R. Driver, *Aramaic Documents* (1956), with D. M. Lewis, *Sparta and Persia* (1977), are ways into the (increasing) evidence of the Persian Empire; compare L. Robert, *C.R.A.I.* (1975) 306, for another cult's Persian regulation. The most relevant seals, of disputed date, are published by N. Avigad, *Bullae and Seals from a Post-exilic Judaean Archive* (1976).

p. 270   *Edicts*: E. J. Bickerman, *Studies in Jewish and Christian History* I (1976) 72–108; on the 'Cyrus Cylinder', A. Kuhrt, *J.S.O.T.* (1983) 83; on Second Isaiah, A. Kuhrt, in M. Beard and J. North, eds., *Pagan Priests* (1990) 128, esp. 144–6, and (an extreme view) G. Garbini, *History and Ideology in Ancient Israel* (1988, E.T.) ch. 7, with bibliography, however, on Persian 'royal style'.

p. 271   *Date*: P. R. Ackroyd, in A. Kuhrt and H. Sancisi-Weedenburg, *Achaemenid History* III (1988) 33, a general survey of method.

p. 272   *Haggai and Zechariah*: evidence and argument in E. J. Bickerman, *Studies* . . . III (1986) 331–6.

p. 272   *Nebuchadnezzar IV*: Darius, Behistun Inscription, Old Persian 49–50: there is a better version, with a greater awareness of the variants between languages, in O. Kaiser, ed., *Texte aus der Umwelt der A.T.* I (1982–5) 419, by W. Hinz and K. Borger.

p. 273   *Aramaic text of Darius's inscription*: J. Greenfield and B. Porten, *The Bisitun Inscription of Darius the Great: The Aramaic Version* (1982).

pp. 273–4   *Beyond the River and its governors*: A. L. Oppenheim, in *Cambridge History of Iran* II (1985) 563–5; on Tattenai, A. T. Olmstead, *J.N.E.S.* (1944) 46. (i) Gubaru/Gobryas was 'governor of Babylon and Beyond the River': he is known there on 12 November 535 and 20 September 525. (ii) Probably, Gubaru continued until the revolt of Nidintu-Bel (Nebuchadnezzar III), attested on 3 October 522. (iii) After the two 'False Nebuchadnezzars', Ustani is holder of this same job, attested on 21 March 520 and in June 516. (iv) Only one tablet attests Ta-at-[tan-ni], on 5 June 502. He is 'governor' (*pahat*) of Beyond the River: see Olmstead, *J.N.E.S.* (1944) 46. It is possible for a *pahat* to be a subordinate to a satrap. Ta-at[. . .] may have been a subordinate in the time of Ustani's satrapy; he may, then, be the biblical Tattenai of Ezra 5:6. It is not, however, certain.

p. 274   *Petitions to Darius*: R. Meiggs, D. M. Lewis, *Greek Historical Inscriptions* (1969) no. 12; with L. Robert *B.C.H.* (1977) 77–98; A. E. Cowley, *Aramaic Papyri of the Fifth Century* BC (1923) no. 30.

V

p. 275   *Jewish names*: E. J. Bickerman, *Studies in Jewish and Christian History* III (1986) 299–326.

p. 276   *Ration documents*: D. M. Lewis, *Sparta and Persia* (1977) ch. 1, for Elamite and Greek evidence, and also (pp. 5–6) G. R. Driver, *Aramaic Documents of the Fifth Century* BC (1956) no. VI.

p. 276   *'Seven counsellors'*: Ezra 7:14 with (e.g.) Herodotus 3.84; Darius, Behistun Inscript. O.P. 68–9 lists six helpers for Darius the Seventh.

p. 277   *Jewish secretary*: A. E. Cowley, *Aramaic Papyri* . . . (1923) no. 26.23 (D. M. Lewis suggests a comparison with Persepolis Fortification Tablets 1561, 1947 for scribes who do not write); compare Cowley, no. 21, perhaps 30.19 and 38.4–10.

p. 277   *Darius and law*: E. Meyer, *Kleine Schriften* II (1924) 91–100, on Egypt in 519; G. Posener, *La Première Domination Perse en Égypte* (1936) 36–41.

p. 277   *Cupbearer*: Hdts. 3.34, with D. M. Lewis, *Sparta and Persia* (1977) 20: on the queen's drinking, Heracleides of Kyme, *ap. Athenaeus* 4.145, suits both Nehemiah's and Esther's picture.

pp. 277–8   *Letters and escort*: A. E. Cowley, *Aramaic Papyri* . . . (1923) no. 26; bread, dinners and land in (e.g.) Hdts. 1.192, Thuc. 1.138; R. Lane Fox, *Alexander the Great* (1973) 515–16.

p. 278   *'Dinaites', etc., at Nehemiah 4:9*: W. Eilers, *Iranische Beamtennamen* (1940) 30–40; against, K. Galling, *Z.A.W.* (1951) 66.

p. 278   *Memoirs*: Solon, in J. M. Edmonds, ed., *Elegy and Iambus* I (1968) 146–54, with translations; the Egyptian Udjahorresnet, in J. Blenkinsopp, *J.B.L.* (1987) 409–21.

p. 279   *Esther and Chiliarch*: E. J. Bickerman, *Four Strange Books* . . . (1967) 206–7, with D. M. Lewis, *Sparta and Persia* (1977) 17–19.

pp. 279–80   *Johanan the Priest*: A. E. Cowley, *Aramaic Papyri* . . . (1923) 30.18 (408 BC), with the small coin in D. Barag, *Biblical Archaeologist* (1985) 166–8, and J. W. Betlyon, *J.B.L.* (1986) 633, esp. 639–40. However, the dating of this type as a 'Group IV' in ?345–332 BC is entirely conjectural: the heads are no less close to those of the Persian king issued earlier at Sidon. C. J. Howgego reminds me that Barag's reading is not yet certain, that a further hoard associates over 100 Hezekiah coins with Ptolemaic coins and that on (subjective) style, the facing heads of these coins suggest, e.g., the small silver dynastic coins from Cilicia, *c.* 380–370 BC. 'Johanan', if true, still floats between *c.* 380 and the early Ptolemaic age.

p. 280   *Sanballats and Papyri*: F. M. Cross, *Wadi Daliyeh* II (1974) 18; *J.B.L.* (1975) 4, for the new evidence. I do not share Cross's reconstruction: G. Widengren in J. H. Hayes, J. Maxwell Miller, *Israelite and Judaean History* (1990, 3rd edn.) 506 ff., refutes it; so, also, the points made by L. Grabbe, *J.B.L.* (1987) 231.

p. 280   *Mission in 445 BC*: H. T. Wade-Gery, *Essays in Greek History* (1958) 201, esp. 219, with D. M. Lewis, *Sparta and Persia* (1977) 51, 153, with notes. On Ezra, O. Margalith, *Z.A.W.* (1986) 110.

p. 281   *Mission in 380s*: troubles on coast, in I. Eph'al, *Cambridge Ancient History* 4 (1988, 2nd edn.) 145, with bibliography.

17 Jesus on Trial

The historical study by A. N. Sherwin-White, *Roman Society and Roman Law in the New Testament* (1963), raises many of the main problems concisely, although the answers and discussions are not always cogent. G. B Caird, *The Apostolic Age* (1987, 2nd edn.), is also clear and positive; among books on the historical Jesus, E. P. Sanders, *Jesus and Judaism* (1985), is outstanding, both in method and scope. On Jesus's arrest and trial, the essential study is by E. J. Bickerman, now in his *Studies in Jewish and Christian History* III (1986) 82.

I

p. 283   *Aphrodisias inscription*: J. Reynolds, R. Tannenbaum, *Jews and Godfearers at Aphrodisias* (*Cambridge Philol. Soc.,* Supplement vol. 1987), with (among others) M. D. Goodman, *J.R.S.* (1988) 261.

p. 284   *Bigamous Jew*: N. Lewis, *The Documents from the Bar Kockha Period in the Cave of Letters: Greek Papyri* (1989) 22–6, 113–15 (text).

p. 284   *Josephus on Jesus*: E. Schuerer, *The History of the Jewish People in the Age of Jesus Christ* I (rev. edn. 1973) 43–63.

p. 284   *'Megistanes'*: Mark 6:21; A. N. Sherwin-White, *Roman Society and Roman Law in the New Testament* (1963) 136–7; F. Cumont, *L'Égypte des astrologues* (1937) 34–9.

p. 284   *Jesus and cities*: G. E. M. de Sainte Croix, in D. Baker, ed., *Studies in Church History* (1975) 3–9.

pp. 284–5   *Provincial context*: most ambitiously pursued in G. Theissen, *Lokalkolorit und Zeitgeschichte in den Evangelien* (1990); also A. N. Sherwin-White, *Roman Society and Roman Law in the N.T.* (1963) 120–43.

p. 285   *Unreal disputes*: I quote E. P. Sanders, *Jesus and Judaism* (1985) 218–21.

p. 286   *'Galilaean holy man'*: I quote G. Vermes, *Jesus the Jew* (1973) 83, by whose 'Jesus' I am seldom persuaded.

pp. 286–7 *Josephus and other criminals*: E. Rivkin, *What Crucified Jesus?* (1986), has the great merit of using Josephus's histories intelligently; Jos., *A.J.* 20.97–8 (Theudas), *A.J.* 20.169–71 and *B.J.* 2.261–3 (the Egyptian), *A.J.* 18.116–19 (the Baptist).

p. 287 *The other Jesus, in 62*: Jos., *B.J.* 6.300–309; E. Rivkin, however, lays too little emphasis on the 'kingdom' in the arrest of the Gospel Jesus.

p. 288 *'Trial of Jesus'*: I owe most to E. J. Bickerman, *Studies in Jewish and Christian History* III (1986) 82; also, now, compare F. Millar, in P. R. Davies and R. T. White, eds., *A Tribute to Geza Vermes* (1990) 355–81. Other versions of importance include A. E. Harvey, *Jesus and the Constraints of History* (1981); J. Bowker, *Jesus and the Pharisees* (1973) 42–52; P. Winter, *On the Trial of Jesus* (1974, 2nd edn.); A. N. Sherwin-White, *Roman Society and Roman Law in the New Testament* (1963) 24–47; and J. Blinzler, *The Trial of Jesus* (1959).

p. 289 *Sanhedrin as court*: Mishnah Sanhedrin, in *The Mishnah*, ed. and transl. H. Danby (1933) 382; 'blasphemy' in Mish. San. 7.5.

p. 289 *Agrippa on Pilate*: Philo, *Embassy to Gaius*, 301, with P. Winter, *On the Trial of Jesus* (1961) 51.

p. 290 *'A' synedrion*: E. Rivkin, *What Crucified Jesus?* (1986), for one such approach; M. D. Goodman, *The Ruling Class of Judaea* . . . (1987) 112–16, for a more extreme one which I do not share; E. P. Sanders, *Jesus and Judaism* (1985) 312 ff., and a subsequent Oxford seminar in 1988, doubting a formal Sanhedrin's role. I attach weight to Acts 21:30 ff. (in my view, of course, a primary source, here).

p. 290 *Papyrus records of trials*: E. J. Bickerman, *Studies in Jewish and Christian History* III (1986) 164–71: p. 166 n. 65, 167 (by implication), 169 n. 87, for governments yielding to crowds.

p. 290 *'Blasphemy'*: E. J. Bickerman, *Studies in Jewish and Christian History* III (1986) 88–90.

p. 291 *Mark 14:64*: E. J. Bickerman, *Studies* . . . III (1986) 91–3.

pp. 291–2 *Trial and Roman law*: A. N. Sherwin-White, *Roman Society and Roman Law in the N.T.* (1963) 24–47, esp. 32, 47; compare E. J. Bickerman, *Studies* . . . III (1986) 164–71, on cognitio and 'pro tribunali'.

p. 292 *The Mockery in Alexandria*: Philo, *Against Flaccus*, 36–9.

p. 292 *'Old clothes' and law*: Digest 48.20.6

p. 293 *Threefold questioning*: Martyrdom of Polycarp 12 (ed. H. Muserillo, *Acts of Christian Martyrs*, 1976); J. Bremmer, *Vig. Christ.* (1985) 112.

p. 293 *Sanhedrin's powers*: E. Schuerer, *History of the Jewish People* II (1973, rev. edn.) 221–3; F. Millar, in P. R. Davies and R. T. White, *A Tribute to Geza Vermes* (1990) 374–6.

II

p. 294   T. Mommsen: Römisches Strafrecht (1899) 240–41.

p. 294   E. J. Bickerman: 'Utilitas Crucis', in R.H.R (1935) 169 = Studies in Jewish and Christian History III (1986) 82.

pp. 294–5   Dating: R. E. Brown, Commentary on Gospel ... St John II (1966) 555–6 (the Last Supper), 882–3 (Passover).

p. 294–304   The Gospel accounts: my discussion is based firmly on Bickerman's op. cit., which should be consulted for each point. The papyrus records matching Mark's story are cited in Bickerman, p. 104, n. 124. To his discussion of Luke (esp. p. 113), I add G. D. Kilpatrick, J.T.S. (1942) 34 (the soldier at the Cross); on 'lawful' at John 18, R. E. Brown, Commentary ... II (1966) 849–50; Augustine, P.L. 35.1937, and F. Millar, in P. R. Davies and R. T. White, A Tribute to Geza Vermes (1990) 374–6, for the view I do not share: I also disagree with Millar, 370–71 (on the 'Trial'). On the opposition's origins, E. P. Sanders, Jesus and Judaism (1985) 270–81; the 'outlawing' is seen by Bickerman, 120–21 (I doubt if it already began at 7:30, not 11:57). 'Friend of Caesar' is paralleled for the Herods in Jos. A.J. 12.7.3, Philo, Against Flaccus 2.40 and Y. Meshorer, Ancient Jewish Coinage II (1982) 55, 247–8 (Herod Agrippa). The 'photograph-portrait' is suggested by A. E. Harvey, Jesus and the Constraints of History (1981) 125; the Lazarus problem, by R. E. Brown, Commentary ... St John I (1966) 414, 428; the broader causes by E. P. Sanders, Jesus and Judaism (1985) 61–76.

III

A. N. Sherwin-White, Roman Society and Roman Law in the N.T. (1963), is particularly good on the Gentile setting of Acts. For alternative chronologies, see C. J. Hemer, The Book of Acts in the Setting of Hellenistic History (1989) 159–75 and 247–77; my main differences are (a) N. Kokkinos's date of 36 for the Crucifixion and (b) my belief that Galatians 1:18 means 'three years after the conversion' and Galations 2:1 'fourteen years after the conversion', not 'fourteen years after Galatians 1:18': Paul is thinking in terms of his own 'great event' and C.E. (Conversion Era) throughout this passage.

p. 304   Gallio inscription: R. P. Oliver, Hesperia (1971) 239–40, is still important; text first in A. Plassart, Fouilles de Delphes III iv.286; E. Haenchen, The Acts of the Apostles (1971) 66; on Acts 1–9, M. Hengel, Between Jesus and Paul (1983) 30–47, at times conjectural.

p. 305   Aretas: Josephus, A.J. 18.115, 120–26, with G. W. Bowersock, Roman Arabia (1983) 51–2, 67–8, on the text and geography.

pp. 305–6   Italic band: F. J. Foakes Jackson and K. Lake, The Beginnings of Christianity 5 (1933) 441–3, for older views.

p. 306   Famine: K. Gapp, H.T.R. (1935) 258; B. M. Levick, Claudius (1990) 109 n. 14.

p. 306   *Agrippa's death*: E. Schuerer, *History of the Jewish People* . . . I (1973) 452.

p. 306–7   *Philippi*: A. N. Sherwin-White, *Roman Society and Roman Law* . . . (1963) 92–3.

p. 307   *Pisidian Antioch and Sergii Pauli*: W. Ramsay, *J.R.S.* (1926) 201, and B. M. Levick, *Roman Colonies in S. Asia Minor* (1967) 112.

p. 308   *Geography and knowledge of Jerusalem*: M. Hengel, *Between Jesus and Paul* (1983) 97–128.

p. 308   *Church and Acts 27:35*: C. K. Barrett, in B. P. Thompson, ed., *Scripture: Meaning and Method, Essays . . . Anthony T. Hanson* (1987) 51; M. Oberweis, *Nov. Test.* (1988) 169.

p. 309   *'Provocatio' and appeal*: A. W. Lintott, *A.N.R.W.* 1.2 (1972) 263–7, decisively against other recent reinterpretations.

18 Back to the Future

J. F. A. Sawyer, *Prophecy and the Prophets of the Old Testament* (1987), is the best of the recent short guides to the subject; R. P. Carroll, *When Prophecy Failed* (1879), is diffuse, but closely related to the themes of this chapter; J. Blenkinsopp, *A History of Prophecy in Israel* (1983), and R. E. Clements, *Prophecy and Tradition* (1975), are studies with a historical context. J. Barton, *Oracles of God* (1986), is a work of major importance on the ways in which prophets were later read.

I

p. 312   *Near Eastern prophets*: R. R. Wilson, *Prophecy and Society in Ancient Israel* (1980) chs. 2 and 3; D. L. Petersen, *The Roles of Israel's Prophets* (1981) esp. 75–6.

p. 312   *Comparative evidence*: M. Loewe, C. Blacker and others, *Divination and Oracles* (1981), a wide-ranging collection; H. H. Rowley, *Prophecy and Religion in Ancient China and Israel* (1956).

p. 312   *Israel and Delphi*: from another angle, J. A. Soggin, *Z.A.W.* 100 Supplement (1988) 255.

p. 313   *Hosea*: I follow the historical case, argued by H. H. Rowley, *B.J.R.L.* (1956–7) 200.

p. 313   *Ezekiel*: 12:5–7; with 24:15–24, I quote G. Josipovici; *The Book of God* (1988) 180–81; for this context, H. H. Rowley, *B.J.R.L.* (1953–4) 146.

p. 314   *Digesting scrolls*: Ezekiel 3:3; Revelation 10:8–11, E. F. Davis, *Swallowing the Scroll* (1989) ch. 3.

p. 314   *Prophets as poets?*: A. G. Auld, R. P. Carroll and H. G. M. Williamson, *J.S.O.T.* (1983) 3–44.

p. 314   *Style of sayings*: G. B. Caird, *Language and Imagery of the Bible* (1980), is full of insights; J. I. Willis, *J.S.O.T.* (1985) 3, on dialogue; D. F. Murray, *J.S.O.T.* (1987) 95, on dispute; P. A. Kruger, *J.N.S.L.* (1988) 143, on Hosea's artistry; L. A. Sinclair, *J.B.L.* (1966) 351, on Amos's.

p. 315 *Prophets as 'insiders'*: W. McKane, *Z.A.W.* (1982) 251, a thoughtful survey.

p. 315 *Visions and Temple cult*: J. Eaton, *Vision in Worship* (1981).

p. 315 *Social and political radicals*: J. Barr, *Scope and Authority of the Bible* (Explorations in Theology 7, 1980) ch. 6, esp. 99–103; on Amos and (traditional) social justice, J. Barton, *Amos's Oracles Against the Nations* (1980) 51. Compare L. Epztein, *Social Justice in the Ancient Near East and People of the Bible* (1986), for a general setting.

p. 315 *Law and prophecy*: A. Phillips, in R. Coggins, M. Knibb, A. Phillips, eds., *Israel's Prophetic Heritage* (1982) 217.

p. 315 *Traditional wisdom*: J. L. Crenshaw, *Z.A.W.* (1967) 42; J. Lindblom, in M. Noth, ed., *Wisdom in Israel and the Ancient Near East* (1960) 19–204; above all, J. Barton, *J.T.S.* (1981) 3 and 11, which I quote; also *J.T.S.* (1979) 1.

p. 316 *Laymen*: I quote E. W. Heaton, *The Old Testament Prophets* (1958) 52.

p. 316 *Foretelling and prophets' heirs*: J. Barton, *Oracles of God* (1986), is of basic importance here.

p. 316 *Aral Sea*: I quote Christian Tyler, *Weekend F. T.* (July 1989)1.

II

p. 317 *Hopeful prophecies*: major study by C. Westermann, *Z.A.W.* (1986) 1–13.

p. 318 *Updating*: Isaiah 45:1 ff., with S. Smith, *Isaiah XL–LV* (1944) 49; on Zechariah, R. Coggins, *Haggai, Zechariah, Malachi* (1987) 40–73; on Christian use, F. F. Bruce, *B.J.R.L.* (1960–61) 336; on Deuteronomists and our Amos book, W. H. Schmidt, *Z.A.W.* (1965) 168; on Jeremiah's editors, E. W. Nicholson, *Preaching to the Exiles* (1970); on Micah, E. W. Heaton, *The O. T. Prophets* (1958) 16, and, in general, pp. 134 ff.

p. 318 *Textual problems*: in Jeremiah, note esp. W. McKane, *A Critical and Exegetical Commentary on Jeremiah* I (1986); E. Tov, in P. M. Bogaert, *Le Livre de Jérémie* (1981) 145, and J. G. Janzen, *Studies in the Text of Jeremiah* (1973); E. Tov, *E.T.L.* 62 (1986) 69, is important, too, on the variant 'Ezekiels'.

p. 319 *Future*: I. T. Ramsay, *Religious Language* (1957) 112–14, for an important statement; on Joel, R. P. Carroll, *When Prophecy Failed* (1979) esp. 171–2.

p. 320 *Prophets' concerns in 760s*: on Amos's originality, R. R. Wilson, *Interpretation* (1978) 3; on (possible) history, M. Haran, *I.E.J.* (1968) 201, with J. Barton, *Amos's Oracles Against the Nations* (1980); religious polemic, H. M. Barstad, *S.V.T.* (1984) 127.

p. 321 *Prophetic logic*: I cite the view of W. H. Schmidt, *Zukunftsgewissheit und Gegenwartskritik* (1973) esp. 55–65: examples of implausible connections between 'crime' and 'punishment' include (he suggests) Hosea 1:4 or Isaiah 5:11. For a thoughtful discussion of this, J. Barton, *Evangelische Theologie* 5 (1987) 427.

p. 321 *Forms of speech*: C. Westermann, *Basic Forms of Prophetic Speech* (1967); H. W. Wolff, *Z.A.W.* (1934) 1.

p. 321 *Repentance*: I disagree with A. Vanlier Hunter, *Seek the Lord* (1982), whose p. 280 I quote; on repentance, Amos 5:4, with A. Soggin, *The Prophet Amos* (1987) 84–8, against (e.g.) R. Smend, *Evang. Theologie* (1963) 404, or H. W. Wolffe, *Z.T.K.* (1951) 129. For good discussion, O. Keel, *Biblische Zeitschrift* (1977) 200.

p. 323 *True/False prophecies*: E. Jenni, *Die Politischen Aussagen der Propheten* (1956), is still basic. On Hosea 1:4, G. I. Emmerson, *Hosea* (1984) 106–13, for various interpretations. On Jehoiakim, J. Hughes, *Secrets of the Times* (1990) 188 n. 60.

p. 324 *Amos's foe*: I follow H. W. Wolff, *Joel and Amos* (1977, E.T.) 89 and notes on Amos 3:9; on Jeremiah's 'northern foe', D. Reimer, *Z.A.W.* (1989) 223.

pp. 324–5 *Isaiah and 701 BC*: I accept R. E. Clements, *Isaiah and the Deliverance of Jerusalem* (1980).

p. 325 *Jeremiah 43:8*: E. W. Nicholson, *Jeremiah 26–52* (1975) 149–52, for details. The Babylonian text for 568/7 is fragmentary and of uncertain scope: D. J. Wiseman, *Nebuchadnezzar and Babylon* (1985) 39–41.

p. 325 *Jews in Egypt*: B. B. Porten, *Archive from Elephantine* (1968), for details.

pp. 325–6 *Isaiah 9*: commentary in *The Interpreters Bible*, vol. 5 (1956) by G. G. D. Kilpatrick, 230 ff., accepting the correct (non–Christian) understanding.

p. 326 *Cyrus*: S. Smith, *Isaiah, XL–LV* (1944) 45 ff., and Herodotus, 1.212–14.

p. 327 *God and lies*: Jeremiah 20:7–12, with the fine study of J. Trigg, in C. Kannengiesser, W. C. Peterson, eds., *Origen of Alexandria* (1988) 147, esp. pp. 162 and 164 ('Truth for O. is not factual information but saving knowledge'!). 1 Kings 22 also repays thought; also J. J. M. Roberts, in J. A. Emerton, ed., *Congress Volume Jerusalem 1986* (1988).

p. 328 *God's vacillation*: Isaiah 38:1–6, another example.

III

The books of Jonah and Daniel are brilliantly discussed by E. J. Bickerman, *Four Strange Books of the Bible* (1967), on which my own discussion depends. On Jonah, I quote D. Daube, *Journal of Jewish Studies* (1984) 36, esp. on Jonah's anger; B. Halpern, R. Friedman, *H.A.R.* (1980) 79, on Jonah and word-play; T. Eagleton, in M. Schwarz, ed., *The Book and the Text* (1990) 231, on Jonah as a self–defeating utterance; R. Payne, *Expository Times* (1989) 131, on Jonah and prayer; B. P. Robinson, *Z.A.W.* (1985) 390, on the botany of Jonah's gourd, with Augustine, *Epistle* 71.3 and 5.

On Daniel, E. J. Bickerman, *Four Strange Books* . . . (1967), is basic, with A. Momigliano, *Alien Wisdom* (1975) 109–112 and his *Settimo contributo alla storia degli studi classici* (1984) 297; on Daniel 7, J. A. Emerton, *J.T.S.* (1958) 225, is still helpful and (less convincing) J. Day, *God's conflict with the Dragon and the Sea* (1985) ch. 4. On Daniel 3, C. Kuhl, *Beiheft 54, Z.A.W.* (1930), esp. 50–65, is excellent.

19 The Old in the New

I

J. Goldingay, *Approaches to Old Testament Interpretation* (1981) esp. ch. 4, gives an up-to-date survey of the questions of this chapter and their treatment by theologians. J. Barr, *Old and New in Interpretation* (1966), is an outstanding critique to which my debt, I hope, is evident. Jewish and Christian uses of scriptural texts are studied in great detail in M. J. Mulder, H. Sysling, eds., *Mikra* . . . (1988) esp. E. E. Ellis, 691 ff. (on early Christianity) and E. E. Ellis, *The Old Testament in Early Christianity* (1991) 53 ff.

pp. 338-9 *Isaiah 7 and Immanuel*: G. B. Caird, *The Language and Imagery of the Bible* (1980) 78–9, for a concise exposition; A. Kanesar, *J.T.S.* (1990) 51, for the development of Christian readings; A. Laato, *Who is Immanuel?* (1988), for a different approach.

p. 339 *Suffering Servant*: I agree with P. Wilcox, D. Paton-Williams, *J.S.O.T.* (1988) 79, rather than with B. Lindars, *B.J.R.L.* (1986) 473, an acute discussion. On the 'situation vacant', G. B. Caird, *The Language and Imagery of the Bible* (1980) 57–8, and W. J. Houston in L. D. Hurst, N. T. Wright, eds., *The Glory of Christ in the N. T.* (1987) 37.

p. 339 *Hosea 6:2*: I quote J. H. Mays, *Hosea* (1969) 95.

p. 340 *Peter at Pentecost*: E. Haenchen, *Acts of the Apostles* (1970, E.T.) 177–85, an important discussion.

p. 341 *Dead Sea scrolls*: M. J. Mulder, ed., *Mikra* . . . (1988); G. Vermes, *The Dead Sea Scrolls* (1977) 167, 213 ff.

p. 341 *Jesus and Paul*: J. Barton, *People of the Book?* (1988) ch. 2; E. P. Sanders, *Paul, the Law and the Jewish People* (1985) 21, on Galatians 3. But we must always remember that our few epistles (all to Christians) are only a tiny sample of Paul's possible techniques.

p. 342 *Types*: J. Daniélou, *From Shadows to Reality* (1960); J. Goldingay, *Approaches to O.T. Interpretation* (1981) 97–115, with bibliography; I quote A. Lowth, *Discerning the Mystery* (1983) 125; on 'sensus plenior', compare D. J.

Moo, in D. A. Carson, J. D. Woodbridge, eds., *Hermeneutics, Authority and Canon* (1986) ch. 5.

p. 343 *Malachi and N.T.*: I quote J. Muddiman, *The Bible: Fountain and Well of Truth* (1983).

p. 344 *Jesus and prophecy*: G. B. Caird, *Jesus and the Jewish Nation* (1965); on Palm Sunday, I do not share the doubts of E. P. Sanders, *Jesus and Judaism* (1985) 306, or the conclusions of D. Catchpole, in C. Moule, E. Bammel, eds., *Jesus and the Politics of His Day* (1984) 317.

p. 344 *Martyr-prophets*: Lamentations 4:13 is important; for the development, G. Garbini, *History and Ideology . . .* (1988) ch. 9, esp. 116 ff.

II

p. 345 *Agabus and famine*: K. Gapp, *H.T.R.* (1935) 258, citing evidence; also B. M. Levick, *Claudius* (1990) 109–11, with notes.

p. 346 *'Kingdom within'*: C. H. Roberts, *H.T.R.* (1948) 1.

pp. 346–7 *Revelation's imagery*: J. Sweet, *Revelation* (1990) 13–21, 113 ff.; G. B. Caird, *Revelation of St John* (1966), a fine account; P. Prigent, *Apocalypse et liturgie* (1964), is compelling; for other approaches, J. M. Court, *Myth and History in the Book of Revelation* (1979).

p. 347 *Revelation's date*: J. Sweet, *Revelation* (1990) 21–7, introduces the problems; the case for the 60s is fully presented by J. A. T. Robinson, *Redating the New Testament* (1976): I reject it, seeing echoes of the past in a work of the 90s.

p. 347 *Bruttius's history*: R. Syme, *Roman Papers* V (1988) 576–7; the persecution falls in 95, certainly after plague, famine at Pisidian Antioch (92/3) and the vine edict of Dom. during a grain shortage (Syme, *Roman Papers* IV, 289).

p. 347 *First Clement*: L. W. Barnard, *Studies in Church History and Patristics* (1978) 139–42.

p. 348 *Food crisis:* W. M. Ramsay, *J.R.S.* (1924) 180–84, with R. Syme, *Roman Papers* IV (1988) 280, 289–90; the governor sets a limit of one denarius per modius for wheat (R. Duncan-Jones, *Economy of the Roman Empire* (1983) 145–6, for comparisons). I forbear to tie in the 'vine edict', although Suet., *Dom.* 7.2, attaches it to a grain-shortage: its date is 90–95, but uncertain (B. M. Levick, *Latomus*, 1982, 68).

p. 348 *Plague*: Dio, 67.11.6, with R. Syme, *Roman Papers* IV (1988) 289 (important): Syme inclines to a sequence of plague years, from 90 on to 93.

p. 349 *Image of the Beast*: S. R. F. Price, *Rituals and Power* (1984) 196–8, important; p. 255 for the statue of Domitian and the Temple at Ephesus, which we cannot yet date exactly.

p. 349 *Mark of the Beast*: C. P. Jones, *J.R.S.* (1987) 139, esp. 144 n. 27 (Isaiah

44:5, and Lucian, *Dea Syria* 59); also p. 152 (with Philo, *Spec. Leg.* 1.58), and bibliography; Lucian, *Peregrinus* 28. For penal marking, p. 148 and Suet., *Calig.* 27.3

p. 350   *'Forthtelling' and repentance*: J. Sweet, *Revelation* (1990) esp. 189 and 307 ff., for a view which I do not share.

PART FOUR

20 The Bible as Story

I

pp. 356–7   *The Brontës*: T. J. Winnifrith, *The Brontës and Their Background* (1988, 2nd edn.) ch. 3, esp. p. 37; for the 'extinct volcano', W. Gerin, *Charlotte Brontë* (1987) 387, which I quote.

pp. 357–8   *San Nicandro*: I quote and use Elena Cassin, *San Nicandro* (1959).

p. 359   *Augustine*: Confessions 9.8–11; 31; 50.

II

p. 360   *Myth, story and fact*; S. Medcalf, in M. Wadsworth, ed., *Ways of Reading the Bible* (1983) 55, on C. S. Lewis, the Gospels and truth in a story; M. F. Wiles, in G. F. Green, ed., *Scriptural Authority and Narrative Interpretation* (1987).

p. 360   *Visions after death*: R. Lane Fox, *Pagans and Christians* (1986) 142–3, for a good example; Livy 1.16, on an ascension (doubted by Livy); E. J. Bickerman, *Entretiens Fondation Hardt* XIX (1973) 1, on the consecration-ascension of emperors.

p. 361   *E. M. Forster*: I quote his *Aspects of the Novel* (1927) 88.

p. 361   *Updating stories*: M. Fishbane, *Biblical Interpretation in Ancient Israel* (1985), is a fundamental, though ill-written, study; on Midrash, J. Neusner, *Midrash in Context* (1988), with bibliography; D. C. Jacobson, *Modern Midrash . . .* (1987), on Hebrew writers in this century; L. H. Feldman, *H.T.R.* (1989) 351, on Josephus, with important bibliography; E. J. Bickerman, *Jews in the Greek Age* (1988) ch. 20.

p. 361   *Sodom and pleading*: C. S. Rodd, *Expository Times* 83 (1972) 137; D. Daube, *Biblical law* (1947) ch. 3.

p. 362   *Genesis 22*: the classic account is by E. Auerbach, *Mimesis* (1953) ch. 1; however, I disagree with several of his points. He misrepresents Homer from one passage in the *Odyssey*, itself not without depth: the contrast between Homer and the Hebrews' Bible derived from H. Gunkel, on whose concern with it see esp. P. Gilbert, *Une Théorie de la légende . . . Herman Gunkel* (1979) esp. 237 ff. There is no necessary connection between monotheism and the biblical reticence of Genesis: contrast the version of Josephus, no mean monotheist, as seen by L. H. Feldman, *J.Q.R.* (1984–5) 212. I also disagree that the story, for its author, was already history 'remorselessly excluding alternatives': C. Westermann, *Genesis 12–36* (1985) 351, gives a valuable survey of the tale's likely origins.

pp. 362–3   *Blanks in Genesis 22*: S. P. Brock, *Le Muséon* (1974) 67, in *Mélanges D. Barthélemy* (1981) 2 and *Expository Times* (1984) 14: R. P. Schmitz, *Aqedat Jishaq* (1979); P. R. Davies, B. R. Chilton, *C.B.Q.* (1978) 514; S. Spiegel, *The Last Trial* (1969).

p. 363–4   *Bible and national 'origins'*: S. Reynolds, *History* (1983) 375; S. Schama, *Embarrassment of Riches* (1987) 93–125.

p. 364   *Esther*: E. J. Bickerman, *Four Strange Books of the Bible* (1967) 169, with my ch. 13 for a different dating; the outstanding study of its literary art is still H. Striedl, *Z.A.W.* (1937) 73, esp. 93–108. For its impact, *Codex Theodosianus 16.8.18* (May 408).

p. 365   *Genesis 30*: M. D. Reeve, *Proc. of Cambridge Philological Society* (1989) 81, a brilliant study.

p. 366   *Moses:* G. Binder, *Die Aussetzung des Konigskindes Kyros and Romulus* (1964), discusses the story's theme.

III

p. 366   *Structuralism and O.T.*: clear introduction by J. Barton, *Reading the Old Testament* (1984) chs. 8, 9, 12; on the use of folk-tales as an analogy, P. G. Kirkpatrick, *The O.T. and Folklore Study* (1988), and P. J. Milne, *Vladimir Propp and the Study of Structure in Hebrew Biblical Narrative* (1988), are important correctives; samples of the approach in R. C. Culley, *Studies in the Structure of Hebrew Narrative*, R. M. Polzin, *Biblical Structuralism* (1977) and R. Barthes, in R. Barthes and F. Bovon, eds., *Analyse structurale et exégèse biblique* (1971) 27 (on Jacob), discussed by H. C. White, *Semeia* 3 (1975) 99. Barthes's analysis of Acts 10–11, now in *The Semiotic Challenge* (1985) 217, is a poor advertisement for the method's value. On structure and thought, E. R. Leach, *Genesis as Myth and Other Essays* (1969) 25 and 113 (Dinah, intermarriage etc.), is a good example, correctly opposed by J. A. Lane-Fox Pitt–Rivers, *The Fate of Shechem* (1977): both are subverted by the more traditional study of J. A. Emerton, *V.T.* (1976) 79, with further bibliography.

p. 367   *Jacob and the 'demon'*: C. Westermann, *Genesis 12–36* (1985) 512: I quote p. 519.

p. 368   *God's/angels' appearances*: R. Alter, *Prooftexts* 3 (1983) 115, for a literary view; J. Scharbert, in G. Rovira, ed., *Der Widerschein des Ewigen Lichtes* (1984) 21, for recent, valuable survey.

p. 368   *Mamre*: C. Westermann, *Genesis 12–36* (1985) 272 on ch. 18; on later readings, W. T. Miller, *Mysterious Encounters at Mamre and Jabbok* (1984); on the cakes, F. Delitzsch, in C. Westermann, p. 279.

p. 369   *Sinai traditions*: Exodus 24, now best in E. W. Nicholson, *God and His People* (1986) 121–33 and 173–8.

p. 369   *God's 'face' and psalms*: M. S. Smith, *C.B.Q.* (1988) 171, whose bibliography I presuppose.

pp. 369–70   *Angel food*: D. Goodman, *J.J.S.* (1986) 160.

p. 370   *Gideon, Samson, Tobit*: Judges 6:11,13; Tobit 5:9, with 12, esp. 12:19.

p. 372   *Pagan epiphanies*: R Lane Fox, *Pagans and Christians* (1986) ch. 4, with bibliography; N. J. Richardson, *Homeric Hymn to Demeter* (1979, 2nd edn.) 207, 252. On sex with a god, P. Maas, *Kleine Schriften* (1973) 66 (not altogether true).

p. 373   *Annunciation stories*: E. W. Conrad, *C.B.Q.* (1985) 656, on 'fear not' with bibliography.

p. 373   *Paul, Acts*: H. S. Versnel, in D. van der Plas, ed., *Effigies Dei* (1987, Supplement to *Numen*, li) 42.

p. 374   *Pan-sacral age*: J. Barton, *J.T.S.* (1984) 301–23, against the famous views of G. von Rad on the Solomonic age and its sequel.

21 *'Divine Letters'*

R. Alter, *The Art of Biblical Narrative* (1981) and *The Art of Biblical Poetry* (1985), are clear, if not altogether convincing, studies in a heavily populated field. F. Kermode, *The Genesis of Secrecy* (1979), has similar qualities among literary studies of the New Testament: the composite volume, *The Literary Guide to the Bible*, eds. R. Alter, F. Kermode (1987), has a wide range and further bibliographies, but the essays vary widely in quality. R. Morgan, with J. Barton, *Biblical Interpretation* (1988) chs. 6 and 7, gives a broad survey of literary study and its application; J. Barton, *Reading the Old Testament* (1984), is a lucid and helpful introduction to theoretical approaches; the essays in M. Schwarz, ed., *The Book and the Text* (1990), are a sample of modern critical readings.

ᵀ

pp. 375–6   *Poetry*: J. Kugel, *The Idea of Biblical Poetry* (1981), is the most challenging, negative account; contrast the review of it by J. Barr, *J.L.S.* (1981) 1506. Among many discussions, F. Landy, W. G. E. Watson, P. D. Miller, in *J.S.O.T.* 28 (1984) 61–107, are helpful, with a reply by Kugel at pp. 107–17. R. Alter, *The Art of Biblical Poetry* (1990, 2nd edn.), for an alternative direction. Josephus, *A.J.* 2.16; 4.8 with Kugel, 140–56 (153, on Jerome and Job).

p. 376 *Scripture and literature*: R. Braun, *Deus Christianorum* (1977) 459, on scripture as 'litterae' in Tertullian; P. Monat, *Lactance et la Bible* (1982) 35.

p. 376 *Juvencus*: O. Bardenhewer, *Geschichte der Altkirchlichen Literatur* III (1912) 429–32.

p. 376 *Biblical style*: S. Prickett, *Words and the Word* (1986) chs. 1–2.

p. 376 *'Modern' appreciation*: I quote G. Josipovici, *The Book of God* (1988) 49.

pp. 376–7 *Literary misreadings*: I cite, as random examples, L. R. Klein, *The Triumph of Irony in the Book of Judges* (1989); J. A. Loader, *Polar Structure in the Book of Qobelet* (1979); M. Sternberg, *The Poetics of Biblical Narrative* (1985), on Uriah.

p. 377 *Esther*: I quote D. J. A. Clines, *Ezra, Nehemiah, Esther* (1984) 319, who is quite wrong. On the book's textual history, E. Tov, *Textus* I (1982) 41, and E. J. Bickerman, *Studies in Jewish Christian History* I (1976) 246–74, are still basic; on its art, H. Striedl, *Z.A.W.* (1937) 73, esp. 98 ff.

p. 377 *David and Goliath*: I quote from R. Alter, *The Art of Biblical Narrative* (1981) ch. 7, esp. 147–54, who is refuted by E. Tov, in D. Barthélemy, D. W. Gooding. J. Lust, E. Tov, *The Story of David and Goliath* (1986) 19–47, 129–38, an unnecessarily tentative research project as Gooding's 'defence' is the misplaced defence of a Homeric scholar (contrast my ch. 5 pp. 105–6), and Barthélemy begins with a prejudice against Tov's correct position.

p. 378 *Biblical language*: G. B. Caird, *The Language and Imagery of the Bible* (1980), is an admirable work of connoisseurship.

p. 378 *Antiphonal song*: J. Kugel, *The Idea of Biblical Poetry* (1981) 116–19.

p. 379 *Exodus*: D. Daube, *The Exodus Pattern in the Bible* (1963).

p. 379 *Ruth*: D. Daube, *Ancient Jewish Law* (1981) 33.

p. 379 *Points of view*: W. P. Ker, *Epic and Romance* (1922, rev. edn.) 239, on 2 Kings: I owe this to S. Medcalf. S. Bar Efrat, *Narrative Art in the Bible* (1989, E.T.), and Adele Berlin, *The Poetics and Interpretation of Biblical Narrative* (1983).

p. 381 *'Fellow pensioners'*: C. S. Lewis, *Reflections on the Psalms* (1967, Fontant edn.) 76.

II

p. 382 *Jesus's sayings*: R. C. Tannehill, *The Sword of his Mouth* (1975), is fundamental here; compare B. Harrison, in M. Wadsworth, ed., *Ways of Reading the Bible* (1981) 190, a fine study of the parables.

p. 383 *Parables*: M. D. Goulder, *J.T.S.* (1968) 51, which I quote as a highly important paper.

III

The fullest modern commentary on the fourth Gospel is R. E. Brown's, in two volumes (1966): I presuppose it on individual passages which I discuss. The most clearly argued recent book is M. Hengel's *The Johannine Question* (1989), whose notes and reasoned bibliography are excellent: I presuppose them too. Literary studies include R. A. Culpeper, *Anatomy of the Fourth Gospel* (1983), but also go back many years. J. Muilenburg, *Literary Form in the Fourth Gospel* (1932), being one of many. As my theme is the author's own shaping of the story, I would emphasize here the more specialized studies of G. van Belle, *Les Parenthèses dans L'Évangile de Jean* (1985), and C. J. Bjerkelund, *Taute Egeneto . . .* (1987), with H. Gese, *Essays on Biblical Theology* (1981) 167, on the ideas of the Prologue. Patrick Grant, *Reading the New Testament* (1989), includes a literary response to the fourth Gospel (pp. 59–78) in a wider, but concise, study of the main New Testament books.

p. 384 *The Gospel's vocabulary*: M. Hengel, *The Johannine Question* (1989) 33, quoting J. Wellhausen, *Dao Evangelium Johannis* (1908) 146, on the 'hieratic' style.

p. 384 *Lazarus*: R. E. Brown, *The Gospel According to St John* I (1966) 414 and 428 for problems; 10:41 picks up 11:47 nicely (11:1–46), the gloss on Bethany at 12:1, 12:9–11 and 12:17–18 can then be marked off as additions to a first version). Some would argue, of course, that Luke 16:28–30 is the origin of the Raising story.

p. 384 *Uniformity of style*: E. Ruckstuhl, *Die literarische Einheit des Johannes-evangelium* (1987, 2nd edn.), rightly endorsed by M. Hengel, *The Johannine Question* (1989) 202–3.

p. 385 *Ageing author*: I quote M. Hengel, *The Johannine Question* (1989) 95.

p. 385 *The Bread at the Supper*: F. Kermode, in R. Alter, F. Kermode, eds., *The Literary Guide to the Bible* (1987) 453–4, makes the most of it.

p. 386 *Night as symbol*: Origen, *Comm. in Joh 34.24* (ed. E. Preuschen, G.C.S., 1903) section 313.

p. 386 *Glory*: G. B. Caird, *N.T.S.* (1969) 265, is an essential study; compare J. Muddiman, in L. D. Hurst, N. T. Wright, eds., *The Glory of Christ in the New Testament* (1987) 51.

p. 387 *Cana miracle*: B. Olsson, *Structure and Meaning in the Fourth Gospel . . .* (1974), for the fullest range of meanings; further discussion by M. Hengel, in L. D. Hurst, N. T. Wright, *The Glory of Christ . . .* (1987) 83.

p. 388 *Testimony and purpose*: John 19:35, 20:31, 21:24.

p. 388 *Threesomes*: I quote P. Grant, *Reading the New Testament* (1989) 72.

p. 388 *The 'protonovelist'*: I quote F. Kermode, in R. Alter, F. Kermode, eds., *The Literary Guide to the Bible* (1987) 454. The allusion to Daniel was suggested by D. F. Strauss in *Das Leben Jesu*.

p. 389 *Jesus and the law of Israel*: S. Pancaro, *The Law in the Fourth Gospel* (1975).

pp. 390–91   *Quotations of Hebrew Scripture*: D. A. Carson, in D. A. Carson, H. G. M. Williamson, *It is Written . . . Essays . . . B. Lindars* (1988).

pp. 391–2   *The misunderstandings*: D. A. Carson, *Tyndale Bulletin* (1982) 59.

p. 393   *Irony*: P. Duke, *Irony in the Fourth Gospel* (1985)

p. 393   *Seeing and believing*: P. Grant, *Reading the New Testament* (1989) 59–78 is very suggestive.

p. 395   *Twofold testimony*: compare the Jewish setting in D. Daube, *Witnesses in Bible and Talmud* (1986).

p. 395   *'Penetrating monomania'*: I quote A. D. Nuttall, *Overheard by God* (1980), and in M. Wadsworth, ed., *Ways of Reading the Bible* (1981) 49.

p. 395   *Uniform style*: esp. A. J. Festugière, *Observations stylistiques sur L'Évangile de S. Jean* (1984) esp. 28 ff.

p. 397   *The synagogues*: I would emphasize Acts 9:2 (AD 36) and on the word aposynagogos, E. Schuerer, *History of the Jewish People* . . . II (1985) 432 and 462.

p. 397   *Idols and 1 John*: correctly understood by M. J. Edwards, *Novum Testamentum* (1989) 164.

22 Human Truth

My choice of theme has been formed by the work of D. Daube, especially his *Biblical Law* (1947) and *Sin, Ignorance and Forgiveness in the Bible* (London, 1960). On social questions, Morton Smith and J. Hoffman, eds., *What the Bible Really Says* (1989), gives a useful, non-ideological summary of the main issues (including war, women and slavery). On women in Hebrew scripture, D. Daube, *La Femme dans le droit biblique* (1962) and his articles in *R.I.D.A.* 25 (1978) 95, and *Juridical Review* (1978) 177, are generous supplements to standard (non-feminist) summaries of the texts; L. J. Archer, *Her Price is Beyond Rubies* (1990), adds social history from later Jewish sources too; A. Cameron, *Greece and Rome* (1980) 60, for the New Testament. In general, K. Stendhal, *Meanings: The Bible as Document and as Guide* (1984) for differing views on a central question of this chapter.

I

p. 400   *Popular capitalism*: Brian Griffiths, *Morality and the Market Place* (1981), for biblical Thatcherism.

p. 400   *Feminism*: L. M. Russell, ed., *Feminist Interpretation of the Bible* (1985), for a selection of varying views; P. Trible, *God and the Rhetoric of Sexuality* (1978), for some influential wishful thinking.

p. 401   *Exodus*: D. Daube, *Biblical Law* (1947) 50.

p. 401   *Kingship and sinfulness*: D. Daube, *J.J.S.* (1959) 1–13.

p. 401   *Slavery*: I quote Morton Smith, in Morton Smith, J. Hoffman, eds., *What the Bible Really Says* (1989) 146, in a valuable chapter on biblical slavery; in Christianity, compare G. E. M. de Sainte Croix, in D. Baker, ed., *Studies in Church History* (1975) 1.

II

p. 402   *'Alternative voices'*: P. Trible, *Texts of Terror* (1984), and *God and the Rhetoric of Sexuality* (1978); R. R. Ruether, *Sexism and God Talk* (1983), and in *J.S.O.T.* (1982) 54; E. S. Fiorenza, *Bread, Not Stone* (1985), and her programme, in *J.B.L.* (1988) 3. The weaknesses are, I trust, obvious.

p. 403   *Genocide*: G. E. M. de Sainte Croix, *The Class Struggle in the Ancient Greek World* (1981) 331–2; on 'holy war', I quote R. de Vaux, *Ancient Israel* (1965; E.T.) ch. 5, esp. p. 262.

p. 404   *Shame-culture*: D. Daube, *Orita* 3 (1969) 27, and *Studi Volterra* II (1971) 1, on Deuteronomy; on Luke, D. Daube in M. D. Hooker, S. G. Wilson, eds., *Paul and Paulinism: Essays . . . C. K. Barrett* (1982) 355; on guilt, J. Barr, in F. C. Grant, H. H. Rowley, eds., *Hastings' Dictionary of the Bible* (1963, one volume).

p. 404   *Absence of accident*: D. Daube, *R.I.D.A.* (1949) 189, esp. 204; *V.T.* (1961) 246; compare the effects of being drunk (always detrimental, in the Bible, to the drinker): D. Daube, *Wine in the Bible* (1975).

p. 405   *Words and error*: D. Daube, *Biblical Law* (1947) 190–200.

p. 405   *Jacob and Rachel*: D. Daube, *Studi Volterra* 2 (1969) 1; *Biblical Law* (1947) 205–17.

p. 406   *Shimei*: D. Daube, *Tulane Law Review* 46 (1972) 653, and *Ancient Jewish Law* (1981) 128–9 (important).

p. 406   *Poetic justice*: J. Barton, *J.T.S.* (1979) 1.

pp. 406–7   *Retaliation*: D. Daube, *Biblical Law* (1947) ch. 3; C. Carmichael, *Biblical Laws of Talion* (Oxford Centre for Hebrew Studies, 1986), with bibliography.

p. 407   *Law and 'ritualism'*: I quote from D. Daube, *Oxford Journal of Legal Studies* 1 (1980) 58; compare his *Studies in Biblical Law* (1947) 200, and *Ancient Jewish Law* (1981) 49 ff. (important).

p. 407   *Right from wrong*: D. Daube, *Oxford Journal of Legal Studies* 1 (1980) 51; also his *Biblical Law* (1947) ch. 5. I disagree with the bold approach of C. Carmichael, *Laws of Deuteronomy* (1974).

pp. 407–8   *Ignorance and guilt*: D. Daube, *Sin, Ignorance and Forgiveness in the Bible* (1960), and in *Festschrift O. Eissfeldt* (1958) 32.

pp. 409–10   *Job*: best survey in J. H. Eaton, *Job* (1989); V. E. Reichert, *Job* (Soncino Commentary, 1946), is still excellent; more recently, N. C. Habel, *The Book of Job* (Cambridge Bible Comm., 1975); also J. Barr, *B.J.R.L.* (1971–

2) 28, on modern interpreters. I have emphasized God's opening gamble which some critics tend to play down. On Prometheus and Job, note Gilbert Murray, in R. B. Sewall, *The Vision of Tragedy* (1959) 58.

p. 411   *Animal symbols of evil*: N. Frye, *The Great Code* (1982) 194.

p. 412   *Einstein*: A. Pais, *Subtle is the Lord: The Science and Life of Albert Einstein* (1982) 443, 462: I owe this to Dr Tony Cox.

III

p. 413   *Elisha and Hazael*: D. Daube, in *Medical and Genetic Ethics* (Oxford Centre for Hebrew Studies, pamphlet 1976).

pp. 413–4   *Joseph and guilt*: D. Daube, *Biblical Law* (1947) 235–57.

p. 414   *Nathan*: D. Daube, *Nov. Testamentum* (1982) 275.

p. 414   *Shimei and conscience*: D. Daube, *Ancient Jewish Law* (1981) 128–9.

pp. 414–15   *Wisdom of Solomon*: I quote the Wisdom of Solomon 2:6–20; on the problems of date and a (possible) Aramaic original, M. D. Goodman, in E. Schuerer, *History of the Jewish People* III.1 (1986, rev. edn.) 568–78.

p. 416   *Forgiveness in Luke*: Luke 23:34, with D. Daube *Studia Patristica*, Oxford (1961) 58.

Index

Index

Suffering Servant, 76, 77, 117, 292, 339, 341, 391

Susannah and the Elders, 163, 332

Tabernacles, Feast of, 85, 116, 118, 206, 287, 299, 300, 303, 390

Tamar, 357–8, 407

Tatian, and Gospel Harmony, 139–40, 150

Tattenai, 273–4

Taylor, J. E., 217

Tekoah, woman of, 189, 190, 380

Tell Mardikh (Ebla), 220

Temple in Jerusalem: destruction of, 69, 109, 111, 137, 169, 246, 284, 346; rebuilding of, 76, 77, 84, 169, 240, 241, 268, 270–74, 302, 318; expatriates, 91; threatened by Antiochus IV, 335

Temple of Herod, 35, 245

Theodotus, 116

Theophilus, 129, 309

Thessalonians, Second Epistle to the: on fakes, 130

Thomas, 249

Thomas, Gospel of, 148–51

Thucydides, 163, 168–71, 173, 174, 210, 211, 311, 362

Timnath-serah, 230

Timothy, First Epistle to, 139; and status of Christian women, 24; quoting Deuteronomy, 124; authorship, 132–3, 134, 136, 151, 153; Jesus called 'God', 140

Timothy, Second Epistle to, 139; authorship, 131, 134, 136, 151, 153; fundamentalism, 136

Titus, Epistle to, 139; stylometric difference, 135; Jesus called 'God', 140; authorship, 153

Tobias, 89, 269, 371, 373

Tobit, Book of 89, 371, 372

Torah see Law

Trial of Jesus, 286–304

Trophimus, 131, 132

Truth, Gospel of, 148, 150

Tudal, Hittite king (Tudhaliya), 253

Turin Shroud, 250–51

Tyndale, William, 138

Tyre, Annals of Kings, 192

United Bible Societies, 156

Unknown Gospel, text of, 148–51

Ur, 217, 218, 225, 270

Uriah, 190, 376, 406, 414

Vespasian, Emperor, 347

Virgil, 261, 342, 381

'Weidner Chronicle', 165

'Western' text, 139, 307

Wisdom of Solomon, 108, 152, 415

Wise Men, 30, 34–8

Witter, H. B., 21

Woolley, Leonard, 217–19, 230

Word of God, unerring, 39–44, 416

Yahweh: origins, 53; meeting with Moses on Sinai, 53; and divine names, 54–5; treated as Number One divinity, 55–6, 61–2, 72, 74; imagery, 57, 74, 84, 372; as Fond Abuser, 59, 61, 122; worship of Yahweh alone, 64, 74, 75, 76, 86, 91, 115, 185; cult ceases, 69; as holy four-letter word, 108–10, 114, 122; *asherah*, 243

Yahwist, The see J

Yaro'am, 225

Yehohanon, 248, 249

Zacchaeus, 214, 402

Zachariah, 214

Zechariah, 117, 118, 268, 271, 273, 318, 326, 338, 340, 344, 348

Zedekiah, 264, 265

Zerubbabel, 271, 272, 273, 275, 326